FOR REFERENCE

Do Not Take From This Room

ENCYCLOPEDIA OF
AMERICAN
IMMIGRATION

Volume 3
Paper sons—*Zadvydas v. Davis*
Appendixes
Indexes

Edited by
Carl L. Bankston III
Tulane University

SALEM PRESS
Pasadena, California   Hackensack, New Jersey

Editor in Chief: Dawn P. Dawson

Editorial Director: Christina J. Moose   *Research Supervisor:* Jeffry Jensen
Project and Development Editor: R. Kent Rasmussen   *Photo Editor:* Cynthia Breslin Beres
Manuscript Editor: Tim Tiernan   *Production Editor:* Andrea E. Miller
Indexer: R. Kent Rasmussen   *Design and Graphics:* James Hutson
Acquisitions Editor: Mark Rehn   *Layout:* William Zimmerman
Editorial Assistant: Brett S. Weisberg

Frontispiece: A man walks along the Mexican side of a portion of the border fence near San Ysidro, California, that was erected to help stem illegal immigration into the United States. (Getty Images)

Cover photo: (The Granger Collection, New York)

Library of Congress Cataloging-in-Publication Data

Encyclopedia of American immigration / edited by Carl L. Bankston III.
    p.   cm.
Includes bibliographical references and index.
  ISBN 978-1-58765-599-9 (set : alk. paper) — ISBN 978-1-58765-600-2 (vol. 1 : alk. paper) —
ISBN 978-1-58765-601-9 (vol. 2 : alk. paper) — ISBN 978-1-58765-602-6 (vol. 3 : alk. paper) —
1. United States—Emigration and immigration—History. I. Bankston, Carl L. (Carl Leon), 1952-
JV6450.E66 2010
  304.8′73003—dc22

2009054334

First Printing

CONTENTS

COMPLETE LIST OF CONTENTS

VOLUME 1

VOLUME 2

VOLUME 3

ENCYCLOPEDIA OF
AMERICAN
IMMIGRATION

PAPER SONS

THE EVENT: Brief period during which Chinese immigrants took advantage of the legal principle of derivative citizenship by using the destruction of government birth records during the San Francisco earthquake of 1906 to enter the United States

DATE: After April, 1906

LOCATION: San Francisco, California

SIGNIFICANCE: The use of faked paperwork identifying new Chinese immigrants as sons and daughters of American-born citizens significantly increased Chinese immigration, which had been severely limited by strict federal immigration laws.

During the several-day fire that followed the great earthquake that nearly leveled the city of San Fran-cisco on April 18-19, 1906, most of the city's official birth records were irretrievably destroyed. Afterward, many Chinese immigrants claimed to have been born in San Francisco. When their claims were recognized, they were regarded as American citizens by birth and permitted to bring their families from China to the United States.

In many cases, nonrelatives entered the United States using falsified paperwork. They became known as "paper sons" because their family ties existed only on paper. These arrangements benefited both the new immigrants and the Chinese who were already in the United States, who were paid money for claiming the immigrants as their kin. Because official birth records had been destroyed during the earthquake, government officials conducted extensive interviews to verify that the immigrants' claims of family connections were valid. The papers the immigrants purchased included detailed information about ancestors and home-

After the 1906 earthquake, parts of San Francisco burn in conflagrations that destroyed the city's official birth records. (Library of Congress)

towns in China. Many Chinese families have continued to use the surnames their ancestors assumed when they immigrated.

The Chinese Exclusion Act of 1882 and the Geary Act of 1892 prohibited Chinese immigration into the United States. California's own Anti-Miscegenation Law of 1906 prevented Chinese and white couples from marrying. These laws to prevent growth in the number of Chinese people in the United States created the conditions that made the paper son arrangements attractive.

Joan Hope

FURTHER READING

Chin, Tung Pok. *Paper Son: One Man's Story.* Philadelphia: Temple University Press, 2000.
Wong, Wayne Hung. *American Paper Son: A Chinese Immigrant in the Midwest.* Champaign: University of Illinois Press, 2006.

SEE ALSO: Angel Island Immigration Station; Asian immigrants; California; Chinatowns; Chinese Exclusion Act of 1882; Chinese immigrants; Families; Geary Act of 1892; San Francisco.

PARACHUTE CHILDREN

DEFINITION: Children sent to the United States by their families to attend American schools while living on their own

SIGNIFICANCE: As children in the United States on student visas, parachute children experience immigration pressures and challenges similar to those of other child immigrants. They must adapt to a new land and learn how to cope in a different educational environment. In addition, however, they are also expected to survive, succeed, and seek educational opportunity in the United States while their parents are overseas.

During the last decades of the twentieth century, many affluent families in Asian nations such as the Philippines, India, Korea, Hong Kong, South Korea, Singapore, Vietnam, and especially Taiwan began sending their children to the United States to attend schools and live essentially on their own. The states to which these children have been most frequently sent are New York, Texas, Washington, and particularly California. Children as young as eight years old have been sent to the United States to live without parental supervision. In some cases, relatives or friends of the families have served as the children's legal guardians. In other cases, boarding arrangements have been made with strangers, and in still other cases, older teenage children have been sent to live alone.

Parents who have sent their children to the United States have continued to support them financially but have not been physically present in their children's daily lives. Parents send children to be educated in the United States and other countries for a variety of reasons. Many hope that access to foreign educational opportunities will provide greater future economic opportunities for the children and their families than they would have if the children were educated in their own countries. Developing English skills and improving the children's chances of gaining American college educations are often considered to be great advantages.

In some cases, parents wish to help their children avoid rigorous educational entrance assessments or stringent military requirements in their homelands. Other parents believe that having their children overseas may improve their own chances of being accepted as immigrants in those countries. Parents who choose to have their children educated in the United States, while they themselves remain in their own countries typically believe that raising transnational families is in the best interests of their children's futures.

Hard statistical data on so-called parachute children are scarce, but it is generally believed that most of these children sent to the United States are well supported financially. Because they are not directly supervised by their parents, many enjoy freedoms that go beyond what is typical for American children of the same ages. However, they also bear everyday responsibilities that their American counterparts rarely have. Typically lonely and homesick, parachute children generally focus their energies on their schoolwork and do well academically. However, their very independence also leaves them vulnerable. Many have been victims of crime, and some have been kidnapped.

In response to the growing numbers of young foreign students studying in public schools in the United States, federal immigration law was changed in 1996. The Illegal Immigration Reform and Immigrant Responsibility Act forbade international students from enrolling in public elementary and middle schools unless the schools were compensated for their educational costs. The law also limited attendance of foreign students in public high schools to one year. However, because the law has not been strictly enforced and does not apply to private schools, parachute children have continued to come to the United States.

Downturns in the American economy have affected parachute children much more than the legal changes. Many parachute children have faced financial hardships as their funding sources have been reduced, and some have returned to their homelands.

Cynthia J. W. Svoboda

FURTHER READING

Lee, Jennifer, and Min Zhou, eds. *Asian American Youth: Culture, Identity and Ethnicity.* New York: Routledge, 2004.

Suarez-Orozco, Carol, Jennifer E. Lansford, Kirby Deater-Deckard, and Marc H. Bornstein, eds. *Immigrant Families in Contemporary Society.* New York: Guilford Press, 2007.

Zhou, Min. "Parachute Kids in Southern California: The Educational Experience of Chinese Children in Transitional Families." *Educational Policy* 12, no. 6 (1998): 682-704.

SEE ALSO: California; Child immigrants; Chinese immigrants; Education; Families; Filipino immigrants; Foreign exchange students; Hong Kong immigrants; Japanese immigrants; Korean immigrants; Taiwanese immigrants.

PASSENGER CASES

THE CASE: U.S. Supreme Court decision concerning state taxation on arriving immigrants
DATE: Decided on February 7, 1849
ALSO KNOWN AS: *Norris v. Boston; Smith v. Turner*

SIGNIFICANCE: Although the case's theoretical foundations were notoriously unclear, in the *Passenger Cases* the Supreme Court held that the individual states did not have the authority to tax immigrants entering the country, nor did they have the right to regulate commerce with foreign nations.

Massachusetts and New York enacted legislation that charged ships' captains with a fee on every incoming passenger, including immigrants and foreign visitors. When the issue reached the Supreme Court, the justices voted 5-4 to strike down the laws, thereby overruling the precedent of *New York v. Miln* (1837). Among the eight separate and confusing opinions, at least three justices based their decision on the commerce clause of the U.S. Constitution, which authorized Congress and not the states to regulate commerce with foreign nations. The two other justices in the majority appeared to base their decisions on other grounds. The four justices in the minority wanted to continue the *Miln* precedent, which had held that such fees were a legitimate application of the states' police power. In subsequent rulings, particularly *Henderson v. Mayor of the City of New York* (1875), a firm majority of the Court would unambiguously rule that the commerce clause prohibited the states from imposing head taxes or bonds on passengers from other countries.

Thomas Tandy Lewis

FURTHER READING

Chuman, Frank. *The Bamboo People: The Law and Japanese Americans.* Del Mar, Calif.: Publisher's Inc., 1976.

Itō, Kazuo. *Issei: A History of Japanese Immigrants in North America.* Seattle: Japanese Community Service, 1973.

SEE ALSO: Capitation taxes; Congress, U.S.; Constitution, U.S.; Due process protections; *Head Money Cases; Henderson v. Mayor of the City of New York*; History of immigration, 1783-1891; Supreme Court, U.S.

PASSPORTS

DEFINITION: Government-issued identification documents carried by international travelers that verify their bearers' nationalities and identities

SIGNIFICANCE: Through much of human history, passports were special documents that were issued by important people to allow merchants and diplomats to move about. Over time, the issuing of passports became a government tool for limiting the ability of citizens to leave their own countries. As pleasure travel increased during the nineteenth century, passports were devised to allow masses of people to move more easily among countries.

Derived from the French words *passer*, meaning "to pass," and *port*, for "port," passports are documents that date back to at least 1500 B.C.E., when ancient Egyptian commoners were required to register themselves with the government. By the time of the Middle Ages, European countries were issuing passports to their citizens to permit them to travel within the countries. At night, gated towns would typically only allow entry to travelers carrying documents attesting to their peaceful intentions. These documents also protected the travelers themselves from harm by conveying discreet threats of reprisals should anything happen to their bearers. Passports of that era were handwritten documents issued by powerful members of the nobility whose names carried weight. After that time, passports continued to be uncommon and privately issued documents until the nineteenth century.

PASSPORTS IN THE UNITED STATES

The first U.S. passports were issued to American travelers in Paris and London during the 1780's. Those one-page documents provided descriptions of their holders and stated the duration of the documents' validity, which was usually three or six months. American travelers could also obtain passports for foreign travel from the cities and states in which they were residents. Foreigners planning to visit the United States during the nineteenth century had various ways of obtaining passports. Some governments refused to allow male citizens of mili-

tary age and those with valuable skills to leave their countries. However, almost any person could walk into a French or Belgian consulate and obtain a passport for travel, as French or Belgian citizenship was not required. This system ended in 1858 when an Italian who fraudulently obtained a French passport by claiming to be British attempted to assassinate the emperor of France. After that date, no nation would issue a passport identifying its holder as a national of another country. This change began the gradual process of formalizing the issuing of passports.

Meanwhile, until 1856, many U.S. cities continued to issue passports to their own citizens who wished to travel abroad. By this time, the U.S. Department of State had become concerned about this practice. Because of the slackness with which passports were being issued, European nations often refused to recognize them unless they were endorsed by local consular officials. In 1856, the U.S. Congress gave the Department of State sole authority to issue passports. Government officials who issued American passports to noncitizens could be fined or fired.

Around that same time, Asian governments had little interest in encouraging their citizens to travel overseas. In systems designed to control commoners for the economic benefit of the ruling class, both China and Japan required would-be travelers to obtain permission from their local lords to move. During the late nineteenth century, as China and Japan began issuing passports, they required travelers to enter their intended plans on the documents.

The British government took a casual attitude toward passports during the nineteenth century. Whereas the passports of most countries required descriptions of their bearers, British passports bore no descriptions at all until the early twentieth century, when they began listing their bearers' ages and occupations. The British attitude was that British subjects should be able to freely travel everywhere. The attitude of the U.S. government toward passports through the nineteenth century was similar. One State Department official even publicly declared that the U.S. government did not impose any law or regulation upon those entering its territory.

NATIONAL SECURITY CONCERNS

The onset of World War I in 1917 forced nations to pay closer attention to who was crossing their

(continued on page 830)

U.S. VISA CATEGORIES

Family-based immigrant visas (all immigrant visa categories except the immediate relative category are subject to numerical restrictions) Visas for immediate relatives: spouses, children, and parents of U.S. citizens

- First preference: unmarried sons and daughters of U.S. citizens

- Second preference: spouses and the unmarried sons and daughters (including children) of permanent resident aliens

- Third preference: married sons and daughters of U.S. citizens

- Fourth preference: brothers and sisters of U.S. citizens

Employment-based immigrant visas

- First preference: "priority workers," which includes aliens of extraordinary ability, outstanding professors and researchers, and certain multinational executives and managers

- Second preference: aliens who are members of the professions holding advanced degrees and aliens of exceptional ability

- Third preference: skilled workers, professionals, and other workers

- Fourth preference: diverse group of "special immigrants," including certain religious ministers, retired U.S. employees, and former U.S. military personnel

- Fifth preference: aliens who come to the United States to create employment opportunities by investing and engaging in a new commercial enterprise

Visas for diversity immigrants (aliens who win a lottery weighted in favor of aliens from countries and regions that have a low immigrant stream to the United States)

Nonimmigrant visas (nonimmigrant visas are designated by the letter of the alphabet preceding the description; for example, an F Visa is a study visa)

- A. Ambassadors, public ministers, other foreign government officials, their spouses, children, and servants

- B. Temporary visitors for business or pleasure

- C. Aliens in transit

- D. Alien crew members

- E. Treaty traders, treaty investors, and their spouses and children

- F. Students attending an academic institution, and their spouses and children

- G. Representatives of foreign governments to international organizations, officers and employees of international organizations, and the spouses, children, and servants of such persons

- H. Temporary workers, including registered nurses, workers in "speciality occupations," agricultural workers, other workers, and the spouses, children, and servants of such persons

- I. Foreign media representatives, and their spouses and children

- J. Exchange visitors, including those participating in academic exchanges, and their spouses and children

- K. Fiancés of U.S. citizens

- L. Certain intracompany transferees, and their spouses and children

- M. Vocational students, and their spouses and children

- N. Officials of the North Atlantic Treaty Organization (NATO), and their spouses and children

- O. Aliens of extraordinary ability in certain fields, their spouses and children, and certain assistants

- P. Certain artists and entertainers, and their spouses and children

- Q. Aliens participating in certain international cultural exchanges

- R. Religious workers, and their spouses and children

- S. Certain aliens who, according to the attorney general or the secretary of state, possess critical reliable information concerning criminal or terrorist organizations and the spouses, unmarried sons and daughters (including children), and parents of such persons borders. After Great Britain executed a German spy who had used a British passport while engaged in wartime espionage in 1914, U.S. secretary of state William Jennings Bryan ordered that all American passports bear photographs of their bearers. Officials suggested that travelers pose for their passport photographs in regular street clothes, instead of the formal wear often worn while posing for studio photographers, and that hats should not be worn unless they were part of daily religious attire.

In 1918, Congress passed legislation requiring that Americans traveling abroad carry passports and that foreign nationals seeking to enter the United States obtain visas. In 1926, the federal government established a standard design for passports: a stiff, dark red cover enclosing a booklet. That design became the worldwide standard. Color photographs were first used in passports in 1958.

As the reality of war had forced the United States to require passports, the reality of terrorism forced the country to pay more attention to worldwide passport security. After the terrorist attacks on the United States of September 11, 2001, the federal government's 9/11 Commission identified flaws in U.S. immigration law that had allowed terrorists to enter the United States. In response, the National Counterterrorism Center developed a strategy to make it harder for terrorists to enter, exit, and travel within the United States. A major part of this strategy has been a tightening of procedures used for issuing and inspecting passports.

The Bureau of Diplomatic Security has implemented the post-9/11 strategy by analyzing the methods of travel used by terrorists, assisting foreign countries in maintaining passport security, and inspecting passport applications. In 2006, the bureau broke up a ring of vendors that had provided fraudulent Indonesian passports to the terrorist group called Jamal Islamyia. Those passports could have been used to enter the United States.

Caryn E. Neumann

FURTHER READING

Bauman, Robert E. *The Complete Guide to Offshore Residency, Dual Citizenship and Second Passports.* New York: Sovereign Society, 2000. Discussion of procedures for obtaining dual citizenship and second passports, written by a former U.S. congressman.

Caplan, Jane, and John Torpey, eds. *Documenting Individual Identity: The Development of State Practices in the Modern World.* Princeton, N.J.: Princeton University Press, 2001. Collection of scholarly essays on issues relating to government-created identification documents, including passports.

Lloyd, Martin. *The Passport: The History of Man's Most Travelled Document.* Phoenix Mill, England: Sutton, 2003. Comprehensive history of the evolution of government-issued travel documents.

Torpey, John. *The Invention of the Passport: Surveillance, Citizenship, and the State.* New York: Cambridge University Press, 2000. Study of how passports have been used by governments to monitor the travels and activities of both aliens and their own citizens.

U.S. Department of State Bureau of Diplomatic Security. *Visa and Passport Security Strategic Plan.* Washington, D.C.: U.S. Department of State, 2006. Government pamphlet outlining the federal government's strategy for tightening passport security.

SEE ALSO: Citizenship; Citizenship and Immigration Services, U.S.; Green cards; 9/11 and U.S. immigration policy; Transit aliens.

PATRIOT ACT OF 2001

THE LAW: Federal legislation designed to increase U.S. security against terrorist threats

DATE: Signed into law on October 26, 2001

ALSO KNOWN AS: Uniting and Strengthening America by Providing Appropriate Tools Required to Intercept and Obstruct Terrorism Act (USA PATRIOT Act)

SIGNIFICANCE: Passed in the wake of the September 11, 2001, attacks on New York City and Washington, D.C., the Patriot Act significantly expanded the ability of U.S. Citizenship and Immigration Services (USCIS) to investigate immigrants with terrorist ties by giving the USCIS greater access to intelligence information regarding terrorist suspects. The act also made it more difficult for non-U.S. citizens to gain citizenship, visas, permanent residency, and work permits.

Prior to the passage of the Patriot Act, the Illegal Immigration Reform and Immigrant Responsibility Act of 1996 was meant to provide accurate information, through an integrated database, regarding the entry and exit information on immigrants. Most of the terrorist acts that occurred on U.S. soil during the 1990's were the result of domestic terrorists or migrants targeting other migrant groups. There were some exceptions, particularly the 1993 World Trade Center bombing and the Islamic terrorist, Ahmed Ressam, who on a false passport, entered the United States from Canada in 1999 with bomb-making materials. Nevertheless, immigration was not considered to be a terrorism issue but a social issue because of the large number of immigrants who entered across the U.S.-Mexico border. Most legislation and immigration control efforts centered on regulating the flow of migrants coming across that border.

IMPACT OF SEPTEMBER 11, 2001

The September 11 terrorist attacks on New York City's World Trade Center and Pentagon building outside Washington, D.C., provoked the U.S. government to reflect on immigration and border security. Mexico and Canada were now viewed as potential sources of terrorist infiltration. Mexico was considered to be incapable of effectively policing its own borders; Canada was viewed as having too lax an immigration policy, enabling terrorists to gain access to the United States by using Canada as an entry point. The U.S. government quickly moved to enact legislation to provide greater security against terrorist threats. With little debate, the House of Representatives and Senate overwhelmingly passed the Patriot Act, and President George W. Bush signed the act into law on October 26, 2001. The act provided a comprehensive restructuring of the capabilities of various federal agencies to combat the threat posed by terrorism to the United States. These reforms included intelligence sharing, expanded powers of surveillance, and tighter border control.

The Patriot Act greatly expanded the ability of border control and immigration agencies to determine who entered the United States and allowed these agencies to locate immigrants with terrorist ties who were already within the United States. The act amended the Immigration and Nationality Act to provide the U.S. Citizenship and Immigration

Services (USCIS) access to the Federal Bureau of Investigation's criminal file databases, allowing the USCIS to run criminal background investigations on any foreign nationals applying for entry into the United States. The USCIS is authorized to refuse admission to any immediate relatives of immigrants with ties to terrorism within the last five years. Any relative found to have an association with terrorist groups or intentions of committing terrorist attacks will be refused entry into the United States. Foreign students in the United States are tracked by a database that records their ports of entry and schools. Additionally, the attorney general must grant approval to foreign students wishing to attend vocational schools, language training schools, or flight schools.

The Patriot Act provided monetary support to triple the number of security personnel on the U.S.-Canada border (since most of the border security was previously centered on the border with Mexico). The act called for investigation of the feasibility of enacting an automated fingerprint identification system to be used at posts abroad and in ports of entry to the United States. Also, any immigrant who was suspected of being a terrorist could be detained for up to six months if the release of the suspect could pose a threat to U.S. national security. The act also called for expediting the integrated entry and exit data system in the Illegal Immigration Reform and Immigrant Responsibility Act by using biometric technology and tamper-resistant documents. In addition, the act provided humanitarian aid to alien spouses and children of deceased U.S. citizens.

The Patriot Act is one of the most controversial U.S. laws in recent history. Some of its provisions have been challenged for their constitutionality. Certain programs, such as biometric identification, have been met with significant resistance from civil rights groups and members of Congress. Many civil rights organizations are critical of Congress's supposed failure to fully debate and explore all the nuances of the Patriot Act before approving it.

Michael W. Cheek

FURTHER READING

Baker, Stewart A., and John Kavanagh, eds. *Patriot Debates: Experts Debate the USA Patriot Act.* Chicago: American Bar Association, 2005. Series of scholarly essays largely relating to provisions of the Patriot Act set to expire in 2005. Includes essays on border security and detention.

Etzioni, Amitai. *How Patriotic Is the Patriot Act? Freedom Versus Security in the Age of Terrorism.* New York: Routledge, 2004. Provides an overview of the security measures of the Patriot Act and contains information surrounding the debate on tracking immigrants.

Ewing, Alphonse B. *The USA Patriot Act.* New York: Novinka Books, 2002. Contains a legal analysis of the Patriot Act as well as an accessible overview of the act.

Foerstel, Herbert N. *The Patriot Act: A Documentary and Reference Guide.* Westport, Conn.: Greenwood Press, 2008. Primary source collection with analysis following each document.

LeMay, Michael C. *Illegal Immigration: A Reference Handbook.* Santa Barbara, Calif.: ABC-CLIO, 2007. Accessible overview of the debates surrounding illegal immigration.

Wong, Kam C. *The Impact of USA Patriot Act on American Society: An Evidence Based Assessment.* New York: Nova Science, 2007. Discussion of the effects of the Patriot Act on immigrant students, universities, and American society.

SEE ALSO: Aviation and Transportation Security Act of 2001; Border fence; Border Patrol, U.S.; Citizenship and Immigration Services, U.S.; Homeland Security, Department of; Immigration law; Muslim immigrants; 9/11 and U.S. immigration policy; Permanent resident status.

PEI, I. M.

IDENTIFICATION: Chinese-born architect
BORN: April 26, 1917; Canton (now Guangzhou), China

SIGNIFICANCE: One of the last great masters of architecture in the high modernist style, Pei is known for his work in stone, concrete, and glass, including the National Center for Atmospheric Research in Boulder, Colorado; the expansion of the Louvre in Paris; the Rock and Roll Hall of Fame in Cleveland, Ohio; and the Museum of Islamic Art in Qatar.

Architect I. M. Pei standing outside a building he designed on the campus of the Massachusetts Institute of Technology in 1983. (AP/Wide World Photos)

Ieoh Ming Pei was born in China in 1917. His family was wealthy, and the home where Pei grew up is in a garden listed as a World Heritage Site. At the age of seventeen, he immigrated to the United States to study architecture. After he graduated from the Massachusetts Institute of Technology (MIT), the outbreak of World War II prevented him from returning to China, so he remained in the United States to work and to earn a master's degree from Harvard. He became a U.S. citizen in 1954.

Pei founded his own firm in 1955 and became known for his creative melding of Eastern and Western ideas of architecture. He has created prize-winning buildings throughout the developed world. His major works in China combine elements of traditional garden architecture with new materials and technology. In 1983, Pei was awarded the prominent Pritzker Architecture Prize. With the

$100,000 prize money, he established a scholarship fund for Chinese students to study architecture in the United States and then return home to work.

Cynthia A. Bily

FURTHER READING

Jodidio, Philip, and Janet Adams Strong. *I. M. Pei: Complete Works.* New York: Rizzoli, 2008.

Von Boehm, Gero. *Conversations with I. M. Pei: Light Is the Key.* New York: Prestel, 2000.

Wiseman, Carter. *I. M. Pei: A Profile in American Architecture.* Rev. ed. New York: Harry N. Abrams, 2001.

SEE ALSO: Art; Asian immigrants; Chinese immigrants; Citizenship; Education; Naturalization.

PENNSYLVANIA

SIGNIFICANCE: To an extent greater than in most other states, Pennsylvania's tradition of immigration in colonial times continued to influence its development for a long period thereafter. During the nineteenth century, the state's iron and steel and coal industries attracted large numbers of immigrants from Europe. The twentieth century saw a slowing of immigration, and at the turn of the twenty-first century, the percentage of the state's residents who were foreign born was much less than one-half the national average.

Founded by William Penn during the late seventeenth century, as a haven for religious freedom and economic self-betterment, Pennsylvania continued to attract immigrants with similar views into the nineteenth century. In 1803, for example, the pietist George Rapp established in Pennsylvania the Harmony Society, whose ideals resembled those of the earlier New England Puritans. These people's mode of living was essentially farm life. Another group, the Sylvania Society, practiced the regimen prescribed by the utopian Fourierist movement. German Amish and Mennonite settlers also entered Pennsylvania during the early nineteenth century. Not all these religious communi-

Fanciful late nineteenth century depiction of William Penn negotiating a land purchase with local Native American leaders. (Gay Brothers)

PROFILE OF PENNSYLVANIA

Region	Northeast
Entered union	1787
Largest cities	Philadelphia, Pittsburgh, Allentown, Erie, Reading
Modern immigrant communities	Asian Indians, Vietnamese, Russians

Population	Total	Percent of state	Percent of U.S.	U.S. rank
All state residents	12,441,000	100.0	4.16	6
All foreign-born residents	637,000	5.1	1.70	13

Source: U.S. Census Bureau, *Statistical Abstract for 2006.*
Notes: The U.S. population in 2006 was 299,399,000, of whom 37,548,000 (12.5%) were foreign born. Rankings in last column reflect total numbers, not percentages.

ties remained in the state, but those who did continued to keep their cultures alive for remarkably long periods. Many of the Amish who began entering the state around 1817 sought the advice of earlier settlers, thereby retaining the wisdom of their sect's past. The Amish have continued to live by their traditional standards into the twenty-first century.

In contrast to the Amish, most of Pennsylvania's many other German immigrants entered the mainstream of society, as did the state's Irish immigrants. As coal fields were developed, Pennsylvania offered many jobs to immigrants, though often of a very difficult kind. Irish immigrants tended to gravitate to the Scranton area to labor in anthracite mines. Other settlers moved to the western part of the state. As early as 1800, boat-building was an important industry where the Allegheny and Monongahela Rivers joined in Pittsburgh to form the Ohio River. As a tributary of the Mississippi, the Ohio River provided a major route for shipping goods to the outside world.

IMMIGRATION, 1830-1914

Immigration to Pennsylvania centered on the industrial area in the western part of the state, the anthracite region in the northeast, and the great city of Philadelphia in the southeast. As steel manufacturing became a major industry in Pittsburgh, Poles, Croatians, Serbians, Slovaks, and other eastern European immigrants found work in the city's mills and the region's bituminous coal mines. By the 1870's, Pittsburgh was producing 40 percent of the nation's iron output and about 50 percent its glass. As the state's bituminous coal industry expanded in the counties of Allegheny, Fayette, and Westmoreland, Polish and Slovak immigrants played increasingly important roles in its labor force. Until after World War II, most of them lived in ethnic enclaves and associated in their ethnic churches and fraternal societies. Eventually, Pennsylvania would be home to the fourth-largest Polish population in the United States.

Irish immigrants who were driven from their homeland by the potato famine of the late 1840's found work in Pennsylvania as laborers and farmers, as in other states. However, many of them worked in the state's anthracite coal mines at jobs that were extremely dangerous and for which no provisions were made for the health and safety of miners. In a long struggle to build effective trade unions, they retaliated against owners by creating a secret society known as the Molly Maguires that conducted a campaign of violence until it was broken up in 1875 by an Irish Pinkerton detective who infiltrated the organization. Other immigrant groups whose members worked in the coal mines included Slavs, Hungarians, and Poles. After 1880, they were joined by Russians. Meanwhile, about 200,000 Italians immigrated to Pennsylvania between 1880 and 1914. Many of them worked in the textile industry, construction trades, and railroad line maintenance.

POST WORLD WAR II IMMIGRATION

Between the two great world wars of the twentieth century, immigration into Pennsylvania declined sharply. After World War II, and especially during the last decades of the century and the first decade of the next, the pattern of immigration into the state differed considerably from that of the rest of the United States. The 2000 U.S. Census found that only 5.1 percent of Pennsylvania residents were foreign born—much less than one-half the national average of 12.5 percent. Likewise, the percentage of state residents of Asian ancestry was only a little more than one-half the national average, and the portion of Hispanic residents was only 4.5 percent—less than one-third the national average of 15.7 percent. Immigrants from the former Soviet Union, India, and Vietnam were the most numerous among the state's foreign born.

Robert P. Ellis

FURTHER READING

Bartoletti, Susan Campbell. *Growing Up in Coal Country.* Boston: Houghton Mifflin, 1996. Social history of Pennsylvania's coal industry from the late nineteenth through the early twentieth centuries. Discusses the role of immigrants in the social structure of coal camps and in early labor movements.

Bell, Thomas. *Out of This Furnace: A Novel of Immigrant Labor.* Pittsburgh: University of Pittsburgh Press, 1976. Originally published in 1941, this historical novel is set in the steel mills and communities of Braddock, Pennsylvania, drawing on three generations of the author's own Slovak family history.

Miller, Randall M., and William Pencak. *Pennsylvania: A History of the Commonwealth.* University Park: Pennsylvania State University Press, 2002. Authoritative general history of the state.

Nolt, Steven M., and Thomas J. Meyers. *Plain Diversity: Amish Cultures and Identities.* Baltimore: Johns Hopkins University Press, 2007. Scholarly study of the unique culture and traditions of the Amish, who settled primarily in Pennsylvania.

Parsons, William T. *The Pennsylvania Dutch: A Persistent Minority.* Boston: Twayne, 1976. Survey of the history of German immigrants in Pennsylvania.

Salinger, Sharon V. *"To Serve Well and Faithfully": Labor and Indentured Servants in Pennsylvania, 1682-1800.* Cambridge, England: Cambridge University Press, 1987. Study of labor through Pennsylvania's colonial era, with special attention to the indentured servant system through which many immigrants came to America.

SEE ALSO: Canals; Coal industry; German immigrants; Irish immigrants; Iron and steel industry; Philadelphia; Philadelphia anti-Irish riots; Polish immigrants; Religions of immigrants; Vietnamese immigrants.

PERMANENT RESIDENT STATUS

DEFINITION: Immigration status permitting foreign nationals to live and work indefinitely in the United States

SIGNIFICANCE: Permanent residence can be either a stepping-stone toward full American citizenship or a status in its own right, suiting the needs of long-term workers and retirees who wish to live indefinitely in the United States but do not want to give up their own citizenship. The status gives foreigners the freedom to work and reside in the United States without forgoing the possibility of eventually returning to their own countries.

Permanent residence, or legal permanent residence (LPR), enables foreign nationals to live and work in the United States for periods of up to ten years and is renewable. Requirements for permanent residency are similar to those for citizenship, and the application process is also similar. Permanent resident status is granted by the U.S. Citizenship and Immigration Services (USCIS; formerly the Immigration and Naturalization Service, INS).

CRITERIA FOR LEGAL PERMANENT RESIDENT STATUS

In 2009, there were five basic ways in which an immigrant could qualify for legal permanent resident status in the United States:

- Obtaining sponsorship from immediate family members who are themselves already American citizens or legal permanent residents (such sponsors may be subjected to financial checks, but cosponsors may be invoked to provide better financial security)

- Accepting a job with an American employer who vouches that no American citizen is available for the position, or accepting a job because of exceptional ability

- Bringing at least one million dollars into the country to start a business that will employ at least ten Americans

- Having success in the diversity lottery

- Being a refugee or asylum seeker

Between the first steps to immigration and the granting of full citizenship and the completion of naturalization, lies a considerable gap, both in the procedures through which applicants must go and in the waiting times required. Waiting periods to become a citizen of the United States have historically ranged from two to seven years. The application procedures are designed to ascertain whether applicants for entry are bona fide, healthy, without criminal records, and with the means to support themselves. Documentation to cover the waiting periods is necessary; the main instrument in modern policy to provide such documentation is legal permanent residence (LPR) or permanent resident status. In the past, this status has gone under a variety of names, from "green card holders" to "resident aliens."

TWENTY-FIRST CENTURY PRACTICES

During the early twenty-first century, the most important differences between permanent resident status and naturalized citizenship were that citizens, unlike permanent residents, could vote, serve on juries, be elected to public office, and hold certain government jobs. Citizens also could not be deported, unless they were proven to have obtained their citizenship fraudulently. The differences between these two statuses have sometimes been subjects of political debate: If the differences are considered to be small, citizenship may be devalued. On the other hand, if the differences are considered too great, then legal questions might be raised about undue discrimination.

LPR status is awarded to immigrants after a complicated procedure similar to that for naturalization. Because the procedure can be costly, many applicants find it best to obtain legal representation. The gaining of LPR status may be begun either through an American embassy abroad, or by adjusting the status of immigrants already in the United States on other kinds of visas. Leaving the country during the application period needs advanced parole documentation. Temporary work permits are available. Temporary status, valid for two years only, is given to those married to American spouses to guard against marriages of convenience.

After five years of continuous residence, legal permanent residents can apply for citizenship. Applicants whose sponsors are spouses have only three-year waiting periods. Those who are in the country on refugee status have only four-year waiting periods. LPR status can be forfeited by residents who remain outside the United States for more than a year without having sought prior permission or who fail to file federal income tax returns. Repeated absences of six months or more may also jeopardize the status. There are set procedures for renouncing LPR status through foreign embassies.

A significant number of LPRs choose not to seek naturalization for any of many possible reasons. For example, some have sentimental attachments to their birth countries. Others have long-term plans to return to their homelands. Many countries recognize dual citizenship, but the United States discourages it. The U.S. naturalization process asks applicants to renounce their previous allegiances, and some are unwilling to swear this.

David Barratt

FURTHER READING

Gania, Edwin T. *U.S. Immigration Step by Step.* 3d ed. Naperville, Ill.: Sphinx, 2006.

Motomura, Hiroshi. *Americans in Waiting: The Lost Story of Immigration and Citizenship.* New York: Oxford University Press, 2006.

Schuck, Peter. *Citizens, Strangers, and In-Betweens: Essays on Immigration and Citizenship.* Boulder, Colo.: Westview Press, 1998.

Waters, Mary C., and Reed Ueda, eds. *The New Americans: A Guide to Immigration Since 1965.* Cambridge, Mass.: Harvard University Press, 2007.

SEE ALSO: Citizenship; Citizenship and Immigration Services, U.S.; Dual citizenship; Green cards; Guest-worker programs; "Immigrant"; "Marriages of convenience"; Naturalization; Resident aliens.

PHILADELPHIA

IDENTIFICATION: Largest city in Pennsylvania and a national political and commercial center since the colonial era

SIGNIFICANCE: Since Philadelphia's founding as one of the first major American cities, immigrants from all over the world have flocked to it. Dutch, Swedes, and English were the first settlers in the area, but modern immigration into the city has been dominated by Asians and Hispanics. By 2006, the greater Philadelphia area was home to more than one-half million foreign-born residents—a figure that was growing at a rate of about 20,000 people a year.

The earliest European settlers in the Delaware River valley arrived during the early seventeenth century. Swedes were the first to inhabit the area, but during the mid-1650's the Dutch effectively took control of the area. Their reign over the area was short-lived, however, as the British soon came and occupied the entire region during the 1660's. Charles II, the king of England at the time, handed over control of the area to William Penn, who named the site of the future city "Philadelphia," from Greek *philos* for "love" and *adelphos* for "brothers"—hence, the city's future nickname of the "City of Brotherly Love."

NINETEENTH CENTURY TRENDS

By the time of the late eighteenth century American Revolution, Philadelphia was one of the most important cities in the British North American colonies. Its prime location as a port city helped it emerge as a hub of the growing country and no doubt helped attract more settlers. The fact that the Declaration of Independence and the U.S. Constitution were both written in Philadelphia cemented the city's reputation as a major metropolitan area.

The first great wave of immigration to Philadelphia occurred during the second half of the nineteenth century, when Italian and Irish immigrants began pouting into the city. The cultural impact of immigrants can be seen in the northwest and south areas of the city. Many of the Irish who came to the United States were fleeing the Great Irish Famine that followed a blight that ruined Ireland's vital potato crop. Many of the Irish who arrived in Philadelphia were farmers and laborers. The Italian immigrants also tended to be farmers and laborers. The Italian immigrant presence can still be seen in the Farmer's Market in the south part of Philadelphia.

TWENTIETH CENTURY DEVELOPMENTS

During the late twentieth century, the composition of Philadelphia's population underwent a shift, as many long-established white families moved from the central city to the outlying suburbs of Greater Philadelphia. As they moved out, many foreign immigrants, especially Asians and Hispanics, moved in. Asian immigrants created an ethnic enclave in central Philadelphia that became known as "Chinatown," although it is actually a multiethnic community, with many Vietnamese, Koreans, Japanese, and Filipinos.

The impact of Hispanic immigration is most evident in the Fairhill district of Philadelphia, an area that has been nicknamed El Centro del Oro (the golden center). By the early twenty-first century, Puerto Ricans constituted nearly 76 percent of the city's Hispanic residents. Since the 1990's, the city has also seen an influx of Mexican, El Salvadoran, Cuban, Brazilian, and Guatemalan immigrants.

TWENTY-FIRST CENTURY TRENDS

In 2005, the U.S. Census Bureau reported that the Greater Philadelphia Metropolitan area was the fifth largest in the United States and had one of the largest and fastest-growing immigrant populations among major American cities. The city was home to the second-largest communities of Irish and Italian ancestry in the United States. In addition to increasing numbers of Asians and Hispanics, Philadelphia has also become home to many Greek, Pakistani, and African immigrants.

P. Huston Ladner

FURTHER READING

Avery, Ron. *A Concise History of Philadelphia*. Philadelphia: Otis Books, 1999.

Davis, Allen Freeman, and Mark H. Haller, eds. *The Peoples of Philadelphia: A History of Ethnic Groups and Lower-class Life, 1790-1940*. Philadelphia: Temple University Press, 1998.

Mauger, Edward Arthur. *Philadelphia Then and Now.* San Diego: Thunder Bay Press, 2002.

SEE ALSO: Asian immigrants; Chinatowns; Civil War, U.S.; Dutch immigrants; German immigrants; Irish immigrants; Italian immigrants; Little Italies; Melting pot theory; Pennsylvania; Philadelphia anti-Irish riots.

PHILADELPHIA ANTI-IRISH RIOTS

THE EVENTS: Violent reactions to the rising number of Roman Catholic Irish immigrants by American-born Protestants who felt their way of life threatened

DATE: May 6-8 and July 6-7, 1844

LOCATION: Philadelphia, Pennsylvania, and the neighboring communities of Kensington and Southwark

SIGNIFICANCE: This major outburst of tension over expanding Irish Catholic populations in northeastern urban cities triggered the national rise of the Native American Party, a growing movement for private Roman Catholic education, and consolidation of some urban government administrations.

As industrialization accelerated during the 1830's and 1840's, more and more Irish Catholics came to America. By the early 1840's, in those neighborhoods and urban areas where the immigrants were rapidly displacing American-born Protestants, anti-Catholic organizations began to develop, fueled by a growing anti-Catholic press.

In 1842, after Philadelphia's Catholic bishop asked to use the Catholic version of the Bible as an option during required school Bible reading, the school board compromised: Catholics could leave the room during Bible reading, but the Protestant King James Version would stay in schools. Within a year, rumors began to circulate that the Catholics had an organized plan to expunge the Bible from public schools. This fed into a continuing fear that the goal of the Roman Catholic immigrants was to bring American political institutions under the political control and authority of the pope in Rome.

On Monday, May 6, 1844, a nativist group called the American Republican Party held a rousing anti-Catholic rally in the heavily Irish Catholic neighborhood of Kensington. Rain forced the planned outdoor meeting into a market house next to a fire company made up of Irish immigrants, and as the rhetoric grew more forceful, shooting and fighting broke out between the opposing groups. During the battle, several area homes were attacked. The Irish eventually drove the nativists out of their neighborhood, but not before a young nativist, George Schiffler, was shot while holding aloft the American flag, which the nativists ardently employed as a symbol of their "America for Americans" ideal. He became a martyr to the anti-immigrant cause.

Title page of one of the Douay Bibles that were at the heart of Philadelphia's anti-Irish riots. The page features an illustration of New York City's first St. Patrick's Cathedral. (Library of Congress)

The next day, an angry mob carried that flag through Philadelphia, calling for retribution on behalf of Schiffler. That enlarged group later marched back to Kensington, attacked the Irish fire company house and the market used the day before, and proceeded to burn down a church, a rectory, and a Catholic school. Two other Catholic churches were also attacked but not destroyed. At least one hundred were wounded, and twenty died. The next Sunday, the bishop ordered all Philadelphia Catholics to stay away from church to avoid violence, and valuable church possessions were taken and hidden in congregants' homes. Tensions eased slightly.

However, when the Fourth of July came, the American Republican Party, by then known as the Native American Party (later known as the American Party, or Know-Nothings), demonstrated its growing political clout in Philadelphia. More than three thousand marched in a holiday parade to display their strength and spread their anti-immigrant beliefs. Alerted that some paraders planned an attack on a Catholic church in the neighborhood of Southwark, the governor allowed the placement of some weapons within the church for its possible defense. The next day, some Protestant locals discovered that an arsenal was in the church, and an angry mob gathered to demand its removal. Some weapons were removed, but the crowd was unsatisfied, and a confrontation developed between the state militia, brought in to protect the church, and the anti-immigrant mob. Two soldiers and at least twelve rioters were killed and twenty-six others were wounded.

Scot M. Guenter

FURTHER READING

Feldberg, Michael. *The Philadelphia Riots of 1844: A Study of Ethnic Conflict.* Westport, Conn.: Greenwood Press, 1975.

Lee, J. J., and Marion R. Casey. *Making the Irish American: History and Heritage of the Irish in the United States.* New York: New York University Press, 2006.

SEE ALSO: Anti-Catholicism; Education; History of immigration, 1783-1891; Irish immigrants; Know-Nothing Party; Nativism; Pennsylvania; Philadelphia; Religions of immigrants; Xenophobia.

PICTURE BRIDES

DEFINITION: Mostly young Japanese and Korean women who became the wives of immigrant laborers from their countries who had preceded them to Hawaii between 1885 and 1920

SIGNIFICANCE: The availability of picture brides made it possible for single Asian male immigrant workers to form families and to make permanent residence in their adopted country, most often Hawaii, but also on the West Coast of North America. After an abbreviated matchmaking process, the bride would be added to her future husband's family register, then sail to meet him, thus complying with the Gentlemen's Agreement of 1907 that allowed only Asians joining family members to immigrate to the United States and its territory of Hawaii.

Between 1848 and 1875, the sugar industry in Hawaii enjoyed meteoric success as a result of four developments: The gold rush created new markets for food products in California, the Great Mahele made private ownership of land possible, the U.S. Civil War boosted the price of sugar, and the Reciprocity Treaty of 1875 guaranteed Hawaii duty-free access to the American markets. The burgeoning sugar market required a vast supply of labor. Between 1875 and 1910, the plantation workforce in the Hawaiian Islands increased from 3,260 to 43,917. Most of these workers were single, male, illiterate Asian immigrants recruited by the sugar agencies and treated as commodities by the white American plantation owners. During the 1880's, "Hawaii Netsu" (emigration fever) swept the economically strained prefectures of southwestern Japan. By 1902, Japanese constituted 73.4 percent of the plantation workforce. Between 1903 and 1905, more than 7,000 Koreans—spurred by Japanese expansion and domination, poverty, and a desire for religious freedom—immigrated to Hawaii. By 1924, almost 200,000 Japanese had migrated to Hawaii (although many eventually returned to Japan and approximately 40,000 remigrated to the West Coast of the United States).

From 1885 to 1889, Asian immigrants were typically bound to three-year work contracts and lived in rudimentary bachelor housing on the plantation grounds, in a paternalistic, highly controlled environment. In 1900, the contract labor system was abolished. Plantation owners found married workers more dependable than bachelors and encouraged the picture bride system as an enticement for male workers to stay. After saving for a bride's trip from his meager wages—a process often taking decades—the laborer would elicit a matchmaker's aid in his home country to arrange a marriage through the exchange of photographs. Commonly, because the man had not been photographed since his original travel papers were issued, the image submitted often pictured a much younger man, a cause of dismay when young brides, many of whom were in their teens, first met their husbands. Segregated by ethnicity, a practice that the plantation management instituted to lessen the likelihood of unification among workers, but a system appealing to the laborers for the comfort of linguistic and cultural sameness, the couples spent ten hours a day in hard labor, working six days a week. Some women did field- or millwork, while others provided domestic needs for single men: washing laundry, housecleaning, sewing, cooking, and operating bathhouses. The families resulting from these unions would become the dominant community of working-class residents of Hawaii in later decades.

The peak period for picture brides in British Columbia, 1910-1920, was approximately twenty years after the surge of brides to Hawaii.

Carolyn Anderson

FURTHER READING

Makabe, Tomoko. *Picture Brides: Japanese Women in Canada.* North York, Ont.: Multicultural History Society of Canada, 1995.

Takaki, Ronald. *Pau Hana: Plantation Life and Labor in Hawaii, 1835-1920.* Honolulu: University of Hawaii Press, 1983.

SEE ALSO: Asian American literature; Asian immigrants; Chinese immigrants; Families; Filipino immigrants; Hawaii; Japanese immigrants; Korean immigrants; Mail-order brides; War brides; Women immigrants.

PILGRIM AND PURITAN IMMIGRANTS

SIGNIFICANCE: During the mid-seventeenth century, thousands of English Puritans escaping from religious persecution immigrated to North America, where they established a society whose ideals and principles would become central to the American concept of civil and religious freedom.

Although the Puritans fled from England during the seventeenth century, the seeds of their migration were sown years earlier with the advent of the Protestant Reformation led by sixteenth century theologians, including Martin Luther, John Calvin, and Ulrich Zwingli. In England, King Henry VIII defied the pope by divorcing his Roman Catholic wife and marrying Anne Boleyn. Henry's archbishop, Thomas Cranmer, continued to loosen Catholicism's hold by forbidding church music, allowing priests to marry, replacing the Latin mass with services in English, and encouraging everyone to read the Bible. These changes within the Anglican Church opened the door to Puritanism, which advanced the foundational doctrine of predestination—the belief that all people were inherently sinful, and the notion that the God is revealed through a personal encounter with the Scriptures and not through the agency of a priest.

ENGLISH ANTI-SEPARATIST SENTIMENT

During the reign of England's King James I (r. 1603-1625), the Separatists, an extreme sect within the Puritan community, wished to sever all ties with the Anglican Church and conduct their own services in accordance with what they claimed were biblical teachings. Their refusal to support the Church of England was illegal under the 1559 Act of Uniformity, which required English citizens to attend the state church. Regarding the Separatists as traitors, James pressured them to conform to the law.

In 1607, a group of Separatists from Scrooby, Nottinghamshire, left England to escape government persecution and eventually settled in Leiden, Holland. Although they enjoyed a prosperous life, they were concerned about the influence of Dutch culture upon their children. In order to preserve their English identity and religious freedom, they decided that they would sail for the New World. Various sites were discussed, including Guiana, Virginia, and the Hudson River area. With the financial support of London merchants and adventurers, they eventually secured a land patent in New England.

THE *MAYFLOWER* AND PLYMOUTH BAY

On September 16, 1620, 102 passengers made up of Leideners and Strangers, non-Puritan colonists who were hired by the investors, set sail from Plymouth, England, in the *Mayflower.* A difficult crossing was made more so by friction between the Leideners and the Strangers, who were wary about living in a community dominated by those they viewed as religious extremists. In order for the new settlement to succeed, both groups realized they would have to work together and abide by the same laws.

After dropping anchor in Provincetown Bay in November, 1620, forty-one male Separatists signed the Mayflower Compact. Exposed to the dangers of theocracy in England, as well as to advantages of a civil government in Holland, the Separatists were aware that formulating "just and equal laws, ordinances, acts, constitutions and offices" that were applicable to every citizen was necessary for the colony's survival. The Mayflower Compact, the forerunner of the Declaration of Independence and the U.S. Constitution, was the germ from which a democratic society based on the separation of church and state would blossom after the American Revolution.

Disembarking from the *Mayflower* on November 21, 1620, the Pilgrims settled in what is now Plymouth, Massachusetts. Their goal was to establish, in Governor William Bradford's words, "a city upon a hill," which they hoped would be a model Christian community founded on biblical principles. Their harsh life in Plymouth Bay gradually eroded the idealism of the colonists, and over the years families drifted to other areas of the region where they could make a better living. When Boston emerged as a major port and economic center, Plymouth diminished in importance and in population.

Pilgrims holding their first Sabbath service after landing at Plymouth, Massachusetts. (Gay Brothers)

THE GREAT MIGRATION

During the years the Pilgrims were struggling to make their Massachusetts a utopia, Puritans in England were increasingly harassed. After succeeding his father, James I, in 1625, King Charles I viewed the Puritans as a threat to his government because they controlled Parliament. In 1629, he dissolved Parliament in an attempt to weaken the Puritans' power, which left them open to further persecution. His actions launched the Great Migration, a mass exodus of English citizens to the Massachusetts Bay Colony. More than twenty thousand people crossed the Atlantic to settle in Massachusetts from 1630 to 1640. In 1640, however, Charles reconvened Parliament, and immigration dropped off sharply.

The Great Migration began with the sailing of the Winthrop Fleet, which comprised eleven ships carrying seven hundred passengers. Most of these immigrants were prosperous, middle class, and well educated. Their primary motivation for settling in the New World was their desire for religious freedom and not for material gain. They possessed a unique set of characteristics that contributed to their success as colonists: They traveled to America in family groups, were highly literate, enjoyed robust health, and were skilled workers who provided well for their typically large families. As the settlers expanded north and south of Boston, they took advantage of land distribution policies, allowing them to purchase large tracts of property that in many cases were kept in families for hundreds of years. The Puritan immigrants' secure family life, shared social and religious values, and stable land distribution system provided a firm foundation on which to build a society whose cultural mores would shape American history in succeeding generations.

Pegge Bochynski

FURTHER READING

Anderson, Virginia DeJohn. *New England's Generation: The Great Migration and the Formation of Society and Culture in the Seventeenth Century.* New York: Cambridge University Press, 1991. Focusing on 693 settlers who arrived in New England between 1635 and 1638, Anderson examines the reasons for the stability of New England society.

Bradford, William. *Of Plymouth Plantation.* 1630. Reprint. New York: Dover, 2006. This firsthand account written by the colony's second governor documents the Pilgrims' life in Holland, their *Mayflower* voyage, their first winter, and the aid they received from Native Americans.

Moore, Susan Hardman. *Pilgrims: New World Settlers and the Call of Home.* New Haven, Conn.: Yale University Press, 2007. Explores the reasons colonists set out from England during the 1630's, their experiences in the Massachusetts colony, and why some chose to return to England.

Philbrick, Nathaniel. *Mayflower: A Story of Courage, Community, and War.* New York: Viking Press, 2006. Examines fifty years of often tenuous relations between the Pilgrims and their Native

THE MAYFLOWER COMPACT

Upon their arrival in Plymouth, the Pilgrims signed the following contract, known as the Mayflower Compact. The compact both formed and declared the signatories' allegiance to the Plymouth Colony.

IN THE NAME OF GOD, AMEN. We, whose names are underwritten, the Loyal Subjects of our dread Sovereign Lord King *James*, by the Grace of God, of *Great Britain, France,* and *Ireland,* King, *Defender of the Faith,* &c. Having undertaken for the Glory of God, and Advancement of the Christian Faith, and the Honour of our King and Country, a Voyage to plant the first Colony in the northern Parts of *Virginia;* Do by these Presents, solemnly and mutually, in the Presence of God and one another, covenant and combine ourselves together into a civil Body Politick, for our better Ordering and Preservation, and Furtherance of the Ends aforesaid: And by Virtue hereof do enact, constitute, and frame, such just and equal Laws, Ordinances, Acts, Constitutions, and Officers, from time to time, as shall be thought most meet and convenient for the general Good of the Colony; unto which we promise all due Submission and Obedience. IN WITNESS whereof we have hereunto subscribed our names at *Cape-Cod* the eleventh of November, in the Reign of our Sovereign Lord King *James,* of *England, France,* and *Ireland,* the eighteenth, and of *Scotland* the fifty-fourth, *Anno Domini;* 1620.

Source: From the Yale Law School Avalon Project. http://www.yale.edu/lawweb/avalon/amerdoc/mayflower.htm. Accessed April 27, 2005.

American neighbors, and shows how the clash of cultures resulted in King Philip's War in 1675-1676.

SEE ALSO: Boston; British immigrants; History of immigration, 1620-1783; Indentured servitude; Massachusetts; Religion as a push-pull factor; Religions of immigrants; Return migration.

PINKERTON, ALLAN

IDENTIFICATION: Scottish-born founder of an American detective agency
BORN: August 25, 1819; Glasgow, Scotland
DIED: July 1, 1884; Chicago, Illinois

SIGNIFICANCE: The founder of one of America's best-known detective agencies, Pinkerton believed in the need to change unjust laws; his principles made him a militant force against slavery.

Allan Pinkerton left school at ten to become a cooper (barrelmaker). A militant Chartist, he advocated reforms such as universal manhood suffrage, then a radical idea in Great Britain. Fearing arrest for his activities, Pinkerton with his wife left for the United States in 1842, settling in Dundee, Illinois.

Pinkerton was successful as a cooper, and his antislavery activities aroused community hostility. His friends included former slave Frederick Douglass, and his home was a stop on the Underground Railroad for escaped slaves. Shortly after exposing the activities of a band of currency counterfeiters in 1846, Pinkerton moved to Chicago, where he became deputy county sheriff and special agent for the U.S. Post Office. In 1850, he formed the North-West Detective Agency (later renamed Pinkerton's National Detective Agency), establishing the first American national law-enforcement agency at a time when public officers honored local and state jurisdictional lines and did not cooperate. In 1856, he hired Kate Warne, the first American female detective. Pinkerton continued abolitionist activities. He thwarted a plot to kill President Abraham Lincoln, created the first American military intelligence unit, and personally spied behind enemy lines.

In 1869, Pinkerton suffered a debilitating stroke, never fully recovering. Because of his increasingly erratic activity and his involvement in the controversial Molly Maguire and Jesse James cases, his sons Robert and William controlled his agency. In his last years, Pinkerton turned to writing; his name appeared on eighteen books, mostly by ghostwriters.

Betty Richardson

FURTHER READING

Josephson, Judith Pinkerton. *Allan Pinkerton: The Original Private Eye.* Minneapolis, Minn.: Lerner, 1996.
Mackay, James. *Allan Pinkerton: The First Private Eye.* 1997. Edison, N.J.: Castle Books, 2007.

SEE ALSO: Abolitionist movement; British immigrants; Chicago; Civil War, U.S.; Molly Maguires.

Allan Pinkerton (front left) during the Civil War. (Library of Congress)

PLYLER V. DOE

THE CASE: U.S. Supreme Court decision concerning children of undocumented aliens

DATE: Decided on June 15, 1982

SIGNIFICANCE: Applying the standard of heightened scrutiny, the Supreme Court ruled that the denial of educational benefits to the children of illegal immigrants is inconsistent with the equal protection clause of the Fourteenth Amendment.

In 1975, the Texas legislature, in a revision of its educational legislation, announced that it would not pay for the education of children who were illegally residing in the country, and it authorized local school districts to deny enrollment to such students. It was widely recognized that the measure was directed at undocumented immigrants from Mexico. According to Texas officials, such persons were not "within the jurisdiction" of the state, and therefore they could not claim the protections of the Fourteenth Amendment. Opponents of the controversial policy brought a class-action suit on behalf of the children.

The Supreme Court, by a 5-4 majority, held that it was unconstitutional for school districts to deny educational benefits to children because of their legal status. Writing for the majority, liberal Justice William J. Brennan insisted that the state had failed to demonstrate that the exclusion was a rational means for furthering a "substantial state interest." Such a denial of educational opportunities would severely restrict the future potentiality of "a discrete class of children not accountable for their disabling status." Because many of the children were likely to become naturalized citizens in the future, the denial could result in "the creation and perpetuation of a subclass of illiterates within our boundaries, surely adding to the problems and costs of unemployment, welfare, and crime." Examining the wording of the Fourteenth Amendment's term "within its jurisdiction," Brennan wrote that it applied "to anyone, citizen or stranger, who is subject to the laws of a state."

As a precedent, the *Plyler* decision failed to answer a number of questions. The Court did not apply the demanding standard of strict scrutiny to the case, because illegal immigrants were not a suspect class and education was not a fundamental constitutional right. Emphasizing the critical importance of education, nevertheless, the Court's majority applied the standard of heightened scrutiny. The compromise left it unclear how future courts would deal with other restrictions on public benefits for illegal immigrants.

In 1986, the amnesty portion of the Immigration Reform and Control Act allowed many of the undocumented children covered under the *Plyler* decision to become legal residents. As the numbers of undocumented immigrants continued to grow, many states continued to complain that the resulting expenses for education and other social programs were unacceptable. In 1994, voters in California passed Proposition 187, which specified that the state would not fund nonemergency services for persons residing in the country illegally. Federal courts, however, refused to allow enforcement of the measure, in large part because it contradicted the *Plyler* ruling.

Thomas Tandy Lewis

FURTHER READING

Chavez, Leo R. *Shadowed Lives: Undocumented Immigrants in American Society.* 2d ed. Fort Worth, Tex.: Harcourt Brace College Publishers, 1998.

Kellough, Patrick H., and Jean L. Kellough. *Public Education and the Children of Illegal Aliens.* Monticello, Ill.: Vance Bibliographies, 1985.

Soltero, Carlos. *Latinos and American Law: Landmark Supreme Court Cases.* Austin: University of Texas Press, 2006.

SEE ALSO: Constitution, U.S.; English as a second language; *Graham v. Richardson*; Proposition 187; Supreme Court, U.S.

POLISH IMMIGRANTS

SIGNIFICANCE: Poles constituted the most numerous Slavic group to immigrate to the United States during the late nineteenth century. A large number of Polish immigrants settled in the Midwest, where they and their descendants played important roles in the politics and industries of cities such as Chicago, Detroit, and Milwaukee.

Polish immigration to the United States can be divided into three primary periods: before 1870, 1870 to World War II, and the decades following the war. The majority of Poles who immigrated to the United States arrived during the early twentieth century, but they were preceded by Poles who joined the British settlers in Jamestown, Virginia, as early as 1608. Most of the Poles who came during the nineteenth century were common laborers searching for job opportunities and better lives for themselves and their families.

EARLY IMMIGRANTS

The Poles who arrived in Jamestown, Virginia, in 1608 were brought in by John Smith to make soap, pitch, tar, rosin, and glass. The earliest name to be recorded was that of Robert the Polonian, who became known as Robert Poole. In 1619, Virginia's Polish workers petitioned for the right to vote. When they were denied, they staged a strike and were granted their petition. That incident was evidently the first recorded workers' strike for voting rights in American history.

By the beginning of the eighteenth century, Pennsylvania had become the primary destination for Polish immigrants. Many arrived with the Moravian Brethren when they came to settle in the area. After Anthony Sadowsky arrived there in 1730, he soon moved to the Ohio River Valley and changed his name to Sandusky—which can now be seen on maps of Ohio. Sandusky and his family became prominent in the exploration of the Ohio territories. Poles continued arriving in small numbers up until the American War of Independence.

The Revolutionary War (1775-1783) attracted the attention of Europeans, including Poles, many of whom came to America to join the struggle against British rule. By 1776, hundreds of Poles were living in the British colonies and many supported the revolutionary cause. Kazimierz (Casimir) Pulaski and Tadeusz (Thadeus) Kosciuszko played particularly important roles as brigadier generals in George Washington's Continental Army.

Pulaski had been a leader of the Poland's Bar Confederacy, which had resisted Russian influence. After leading a failed revolt against the Russian Empire, he fled from Europe to North America, where he volunteered to help train the fledgling American cavalry and tried to create elite cavalry and

PROFILE OF POLISH IMMIGRANTS	
Countries of origin	Poland, Lithuania, Russia
Primary language	Polish
Primary regions of U.S. settlement	Upper Midwest and Northeast
Earliest significant arrivals	1608
Peak immigration periods	1920's, 1990's
Twenty-first century legal residents*	100,427 (12,553 per year)

*Immigrants who obtained legal permanent resident status in the United States.
Source: Department of Homeland Security, Yearbook of Immigration Statistics, 2008.

infantry units similar to modern rapid response forces. He was eventually killed while leading a cavalry charge against the British forces in Georgia and has become recognized as the founder of American cavalry.

A graduate of the newly formed Polish Military Academy, Tadeusz Kosciuszko found his opportunities limited in Poland, so he decided to join the American revolutionary cause. He became a good friend of the Marquis de Lafayette and Thomas Jefferson. Kosciuszko was an engineer and artilleryman by training and was assigned to design the fortifications at West Point in New York. He later wrote the first manual for American artillery. After surviving the war, he was awarded a plantation and slaves by the new American government. However, he freed his slaves, sold the plantation, and gave the money from the plantation sale to the former slaves for their education.

In 1795, Poland was partitioned among its more powerful neighbors and ceased to exist as a sovereign country. Throughout the nineteenth century, Polish nationalists struggled to re-create their homeland. Between 1807 and 1813, the French emperor Napoleon Bonaparte resurrected a truncated Poland, but it soon fell back under Russian, Austrian, and Prussian control. Over the next five decades, Poles staged several failed revolts against their foreign masters. After each rebellion failed, Polish refugees fled west and many came to America. In 1834, 234 Polish refugees arrived in New York, where they formed the Polish Committee in America. In 1852, the Democratic Society of Polish Émigrés was formed and became affiliated with the antislavery movement.

THE U.S. CIVIL WAR AND AFTERWARD

When the U.S. Civil War broke out in 1861, Poles found themselves on both sides of the conflict. In Louisiana a Polish Brigade was formed to fight for the Confederacy, while in New York Wlodziemierz Krzyzanowski organized the Fifty-eighth New York Infantry for the Union Army. Known as the Polish Legion, Krzyzanowski's infantry unit dressed in Polish-style uniforms. Both units saw action in Virginia and eventually faced each other at the Battle of Gettysburg in July, 1863. Overall, an estimated 4,000-5,000 Poles served in the Union Army and 1,000 in the Confederate Army.

The decades immediately following the Civil War began the first major period of Polish immigration. The Polish regions of central Europe were still disrupted by warfare and political uncertainty, and all of Europe fell into an economic depression during the 1870's. Consequently, the lure of America became ever stronger. Most of the Poles who began immigrating to the United States during this period settled in the states of the industrial north, but some also went farther west. In Texas, Polish immigrants founded a settlement known as Panna Maria.

Most Polish immigrants gravitated to the industrial North, attracted by expanding employment opportunities in factories and the coal and iron mines that fed the industries. Buffalo, Detroit, Milwaukee, and Chicago became especially strong magnets to Polish peasants, who had limited education, few industrial skills, and little or no ability to speak English. Most filled lower-rung jobs left by earlier Irish and German immigrants who had moved up the labor ladder. As Irish and German workers moved into managerial and foreman positions, the Poles and other immigrants from central and eastern Europe became common laborers in factories and mines.

Because Polish immigrants were sometimes seen as competitors responsible for lowered wages, they were not always welcomed with open arms. Signs with slogans such as "No Polaks Wanted" became commonplace in shop and factory windows.

Many Polish immigrants had to pay bribes to find work. Nevertheless, despite these handicaps and ethnic bias, Polish immigrants generally succeeded in finding work.

Polish immigrants initially settled into communities among other central Europeans, such as Germans, until their numbers grew large enough to form ethnic enclaves of their own such as "Poletown" in Detroit. The largest concentration of Poles formed in Chicago, around the city's Milwaukee Avenue. Polish shops, churches and social clubs were soon to follow.

While many immigrants settled in cities, others chose rural communities so they could continue their familiar agricultural lifestyles. Many saved their earnings from factory work to purchase midwestern farms. Central Wisconsin's Portage County attracted such a large number of Poles that the majority of its residents were still Poles into the twenty-first century.

THE ROMAN CATHOLIC CHURCH

As the number of Poles in the United States grew, they began to push for social organizations of their own rather than sharing with other ethnic groups. Having their own Roman Catholic parishes became a major priority. The Catholic Church had played an important role in Poland society in Europe so it was only natural for immigrants to want their own Polish parishes in America. Chicago's St. Stanislaus Kostka Church, which formed in 1867, was the first Polish parish to form in the upper Midwest. The following year, 1868, saw the opening of the first Polish parochial school in the United States in Milwaukee.

During the late nineteenth century, demands for Polish parishes grew at such a rate that they began to trouble the Roman Catholic hierarchy. In South Bend, Indiana, a Polish parish formed directly across a street from an Irish parish. To avoid wasteful redundancy, the church's hierarchy worked to discouraged ethnic-based parishes by portraying Catholic churches as vehicles for the Americanization of immigrants. However, many Polish immigrants regarded this attitude as a form of discrimination because German and Irish immigrants had already been allowed to form their own parishes. In 1904, a group of disaffected Poles decided to split from the main body of the Roman church by forming the Polish National Catholic

Church (PNCC), which allied with the Episcopalian Church. Within a dozen years, PNCC membership grew to more than 30,000 members. Father Francis Hodur was consecrated as the first bishop of the PNCC in 1907.

Meanwhile, within the Roman Catholic Church, Polish parishes were quickly followed by Polish religious orders, the most prominent of which was the Felician Sisters. The Felician Sisters formed their first base of operation in New York City to aid newly arriving immigrants in 1877. By 1882, they had moved to Detroit as Polish immigrants moved west. The Felician Sisters became the bulwark of the Polish parochial school system. Other orders soon followed, such as the Sisters of the Holy Family of Nazareth.

ADJUSTING TO AMERICAN LIFE

With their spiritual lives safely provided for, Polish immigrants turned more toward self-help organizations and Polish language newspapers for information on their specific concerns and needs. As early as 1852, the Democratic Society of Polish Émigrés in America was formed in New York City. It continued until 1858, when its name was changed to the Polish Committee. During the 1860's, the St. Stanislaus Kostka Society was formed to aid Polish Catholics, and the Gmina (Commune) Polska was formed to aid Poles without regard to their religious or political affiliation.

In cities from New York to Philadelphia to Milwaukee, organizations named after saints and Polish national heroes, such as the American Revolu-

Polish immigrant family working together on a Maryland farm in 1909. (Library of Congress)

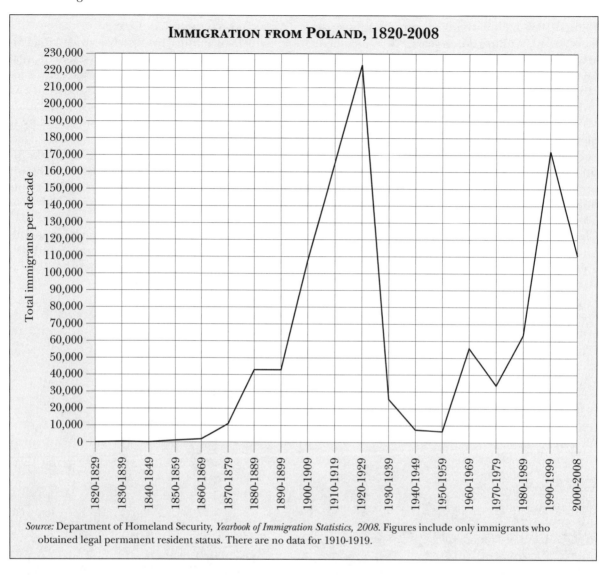

IMMIGRATION FROM POLAND, 1820-2008

Total immigrants per decade

Source: Department of Homeland Security, *Yearbook of Immigration Statistics, 2008.* Figures include only immigrants who obtained legal permanent resident status. There are no data for 1910-1919.

tionary War general Tadeusz Kosciuszko, sprang up during the 1870's and 1880's. To coordinate efforts on shared Polish concerns, several national bodies were formed during this period. The Polish Roman Catholic Union was formed in 1873, and the Polish National Alliance appeared in 1882. However, the members of these two organizations did not agree on all issues because of a religious/secular divide, and the organizations were often in conflict with each other.

The Poles also created their own athletic clubs, similar to the German Turner's Clubs, that were called Sokols or Falcons. The initial purpose of these clubs was often to train future soldiers to fight

for a reborn Poland. The creation of fighting squads known as Bojowki was popular in the socialist-oriented Sokols but condemned in the Catholic-oriented halls. The goals of the Sokols revealed a basic division within the nation's Polish communities between those who considered themselves "Poles in America" and those who saw themselves as "Polish Americans."

Polish-language newspapers became immigrants' primary sources of information about what was happening in the Old World as well as what was happening in their New World. One of the earliest newspapers was Buffalo's *Polak w Ameryce,* which began publishing in 1887. It was quickly followed by

Kuryer Polski in Milwaukee, Wisconsin; *Ameryka Echo* in Toledo, Ohio; *Dziennik Polski* in Detroit; and one of the longest-enduring Polish newspapers, *Gwiazda Polarna* in Stevens Point, Wisconsin. By 1907, even Polish socialists were publishing their own paper, *Dziennik Ludowy*, in Chicago.

During the 1880's, Poles began making their presence felt in American politics with the election of Polish city and state officials in Illinois, Wisconsin, and Michigan. Polish women also took an active part in politics by working in the women's suffrage movement. To coordinate their efforts, the Polish Women's Alliance was created in 1898 in Chicago.

TWENTIETH CENTURY DEVELOPMENTS

When World War I broke out in 1914, Polish immigrants in the United States formed the Polish Defense Committee to support the Polish Legions of Józef Pilsudski, who was working to get the Central Powers to guarantee the re-creation of the Polish state. By 1917, however, when the United States entered the war against the Central Powers, Poles were shifting their support to a Polish army formed in France under Józef Haller. Polish Americans sent both money and volunteers to France to fight for a free Poland.

Many Poles volunteered for the U.S. Army after the United States entered the war. The conflicting efforts of Polish immigrants during the war reemphasized the split personality of the Polish community. When U.S. president Woodrow Wilson aided in the rebirth of Poland after the war, immigrants not ready to think of themselves as "Polish Americans" had the opportunity to return to their homeland and resume being Polish citizens.

For those immigrants who opted to remain in the United States, Polish social and fraternal organizations played a major role in helping them become Polish Americans. Poles also began playing larger roles on the American scene. They became leaders in the labor protests of the 1920's and 1930's, most notably Chicago's stockyard strikes during the 1920's and Detroit's auto worker strikes of the 1930's. Poles began to break into the arts and sports, especially baseball, the quintessential American game. Stanley Coveleski was an integral member of the Cleveland Indians during the 1920's and eventually made it into the Baseball Hall of Fame. He was followed shortly thereafter by Stan

Musial of the St. Louis Cardinals. Poles were also making their way in professional football.

MAINTAINING POLISH IDENTITY

Despite efforts to become more American, Polish Americans still wanted to maintain some elements of their ancestral identity. Polish cultural clubs helped maintain that identity by sponsoring concerts of Polish music, art exhibits, and weekend classes in Polish language and history. Nevertheless, within each new generation, ties to Poland and Polishness (*Polkosc*) became weaker. During the 1920's, the numbers of new Polish immigrants were severely diminished by new federal anti-immigrant legislation.

World War II started in Europe in 1939 when Nazi Germany invaded Poland. The response of the American Polish community showed how much it had changed in only two decades. This time, Polish Americans did not enlist in a Polish army in exile as they had in 1917. Instead they enlisted in the U.S. military forces that they thought would contribute to the liberation of Poland while defending the United States. Now, their first loyalties lay with the United States, but many of them still gave moral and monetary support for a free Poland. Large numbers of Polish American men served in the European and Pacific theaters, while many women worked in the factories throughout the war.

Following the war, a new wave of Polish immigrants came to America fleeing communism in Eastern Europe. The new migration was split between the well educated who found their way into the fields of education, medicine, and business and became leaders in the Polish American community, while the less educated took the routes of their predecessors into factories and mines as common laborers. However, members of both groups picked up the banner of maintaining Polishness in the United States through cultural and arts societies. They also became leaders in the anticommunist movement in the United States.

From the mid-1950's through the 1970's, Polish immigration to America was severely curtailed due to the Cold War. Following the crushing of the Solidarity Labor Union in 1981, a fresh wave of Polish refugees made their way to the United States. These new immigrants did not mesh well with the older generations of immigrants. The new immigrants were, for the most part, well educated and saw their predecessors as frozen in time—not seeing the world or Poland as it actually was, but as it once had been. Many of these newcomers would return to Poland after 1989. They resembled the early Poles in America's mindset around the turn of the twentieth century.

With each new generation, the Polish American community has moved farther from its Polish cultural roots. Although fraternal organizations continue to operate local organizations and Polish language newspapers, they are quickly disappearing as more and more Poles begin to see themselves not as Poles in America or Polish Americans but as Americans of Polish descent.

David R. Stefancic

FURTHER READING

Bukowczyk, John J. *And My Children Did Not Know Me.* Bloomington: Indiana University Press, 1987. Concise but useful history of Polish immigrant history.

_____, ed. *Polish Americans and Their History: Community, Culture, and Politics.* Pittsburgh, Pa.: University of Pittsburgh Press, 1996. Collection of articles about Polish immigrants with papers focusing on such subjects as labor, family issues, women and gender issues, religion, and politics.

Pacyga, Dominic A. *Polish Immigrants and Industrial Chicago: Workers on the South Side, 1880-1922.* Chicago: University of Chicago Press, 2003. Excellent study of Polish immigration focusing on Poles working in Chicago's steel mills, slaughterhouses, and meatpacking plants.

Pula, James. *Polish Americans.* New York: Twayne, 1995. Popular history of Polish Americans.

Renkiewicz, Frank, ed. *The Poles in America, 1608-1972.* Dobbs Ferry, N.Y.: Oceana, 1973. Excellent collection of primary documents related to Polish American history.

Wytrwal, Joseph A. *America's Polish Heritage.* Detroit: Endurance Press, 1961. Broad survey of Polish immigration to the United States, which Wytrwal divides into three major periods: adventurers of 1608-1776, political emigrants of 1776-1865, and economic refugees of the 1860's to 1920's.

_____. *Poles in American History and Tradition.* Detroit: Endurance Press, 1969. Classic work on Polish American history.

SEE ALSO: Chicago; Czech and Slovakian immigrants; Hungarian immigrants; Jewish immigrants; Rickover, Hyman G.; Russian and Soviet immigrants; Wisconsin; Yezierska, Anzia.

POLITICAL PARTIES

DEFINITION: Organizations that reflect the various beliefs and views of a country and in an organized fashion put forth candidates for elective offices

SIGNIFICANCE: Political parties have impacted immigration in both positive and negative ways. Most American political parties have opposed unrestricted immigration and when in power have passed laws to restrict immigration and, at times, make naturalization more difficult. In contrast, membership in political parties and active participation in politics have provided one of the means by which members of some immigrant groups—particularly Irish and Germans—have been able to preserve their culture while becoming upwardly mobile in American society.

Throughout American history, the stances of political parties toward immigrants have been affected by a number of factors, including the naturalization status of the immigrants, the sizes of particular immigrant populations, and the general attitudes of the American voting constituency toward immigrants. From the late eighteenth century through the greater part of the twentieth century, parties mirrored the American distrust of foreigners, their languages, their religions, their cultures, and their physical appearances. Through that long period of time, the American population in general viewed immigrants as threats to the maintenance of their religious and cultural traditions as well as their jobs.

The platforms of almost all political parties have advocated restrictions on immigration and often have proposed more stringent requirements for naturalization. However, from 1850 through the last years of the twentieth century, the Democratic Party has been the one exception to this generalization. During the years surrounding the turn of the twenty-first century, as the composition of the

American voting population was changing, with ever-increasing numbers of nonwhite and non-Anglo-Saxon voters, the political parties began to recognize the importance of immigrants as voters and became more aware of issues important to immigrants.

NINETEENTH CENTURY POLITICAL PARTIES

The nineteenth century witnessed massive immigration to the United States from Europe. Driven by famine, poor economic conditions, and political and religious persecution, immigrants arrived from Ireland, Germany, Italy, Poland, Belgium, and central and eastern European countries. Their customs and lifestyles were different from those of native-born Americans, and most of them did not speak English. American citizens, who tended to be isolationist and distrust anything or anyone not American, reacted negatively to the influx of immigrants. Of particular concern were the large numbers of Irish Catholic immigrants who were entering the country. The primarily Protestant Anglo-Saxon population was particularly apprehensive about Irish Catholic allegiance to the Roman Catholic pope. Limiting immigration or stopping it completely became a central issue. The political parties who had members seated in Congress called for restrictions on immigration and passed laws to that end.

Nativism, which advocated the perpetuation of the established Anglo-Saxon culture and the prevention of any foreign culture being established, resulted in the founding of a number of small political parties and secret societies who were anti-immigration and anti-immigrants. These included the Order of the Star Spangled Banner, the American Party (also called the Know-Nothing Party) and the Greenback Labor Party. Members of these organizations were of Protestant faiths and came from the middle and working classes of society. They insisted that Roman Catholic immigrants, especially the Irish Catholics, intended to gain elected offices and then place the country under the rule of the pope.

The other main tenet of their anti-immigrant stance was that immigrants should not be given jobs, that employers should only hire what the nativists called "true Americans." In addition to restrictions on immigration, their campaign platform included proposals to increase the length of time immigrants had to live in the United States before becoming eligible to apply for naturalization. The American Party enjoyed considerable success in areas where large numbers of immigrants had settled. In 1854, the party gained control of the Massachusetts legislature. The Whig Party, one of the two major parties of the time, also advocated placing restrictions on immigration and looked upon immigrants as outsiders. In contrast, the other major party, the Democrats, was favorable to immigrants and recruited urban Irish and German immigrants into their party.

IRISH IMMIGRANTS AND THE DEMOCRATIC PARTY

The Democrat Party was already looked upon favorably by Irish immigrants, who were for the most part laborers in factories, slaughterhouses, and steel mills in large cities such as Chicago, Boston, and New York. The party's platform emphasized programs to provide government aid and protection to immigrants, the unemployed, and the impoverished. As the primary immigrant group targeted by the nativists, the Irish were well aware that they needed to have input into the political system in order to counter and prevent the type of legislation proposed. Becoming politically active was easier for the Irish than for the majority of the immigrant groups. They spoke English as well as Gaelic and were familiar with a political system that had many similarities to that of the United States. The Irish appeared to the Democratic Party as a population to be recruited because they were the largest ethnic group and their resistance to English oppression had developed a sense of unity among them. Thus the recruiting of the Irish in the United States would open the way to the winning of new arrivals for the party as well.

In addition to wanting to offset the attacks of the nativists, the Irish laborers were seeking to improve their economic situation and their lifestyle by acquiring better jobs. Membership in the Democrat Party was on way to achieving this goal. The Party offered jobs in city government and services to its loyal party workers. Helping to get out the vote and win the election meant better jobs and upward social mobility. So many Irish joined the Democratic Party that they actually came to dominate it and maintained that dominance from 1860 through the 1920's. Although the patronage system of so-called "machine politics" has been severely criticized for its cronyism and nepotism and for awarding of offices in return for political support rather than on the basis of merit, it did much to disperse the Irish throughout the various economic classes and to assimilate them into the general population of the United States.

German Immigrants and the Republican Party

Between 1840 and 1920, a strong wave of anti-German feeling swept the United States. This was due in great part to the fact that the Germans, while assimilating in many ways, insisted upon maintaining their social culture and their language. They established German language elementary schools in their communities and taught their children in their native language. Taking the traditional Republican Party position regarding immigrants as outsiders, Republicans in Illinois and Wisconsin attempted to pass laws in 1890 that would close the German language elementary schools. The laws did not pass, however, and German voters helped bring about the defeat of many Republican candidates in 1890. As active participants in the labor movement, the German immigrants were the major founders of the Socialist Party of America in 1901. Thus the German immigrants, like the Irish immigrants, did not remain a "foreign" population outside the American political process. Instead, they became American citizens involved in American political parties and the political life of the country.

Asian Immigrants

From the mid-nineteenth century until after World War II during the 1940's, Asian immigrants were excluded from the political life of the United States by a variety of laws restricting their rights and even excluding them from citizenship. During and after World War II, these laws were repealed and other laws favoring Asian immigrants were passed. By 1962, Asian immigrants were playing an active role in American politics as members of both major parties and increasing numbers of them were elected to public offices.

Late Twentieth and Early Twenty-first Century Trends

The twentieth century was a time of significant change in both the attitudes of Americans and the role of the United States in world affairs. The isolationism that had been popular in the United States since its founding was no longer a sustainable position for the country after two world wars. International cooperation became important and changed attitudes toward immigrants. The Civil Rights movement of the 1960's also helped to change public attitudes. The concept of an exclusively white Anglo-Saxon electorate was challenged and began to be replaced by one that included individuals of other racial and ethnic ancestries.

Political parties began to recognize and target the African American population of voters and potential voters. Issues important to these voters became part of the platforms of the major political parties. At first, the major political parties focused more on African Americans than on immigrant populations, although many of the latter had ancestors who had immigrated from Europe and had already become members of political parties.

Due in large part to changes in U.S. immigration laws during the second half of the twentieth century, the composition of the population of the United States has changed significantly. During the early years of the twenty-first century, one out of every five adults living in the United States had been born in a foreign country. Approximately one-third of the population was of nonwhite and non-European descent. The largest of these groups was the Mexican American community, which was by then becoming recognized by both major political parties as a significant and important sector of the voting population. In the 2004 and 2008 presidential elections, the Democratic Party and the Republican Party targeted and made special efforts to attract the Mexican American voters.

Shawncey Webb

Further Reading

Aldrich, John H. *Why Parties: The Origin and Transformation of Political Parties in America.* Chicago: University of Chicago Press, 1995. Good, comprehensive look at political parties, why they were formed, and how they have changed.

Gerring, John. *Party Ideologies in America, 1828-1996.* New York: Cambridge University Press, 2008. Excellent for information on the political parties and the changes they underwent during various historical periods. Discusses how party ideologies have affected attitudes toward immigrants.

Higham, John. *Strangers in the Land: Pattern of American Nativism, 1860 to 1925*. New Brunswick, N.J.: Rutgers University Press, 2002. Excellent for understanding the anti-immigrant thinking of the late nineteenth and early twentieth centuries and the formation of political parties based on nativism.

Junn, Jane, and Kerry L. Haynie, eds. *New Race Politics in America: Understanding Minority and Immigrant Politics*. New York: Cambridge University Press, 2008. Excellent coverage of how the American electorate has changed, with chapters on political party efforts to incorporate immigrants, and Asian and Mexican Americans, their political activities, and party attitudes toward them.

McLaughlin, John. *Irish Chicago*. Charleston, S.C.: Arcadia Publishing, 2003. Good look at the Irish immigrant population in Chicago and their political activity, from mayors to ward politicians.

Magaña, Lisa. *Mexican Americans and the Politics of Diversity*. Tucson: University of Arizona Press, 2005. Excellent for understanding how political issues affect Mexican Americans. How Mexican Americans impact political parties and reasons for interest of major political parties in this ethnic community.

Tolzmann, Don Heinrich. *The German-American Experience*. New York: Humanity Books, 2000. Thorough study of the German immigrants in the United States, with sections on politics and nativism, German rural and urban communities, and German-speaking communities.

SEE ALSO: Congress, U.S.; Immigration waves; Irish immigrants; Know-Nothing Party; Machine politics; Nativism; Presidential elections; Tammany Hall.

PONZI, CHARLES

IDENTIFICATION: Italian-born American swindler
BORN: March 3, 1882; Lugo, Italy
DIED: January 18, 1949; Rio de Janeiro, Brazil

SIGNIFICANCE: In 1920, fewer than twenty years after Ponzi came to the United States with little money and unable to speak English, his wealth seemed to make him the embodiment of the immigrant's dream. Instead

Charles Ponzi. (Library of Congress)

of creating wealth, however, Ponzi became a master of a type of elaborate swindle that became known as a "Ponzi scheme."

Charles Ponzi identified with stories of his family's past glory. Having a taste for the good life and a disdain for the type of work available to him in Italy, he immigrated to the United States to seek his fortune. After gambling away his money en route to Boston in 1903, Ponzi quickly found that the streets were not paved with gold, and he was forced to take the types of jobs he spurned in Italy. In search of easy money, Ponzi moved and switched jobs frequently, finding himself in trouble with the law in both the United States and Canada.

By December, 1919, Ponzi was back in Boston, a married man about to embark on a venture that would make him both rich and infamous. His seemingly plausible investment scheme attracted investors by offering a high return. Within seven months, he had collected nearly $10 million. In August, 1920, it was discovered that Ponzi was actually paying the high returns with the money of new investors. With that, his pursuit of the immigrant's dream came to an end. After serving over a decade in state and federal prisons for his crimes, Ponzi was deported to Italy. He later died in the charity ward of a Brazilian hospital.

Randall Hannum

FURTHER READING

Dunn, Donald. *Ponzi: The Incredible True Story of the King of Financial Cons.* New York: Broadway Books, 2004.

Zuckoff, Mitchell. *Ponzi's Scheme: The True Story of a Financial Legend.* New York: Random House, 2005.

SEE ALSO: Boston; Crime; Criminal immigrants; Italian immigrants; Massachusetts.

PORTUGUESE IMMIGRANTS

SIGNIFICANCE: Portuguese immigrants to the United States have tended to cluster in the New England and mid-Atlantic states, upper California, and Hawaii. Most came from Portugal's Azores and Madeira island provinces in the Atlantic Ocean; only the most recent waves have come directly from the European mainland. A seafaring people, the earliest Portuguese in the United States engaged in the whaling and fishing industries, from which they progressively moved into manufacturing and agricultural work.

The Portuguese were among the earliest European explorers and settlers of the New World. A Portuguese expedition along the Atlantic coast of North America identified and named the island of Labrador in 1498. Two years later. Portuguese navigators explored the eastern coast of South America, where they settled Brazil and sent to it by far the largest numbers of Portuguese people in the Western Hemisphere. Portuguese immigrants to the United States originated not only from the Portuguese island provinces of the Azores and Madeira but also from continental Portugal itself. Portugal's seafaring traditions prompted the Portuguese to navigate throughout the Atlantic, Pacific, and Indian Oceans.

EARLY PORTUGUESE IN NORTH AMERICA

Two small Portuguese communities appeared in the mid-seventeenth century British North American colonies—in New York and Rhode Island. Portuguese immigrants to the latter colony were mostly Sephardic Jews. The earliest known documented reference to an immigrant of Portuguese descent was recorded in Maryland in 1634. An eighteenth century descendant of a Portuguese immigrant was a founder of the New York Stock Exchange. During the early nineteenth century, the growing importance of whale oil as a fuel brought seamen from the Azores and Madeira, settling in Rhode Island and Massachusetts. The abundance of cod fish in the North Atlantic also attracted them.

Portuguese seamen sailing the Pacific during the nineteenth century established small settlements in Hawaii, Alaska, and California. The gold rush in the latter state prompted a ten-fold increase in the Portuguese population of the state's northern region between 1850 and 1860. California's development of a fish-canning industry attracted more Portuguese. During the nineteenth century the number of immigrants from Portugal and its islands became sufficient to establish several Portuguese mutual benefit societies in various cities. In 1877, the first Portuguese newspaper, the

PROFILE OF PORTUGUESE IMMIGRANTS

Country of origin	Portugal
Primary language	Portuguese
Primary regions of U.S. settlement	New England, Mid-Atlantic and West Coast states, Hawaii
Earliest significant arrivals	1630's
Peak immigration periods	1900-1920's, 1970's
Twenty-first century legal residents*	9,124 (1,141 per year)

*Immigrants who obtained legal permanent resident status in the United States.
Source: Department of Homeland Security, *Yearbook of Immigration Statistics, 2008.*

Two Portuguese girls working in the Royal Mill in Rhode Island, 1909. (Library of Congress)

Jornal de Notícias (News Journal), appeared in the United States, prompting the appearance of several other such publications in the next decade.

FLUCTUATING IMMIGRATION RATES

By the turn of the twentieth century, Portuguese immigrants were arriving in the United States by the tens of thousands, expanding the clusters already established in New England, the mid-Atlantic states, and California. Their numbers, however, have probably been underestimated because immigrants from the Azores and Madeira were not always counted as Portuguese by U.S. immigration officials. Indeed, Portuguese immigrants were often identified as Spanish. Moreover, many immigrants arrived clandestinely, declaring no nationality.

On the eve of World War I (1914-1918), New England had a population of Portuguese descent numbering approximately 150,000. Working mainly in textile mills, these people formed the second-largest Portuguese population in the Americas after Brazil. The Portuguese population in California expanded from the San Francisco Bay area into the San Joaquim Valley, aiding in the development of its agricultural abundance. Some Portuguese in Hawaii moved to California although the number on the islands remained considerable and influential.

Postwar immigration restrictions reduced the number of Portuguese who could enter the country to only a few hundred per year. However, those who did succeed in immigrating now originated principally from mainland Portugal. During the decades after World War II, Portuguese immigration quotas were raised, and 100,000 immigrants entered the United States between 1950 and 1970. They left a country that had become one of the poorest in Europe, burdened with a fascist regime that had been in power for a half-century and mired in warfare to suppress the independence

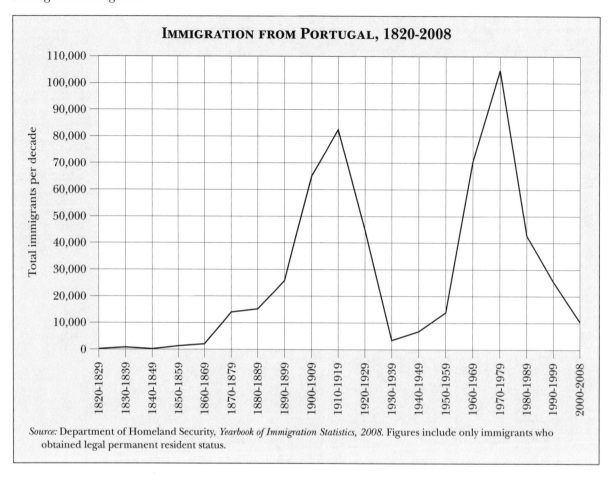

IMMIGRATION FROM PORTUGAL, 1820-2008

Source: Department of Homeland Security, *Yearbook of Immigration Statistics, 2008.* Figures include only immigrants who obtained legal permanent resident status.

movements of its African colonies. By 1980, the U.S. Census registered more than one million Americans of Portuguese descent. Several American universities now had Portuguese studies centers, including Brown University, the University of Massachusetts at Dartmouth, Columbia University, and the University of California at Santa Barbara.

Edward A. Riedinger

FURTHER READING

Baganha, Maria Ioannis Benis. *Portuguese Emigration to the United States, 1820-1930.* New York: Garland, 1990. Examines the earliest waves of Portuguese immigrants and their settlement and occupation patterns along the Atlantic and Pacific coasts.

Higgs, David. *Portuguese Migration in Global Perspective.* Toronto: Multicultural History Society of Ontario, 1990. Places the history of Portuguese immigrants to the United States in the context of their global diaspora after the fifteenth century, with attention to Brazil, Africa, and Asia.

Mira, Manuel. *The Forgotten Portuguese.* Franklin, N.C.: Portuguese American Historical Research Foundation, 1998. Offers a clearer role of the Portuguese in the United States as a minority ethnic group overshadowed by much larger groups such as the English, Germans, Irish, and Italians.

_____. *The Portuguese Making of America.* Franklin, N.C.: Portuguese American Historical Research Foundation, 2001. Highlights the contributions of Portuguese immigrants to American society.

Pap, Leo. *The Portuguese-Americans.* Boston: Twayne, 1981. Defines the unique character and achievements of Portuguese immigrants in the United States in comparison with other immigrant groups.

Wiarda, Iêda Siquera, et al. *Handbook of Portuguese Studies.* Philadelphia: Xlibris, 1999. Annotated guide to works in the humanities and social sciences dealing with Portugal and the lusophone world, providing detailed background materials on immigration.

Williams, Jerry R. *In Pursuit of Their Dreams: A History of Azorean Immigration to the United States.* North Dartmouth: Center for Portuguese Studies and Culture, University of Massachusetts Dartmouth, 2005. Traces the conditions in the Azores that prompted many islanders to immigrate to the United States and the factors determining their decisions regarding where to settle there.

SEE ALSO: Brazilian immigrants; California; California gold rush; Economic consequences of immigration; Economic opportunities; European immigrants; Massachusetts; Push-pull factors; Rhode Island.

POWDERLY, TERENCE V.

IDENTIFICATION: American labor leader
BORN: January 22, 1849; Carbondale, Pennsylvania
DIED: June 24, 1924; Washington, D.C.

SIGNIFICANCE: Although he was the son of immigrants, Powderly believed that immigrant workers had a detrimental effect on the national economy and spent much of his adult life working to combat immigrant labor. As a union leader he supported legislation barring Chinese workers from entering the United States, and he later campaigned for broad bans on immigration. Later, however, he worked on behalf of immigrant welfare.

Born to Irish immigrants, Terence Powderly began his career by following in his father's footsteps as a railroad mechanic. After losing a job, he found new work through a machinists' union and later became a union organizer. In 1879, he was elected to lead the Knights of Labor, a national workers' union. Realizing that employers were recruiting immigrants to work for low wages, he supported the Chinese Exclusion Act of 1882. In 1885, with the Knights of Labor's 700,000 members behind

him, Powderly backed further federal legislation to bar American employers from recruiting workers overseas.

While he was a member of Knights of Labor, Powderly was three times elected mayor of Scranton, Pennsylvania. After leaving the union in 1893, he established a successful legal practice. In 1907, he became chief of the new Division of Information in the Bureau of Immigration. In 1911, he was named honorary president of a National Conference of Immigration, Land, and Labor Officials. Both agencies helped immigrants find work and promoted cultural assimilation. Powderly served as Commissioner of Conciliation in the Department of Labor from 1921 until his death three years later.

Maureen J. Puffer-Rothenberg

FURTHER READING

Phelan, Craig. *Grand Master Workman: Terence Powderly and the Knights of Labor.* Westport, Conn.: Greenwood Press, 2000.

Powderly, Terence Vincent. "A Menacing Irruption." *The North American Review* 147, no. 381 (1888): 165-174.

Watson, Martha S., and Thomas R. Burkholder, eds. *The Rhetoric of Nineteenth-Century Reform.* East Lansing: Michigan State University Press, 2008.

SEE ALSO: Anti-Chinese movement; Bureau of Immigration, U.S.; Chinese Exclusion Act of 1882; Chinese immigrants; History of immigration, 1783-1891; Immigration law; Labor unions.

PRESIDENTIAL ELECTIONS

DEFINITION: Quadrennial national elections held to select U.S. presidents

SIGNIFICANCE: After attaining American citizenship, immigrants can vote in national elections. However, because they tend to identify with their ethnic, racial, or religious groups, they tend to vote in blocs. This makes them prime targets for the attention of political campaign strategists. Throughout American history, immigrants have been alternatively courted and attacked by organized political parties embroiled in presidential campaigns. At times, immigrant issues have dominated national policy agendas; at other times, such issues have been ignored or shunned as political hot potatoes.

The nexus of immigration and national-level politics is the presidential campaign. The United States has, at best, a mixed record of embracing immigrants in this important electoral process. Because of ongoing neglect, the voices of immigrant groups have often been quiet in American public policy-making. Moreover, presidential elections by their very nature have tended to reinforce strong intra-group bonds of new American citizens. During the late nineteenth century, urban political machines sprang up as informal organizations serving the political interests of immigrants on both the national and local levels. By the twenty-first century, urban machines were nearly extinct, and immigration issues were alternately on and off national political agendas.

MIXED ENFRANCHISEMENT

The United States has been called the "first new nation," which is to say it is the first modern Western country formed without a European feudal and aristocratic past as its historical bedrock. This means that at some basic level, American presidential elections have always hinged upon the voting efforts of immigrants. However, despite America's status as the first new nation, the degree of success in extending voting rights to immigrants since the American Revolution can be fairly described as mixed.

During the early decades after the creation of the American nation, the drafting of the U.S. Constitution, and the early elections of George Washington, John Adams, and Thomas Jefferson, the rate of foreign immigration into the United States was steady but slow. During the decades-long lull in significant immigration, the political identity of the United States matured. The immigrants and descendants of immigrants already on American shores began to recognize themselves as a distinct group. In terms of American political development, this was very important. Perhaps ironically, the immigrants who would later come from Europe would be seen as "outsiders" to an established political process.

Early American voting laws began to reflect this newfound electoral xenophobia. In a nation that

fewer than seventy-five years earlier had been started by foreign immigrants seeking new beginnings, rules and regulations began to take shape to limit the voting rights of new immigrants. Enfranchisement is the right of a person to cast a ballot for an elected official. Its opposite, "disenfranchisement," began emerging in the United States during the 1830's and 1840's.

Prior to the U.S. Civil War of 1861-1865, a partisan battle between the emergent Whigs and the Democratic Party spilled over into public law. The Democratic party of Thomas Jefferson and Andrew Jackson had thrived. The Democrats had created something known as the spoils system in which party backers were rewarded with government jobs. The Whigs stood in opposition to this Democratic success and somewhat effectively united native-born voters against immigrant voting rights. In 1840, the Whigs chose as their candidate for president William Henry Harrison, a decorated leader in the war against Native Americans on the western frontier.

The Whigs perceived that the Democrats had developed an advantage over them by supporting laws allowing immigrants to vote. Indeed, the Whigs represented the more affluent and established members of American society. In early American elections, there were no voting registration laws, but as the sense of community felt by existing American residents grew, registering voters began to make sense to them. The idea of transients voting in elections was seen as something to stop by this reactionary element of the electorate. It can be argued that registration laws were first developed as a reasonable method of stopping voting fraud, but such laws were more likely enacted to discourage poor people from voting.

During the nineteenth century, the American poor were most frequently immigrants. With the potato blight in Ireland during the 1840's and the rapid influx of Irish Catholics to eastern urban centers, "native" Americans began to lobby for voter registration laws. Without a doubt, some of these laws were blatantly aimed at new waves of Irish, German, French, and Dutch immigrants. One anti-immigrant proposal sought to extend the length of time immigrants had to wait before they could qualify for citizenship and vote. Some anti-immigrant leaders even pushed for waiting periods as long as twenty years of citizenship before naturalized citizens could vote.

MID-NINETEETH CENTURY CHANGES

After a few years of success, the Whig Party began to fade from the national political scene during the 1850's. However, it was quickly replaced by a more insidious body—the Know-Nothings. The Know-Nothing Party had begun as a secret nativist society called the Order of the Star Spangled Banner. The party was strangely progressive on some issues, such as women's rights, but in general, it stood for unabashed bigotry. The Know-Nothings openly expressed fear over Irish Catholic workers settling in Boston and New York. They saw the Irish as un-American and feared that they took their marching orders from the Roman Catholic pope.

Along with the surging Republicans and the fading Whigs, the Know-Nothings pushed for state voting laws establishing literacy tests and grandfather clauses. These laws required such things as civics tests and minimum-residency requirements before individuals could vote. During the nineteenth century, the legal hurdles placed in front of voters, which would later become known as "Jim Crow" laws, were not aimed solely at African Americans. Rather they were directed toward eastern European immigrants and others who were not established property-owning Protestants.

At various times in American history, members of very different immigrant groups have been feared for their possible political influence. The Chinese in California, Italians in New York, and Cubans in Florida have all held this distinction. However, some regions of the United States have been more tolerant toward immigrants than others. For example, Minnesota and Wisconsin, perhaps because of their residents' heritage of Scandinavian egalitarianism, have generally been more embracing of the foreign born. Likewise, immigrants who moved to the western frontier during the nineteenth century and stayed away from the eastern seaboard had a bit easier go gaining political acceptance.

URBAN POLITICAL MACHINES

In contrast, political life during the nineteenth century could be harsh for many urban immigrants. Low-paying factory jobs and thick foreign accents did not easily gain them entry into the landed classes. The importance of property-owning status and high educational achievement made it difficult for immigrants to gain political acceptance. Consequently, local elections were often sealed off from members of poorly organized and politically naive immigrant groups, and presidential elections were generally completely out of reach of new Americans. Moreover, immigrants typically could neither run for office nor get their issues onto the political agenda.

Because immigrants lacked representation in both public candidacy and voting, their political problems were only compounded. Muckraking works such as Upton Sinclair's 1906 novel *The Jungle* documented the harsh work and living conditions of the immigrant working poor. Their oppressed, low-class status was directly linked to the lack of political representation in a supposedly democratic nation. Most often presidential candidates of the late nineteenth and early twentieth centuries, such as James Garfield and Benjamin Harrison, did not stand strongly for immigrant and minority rights.

However, at least one political tide was turning. After the Civil War and the onset of urban industrialization, European immigrants formed close-knit communities that housed their own forms of political expression. For example, Slavic communities that provided labor for the coal industry in Pennsylvania, embraced one another in insular neighborhoods. Soon enough the close-knit nature of immigrant communities, usually centered on ethnically flavored churches, lent itself naturally to political organization.

Urban political machines were born not only to clutch onto political power, but also to give a voice to immigrants. Machine politics was indeed a locally born phenomenon, but it also provided the first roots of immigrant political power exercised on a national level. Political machines taught immigrants that they could organize and help change government policies. Through the machines, immigrants learned about their civil rights and were even encouraged to cast votes for their preferred candidates. By supporting the political candidates put forward by political machines, immigrants gained patronage jobs in government. At the turn of the nineteenth century waves of new Americans were learning the lessons of politics.

American presidential elections are actually not monolithic national elections. It would be more accurate to describe them as accumulations of individual state elections that are held on the same day. The electoral votes of the individual states are aggregated to determine who the president will be, but the federal system has always granted king-making power to state electoral systems. During the nineteenth century, the individual state systems were dominated by political machines in large urban centers in which immigrants played increasingly important roles.

As urban machines composed of distinct ethnic groups gained political ground in cities such as Chicago, Philadelphia, and San Francisco, they became national-level power brokers. Because immigrant political power was nested in urban centers, these machines could "deliver" votes for federal level candidates, including the presidents. Many political historians have noted that President John F. Kennedy's electoral victory in 1960 was delivered with the blessing of the Daley machine in Chicago. However, the political power of European immigrants peaked with Kennedy's victory.

IMMIGRATION POLICY

Public policy scholars have long known that when an ethnic or racial minority candidate wins elected office, new public policy tends to more closely follow the particular needs of the candidate's group. As European immigrants assimilated into the greater American melting pot during the mid-twentieth century, the unique needs of other immigrant groups have become more visible.

By the late twentieth century, American immigration policy debate was focusing sharply on the trials of recent Hispanic immigrants. While some immigration policy issues have diverged from their counterparts of a century earlier, commonalities have remained. For example, Hispanic immigrants have faced the same kinds of workers' rights issues that daunted European immigrants during the nineteenth century. Perpetually assuming the role of the newcomer in a developed American economy, immigrants have always had acute concerns about workplace safety and fair wages.

Issues of political representation have remained as well. Hispanic Americans have gained ground in winning public offices, but white native-born Americans have continued to dominate campaign politics. New Mexico's Hispanic governor Bill Richardson was a possible candidate for president in the 2008 election, but he constantly trailed fel-

Chinese man reading a Shanghai newspaper story about the January, 2009, inauguration of Barack Obama, the first black U.S. president. (AP/Wide World Photos)

low Democratic Party nominees Hillary Clinton and Barack Obama.

No Asian has ever been a viable candidate for the presidency. Under the U.S. Constitution, only natural-born American citizens are eligible to become president, but the children of naturalized citizens can hold the highest office. President Barack Obama himself had a Kenyan father. However, in 2009, it remained to be seen whether Obama's election would mark an ascendancy of immigrant and ethnic minority candidates. It could be that Obama's status as an African American, and the long history of unequal treatment of African Americans, will supersede the notion of a candidate for immigrants.

It could very well take a Hispanic president to capture the mantle of an "immigrant" president. Because immigration was strongly associated in public perceptions with Latin countries to the south during the early twenty-first century, immigrant issues have become most salient in Mexican-border states such as Arizona, New Mexico, California, and Texas. It came as little surprise, therefore, that Bill Richardson ran for president as the sitting governor of New Mexico.

The immigration issue that stood out during the first decade of the twenty-first century was indeed tied to border states and immigrants from Latin America: illegal immigration. Illegal immigration has been a thorny topic for American citizens living along the Mexican border, but it has usually been of less concern to those who live elsewhere. Coping with illegal immigration issues can be a difficult challenge for politicians who face uncaring electorates. Humane treatment of apprehended illegal immigrants, as well as fundamental questions of the requirements of citizenship, are topics that will not disappear from the political landscape until they are dealt with more soundly.

U.S. immigration policy has become a bit schizophrenic. Both members of Congress and presidents have been torn between building a wall along the Mexican border and strictly enforcing existing immigration statutes and providing a more compassionate treatment of illegal immigrants as people with inherent rights. Solutions to such a complicated issue are likely to possess subtleties that do not lend themselves well to the simple discourse of modern presidential campaigns. By 2008, the Republican Party had lost much of its appeal among Latin American immigrants because of its harsh stance on immigration. Consequently, Democratic Party candidates for president have enjoyed broader support among immigrant voters—as was the case in the days of Andrew Jackson.

R. Matthew Beverlin

FURTHER READING

Asian American Legal Defense and Education Fund. *Asian American Access to Democracy in the 2008 Elections.* New York: Author, 2009. Report presented to the U.S. Congress about problems faced by Asian Americans in several states while voting during the 2008 elections. Available online in PDF format.

Erie, Steven P. *Rainbow's End.* Berkeley: University of California Press, 1988. Perhaps the best available book on Irish American political machines.

Greenblatt, Alan. "Immigration Debate." In *Urban Issues,* edited by CQ Press Publishing Group. Washington, D.C.: CQ Press, 2009. The product of Congressional Quarterly's research staff, this excellent essay from an edited collection provides an overview of the contemporary immigration policy debate.

Greene, Victor R. *American Immigrant Leaders.* Baltimore: Johns Hopkins University Press, 1987. Covers the political leadership of a number of ethnic immigrant groups including Italians, Poles, and Swedes.

_____. *The Slavic Community on Strike.* Notre Dame, Ind.: University of Notre Dame Press, 1968. Illustrates the importance of labor issues to the tightly woven Slavic immigrant group.

Keyssar, Alexander. *The Right to Vote.* New York: Basic Books, 2000. Well-written historical overview that provides a sweeping perspective of the American tendency to limit enfranchisement, with particular attention to the Whig and Know-Nothing parties.

Vought, Hans Peter. *Redefining the "Melting Pot": American Presidents and the Immigrant, 1897-1933.* Ann Arbor, Mich.: UMI, 2001. Study of the role of U.S. presidents in American immigration policy through an era of heavy European immigration and convulsive changes in U.S. immigration policy.

SEE ALSO: Congress, U.S.; Constitution, U.S.; Immigration waves; *The Jungle*; Latinos and immigrants; Machine politics; Political parties.

PRISONERS OF WAR IN THE UNITED STATES

THE EVENT: Holding of large numbers of enemy military personnel captured during World War II in camps within the United States

DATE: 1943-1946

SIGNIFICANCE: U.S. prisoner of war camps exposed foreign nationals to a humane system of mass incarceration. Through contract-labor and reeducation programs, the camps played an important role in deepening foreign understanding of life within a democratic society. They also aided in creating an atmosphere of renewed acceptance for immigration in postwar America.

When the United States entered World War II in late 1941, its leaders resisted the idea of holding foreign prisoners of war (POW) on domestic soil. Internment camps built by the War Relocation Authority to house first and second-generation Japanese Americans did, however, hold some German "enemy aliens" from various Central American countries, as well as some captured German sailors. Because Great Britain's capacity for holding POWs was becoming severely overtaxed, the United States began accepting prisoners captured by the British after Operation Torch, the Allied landing in November, 1942. By the end of the war, the number of foreign prisoners of war—mostly Germans—on American domestic soil exceeded 425,000. Italians made up less than one-eighth of the total. Japanese prisoners of war, as distinct from interned Japanese Americans, numbered only 5,435.

The camps themselves were designated as "internment camps" until June, 1943, and afterward as "prisoner of war camps." Most were designed to hold 2,000 to 4,000 prisoners. Two-thirds of the camps, 340 out of 511, were located in southern states, with 120 in Texas alone.

GERMAN PRISONERS

German prisoners held on U.S. soil numbered almost 379,000. Arriving in increasing numbers from May, 1943, to May, 1945, they received humane treatment. Their camp facilities included hobby workshops, recreational areas, and PX stores. Meals that met high standards of nutrition were served regularly, until Germany's surrender, when the U.S. military responded to public charges that it been coddling prisoners by lowering standards. Some of the most severe discomforts in the camps were due not to U.S. guards or policies, however, but to internal political strife among the Germans themselves.

Both German and Italian prisoners interacted with local farmers and industry workers early during their incarceration. Initially, prisoners were allowed to work at paid jobs within the camps themselves on a voluntary basis. Over time, they were allowed to work on military bases, and later they could work outside the camps on a contract-labor basis. In Florida, for example, many became fruit-pickers and packers, sugar cane harvesters, and potato diggers. In the sole New Hampshire prisoner of war camp, Camp Stark, on the other hand, logging supplied outside employment.

Of all the prisoners who participated in paid labor, 58 percent worked on U.S. Army posts and about 30 percent in contract work. The rest held jobs within the prisoner of war camps themselves.

German prisoners disembarking at a New York City pier in 1945, under the guard of returning American soldiers. (AP/Wide World Photos)

862

In conjunction with this effort, the military's Prisoner of War Special Projects Division undertook an ambitious plan for reeducating 372,000 of the German prisoners. Rather than attempt to discredit Germany's National Socialist (Nazi) system, the program fostered respect for the American democratic alternative and encouraged positive, unselfish behavior.

Although many German prisoners developed a taste for American life, all were required to leave U.S. soil after the war. The last large group of Germans left the United States on July 22, 1946. However, before being finally repatriated to Germany, many were assigned to rebuilding war-damaged areas in England and France. The number of former prisoners of war who later returned to the United States from Germany to stay is impossible to determine exactly; however, their number has been estimated at about 5,000.

ITALIAN PRISONERS

Of the 500,000 Italian soldiers, sailors and airmen captured by the Allies during World War II, only 10 percent were transferred to the United States. Although American troops captured Tunis and other North African positions from Italian forces by June, 1943, virtually all the Italian prisoners brought to the United States had been captured by British forces in North Africa and Sicily. They arrived during a six-month period in the spring and summer of 1943, and remained in the United States through most of the next three years.

The political status of these Italians became less clear than that of the German prisoners, because of the Armistice that Italy signed with the Allies in September, 1943, shortly before Germany began its own invasion and brutal occupation of Italy. In Allied hands, the Italian prisoners generally found camp life a benign experience. As with the Germans, some of their worst experiences were caused by internal political clashes.

Before being shipped to the United States, Italian prisoners were divided into groups of high and low security risks, with the former predominating among the prisoners brought to the United States. Few of these high-security risks caused actual security problems, however.

The popular American attitude toward the Italian prisoners was more positive than the public attitude toward the German and Japanese prisoners. This may have been due to the fact that Italians constituted the largest foreign-born fraction of the U.S. population. Moreover, the U.S. military encouraged public portrayals of the Italians as congenial, cheerful, and sociable, to further its plans to organize the prisoners into Auxiliary Service Units. Three-fifths of the prisoners eventually participated in these units.

Because of greater freedoms enjoyed by Italian prisoners, in and outside the camps, many enjoyed social lives that brought them into regular contact with the neighboring American communities. Despite the mandatory repatriation of all the prisoners after the war ended, some marriages resulted from social interactions between Italian prisoners and American women. In some cases, the American brides moved to Italy. However, many of these postwar couples subsequently returned to the United States.

The small number of Japanese prisoners held in the United States were incarcerated under higher security than the German and Italian prisoners, primarily in Wisconsin and Iowa. Because of the highly negative public opinions of Japanese soldiers, they had few opportunities for engaging in contract labor or outside socializing.

Mark Rich

FURTHER READING

Billinger, Robert D., Jr. *Hitler's Soldiers in the Sunshine State.* Gainesville: University Press of Florida, 2000. Area study of camps including early enemy-alien internments.

_____. *Nazi POWs in the Tar Heel State.* Gainesville: University Press of Florida, 2008. Detailed examination of state's camp system within larger historical and political context.

Bosworth, Allan R. *America's Concentration Camps.* New York: W. W. Norton, 1967. Classic study of the forced relocation of immigrant and second-generation Japanese Americans.

Gansberg, Judith M. *Stalag: USA.* New York: Thomas Y. Crowell, 1977. Overview of U.S. prisoner of war camp system, covering its development, the problems encountered, and reeducation programs.

Keefer, Louis E. *Italian Prisoners of War in America, 1942-1946: Captives or Allies?* Westport, Conn.: Praeger, 1992. Covers Italian prisoner populations from the time of their surrender to Allied troops until their release, with discussion of their awkward political situation during Germany's occupation of Italy.

Robin, Ron. *The Barbed-Wire College: Reeducating German POWs in the United States During World War II.* Princeton, N.J.: Princeton University Press, 1995. Study of reeducation efforts in U.S. camps for German POWs.

Smith, Arthur L., Jr. *The War for the German Mind.* Providence, R.I.: Berghahn Books, 1996. Places U.S. reeducation efforts in the context of similar programs in Great Britain and Russia.

See also: Asian immigrants; German immigrants; Italian immigrants; Japanese American internment; Marriage; War brides; World War II.

Progressivism

Definition: Social and political reform movement that lasted roughly from the 1890's to 1920, coinciding with America's early twentieth century immigration surge

Significance: Because of its political and social dominance, Progressivism shaped policies regarding immigration and the treatment of immigrants. By linking immigration to other national problems, reformers successfully advocated for new restrictions on immigration and for the rapid assimilation of immigrants already arrived.

Progressivism and immigration, two crucial components of United States history, are so tightly linked that it is difficult fully to understand one independently of the other. The Progressive Era, in which the movement's reform ideals were ascendant in both politics and society at large, neatly coincided with the early twentieth century's immigration surge. Furthermore, the somewhat inconsistent ideals of Progressive reform largely shaped decisions on whether and how to reduce the flow of immigration as well as decisions regarding the treatment of new arrivals.

The Progressive Era was marked by increasingly successful efforts to restrict immigration. Over the course of these years, several federal restriction laws were passed; early legislation barred immigrants with particular characteristics, such as certain diseases or criminal backgrounds, and later laws imposed general head taxes and literacy tests. Although the national origins quota system was not passed until 1921, after the Progressive Era had ended, the idea had its roots in Progressivism, having been proposed years prior to passage.

The link between the movement and immigration restriction is the product of Progressivism's focus on improving social conditions and restoring order following a period of rapid national industrialization and urbanization. To a degree, restriction efforts were based on blatant discrimination toward the new immigrants—southern and eastern Europeans and Asians. Some reformers saw them as culturally and physically inferior to the northern and western Europeans who constituted earlier immigration waves. Others thought that their native loyalties might represent a security threat to the United States during a time of heightened concerns over the global balance of power.

A more indirect link between Progressivism and immigration had to do with a perceived connection between immigrants and many of the other problems targeted by reformers. For example, Progressives fought municipal corruption in the form of powerful political machines and their bosses. Because the immigrant population was a key foundation of the typical machine's power base, an argument was made that reducing immigration levels was the first step toward cleaning up politics. Relatedly, immigrants were seen as contributing to other social ills such as a lower national literacy rate (because many arrived with relatively little schooling), worker exploitation (because some were willing to accept nonunion wages), and the evils of alcohol (because many immigrants were Roman Catholic, and prohibition in America was pushed by Protestant groups). While more enlightened reformers understood that immigrants were just as likely the victims of these social conditions as native-born Americans, it became common simply to premise progress on some reduction in the immigrant surge.

Progressives also targeted immigrants already arrived, basing their efforts on a belief that rapid assimilation, through mandatory education in the English language and American culture, would diminish the deleterious impact of immigrants on society. Some Progressives, however, particularly those associated with Jane Addams and the settlement house movement, were more likely to treat immigrants with dignity and human kinship. These reformers, while seeking to ameliorate poverty, illiteracy, and other problems of the immigrant community, also appreciated the contributions of these newcomers and encouraged the retention of native customs and traditions.

Francine Sanders Romero

FURTHER READING

Higham, John. *Strangers in the Land: Patterns of American Nativism, 1860-1925.* New Brunswick, N.J.: Rutgers University Press, 2002.

Hofstadter, Richard. *The Age of Reform.* New York: Alfred A. Knopf, 1955.

McGerr, Michael. *A Fierce Discontent: The Rise and Fall of the Progressive Movement in America, 1870-1920.* New York: Free Press, 2003.

SEE ALSO: Americanization programs; Dillingham Commission; Eugenics movement; Immigration Act of 1907; Immigration Act of 1917; Immigration Act of 1921; Literacy tests; Machine politics; Nativism; Settlement houses; World War I.

PROPOSITION 187

THE LAW: California state initiative approved by 60 percent of voters to limit public services available to illegal immigrants

DATE: Passed in 1994

ALSO KNOWN AS: Save Our State initiative

SIGNIFICANCE: The first legislation to focus on the public costs of illegal immigration, California's Proposition 187 was written to prevent illegal immigrants from receiving benefits or public services from the state. It

Anti-Proposition 187 demonstrators outside a building in which California governor Pete Wilson was speaking in January, 1996. (AP/Wide World Photos)

arose because of the belief that illegal immigrants caused hardships to California citizens. Critics charged that measure arose out of racism.

The movement to place Proposition 187 on California's ballot began in November, 1993, as the "Save Our State" initiative. Promoted by former agents of the U.S. Immigration and Naturalization Service (INS) as well as several politicians, the measure proposed stricter penalties for false residency documents. It also reversed existing laws by mandating cooperation between the police and the INS. The sections of the law that triggered a bitter public debate denied social services, including nonemergency health care and public education, to illegal immigrants. Officials who delivered public services were also required to report any suspected undocumented person to the INS. The initiative appeared on the November, 1994, ballot as Proposition 187. Proponents had gathered more than 385,000 signatures to place the measure on the ballot.

After the introduction of Proposition 187, much political debate in California focused on the measure. According to the opposition, the measure was the result of white racism and specifically targeted Latinos. Its supporters insisted that they were concerned only with immigration status, a race-neutral phenomenon, and that their opponents were racist in their narrow assessment of the measure. These mutual accusations of racism led to an extremely polarizing debate.

At the time of Proposition 187's introduction, California faced a huge budget deficit. Governor Pete Wilson had requested a $2.3 billion reimbursement from the federal government to cover the state's expenses related to illegal immigration. Wilson also filed lawsuits against the federal government to retrieve money spent for incarcerating, educating, and providing emergency medical care for illegal immigrants. Wilson's requests served to highlight the costs associated with illegal immigrants.

California voters overwhelmingly approved Proposition 187, with many people stating that they had gone to the polls expressly to vote on the measure. In the immediate wake of passage, opponents filed lawsuits and U.S. district court judge Mariana Pfaelzer placed an injunction on enforcement of the measure, ruling Proposition 187 to be unconstitutional on the grounds that the state attempted to regulate immigration, a federal responsibility. The state did not appeal. Undocumented immigrants were never denied public services in the state of California.

Nevertheless, other states tried to copy Proposition 187. The legislation is credited with triggering conservative changes in the Republican Party platform on immigration as well as sparking provisions in federal welfare reform that denied services to legal immigrants. It may have also prompted increases in rates of naturalization and contributed to the politicization of Latinos.

Caryn E. Neumann

FURTHER READING

Jacobson, Robin Dale. *The New Nativism: Proposition 187 and the Debate Over Immigration.* Minneapolis: University of Minnesota Press, 2008.

Ono, Kent A., and John M. Sloop. *Shifting Borders: Rhetoric, Immigration, and California's Proposition 187.* Philadelphia: Temple University Press, 2002.

Wroe, Andrew. *The Republican Party and Immigration Politics: From Proposition 187 to George W. Bush.* New York: Palgrave Macmillan, 2008.

SEE ALSO: California; Citizenship; Economic consequences of immigration; Education; Farm and migrant workers; Illegal immigration; Latinos and immigrants; Los Angeles; Mexican American Legal Defense and Educational Fund; *Plyler v. Doe*; Univision; Welfare and social services.

PUERTO RICAN IMMIGRANTS

SIGNIFICANCE: A small island with more than 4 million people, Puerto Rico has long been seriously overcrowded, making migration to the mainland United States a useful means of reducing population pressures. As a U.S. commonwealth, Puerto Rico has had an open border with the United States that has allowed Puerto Ricans—who are U.S. citizens by law—to move so easily to the mainland that by 2003, emigrants from the tiny Caribbean island had become the second-largest

Workers on a Puerto Rican sugar cane plantation around 1900. (Library of Congress)

PUERTO RICO'S AMBIGUOUS FUTURE

For many decades, Puerto Rican political debates have focused on one defining question: Should the island declare its independence, apply for U.S. statehood, or continue its hybrid "commonwealth" status. Puerto Ricans were granted U.S. citizenship by birthright in 1917. Their island's commonwealth status allows them free access to the United States and many federally provided social services but denies them the right to vote in U.S. elections. Puerto Rico has one nonvoting representative in the U.S. Congress; its citizens can vote in U.S. primary elections of political parties but not in national general elections. At the same time, Puerto Ricans are subject to U.S. military service, and they have served in all American wars since 1900.

Puerto Rico has been a multicultural society for several centuries. When the Spanish first arrived, it was inhabited by Arawak and Taino people, most of whom were killed by European diseases and weapons. Spain formally occupied the island in 1511, a full century earlier than England began colonizing North America. By the time the island was acquired by the United States, it already had a university with degrees recognized in Spain and well-defined cultural traditions of its own.

Puerto Ricans began immigrating to the United States even before the Spanish-American War. Indeed, by 1898, New York City was already home to a small but vigorous community of Puerto Ricans, many of whom were exiles who supported U.S. aid as a measure of liberation from Spain. Some of them cited the American struggle for independence against Great Britain in their calls for greater autonomy for Puerto Rico. Advocates of Puerto Rican independence were profoundly disappointed by the lack of American interest in that goal. The commonwealth status that the United States later granted to Puerto Rico actually restricted Puerto Rican autonomy more severely than the 1897 Charter of Autonomy granted by Spain, especially in extranational matters, such as trade. However,

Latino ethnic group in the United States, trailing only immigrants from vastly larger Mexico. Although most Puerto Ricans are bicultural and speak both English and Spanish, they also have worked to retain their ethnic identity in the United States both collectively and individually, even after more than a century of increasing immigration, provoked mainly by the lure of employment.

Before the Spanish-American War of 1898, the people of the Spanish island colony of Puerto Rico had started to evolve a sense of national identity. In 1897, after four centuries Spanish rule, the island's rich hybrid mixture of Spanish, African, and native Taino and Arawak peoples had acquired a Charter of Autonomy from the Spanish government. Spain's defeat in the Spanish-American War passed control of Puerto Rico to the United States. Since that time, the island's people have faced paradoxical tendencies. While a powerful nationalistic streak has continued to imbue islanders with a strong sense of Puerto Rican identity, large numbers of Puerto Ricans have flocked to the United States.

commonwealth status offers Puerto Ricans the advantages of unrestricted immigration to the United States and integration into the U.S. trade and cultural networks.

New York City as a Point of Entry

After the U.S. occupation of Puerto Rico, immigration to the United States developed slowly. As late as 1910, fewer than 2,000 Puerto Ricans lived in the country, and almost all of them were in New York City. By 1930, the Puerto Rican population of the United States had risen to about 40,000. Soon thereafter, however, the main entry-port of New York City was flooded by Puerto Ricans. Substantial Puerto Rican communities were soon established in Brooklyn, the South Bronx, and Manhattan's East (Spanish) Harlem, lower East Side, parts of the upper East Side, and Chelsea.

Around this same time, Puerto Rico's economy was undergoing an important shift. During the last years of Spanish rule, the island had produced four main export products: sugar cane, coffee, cattle, and tobacco. However, the island's close association with the United States elevated the importance of sugar, which was cheaper to produce in Puerto Rico than in Hawaii or the southern United States, which had previously provided most of the sugar consumed in the United States. The shift to a primarily sugar-based economy under U.S. corporate control took place during the second decade of the twentieth century.

The expansion of large-scale sugar production in Puerto Rico drove many small farmers off their land and into shantytowns in San Juan and other cities, while also creating new pressure for emigration. This powerful "push factor" was intensified during the 1920's and 1930's, when the island's sugar cane industry declined, creating even more unemployment, poverty, and emigration to the United States. As increasing numbers of Puerto Ricans went north, shipping lines established regular routes on which to ferry large numbers of Puerto Ricans between San Juan and New York City, a trip that required four to five days.

Push-Pull Factors, 1940's-1950's

Between 1940 and 1950, the number of Puerto Ricans living in the United States grew by more than 400 percent, from about 70,000 to more than 300,000, including roughly 75,000 children born after their parents' arrival. After the United States entered World War II in 1941, expanding war production drew still more Puerto Ricans to the mainland, providing the island some relief from widespread unemployment. Meanwhile, the Puerto Rican government sought to diversify the island's economy by subsidizing industries such as glass, pulp and paper, shoe leather, and other products through the Puerto Rican Development Corporation. This effort, which began as the Fomento Program in 1942, utilized state capitalism. Later, it was reconstituted as "Operation Bootstrap," under the aegis of private ownership.

The "Bootstrap" program was designed to create jobs and provide an independent economic base that would reduce emigration pressures. Companies, mostly from the United States, were invited to set up plants on the island to take advantage of relatively low wages and tax incentives. With the advent of large-scale jet air travel during the 1960's, the government also promoted tourism, again mainly from the United States. The program enjoyed mixed success, but it had several side benefits, including improvement of the island's roads, water supplies, sewage systems, education, and electrical utilities. Medical care also improved, allowing many Puerto Ricans to live longer. Even with these efforts, the number of new jobs created fell short of needs as continuing evictions of small farmers and steady, natural population growth continued to propel emigration to the United States into the 1950's and early 1960's. More than 69,000 Puerto Ricans moved to the United States in 1953 alone.

Rising prosperity in the United States during those years also played a role in drawing immigrants from Puerto Rico. Net annual immigration, which had averaged between a few hundred and 8,000 from 1920 through the early 1940's, rose quickly to 40,000 during the early 1950's. It peaked at almost 80,000 per year during the mid-1950's then declined rapidly to fewer than 10,000 by the mid-1960's, as new jobs opened in Puerto Rico's own Bootstrap industries. However, many companies that established plants on the island later abandoned them, as even cheaper labor became available in other countries. As unemployment again rose, so also did emigration from the island.

The large amount of Puerto Rican immigration between the end of World War II and the mid-

1960's caused Puerto Rican communities within the United States to grow rapidly. Most new arrivals gravitated to New York City, but Puerto Ricans were beginning to spread out to nearby parts of New Jersey and Connecticut and as far afield as Illinois, Los Angeles, California, and Miami, Florida.

IMMIGRATION AND LABOR

Most Puerto Ricans immigrated to the United States to find jobs. U.S.-based corporations often played an active role in their immigration by advertising stateside employment on the island. Some basic American industries such as cement making and steel manufacturing actively recruited workers from the island. Waves of migration resulted from labor requirements in specific industries, such as textiles in New York City and steel mills in Ohio. Many thousands of immigrants also held jobs in seasonal industries, such as farmwork. The idle season in Puerto Rico's sugar cane industry is summer, which also happens to be the peak season for agricultural labor in the United States.

DEMOGRAPHIC TRENDS

By the time of the 1980 U.S. Census, most Puerto Ricans living in the United States were still concentrated in the Northeast, with 986,802 in New York State alone—an increase of about 50 percent over the figure for 1960. Another 243,540 lived in New Jersey, a 400 percent increase over 1960; 129,165 in Illinois, mostly in and near Chicago, a 400 percent increase over 1960; 88,361 in Connecticut; and 91,802 in Pennsylvania, with a notable community in Philadelphia.

Large Puerto Rican communities in other parts of the United States in 1980 included 94,775 people in Florida, mostly in and near Miami; and 93,038 in California, mostly centered in the Los Angeles area. By 1980, Puerto Ricans were living in every state, with significant numbers even in Alaska (965), Hawaii (19,351), Washington State (5,065), Wisconsin (10,483), and Kansas (2,978).

Between 1960 and 1980, the total Puerto Rican population in the United States rose about 880,000 to almost 2 million. However, only part of this increase was the result of immigration. The rest reflected natural population growth within the United States. By the year 2000, the total Puerto Rican population in the United States was about 3.4 million—a 70 percent increase since 1980.

PROFILE OF PUERTO RICAN IMMIGRANTS

Country of origin	Commonwealth of Puerto Rico
Primary languages	Spanish, English
Primary regions of U.S. settlement	New York City
Earliest significant arrivals	Mid-nineteenth century
Peak immigration periods	1948-1958, 1980's-2008

Source: Department of Homeland Security, *Yearbook of Immigration Statistics, 2008.* Note that as U.S. citizens, Puerto Ricans are not regarded as foreign immigrants when they come to the United States.

Beginning during the 1990's, the Puerto Rican population dispersed from New York City, which had been the overwhelming center of demographic gravity, with more than 80 percent of the group's population within the United States. By 2000, Puerto Ricans in New York City represented only one-quarter of all Puerto Ricans in the United States. However, despite that declining proportion, about 800,000 Puerto Ricans still lived in the city. At the same time, Puerto Ricans in Florida nearly doubled from 247,016 to 482,027 between 1990 and 2000, a 95.1 percent increase. In 2003, a U.S. Census survey found an estimated 760,127 Puerto Ricans in Florida, a 57.7 percent increase in only three years.

Puerto Rico's population in the 2000 Census was 3,808,610, an 8.1 percent increase over 1990. The Census estimated 3,855,000 by 2003, and 4,120,205 in 2007. In 2003, for the first time, the Puerto Rican population in the United States exceeded the number living on the home island. Close to 4 million Puerto Ricans lived in the United States full or part-time by 2008. In Puerto Rican communities, the phrase *aqui y alla* ("here and there") has been used to describe this mass migration back and forth.

PUERTO RICANS IN THE UNITED STATES

By the year 2000, Puerto Ricans in the United States were earning about $54.5 billion a year—

28 percent more than the $42.6 billion earned by fellow Puerto Ricans still on the island. However, immigrants were supplementing island incomes by remitting an estimated $1 billion a year to relatives in Puerto Rico.

Puerto Ricans have maintained collective advocacy for political and social rights, preserving their cultural heritage within the context of broader U.S. society. In New York City, for example, many Puerto Ricans have run for elective offices since the 1920's. In 1937, a Puerto Rican was elected to the New York State Assembly for the first time. By 2008, three Puerto Ricans were serving in the U.S. House of Representatives—two from New York City and one from Chicago. Puerto Rican mayors have also been elected in such American cities as Miami, Florida; Hartford, Connecticut; and Camden, New Jersey—all with the support of large immigrant populations. Puerto Ricans have been targeted by national political parties as a potential swing vote in New York City and Florida.

Advocacy groups for Puerto Rican immigrants including the educational organization Aspira, began in New York City in 1961. Others include the National Conference of Puerto Rican Women, the National Puerto Rican Coalition, the National Puerto Rican Forum, and the Puerto Rican Legal Defense and Education Fund. Puerto Rico's government also maintains services "stateside." Its Department of Labor has maintained an office in New York City since 1930; its Migration Division, which opened in New York City during 1948, by 2005 had offices in 115 American cities.

Bruce E. Johansen

FURTHER READING

Acosta-Belén, Edna, and Carlos Enrique Santiago. *Puerto Ricans in the United States: A Contemporary Portrait.* Boulder, Colo.: Lynne Rienner, 2006. Richly descriptive account of Puerto Rican lives in the United States through the early twenty-first century.

Centro de Estudios Puertorriqueños. *Labor Migration Under Capitalism: The Puerto Rican Experience.* New York: Monthly Review Press, 1979. Socialist perspective of Puerto Rican migration to the United States with an emphasis on immigrants' roles as surplus labor.

Fitzpatrick, Joseph P. *Puerto Rican Americans: The Meaning of Migration to the Mainland.* Englewood Cliffs, N.J.: Prentice-Hall, 1987. Broad survey of Puerto Rican migration to the United States from cultural, sociological, and economic perspectives, with attention to effects of this migration on both Puerto Rico and the United States.

Flores, Juan. *Puerto Rican Arrival in New York: Narratives of the Migration, 1920-1950.* Princeton, N.J.: Markus Wiener, 1997. Individual and family stories of migration, mainly between the two world wars, emphasizing the growth of Puerto Rican communities in and near New York City.

Friedlander, Stanley L. *Labor Migration and Economic Growth: A Case Study of Puerto Rico.* Cambridge, Mass.: MIT Press, 1965. Scholarly study of labor mobility and its relationship to economic growth, using Puerto Rico—with its open border with the mainland United States—as an example of how fluidity of labor flow can enhance productivity and cause problems in all areas that participate.

Hernández Alvarez, José. *Return Migration to Puerto Rico.* Berkeley: Institute of International Studies, University of California, 1967. While most studies of migration between Puerto Rico and the U.S. mainland focus on U.S. immigration, this one concentrates on the reasons why some Puerto Ricans return to the island.

Maraniss, David. *Clemente: The Passion and Grace of Baseball's Last Hero.* New York: Simon & Schuster, 2006. Definitive biography of Roberto Clemente, arguably the greatest Puerto Rican player in Major League Baseball. Looks at Clemente as a social activist as well as a baseball player.

Morales, Julio. *Puerto Rican Poverty and Migration: We Just Had to Try Elsewhere.* New York: Praeger, 1986. Poverty and other "push factors" as major provocations of migration from Puerto Rico to the United States.

Pérez, Gina M. *The Near Northwest Side Story: Migration, Displacement, and Puerto Rican Families.* Berkeley: University of California Press, 2004. Study integrating economic and cultural factors in immigration into the matrix of family relations.

Pérez y González, María. *Puerto Ricans in the United States.* Westport, Conn.: Greenwood Press, 2000. College-level reference book that surveys Puerto Rican history and communities in the United States.

Torre, Carlos Antonio, and Hugo Rodríguez Vecchini. *The Commuter Nation: Perspectives on Puerto*

Rican Migration. Río Piedras, Puerto Rico: Editorial de la Universidad de Puerto Rico, 1994. Wide-ranging description of immigration's role in the history of Puerto Rico, with a focus on shifting demands for labor as a "pull" factor from the island to the United States.

Whalen, Carmen. *From Puerto Rico To Philadelphia.* Philadelphia: Temple University Press, 2001. History of Philadelphia's Puerto Rican community in the context of broader immigration issues.

SEE ALSO: Citizenship; Garment industry; History of immigration after 1891; Latin American immigrants; Latinos and immigrants; New York City; New York State; Santiago, Esmeralda; West Indian immigrants.

PULITZER, JOSEPH

IDENTIFICATION: Hungarian-born American newspaper publisher
BORN: April 10, 1847; Makó, Hungary
DIED: October 29, 1911; Charleston, South Carolina

SIGNIFICANCE: An editor and newspaper proprietor who owned the *New York World* and gave modern journalism its pulse and success, Pulitzer fought against injustice, special privilege, and corruption, claiming support for "the people" and representing immigrants, workingmen, tenement dwellers, and middle-class taxpayers. He introduced pictures, large headlines, and sensationalism to the newspaper world, making the *World* the most widely read daily in the Western Hemisphere.

Joseph Pulitzer was born to Philip Pulitzer, a grain merchant, and Louise Berger near Budapest, Hungary. After being educated privately, he came to the United States as a recruit for the Union Army during the U.S. Civil War. Following his discharge in 1865, he went to St. Louis, Missouri, where he became a reporter for and part owner of the German-language newspaper the *Westliche Post* through his friendship with the paper's German immigrant owner, Carl Schurz. After Pulitzer was naturalized

Chromolithograph of Joseph Pulitzer superimposed over pages from his newspapers. (Library of Congress)

in 1867, he was elected in 1869 to the Missouri House of Representatives. A liberal reformer, he was appointed for a term as police commissioner of St. Louis. He studied law and was admitted to the bar in Washington, D.C., in 1874. That year, having sold his newspaper interest in the *Westliche Post*, he purchased the *St. Louis Staats-Zeitung.* He then sold his interest and its Associated Press franchise to the St. Louis *Globe* (later the *Globe-Democrat*) for a substantial profit. In 1878, he purchased the *St. Louis Dispatch* at auction and merged it with the *St. Louis Post*, which became the *Post-Dispatch.* That year, he married Kate Davis, and they had three sons. In 1880, he became the sole owner of the *Post-Dispatch.*

In 1883, Pulitzer moved east, purchased the *New York World* from Jay Gould, and increased its circulation tenfold. His dedication to truth and accuracy combined with sensational stories and campaigns—sending journalist Nellie Bly around the world, raising funds for the Statue of Liberty's pedestal, competing with William Randolph Hearst for circulation and support for the Spanish-American

War—made Pulitzer one of the most prominent names in American journalism. His newspaper was the democratic podium for his liberal reform politics as he sought protection for immigrants and their socioeconomic interests. He posthumously endowed the Pulitzer Prizes and the School of Journalism at Columbia University (1912).

Barbara Bennett Peterson

FURTHER READING

Barrett, James Wyman. *Joseph Pulitzer and His World.* New York: Vanguard Press, 1941.

Juergens, George. *Joseph Pulitzer and the New York World.* Princeton, N.J.: Princeton University Press, 1966.

SEE ALSO: German American press; German immigrants; Huffington, Arianna; Jennings, Peter; Jewish immigrants; Literature; Melting pot theory.

PUSH-PULL FACTORS

DEFINITION: Factors explaining movements of people across geopolitical boundaries, with push factors being aspects of homelands that motivate nationals to emigrate, and pull factors being aspects of other countries that attract immigrants

SIGNIFICANCE: Push-pull factors are important aspects of migration theory. Since the late nineteenth century, researchers have utilized these models with increasing theoretical and statistical complexity. Push-pull factors help to explain why migrants relocate, in both contemporary times and the past.

Push-pull factors are applied by demographers, geographers, anthropologists, economists, and other social scientists who study human migrations and resettlement. Population movements may occur across regional political boundaries, such as American state lines, or between nations, such as the United States and Canada. They may involve individual migrants moving alone or migrations of entire families or larger groups. Population relocation is important to understand because of its relevance to planning decisions and the well-being of donor regions, host populations, and the new immigrants themselves. Investigation of push factors may, for example, reveal such information about a donor nation as its loss of skilled workers, while investigation of pull factors may yield insights into future issues for the host nation, such as an increase in language instructional needs among adults.

Historians of demography typically trace the origin of migration theory and the development of push-pull factors to Ernest George Ravenstein, who published *The Laws of Migration* in 1885. Ravenstein's concepts were further developed by Everett S. Lee in a 1966 article titled "A Theory of Migration." Lee suggested that pull factors are evaluated by individuals, who appraise their individual benefits at the new locations. For example, if several people consider moving to Washington, D.C., for tertiary education, such a move may be tempting only to those who are likely to be accepted into a Washington, D.C., university. In contrast, push factors often act on entire populations. For example, if a destructive earthquake were to strike Guatemala, all the people affected by the quake might try to leave the area, although only a few might succeed in reaching the United States.

AMERICAN PULL FACTORS

While specific geographic, economic, and political conditions may have immediate application to push-pull factors and population movements, certain characteristics of the United States have influenced immigration for many years. For example, a notable long-term pull factor has been the internal political stability of the United States, which is notably different from many areas of the world. Even when the United States has been involved in major international military conflicts, the conflicts have had limited effects on the nation's internal political stability. American stability during wartime contrasts sharply with many other nations' experiences in world wars and other conflicts. Consequently, the United States is typically viewed as a safe refuge by many people around the world, especially members of oppressed minorities and political refugees.

Aspects of the American legal system have also appealed to people experiencing political harassment and persecution in their homelands. The United States endorses human rights protections, including freedom of religion, which is not the case in all nations. Also, American support of cultural pluralism is seen as a positive trait by people from minority communities in other countries who may not feel free to express their ethnicity, gender, or sexual orientation without repercussions, sometimes even torture or death.

Another attractive long-term characteristic of the United States has been the high level of prosperity enjoyed by its citizens, with the notable exception of the Great Depression of the 1930's, when the United States actually experienced negative immigration. Economic opportunities, including advancement for skilled professionals, have been a major pull factor since the American colonies were first founded, and they continue to attract immigrants. Economic well-being in the United States also correlates with educational opportunities, especially in tertiary education, and with access to modern health care. Many first-generation immigrants to the United States are highly motivated to ensure that their children get first-rate educations and progress to university-level education.

As immigrant populations within the United States grow, members of ethnic communities themselves exert some pull on their compatriots overseas. For example, the significant number of Tongans living in Salt Lake City, Utah encourages fellow Tongans living on Pacific islands to immigrate to Utah, where on arrival they can count on assistance with accommodations, language issues, finding jobs, and other concerns of new immigrants.

PUSH FACTORS IN OTHER COUNTRIES

In contrast to pull factors drawing immigrants to the United States, many often highly specific regional issues encourage people to leave their homelands. North America was first settled by the ancestors of modern Native Americans who immigrated to the New World long before the Europeans arrived. Little is known about the push-pull factors underlying these population movements. However, in the case of later European immigration, it is possible to identity several push factors. Traditional class structures and the economic organization of the European nations kept the lower classes subordinated and living in poverty. Immigration to the American colonies allowed people to transform their socioeconomic standing for the

better. In addition, some early immigrants came to America to escape religious persecution, and others to escape legal sanctions. Still others came to the New World to flee regional food shortages, such as the Great Irish Famine (1845-1852), which drove more than 1.5 million people to leave Ireland for North America.

In contrast to individuals who migrated to the United States to escape problems in their homelands, enslaved immigrants, primarily from West and central Africa, possessed almost no control over their destinies. They were forcibly moved from Africa to the American South before the U.S. Civil War. Treated as chattel, or nonpersons by local laws, many of these people strove to escape from bondage and migrate north to freedom. Despite the risks of harsh penalties, some slaves did manage to escape to the northern states and Canada. The pull of freedom in the North and economic improvement, combined with greater social freedom, became stronger after slavery was abolished when the Civil War ended. Many African Americans moved north to urban locations, including Canadian cities.

In addition to the sharp separation between southern slave states and northern free states before the Civil War, other regional differences influenced immigration patterns. For example, the American Northeast was settled by English-speakers, and other northern Europeans, while the Southeast was initially populated by the French and the Spanish, and the Southwest by the Spanish. These broad trends were augmented by other settlement patterns as the nation grew in geographical extent, political cohesion, and total population. For example, after the 1880's, there was a massive influx of southern and eastern Europeans, including many Jewish people, into the United States. This was the result of social, economic, and political upheaval in Europe that motivated people to leave, although they were often delayed and frustrated by the restrictive U.S. immigration policies and selective naturalization acts typical of the late nineteenth and twentieth centuries.

Twentieth century push factors continued to be poverty, often augmented by civil unrest, or wars, which resulted in many specific populations immigrating in high numbers immediately after regional warfare or disasters. For example, after the communist Cuban Revolution of 1959, hundreds of thousands of Cubans immigrated to the United States. The disruptions of World War II impelled many Pacific Islanders to immigrate to the United States. Many Hungarians fled their homeland after its invasion by the Soviet Union in 1956. Vietnamese, Laotian, and Cambodian refugees came to the United States during the 1970's, after the Vietnam War. Somali civil wars during the 1990's resulted in major movements of refugees and displaced people to the United States.

In addition to civil unrest, natural and human-made disasters have prompted movements of people. In addition to the Great Irish Famine, other examples include a massive earthquake and tidal wave that prompted departures from Italy in 1908, the Halifax explosion in Canada in 1917, and a series of late twentieth century famines in Africa.

POPULATION MOVEMENTS WITHIN THE UNITED STATES

Push-pull factors may also play a role in interstate population movements within the United States. The United States is highly diverse geographically, culturally, and economically, so many of the same types of factors that encourage people to change countries may also induce Americans to migrate across state boundaries. Americans are frequently drawn to new regions by work and educational opportunities. Climate differences also help drive internal migrations. For example, many retirees flee the frigid winters of northern states by migrating to the South. Indeed, northerners who migrate to Florida have been dubbed "snowbirds." Health needs can also drive internal migration, as people with lung disorders might seek out less polluted or drier regions.

The massive migrations of African Americans from the South to northern cities dramatically altered the demographic profile of many American states. Another example was the movement of Pacific Islanders from Hawaii to the mainland, especially California, during the mid-twentieth century.

Americans have also been pushed to leave regions because of natural disasters. The devastation left by Hurricane Katrina and the ensuing floods and civil unrest in 2005 resulted in massive emigration from New Orleans and other affected areas of Louisiana. Many people resettled in Baton Rouge and other locations in Louisiana, and in Texas and Mississippi. People with family or connections in other parts of the United States moved to be near their kin. It was expected that New Orleans would require many years to recover from its population loss.

Susan J. Wurtzburg

FURTHER READING

Boisson, Steve. "When America Sent Her Own Packing." *American History* 41, no. 4 (2006): 20-27. Study of the Great Depression, anti-immigrant sentiment, and other push factors that resulted in a massive migration of people southward into Mexico from the United States.

Grigg, David B. "E. G. Ravenstein and the 'Laws of Migration.'" *Journal of Historical Geography* 3, no. 1 (1977): 41-54. Covers the early history and application of Ernest George Ravenstein's push-pull theory.

Lee, Everett S. "A Theory of Migration." *Demography* 3, no. 1 (1966): 47-57. Definitive article that formulated the concept of push-pull factors for understanding migrations.

Parrado, Emilio A., and Chenoa A. Flippen. "Migration and Gender Among Mexican Women." *American Sociological Review* 70, no. 4 (2005): 606-632. Article examining the complex push-pull involved in individual decisions of Mexicans who immigrated to Durham, North Carolina.

Syed, Nadir Ali, Farhad Khimani, Marie Andrades, Syeda Kausar Ali, and Rose Paul. "Reasons for Migration Among Medical Students from Karachi." *Medical Education* 42, no. 1 (2008): 61-68. Results of research with final-year medical students in Karachi, Pakistan, documenting their reasons for remaining in Pakistan and the factors encouraging them to depart for the United States and other destinations.

Yaukey, David, Douglas L. Anderton, and Jennifer Hickes Lundquist. *Demography: The Study of Human Population.* 3d ed. Long Grove, Ill.: Waveland Press, 2007. Excellent text for learning about demography, and the application of push-pull factors in population research.

SEE ALSO: Chain migration; Economic opportunities; Education; Families; Great Depression; Health care; Natural disasters as push-pull factors; Religion as a push-pull factor; Settlement patterns.

Q

QUOTA SYSTEMS

DEFINITION: Laws setting limits on the numbers of specific nationalities who could immigrate to the United States

SIGNIFICANCE: National quotas set by U.S. immigration laws during the 1920's directly controlled the flow of immigrants from individual countries and effectively banned all Asian immigration for many years. The quotas also prevented many Jews seeking refuge from Nazi genocide during the 1930's from finding safe havens in the United States. In 1965, national quotas were replaced by much more flexible hemispheric quotas.

The first numerical limits on immigrants from specific countries in U.S. immigration law appeared in the 1921 Emergency Immigration Act. During the late 1910's and early 1920's, a serious anti-immigrant fever swept the United States, and many Americans came to believe that too many undesirable immigrants were coming to America. This concern helped lead to enactment of the 1921 law, which set quotas for numbers of immigrants from individual foreign countries. Under the law, only 3 percent of the number of people from a country who had been counted in the 1910 U.S. Census could immigrate each year after 1921.

The Immigration Act of 1924 was even more restrictive. It added a total ban on Asian immigration. This ban targeted primarily Japanese immigrants, as Chinese immigration had been banned since 1882. The new act also lowered the quota percentage from 3 to 2 percent and pushed the baseline year from 1910 back to 1890. This change had a dramatic impact on immigration from countries in eastern and southern Europe, from which much smaller numbers of immigrants had come before 1890. After 1924, all immigration dropped precipitously, even though some favored nations did not even fill their annual quotas. During the Depression years of the early 1930's, the United States even experienced negative immigration, with more people leaving the country than entering it.

The quotas had their most significant impact upon eastern Europeans, particularly Jews, during the 1930's. This was the period when Adolf Hitler's Nazi government came to power in Germany and began adopting anti-Jewish legislation and fostering anti-Jewish violence that made many people want to leave the country. However, U.S. immigration quotas closed the door to significant Jewish immigration, leaving thousands of Jews to perish in the coming Holocaust. Attempts made in the U.S. Congress to pass legislation that would admit an additional 20,000 Jews into the United States failed. The only significant U.S. action that was taken was President Franklin D. Roosevelt's order to have the visas of 15,000 political refugees already in the United States extended indefinitely.

LOOSENING OF THE RESTRICTIONS

After the United States entered World War II during the early 1940's, there was some loosening of quota restrictions. In 1943, for example, China, a U.S. ally in the war, was allowed to send 105 immigrants. During the same year, the Chinese Exclusion Act of 1882 was repealed. The Philippines and British India were also granted small quotas in this period.

During the late 1940's and 1950's, the government continued to loosen the quota system. It also created mechanisms that allowed people to immigrate outside the quota system. For example, the Displaced Persons Act of 1948 allowed refugees from political persecution to immigrate without regard to quotas. The Immigration and Nationality Act of 1952 (also known as the McCarran-Walter Act) made the naturalization system color-blind, thereby allowing more countries to fulfill their quotas. Meanwhile, the Central Intelligence Agency (CIA) managed to sneak foreign scientists into the United States under a 1945 program dubbed Operation Paperclip.

The quota system underwent its most serious alteration with passage of the Immigration and Nationality Act of 1965, in which the entire national origins system was scrapped. Hemispheric quotas then replaced national quotes. A system of preferences was also established, and persons with family ties to American citizens and permanet residents were let in without regard to quotas. These changes greatly increased the numbers of immigrants entering the United States, particularly from countries that had previously had the most severe restrictions. The hemispheric quota system continued into the twenty-first century, but a number of post-1965 laws allowed refugees from communist countries to enter as political refugees without being counted under the quotas.

Scott A. Merriman

FURTHER READING

Barde, Robert Eric. *Immigration at the Golden Gate: Passenger Ships, Exclusion, and Angel Island.* Westport, Conn.: Praeger, 2008. While much of immigration history focuses on the East Coast, Barde focuses on the West Coast, including Angel Island in California, which was the entry point for most who immigrated from Asia and who were also the most often targeted by quotas and bans.

Daniels, Roger. *Coming to America: A History of Immigration and Ethnicity in American Life.* New York: Harper Perennial, 2002. A leading historian, Daniels examines the various peoples who have immigrated to American over the years, combining broad discussions with vignettes about many famous immigrants. He also details the native-born reaction to those immigrants and includes a discussion of the twentieth century immigration quota systems.

Graham, Otis. *Unguarded Gates: A History of America's Immigration Crisis.* Lanham, Md.: Rowman & Littlefield, 2004. General history of immigration, focusing mostly on the twentieth century. Argues that immigration needs to be limited, particularly for national security reasons, and suggests that unchecked immigration will lead to a population explosion.

King, Desmond. *Making Americans: Immigration, Race, and the Origins of the Diverse Democracy.* Cambridge, Mass.: Harvard University Press, 2000. King points out that quotas and categories were used to exclude many immigrants during the 1880 to 1960 period. He also argues that these exclusions had lasting effects on America.

Shanks, Cheryl. *Immigration and the Politics of American Sovereignty, 1890-1990.* Ann Arbor: University of Michigan Press, 2001. Examines how people have defined their Americanness, and how this relates to sovereignty and immigration.

SEE ALSO: Anti-Semitism; Asian immigrants; Chinese Exclusion Act of 1882; Citizenship and Immigration Services, U.S.; Displaced Persons Act of 1948; *Henderson v. Mayor of the City of New York*; History of immigration after 1891; Immigration Act of 1921; Immigration Act of 1924; Immigration and Nationality Act of 1965; Jewish immigrants.

R

RAILROADS

DEFINITION: Transportation networks on which trains carried passengers and cargoes

SIGNIFICANCE: Many of the canals, railroads, and other vast infrastructure projects of the early and mid-nineteenth century were built primarily by immigrant labor. As the rail lines were extended, immigrant workers created ethnic neighborhoods in many American cities and entirely new settlements in the West. After the Civil War, the federal government awarded to railroad corporations large grants of undeveloped land that was eventually parceled and sold to settlers, many of whom were immigrants.

When American railroad construction began during the early nineteenth century, the pool of unskilled native-born labor on which to draw was too small to meet the railroads' needs. At that time, most Americans were farmers, and many urban workers were skilled craftsmen or artisans working in small shops. Consequently, the railroads, like the canals built in earlier years, were built primarily by immigrant labor.

Most of the early railroad workers were German and Irish immigrants, nationalities that accounted for nearly 75 percent of all immigration between 1845 and 1860. Indeed, Irish workers became so common on the railroads and suffered so many fatal injuries that the saying "There is an Irishman buried under every tie" became a common expression. Many of these workers were recruited by agents working for the railroads in the large port cities of the East Coast and in New Orleans. Initially, there was little effort to recruit workers in Europe.

As the railroads extended their lines across vast open spaces between big cities, workers typically lived in makeshift labor camps, and sometimes in railroad cars. Maintaining an adequate supply of workers in these remote places was a continuing challenge for the railroads.

TRANSCONTINENTAL RAILROAD

In 1862, Congress passed the Pacific Railroad Act, which authorized construction of a railroad stretching across the western United States. Two companies built this line. The Union Pacific started building its lines at Omaha, Nebraska, and worked its way west. The Central Pacific built eastward from Sacramento, California. Little construction was done until after the Civil War ended in 1865. The first transcontinental line was completed in May, 1869, when the Union Pacific and Central Pacific lines were joined at Promontory Point in northern Utah. Both railroads used large numbers of immigrant workers. The Union Pacific's labor force included many Civil War veterans, some former slaves, and many immigrants from Germany, Italy, and, most notably, Ireland. It is estimated that between 8,000 and 10,000 immigrants worked on the Union Pacific lines.

At the California end of the railroad, maintaining a constant supply of labor was a continual problem. Although the state's gold rush was essentially over by the 1860's, prospecting still attracted interest in California. Whenever word of new mining strikes came, many railroad workers abandoned their jobs and headed for the mining fields. Eventually, the Central Pacific decided to employ Chinese workers. At first, it hired Chinese men who were already living in California, many of whom had come to prospect and work in the gold mines. Later, the company began recruiting workers in China. Eventually, about 6,000 Chinese worked for the Central Pacific. Many Americans initially doubted the ability of the Chinese to do heavy labor because of their small stature and because of general American racial prejudices against Asians. However, the Chinese proved to be capable, hard workers who quickly learned new skills. Because they often drank tea made with water purified by boiling and ate more healthful diets of food they purchased and prepared themselves, they avoided many of the illnesses that plagued other workers on the line.

Because the Central Pacific lines crossed rugged mountains, the company faced greater construction challenges than the Union Pacific, most of whose lines crossed relatively flat and featureless

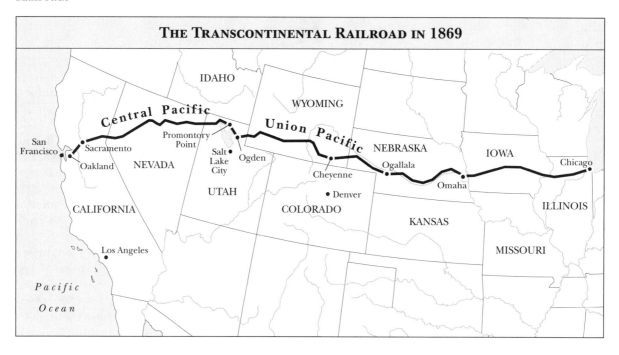

THE TRANSCONTINENTAL RAILROAD IN 1869

plains. As the Central Pacific line extended across the Sierra Nevada range in eastern California and western Nevada, numerous tunnels had to be cut, often through sheer rock faces. Cornish miners from Great Britain were imported to direct this work, in which progress was sometimes measured in inches per day. It was expected that the experienced miners would be able to do this specialized work more efficiently than the Chinese, but the latter soon proved otherwise, and the Cornish workers were paid off and sent home.

In addition to the Union Pacific and Central Pacific lines, four other railroads were built across the western United States during the late nineteenth century. Three lines, which received large land grants similar to those given to the Union Pacific and Central Pacific, were finished in 1883. These included the Northern Pacific, from Lake Superior to the Pacific coast, through Washington Territory; the Southern Pacific, from New Orleans to Los Angeles, California; and the Atchison, Topeka and Santa Fe, from Kansas City, Missouri, along much of the old Santa Fe Trail and then westward to California. In 1893, the Great Northern was completed on a line roughly paralleling the Northern Pacific but about one hundred miles farther north. The Great Northern, however, did not receive a federal land grant.

IMMIGRANT WORKERS

The experience of immigrant railroad workers illustrates two common themes in American immigration history: chain migration and ethnic succession. Chain migration occurred when immigrants came, found work and settled in communities, and then encouraged others from their homelands to join them in America. In this way, ethnic neighborhoods grew up among railroad workers in many large cities, and whole new communities were created by immigrant settlers throughout the West.

Ethnic succession describes the process whereby native-born workers and earlier immigrants gradually moved up to better-paying jobs, and the places they vacated on the lower levels of the economic ladder were taken by newer immigrants. During the late nineteenth century, observers often noted that Italian laborers had largely supplanted the Irish workers in railroad construction and track maintenance jobs. One New York labor agency that specialized in placing railroad workers reported that 75 percent of the workers it was placing on railroads in the north central states around 1900 were Italian immigrants.

As the western railroads were completed, they hired many recently arrived immigrants from southern and eastern Europe. The Western Employment Company had offices in several cities in north central and Pacific Northwest states, and it supplied thousands of workers from Greece, Bulgaria, and Austria to the Great Northern and Northern Pacific railroads. In the Pacific Northwest, the railroads also hired large numbers of Asian workers.

In 1882, the Northern Pacific employed 15,000 Chinese workers on its line in Washington Territory, and another 6,000 worked in Idaho and Montana territories. During the early twentieth century, the Great Northern, the Northern Pacific, and several other lines in the Pacific Northwest employed about 13,000 Japanese workers. These Asian workers faced considerable discrimination and were generally paid less than other workers. The railroad labor pay scales were highest for native-born white workers, slightly less for European immigrants, and still less for Asians, Mexicans, and African Americans. When the railroad work was finished and the Asian workers began looking for

work in the cities of the West Coast, they excited much anti-Asian prejudice and concerns over the "flooding" of the job market. In the Southwest, the Southern Pacific railroad and the Santa Fe employed many Hispanic workers, both American-born and Mexican immigrants, during the late nineteenth and early twentieth centuries.

The western railroads that received large land grants from the federal government had great incentives to recruit settlers. The government made the grants with the idea that most of the land not actually needed for the railroad lines themselves would eventually be sold to settlers. The sales would pay for the construction of the railroads, and the settlers would develop the land. All the western railroad companies had active land departments that advertised widely throughout the eastern United States and in Europe for settlers to come and buy farms or start businesses in towns along the rail-

Illustration from an August, 1869, issue of Harper's Weekly *depicting the completion of the Pacific Railroad, which employed large numbers of Chinese workers.* (Library of Congress)

roads. Recruitment of workers and recruitment of settlers often went hand in hand. Indeed, some people immigrated to work on the railroads with the goal of earning enough money to buy land and then bought railroad land and settled near the tracks.

LIFESTYLES OF THE RAILROAD WORKERS

Construction jobs on the railroads, especially through the northern parts of the country, were largely seasonal, as most work had to stop during winter months. One immigrant worker later recalled how the man who had recruited him had spoken of the big wages awaiting workers, while neglecting to mention they would not earn any money during winter months. Many railroad workers found additional work in other industries such as lumbering, or went south to work in agricultural jobs. Others, however, simply endured the hard winters while waiting for construction work to resume in the spring.

Construction work was largely seasonal, but maintenance of the tracks that had been laid went on year round, as did the repair of cars and locomotives and actual operation of the trains. Many construction workers who remained with the same companies for substantial lengths of time gradually moved into the more permanent jobs in maintenance and operations and then enjoyed steadier work schedules. Some moved into the actual operating service as conductors, firemen, and engineers. These positions were considered skilled jobs and were among the earliest to unionize along craft lines. These craft unions showed little interest in trying to organize or represent the unskilled immigrant workers.

IMMIGRANT TRANSPORTATION AND TRAVEL

Many immigrants who settled in the West were transported to their new homes by railroads. In addition to those who bought land directly from the railroads, many became homesteaders and bought their land directly from the federal government. Although these settlers did not buy railroad land, they represented potential future shippers who would eventually bring farms and ranches into production and use the railroads to carry their produce.

Every western railroad had a large operation aimed at recruiting settlers from Europe. Potential land buyers were given special rates, or sometimes free transportation, to inspect the lands available for purchase. Many railroads built hotels or reception houses to serve these potential land purchasers. Special rates were often given for "immigrant cars," in which migrating families could transport everything they carried to their new homes. Most "new immigrants" of the post-Civil War era remained in the large cities of the East and the Midwest, but those who came specifically with the intention of going to the frontier to farm were the exceptions to this rule. These agrarian immigrant settlers, such as the Scandinavians in Iowa, Minnesota, and the Dakotas; the Germans from Russia in the Plains states; and the Russian Mennonites who settled along the Santa Fe Railroad in Kansas, contributed greatly to the economic development and ethnic diversity of the West and the North Central states.

Mark S. Joy

FURTHER READING

Ambrose, Stephen E. *Nothing Like It in the World: The Men Who Built the Transcontinental Railroad, 1863-1869.* New York: Simon & Schuster, 2000. Highly readable account by a renowned American historian of the building of the Union Pacific-Central Pacific line.

Bain, David Haward. *Empire Express: Building the First Transcontinental Railroad.* New York: Penguin Books, 1999. Deeper than Ambrose's book, this history of the transcontinental railroad is also extensively illustrated and has a full bibliography.

Erickson, Charlotte. *American Industry and the European Immigrant, 1860-1885.* Cambridge, Mass.: Harvard University Press, 1957. Excellent study of the employment of immigrant labor during the Civil War and postwar era.

Michaud, Marie-Christine. *From Steel Tracks to Gold-Paved Streets: The Italian Immigrants and the Railroad in the North Central States.* New York: Center for Migration Studies, 2005. Excellent regional study of Italian railroad workers in upper midwestern states.

Ray, Kurt. *New Roads, Canals, and Railroads in Early Nineteenth-Century America: The Transportation Revolution.* New York: Rosen Publishing Group, 2004. Exploration of how new transportation systems opened the western frontier to settlement. Written for younger readers.

White, W. Thomas. "Race, Ethnicity and Gender in the Railroad Work Force: The Case of the Far Northwest, 1883-1918." *Western Historical Quarterly* 16, no. 3 (July, 1985): 265-283. Detailed regional study of the use of African Americans, immigrants, and women in the labor force in the Pacific Northwest during the period after the completion of the Northern Pacific and Great Northern railroads.

SEE ALSO: Canals; Chain migration; Chinese immigrants; Employment; History of immigration, 1783-1891; Irish immigrants; Italian immigrants; Mexican immigrants; Transportation of immigrants.

RAPP, GEORGE

IDENTIFICATION: German-born founder of the Rappite religious community
BORN: November 1, 1757; Iptingen, Duchy of Württemberg (now in Germany)
DIED: August 7, 1847; Economy, Pennsylvania

SIGNIFICANCE: After emigrating from Germany to the United States in 1803, George Rapp established a religious commune near Pittsburgh, Pennsylvania, with six hundred followers, believing that God had told him to form a radical pietist Christian community. The community was successful in its commercial activities, including farming, silk production, banking, and the manufacture of various crafts.

While he was living in Germany, George Rapp advocated a social order derived from the New Testament that led to him. After suffering local persecution, Rapp led his followers to the United States to avoid both religious persecution and military conscription, as his movement held pacifist beliefs. Rapp initially planned to move to Louisiana because of the influence that John Law previously had in populating that area with Germans. On French maps, the area between New Orleans and Baton Rouge was called the German Coast. However, upon applying to the French emperor Napoleon I for permission to settle in the French territory, Rapp was told that the area had been sold to the United States government as part of the Louisiana Territory.

Upon relocating in Baltimore, Rapp and his followers were given generous assistance by German residents of that city. In 1804, Rapp purchased five thousand acres in Pennsylvania, where he transformed his following into the Harmony Society. Because the society had members who were too old to work, a communal life was adopted. On February 15, 1805, all possessions were conveyed to Rapp and placed in a common fund. Because members believed in the imminence of the end of the world, they were willing to give up possessions. Throughout the group's history, February 15 was to be celebrated as a holiday called Harmoniefest.

The Rappites' move to Indiana in 1814 was prompted by a shortage of good soil for vine growing in Pennsylvania. After buying 30,000 acres in southwestern Indiana. the group prospered, and its prosperity attracted new immigrants from Germany. When the Rappites had first come to America, their wealth had averaged only twenty-five dollars each; by 1824, that figure had increased to two thousand dollars—an amount thirteen times greater than that of the average Indianan. This disparity aroused local envy. Increasing persecution by neighbors moved the Rappites to sell their land to Robert Owen in 1824 and buy new land near Pittsburgh, close to their original location.

The progress of the Rappites was closely monitored in the United States and Europe, because they had become famous for their achievements. Meanwhile, a religious schism arose within the group because Rapp's prophecy about Christ's return to Earth never materialized. In 1831, Rapp thought his prophecy had come true because of the appearance of a man named Count Leon. However, Leon proved to be merely a competitor who worked to draw Rapp's followers to his own utopian community. When Leon eventually left, he took with him about 250 of Rapp's followers. Afterward, dissension remained within Rapp's community. After Rapp died in 1847, the Rappite community gradually broke up and disappeared.

Dale L. Flesher

FURTHER READING
Arndt, Karl J. R. *George Rapp's Harmony Society, 1785-1847.* Philadelphia: University of Pennsylvania Press, 1965.

_____. *Harmony on the Connoquenessing, 1803-1815: George Rapp's First American Harmony.* Worcester, Mass.: Harmony Society Press, 1980.

_____. *Harmony on the Wabash in Transition, 1824-1826.* Worcester, Mass.: Harmony Society Press, 1982.

Wilson, William E. *The Angel and the Serpent: The Story of New Harmony.* Bloomington: Indiana University Press, 1964.

SEE ALSO: Economic consequences of immigration; Economic opportunities; European immigrants; German immigrants; Indiana; New Harmony; Pennsylvania; Religion as a push-pull factor; Religions of immigrants.

RED SCARE

THE EVENT: Brief period during which post-World War I public hysteria fueled by Russia's Bolshevik Revolution led to government harassment of radicals, trade unionists, and political dissidents—particularly those of foreign birth, many of whom were deported

DATE: 1919-1920

SIGNIFICANCE: Growing out of efforts to silence antiwar voices during World War I, the Red Scare became a means of justifying government repression and disregard for civil liberties against revolutionary, labor, and pacifist groups. The assault fell hardest on immigrant laborers and sought to divide presumably loyal, native-born workers from less-trustworthy foreign-born workers.

After American entry into World War I in early 1917, a number of developments combined to create the conditions for a red scare that would result in illegal searches and seizures and ultimately the deportation of hundreds of immigrants without due process of law. Active antiwar agitation, led by the Socialist Party, among others, was attacked as being akin to giving aid and comfort to the enemy. Moreover, the comparatively large number of German Americans who were active in radical movements made it easier to paint a picture of disloyal and ungrateful immigrants.

In 1917, the U.S. Congress passed the Espionage

A. Mitchell Palmer before he became U.S. attorney general. (Library of Congress)

Act to create a legal tool for suppressing any kind of action that could construed as interfering with the national war effort. A year later, it passed the Sedition Act of 1918, which allowed the government to punish any form of speech expressing disloyalty toward or abuse of the government. The government's readiness to enforce these draconian laws was increased by the success of the radical Bolshevik Revolution of October, 1917, an event that greatly alarmed American industrialists. By the following year, the postmaster general was ordering the confiscation from the U.S. mails massive amounts of Socialist Party literature, which he had publicly burned.

Into this climate of fear and suppression of civil liberties came A. Mitchell Palmer, the U.S. attorney general under President Woodrow Wilson. Palmer was determined to rid American society of all political radicals. In August, 1919, Palmer established the antiradical General Intelligence Division with the U.S. Department of Justice. He appointed as its head a very young J. Edgar Hoover, the future long-term director of the Federal Bureau of Investigation. Hoover promptly began assembling an elaborate card index of radical organizations, publications, and leaders.

In November, 1919, agents working under Hoover raided the headquarters and branches of a labor society known as the Union of Russian Workers. Throughout the United States, state and local officials carried out smaller actions, which came to be known as Palmer raids, on suspected radicals. While these raids were going on, members of Congress began introducing bills to deport foreign radicals. When 249 foreign deportees were placed aboard an old army transport ship to be returned to Europe, the ship was dubbed the "Soviet Ark" in the news media. The last and largest of what became known as the Palmer raids were carried out in January, 1920. Afterward, antiradical hysteria abated, and the Red Scare ended.

Ethnic and racial prejudices seemed to feed the Red Scare hysteria, as Russians, Italians, Germans, and Jews were singled out as unworthy of American residence. Another prime target of the Red Scare was trade unionists, particularly immigrants, leftist militants, and even those who merely went out on strike. During the height of the Red Scare, one U.S. senator even went so far as to propose sending radicals who were native-born American citizens to a penal colony that was to be established on Guam.

The antiradical paranoia spread by much of the mainstream press contributed to harassment, physical attacks, and even murders of immigrants. Eventually, however, the increasingly extreme claims made about radical threats tended to backfire and dampen public antiradical fervor. Some historians have suggested that the end of the Red Scare can be dated to May 1, 1920, when A. Mitchell Palmer predicted a massive communist uprising that never materialized.

William A. Pelz

Further Reading

Ackerman, Kenneth. *Young J. Edgar Hoover: The Red Scare and the Assault of Civil Liberties.* New York: Da Capo Press, 2008.

Gengarelly, W. Anthony. *Distinguished Dissenters and Opposition to the 1919-1920 Red Scare.* Lewiston, N.Y.: Edwin Mellen Press, 1996.

Murray, Robert K. *Red Scare: A Study in National Hysteria, 1919-1920.* Reprint. Minneapolis: University of Minnesota Press, 2009.

Post, Louis F. *The Deportations Delirium of Nineteen-Twenty.* 1923. Reprint. Seattle: University Press of the Pacific, 2003.

See also: Alien and Sedition Acts of 1798; Deportation; Espionage and Sedition Acts of 1917-1918; German immigrants; Goldman, Emma; Jewish immigrants; Labor unions; Russian and Soviet immigrants; Sacco and Vanzetti trial; World War I.

Refugee fatigue

Definition: Reluctance of countries to host growing numbers of refugees and asylees

Significance: There is a rift between the growing number of refugees and displaced persons in the world and the countries that are able to assist them. Refugees are in limbo, living in camps that are constructed along national borders and supported by international humanitarian aid. Host nations face economic uncertainty, and, because of national security threats, immigration restrictions are heightened.

Refugees are the victims of oppression and human rights abuses in their home countries. Their ways of life are typically threatened by their own governments or violent rebel groups. During the first decade of the twenty-first century, the majority of the world's refugees emigrated from Southeast Asia and Africa and sought assistance from both neighboring countries and developed nations.

While fleeing from persecution, refugees often find themselves fighting through red tape to find stable places in which to relocate. Camps are constructed along borders of neighboring states, with refugees living day to day on humanitarian aid services. Some camps are intended as temporary refuge until political unrest and violence dissipates, allowing citizens to return to their homes. These camps often remain under threat from oppressors. During the first decade of the twenty-first century, the Janjaweed militiamen in the Darfur region of Sudan continually attacked camps of people fleeing the genocide. Other camps, such as those on the Thai-Burmese border, have been in place for more than twenty years. In cases like this one, the younger generations are unaware of life outside refugee camps. Although food is made available to the refugees, education and additional resources are limited. Regulations make it virtually impossible to travel outside the camp or to obtain employment.

With growing numbers of refugees seeking places to live during the early twenty-first century, the international community has struggled to find countries willing to take them. Border countries already feel the strain on their economy from border camps and illegal immigration. In the United States, national security concerns and a recession (beginning in late 2007) are major factors that limit the number of refugees admitted. Few applicants have family already in the United States, and their education and English-language skills are limited. Efforts are made to return refugees to their home countries when it is safe, but it is difficult to estimate how long refugees will remain in the United States or how many will seek permanent legal status once they have arrived.

The terrorist attacks on U.S. soil on September 11, 2001, led to stricter immigration standards, established in the Patriot Act of 2001. In 2000, the United States accepted 68,925 refugees; in 2002, the number of admitted refugees fell sharply to 26,773. Some of these standards have been relaxed, but national security remains a high priority. About half a million refugees were relocated to the United States during the first decade of the twenty-first century, but the numbers are in decline despite the increasing number of refugee applicants. Potential host countries face a moral dilemma: whether to host refugees whose lives are threatened and who are without homes, or to limit the number of refugees allowed in the country because of national security and economic issues.

Tessa Li Powell

FURTHER READING

Lischer, Sarah Kenyon. *Dangerous Sanctuaries: Refugee Camps, Civil War, and the Dilemmas of Humanitarian Aid.* Ithaca, N.Y.: Cornell University Press, 2005.

Martin, Susan F., et al. *The Uprooted: Improving Humanitarian Responses to Forced Migration.* Lanham, Md.: Lexington Books, 2005.

Whittaker, David. *Asylum Seekers and Refugees in the Contemporary World.* New York: Routledge, 2006.

SEE ALSO: Economic consequences of immigration; Refugee Relief Act of 1953; Refugees; Select Commission on Immigration and Refugee Policy; Welfare and social services; World migration patterns.

REFUGEE RELIEF ACT OF 1953

THE LAW: Federal legislation that created a means of admitting displaced persons outside the national quota system on an emergency basis

DATE: Enacted on August 7, 1953

SIGNIFICANCE: Five years after passage of the Displaced Persons Act of 1948, the Refugee Relief Act of 1953 allowed anticommunist refugees, or those who had reason to fear living under communist control, entry into the United States under a special set of regulations. Anticommunist refugees, ethnic Germans who had previously resided in non-German countries but who had been expelled after the collapse of Nazi Germany, war orphans, and members of military forces who had fought on the Allied side during World War II all became eligible for immigration to the United States under special quotas. However, with the exception of war orphans, these refugees had to prove that if they were unable to emigrate, they would become subject to government persecution in their own countries.

The Refugee Relief Act of 1953 provided an additional 205,000 immigration visas for specific categories of aliens, their spouses, and their dependent children. An additional 4,000 visas were made available for orphans under the age of ten whom U.S. citizens had agreed to adopt. The law made these visas available until the end of 1956 in order to allow U.S. immigration officials time to investigate individual immigrants' applications. The lengthy application and investigation process also allowed immigrant assistance groups in the United States time to raise sufficient funds to cover the transportation and resettlement of refugees in the United States.

Under the law, every adult applicant had to provide suitable proof of identity. Those who claimed they were threatened by persecution or feared they would be persecuted on the basis of their race, religion, or ethnic origin, also had to provide sufficient documentation of those threats to warrant their emergency immigration. Applicants also had to provide evidence of their employability in the United States and assurances that neither they nor any members of their families immigrating with them would go on welfare in the United States. Finally, applicants had to show that whatever jobs they took would not displace American workers.

The largest number of visas, 55,000, was reserved for ethnic Germans then residing in Allied-controlled sections of Germany who had been expelled from their homes in eastern European countries at the end of World War II. The second-largest number of visas, 45,000, was reserved for Italians who found themselves living in Soviet-controlled portions of Yugoslavia after the end of the war. Another 35,000 visas were reserved for applicants of any ethnic origin who had managed to escape from territories controlled by the Soviet Union immediately following the war. These people had to reach Austria or Allied-controlled sectors of Germany in order to become eligible to apply. Up to 10,000 refugees who escaped from communist-controlled territories and reached Turkey, Sweden, or Iran were also eligible to apply.

IMPLEMENTATION OF THE LAW

Unlike the Displaced Persons Act of 1948, which directly addressed the problems of persons displaced by World War II, the Refugee relief Act of 1953 addressed cases of persons whose military service or political activities in the war were still causing them problems, as they ended up in Soviet-controlled territories as Cold War tensions between the United States and the Soviet Union were rising. For example, former soldiers in the Free Polish Forces were allotted 2,000 visas, and about 17,000 visas were allotted to Greeks due to problems stemming from the Greek civil war against communism that began after World War II. Another 5,000 visas were reserved for Chinese anti-communists. Jewish refugees still resident anywhere in Europe were granted a special allotment of 2,000 nonquota visas to immigrate to the United States instead of Israel.

U.S. immigration officials worked with the Intergovernmental Committee for European Migration to standardize financial arrangements for transportation to the United States for applicants who had been approved for immigration and had proof of employment and housing awaiting them. Family members in the United States or immigrant assistance groups had to furnish evidence of support for sponsored immigrants. In order to help immigrant assistance groups in the United States, the act allowed the U.S. Department of the Treasury to lend these groups up to five million dollars to aid in resettlement costs. Indigent applicants were not eligible to apply. To be considered, applicants had to produce documentation to support their personal histories for at least two years prior to application. Anyone found guilty of misrepresentation of facts on the application was permanently denied consideration. Applicants already in the United States who falsified their applications were subject to immediate and permanent deportation.

In an effort to prohibit former Nazis and members of certain other groups from applying, anyone who advocated or participated in any form of racial or religious persecution was automatically and permanently denied consideration. Applicants with job skills in demand in the U.S. workforce were given priority consideration, as were those who had family members who were U.S. citizens and were willing to sponsor the applicant.

Victoria Erhart

FURTHER READING

Bon Tempo, Carl J. *Americans at the Gate: The United States and Refugees During the Cold War.* Princeton, N.J.: Princeton University Press, 2008. Examines the Refugee Relief Act of 1953 in terms of massive changes in immigration policies and law in the United States following World War II.

Freedman, Jane. *Gendering the International Asylum and Refugee Debate.* New York: Palgrave Macmillan, 2007. Wide-ranging examination of the experiences of women refugees that focuses on differences between what male and female refugees go through.

LeMay, Michael, and Elliott Robert Barkan, eds. *U.S. Immigration and Naturalization Laws and Issues: A Documentary History.* Westport, Conn.: Greenwood Press, 1999. Collection of one hundred primary documents on immigration issues, with analyses.

Whittaker, David. *Asylum Seekers and Refugees in the Contemporary World*. New York: Routledge, 2006. Broad discussion of issues arising from the growing numbers of refugees around the world.

SEE ALSO: Displaced Persons Act of 1948; German immigrants; Immigration and Nationality Act of 1952; McCarran Internal Security Act of 1950; Quota systems; Refugee fatigue; Refugees; World War II.

REFUGEES

DEFINITION: People forced to live outside their homelands because of government persecution or high risks of maltreatment based on their ethnicity, race, religion, or associations with social or political groups

SIGNIFICANCE: Government persecution, and its most severe form, genocide, is a major violation of individual human rights and group welfare. It is signified by humanitarian crises and population migrations that generally require international collaboration to ameliorate.

It is important to distinguish refugees who cross international borders from internally displaced persons (IDPs) who migrate within their own countries' boundaries to escape high levels of persecution or other harms, such as civil wars or natural disasters. Worldwide aid agencies, such as the International Red Cross and Médecins Sans Frontières (Doctors Without Borders), often work in conjunction with the United Nations High Commissioner for Refugees (UNHCR) on behalf of people in both these groups.

The UNHCR was established by the United Nations (U.N.) General Assembly in December, 1950, in response to the post-World War II European humanitarian crisis. The mandate of the agency has always been to safeguard refugees and to assist with relocation. During the early twenty-first century, the UNHCR employed approximately 6,500 people in 116 different nations and had assisted more than 34.4 million refugees. The UNHCR also con-

nects with other international and national agencies to help refugees and displaced peoples: organizing camps for people in exile, providing transportation, and assisting with resettlement in host nations.

The term "refugee" was defined in the 1951 U.N. Convention Relating to the Status of Refugees. Key tenets of the convention are that refugees should be provided with procedures for obtaining passports and should be assured they will not be returned to the countries in which they have experienced persecution. This international codification was important because it provided uniformity to a confusing array of national laws focusing on refugee issues. For example, the United States had enacted the Displaced Persons Act of 1948, and other countries had their own individual legislation, but there was little uniformity among different legal jurisdictions. The U.N. ratification process ensures that as member nations become signatories to conventions, there is movement toward international legal conformity.

During the early 1950's, U.N. members were highly aware of World War II atrocities, encouraging a treaty focus on nationality, race, religion, and sociopolitical groups, with little attention to gender, sexual orientation, or other human differences that may result in persecution. The 1951 U.N. convention granted rights to refugees and provided them with a process for formalizing new citizenship statuses. However, it applied only to people who had become refugees because of events occurring before 1951. Ongoing wars and humanitarian crises during the 1950's and 1960's meant that the original convention needed an extension. For this reason, the 1967 Protocol Relating to the Status of Refugees removed the 1951 cutoff date and ensured ongoing protection of refugees.

TWENTY-FIRST CENTURY REFUGEES

By the early twenty-first century, widespread political and social unrest around the world was placing large numbers of people at risk of harm. A 2005 estimate by the UNHCR suggested that approximately 8.4 million of the estimated 191 million migrants of that year could be considered refugees. In early 2008, the UNHCR stated that 31.7 million people were of concern to the international organization, including 11.4 million refugees, 13.7 million internally displaced people, 3 million stateless people, 2.8 million returned refugees and IDPs, 740,100 asylees, and 68,700 unspecified others. Despite its huge size, this number of people was lower than that for the previous year, when 32.9 million were estimated to be at risk worldwide.

In 2008, the highest number of refugees was from Afghanistan (3 million), followed closely by Iraq (2.3 million). These people and many of the others at risk of persecution, and protected by the UNHCR, hoped to receive residential status from one of the many nations that accept refugees, including the United States.

REFUGEES IN THE UNITED STATES

The United States is one of a group of forty-four countries that provide monthly asylum data to the UNHCR. The other non-European nations that provide such information are Australia, Canada, Japan, New Zealand, and South Korea. In both 2007 and 2008, asylum requests increased dramatically throughout the reporting countries, reflecting increased unrest around the world. For the period 2006-2008, the United States received the largest number of applications for asylum, and in 2008, the United States also ranked first in the world in the number of asylum seekers it accepted.

The United States has not always welcomed asylum seekers. An infamous example was the attempt by the German vessel *St. Louis* to carry 937 Jewish refugees from Nazi persecution in Europe to the United States in May, 1939. After crossing the Atlantic, the ship docked in Havana, Cuba, where its captain tried to disembark all his passengers so they could await U.S. immigration decisions while in a safe location. Cuba refused entry to all but twenty-eight of the passengers. A few days later, the U.S. State Department denied entry to the remaining travelers. The refugees were shipped back to Europe, where more than six hundred of them later died in Nazi death camps. Later U.S. governmental initiatives, however, have been more welcoming to refugees. Indeed, many international treaties focusing on refugees have been mirrored by American legislative initiatives. For example, the Refugee Relief Act of 1953 was signed into law by President Dwight D. Eisenhower only a few years after the U.N. Convention Relating to the Status of Refugees was drafted. This U.S. law upheld the U.N. definition of refugee and allocated quotas to

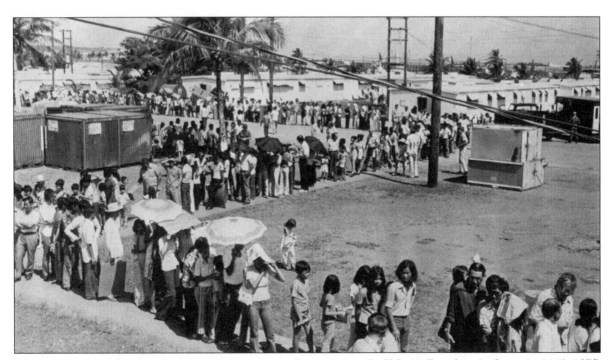

Vietnamese refugees lined up for food at the temporary refugee camp at the U.S. Air Force base in Guam in April, 1975. Most of these people were later relocated to the United States. (AP/Wide World Photos)

different refugee groups, focusing primarily on Europe but also covering some regions in the Middle East and Far East. Almost two decades later, another special refugee act was signed by President Gerald R. Ford. The Indochina Migration and Refugee Assistance Act of 1975 was enacted in response to conditions in South Vietnam immediately after the Vietnam War ended and Saigon was occupied by communist forces. The 1975 law provided additional refugee quotas and funds for Vietnamese and Cambodian refugees seeking to escape violence directed toward them because of their collaboration with the U.S. military.

Within a few years of passage of the 1975 act, it became apparent to American government employees that it was inefficient for the United States to enact individual pieces of legislation to deal with each humanitarian crisis that arose. It made more sense to devise an overarching law that would always be in place to provide a process for dealing with new crises as they arose, in an efficient and timely manner. For this reason, the Refugee Act of 1980 came into being. This act created the Office of Refugee Resettlement, which administers programs and services for refugees within the United States. The new law also established a method for setting refugee quotas by empowering the president and Congress to perform this task. For the period 2003-2008, the American refugee quota was set at 70,000 per year. Refugees and asylees are treated slightly differently in the act, which does not set a quota for the latter.

The United States recognizes two types of exile status: refugees and asylees. Refugees receive their designation outside the United States and often reside in refugee camps for many years prior to acceptance by the United States. Asylees are individuals who announce their status at the U.S. border when they arrive by land, sea, or air. They then often live in detention facilities for many months, if not years, while their claims are processed. Between 1997 and 2006, the United States accepted an average of approximately 98,000 refugees and asylees each year. Since the creation of the U.S. Department of Homeland Security in 2003, refugee and asylee claims have been processed by the department's U.S. Citizenship and Immigration Services branch.

Refugees and asylees have come to the United States from around the world. A small number of source countries generally predominate each year,

depending on the locations of global trouble spots. In 2008, 90,030 refugees and 76,362 asylees were admitted to the United States as legal permanent residents. They made up 15 percent of the legal permanent residents accepted in that year.

The 2007 data demonstrate that 48,217 refugees and 25,270 asylees were accepted by the United States. The primary donor nation was Burma, followed by Somalia and Iran. The previous year, most asylees were from China, followed by Colombia and Haiti. The primary nations from which refugees came were Somalia, Russia, and Cuba. All of these disparate groups have to find a way of living together in the United States once they are accepted as legal permanent residents.

REFUGEE CHALLENGES IN THE UNITED STATES

Living in the United States can be difficult for refugees. They typically arrive after experiencing considerable hardship in both their home countries and countries in which they have resided while awaiting acceptance into the United States. When they finally reach the United States, they generally have little money, few possessions, and limited understandings of American culture and what they need to know to find homes, food, education, and social services. The support they receive from government and private aid agencies seldom lasts for more than a few months, and within a short period of time, they must find work to support their families. This can be incredibly difficult for individuals who may have spent years living in refugee camp, especially if they possess minimal fluency in English and have limited job skills.

Refugee families often have young children who have received negligible schooling for several years and are consequently completely baffled by what they are expected to do in American schools, often in an unfamiliar language. Refugee families also generally have little understanding of the American legal system, and may unknowingly contravene laws of which they are unaware, such as driving license requirements and child-abuse codes. Parents who were powerful figures in their homelands can easily become marginalized in the United States, where they receive little respect from either Americans or their own offspring.

For all of these reasons, the settlement process can be demoralizing for refugees who have newly arrived in the United States. In fact, some refugees find that life in the United States is so difficult that they choose to return to the dangerous circumstances of their home nations, rather than struggle to rebuild their lives in a culture that is almost completely alien to them. The early twenty-first century saw some highly publicized accounts of Iraqi refugees who left the United States for the uncertainties of life back in Iraq.

Susan J. Wurtzburg

FURTHER READING

Chang-Muy, Fernando, and Elaine P. Congress, eds. *Social Work with Immigrants and Refugees: Legal Issues, Clinical Skills, and Advocacy.* New York: Springer, 2009. Excellent resource for understanding a wide range of issues affecting refugees who come to the United States.

Daniels, Roger. *Coming to America: A History of Immigration and Ethnicity in American Life.* 2d ed. New York: HarperCollins, 2002. Excellent history of immigration and refugee law in the United States with very useful supporting data.

Freedman, Jane. *Gendering the International Asylum and Refugee Debate.* New York: Palgrave Macmillan, 2007. Examination of women's experiences, focusing on differences between men's and women's refugee pathways.

Goździak, Elżbieta, and Micah N. Bump. *New Immigrants, Changing Communities: Best Practices for a Better America.* Lanham, Md.: Lexington Books, 2008. Practical consideration of the kinds of issues that refugees face after they arrive in the United States.

Hollenbach, David, ed. *Refugee Rights: Ethics, Advocacy, and Africa.* Washington, D.C.: Georgetown University Press, 2008. Collection of essays on African refugees and the challenging conditions that they face in refugee camps.

Loescher, Gil, Alexander Betts, and James Milner. *The United Nations High Commissioner for Refugees (UNHCR): The Politics and Practice of Refugee Protection into the Twenty-first Century.* New York: Routledge, 2008. Broad coverage of refugee issues, including the history of international collaboration, and refugee conventions.

McKay, Sonia, ed. *Refugees, Recent Migrants and Employment: Challenging Barriers and Exploring Pathways.* New York: Routledge, 2008. Edited collection of recent research on a wide variety of aspects of refugee issues.

Pipher, Mary. *The Middle of Everywhere: The World's Refugees Come to Our Town.* New York: Harcourt, 2002. Empathetic narration of American refugee stories.

SEE ALSO: Censuses, U.S.; Citizenship and Immigration Services, U.S.; Congress, U.S.; Holocaust; Indochina Migration and Refugee Assistance Act of 1975; Refugee fatigue; Refugee Relief Act of 1953; Stereotyping.

RELEASED RE-EDUCATION DETAINEE PROGRAM

IDENTIFICATION: Federal program implementing an agreement with the government of Vietnam to resettle Vietnamese who had been interned in reeducation camps in the United States

DATE: Established on July 30, 1989

ALSO KNOWN AS: Humanitarian Operation

SIGNIFICANCE: The Released Re-education Detainee Program provided a pathway for Vietnamese who had been sent to reeducation camps by the communist government of Vietnam after the fall of the South Vietnamese government in 1975 to emigrate to the United States with their families.

After the fall of the South Vietnamese government in 1975, thousands of Vietnamese fled the country to escape possible reprisals from the new communist government. Many of these people died at sea while trying to flee in small boats, and in poorly supported refugee camps in Southeast Asia. Meanwhile, many of those unable to leave Vietnam were interned by the national government in "reeducation" camps, which were actually prison camps aimed at punishing those who had worked for the South Vietnamese government or U.S. forces and indoctrinating them in communist ideology.

By 1979, the United Nations persuaded the new national government of Vietnam to participate in what became known as the Orderly Departure Program. Over the next two decades, various humanitarian efforts were launched to help Vietnamese wishing to emigrate to find homes in other countries. Many Vietnamese successfully relocated to various countries around the world, including the United States. However, little progress was made in persuading Vietnam's government to alleviate the condition of current and former internees of its reeducation camps.

Feeling a special obligation to certain groups of Vietnamese, during the 1980's the U.S. government developed programs to encourage immigration of Vietnamese children of American servicemen, families of those children, and former employees of the South Vietnamese and U.S. government and their families. In 1984, U.S. secretary of state George Schultz negotiated an agreement to allow members of these groups to come to the United States. However, the Vietnamese government dragged its feet in signing onto the program and permitting its people to leave the country legally. While some Amerasian children were allowed to depart, adults who had served time in reeducation camps were usually blocked from leaving, frequently as a result of inordinately complicated bureaucratic requirements. Eventually, however, back-and-forth negotiations between the U.S. and Vietnamese governments resulted in passage by the U.S. Congress of a new law, the Released Re-education Detainee Program, in July, 1989. Under the provisions of that law, Vietnamese who had spent at least three years in reeducation camps were eligible for expedited processing to emigrate to the United States.

The Released Re-education Detainee Program quickly became known as Humanitarian Operation. Frequently this term was used to designate the efforts to resettle former internees as well as those designed to assist children of American servicemen. Both initiatives were particularly successful. Through the five years following passage of the law, the number of individuals in these categories taking advantage of the program increased steadily.

By 1994, when the program expired, more than 70,000 former internees and their families, as well as thousands of Amerasian children and their fami-

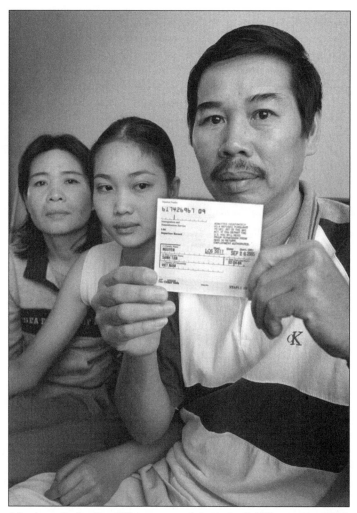

Members of a family of Vietnamese refugees who fled Vietnam in 1989. As stateless refugees, they had to spend many years in a Philippines refugee camp before they reached the United States, where they finally achieved legal immigrant status in 2005. Here, the father holds the document certifying their legal immigrant status. (AP/Wide World Photos)

lies, had resettled in the United States. It is estimated that more than 160,000 people entered the United States under the provisions of these programs. Ten years later, the U.S. government began negotiations to resurrect Humanitarian Operation initiatives to assist Vietnamese who had been eligible for these programs but had not been able to take advantage of them. Leading this new initiative was U.S. senator John McCain, who had been a prisoner of war in Vietnam for more than five years.

Laurence W. Mazzeno

FURTHER READING

Chan, Sucheng, ed. *The Vietnamese American 1.5 Generation: Stories of War, Revolution, Flight, and New Beginnings.* Philadelphia: Temple University Press, 2006.

Do, Hien Duc. *The Vietnamese Americans.* Westport, Conn.: Greenwood Press, 1999.

Nguyen, Kien. *The Unwanted.* Boston: Back Bay Books, 2001.

Zhou, Min, and Carl L. Bankston III. *Growing Up American: How Vietnamese Children Adapt to Life in the United States.* New York: Russell Sage Foundation, 1998.

SEE ALSO: Asian immigrants; Families; History of immigration after 1891; Immigration waves; Vietnam War; Vietnamese immigrants.

RELIGION AS A PUSH-PULL FACTOR

SIGNIFICANCE: Most immigrants to America from earliest colonial times have had specific religious affiliations, and many have sought American residence because of their beliefs and practices. Hostile attitudes and policies in native countries often alienated and pushed out religious minorities, while America's reputation for freedom drew them to its shores. Developed or developing American faith communities continued to draw foreign coreligionists, even in the face of sporadic or endemic prejudice by some Americans.

COLONIAL PATTERNS

From 1620 to roughly 1800, most immigrants who established and developed the thirteen English colonies—and later the United States—were from the British Isles. There Christianity was the dominant, and official, religion, but it took several forms in the wake of the Reformation. Jamestown and later Virginia colonists, drawn largely by economic motives, tended to be members of the Protestant Church of England, headed by the English monarch. Roman Catholics who resisted the royal religious reforms remained a distinct, untrusted, and sometimes persecuted minority, while other Protestants who were influenced by the more radical ideas of John Calvin, including Scottish Presbyterians, English Puritans, Separatists, and Baptists, lived more or less comfortably with the state church.

The Pilgrims of 1620 were Separatists who sought the freedom to worship as they pleased, first in Holland, and then in America. They were soon followed by large numbers of Puritans, who abandoned an increasingly hostile king for new shores on which they could establish a church and community that could serve as a model for purifying the English (Anglican) Church. During the Great Migration of 1630-1640, as many as 20,000 Pilgrims may have crossed the Atlantic. Massachusetts Bay Colony grew with the flow of other disaffected Puritans in the lead-up to and during the English Civil War (1642-1651). The earliest Jewish community in America was founded by twenty-three Sephardic refugees from Brazil who fled Portuguese Roman Catholic authorities to settle in New Amsterdam (later New York City) in 1654. Despite opposition by the colony's director-general, Peter Stuyvesant, the Dutch West Indies Company insisted on their being allowed to settle among the Dutch Reformed Christians.

Puritan intolerance that continued to characterize Massachusetts led to the founding of Rhode Island Colony by the freethinking and unusually tolerant Roger Williams. Royal support created havens for beleaguered English Catholics in Maryland (1630's) and newly emerging Protestant Quakers in Pennsylvania (1680's). Above all colonies, Pennsylvania, with burgeoning Philadelphia, opened itself to a wide range of immigrants who had suffered as Protestant religious minorities back home. These included the Pennsylvania "Dutch" (from Deutsch, meaning "German"); German Anabaptists such as the Amish and Mennonites, who had suffered prejudice and persecution since the 1520's; and French Calvinists (Huguenots) who sought refuge after King Louis XIV revoked the Edict of Nantes in 1685. The failure of the Puritan Commonwealth in England and the restoration of the Stuart monarchy in 1660 created another wave of Puritan emigration to New England, along with that of a large number of Scottish and English Presbyterians.

Middle- and upper-class Irish Protestants, Anglicans, and especially Presbyterians (usually Scotch-

Religion as a push-pull factor

Mennonite teacher in a Lancaster County, Pennsylvania, school during the early 1940's. Her students included Mennonite, Amish, and Pennsylvania Dutch children. (Library of Congress)

Irish) began leaving Ireland in the wake of the Irish campaigns of the Glorious Revolution of 1688-1689. Drawn more by freedom of opportunity than by religious motives, these pioneers placed their stamp especially on the southern colonies of the Carolinas and Georgia. Irish Catholics, though impoverished and oppressed by Parliament's Penal Laws, were generally unwelcome and too poor to emigrate. Along the fringes of British colonial territory, French Jesuits in Canada and Louisiana and Spanish Franciscans in Florida, the southwestern interior, and the California coast served as Roman Catholic missionaries among the Native Americans, as did Russian Orthodox monks along the coastal northwest from Canada to California.

NINETEENTH CENTURY

American independence and constitutional guarantees established a framework for a religiously neutral nation, though many states initially retained official denominations and civil rights associated with them. In 1785, only 1 percent of the American population was Roman Catholic, a situa-

tion steadily expanded with Irish—and later Continental—immigration from the 1820's. Although English Parliaments had lifted most of the anti-Irish Catholic Penal Laws by the 1820's, Irish Catholic peasants still suffered the effects of economic oppression rooted in religious prejudice. Many sought out America for its economic and religious opportunities. The infamous Great Irish Famine (1845-1852), which killed and scattered millions of Irish, was exacerbated by British Protestant anti-Catholicism and resulting poverty.

Although American anti-Catholic nativists opposed free immigration, hundreds of thousands of refugees joined family members or started new lives in cities such as New York, Boston, and Philadelphia. The blight that struck Ireland also destroyed crops in central and eastern Europe. German and Polish German Catholic peasants living under officially Lutheran rule suffered social as well as economic hardship and shipped off to America in increasing numbers. As pioneer communities became established, especially in the upper Midwest, chain migration brought relatives and fellow villagers to the American frontier.

The same pattern affected Scandinavian immigration from the 1820's. The official Lutheran Church in Norway made life hard for Quakers, many of whom became Americans. Lutherans who chafed under the strictness of the official churches also gravitated to the United States. Before 1860, there were about 15,000 Swedes in America, but between 1868 and 1893 the number grew to 600,000. Orthodox and other Christians in eastern Europe and the Ottoman Empire suffered intolerance and outright persecution, and many fled to America. Roman Catholic authorities in the eastern lands of the Austro-Hungarian Empire failed to understand the nuanced identities of Uniate Christians, whom they lumped with Orthodox and treated as outsiders. Muslim Turks particularly oppressed their Orthodox populations from the 1890's, culminating in the infamous Armenian genocide and the emigration of 300,000 Greek Orthodox between 1890 and 1910, and another 300,000 from 1910 to 1920.

At the same time, large numbers of Jews living under oppressive Christian regimes in central and eastern Europe began migrating to the United States. In 1820, America was home to about 4,000 Jews, many of whom retained ties to their homelands. Over the following six decades, the number swelled to 150,000, most from central Europe. Societal anti-Semitism as well as political activities (Russian pogroms, Germany's Kulturkampf) made life miserable for entire Jewish communities, spurring many to migrate. Existing Jewish American communities along the East Coast promised and provided a new home. As ever a despised minority in Europe, Jews flocked to America, which many came to see as a new Promised Land. Between 1881 and 1900, a period of increased Russian anti-Jewish violence, two-thirds of eastern Europe's Jewish population, an estimated 675,000 people, emigrated to America, often as full families. As Europe grew more bellicose, another 1,346,000 Jews fled its shores for the United States between 1900 and 1914.

Southern Italian Catholics experienced famine and great poverty rather than intolerance, and they came to America by the thousands. About 300,000 arrived from 1880 to 1890, and average annual numbers doubled during the 1890's. A large percentage of these were young men seeking work, who expected to return to Italy later in life. Instead, the well-established Italian American communities, and especially the ethnic Catholic churches, helped retain many of these immigrants, who often called for their families to join them.

TWENTIETH CENTURY

The twentieth century was marked by religious persecution that served the purposes of totalitarian ideologies and regimes. Many of those who suffered sought refuge in America. Anti-immigration laws passed in 1921 and 1924, however, set the tone for the next four decades by severely limiting annual numbers. Bolshevik victories in the Russian Revolution (1917) and ensuing civil war sent many Russian Orthodox Christians and Jews fleeing westward. Nazi Germany's campaign to eradicate European Jews during World War II, first in Germany and then in conquered territories, ran up against America's very restrictive Johnson Act of 1924. As well, popular, if understated, American anti-

Semitism blamed the Great Depression on powerful Jewish economic interests, which damped American sympathy. A rather small portion of those who fled the Third Reich during the 1930's found a welcome in the United States, and these all required American sponsors who oversaw their transition into productive Americans. Between the onset of World War II and the establishment of the state of Israel in 1948, the United States did absorb some 140,000 Jews fortunate enough to flee or survive the Holocaust.

Though theoretically tolerant of Jews and sponsors of a puppet Orthodox Church, the Soviet regime from Vladimir Lenin to Mikhail Gorbachev oppressed the faithful of both religions. During the Cold War following World War II, many exceptions to official immigration policies were made on behalf of high-profile figures and groups. During the 1970's and again during the 1990's, large numbers of Jews—totaling some 300,000—fled first official anti-Semitic state activity and then popular resentment and bigotry unleashed by the fall of the communist regime. In 1968, American coreligionists and sympathizers formed the Jewish Defense League, which applied pressure on the Soviets to end mistreatment of Jews in the Soviet Union and urged the U.S. government to apply diplomatic pressure to the same end.

By its nature officially atheistic, communism sparked religious as well as political refugee movements across the globe, and, after 1965, America again began drawing many of the victims. Chinese Christians and Buddhists fled before Mao Zedong's armies during the late 1940's; hundreds of thousands of oppressed Catholic Cubans sought American soil in several waves from 1959. After China's invasion of Tibet in 1950, Tibetan Buddhists followed their Dalai Lama into exile, many choosing the United States as a new home. After the Vietnam War, countless South Vietnamese "boat people," many of whom were Catholic or Buddhist and expected antireligious persecution from the triumphant North Vietnamese communists, floated in search of transport to the United States. Early waves established religious and ethnic communities that have continued to draw emigrants pushed out by religious as well as political and economic conditions.

During the late twentieth century, wars in Somalia and other parts of Africa pitted well-supplied

Muslims against minority Christians, and many of the latter fled to the United States as a result. Other African or Afro-Caribbean religious minorities in the United States faced legal restrictions on traditional practices. However, the U.S. Supreme Court's 1993 decision in *Church of the Lukumi Babalu Aye v. City of Hialeah* sanctioned animal sacrifice by practitioners of Caribbean Santeria. Such liberalization encouraged the migration of as many as 800,000 Haitians, many of whom practice voodoo.

Joseph P. Byrne

FURTHER READING

Carroll, Brett E. *The Routledge Historical Atlas of Religion in America.* New York: Routledge, 2000. Record of major influxes and shifts of religious groups in America, from the precolonial era to the late 1990's.

Gaustad, Edwin S., and Leigh Schmidt. *The Religious History of America: The Heart of the American Story from Colonial Times to Today.* Rev. ed. New York: HarperOne, 2004. Standard overview of the topic that emphasizes the relationships of multifaith immigration to major trends in American religious developments.

Haddad, Yvonne Yazbeck, Jane I. Smith, and John L. Esposito, eds. *Religion and Immigration: Christian, Jewish, and Muslim Experiences in the United States.* Walnut Creek, Calif.: AltaMira Press, 2003. Collection of articles focusing on the period after 1965, surveying religious conditions in immigrants' native countries as well as experiences in the United States.

Joselit, Jenna Weissman. *A Parade of Faiths: Immigration and American Religion.* New York: Oxford University Press, 2008. Short, illustrated overview of the interplay of immigrant religious expectations and the interplay with American social and cultural history from the *Mayflower* voyage of 1620 to the 1990's.

Levitt, Peggy. *God Needs No Passport: Immigrants and the Changing American Religious Landscape.* New York: New Press, 2007. Sociological study that emphasizes the ways in which religious identities ensure strong self-identification with native countries.

Olupona, Jacob, and Regina Gemignani. *African Immigrant Religions in America.* New York: New York University Press, 2007. Studies the range of native African religious traditions transplanted to America, especially the effects on American black communities such as the interactions of African American Christians with African immigrants.

Tweed, Thomas A., and Stephen Prothero, eds. *Asian Religions in America: A Documentary History.* New York: Oxford University Press, 1999. Collection of more than one hundred reflections by native American and immigrant cultural and political figures on the place of major Asian religions within the broader American Judeo-Christian religious landscape.

SEE ALSO: American Jewish Committee; Anti-Catholicism; Anti-Semitism; Holocaust; Jewish immigrants; Missionaries; Mormon immigrants; Muslim immigrants; Pilgrim and Puritan immigrants; Religions of immigrants.

RELIGIONS OF IMMIGRANTS

SIGNIFICANCE: Religion has historically played important roles in the lives of immigrants to the United States. The many different faiths have served as links with familiar traditions, community focuses, and sources of moral support for families adrift amid an alien culture. Some immigrants came to America primarily in order to practice their faiths without government interference or persecution. The diversity of religions in the United States has operated as a laboratory in supporting democracy along with respect for minority rights.

As a nation of immigrants, the United States is also a place in which diverse cultures collide with one another. The results of these collisions have been forms of alchemy that have rearranged some elements and transformed others. These processes have repeatedly happened with the religions brought by immigrants to America. Although the faiths brought by immigrants have had many important differences, the basic religious attitudes of immigrants have shared a number of common traits. For example, early immigrants prized individual conscience—an attitude that allowed new denominations to spring up, and a diversity of special groups to form even within faiths that had lacked them before.

Also, the need for ongoing moral and practical support among new immigrants ensured that their places of worship would become de facto community centers for their parishioners. This tendency almost necessitated professional clergy, even within religious traditions that previously did not have them. In the absence of an established church in the United States, all religions shared a level ground and a modicum of respect in the marketplace of religious ideas. Finally, while these developments were first evident among Christians, as immigration from non-European countries increased, they came to apply to the non-Christian faiths of new immigrants as well.

CALVINIST TRADITION

In many ways, Protestant Calvinism is the "default standard" for American religions. It set a pattern for future American expectations of what religion is and does. Because the British North American colonies were established shortly after a great split in European Christianity, the various different colonies tended to be settled by adherents of different theological foundations. Every American schoolchild learns that New England was first settled by English Puritans, seeking a place to worship in their own way. The Puritans believed in Calvinism, one of the two original Protestant forms taken by the Reformation in reaction against the practices and doctrine of the medieval Roman Catholic Church. Its most influential advocate, John Calvin of Geneva, Switzerland, held that salvation was accessible to all believers, without the need for a church or saints to act as intermediaries. Calvinists generally discounted the importance of ritual and church tradition and stressed the importance of faith and grace in the individual's life.

The *Mayflower* Puritans were separatists, English Christians whose quest for righteousness had led them to break entirely with the Church of England. The nearby Massachusetts Bay Colony was settled by dissenters, Puritans who had not entirely lost their ties with the established church but whose outlook and worship practices were primarily Calvinistic. Both groups believed in the autonomy of individual church congregations, the primacy of an individual's faith, the importance of Scripture,

and certain strict behavior standards. They also believed civil authority should reflect the same standards. This is what permitted the witchcraft trials to take place and unorthodox preachers such as Roger Williams to be expelled from the colony. There was a huge potential contradiction between the two ideals: the value of the individual Christian's own connection with God, and church-imposed interpretations and rules of behavior. This conflict was to lead to a whole "marketplace" of churches in the New World, each expressing a slightly different understanding of Christianity.

As time went on, the New England Puritans—and other settlers of directly Calvinistic faiths, such as the Dutch Reformed settlers of New York—were numerically outpaced by other colonists. So strong was the influence of Calvinism in western Europe, however, that most of these colonists—Presbyterians, Congregationalists, Baptists, and others—held basically the same views on the relationship of the individual to the divine. Many people were needed for the work of "taming the wilderness" and building a new nation, and there were enough similarities of belief to allow the differences to be ignored. Respect for the demands of individual conscience spread. A sort of pan-Protestantism developed, in which anyone who professed to be Christian was recognized as such. By the time of the late eighteenth century American Revolution, most Americans agreed with the following assumptions, drawn from a Calvinistic base:

- Conscience and spiritual truths are integral to an individual's soul.
- Religious liberty is essential in a democracy.
- Congregations are the primary units of a religion's presence.

These attitudes were uniquely helpful for building religious comity within a nation of immigrants.

ROMAN CATHOLICS

The experience of Catholic immigrants in America raised many issues that also faced other immigrants of minority faiths. Roman Catholics were among the early settlers of British North America, but few of the original colonies welcomed them. Both the New England colonies that had been established by dissenters to build a "godly" society and the southern colonies based on Anglican traditions saw only trouble coming from the presence of "papists." A few colonies, however, were more hospitable. The second Lord Baltimore, himself a well-connected and wealthy Roman Catholic peer, founded Maryland in 1634 as a refuge colony for his coreligionists. Rhode Island and Pennsylvania both had policies of toleration that benefited Catholics. However, Catholics never became a majority even in those colonies. Like Catholics who settled in other colonies, they were circumspect and "blended in" for their own safety.

"Blending in" was actually not difficult for Roman Catholics in the English colonies. Most Catholic immigrants in the colonies were English and thus able to navigate the colonies' social worlds readily. Catholic priests were scarce in the colonies and had to travel widely to conduct masses for Catholics in scattered settlements. By the time of

the Revolution, about 30,000 Roman Catholics were living in the original thirteen colonies. Almost all were of English, French, or Scotch-Irish descent. Many were landed gentry. Charles Carroll of Maryland, a signer of the Declaration of Independence, led his coreligionists in support of the colonists' cause during the war. Soon after independence John Carroll, his cousin, was named "superior of the mission," in charge of the Catholic church in the United States. Six years later he became its first bishop.

After the United States achieved its independence, Roman Catholics seemed poised for uneventful coexistence with other citizens of the new nation. However, that did not happen, During the early nineteenth century, a large stream of Irish immigrants began arriving in America. These Irish were overwhelmingly Roman Catholic and somewhat bewildered by their new surroundings. Early on, a number of cultural gaps drove wedges between already established Catholic priests and their new Irish parishioners. The existing clergy were mostly French, many in flight from the late eighteenth century French Revolution and its aftermath, and were culturally much more sophisticated than the Irish farm folk. The latter badly needed help in the transition to American life, but language differences and other barriers meant that their French priests were often ill equipped to provide it. Eventually, the Irish developed their own subculture and communities within the larger cities, centered around the church and school, and during their next generation produced their own priests.

New immigrants desperately sought to live and worship in a setting that reflected their own traditions. Despite the many gaps and misfires, the Roman Catholic Church did eventually provide this. Church and parish came to serve as a bridge and buffer between the immigrant home cultures and the new nation's confusing ways. To immigrant workers in the factories and mills, or in service occupations in the city, the Catholic Church was a haven. It supplied the

Bishops of the Syrian and Russian Orthodox churches in Alaska during the early twentieth century. First colonized by Russia during the late eighteenth century, Alaska still has remnants of Russian culture. (Library of Congress)

comforts of familiar ritual and belief, and often offered material and spiritual aid as well. Priests could mediate with outside entities when immigrants did not know how to navigate American institutions. Such help was needed all the more as distrust of the growing Catholic population rose in primarily Protestant America.

These processes repeated themselves as the mix of national origins changed during the late nineteenth century and later. By the late nineteenth century, it Irish priests were often trying to connect with new Catholic immigrants from Italy, Poland, and the Balkan countries.

One lasting result of the Catholic influx was the parochial school system. Parents—and even more, the church's hierarchy—objected to their children being exposed to generic Protestant prayers and values in the era's public schools and built their own alternative system. Many Catholic elementary schools were run by parish priests and maintained the ethnic identities and even the languages of the families whom they served. Other schools were operated by Catholic religious orders or local dioceses. Status differentials among schools existed as well. Parochial schools educated many generations of immigrant children and are one of the major reasons that the descendants of Roman Catholic immigrants have tended to stay loyal to their religious heritage.

During much of the twentieth century, immigration from Roman Catholic countries slowed to a trickle. Meanwhile, the children of the previous era's Catholic immigrants scaled the socioeconomic ladder, assimilating to American norms even as most kept their ancestors' faith. However, many of these Catholics claimed a very Calvinistic right to follow their own consciences on many matters, living as what became known as "cafeteria Catholics," which the church's hierarchy has deplored. On the other hand, it is hard to imagine some of the changes made by the Vatican II Council without the democratizing influence of American Catholics on the church.

Reforms in U.S. immigration enacted in 1965 brought large numbers of new immigrants into the United States from parts of the world that had not previously provided many immigrants. Many of these newcomers were Roman Catholics from Latin American countries and the Philippines. Like previous Catholic immigrants, these people have tried to maintained their cultural traditions and festivals, even as they have become Americans.

LUTHERANS

The Lutheran Church was one of the major divisions of Protestant Christianity to arise out of the Reformation. Indeed, its founder, Martin Luther, is regarded as the leader of the Protestant movement. However, Lutheran ties predominated only in Germany and the Scandinavian countries. The tradition was brought to the United States mostly by German immigrants. In colonial times, they settled in Pennsylvania and adjacent areas. A large German influx during the nineteenth century cut a wide swath west through the rich farming states. Scandinavian immigrants—Swedes, Norwegian, Danes—came soon after and settled in the northern Midwest region.

Lutherans were a small minority among preindependence Americans, but so many immigrated during the following century that they were the third-largest Protestant denomination by 1910, when they were outnumbered only by Baptists and Methodists. Their influence in the United States was less than their numbers would suggest, however, for several reasons. Lutheran immigrants tended to live mostly in rural areas and small cities. Many congregations clung to the German language, and Lutherans were preoccupied with their own internal differences.

In contrast to Europe, where united national churches existed, American Lutherans splintered into at least twenty separate groups. Some splits derived from national origins and cultures, but many revolved around doctrinal differences. Strict or conservative Lutherans generally adhered to the Augsburg Confession and believed in the "Real Presence" in the Eucharist, which struck more liberal Lutherans as too close to Roman Catholic beliefs. Overall, Lutheranism remained a liturgical church, but the more theologically strict groups retained more ritual, and the more open churches put more emphasis on preaching. Many of the same strategies used by Roman Catholics to maintain an immigrant faith community were also followed by Lutherans where they had the resources. However, members living in the countryside were harder to reach this way, and a pastor shortage also existed during the mid-nineteenth century.

Unlike Protestant denominations that brought

in many adult converts, the rolls of Lutheran churches were built largely on immigrants and their descendants. The result was loyal and religiously educated members who knew their church's theology thoroughly. After World War I, the German language was no longer used in worship, and Lutheran churches began to resemble mainstream Protestant denominations more closely. Later during the twentieth century, the denomination consolidated into two major groups: the Missouri Synod, which remains doctrinally and socially conservative, and the Lutheran Church in America, which became involved in ecumenical efforts.

ANGLICAN AND ORTHODOX TRADITIONS

Although Anglicanism and Orthodox Christianity differ widely on many matters, they also share some similarities. Both reflect a historic break from the Roman Catholic Church and its claims to universal Christian authority. Both traditions became the established churches in the countries in which they arose and remained closely tied to those countries' political power structures. These facts meant that the adherents and clergy of these religions had to undergo a considerable readjustment when they immigrated to America.

Virginia and the Carolinas from their beginnings were officially Anglican colonies because of their status as colonies under Royal authority. However, in those colonies, as in others, Anglicans were outnumbered by settlers with other religious allegiances, as well as those with none. During the Revolutionary War, Anglicans were suspect because of their church's ties to the British Crown and the fact that political maneuvering on both sides of the Atlantic had kept an American bishop from ever being named. However, several major revolutionary leaders were Anglicans. George Washington himself was a vestryman of his local church. Control of Anglican church affairs remained in the hands of local clergy and parishioners. While the U.S. Constitution was being framed in 1787, Anglican delegates met after convention sessions to work out a structure for their new church. This resulted in a more democratic structure than the American Anglican church had had before. Although the reformed church remained a strongly hierarchal organization, every level of the church, from local governing boards to bishops, was chosen by election.

In postrevolutionary America, the new Episcopal Church, as it became known, had to struggle for survival. It had lost its royal privileges and much of its support. The church was also challenged by the Methodist movement that had been started by Church of England clergyman John Wesley. Wesley first advocated a methodical approach to the spiritual life (therefore the name), but his later experience of "a heart strangely warmed" became a benchmark for authentic spiritual transformation. John Wesley's lone visit to America during the 1730's had been a disaster, but his colleague George Whitfield sparked a great missionary effort, with more than eighty traveling preachers covering the backwoods settlements. The Methodist movement soon became independent of its Anglican origins.

Methodism drew in many immigrants, from nineteenth century Swedes to late twentieth century Koreans. It also spun off many "daughter" churches, from African American denominations to the Disciples of Christ/Christian Church movement that aimed at simplicity. The Episcopal church eventually regrouped and regained its share of members. Its direct outreach to immigrants was less than that of the Methodists, but both offered a "middle way" between highly ceremonial worship and the spontaneity of "gospel"-oriented churches.

The first American Eastern Orthodox diocese was established in Alaska in 1867, but missionary monks from Russia came even earlier to work with the native inhabitants. Orthodoxy, however, did not reach America as a significant religious group until the early twentieth century, when Greek and Slavic immigrants flocked to work in mining and factories in Pennsylvania and the Great Lakes states.

In Europe and the Middle East, Orthodoxy existed as independent national churches, but the first U.S. immigrants all were overseen by the already functioning Russian church. After World War I this unity fragmented, with each church tending to emphasize its own national origins. As with other immigrant groups, these churches found themselves adding new functions: church suppers, special-purpose societies, ethnic festivals, and the like. Orthodox communicants have always been a minority in America, but they have brought to their new home pride in their heritages and a reminder of another Christian tradition, outside the

Members of a Los Angeles Korean Methodist church on Easter Sunday in 1950. Christian churches play an important role in promoting fellowship among Korean immigrants and their families. (University of Southern California, East Asian Library)

Protestant-Roman Catholic dichotomy, with historical and theological depth.

Non-Christian Faiths

Although the United States always had a majority-Christian population, believers in other faiths have immigrated to America since early colonial times. The first Jewish immigrants were twenty-three Sephardic refugees who came to New Amsterdam in 1654 from Recife in Brazil. Others arrived directly from Europe. After American independence, some were drawn by the new nation's principle of religious liberty. Jewish immigrants made homes in the eastern seaboard cities. The first synagogue was established in Providence, Rhode Island, a state with a long heritage of religious openness, due to its founder Roger Williams's tolerant philosophy.

The nineteenth century saw massive immigration waves from Germany and central Europe that brought many Jewish families. Along with the general chaos in their homeland, the Jews had the added burden of persecution, and the New World promised a hopeful new start. These immigrants spread out to frontier areas where opportunity beckoned. The Judaic rule that twelve adult men can constitute a congregation made founding new Jewish groups relatively easy. However, American models of religious life percolated to newcomers, so that many Jewish groups sought trained rabbis to lead them and made other innovations. Reform Judaism was introduced in Charleston, South Carolina, by a group of young Jews hoping to revitalize their faith by emphasizing its philosophical and ethical components over its many ritual requirements. This movement later became the dominant branch of Judaism in America.

After 1880, a flood of Russian and eastern European Jews emigrated to America, fleeing from Russian-instituted pogroms. These immigrants were used to living in enclaves and spoke mostly Yiddish. Already established Jewish Americans felt themselves outnumbered but nevertheless tried to help assimilate the newcomers and provide them with moral support. A third wave of Jewish migration developed during World War II. Because of Americans' reaction to the horrors of the Nazi regime, and because these newcomers tended to be highly educated, they had an easier time of fitting into American life.

After 1965, legislation opened up the United States to immigration from all over the world. The nation's life was enriched by the presence and growth of even more religious traditions. Muslims came from the Middle East and Pakistan, Buddhists from the Far East, Hindus from India, and even faiths such as Baha'i (of Iranian origin) and West Indian Santeria became visible.

The American constitutional guarantee of freedom of religion has worked to ensure that the United States welcomes religious diversity that may eventually reflect the whole spectrum of world religions. If this trend has shocked some old-line Christian Americans, it has also surprised newcomers who have found themselves becoming more religiously observant than they were at home, if only to keep in touch with their home cultures. American traditions are changing too, as public life opens up to input from the new immigrants' religions. "Interfaith" efforts have had to expand enormously, and American culture is the richer for it.

Emily Alward

FURTHER READING

Alba, Richard, et al., eds. *Immigration and Religion in America: Comparative and Historical Perspectives.* New York: New York University Press, 2008. Collection of thoughtful articles by notable scholars on how past and present immigrants have adapted to American life through experiences in their faith groups.

Foley, Michael W., and Dean Hoge. *Religion and the New Immigrants.* New York: Oxford University Press, 2007. Study of twenty worship communities in the Washington, D.C., area. Shows varied connections between religious identities and civic involvement.

Joselit, Jenna Weissman. *A Parade of Faiths: Immigration and American Religion.* New York: Oxford University Press, 2007. Short historical survey of religion in the United States with representative case studies of immigrants.

Orsi, Robert A. *The Madonna of 115th Street.* New Haven, Conn.: Yale University Press, 2002. Multidimensional study of "lived religion" as exemplified by a festival unique to Italian Harlem.

Williams, Peter W. *American Religions: From Their Origins to the Twenty-first Century.* Champaign: University of Illinois Press, 2002. Massive compendium of churches and religious developments in each era of American history.

SEE ALSO: Anti-Catholicism; Immigration and Nationality Act of 1965; Immigration waves; Jewish immigrants; Military conscription; Missionaries; Muslim immigrants; Pilgrim and Puritan immigrants; Religion as a push-pull factor.

REMITTANCES OF EARNINGS

DEFINITION: Money or goods sent by immigrants to relatives and friends in their home countries

SIGNIFICANCE: The ability to send substantial financial assistance to friends and relatives at home has been a strong incentive for both legal and illegal immigration to the United States. Remittances have also become an important component of global financial markets, and the substantial sums received in some impoverished countries often make important contributions to the local economies.

The sending of part of one's wages to friends or family back home, known as remittances, is a common practice for many immigrants, especially those from Latin America and the Caribbean. Remittance-sending is a worldwide practice, but the United States leads the world in the total amounts of money annually sent out of the country by its immigrant residents. Many legal and illegal immigrants come to the United States from poorer countries not merely to better their own economic condition but also to contribute to relatives in their homelands.

Immigrants who send remittances typically send a few hundred dollars per month, using both formal and informal financial channels. Popular methods have included deliveries made in person during home visits, regular postal services, and wire-transfer companies such as Western Union and MoneyGram. Immigrants are often reluctant to deal with banks and credit unions to send remittances because of problems with their own immigration status or a lack of required identification documents.

The amounts of money sent in remittances tend to fluctuate with changing immigration policies, dropping during times of immigration restrictions. However, the general trend has been steady growth over the years. Sending remittances has become so popular that it has inspired the development of a sizable international remittance market. At the same time, many poor and developing countries have come to rely on remittances from the United States as key sources of hard currency and development capital, especially in Latin America, the Caribbean, India, and the Philippines. Mexico is the largest beneficiary of remittances sent from the United States. Remittance money provides a major source of income for many families in Mexico, giving Mexico a strong incentive to encourage the United States to loosen its restrictions on immigration. Recipients of remittances use the money for basic necessities such as food, clothing, and housing costs as well as for educational purposes and to build savings.

The popularity of remittances among U.S. immigrants has had both positive and negative impacts. Remittances provide an incentive to immigration and allow immigrants to maintain close links with family members back home. However, critics have argued that immigrants cost American workers needed jobs and their remittances drain money from the U.S. economy that should be spent within the United States. An additional criticism is that remittances can promote a dependence on outside charity without contributing to local development.

Marcella Bush Trevino

FURTHER READING

Borjas, George J., and Richard B. Freeman. *Immigration and the Work Force: Economic Consequences for the United States and Source Areas.* Chicago: University of Chicago Press, 1992.

Maimbo, Samuel Munzele, and Dilip Ratha. *Remittances: Development Impact and Future Prospects.* Washington, D.C.: World Bank, 2005.

Özden, Caglar, and Maurice W. Schiff, eds. *International Migration, Remittances, and Brain Drain.* Washington, D.C.: World Bank, 2005.

SEE ALSO: Economic consequences of immigration; Economic opportunities; Employment; Globalization; Honduran immigrants; Latin American immigrants; Mexican immigrants; Pacific Islander immigrants.

RENO V. AMERICAN-ARAB ANTI-DISCRIMINATION COMMITTEE

THE CASE: U.S. Supreme Court decision on deportation procedures
DATE: Decided on February 24, 1999

> **SIGNIFICANCE:** The *American-Arab Anti-Discrimination Committee* decision upheld and broadly interpreted a federal statute that severely restricted the rights of alien residents to challenge deportation orders in court, even in cases when the defendants claim a violation of their constitutional rights.

The U.S. government characterized the Popular Front for the Liberation of Palestine (PFLP) as an international terrorist organization. In 1987, the Immigration and Naturalization Service (INS) ordered the deportation of eight resident aliens who were members of the PFLP, even though none of the eight had been accused of committing a criminal act. In response, they filed suit, alleging that Attorney General Janet Reno and other federal officials had targeted them for deportation because of their political opinions and political affiliation—a violation of the freedoms protected by the First Amendment. In 1996, while the case was still being adjudicated in the lower courts, Congress enacted the Illegal Immigration Reform and Immigrant Responsibility Act (IIRIRA), which eliminated judicial review of the Justice Department's deportation proceedings against several classes of aliens.

Based on the new law, Reno filed a motion asserting that the federal courts no longer had jurisdiction to review the validity of the selective enforcement claim. Both the district court and the court of appeals rejected the motion. By an 8-1 margin, the U.S. Supreme Court reversed these rulings and upheld Reno's motion. In the majority opinion, Justice Antonin Scalia wrote that "an alien unlawfully in this country has no constitutional right to assert selective enforcement as a defense against his deportation." In a strong dissent, Justice David Souter argued that a complete preclusion of judicial review would "raise the serious constitutional question of whether Congress may block every remedy for enforcing a constitutional right." In subsequent cases, the application of the IIRIRA has continued to be controversial.

Thomas Tandy Lewis

FURTHER READING

Kanstroom, Daniel. *Deportation Nation: Outsiders in American History.* Cambridge, Mass.: Harvard University Press, 2007.

Miyamoto, Maryam K. "The First Amendment After *Reno v. American-Arab Anti-Discrimination Committee*: A Different Bill of Rights for Aliens?" *Harvard Civil Rights-Civil Liberties Law Review* 35 (Winter, 2000): 183-224.

SEE ALSO: Arab immigrants; Congress, U.S.; Deportation; Due process protections; Illegal Immigration Reform and Immigrant Responsibility Act of 1996; Supreme Court, U.S.

RESIDENT ALIENS

DEFINITION: Term informally applied to immigrants who reside in the United States for long periods without obtaining citizenship

SIGNIFICANCE: Definitions of "resident aliens" vary among different users. According to the U.S. Department of Homeland Security, resident aliens are immigrants who en-

ter the United States legally and obtain valid green cards. In contrast, the U.S. Department of the Treasury applies the term to all immigrants who remain in the country for significant periods of time, whether they enter the country legally or illegally.

Although the term "resident alien" does not have the official recognition in U.S. government usage that its cousin, "permanent resident," possesses, the term is generally understood to convey essentially the same meaning: an immigrant residing in the United States for an indefinite duration. Under this view, resident aliens can be divided into three categories:

- immigrants intending to stay permanently who are in the process of meeting naturalization requirements to become citizens
- immigrants allowed to stay in the country indefinitely although they do not meet naturalization requirements
- immigrants who meet requirements but do not desire to become U.S. citizens

With the establishment of the United States during the late eighteenth century, it became necessary to define who were American citizens, with all the rights and privileges of citizenship outlined in the U.S. Constitution, and who were not. Over the years, Congress passed immigration laws outlining how persons born outside the United States could naturalize to become American citizens. Foreigners who move to the United States with the intention of remaining indefinitely can obtain green cards that give them permanent residence status. They are often known as resident aliens. Legal permanent residents of the United States have certain restrictions placed upon them, such as not being able to reside outside the United States for more than a year without special permission from the government.

Donald A. Watt

FURTHER READING

Bray, Ilona, et al. *U.S. Immigration Made Easy.* Berkeley, Calif.: Nolo, 2009.

Tichenor, Daniel. *Dividing Lines: The Politics of Immigration Control in America.* Princeton, N.J.: Princeton University Press, 2002.

SEE ALSO: Assimilation theories; Citizenship; Citizenship and Immigration Services, U.S.; Green cards; "Immigrant"; Immigration and Naturalization Service, U.S.; Naturalization; Permanent resident status; Transit aliens.

RETURN MIGRATION

DEFINITION: Reverse form of migration in which immigrants go back to their original homes

SIGNIFICANCE: Return migration can be important to original homelands, when returnees come back with money to invest and with new skills and education acquired while living in the United States. At the same time, however, the United States can lose people with valuable knowledge and skills.

People who choose to emigrate to other lands, no matter what their reasons, generally do not plan on returning to their homelands. Consequently, if they later to return to their original homes, they do so for unexpected reasons. Return migration thus differs from movements of migrants who move back and forth between countries to do seasonal work or to take on short-term jobs. The concept of return migration as a special phenomenon was first articulated in E. G. Ravenstein's seminal 1885 book *The Laws of Migration.*

Studies have shown that the longer immigrants remain in the United States, the less likely they are to leave. Those who do return home are generally influenced by several factors. Sometimes they are weary of being treated poorly or suffering from racial prejudice and discrimination. Language barriers and difficulty with cultural assimilation can also be factors in deciding to return home. Even some-

Greek immigrants leaving New York City in 1912 to return home to fight for Greece in the first Balkan war. (Library of Congress)

thing as basic as climate may cause immigrants to leave; people used to warm tropical climates may not be able to adjust to cold North American winters. Immigrants naive enough to have expected to find easy riches in America may find the economic reality too harsh to bear.

Positive factors can be at play, too. For example, some immigrants find that the skills they have acquired in America are badly needed in their home countries. Immigrants who leave their homelands for political reasons may find that improvements in their homelands' political climates are incentives to return. However, the principal reason most immigrants return is strong family ties in their homelands.

After immigrants return to their homelands, some settle with other returnees when they find they are unable to live as they did before they left their countries, particularly as many of them have become used to more prosperous lifestyles. Moreover, returnees often find they have more in common with fellow returnees than they do with former friends or even relatives. Women returnees often have difficulties readjusting to societies that place restrictions on their roles. For this reason, Latin American women have shown an especially strong reluctance to return home. Not all returnees go home as successes, particularly those who originally intended to return who have made little effort to adapt to American ideas. However, returnees are seldom economically worse off when they return than they were before they left.

Some immigrants who remain in the United States for long periods of time before returning to their homelands send money home to build up savings for their planned retirement in their homelands. Others return home but maintain residencies in the United States. Some countries, such as Jamaica and Portugal, offer financial incentives and other inducements to persuade emigrants to return.

Marcia B. Dinneen

FURTHER READING

Bernstein, Nina. "No Evidence of Return Migration Is Found." *The New York Times*, January 15, 2009, p. 20.

Brettell, Caroline. *Anthropology and Migration*. Walnut Creek, Calif.: AltaMira Press, 2003.

Sowell, Thomas. *Migrations and Culture*. New York: Basic Books, 1996.

SEE ALSO: "Brain drain"; Chain migration; Deportation; Economic opportunities; Emigration; Permanent resident status.

RHODE ISLAND

SIGNIFICANCE: Though an exceptionally small state, Rhode Island has had a history of diverse immigration, and immigration and politics have long been closely intertwined in the state. The state's first major immigrant group was the Irish, who crowded into growing industrialized and urbanized areas during the nineteenth century. Because the state's charter gave much greater representation to the declining rural areas, a political struggle began during the 1840's that has continued to affect immigrant life in the state into the twenty-first century.

In 1790, the same year in which Rhode Island became a state, a mill at Pawtucket Falls on the Blackstone River mounted a cotton-spinning frame. This ostensibly minor event actually portended the rise of the state's textile industry that would draw immigrant workers through the century to come. The first major immigrant wave was made up predominantly of Irish. Many of them happened to arrive during the 1840's, when Rhode Island was experiencing a constitutional crisis. This crisis reached a head in the 1843 Dorr Rebellion, which forced a change in the state's electoral laws. The rebellion forced a major liberalization of the state's voting laws. This change did not immediately benefit working-class immigrants, but it pointed the way toward further liberalization that would eventually allow immigrants—particularly the Irish—to play major roles in state politics.

Meanwhile, French Canadian immigrants became an important and stable part of the workforce in Blackstone Valley textile mills at Woonsocket, Central Falls, and Pawtucket. Around 1890, Italians began entering Rhode Island. By 1910, they were almost as numerous as French Canadians. Those who did not work in the mills on the Blackstone River settled in Providence. By this time the Irish had a firm grip on local political power. In 1907, Rhode Island elected its first governor with an Irish background. Franco-Americans and those of Italian and Jewish heritage gravitated to the Republican Party until those affiliations were weakened by the economic unrest of the Great Depression of the 1930's.

INCREASING DIVERSITY IN IMMIGRATION PATTERNS

During World War II, Rhode Island prospered from the development of defense-related industries. These, in turn, attracted new immigration to the state. After the war, the mix of immigrants became very diverse. Among the newcomers were Portuguese-speakers from Europe, Cape Verde, and Brazil; Latinos from Puerto Rico, Colombia, and the Domin-

ican Republic; Asians from Vietnam, Cambodia, and Laos; and Africans from Liberia, Nigeria, and Ghana. Generally more prosperous than the others, the Portuguese speakers lived mostly in suburban

PROFILE OF RHODE ISLAND

Region	New England
Entered union	1790
Largest cities	Providence (capital), Warwick, Cranston, Pawtucket
Modern immigrant communities	Portuguese, Hispanics, Asian Indians, Africans

Population	Total	Percent of state	Percent of U.S.	U.S. rank
All state residents	1,067,000	100.0	0.36	43
All foreign-born residents	134,000	12.6	0.36	32

Source: U.S. Census Bureau, *Statistical Abstract for 2006.*
Notes: The U.S. population in 2006 was 299,399,000, of whom 37,548,000 (12.5%) were foreign born. Rankings in last column reflect total numbers, not percentages.

Roger Williams, the founder of Rhode Island, being welcomed by Narragansett Indians while making his first landfall. (Francis R. Niglutsch)

areas near Providence. Other recent immigrants tended to settle in cities, particularly in Providence.

With growing populations of linguistically isolated families in which no members over the age of fourteen years could speak English well, the need for English as a second language and bilingual instruction grew in the schools. At the same time, a growing public conviction that many new immigrants had entered the country illegally led to strong efforts to root out undocumented immigrants and opposition to increased spending on English-language instruction and social services for immigrants.

Robert P. Ellis

FURTHER READING

Brault, Gerard J. *The French-Canadian Heritage in New England.* Hanover, N.H.: University Press of New England, 1986.

McLoughlin, William G. *Rhode Island: A Bicentennial History.* New York: W. W. Norton, 1978.

Perlmann, Joel. *Ethnic Differences: Schooling and Social Structure Among the Irish, Italians, Jews, and Blacks in an American City, 1880-1935.* New York: Cambridge University Press, 1988.

Smith, Judith E. *Family Connections: A History of Italian and Jewish Immigrant Lives in Providence, Rhode Island, 1900-1940.* Albany: State University of New York Press, 1985.

SEE ALSO: *Chae Chan Ping v. United States*; Connecticut; English as a second language; Irish immigrants; Italian immigrants; Know-Nothing Party; Maine; Massachusetts; Political parties; Portuguese immigrants.

RICKOVER, HYMAN G.

IDENTIFICATION: Polish-born American Navy admiral

BORN: January 27, 1900; Makov, Russian Empire (now Máków, Poland)

DIED: July 8, 1986; Arlington, Virginia

SIGNIFICANCE: Known as the founder of the modern American nuclear Navy, Rickover pioneered the use of nuclear power for the Navy and was also an influential critic of the U.S. educational system.

Born to a Jewish family in a part of Poland under Russian rule in 1900, Rickover fled with his parents to the United States in 1905 in an effort to avoid Russian-instigated pogroms. The family settled in the lower East Side of New York City. Despite working several part-time and full-time jobs to help support the family, Rickover graduated high school with honors and was accepted to the U.S. Naval Academy. Commissioned as an ensign in 1922, he served on both destroyers and battleships, becoming convinced that smaller ships and submarines were the future of the Navy.

Rickover's naval career was a successful one, but it was his service in World War II that defined both his career direction and, in many ways, the future of the U.S. Navy. As head of the Electrical Section of the Bureau of Ships, he directed salvage operations, worked with private industry, and pioneered the use of advanced technology in the outfitting of naval vessels. During the 1950's, Rickover directed the Navy's development of its nuclear submarine program. His accomplishments were not without controversy, however, as Rickover's rather abrasive personality and bluntness often alienated those with whom he worked.

In his typically outspoken fashion, Rickover published a best-selling book, *Education and Freedom,* in 1959 and subsequently lobbied the administration of President John F. Kennedy to enact changes that he believed would strengthen the public school system. After having a sixty-three-year military career that was longer than that of any military officer in history—thanks in part to the ascension of one of his protégés, Jimmy Carter, to the presidency—Rickover was forced to retire in 1982. He died at his Virginia home in 1986.

William Carney

FURTHER READING

Allen, Thomas B., and Norman Polmar. *Rickover: Father of the Nuclear Navy.* Washington, D.C.: Potomac Books, 2007.

Rockwell, Theodore. *The Rickover Effect: How One Man Made a Difference.* Annapolis, Md.: Naval Institute Press, 1992.

SEE ALSO: Education; European immigrants; Jewish immigrants; Polish immigrants.

ROCKNE, KNUTE

IDENTIFICATION: Norwegian-born college football coach

BORN: March 4, 1888; Voss, Norway

DIED: March 31, 1931; near Bazaar, Kansas

SIGNIFICANCE: Rockne's innovative coaching skills and ability to use the media for publicity helped popularize both the college football game and the University of Notre Dame, and the Norwegian-born Rockne became an American icon.

Born in Norway, Knute Rockne came to America with his family when he was five years old. As he grew up in late nineteenth century Chicago, he rapidly assimilated into the midwestern city's multiethnic melting pot and quickly discovered such American pastimes as the game of football.

Knute Rockne. (Hulton Archive/Getty Images)

After graduating from Indiana's University of Notre Dame with honors, Rockne accepted a position as a graduate assistant in chemistry on the condition that he be allowed to help coach football. When head coach Jesse Harper retired in 1917, Rockne took over the team, which he coached through the remainder of his life. Over the ensuing twelve seasons, his teams compiled an exceptional record of 105 victories, 12 losses, and 5 ties, and were honored with six mythical national championships.

Rockne transformed college football into a game that was exciting for spectators to watch by employing forward passes and motion backfields more than they had ever been used before. He changed what had previously been primarily a running game into a contest that favored speed and intelligence. His teams "stretched" the field by constantly threatening to score. Moreover, his personal gift for showmanship and ability to manipulate the media helped bring enormous crowds to see Notre Dame play. His innovations laid the groundwork for the modern popularity of both collegiate and professional football.

Under Rockne's coaching, the University of Notre Dame's Fighting Irish teams were also an important symbol of hope to the nation's Roman Catholic communities, who were predominantly immigrants during his time, as he showed them that "their boys" could beat the best teams in the nation. He died at the early age of forty-three, in a plane crash in Kansas.

B. Keith Murphy

FURTHER READING

Maggio, Frank P. *Notre Dame and the Game That Changed Football: How Jesse Harper Made the Forward Pass a Weapon and Knute Rockne a Legend.* New York: Carroll & Graf, 2007.

Robinson, Ray. *Rockne of Notre Dame: The Making of a Football Legend.* New York: Oxford University Press, 1999.

Rockne, Knute, and Bonnie Skiles Rockne. *The Autobiography of Knute K. Rockne.* Indianapolis: Bobbs-Merrill, 1931.

Steele, Michael R. *Knute Rockne: Portrait of a Notre Dame Legend.* Champaign, Ill.: Sports Publishing, 1998.

SEE ALSO: Higher education; Scandinavian immigrants; Soccer; Sports.

RUSSIAN AND SOVIET IMMIGRANTS

SIGNIFICANCE: Between 1870 and 2004, a time span encompassing the nineteenth century Russian Empire, seven decades of the Soviet Union, and the post-Soviet Russian Federation, roughly 4 million people immigrated to the United States from Russia. Of the more than 75 percent of those immigrants who came between 1890 and 1915, 44 percent were Jewish. An even larger percentage of post-Cold War immigrants from Russia have been Jewish. Because of the ethnic diversity of the Russian domains, many of their immigrants have not been ethnic Russians. Because of this ethnic diversity, immigrants of Russian origin, although numerous, have never been a strong political or cultural force as a group in the United States. Nevertheless, many of them have made significant contributions to science and the arts.

There have been three waves of immigration from the various Russian domains since the late nineteenth century. The first and largest wave occurred between 1870 and 1915 and included mainly peasant and working-class families from western Russia and the Ukraine. After the Russian Revolution of 1917 and the subsequent Civil War (1917-1921), large numbers of nobility, intellectuals, and members of the middle class fled or were deported. Some immigrated directly to the United States. The third wave began in 1969, when the Soviet Union eased its emigration policies to allow Jews to emigrate to Israel, and the United States granted these migrants refugee status.

EARLY RUSSIAN IMMIGRATION

The earliest immigrants from Russia to what is now the United States settled in Alaska between 1733 and 1867, when Alaska was a Russian territory. Russian fur trappers and traders married to native Alaskan women established permanent settlements at Kodiak in 1790 and at Sitka in 1795. Although they exerted a cultural influence on the native population that has persisted into the twenty-first century, the total number of ethnic Russians who settled in Alaska never exceeded

one thousand, and most of them returned to Siberia after Russia sold Alaska to the United States in 1867.

During the eighteenth and nineteenth centuries, Russia, like the United States, needed people to develop large tracts of thinly populated territory. Needing manpower, the czarist government actively discouraged immigrant brokers, favoring voluntary and involuntary relocation from European Russia to Siberia and Central Asia. The Russian government had a system of penal transportation throughout the eighteenth and nineteenth centuries and provided relocation subsidies to farmers wanting to homestead during the late nineteenth and early twentieth centuries. Settlers in Siberia enjoyed more political and religious freedom than those who remained in European Russia. In 1885, the czarist government passed a law prohibiting emigration of Russian citizens other than Jews and Poles.

Until 1863, the mass of Russian peasantry consisted of serfs whose landlords controlled their movements and places of residence. Reforms instituted during the next decade increased peasant autonomy. However, the paternalistic system of village councils that replaced serfdom left Russia's rural masses with little incentive to migrate to cities in search of industrial employment, relocate to the

PROFILE OF RUSSIAN IMMIGRANTS

Countries of origin	Russian Empire, Soviet Union, Russian Federation
Primary language	Russian
Primary regions of U.S. settlement	Central Atlantic states
Earliest significant arrivals	1870's
Peak immigration periods	1890-1915, 1990's
Twenty-first century legal residents*	124,764 (15,596 per year)

*Immigrants who obtained legal permanent resident status in the United States.
Source: Department of Homeland Security, *Yearbook of Immigration Statistics, 2008.* See also the article on Former Soviet Union immigrants.

Siberians preparing to emigrate to America in 1910. (Library of Congress)

country's own frontier areas, or emigrate to America. The extreme inertia of Russian peasants was one reason why the czars relied so heavily on convict labor to develop Siberia.

Nearly one-half of all immigrants from Russia who arrived in the United States before 1917 were Yiddish-speaking Jews from communities within the Pale of Settlement, a region that had been part of Poland until Russia annexed it during the late eighteenth century. After annexation, the social and economic position of Jewish inhabitants deteriorated. Increased discrimination, restrictions, and hostility on the part of ethnic Russians and Ukrainians culminated in waves of pogroms. The czarist government ignored and sometimes encouraged these organized, brutal attacks on Jewish communities. In response to the pogroms, poverty, and increasing intolerance, roughly one-half of Russia's estimated 4 million Jews emigrated between 1890 and 1915, 1.4 million of them to the United States.

Most of these immigrants settled in urban areas in the Middle Atlantic states, especially in New York City. A large majority, 88 percent, had been town-dwelling artisans and service workers in Russia, not agricultural workers. Many found employment in the garment industry. Russian Jewish immigrants brought with them a strong work ethic, a tradition of caring for their own in a tightly knit community, and respect for education—all traits that served them well in the New World. Within a generation they were almost completely integrated into the economic life of America. In 1970, the median income of Americans of Russian descent was 130 percent of the median for white Americans as a whole. Except for their religious observances, Russian Jews as a group have retained relatively little of their Old World heritage, and of what they have retained, almost none of it is Russian.

Slavic immigrants from the Russian Empire gravitated toward American cities with heavy industries, mainly in the Midwest. As with many immigrant groups, continued cultural identity centered around religious affiliation, which gave Poles and Ukrainians who were Roman Catholics a distinct advantage over Russian Orthodox immigrants, whose own church had no official head in the United States between 1917 and 1960.

Only about 65,000 of the 3 million immigrants from the Russian empire to the United States between 1870 and 1915 were ethnic Russians. Most modern Americans who claim Russian cultural roots are, in fact, Carpatho-Russians, whose ancestors immigrated from the Galicia region of the Austro-Hungarian Empire. The Carpatho-Russians converted from Roman Catholicism to Eastern Orthodoxy after coming to America and form the backbone of the Russian Orthodox Church in America.

Immigrants from Russia during the early twentieth century tended to be left-wing in their political leanings and active in trade unions. This association of Russians with political radicalism reinforced prejudices against people already considered alien and undesirable on the grounds of language and customs. After the Russian Revolution, during the Red Scare of 1919-1920, anti-Russian xenophobia included a supposed threat of violent revolution. Fear of political radicalism helped frame immigration quotas based on America's ethnic makeup in 1890, before significant immigration from Russia had taken place.

SECOND WAVE, 1920-1960

The Russian Revolution of 1917, subsequent bitter civil war, political repression, and extreme economic hardship produced a flood of refugees from Russia during the early 1920's. Because the U.S. Immigration Act of 1924 set the quota for Russia at only 2,248 immigrants per year, few refugees from that period were admitted directly as permanent residents. Over the next decade, however, many more managed to circumvent the quota. Fourteen thousand of the 30,000 immigrants in the second wave entered the United States as refugees from Western Europe and Manchuria on the eve of World War II. Among the arrivals from Manchuria were Russian Old Believers. Members of this religious sect who had earlier settled in Alaska and Oregon still speak Russian and retain customs dating back to the seventeenth century.

Though numerically the smallest of the three waves of Russian immigration, the second wave included a number of prominent figures, including Alexander Kerensky, Russia's head of state between February and November of 1917, who be-

came a professor at Stanford University in California; the author Vladimir Nabokov; the television pioneer Vladimir Zworykin; the inventor of the helicopter, Igor Sikorsky; and Wassily Leontieff, who would win the Nobel Prize in Economics in 1973.

At the end of World War II, nearly 1 million Soviet citizens remained in Germany as prisoners of war and conscript laborers. Most were forcibly repatriated to the Soviet Union, but approximately 30,000 were admitted to the United States.

THIRD WAVE, 1969-2005

Except for an occasional highly publicized defector, restrictive Soviet emigration policies prevented further Russian emigration to the United States between 1945 and 1969. In 1969, pressure from the United States resulted in the Soviet Union's agreeing to permit Soviet Jews to emigrate to Israel, as a condition of a general treaty establishing more normal commercial relations. The United States classified Soviet Jews as refugees from political and religious persecution, which exempted them from overall annual limits on immigrant visas.

For many Soviet Jews, the principal reason for emigrating was economic advancement, and the ultimate destination was the United States. Between 1969 and 1985, when Soviet immigration policies relaxed and citizens of other ethnic backgrounds became free to leave the country, 300,000 Jews from the Soviet Union were admitted as permanent residents to the United States. These third-wave immigrants were typically well educated and eager to make the most of increased economic opportunities. Most were nominal Jews who had not actively sought to practice their religion in the Soviet Union. The new immigrants disappointed their Jewish American sponsors by having little interest in the faith-based cultural practices that still form an important part of the lives of many descendants of first-wave Russo-Jewish immigrants. A majority of them settled initially in the Middle Atlantic states; later years have seen increasing numbers of them relocate to the West Coast and the Sun Belt states. Areas with high concentrations of technology-intensive industries have also been magnets for people with degrees in mathematics and engineering.

At first these third-wave immigrants tended to be politically conservative. This changed after several decades of experience tempered their unques-

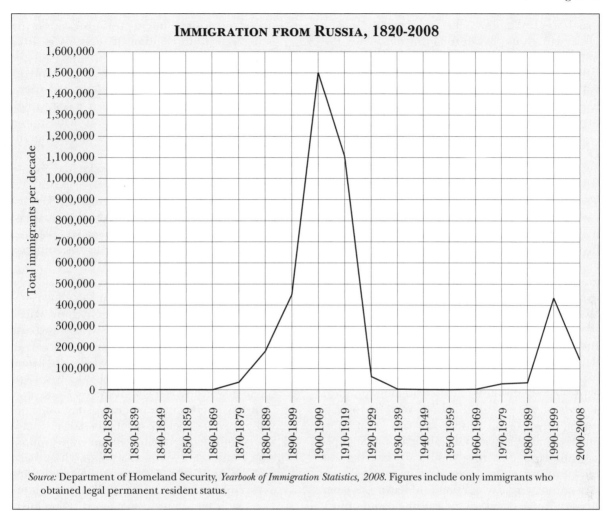

IMMIGRATION FROM RUSSIA, 1820-2008

Source: Department of Homeland Security, *Yearbook of Immigration Statistics, 2008.* Figures include only immigrants who obtained legal permanent resident status.

tioned early enthusiasm. In contrast to the experience of earlier Russian immigrants, these new Americans have seen their children face declining opportunities and a poor social safety net for those who fail to prosper. Many of them have expressed a desire to return to Russia—if it were still the country they had left during the 1970's. Although no legal barriers prevent their remigration, the collapse of Soviet communism gutted Russia's own social safety net and the excellent Russian education system that had prepared these people to be successful in a competitive economy, without a compensatory change in the overall standard of living.

POST-SOVIET CHALLENGES FOR IMMIGRANTS

After the collapse of Soviet communism, prospective immigrants from Russia lost their status in the United States as political refugees and had to begin competing for scarce work and residency visas on an equal footing with immigrants from most other countries. Consequently, the number of legal immigrants from Russia dropped dramatically.

Russia has also become a source of undocumented immigrants to the United States, although the numbers are low compared to undocumented migrants from Latin America. The "Russian mafia" has become, in the popular imagination, synonymous with organized techno-crime. While organized crime is rampant in the former Soviet Union, its influence in America appears to be limited.

One area of questionably legal to frankly criminal immigration operations is the mail-order bride industry. Nearly half of the women advertised as mail-order brides since 1990 have been Russian or Ukrainian. At its peak, during the mid-1990's, the mail-order bride industry brought a maximum of 6,000 Russian women into the United States on legal visas, or perhaps 3,000 Russians and Ukrainians. Since then, the U.S. government has made it much more difficult for American citizens to obtain visas for prospective spouses of foreign origin. Consequently, the mail-order bride industry has evolved into a cover for prostitution.

TWENTY-FIRST CENTURY TRENDS

Immigration from Russia to the United States has lost its value as a propaganda tool for reinforcing American stereotypes of Russia as a totalitarian country. The numbers and proportions of new migrants from Russia are both steadily declining and expected to continue to do so, especially as Russia has a low birthrate and has itself became a destination for numerous immigrants from East Asia, the Indian subcontinent, and the former Soviet republics of Central Asia.

To the extent that Americans of Russian or Russo-Jewish descent have a common political agenda—and, except in certain areas of foreign policy, there is little evidence for this—that influence is likely to lessen. With minimal ongoing Russian immigration and a historically low Russian birthrate, the proportion of Russians in the American population may continue to decline, leaving the persuasive effects of the existing community's economic clout and superior education as these immigrants' only competitive advantage.

Martha A. Sherwood

FURTHER READING

Davis, Jerome. *The Russian Immigrant.* New York: Arno Press and New York Times, 1969. Sketches the history of Russian immigration from the mid-eighteenth century; provides data on the geographical distribution of Russians in 1910 and their means of livelihood.

Finckenauer, James, and Elin Waring. *Russian Mafia in America: Immigration, Culture, and Crime.* Boston: Northeastern University Press, 1998. Thorough academic study that concludes that most crime in America's Russian immigrant community is not organized.

Gloecker, Olaf, Evgenija Garbolevsky, and Sabine von Mering, eds. *Russian-Jewish Emigrants After the Cold War.* Waltham, Mass.: Brandeis University Center for German and European Studies, 2006. Collection of conference papers, the majority of which treat the role of Russian immigrants in American society.

Nabokov, Vladimir. *Speak, Memory.* Rev. ed. New York: G. P. Putnam's Sons, 1966. Personal reminiscences of a famous Russian immigrant writer, who describes his experiences as an immigrant to the United States.

Portes, Alejandro, and Rubén Rumbaut. *Immigrant America: A Portrait.* 3d ed. Berkeley: University of California Press, 2006. College-level textbook focusing on recent immigration issues; especially useful for comparisons of Soviet immigrants with members of other immigrant groups.

Shasha, Dennis, and Marina Shron. *Red Blues: Voices from the Last Wave of Russian Immigrants.* New York: Holmes & Meier, 2002. Collection of interviews with men and women who immigrated from the Soviet Union to America, documenting the varieties of experience.

SEE ALSO: Alaska; American Jewish Committee; Antin, Mary; Brin, Sergey; European immigrants; Former Soviet Union immigrants; Jewish immigrants; Mail-order brides; Polish immigrants; Red Scare; Yezierska, Anzia.

S

SACCO AND VANZETTI TRIAL

THE EVENT: Celebrated murder trial of two
   Italian immigrants
DATE: May 31-July 14, 1921; appeals continued
   until August 23, 1927
LOCATION: Norfolk County, Massachusetts

SIGNIFICANCE: The trial of the Italian immigrants Nicola Sacco and Bartolomeo Vanzetti
illustrates the extreme nativism pervading
American society during the 1920's. Through
the questionable investigation that led to
their arrest, the lack of concrete proof against
them, the questionable methods of the pre-
siding judge, and the subsequent public outrage at their conviction, it is clear that an injustice was wrought.

American participation in World War I (1914-1918)
engendered an extraordinary level of patriotism
that fostered public xenophobia and government
curbing of civil liberties. The Russian Revolution of
1917 exacerbated this trend and helped create a
"Red Scare" during which both the public and the
government—through the office of U.S. attorney
general A. Mitchell Palmer—sought to eradicate
the country of communists, socialists, anarchists,
and all others deemed threats to the capitalist democratic way of life. Immigrants became prime targets of nativist hysteria, as they collectively represented all that was "foreign" and antithetical to
Americanism. Social and political groups of immigrants had their meetings disrupted, their members beaten, their newspapers censored, and their
supporters thrown in jail.

IMPACT OF THE RED SCARE

In 1917-1918, the U.S. Congress passed the Espionage Act and the Sedition Act, two pieces of cen-
sorial legislation unlike any seen since the 1798
Alien and Sedition Acts. Combined, these laws
punished virtually anyone deemed disloyal to the
U.S. government, whether through actual treason-
ous actions, resistance to federal law, or even simply the use of defamatory language against the
government or military. Persons who obstructed

the government's conduct of the war or interfered
with military recruitment were also in violation of
these laws.

Because the U.S. postmaster general had the
power to prevent the distribution of defamatory
and abusive material through the U.S. mail, it was
relatively easy to shut down radical presses that
depended on the mail to distribute their publications. In this climate, the anarchist newspaper
Cronaca Sovversiva—founded by well-known Italian
anarchist Luigi Galleani—became a mouthpiece
for the Italian immigrant community. Its contributors touted the end of capitalism—even through violent means. The newspaper's criticism of U.S.
draft laws made it a prime target for censorship.
The Italian immigrants Nicola Sacco and Bartolomeo Vanzetti were known to be anarchists because they wrote for *Cronaca Sovversiva* and gave
money to it. Their connections with the newspaper
probably drew early government attention to them.

THE CRIMES

Between December, 1919, and April, 1920, a series of unexplained robberies and two murders occurred in Massachusetts. These events, along with
bombing incidents, prompted public outrage
against anarchists, who were believed to be out of
control. Law-enforcement officials fell under
heavy public pressure to take action. A veritable
witch hunt ensued as U.S. attorney general Palmer's Department of Justice demanded the roundup
and deportation of suspected anarchists and
"Reds." In the investigations that followed, similarities were found in two unsolved crimes—a robbery
case in Bridgewater, Massachusetts, and a robbery/
murder case in South Braintree, Massachusetts.
These clues led detectives to a garage owner named
Simon Johnson.

Because eyewitnesses declared they saw Italian
men leaving the scene of the Bridgewater robbery
in a car, the Bridgewater police chief tried to round
up all Italians in the vicinity who owned cars. No
consideration was given to how eyewitnesses determined the suspects were Italians; they were simply
taken at their word. On May 5, 1920, Sacco, Vanzetti, and a man named Orciani were arrested
when they showed up at Simon Johnson's garage to

collect a car, whose owner fled without being arrested. Orciani was later released because he had solid alibis for the times when the crimes that were being investigated had occurred.

At the moment when Sacco and Vanzetti were arrested, both men were armed. They then lied to the police and later the district attorney about their politics and affiliations with other anarchists and *Cronaca Sovversiva*. The following month, Vanzetti was indicted for the Bridgewater robbery, for which he was later convicted; Sacco had an alibi for that incident. In September, 1920, both Sacco and Vanzetti were indicted for the South Braintree robbery and murders.

THE TRIAL

When Sacco and Vanzetti were brought to trial for murder in May, 1921, several people who had earlier deposed either that they were unsure of the culprits' identities or that Sacco and Vanzetti did not resemble the culprits they saw changed their testimonies by swearing they were certain they had seen Sacco and Vanzetti at the scene of the crime or fleeing it, or that they knew the men were somehow associated with the crime. During cross-examination, both defendants were repeatedly questioned about their political views—an issue that had nothing directly to do with the crimes for which the men were charged. In fact, more time was spent asking Sacco and Vanzetti about their avoiding the draft, their feelings about America, and deportations of their friends than about evidence actually relating to the criminal case.

When Judge Webster Thayer instructed the jury about deliberations, he reminded them that as members of the jury they were proving their "loyalty" to the U.S. government and that their duty was sacred in this respect. He went on to explain that there never would have been a trial had not a grand jury ruled there was sufficient evidence for an indictment. His implication was that if the jury did not convict, it would, in effect, be declaring that the grand jury had been prejudiced. He also added that the law did not require jury members to be certain of the defendants' guilt to convict them. While the members of the jury were deliberating, the foreman, named Ripley, brought .38 caliber cartridges into the room to show other jurors. While admitting there was not much evidence against the men, he said, "They outta hang anyway."

After the jury returned with two convictions, the defense tried to argue for a new trial based on using the "Ripley motion" that unfair and unjust proceedings had occurred. Several other motions, mostly directed against Judge Thayer, were made for new trials, citing retractions by eyewitnesses and discoveries that certain witnesses had testified under false pretenses. These motions were all denied, as Thayer felt the new evidence was not substantial enough to overturn the convictions. When Sacco was in prison, a Portuguese man named Celestino Medeiros admitted to him that he had been involved in the South Braintree holdup and murders; however, a motion for

---

SACCO AND VANZETTI ON TRIAL

Many of Sacco and Vanzetti's supporters argued that neither man spoke fluent English and that the defendants' inability to understand the questions asked during the trial placed them at an unfair disadvantage. This excerpt from the 1926 trial proceedings gives an indication of Nicola Sacco's familiarity with English.

The testimony of the defendant Sacco to which the remarks of the district attorney . . . referred was as follows: He was shown exhibit 43 and was asked if he knew whose cap it was. He answered, "It looks like my cap." He then was asked, "Did you have such a cap as that in your house at the time of your arrest?" and answered, "Yes, sir, something like. . . . I think it is my cap, yes." Asked to "look at it carefully," he reiterated, "Yes," and in answer to the question, "There isn't any question but what that is your cap, is there?" he answered, "No, I think it is my cap." He then was asked to try it on, and stated, "I don't know. That cap looks too dirty to me because I never wear dirty cap. I think I always have fifty cents to buy a cap, and I don't work with a cap on my head when I work. I always keep clean cap. Right when I go to the factory, take all my clothes off and put overalls and jump. It look to me pretty dirty and too dark. Mine I think was little more light, little more gray." He then was asked, "Is it your cap?" and stated, "I think it is. It look like, but it is probably dirt—probably dirty after."

Source: Supreme Judicial Court of Massachusetts, *Commonwealth v. Nicola Sacco & Another,* 255 Mass. 369; 151 N.E. 839 (1926).

Bartolomeo Vanzetti (left) and Nicola Sacco, manacled together and surrounded by guards as they approach the Massachusetts courthouse in which they were about to be sentenced. (Library of Congress)

a new trial based on this information was also denied.

Public agitation on behalf of Sacco and Vanzetti by radicals, workers, immigrants, and Italians became international in scope, as demonstrations protesting the unfairness of their trial were held in major world cities Mounting public pressure, combined with influential behind-the-scenes interventions, eventually persuaded Massachusetts governor Alvin T. Fuller to consider the question of clemency. He appointed an advisory committee under the leadership of Harvard University president A. Lawrence Lowell. In a decision that became notorious, the Lowell committee reported that Sacco and Vanzetti's trial had been fair, so clemency was not warranted. After Fuller ignored a request for a stay of execution plea, Sacco and Vanzetti were electrocuted on August 23, 1927, slightly more than six years after their conviction. Fifty years later, Sacco and Vanzetti were pardoned by Massachusetts governor Michael Dukakis, who declared August 23 a memorial day.

Noelle K. Penna

FURTHER READING

Avrich, Paul. *Sacco and Vanzetti: The Anarchist Background.* Princeton, N.J.: Princeton University Press, 1996. Offers a fresh look at the case that paints a more circumspect picture of the two men. Rather than portraying them as purely innocent, Avrich reveals how their substantial role in the Italian anarchist movement was a major factor in their arrest, conviction, and execution.

Bortman, Eli C. *Sacco and Vanzetti.* Beverly, Mass.: Commonwealth Editions, 2005. Brief, dramatic, and evenhanded account of the Sacco and Vanzetti trial and its circumstances.

Ehrmann, Herbert. *The Case That Will Not Die: Commonwealth vs. Sacco and Vanzetti.* Boston: Little, Brown, 1969. Liberally illustrated account by the case's assistant defense attorney during the period 1926-1927.

Frankfurter, Felix. "The Case of Sacco and Vanzetti." *The Atlantic Monthly*, March, 1927. Primary-source document written when nearly all hope of overturning the convictions of Sacco and Vanzetti had been lost. U.S. Supreme Court justice Frankfurter—who was himself an immigrant—openly criticized the procedures of the trial, being especially critical of Judge Thayer's conduct. The article can be found online in the archives section of *The Atlantic Monthly*.

Topp, Michael M. *The Sacco and Vanzetti Case: A Brief History with Documents*. Boston: Bedford/St. Martin's, 2004. Good resource for those interested in primary-source material on the Sacco and Vanzetti case.

SEE ALSO: Crime; Frankfurter, Felix; History of immigration after 1891; Italian immigrants; Massachusetts; Nativism; Red Scare.

SALE V. HAITIAN CENTERS COUNCIL

THE CASE: U.S. Supreme Court decision concerning Haitian refugees
DATE: Decided on June 21, 1993

SIGNIFICANCE: The *Sale* decision allowed the U.S. government to capture fleeing Haitian refugees before they reached the shores of the United States and to return them to Haiti, where they possibly faced political persecution.

During the early 1990's, political instability and poverty caused large numbers of Haitians to attempt to flee to the United States in makeshift boats. In response, both the George H. W. Bush and Bill Clinton administrations pursued a policy of intercepting the refugees at sea and returning them to Haiti. In 1992, a federal appeals court in New York ruled that the policy violated the Refugee Act of 1980 and the United Nations Protocol Relating to the Status of Refugees. Before the Supreme Court, the government defended the policy as necessary to prevent a "humanitarian tragedy at sea," which

would result from tens of thousands of Haitians drowning in boats that were not seaworthy.

The Supreme Court upheld the government's policy by an 8-1 margin. Writing for the majority, Justice John Paul Stevens concluded that the treaty could not be read to say anything about "a nation's actions toward aliens outside its own territory," even though the policy possibly violated the "spirit" of the treaty. Regarding the federal law, moreover, there was "not a scintilla of evidence" that Congress had intended to protect refugees beyond the national borders. Stevens also mentioned that a U.S.-Haitian treaty of 1981 authorized the U.S. Coast Guard to intercept vessels engaged in illegal transportation of undocumented aliens. In a strong dissent, Justice Harry A. Blackmun asserted that the 1980 law prohibited the government from returning refugees to their persecutors, whether or not they were on American soil.

Thomas Tandy Lewis

FURTHER READING

Legomsky, Stephen. *Immigration and Refugee Law and Policy*. New York: Foundation Press, 2005.

Loescher, Gil, and John Scanlan. *Calculated Kindness: Refugees and America's Half-Open Door*. New York: Free Press, 1986.

SEE ALSO: Congress, U.S.; Haitian boat people; Haitian immigrants; Immigration law; Refugees; Supreme Court, U.S.

SALVADORAN IMMIGRANTS

SIGNIFICANCE: One of the smallest Central American nations, El Salvador has supplied a disproportionate number of immigrants to the United States. By the early twenty-first century, roughly 20 percent of all Salvadorans were living in the United States, where they constituted the largest Central American immigrant community and the fourth-largest Latin American group, behind Mexicans, Cubans, and Puerto Ricans.

Salvadorans have immigrated to the United States since the late nineteenth century, but substantial Salvadoran immigration did not begin until after a bloody civil war exploded in the tiny Central American nation in 1979. Since then, deteriorating economic conditions and natural disasters have pushed more than one million Salvadorans to seek better lives in the United States. Most have come as undocumented workers.

PRE-CIVIL WAR IMMIGRANTS

The first wave of Salvadoran migration can be traced to the late nineteenth century, when San Francisco-based companies established business contracts with Salvadoran and other Central American coffee growers. The migration networks then established were initially limited to the elite but were later extended to Salvadorans who were recruited to work in California coffee factories and other industries. During the 1930's, a combination of harsh economic conditions and political instability drove many Salvadorans to leave their homeland. The military regime of Maximiliano Hernández forced into exile middle- and upper-class Salvadorans, who resettled mostly in the San Francisco Bay Area, Los Angeles, and New York City, where they found employment in the cities' industrial sectors.

Another important immigration wave took place during the 1940's, as World War II created a significant demand for labor. Some Salvadorans went to work in the Panama Canal Zone, and many others got contracts to work in Southern California. After passage of the U.S. Immigration and Nationality Act of 1965 opened immigration to many countries that had not been historically included, some 100,000 Central Americans, many of them Salvadorans, immigrated to the United States. They settled not only in California, but also in Texas, New Jersey, and Washington, D.C.

POST-1979 IMMIGRATION

The migration of Salvadorans to the United States between 1979 and the late 1990's was prompted mainly by political instability resulting from the civil war that ravaged the country from 1979 to 1992. During this period, the left-leaning Farabundo Martí National Liberation Front escalated its armed insurgency against the conservative oligarchy and military government ruling El Salvador. During the conflict, military and right-wing paramilitary death squads targeted labor leaders, intellectuals, religious leaders who were deemed

PROFILE OF SALVADORAN IMMIGRANTS	
Country of origin	El Salvador
Primary language	Spanish
Primary regions of U.S. settlement	Southern California, Washington, D.C.
Earliest significant arrivals	Late nineteenth century
Peak immigration period	1980's-1990's
Twenty-first century legal residents*	214,114 (26,764 per year)

*Immigrants who obtained legal permanent resident status in the United States.
Source: Department of Homeland Security, Yearbook of Immigration Statistics, 2008.

subversive because of their adhesion to Liberation Theology, and other sympathizers with the uprising. By the time peace accords were signed in 1992, some 75,000 Salvadorans had died.

Throughout the civil war, hundreds of thousands of Salvadorans fled the country. Some left because of persecution and death threats from both the government and leftist guerrillas, while many rural laborers whose livelihood was disrupted by the conflict emigrated in search of economic opportunities. The war's impact on immigration to the United States was significant. Between the early 1980's and 1990, the number of Salvadorans residing in the country rose from 213,000 to 565,000. Immigrant settlement patterns followed those of earlier migration waves, with Los Angeles, Washington, D.C., and New York continuing to be the top destinations. However, Salvadorans also settled in other cities with substantial Hispanic populations, such as Miami and Boston. In Los Angeles, Salvadorans soon became the second-largest immigrant community.

The immigration of Salvadoran refugees into the United States during the civil war was mired in political controversy. The Salvadorans were not given the same refugee status that refugees from many other nations had enjoyed, so most entered the country illegally and experienced a long, painful journeys toward legal residency. During the

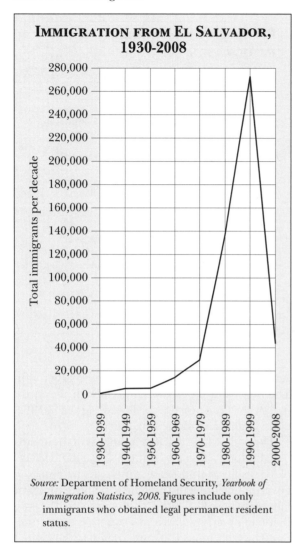

IMMIGRATION FROM EL SALVADOR, 1930-2008

Source: Department of Homeland Security, *Yearbook of Immigration Statistics, 2008.* Figures include only immigrants who obtained legal permanent resident status.

jobs or family reunification in the United States. Earthquakes in 2001 left 1.5 million Salvadorans without homes, further disrupting economic recovery and fueling emigration. This time, however, immigrants who reached the United States settled in states that had not traditionally received many Hispanic immigrants in search of agricultural and construction jobs, such as North Carolina and Arkansas. A revised 2000 U.S. Census study put the number of Salvadorans in the United States at 1,010,740. However, estimates made by the Salvadoran embassy in Washington, D.C., placed that figure at about 1.7 million.

Salvadorans have contributed to the U.S. economy by engaging in both high- and low-skilled occupations. Their remittances ($3.7 billion in 2007) have become vital to El Salvador, representing 18 percent of the country's gross domestic product.

Mauricio Espinoza-Quesada

FURTHER READING

Cordova, Carlos. *The Salvadoran Americans.* Westport, Conn.: Greenwood Press, 2005. Overview of El Salvador, Salvadoran immigration, and various aspects of the Salvadoran community in the United States.

Coutin, Susan Bibler. *Legalizing Moves: Salvadoran Immigrants' Struggles for U.S. Residency.* Ann Arbor: University of Michigan Press, 2000. Analysis of the fight by Salvadorans to normalize their residency situation in the United States.

Hamilton, Nora, and Norma Stoltz Chinchilla. *Seeking Community in a Global City.* Philadelphia: Temple University Press, 2001. Study of the struggle for survival and efforts to build their own communities by Salvadorans and Guatemalans.

Kowalski, Kathiann. *Salvadorans in America.* Minneapolis: Lerner Publications, 2006. Concise history of the nation of El Salvador, its civil war, and Salvadoran experiences in the United States.

Mahler, Sarah. *Salvadorans in Suburbia: Symbiosis and Conflict.* Needham Heights, Mass.: Allyn & Bacon, 1995. Study of the settlement patterns and interaction of Salvadoran immigrants in the Long Island suburb of New York City.

SEE ALSO: Illegal immigration; Latin American immigrants; Latinos and immigrants; Los Angeles; Natural disasters as push-pull factors; Refugees; Washington, D.C.

1980's, fewer than 3 percent of Salvadoran applicants were granted refugee status. In 1985, religious and refugee-service organizations sued the U.S. government for discrimination against Salvadoran and Guatemalan asylum seekers. The U.S. Immigration Act of 1990 created a temporary protected status (TPS) and designated Salvadorans as its first recipients. Salvadorans were later allowed to register for "deferred enforced departure" between 1992 an 1996, but even those provisions left many Salvadorans in legal limbo.

Salvadoran immigration to the United States did not stop with the settlement of El Salvador's civil war. A devastated economy, poverty, and insecurity propelled even more Salvadorans to seek

SAN FRANCISCO

IDENTIFICATION: Third-largest city in California and the state's primary commercial center, transportation hub, and immigrant-receiving center during the nineteenth century

SIGNIFICANCE: Northern California's major port city, San Francisco, has been a reception center and place of settlement for many immigrant groups since the mid-nineteenth century. Its rapid growth during the years before the U.S. Civil War was a direct result of California's gold rush, but its status as one of the best natural harbors on the Pacific Coast ensured that it would continue to attract immigrants long after the gold rush ended.

California became a U.S. territory after the United States won the Mexican War of 1846-1848, and it became a state in 1850. At the time gold was discovered near Sacramento in 1848, San Francisco was little more than a sleepy waterfront village with about 800 mostly Spanish-speaking inhabitants. By the end of 1849, it had become a city with 30,000 residents from all over the United States and the world. Between 1849 and 1860, another 40,000 people arrived in San Francisco by sea. By 1880, the city had 100,000 residents, about 45 percent of whom were foreign born.

ASIAN IMMIGRANTS

In 1849, a few hundred Chinese men arrived in San Francisco hoping to work in the gold fields; another thousand arrived the following year. In 1860, official U.S. Census records showed that 2,719 Chinese were living in the city; that figure rose to 12,022 in 1870, 21,745 in 1880, 25,833 in 1890, and 13,954 in 1900. Through those years, thousands more Chinese passed through the city on their way to jobs in the gold fields, on railroads, and in other industries. Records of the city's customs office show that 233,136 Chinese arrived in San Francisco between 1848 and 1876 alone; 93,273 of these immigrants later returned to China. The overwhelming majority of these early Chinese immigrants were men from the Pearl River Delta region of China that includes Canton, Macao, and Hong Kong.

Most of the Chinese who remained in San Francisco lived within the fifteen-square-block area that became known as Chinatown. The city's Chinese worked primarily in service industries, such as laundries and domestic service. Chinese women were few, and many of them were prostitutes who serviced the large number of single men. Most of the prostitutes came from the lower classes in China and had been sold into the sex trade involuntarily or had been tricked into coming to America.

In 1877, five years before passage of the Chinese Exclusion Act, Harper's Weekly *published this cover, which gives the impression that an unending stream of Chinese are pouring into San Francisco.* (Hulton Archive/Getty Images)

During the 1880's, Japanese immigrants, mostly students, began arriving in San Francisco. By 1900, the city had more than 1,700 Japanese residents, but these immigrants did not congregate in any one neighborhood.

EUROPEAN IMMIGRANTS

During the 1850's, Italians began settling in an area next to Chinatown known variously as the North Shore, the Italian Section, and Little Italy. Many were fishermen from Liguria, the northwest region of Italy that includes Genoa. These immigrants dominated the San Francisco Bay Area's important fishing industry for many years, and strong Italian influences can still be seen in the city's Fisherman's Wharf area, a popular tourist site.

California's American development began at the same time Irish immigrants were starting to immigrate to the United States in massive numbers. As early as 1852, 4,200 Irish were living in San Francisco, accounting for 9 percent of the city's entire population. By 1880, the Irish accounted for 37 percent of the residents, but that figure had dropped to 25 percent by 1900. Many Irish immigrants congregated in the area that became known as Irish Hill during the 1880's so that they could be close to the factories in which they worked. Irish men also constituted about 90 percent of the city's small police force during this time.

THE 1906 EARTHQUAKE AND ITS AFTERMATH

In early 1906, San Francisco suffered one of the most devastating earthquakes that any American city has ever experienced. Later estimated to have been as strong as 8.4 on the modern Richter scale, the quake flattened much of the city and was then followed by an equally destructive fire. Because of the cataclysmic impact of the earthquake, standard histories of San Francisco divide their narratives into two parts: before and after the quake.

San Francisco was completely rebuilt by the time of American's entry into World War I in 1917, but by then significant changes had occurred. The city's Japantown was established, but one-third of its residents would choose not to return after they were interned during World War II. An attempt had been made to dismantle Chinatown, but its residents successfully rebuilt the enclave using Chinese architectural designs. Although San Francisco's Chinese population fell to 11,000 by 1920, Chinatown became a major tourist destination after government authorities closed its brothels and suppressed the criminal gangs known as tongs. Meanwhile, the city's Irish residents had become so thoroughly assimilated that there were few traces of distinctly Irish neighborhoods.

During the second half of the twentieth century, San Francisco's population remained relatively stable, and most people who immigrated to the city came for lifestyle reasons, to enjoy its picturesque setting, cultural attractions, and tolerance of all kinds of diversity. During the 1970's, the city became a magnet for gay and lesbian people.

As with the United States as a whole, San Francisco began experiencing a large influx of Asian and Latin American immigration after the 1960's. By the early twenty-first century, about 35 percent of its residents were foreign born. In 2007, residents of Asian descent constituted about 33 percent of the city's estimated population of 800,000. and Hispanics constituted about 14 percent.

Thomas R. Feller

FURTHER READING

Brook, James, Chris Carlsson, and Nancy Joyce Peters, eds. *Reclaiming San Francisco: History, Politics, Culture.* San Francisco: City Lights Books, 1998. Collection of essays on San Francisco.

Chen, Yong. *Chinese San Francisco, 1850-1943: A Trans-Pacific Community.* Stanford, Calif.: Stanford University Press, 2000. Comprehensive history of Chinese immigration to San Francisco from the time of the gold rush to the year in which the Chinese Exclusion Act of 1882 was finally repealed.

Cinel, Dino. *From Italy to San Francisco: The Immigrant Experience.* Stanford, Calif.: Stanford University Press, 1982. Thorough history of Italian immigration to San Francisco.

Dillon, Richard H. *Hatchet Men: The Story of the Tong Wars in San Francisco's Chinatown.* Fairfield, Calif.: James Stevenson, 2005. History of organized crime in San Francisco's Chinatown during the late nineteenth and early twentieth centuries.

Garvey, John, and Karen Hanning. *Irish San Francisco.* Mount Pleasant, S.C.: Arcadia Publishing, 2008. History of Irish immigration to San Francisco.

SEE ALSO: Angel Island Immigration Station; Anti-Chinese movement; Asian immigrants; California; California gold rush; Chinatowns; Chinese immigrants; *I Remember Mama*; Mexican immigrants; Paper sons; Spanish immigrants; "Yellow peril" campaign.

SANCTUARY MOVEMENT

THE EVENT: Movement within the United States in which religious congregations and other bodies provided aid to mostly undocumented refugees fleeing Central America

DATE: Began in 1980

SIGNIFICANCE: The Sanctuary movement was part of a broader antiwar movement against President Ronald Reagan's foreign policy in Central America. By 1987, 440 Christian congregations, Jewish temples, and other religious meeting sites were granting asylum to undocumented political refugees primarily from El Salvador, Guatemala, and Nicaragua. The Reagan administration's support of military governments in countries implicated in assassinations of hundreds of religious workers motivated religious communities in the United States to offer sanctuary to Central Americans denied refugee status by the U.S. government. The Reagan administration could not have given them refugee status without undermining its support of the Central American military regimes it supported in its broader Cold War struggle against communism.

The year 1980 marked the beginning of public controversy over U.S. policy in Central America, when national refugee policy was being tested by the civil wars engulfing Central America. During the last months of the Carter administration, the U.S. Congress passed the Refugee Act of 1980, which was intended to expand eligibility for political asylum in the United States. The 1980 law brought the United States into line with the United Nations' 1951 protocol relating to the status of refugees. Previous U.S. law had dealt only with refugees from communism. The new law classified refugees as persons with a "well-founded fear of persecution."

The fact that the Refugee Act was passed at the same time Central Americans were fleeing civil wars set the stage for a decades-long controversy that ultimately involved thousands of Americans. On one side of the controversy were immigration lawyers, religious activists, and liberal members of Congress and the public. On the other side were the U.S. Immigration and Naturalization Service (INS), the Federal Bureau of Investigation (FBI), and the U.S. Departments of Justice and State. Members of the first side sought to protect the lives of the fleeing refugees, while representatives of the federal government agencies claimed to be focused on national security.

The religious congregations that became known as the Sanctuary movement began in Arizona in 1980, when Presbyterian and Quaker groups began aiding refugees from El Salvador and Guatemala. The movement was motivated in its effort by the fact that the military regimes the Reagan administration supported in Central America were wantonly assassinating religious workers. American priests and nuns were also assassinated in El Salvador and Guatemala. With the assassination of Archbishop Oscar Romero by elements of the Salvadoran military in March, 1980, the movement went into high gear.

Eventually, more than one thousand Roman Catholic, Protestant, and Jewish congregations supported the movement. A modern-day "underground railroad" was assembled with the aid of supporters in Mexico who helped Central American refugees reach the safety of Sanctuary sites in the United States. While the Reagan administration attempted to prosecute some of those involved in the movement, the accompanying publicity of trials in Texas and Arizona ultimately resulted in the indictment of Reagan's war in Central America.

Raymond J. Gonzales

FURTHER READING
Bau, Ignatius. *This Ground Is Holy: Church Sanctuary and Central American Refugees*. Mahwah, N.J.: Paulist Press, 1985.
Golden, Renny, and Michael McConell. *Sanctuary: The New Underground Railroad*. Maryknoll, N.Y.: Orbis Books, 1986.
Gonzales, Raymond J. "Secret Cable: The Roman Catholic Church as a Factor in Guatemalan Politics." In *A Lifetime of Dissent*. New York: Xlibris, 2006.

SEE ALSO: Catholic Charities USA; Civil Rights movement; Guatemalan immigrants; Honduran immigrants; Illegal immigration; Immigration law; Immigration lawyers; Religions of immigrants; Salvadoran immigrants.

SANTIAGO, ESMERALDA

IDENTIFICATION: Puerto Rican author
BORN: May 17, 1948; San Juan, Puerto Rico

SIGNIFICANCE: Since the publication of her memoir in 1993, Santiago has become one of the most studied Latina writers in the United States. Her work illuminates the reasons Puerto Ricans have immigrated to the United States and the challenges immigrants—particularly women—face in negotiating their cultural identity.

Born in Puerto Rico in 1948, Esmeralda Santiago was the eldest of eleven children of her single mother, Ramona Santiago. In 1961, she moved with her family to New York City. Her first book, *When I Was Puerto Rican* (1993), is a memoir of her childhood in Puerto Rico, in particular the effects of Operation Bootstrap, a U.S. policy during the 1950's and 1960's that transformed the island's agricultural economy into one based on manufacturing. Her narrative describes the colonial status of the island and the policy that resulted in the displacement of rural Puerto Ricans to San Juan, which eventually led to their migration to the mainland United States. Santiago concludes her story describing her own displacement in Brooklyn, her struggles to adapt, and her ultimate triumph, as she not only is accepted to the Performing Arts High School despite knowing little English but also graduates from Harvard University.

In 1997, Santiago published her first novel, *América's Dream*, an alternate selection of the Literary Guild that was published in six languages. The protagonist of this novel, América, is a hotel housekeeper who escapes her alcoholic mother, abusive boyfriend, and resentful daughter to come to the United States in search of a new life. As a live-in nanny for a wealthy family, América struggles to es-cape her past and understand her devalued position in her new country. The novel deals with not only the search for identity but also the desire for independence, while at the same time providing a profound reflection on the relationships between mothers and daughters.

Santiago next published *Almost a Woman* (1998), a continuation of her first memoir that details her search for independence and the struggles of growing up bicultural, both of which are tied to her relationship with the women in her family. *Almost a Woman* won numerous awards from the American Library Association, was adapted into a film for the Public Broadcasting Service's Masterpiece Theater, and was awarded a Peabody Award. In 2004, Santiago released her third memoir, *The Turkish Lover.* Picking up where she left off in *Almost a Woman*, Santiago describes her years after high school, her independence from her mother, and her seven-year romance with her domineering lover, Ulvi. Despite the obstacles, Santiago once again emerges triumphant.

Santiago's books share common themes: the experience of immigration, the negotiation between two cultures and languages, the struggles of women living in a patriarchal society, and the difficult journey of women in search of independence. Her work shares much in common with that of other Puerto Rican writers in the United States; at the same time, it has much in common with the larger body of American Latina literature that, while also negotiating biculturalism, challenges patriarchal society. Santiago is also the author of the children's book *A Doll for Navidades* (2005) and is the editor of two anthologies, *Las Christmas: Favorite Latino Authors Share Their Holiday Memories* (1998) and *Las Mamis: Favorite Latino Authos Remember Their Mothers* (2000).

Stephanie M. Alvarez

FURTHER READING

Hernández, Carmen. "Esmeralda Santiago." In *Puerto Rican Voices in English: Interviews with Writers.* Westport, Conn.: Praeger, 1997.

Keavane, Bridget. "Puerto Rican Existentialist in Brooklyn: An Interview with Esmeralda Santiago." In *Latina Self-Portraits: Interviews with Contemporary Women Writers*, edited by Juanita Heredia and Bridget Kevane. Albuquerque: University of New Mexico Press, 2000.

Rodríguez-Mangual, Edna. "Esmeralda Santiago." In *Latino and Latina Writers*, edited by Alan West-Durán. New York: Charles Scribner's Sons, 2004.

SEE ALSO: Alvarez, Julia; Danticat, Edwidge; Families; Latin American immigrants; Latinos and immigrants; New York City; Puerto Rican immigrants; Women immigrants.

SCANDINAVIAN IMMIGRANTS

SIGNIFICANCE: The large numbers of Scandinavians who immigrated to the United States during the nineteenth century were driven primarily by economic motives. Most settled in the upper Midwest as homesteaders, and many later moved to the Pacific Northwest. As northern European Protestants, they were readily accepted in America and assimilated easily. Scandinavian immigration was also a classic example of chain migration, as many immigrants were drawn to America by the enthusiastic letters they received from friends and relatives who preceded them to the New World.

The term "Scandinavian" has three different but overlapping meanings. In its narrowest, geographical sense, it applies to northern Europe's Scandinavian Peninsula, which encompasses only Norway and Sweden. In a broader, primarily linguistic sense, it applies to the countries in which members of the Scandinavian language group are spoken—Denmark, Norway, and Sweden. Iceland and the Faroe Islands are also sometimes included within this meaning of the term. Finally, in its broadest, cultural sense, it encompasses all those countries, plus Norway and Sweden's eastern neighbor, Finland. Whereas the Scandinavian languages Danish, Icelandic, Norwegian, and Swedish are part of the Northern Germanic group, Finnish is a Finno-Ugric language closely related to Estonian and Hungarian. However, apart from their language, Finns are culturally closely allied with the speakers of Scandinavian languages and for that reason are commonly regarded as Scandinavians.

HISTORY OF SCANDINAVIAN IMMIGRATION

Scandinavians were probably the first Europeans to settle in the Western Hemisphere, but their earliest explorations and settlement attempts left few lasting traces. Viking expeditions from Iceland reached eastern Canada as early as 1000 C.E., and some early Viking navigators may have reached as far south as what is now known as New England. After these early explorations failed to create permanent settlements, Scandinavians would not reappear in North America until the British began founding colonies. However, while small numbers of Scandinavians joined the British settlements, no substantial groups came. In 1638, Swedes participated in a trade expedition with Germany and the Netherlands that established a settlement called New Sweden at the mouth of the Delaware River. Afterward, however, few additional Swedes immigrated for more than a century because of Swedish laws restricting emigration.

Small numbers of Norwegians settled in Dutch American colonies during the seventeenth century because Holland had commercial ties with Norway. Some Norwegians also settled in colonial Pennsylvania. The first organized group of Norwegian im-

PROFILE OF SCANDINAVIAN IMMIGRANTS

Countries of origin	Denmark, Finland, Iceland, Norway, and Sweden
Primary languages	Danish, Finnish, Icelandic, Norwegian, Swedish, English
Primary regions of U.S. settlement	Upper Midwest
Earliest significant arrivals	Seventeenth century
Peak immigration period	1880's-1920's
Twenty-first century legal residents*	22,688 (2,836 per year)

*Immigrants who obtained legal permanent resident status in the United States.

Source: Department of Homeland Security, *Yearbook of Immigration Statistics,* 2008.

migrants was the Sloopers, a group of fifty Norwegians led by a Norwegian Quaker on the ship *Restauration*. This group settled in Kendall, New York, in 1825 but later many moved to Illinois, where they founded the Fox River settlement.

From the early nineteenth century through the first years of the twenty-first century, more than 2.5 million Danes, Finns, Icelanders, Norwegians, and Swedes immigrated to the United States. Most came between 1840 and 1924. Chain migration had a snowballing effect on their immigration: Early migrants actively encouraged and helped later migrants, and their numbers steadily increased. The help included not only practical advice and encouragement but also transatlantic steamer tickets. The largest influx of Scandinavians occurred during the 1880's, but an economic downtown during the 1890's caused a temporary decline.

During the late nineteenth century, the numbers of Scandinavian immigrants grew as whole families traveled together. The journeys of the earliest emigrants began in Scandinavian port cities, from which they sailed to other European ports in which they could find ships to carry them across the Atlantic. As Scandinavian migration increased, immigrants were able to sail directly to North America from their own countries. Voyages on sailing ships could take months, but as steamships replaced sailing vessels during the 1870's, the lengths of the voyages dropped under two weeks. Many Scandinavians traveled by steerage class. Most immigrants arrived in New York City; others landed in Boston and Quebec City.

Most early nineteenth century Scandinavian immigrants were peasants. However, by 1900, wealthier urban Scandinavians were settling in U.S. cities. The rate of Scandinavian immigration picked up again during the early years of the twentieth century, but the onset of World War I in 1914 and more restrictive U.S. immigration laws passed during the 1920's again slowed Scandinavian immigration.

PUSH-PULL FACTORS

Economic problems, such as major crop failures, in the Scandinavian countries were the primary factors that pushed emigration to North America during the nineteenth century. Medical advances such as smallpox vaccination helped populations to grow faster than food production could keep up. Many Scandinavian immigrants had been peasants in their homelands, working tiny plots of land whose small harvests they had to share with landlords. In their harsh northern climes, they struggled to grow crops on tired soil during short summer growing seasons and typically were only one harvest away from starvation. Other immigrants had been skilled craftsman who had insufficient markets for their goods. Many Scandinavians faced the additional burden of having to pay church ministers head taxes.

Elements of Scandinavian political systems also helped push people to emigrate. Some Scandinavians were denied the right to vote or wished to avoid compulsory military service. Many chafed under monarchic rule and yearned for democracy. Another source of grievance was the fact that both Sweden and Norway had state religions.

Meanwhile, the United States appeared to offer compelling economic opportunities that pulled immigrants already dissatisfied with their homelands. Peasants looked forward to abundant free, fertile land available under the federal Homestead Act of 1862. This legislation allowed settlers to claim virtually free 160-acre parcels of land in return for living on the land and making modest improvements. Immigrants who were not farmers felt the pull of good jobs in many industries. The letters that immigrants sent home were circulated among family and friends and were sometimes published in newspapers. "America Fever" also spread via advertising by steamship companies.

SETTLEMENT PATTERNS

Some Scandinavian immigrants settled in eastern states, but most farmers chose to homestead in the upper Midwest, whose physical terrain of abundant lakes and verdant farmlands was similar to that of the Scandinavian countries. After arriving in eastern port cities, the immigrants took steamboats up the Hudson River, through the Erie Canal, and across the Great Lakes to the Midwest. Some Scandinavians settled around Chicago, but most continued farther west to Minnesota, Iowa, Wisconsin, North Dakota, and South Dakota.

Meanwhile, Chicago became such a popular Swedish destination that one of its neighborhoods was dubbed Swede Town. Swedes worked in lumber mills that manufactured building material for the growing city and were so important in the rebuilding of Chicago after the city's great 1871 fire that observers said that Swedes built Chicago. Eventually, however, Minneapolis became a more popular urban destination for Swedish immigrants.

After establishing themselves firmly in the upper Midwest, many Scandinavians turned their sights still further west to Washington, Oregon, and California, where they took jobs in shipbuilding, lumber, salmon fisheries, and canning. So many western loggers were Swedish that "Swedish fiddle" became a nickname for the crosscut saw.

Several western cities became Scandinavian centers, such as Tacoma and Seattle in Washington. Scandinavians participated in the major events of nineteenth century America, such as the gold rush and the building of the transcontinental railroad. They fought on the Union side in the U.S. Civil War. While farmers predominated, many immigrants were craftsmen or in the maritime trades. Many were active in the labor union movement. Most first-generation immigrants took blue-collar

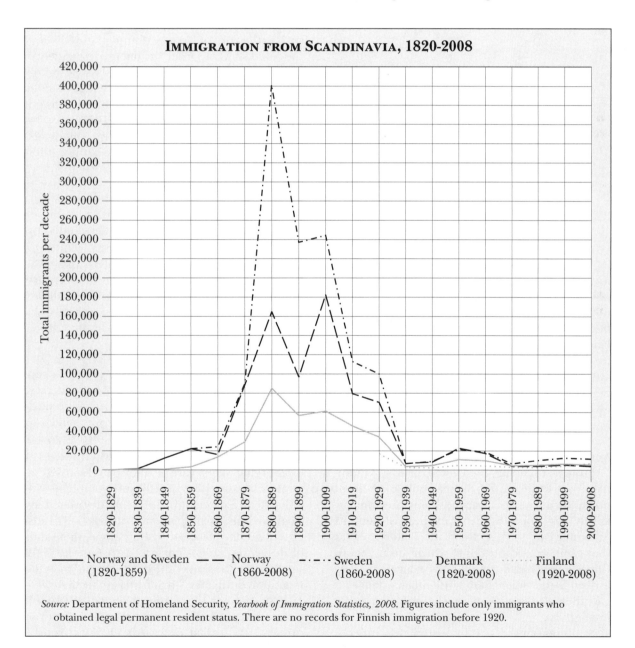

IMMIGRATION FROM SCANDINAVIA, 1820-2008

Legend:
— Norway and Sweden (1820-1859)
– – Norway (1860-2008)
–·· Sweden (1860-2008)
— Denmark (1820-2008)
····· Finland (1920-2008)

Source: Department of Homeland Security, *Yearbook of Immigration Statistics, 2008.* Figures include only immigrants who obtained legal permanent resident status. There are no records for Finnish immigration before 1920.

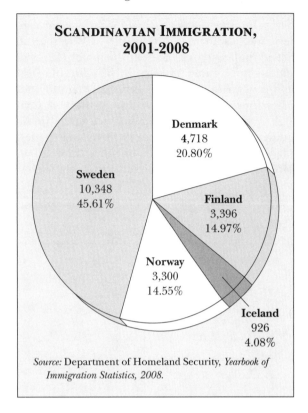

SCANDINAVIAN IMMIGRATION, 2001-2008

Denmark
4,718
20.80%

Sweden
10,348
45.61%

Finland
3,396
14.97%

Norway
3,300
14.55%

Iceland
926
4.08%

Source: Department of Homeland Security, *Yearbook of Immigration Statistics, 2008.*

jobs, but many second- and third-generation family members held skilled blue-collar and white-collar positions.

Other Scandinavians, particularly Swedes, settled in eastern cities, such as Providence, Rhode Island, and Boston, Massachusetts, in which they found skilled industrial jobs. Worcester, Massachusetts, developed a Swedish enclave whose immigrants worked in factories making abrasives and wire. The immigrants' influence on the neighborhood can still be seen in Swedish street names.

ACCEPTANCE AND ASSIMILATION

From its founding, the United States was dominated by white, Anglo-Saxon Protestants from northern and western Europe. It was thus comparatively easy for northern European Protestant Scandinavians to find acceptance. Moreover, as they came from countries in which the Lutheran Church demanded compulsory education, they arrived in the United States with literacy skills that gave them a competitive advantage over many other immigrants.

Scandinavians generally assimilated quickly.

However, members of their various nationalities varied somewhat in the speed of blending. The Danes assimilated the fastest, followed by Swedes, Norwegians, and Finns. The latter were probably slightly handicapped by speaking a language outside the Indo-European family of languages.

Despite their high degree of assimilation, Americans of Scandinavian heritage have retained some characteristics of their traditional cultures. For example, old cultural traditions can still be seen in Christmas cookie recipes and jokes about lutefisk, the codfish soaked in lye. Fraternal organizations such as the Sons of Norway (founded in 1895) and the Swedish Vasa Order of America (founded in 1896) remind members of the old ways. Scandinavian Americans are seen as celebrating symbolic ethnicity, in which they retain a few traditions but do not take them very seriously. They enjoy hyphenated identities such as "Swedish-Americans" and "Danish-Americans," but these do not interfere with their more serious identities as Americans.

SWEDISH IMMIGRANTS

Sweden contributed the largest number of Scandinavian immigrants to America, with more than 1 million coming between 1851 and 1930. During the first years of the twenty-first century, slightly fewer than 5 percent of Americans claimed Swedish ancestry. The states with the largest Swedish American populations were Minnesota, California, Illinois, and Washington.

Significant Swedish immigration began after 1840, when Sweden relaxed its restrictions on emigration. A group of religious dissenters known as Jansenists established a community in Illinois called Bishop Hill that lasted from the 1840's into the 1860's. Major Swedish immigration, however, did not begin until the late 1860's, when a series of disasters in Sweden gave people new reasons to emigrate. Excessive rains in 1867 were combined with a destructive drought in 1868 that devastated agriculture. In 1869, epidemics caused the deaths of thousands of Swedes. In 1869 alone, thousands of desperate Swedes emigrated to America, in a smaller-scale version of the great surge of Irish immigration during the Great Irish Famine of the late 1840's. Another development spurring Swedish emigration was an 1877 law raising the amount of property Swedes had to own to be eligible to vote.

By the 1920's, the rate of Swedish immigration was beginning to drop. During the Great Depression years of the early 1930's, more Swedes returned to their homeland than immigrated to the United States. Since that era, Swedish immigration to the United States has been modest. The small numbers of Swedes coming during the early twenty-first century tended to settle in the suburbs of New York City and Los Angeles.

Most Swedes adapted quickly to American ways. The homesteaders dressed much like American farmers, used similar dugouts and log cabins, and were quick to adopt American farming methods. In other respects, however, they were slower to assimilate. Some farm families remained paternalistic, retained the Swedish language in the home, preferred in-group marriage, and opposed such leisure pursuits as pool halls and movies. Even during the twenty-first century, some of these holdovers remain among older rural Swedes.

NORWEGIAN IMMIGRANTS

Among the Scandinavian countries, Sweden sent the largest number of immigrants to the United States, but Norway sent a larger proportion of its population. Among European countries, only Ireland lost a larger share of its population to emigration. By 1925, about 800,000 Norwegians had immigrated to the United States. The force pushing Norwegian emigration was economic. During the nineteenth century, Norway's population growth outstripped its agricultural production, which was limited by the scarcity of tillable land. Another factor that attracted Norwegians to the United States was the 1839 publication of Ole Rynning's *A True Account of America for the Information and Help of Peasant and Commoner*, which painted an enthusiastic picture of life in North America for immigrants.

Significant Norwegian immigration began around 1850. Early immigrant ships usually disembarked in New York City. Later, however, most Norwegians traveled through Canada because transatlantic fares to Canada were cheaper, and British navigation permitted ships of all nationalities to land in Canadian ports. The most common route to the American Midwest began in Quebec City, from which immigrants went by ships to Toronto. From there, they traveled overland by rail to Collingwood, Ontario. Then they took steamers across Lake Huron and Lake Michigan to disembark in Green Bay or Milwaukee in Wisconsin or in Chicago, Illinois, from which they continued to the upper Midwest.

Norwegian immigration slowed temporarily during the U.S. Civil War (1861-1865), then picked up again. As homesteaders, the Norwegians quickly adapted, changing from their crude ox-driven wagons with wheels made from tree trunk slices to modern horse-drawn wagons. Many Norwegian immigrants later moved to California, Washington, Oregon, and Alaska. Not all followed this path, however. Some remained in the Canadian provinces. Others took copper and iron mining jobs in Michigan. Some Norwegians established a large ethnic enclave in Brooklyn, New York, where they worked in shipbuilding trades and bridge construction. The women ran rooming houses and worked in domestic service. Large numbers of single Norwegian women immigrated alone, settling in cities as domestic workers.

Norwegians assimilated comparatively quickly. At first, many continued to speak Norwegian in their homes and churches, and dozens of Norwegian-language newspapers were published. However, the language usually was not passed on to the second and third generations. Norwegians also established colleges that have kept some of the culture alive, such as St. Olaf College in Northfield, Minnesota. Some celebrate Norwegian Constitution Day, or *Syttende mai*, each May 17, an instance of symbolic ethnicity.

Nancy Conn Terjesen

FURTHER READING

Gerber, David A., and Alan M. Kraut, eds. *American Immigration and Ethnicity: A Reader.* New York: Palgrave Macmillan, 2005. Collection of articles on ethnic identity, many of which compare modern immigration with immigration in the past.

Gesme, Ann Urness. *Between Rocks and Hard Places.* Hastings, Minn.: Caragana Press, 1993. Describes living conditions and cultural practices in nineteenth century rural Norway.

Kivisto, Peter, and Wendy Ng. *Americans All: Race and Ethnic Relations in Historical, Structural, and Comparative Perspectives.* 2d ed. New York: Oxford University Press, 2005. Explores leading sociological perspectives on race and ethnic relations, with many Scandinavian examples.

Lewis, Anne Gillespie. *Swedes in Minnesota: The People of Minnesota.* St. Paul: Minnesota Historical Society Press, 2004. Traces the founding of Swedish churches and other organizations in Minnesota.

Lovoll, Odd. *The Promise of America: A History of the Norwegian American People.* Minneapolis: University of Minnesota Press, 1984. Scholarly study of Norwegian immigration that examines the lives of immigrants in both their homeland and America.

Rasmussen, Janet E. *New Land, New Lives: Scandinavian Immigrants to the Pacific Northwest.* Seattle: University of Washington Press, 1993. Study drawing on oral histories collected around 1980. Emphasizes the lives of women immigrants.

Semmingsen, Ingrid. *Norway to America: A History of Immigration.* Minneapolis: University of Minnesota Press, 1978. A Norwegian history professor describes how migration affected both Norway and America.

SEE ALSO: Chain migration; Chicago; Economic opportunities; European immigrants; Homestead Act of 1862; Minnesota; Mormon immigrants; Push-pull factors; Settlement patterns; Westward expansion.

SCHURZ, CARL

IDENTIFICATION: German-born American journalist, lawyer, social activist, Civil War general, and statesman

BORN: March 2, 1829; Liblar, Prussia (now in Germany)

DIED: May 14, 1906; New York, New York

SIGNIFICANCE: Schurz was one of the most influential foreign immigrants in American history. In exile since the failed German Revolution of 1848, he came to the United States in 1852. As an antislavery activist, he campaigned heavily for Abraham Lincoln in the 1860 presidential election and eventually served as envoy to Spain, a Union general during the Civil War, a U.S. senator, and secretary of the interior. Ever the reformer, he supported the rights of freed slaves and Native Americans, attacked the "spoils system," and was a staunch conservationist.

Born to middle-class parents in the tiny village of Liblar in the Rhineland, Carl Schurz rose from humble beginnings to become one of the premier American statesmen of the nineteenth century. His schoolteacher father taught him to read and write at a very young age. His intellectual abilities eventually led him to attend university in Bonn.

In 1848, working-class discontent over low wages and unemployment pervaded European society, and uprisings against governments were common but often short-lived due to lack of military strength. The Germanic states had a secret weapon in the Prussian army—arguably the most powerful army in Europe at the time—and so the Frankfurt Assembly elected Prussia's King Frederick William IV emperor of a new German Reich. Not wanting to accept the crown from commoners, Frederick William IV simply took the crown and dismissed the Frankfurt Assembly, establishing himself as absolute ruler. Angered by this turn of events, Schurz joined a revolutionary movement to restore liberty and the rights declared by the Frankfurt constitution.

After being captured by Prussians, Schurz made a daring escape and ended up in exile in Switzerland and France. In 1850, he returned to Berlin under an alias to rescue his former professor Gottfried Kinkel from prison. After fleeing Germany for the last time, Schurz went to London, where in 1852 he met and married Margarethe Meyer. When Louis Napoleon's coronation as Emperor Napoleon III in France that same year aroused almost no protests anywhere in Europe, Schurz realized that the reactionaries were once again fully in control and decided to emigrate to America, where he believed true freedom for all could be achieved. He and Margarethe landed in New York in September, 1852.

POLITICAL AND ACTIVIST LIFE IN AMERICA

While touring New York, Philadelphia, and Washington, D.C., Schurz acquainted himself with the ways of American politics. He immediately despised the "spoils system" for its resemblance to the Old Regime political order in Europe and became interested in the plights of African American slaves and Native Americans. He eventually settled in Wisconsin, where he found a strong community of German immigrants. In 1858, he became a naturalized American citizen—*after* he had already run for lieutenant governor of Wisconsin.

The recently created Republican Party attracted Schurz, in large part because its antislavery position meshed with the anti-reactionary ideals he held since his days as a young revolutionary. He was soon asked to give speeches on the party's behalf at local meetings, mostly on the question of slavery. Eventually, his rhetorical skills gained greater notice, and he was asked to speak in other parts of the country, including in Illinois, where Abraham Lincoln and Stephen A. Douglas were conducting their famous debates during their campaigns for the U.S. Senate. Meeting Lincoln on this occasion would prove fruitful to Schurz's future political career.

While becoming a well-known lawyer, antinativist speaker, and member of a literary crowd that included Oliver Wendell Holmes and Henry Wadsworth Longfellow, Schurz served as a delegate at the 1860 Republican National Convention and contributed to the party's platform. Lincoln shrewdly recognized that close ties to Schurz endeared him to the country's large German American population. After he was elected, he rewarded Schurz for his support with the ambassadorship to Spain. During the Civil War, Schurz was probably the first high-ranking Union official to declare that an antislavery position would actually assist the Union in preventing international support for the Confederacy. It would be difficult for foreign powers, he argued, to take a proslavery stance by supporting the South if the North were to stand for freedom.

Eventually, Schurz felt called to return to the tumultuous situation in America and was commissioned a brigadier general in the Union Army, in which he became more known for his bravado than for his tactical skills. A groundswell movement to remove Lincoln from office pushed Schurz to get involved in the election of 1864 and return to oratory. General William T. Sherman's march on Atlanta and Lincoln's triumph over Democratic nominee George B. McClellan took Schurz back to the Army—but not for long, as the Confederacy surrendered in April, 1865, shortly before Lincoln was assassinated. The new president, Andrew Johnson, then sent Schurz to the South to assess postwar

Carl Schurz in his Union Army uniform during the Civil War. (Library of Congress)

conditions. What Schurz found there was a vengeful population prone to violent uprisings against northern interlopers and newly freed slaves. However, his scathing report on the South was all but ignored by Johnson because it did not contain the information he wanted to hear. Schurz was especially appalled by the poor treatment of newly freed slaves by both the men and the women of the South. Deeming it the public's right to hear the truth, Schurz published his observations and thus began a new career as a journalist.

In 1868, Schurz campaigned for Ulysses S. Grant's election to the presidency and was himself successful in a bid to represent his new home state of Missouri in the U.S. Senate. As a senator Schurz made a point of declaring war on the spoils system in American politics and resurrecting his revolutionary fervor against established protocol. Fortified by the Whiskey Ring and Belknap scandals of the Grant administration, Schurz's Liberal Republican movement gained momentum during Grant's second term, but it was not enough to keep the Democrats from retaking Congress in 1874. Thus, Schurz returned to Missouri and civilian life. During this time, Margarethe died, and Schurz's anguish threatened to stifle his zealous campaign against political corruption. He found a compatriot in Ohio governor Rutherford B. Hayes and soon stumped for Hayes's presidential campaign. After Hayes was elected, he appointed Schurz secretary of the interior in his cabinet.

CABINET SECRETARY AND JOURNALIST

As secretary of the interior, Schurz directly confronted the issue of Native American rights and was instrumental in preventing the Indian Bureau from being transferred to the War Department. He believed that the best course of action was assimilation of Native Americans into the "white man's" world, largely through property ownership. If Indians owned their own land, he surmised, then they would be motivated to work and contribute to the economy, and their tribal affiliations would gradually fade away. This view aligned with his belief that anyone could become a loyal and steadfast American citizen as he had himself. However, whereas he decried tribalism, he was more than supportive of European cultural pluralism and never ceased to champion his German homeland's every triumph. He also believe that while immigrants could assimilate to American life, they could never completely sever their connections to their homelands. Schurz also made great headway in civil service reform by implementing examinations for entrance into the civil service and applying the merit system when dispensing promotions, a cause near to his heart since his days in the student government at Bonn.

With the election of James A. Garfield in 1880, Schurz settled in New York and returned to writing. He served anonymously as the editor of *Harper's Weekly* for more than five years and used that position to tout further civil service reform and less restrictive immigration laws. However, with the election of William McKinley in 1898 and growing American expansionist fervor, Schurz fell outside popular sentiment and broke ties with the influential weekly. He then dedicated himself to writing his memoirs: He wrote about his youth in German and switched to English for the remainder of his life, ever true to his German American pride.

In 1902, Schurz moved to a new home on Manhattan's East Ninety-first Street in New York City, a traditional German American neighborhood. There he remained until his quiet, peaceful death in 1906. Carl Schurz Park, overlooking the northern edge of Manhattan's East River, forever associates this legendary statesman with his beloved German American heritage.

Noelle K. Penna

FURTHER READING

Easum, Chester V. *The Americanization of Carl Schurz.* Chicago: University of Chicago Press, 1929. Early study of Schurz upon which much of the later scholarship on him has depended.

Fuess, Claude M. *Carl Schurz, Reformer: 1829-1906.* Edited by Allan Nevins. New York: Dodd, Mead, 1932. Gentlemanly biography by a scholar of German American parentage.

Kennedy, David M., and Thomas A. Bailey. *The American Spirit.* 2 vols. Boston: Houghton Mifflin, 2006. Collection of primary source documents dating from Reconstruction to the early twenty-first century.

Schurz, Carl. *Carl Schurz: Revolutionary and Statesman.* München, Germany: Heinz Moos, 1979. Autobiographical collection of materials based on Schurz's memoirs, with additional material on his public service, including photographs, sketches, and speeches.

Trefousse, Hans L. *Carl Schurz: A Biography.* New York: Fordham University Press, 1998. Biography of the German American statesman that focuses on his rise in American politics while maintaining a strong connection to his cultural heritage. Based on an exhaustive study of printed and manuscript sources in both the United States and Europe. Excellent notes and bibliography.

Wallman, Charles J. *The German-Speaking Forty-eighters: Builders of Watertown, Wisconsin.* Madison: Max Kade Institute for German American Studies, University of Wisconsin-Madison, 1990. Chronicles the experiences of Schurz and other German emigrants who left Europe after the revolutions of 1848 and eventually settled in Watertown, Wisconsin.

SEE ALSO: European revolutions of 1848; German immigrants; History of immigration, 1783-1891; New York City; Pulitzer, Joseph; Wisconsin.

SCHWARZENEGGER, ARNOLD

IDENTIFICATION: Austrian American bodybuilder and film star who became governor of California

BORN: July 30, 1947; Graz, Austria

SIGNIFICANCE: Already a champion bodybuilder when he came to America to advance his career, Arnold Schwarzenegger became a major film star and multimillionaire businessman, married into one of the most famous political families in the United States, and was twice elected governor of California.

Born in Austria in 1947, Arnold Schwarzenegger was the son of a small-town police chief and a housewife. He became enamored with bodybuilding when he was thirteen and won his first major bodybuilding title when he was only eighteen. After winning his second Mr. Universe title in 1968, he emigrated to the United States and settled in Southern California, the center of the national bodybuilding subculture. He initially planned to stay for only one year but ultimately remained there. He spoke English poorly at first, and although he eventually became fluent in the language, he never rid himself of his heavy Austrian accent.

Schwarzenegger's first film, *Hercules in New York* (1970), was both a commercial and critical failure. He was billed as "Arnold Strong," and his accent was so thick that his dialogue had to be dubbed by another actor. A few years later, his English had improved sufficiently for him to win a Golden Globe Award from the Los Angeles Press association as new star of the year for his role as a bodybuilder in the film *Stay Hungry* (1976). He then starred in the documentary *Pumping Iron* (1977) and invested his earnings in real estate.

The year 1980 was a transitional time for Schwarzenegger. That year he won his last bodybuilding title and was cast as Mickey Hargitay, the husband of actor Jayne Mansfield, in a television film about Mansfield's life. Because Hargitay had been a Hungarian-born champion bodybuilder, the Austrian bodybuilder Schwarzenegger was the obvious choice for the role. However, Schwarzenegger's breakthrough role came when he played the title character in *Conan the Barbarian* (1982).

Because he was playing a fantasy character, his thick accent was irrelevant, as it also was for *The Terminator* (1984), in which he created his most famous character, an android from the future. Other action film roles followed, and Schwarzenegger established himself as one of the leading box office draws in Hollywood.

Meanwhile, in 1977, Schwarzenegger met Maria Shriver, the daughter of Sargent Shriver, the first director of the Peace Corps and the 1972 Democratic nominee for vice president, and Eunice Shriver, the sister of former president John F. Kennedy and Senators Robert F. and Edward Kennedy. He married Shriver in 1986.

Despite his marriage into the most famous Democratic family in America, Schwarzenegger chose to become a Republican after he became an American citizen in 1983, because of the party's stronger

California governor Arnold Schwarzenegger addressing farmworkers on water issues outside the state capitol in October, 2009. (AP/Wide World Photos)

probusiness stances. At the Republican National Convention the following year, he spoke on President Ronald Reagan's behalf, and he campaigned for George H. W. Bush during the presidential elections of 1988 and 1992.

In 2002, Schwarzenegger considered running for governor of California but decided to reprise his android role in the film *Terminator 3*. Fortuitously, however, he had another chance to run for governor in 2003, when the Democratic incumbent, Gray Davis, was subjected to a recall election at the same time a new election for his possible replacement was held. Davis lost his bid to retain his governorship, and Schwarzenegger won the second election over a field of more than two hundred candidates, including another immigrant, journalist Arianna Huffington. Three years later, Schwarzenegger was reelected after completing Davis's original four-year term.

Schwarzenegger was sufficiently popular as governor to inspire a movement to amend the U.S. Constitution to allow a foreign-born citizen such as Schwarzenegger to run for president, beginning in 2004. However, the idea lost momentum after a few years.

Thomas R. Feller

FURTHER READING

Andrews, Nigel. *True Myths: The Life and Times of Arnold Schwarzenegger.* Secaucus, N.J.: Birch Lane Press, 1996.

Leamer, Laurence. *Fantastic: The Life of Arnold Schwarzenegger.* New York: St. Martin's Press, 2005.

Mathews, Joe. *The People's Machine: Arnold Schwarzenegger and the Rise of Blockbuster Democracy.* New York: Public Affairs, 2006.

SEE ALSO: Atlas, Charles; Austrian immigrants; California; Huffington, Arianna.

SCIENCE

> **SIGNIFICANCE:** Scientists who escaped from dictatorships in Hungary, Germany, Italy, and other European countries during the 1930's played a major role in the successful development of the American atomic bomb and other projects during World War II.

European immigrants who came to America during the nineteenth century were mostly farmers, construction workers, domestic servants, or day laborers. Only very few scientists with professional training came over, usually to take advantage of broader opportunities than were available in their homelands. For example, the Scottish inventor Alexander Graham Bell came from London, England, to an innovative school in Boston, where he worked with deaf children to teach them the rudiments of speech. His research on using vibrating reeds to duplicate the sounds of words made by the human voice led to his invention of the telephone in 1876. Nikola Tesla, an electrical engineer from Serbia, was inspired to come to America after reading about Thomas Alva Edison's ingenious inventions of electrical apparatuses. Tesla's specialty became the development of alternating current (AC). He designed the first hydroelectric power plant built at Niagara Falls, New York, in 1897, making the United States the world leader in electricity production and use. Bell and Tesla should be viewed as rare exceptions among the multitude of blue-collar workers who immigrated to the United States.

PERSECUTION OF EUROPEAN SCHOLARS DURING THE 1930'S

Adolf Hitler came to power in Germany in 1933 as a fascist dictator. It is noteworthy that in the chaos following World War I, a substantial number of other European countries had already become dictatorships before Germany. They included Hungary under Admiral Nicholas Horthy, Italy under Benito Mussolini, Spain under General Miguel Primo de Rivera and later under Generalissimo Francisco Franco, Poland under Marshall Józef Piłsudski, Russia under Joseph Stalin, and Portugal under António de Olivera Salazar. In order to gain control over their people, these dictators appealed to nationalistic pride and made scapegoats out of foreigners and Jews.

In Hungary, the Horthy regime made anti-Semitism a legal doctrine, dismissing Jews from employment in public schools and universities. In Italy, Mussolini demanded that all university faculty members sign a loyalty oath that was designed to stifle criticism of the government. During the mid-1930's, Stalin and Hitler both instituted reigns of terror to enforce obedience. Jews and other people whose names had gotten on a list of undesirables could be arrested and deported to labor camps without warning.

It should be pointed out that many Jews had separated themselves from the religious tradition of their parents or grandparents and in some cases had been baptized as Roman Catholics or Protestants. Nevertheless, these governments classified all people of Jewish heritage into the same category.

University scholars who had lost their livelihood in Europe anxiously looked to the United States for employment. American universities would have liked to add distinguished Europeans to their faculty, but the Great Depression limited the availability of funds for new positions. An organization of American university presidents, the Emergency Committee in Aid of Displaced Scholars, provided notable help to refugees. It was able to find employment for some three hundred scholars out of more than six thousand applicants. The Institute for Advanced Study at Princeton, New Jersey, opened in 1933 with a large private endowment. The institute was able to bring over the world-renowned physicist Albert Einstein from Berlin during its first year of operation. The National Refugee Service was the largest American organization that provided financial aid to Europeans in many occupations.

One interesting immigration anecdote relates to the Italian physicist Enrico Fermi, who had been selected to receive the Nobel Prize in Physics in 1938. Mussolini boasted publicly about the excellence of scientific research under his Fascist rule. However, Fermi's wife was of Jewish heritage, which meant that the Fermis' children were not permitted to attend public school, so they quietly planned to emigrate to America. When the Fermi family went to Sweden to accept the Nobel award, they did not return to Italy but used the prize money to pay for their boat trip to America and to get settled in their new home.

DISCOVERY OF NUCLEAR FISSION

In January of 1939, a dramatic discovery was announced by two scientists in Germany: the fission of the uranium nucleus into two pieces, accompanied by a large release of energy. The amount of nuclear energy emitted per atom is a million times greater than the chemical energy that is released by traditional explosives. That meant that if uranium could be purified sufficiently, it might be possible to build a weapon of terrifying power. Two Hungarian physicists who had immigrated to America earlier, Leo Szilard and Eugene Wigner, realized the danger to the world if Hitler's scientists were able to develop an atomic bomb. They wrote a letter addressed to President Franklin D. Roosevelt to warn him and to urge him to establish a scientific team to investigate the feasibility of such a weapon. They took the letter to Einstein for his signature, thinking that only Einstein's prestige would carry enough weight to get the message through to the president.

The story of the subsequent development of the atomic bomb during World War II has been told by numerous authors. As in any research project, there was uncertainty at many points about the eventual outcome. The large reactor that was built for plutonium production at Hanford, Washington, almost failed because of an unanticipated problem with a previously unknown neutron absorber. At Oak Ridge, Tennessee, three different technologies for uranium isotope separation were attempted with no guarantee that any of them could be made to work. The test explosion at Alamogordo, New Mexico, in June of 1945 could have been a dud if the unusual detonation mechanism of an implosion had fizzled. A spirit of cooperation developed among the scientists, the Army, and the private contractors, without which the project could not have been completed within four years.

CONTRIBUTIONS BY EUROPEAN SCIENTISTS

European scientists were few in number in comparison to the many Americans who worked on the atomic bomb and other war research projects. However, the Europeans made major contributions, often in leadership roles. The magnitude of the immigrants' contributions can be appreciated by listing the accomplishments of some of the most prominent individuals.

Enrico Fermi, a refugee from Italy, was the world's foremost expert on nuclear reactions by neutron bombardment. He was the chief designer of the first nuclear reactor using natural uranium fuel. The successful operation of the reactor in 1942 was an essential step toward the crash program to develop an atomic bomb.

Leo Szilard was a physicist who left Hungary during the 1920's to escape from the open anti-Semitism of the government. After a period in Berlin, he immigrated to the United States in 1937 and was one of the first scientists to envision the possibility of an atomic bomb. He wrote the letter that alerted President Roosevelt to the potential danger of a nuclear Germany. He worked closely with Fermi on the construction of the first nuclear reactor and other projects.

Russian-born physicist George Gamow in 1961. (AP/ Wide World Photos)

Eugene Wigner also was a physicist and a refugee from Hungary. His major contribution to the atomic bomb project was to design the large nuclear reactor at Hanford, Washington, which produced plutonium. He was a cowinner of the Nobel Prize in Physics in 1963.

Hans Bethe was a theoretical physicist who fled Germany in 1933, went to England, and then joined the faculty at Cornell University in 1935. He developed a theoretical model for energy production in stars for which he received the Nobel Prize in Physics in 1967. At the Los Alamos National Laboratory in New Mexico, J. Robert Oppenheimer chose him to head the Theoretical Physics Division. During the 1950's, he served on the President's Science Advisory Committee.

Felix Bloch was a Swiss physicist who came to Cornell University in 1934. During World War II, he contributed to the development of radar. In 1952, he shared the Nobel Prize in Physics for his work on nuclear magnetic resonance, which is the basis for magnetic resonance imaging (MRI), now widely used by the medical profession.

James Franck was a German physicist who received the Nobel Prize in Physics in 1925. In 1935, he resigned his university position at Göttingen in protest over the dismissal of Jewish faculty and came to the University of Chicago. He headed the chemistry division that prepared the materials for Fermi's reactor. In 1945, he was a leading voice among scientists who recommended a demonstration of an atomic explosion as a warning to Japan before military use.

George Gamow was a physicist refugee who fled from Russia during the 1920's. He established his reputation in physics by providing an explanation of the mechanism of radioactive decay. After coming to the United States in 1933, he developed a theory of energy production in stars by nuclear fusion, which later became important in the design of the hydrogen bomb.

Edward Teller, a Hungarian physicist, was able to immigrate to the United States in 1935. While working at Los Alamos, he conceived the idea of a superbomb using hydrogen fusion (the so-called H-bomb) that would be detonated by an atomic bomb. In 1952, the Atomic Energy Commission set up a new laboratory at Livermore, California, specifically to pursue H-bomb research, with Teller as its head. Another Hungarian immigrant, John von

Edward Teller. (Lawrence Radiation Laboratory/ AIP Niels Bohr Library)

Neumann, was a talented mathematician. At the age of thirty, he came to America at the invitation of the prestigious Institute for Advanced Study at Princeton. He designed the first electronic computer, at Los Alamos to replace the slow mechanical calculators. As a respected technical adviser, he contributed his expertise to the H-bomb and long-range missile programs.

Theodore von Karman was a Hungarian who became an outstanding aeronautical engineer. After immigrating to America, he improved the performance of high-speed military aircraft and designed rocket engines for spaceflight. For ten years, he served as director of the Jet Propulsion Laboratory for the National Aeronautics and Space Administration (NASA).

Samuel Goudsmit was a Dutch physicist who was chosen to head the Alsos mission, which followed Allied forces in Europe in 1944 to determine just how far Germany had come toward building an atomic bomb.

Emilio Segrè was a colleague of Fermi at Rome but found the rise of Fascism in Italy intolerable. He joined the cyclotron group at the University of California, Berkeley, which produced the first tiny samples of plutonium in 1942, and later worked at Los Alamos. He shared the Nobel Prize in Physics in 1959 for the discovery of the antiproton.

Hans G. Graetzer

FURTHER READING

Compton, Arthur H. *Atomic Quest: A Personal Narrative.* New York: Oxford University Press, 1956. The best account of the American atomic bomb development written for a nontechnical audience. The author knew all the leading scientists personally and describes their contributions.

Fermi, Laura. *Atoms in the Family: My Life with Enrico Fermi.* Chicago: University of Chicago Press, 1954. Describes the difficult conditions in Italy under Mussolini's Fascism and the Fermi family's escape to America, with perceptive personality sketches of the author's husband's scientific colleagues.

_____. *Illustrious Immigrants: The Intellectual Migration from Europe, 1930-1941.* 2d ed. Chicago: University of Chicago Press, 1971. Overview of the large wave of notable scientists and other professionals who came to America to escape fascism. Discusses how they contributed to their new homeland.

Groves, Leslie R. *Now It Can Be Told: The Story of the Manhattan Project.* New York: Da Capo Press, 1962. General Groves was the chief military officer for all aspects of the American bomb project from 1942 to 1946. He had responsibility for the construction of the three atomic laboratories at Oak Ridge, Hanford, and Los Alamos, while maintaining secrecy for the whole project.

Hargittai, István. *The Martians of Science: Five Physicists Who Changed the Twentieth Century.* New York: Oxford University Press, 2006. Biographies of five extraordinary Hungarians: Leo Szilard, Eugene Wigner, John von Neumann, Edward Teller, and Theodore von Karman. All were born in Budapest, immigrated to America, and had leading scientific roles during and after World War II. Contains much personal information not found elsewhere.

Sayen, Jamie. *Einstein in America: The Scientist's Conscience in the Age of Hitler and Hiroshima.* New

York: Crown, 1985. This biography describes Einstein's many nonscientific, social involvements from 1933 to 1955, including his assistance to refugees, his letter to President Roosevelt, and his opposition to military H-bomb test explosions.

SEE ALSO: Anti-Semitism; Bell, Alexander Graham; "Brain drain"; Einstein, Albert; European immigrants; German immigrants; Higher education; Hungarian immigrants; Jewish immigrants; Tesla, Nikola.

SEI FUJII V. STATE OF CALIFORNIA

THE CASE: California Supreme Court decision on immigrant rights
DATE: Decided on April 17, 1952

SIGNIFICANCE: Ending a long legal struggle, California's highest court struck down the state's Alien Land Law as a violation of the equal protection clause of the Fourteenth Amendment. While the direct beneficiaries of the ruling were Japanese immigrants, it had the long-term impact of promoting the Civil Rights movement.

When World War II ended in 1945, the state of California continued to have its infamous Alien Land Law, which prohibited land ownership by aliens ineligible for citizenship. By that time, the law applied almost exclusively to immigrants from Japan. In the case of *Oyama v. California* (1948), the U.S. Supreme Court ruled that Fred Oyama, a U.S. citizen, had the equal rights to own land without having to explain why his father, a noncitizen, had purchased it in his name. The ruling, however, did not address whether noncitizens had a constitutional right to land ownership. During that same year, Sei Fujii, a first-generation immigration from Japan, purchased land in East Los Angeles in order to test the constitutionality of the law. When the state initiated an escheat action to take possession of his property, Fujii argued that the Alien Land Law was void because it violated the Fourteenth Amendment as well as the United Nations Charter.

By a 4-3 vote, the California Supreme Court ruled in Fujii's favor. Although the majority opinion rejected the relevance of the United Nations Charter, it determined that the law violated the equal protection and due process components of the Fourteenth Amendment. Applying a "most rigid scrutiny" standard of review, the court found the law to be arbitrary and unreasonable, because it "was not reasonably related to any legitimate government interest." The state chose not to ask the U.S. Supreme Court to review the ruling. Four years later, California voters repealed the Alien Land Law in a referendum.

Thomas Tandy Lewis

FURTHER READING
Bosniak, Linda. *The Citizen and the Alien: Dilemmas of Contemporary Membership*. Princeton, N.J.: Princeton University Press, 2008.
Hyung-chan, Kim, ed. *Asian Americans and the Supreme Court: A Documentary History*. Westport, Conn.: Greenwood Press, 1992.

SEE ALSO: Alien land laws; Asian immigrants; California; Due process protections; History of immigration after 1891; Japanese immigrants; *Oyama v. California*; Supreme Court, U.S.

SELECT COMMISSION ON IMMIGRATION AND REFUGEE POLICY

IDENTIFICATION: Commission created by the U.S. Congress to assess the impact of both legal and illegal immigration on the United States and make policy recommendations
DATE: October 5, 1978-March 1, 1981
ALSO KNOWN AS: Hesburgh Commission

SIGNIFICANCE: The commission's report provided data used in the late twentieth century immigration reform debate. Its recommendations were reflected in such subsequent immigration legislation as the Immigration Reform and Control Act of 1986 and the Immigration Act of 1990. The commission's work was still being used by Congress in twenty-first century immigration policy debates.

Despite the long-held belief that the United States, being a nation of immigrants, has historically encouraged immigration, much of U.S. immigration policy has actually been designed to limit immigration flows. The Dillingham Commission of 1907 paved the way for the immigration quota laws of the 1920's that capped overall annual immigration and severely restricted the numbers of visas issued to people in regions other than western and northern Europe. The Immigration and Nationality Act of 1965 ended what were essentially racial and ethnic quotas imposed during the 1920's and increased the overall number of annual visas. By the 1970's, however, renewed restrictionist sentiments were being voiced. Some members of Congress and their constituents were concerned about the perceived negative cultural and economic impacts of a large and growing foreign-born population, and the inadequacy of federal laws in addressing illegal immigration.

CREATION OF THE COMMISSION

The significant increase in illegal immigration flows during the 1970's led to the call for a study of the overall impact of immigrants on America. U.S. immigration laws made unauthorized entry and the harboring of undocumented aliens illegal, but failed to address the employment opportunities that were attracting undocumented immigrants. Historically, immigration law enforcement generally ignored the employers of illegal immigrants because businesses benefited from low-wage labor. Indeed, in 1952, Congress passed the "Texas Proviso," which specifically stated that employing illegal immigrants was not illegal. During the 1970's, Congress voted down all immigration bills that included employer penalties. One such proposal by President Jimmy Carter in 1977 also contained an amnesty provision. The public response indicated that restrictionist sentiment was widespread. On October 5, 1978, Congress passed a bill to establish the Select Commission on Immigration and Refugee Policy (SCIRP).

MANDATE, COMPOSITION, AND RESEARCH OF THE COMMISSION

SCIRP was charged with conducting research designed to determine the political, social, and economic impacts of immigrants and the effects of immigrants on population size and composition and unemployment of the indigenous labor force. The commission was also asked to make recommendations for policy initiatives based on an evaluation of immigration laws. The commission was chaired by the Reverend Theodore Hesburgh, the president of the University of Notre Dame. Among the commission's other sixteen members were four prominent citizens, eight members of Congress, and the secretaries of state, labor, justice, and health and human services.

The commission compiled and analyzed databases on the testimony of hundreds of witnesses in public hearings conducted in twelve cities, meetings with experts on immigration issues, twenty-two studies of the economic and social assimilation of immigrants and refugees, and consultations with special interest groups. This two-year effort resulted in nine volumes of appendixes and a 916-page report.

FINDINGS AND RECOMMENDATIONS

Issued on March 1, 1981, the SCIRP report recommended that the global cap on annual visas be increased to 350,000, with preferences for immigrants who were highly skilled or who had capital to invest in the United States, and persons with family members who were American citizens. The report also recommended that an additional 100,000 visas be awarded annually for five years to reduce the pressure for illegal immigration, Finally, it recommended the extension of quota-exempt status to relatives of American citizens other than the currently exempted spouses, parents, and minor children.

Because of the large annual number of refugees seeking asylum who claimed to be fleeing persecution or to have been forcefully expelled from their homelands, the commission recommended that asylum should be considered on a group basis, with individuals being required to establish their eligibility. Failure to meet the criteria should result in deportation.

Based on its research, the commission found that the impact of illegal immigrants on American salary and unemployment levels could not be determined. It also found that undocumented workers were reluctant to apply for social services for which they were paying with money withheld from their paychecks, for fear of being detected. Consequently, social services were enjoying net funding gains.

On the other hand, the report also charged that illegal immigration had spawned huge enterprises in human smuggling and document forgery, and a general disregard for law. The commission therefore recommended legal penalties for employers of illegal immigrants and increasing the personnel and equipment used for border enforcement. It also recommended that amnesty and an opportunity to apply for immigrant status be extended to undocumented immigrants who had arrived before January 1, 1980, while rejecting the idea of a large-scale guest-worker program.

The commission's recommendations for increasing legal immigration flows while curbing illegal immigration had a clear impact on immigration policy debates and legislation that Congress passed after the commission issued its report. For example, the Immigration Reform and Control Act of 1986 featured employer sanctions and amnesty for illegal immigrants who had been in the country since January 1, 1982, and the Immigration Act of 1990 increased the number of annual "quota visas" to 700,000 for three years and 675,000 thereafter.

Jack Carter

FURTHER READING

Graham, Otis L., Jr. *Immigration Reform and America's Unchosen Future*. Bloomington, Ind.: Author House, 2008. Call for decisive action in reducing flows of illegal and legal immigrants that discusses the role SCIRP has played in affecting immigration debates and legislation.

Jacobson, David. *Rights Across Borders: Immigration and the Decline of Citizenship*. Baltimore: Johns Hopkins University Press, 1997. Describes the contribution of SCIRP to the immigration reform movement and its effect on the erosion of traditional national sovereignty.

Laham, Nicholas. *Ronald Reagan and the Politics of Immigration Reform*. Westport, Conn.: Praeger, 2000. Critique of the Reagan administration's immigration policies, including the impact of SCIRP.

Newton, Lina. *Illegal, Alien, or Immigrant: The Politics of Immigration Reform*. New York: New York University Press, 2008. Describes how SCIRP affected immigration policy changes, including the passage of the Immigration Reform and Control Act of 1986, in the context of a discussion of the way that political dynamics and rhet-

oric have altered American perceptions of immigrants and driven policy agendas.

Tichenor, Daniel. *The Politics of Immigration Control in America*. Princeton, N.J.: Princeton University Press, 2002. Comprehensive examination of the history of U.S. immigration policy that shows the back-and-forth shifts from restrictionist to more open-border policies, including the effect of SCIRP on important changes during the 1980's and 1990's.

SEE ALSO: Censuses, U.S.; Dillingham Commission; Economic consequences of immigration; Economic opportunities; Illegal immigration; Immigration Act of 1990; Immigration and Nationality Act of 1965; Immigration Reform and Control Act of 1986.

SETTLEMENT HOUSES

DEFINITION: Neighborhood centers that provided community services to residents of economically depressed areas of cities during the late nineteenth and early twentieth centuries

SIGNIFICANCE: Settlement houses assisted immigrants struggling to cope with meager incomes, new social customs, and unhealthy living conditions. Settlement house workers laid the foundation for government-sponsored social work as a profession by offering assistance to the poor and by gathering data to prove the need for societal reform.

Settlement houses in slum neighborhoods were established and run by young, primarily female, college-educated members of the middle class who hoped to improve the lives of immigrants and other poor city dwellers. With the rapid expansion of factory-based employment, such city dwellers suffered from devastating poverty, a situation that settlement workers hoped to remedy through education and charitable relief.

THE SETTLEMENT MOVEMENT

Two of the original leaders of the settlement house movement, Stanton Coit and Jane Addams, were inspired by a visit to the London settlement

Hull-House founder Jane Addams (second from left) aboard the Noordam, *which auto manufacturer Henry Ford chartered in 1915 to send a peace delegation to The Hague during World War I. Addams was the head of the forty-two delegate group, whose members include three settlement workers, six teachers, three writers, two poets, and a variety of other people.* (The Granger Collection, New York)

house of Toynbee Hall. Coit went on to open the first settlement house in the United States, the Neighborhood Guild of New York City, in 1886, and Addams and her friend Ellen Gates Starr opened Hull-House in Chicago in 1889. Coit envisioned a settlement that would offer relief, education, and recreation, a combination that he hoped would stimulate the intellectual and moral life of slum residents and bring neighbors to recognize their interdependence. The founders of Hull-House aimed to educate the public and to strengthen the social functions of democracy—a quest that soon led to a pattern of service, research, and reform that influenced the entire settlement movement. Settlements proceeded to grow rapidly in number, expanding from a total of six in 1891 to more than one hundred by 1900. More than four hundred centers were operating in over thirty states by 1913, with the largest and most influential located primarily in northern and midwestern cities.

The settlement house movement represented an adherence to a "social gospel" calling for a more Christian society that would minimize the increasing gap between the upper and lower classes. Concerned religious and civic leaders designated church and "Community Chest" funds to finance settlement houses staffed by trained workers as a means of granting charitable relief to the poor, many of them immigrants from southern and eastern Europe. Settlement workers agreed to reside in the neighborhoods they served in order to obtain the fullest possible exposure to the plight of the urban poor, who were forced to live in overcrowded tenement housing with inadequate sanitation.

Settlement workers offered immigrants opportunities in music, dance, and cultural productions as well as classes in cooking, sewing, child care, and personal hygiene. Some settlements even established public bathing facilities. Many added day care, kindergarten, and English-language classes to their services. In addition, settlements supported clubs, lending libraries, and lecture series as well as providing space for laborers to organize. The wide variety of settlement house services reflected a pragmatic response to local needs.

RESEARCH AND REFORM

Settlement workers kept detailed records of their accomplishments and of their observations of neighborhood problems in order to substantiate specific cases in which immigrants deserved more equitable treatment. As settlement leaders struggled to develop more accurate assessments of the pressures of poverty, they relied upon the data that they had gathered to support calls for reform. The most successful campaigns for urban improvement centered on subjects such as garbage removal and the creation of parks and playgrounds. Ironically, legislation requiring improvements in tenement houses tended to increase property values and at times displaced immigrant families unable to pay higher rents.

Settlement houses generally proved inadequate to deal with the escalating difficulties immigrants experienced, in part because their philanthropic status rendered them ill-equipped to address deep-seated political and economic issues. Immigrants were forced to contend with unfamiliar institutions, language barriers, isolation, low wages, and unemployment. These challenges prevented the majority of them from achieving the self-improvement that settlement founders expected. Most immigrants utilizing settlement services were women, and settlement organizers seldom recruited them to assess neighborhood needs or to participate in program planning. Although immigrant leaders viewed settlements positively and encouraged cooperation with them, newcomers relied on local politicians and contacts in religious and ethnic communities to provide key resources.

Settlement house workers soon extended their efforts beyond neighborhoods, pressing for progressive reform through legislation at city, state, and national levels. As reforms took hold, alternate employment opportunities for settlement workers increased and they continued relief efforts as researchers, union organizers, lobbyists, and administrators of charitable foundations. Others served as teachers in expanded nursing schools and social work programs.

Settlement houses were institutions that called for an American ideal of personal service and moral responsibility, and in so doing they encouraged cities to become more responsive to the needs of their immigrant populations. After World War I, the importance of settlement houses declined as government-sponsored social programs developed and efforts to build cooperative neighborhoods came under the auspices of nonprofit organizations and other sponsors. In the modern era, community centers, shelters, and organizations such as the Young Men's Christian Association (YMCA) continued to facilitate similar neighborhood cooperatives.

Margaret A. Koger

FURTHER READING

Carson, Mina. *Settlement Folk: Social Thought and the American Settlement Movement, 1885-1930.* Chicago: University of Chicago Press, 1990. Social and intellectual history portraying the shift from charismatic leadership to scientific procedures in the settlement movement.

Davis, Allen F. *Spearheads for Reform: The Social Settlements and the Progressive Movement, 1890-1914.* New Brunswick, N.J.: Rutgers University Press, 1984. Traces the expanding influence of settlement workers, especially in Boston, Chicago, and New York.

Friedman, Michael, and Brett Friedman. *Settlement Houses: Improving the Social Welfare of America's Immigrants.* New York: Rosen, 2006. Reveals the broad influence of settlement house reformers. For younger readers.

Koerin, Beverly. "The Settlement House Tradition: Current Trends and Future Concerns." *Journal of Sociology and Social Welfare* 30, no. 2 (2003): 53-68. Reports on a national survey of current settlements and their services.

Trolander, Judith Ann. *Professionalism and Social Change: From the Settlement House Movement to Neighborhood Centers, 1866 to the Present.* New York: Columbia University Press, 1987. Detailed assessment of the settlement house movement and its extended influence in the United States.

SEE ALSO: Americanization programs; Chicago; Cultural pluralism; Education; Hull-House; Progressivism; Welfare and social services; Women immigrants; Women's movements.

SETTLEMENT PATTERNS

DEFINITION: Changing geographical distribution of immigrants in the United States

SIGNIFICANCE: Immigrants to the United States from all regions of the world have generally tended to settle among communities that already have people from their own homelands, making the United States a land of enclaves, neighborhoods, and districts with both American and foreign flavors. Although such communities may slow the assimilation of immigrants into American culture, they also help newcomers make easier transitions to American life and even become places in which other people can learn about immigrant cultures.

Because all the people who have come to the shores of what is now the United States were immigrants, every place they settled was originally an immigrant settlement. The British North American colonies that would become the first thirteen American states were settled almost exclusively by European immigrants, along with substantial numbers of involuntary immigrants imported from Africa as slaves. After independence, with the states established, American settlements began expanding west beyond the Mississippi River. By this time, the total population of native-born Americans was about four million, including African slaves.

EUROPEAN IMMIGRANT PATTERNS

The vast majority of the Irish, Italian, and British immigrants who came during the early to mid-nineteenth century settled in cities. Most of them came from rural communities, but when they arrived in the United States, few of them had funds with which to buy farmland. In any case, some had been so badly treated by their landlords in their native countries that they wanted nothing more to do with farming. Moreover, their unfamiliarity with American farming practices put them at a disadvantage. At the same time, wage-paying jobs were usually more plentiful in the cities than in the countryside. In urban centers, they met fellow countrymen who had immigrated before them and established lives and communities in cities, to which the newcomers naturally gravitated.

During the 1860's, two new developments enhanced the attractions of farming for immigrants. In 1862, the U.S. Congress passed the Homestead Act, which made available to both Americans and immigrants plots of land of up to 160 acres in return for residing on and developing the land. The same decade saw the construction of the first transcontinental railroad line, which was completed in 1869. Additional transcontinental lines soon followed. To help the railroad companies finance construction and to spur settlement and development of the relatively empty expanses through which many of the railroad lines passed, the federal government gave the companies vast tracts of land surrounding the tracks. The railroads in turn sold much of the land to settlers—some of whom helped to build the railroad lines—and actively encouraged European immigrants to come to the United States. The available of free and cheap land was a powerful lure to many immigrants.

German immigrants who preferred urban life established large communities in St. Louis, Cincinnati, Chicago, and Milwaukee. Those who wanted to farm went on westward to the Old Northwest Territory or the Great Lakes region, which were still largely unsettled.

Italian immigrants initially settled mostly along the East Coast, but they soon fanned out to the Midwest and eventually all the way to the West Coast. In many large cities, they established enclaves that became known as Little Italies. These were close-knit neighborhoods in which familiar foods and customs prevailed. By the twentieth century, however, as Italians became more Americanized, they tended to disperse, often leaving only their restaurants as reminders of the Italian neighborhoods.

Scandinavian immigrants tended to go to unsettled rural areas in the upper Midwest, rather than cities, where the climate and terrain were similar to those of their homelands. Swedes and Danes spread out over especially vast regions. Finnish immigrants tended to settle mostly in Michigan and Minnesota. Danes had little hesitation about intermarrying with non-Danes and consequently nearly disappeared as a recognizable ethnic group. In contrast, Finns were more clannish and stayed pretty much with their own kind. Norwegians and Swedes tended to maintain their distinctively rural character longer than the other Scandinavian immigrant groups, but even they were becoming primarily urban dwellers by the twentieth century. Meanwhile, Scandinavian settlements continued to attract new immigrants from the old countries.

ASIAN IMMIGRANT SETTLEMENTS

The first significant numbers of Asians to immigrate to the United States were Chinese who came to California to work in the gold mines opening during the 1850's and to Hawaii to work on sugar cane plantations. Shunned and ill-treated by the non-Asians who surrounded them, the Chinese soon established strong communities within Northern California and Hawaii. As they spread out across the United States, they established Chinatowns in virtually every city in which they settled in significant numbers. These enclaves featured distinctively Chinese architecture and Chinese shops and restaurants that not only served the communities' own residents but also attracted tourists.

The Japanese immigrants who came later followed a similar pattern. "Little Tokyos" and "Japantowns" began appear in cities in Hawaii and California during the 1870's. As these communities grew in size, they added ethnic shops, restaurants, theaters, hotels, Japanese baths, and sushi bars.

LATE TWENTIETH TO TWENTY-FIRST CENTURY PATTERNS

After the great waves of immigration from Europe crested during the first decades of the twentieth century, new immigration slowed considerably for many decades. In some years during the Great Depression of the 1930's, the United States actually experienced net negative immigration, with more immigrants leaving the country than entering it.

Ceremony commemorating the completion of the first transcontinental railroad at Promontory, Utah, on May 10, 1869. Completion of the cross-country line greatly accelerated the settlement of the Far West. (Getty Images)

During the 1940's, as the U.S. government began relaxing restrictions on immigration, the rates of immigration began climbing again. Passage of the Immigration and Nationality Act of 1965 was a turning point in U.S. immigration history. That law removed restrictions on nationalities that had been effectively blocked from entering the United States since the 1920's and triggered a huge surge in total immigration. Since the 1960's, immigrants from all over the world have settled in every American state, but seven states have received disproportionate shares of new immigration: California, New York, Florida, Texas, Pennsylvania, New Jersey, and Illinois.

Thanks to the 1965 immigration law's removal of national origins quotas, Asians began entering the country in unprecedented numbers, especially Chinese, Filipinos, Koreans, and Asian Indians. After the Vietnam War ended in 1975, Vietnamese and other Southeast Asian peoples began immigrating in large numbers. Many of these new Asian immigrants expanded existing enclaves of earlier immigrants or established new ones. Consequently, in addition to existing Chinatowns and Little Tokyos, most large American cities soon had districts known as Koreatowns, Little Manilas, Little Saigons, and Little Indias. By the mid-1980's, the well-known Chinatown in New York's Manhattan grew so large that it no longer had room to expand, and new Chinatowns began arising in other parts of New York City, including the boroughs of Brooklyn and Queens.

Filipinos, most of whom first came to the western United States and Hawaii during the early twentieth century to do agricultural work, also established enclaves in many American cities. However, their largest concentrations have been in Southern California's Los Angeles and Orange counties. By the early twenty-first century, the city of Los Angeles was home to the largest concentration of Filipinos outside the Philippine Islands. In contrast to the early Filipino immigrants, who were mostly farmworkers, a large proportion of the Filipinos who began immigrating to the United States during the late twentieth century have been professionals, especially in the medical professions. In fact, so many Filipinos with medical training have settled in Illinois that they have established a small Filipino enclave in north Chicago.

Another previously underrepresented part of the world from which immigrants have come since the 1960's is the predominantly Muslim Middle East, including North Africa, a large region that encompasses Algeria, Egypt, Iraq, Lebanon, Libya, Morocco, Palestine, Saudi Arabia, Syria, Tunisia, and many other countries. Immigrants from that part of the world have tended to settle in major American cities, such as New York, Boston, Miami, Los Angeles, and Washington, D.C. Many Middle Eastern immigrants have come seeking educational opportunities. Consequently, they have established communities in many cities known for their institutions of higher living. African immigrants have also tended to be concentrated in cities with colleges and universities.

One of the largest categories of modern immigrants have been Hispanic peoples from Mexico, Central America, South America, and the Caribbean. Many of these people, especially those from Mexico and Central America, have come to the United States to do farmwork and have tended to go wherever they can find work. Those who have come with the intention of settling permanently in the United States have tended to go to regions close to where they enter the country. For example, Mexicans and Central Americans have tended to settle in American border states, and Cubans in South Florida. However, there has also been a growing trend for Hispanic immigrants to disperse throughout the United States in unprecedented numbers. By the early twenty-first century, sizable Mexican communities could be found not only in western and southwestern border states but also throughout the Southeast and the Midwest and even in such eastern and northern metropolitan centers as New York City, Philadelphia, and Washington, D.C.

Jane L. Ball

FURTHER READING

Daniels, Roger. *Coming to America: A History of Immigration and Ethnicity in American Life.* Princeton, N.J.: Visual Education Corporation, 1990. Comprehensive overview of the major immigrant groups who have come to the United States, emphasizing demographic data and socioeconomic settlement patterns.

Massey, Douglas S. *New Faces in New Places: The Changing Geography of American Immigration.* New York: Russell Sage Foundation, 2008. Explores relatively recent changes in immigrant settlement sites, from large cities to small towns, and the resulting concerns.

Olesker, Michael. *Journeys to the Heart of Baltimore.* Baltimore: Johns Hopkins Press, 2001. Stories about Baltimore, Maryland, as a melting pot of generational ethnic enclaves and neighborhoods of Italians, African Americans, and other groups.

Pedraza, Silvia, and Rubén G. Rumbaut, eds. *Origins and Destinies: Immigration, Race, and Ethnicity in America.* New York: Wadsworth, 1996. Collection of stories of European, Latin American, Asian, and African immigrants through the twentieth century.

Rodriguez, Gregory. *Mongrels, Bastards, Orphans, and Vagabonds.* New York: Random House, 2007. Describes the movement and settlement of various Hispanic groups who immigrated to America, from colonial to modern times.

Wheeler, Thomas C., ed. *The Immigrant Experience: The Anguish of Becoming American.* New York: Dial Press, 1971. Chronicles the stories of immigrants from Ireland, Italy, Norway, Puerto Rico, China, England, and Poland, with chapters on African American and Jewish immigrants.

See also: Alien land laws; Asian immigrants; Canals; Chinatowns; Coal industry; Coolies; Gentlemen's Agreement; Immigration and Nationality Act of 1965; Quota systems; Social networks.

Sidhwa, Bapsi

Identification: Pakistani-born American author

Born: August 11, 1938; Karachi, India (now Pakistan)

Significance: As one of the first major Pakistani authors to write in English and to describe life in the Parsi community, Sidhwa has made significant contributions to the literature of diaspora. Her novel *An American Brat* (1993) is an important exploration of Pakistani immigrants in the United States.

Bapsi Sidhwa was born Bapsi Bhandara in what is now Pakistan in 1938. Her parents, who ran a brewery, were Parsis, members of a religious minority group in India. Karachi, where she was born, and Lahore, where she was raised, were the two centers of the Pakistani Parsi community. Because she suffered from polio for much of her childhood, Sidhwa was educated mostly by private tutors, who encouraged her love of reading and introduced her to classic works of British literature. In 1957, she graduated from the Kinnaird College for Women in Lahore with a degree in ethics and psychology. She married in 1958 and moved to India, where her son and first daughter were born; after a divorce, she returned to Lahore. In 1963, she married Noshir Sidhwa, who became the father of her second daughter.

Sidhwa published her first novel, *The Crow Eaters,* in 1978. This comic novel about Parsi life was followed by *The Bride* in 1983, a narrative that begins with the India-Pakistan partition of 1947. Fluent in four languages, Sidhwa wrote the novels in English, believing that they would be more popular in England and the United States than in Pakistan; she thus became one of the first writers to introduce Western audiences to life in Pakistan. When her third novel, *Ice-Candy Man* (1988; published in the United States as *Cracking India,* 1991), was published, Sidhwa was living in the United States, teaching creative writing at the University of Houston. This novel, like *The Bride,* focuses on the India-Pakistan partition and deals with violence against women in Pakistani society.

Sidhwa next turned her attention to the experiences of Pakistanis and Indians living in the United States with the short story "Defend Yourself Against Me" (1990) and her fourth novel, *An American Brat* (1993). In this novel, a young woman from Lahore comes to the United States and negotiates the difficult terrain between traditional Parsi culture and American free-spiritedness. Sidhwa adapted the novel as a play, which was produced in 2007. In these fictional works, Pakistani and Indian immigrants live and work together as they were unable to do in Asia.

Sidhwa collaborated with Indian Canadian filmmaker Deepa Mehta on two films: *Earth* (1998), based on *Cracking India,* and *Water* (2005), upon which Sidhwa based her 2006 novel of the same title. The winner of several literary prizes, Sidhwa won the Lila Wallace-Reader's Digest Award (worth more than $100,000) in 1993, which she used to fund programs to bring together Pakistani, Indian, and Bangladeshi immigrants for scholarly and social events. Sidhwa, who became a U.S. citizen in 1992, lives in Houston, Texas, but travels often to Pakistan, where she campaigns for women's rights.

Cynthia A. Bily

FURTHER READING

Dhawan, R. K., and Novy Kapadia, eds. *The Novels of Bapsi Sidhwa.* New Delhi: Prestige Books, 1996.

Jussawalla, Feroza, and Reed Way Dasenbrock, eds. *Interviews with Writers of the Post-colonial World.* Jackson: University Press of Mississippi, 1992.

Ray, Sangeeta. *En-Gendering India: Woman and Nation in Colonial and Postcolonial Narratives.* Durham, N.C.: Duke University Press, 2000.

SEE ALSO: Anglo-conformity; Asian American literature; Asian immigrants; Films; Lahiri, Jhumpa; Literature; Mukherjee, Bharati; Pakistani immigrants.

SIMON, JULIAN LINCOLN

IDENTIFICATION: American economist who advocated liberal policies on immigration and population growth

BORN: February 12, 1932; Newark, New Jersey

DIED: February 8, 1998; Chevy Chase, Maryland

SIGNIFICANCE: Perhaps the foremost American academic advocate for liberal immigration policy, Simon argued that immigration's economic benefits exceed its costs for both native persons and immigrants alike.

An optimist about the future of humankind, Julian Lincoln Simon was an advocate for liberal policies on immigration, population growth, and economic growth. A believer in the positive value of additional human beings both as newborns and as immigrants, he was a leading advocate of economic and political freedom.

Simon was the scion of immigrant Jewish grandparents from Austria and Poland. The family name, originally Sczymschak, was changed to Simon by officials at Ellis Island. After graduating from Harvard University in 1953, Simon served in the U.S. Navy for three years. He received his master's degree in business administration in 1959 and a doctorate in business economics in 1961, both from the University of Chicago. He held academic positions at the University of Illinois, Hebrew University in Israel, and the University of Maryland, where he worked from 1983 until his death.

In 1989, Simon published *The Economic Consequences of Immigration,* in which he argued that immigrants to the United States increase welfare not just for themselves but also, on average, for native-born Americans. He stressed that immigrants come to the United States not only for economic reasons but also to live in freedom and dignity. Acknowledging that immigration will displace some native workers, he argued that the increased returns to capital that immigrants provide inure to the benefit of workers generally, most of whom have investments in pension funds, thus contributing to making workers as a group better off. He argued that any short-run negative effects on workers will ultimately be dominated by the positive effect of immigration on productivity. His analysis of the data indicated that immigrants use less public welfare services per capita than do native families.

Simon nevertheless understood that the most influential issues in the immigration debate might be noneconomic ones. For example, some immigration opponents worry about how culturally diverse American society can become before it begins to lose its fundamental identity. Simon did not support a policy of open borders, and he granted that when the proportion of immigrants from a particular country makes up too large a proportion of the population to be readily assimilated, the costs might outweigh the benefits for native persons. Even then, he argued, it was important to consider the benefits of immigration to the immigrants themselves, many of whom are desperate to escape tyranny and deprivation.

Simon was perhaps best known for advocating the view that humanity will never exhaust the world's essential resources. He authored books on diverse subjects, including immigration, demography, business, statistics, advertising, psychology, and managerial economics. He was the author of almost two hundred articles in professional journals and numerous articles in newspapers and magazines. Though his record of accomplishment was formidable, Simon was never offered a prestigious academic post. He believed to the end that his predictions that the world would continue to become materially better off for the foreseeable future earned him the vilification of his academic peers, for whom Simon's optimism was a challenge to their orthodox beliefs that the world is running out of resources and that each additional person in the world creates more harm than good.

Howard C. Ellis

FURTHER READING

Moore, Stephen, and Julian L. Simon. *It's Getting Better All the Time: One Hundred Greatest Trends of the Last One Hundred Years.* Washington, D.C.: Cato Institute, 2001.

Simon, Julian. *The Economic Consequences of Immigration.* 2d ed. Ann Arbor: University of Michigan Press, 1999.

_____. *The Ultimate Resource 2.* Princeton, N.J.: Princeton University Press, 1996.

SEE ALSO: Assimilation theories; Economic consequences of immigration; Identificational assimilation; Multiculturalism; Nativism; Welfare and social services.

SLAVE TRADE

THE EVENT: Forcible transportation of Africans to North America

DATE: Early seventeenth century to 1862

LOCATION: Primarily between southern United States and West and West-Central Africa

SIGNIFICANCE: Mass importation of African slaves into the thirteen British colonies became established practice during the mid-seventeenth century. Although slavery existed in every colony, the greater portion of the African population resided in the plantation South. The slave trade was carried on legally until 1808, when Congress outlawed it; afterward, it continued illegally until the time of the Civil War. The most lasting impact of the slave trade was the creation of a large African American population that has made an immeasurable impact on every profession, field, and discipline in the United States.

The first documented instance of African slaves being carried to what is now the United States occurred in 1526 in a Spanish attempt to establish a coastal colony that failed so completely it is no longer known whether the attempt was made in present-day Georgia or South Carolina. In any case, when Lucas Vázquez de Ayllón, the Spanish explorer and former follower of Hernán Cortés, led six hundred settlers to the site where he had received a large land grant from the Spanish crown, an unknown number of African slaves were among the colonists. At some point before the colony was abandoned, the Africans escaped—possibly to join some Native American community. Four decades later, Pedro Menéndez de Avilés led a successful effort to establish what would prove to be a permanent settlement at St. Augustine, Florida. African slaves made up a small portion of St. Augustine's original population, but they may have numbered close to 600 by the end of the eighteenth century.

BRITISH SLAVE TRADE

The first Africans known to arrive in British North America were among the original settlers of Jamestown, Virginia, in 1619. That much is known. Less certain, however, is the status of these Africans. Because chattel slavery was not then recognized under English law, it has been argued that these early black Virginia colonists were indentured servants with the same legal rights and obligations as white indentured servants in the colonies. However, regardless of what the true status of those colonists was, chattel slavery was soon to be recognized in the British colonies.

As the southern colonies developed labor-intensive plantation systems to produce cash crops, such as tobacco, a transition was eventually made from indentured servitude to a form of racially based chattel slavery. This development mirrored the existing model for Spanish and Portuguese colonies. The tendency to move toward this Iberian American conception of slavery can be seen in Virginia as early as 1640, merely two decades after the founding of Jamestown. From that time, one after another, the British colonies legalized slavery, thereby opening the door to the involuntary immigration of Africans via what would become notorious as the "Middle Passage" that linked Africa to the New World.

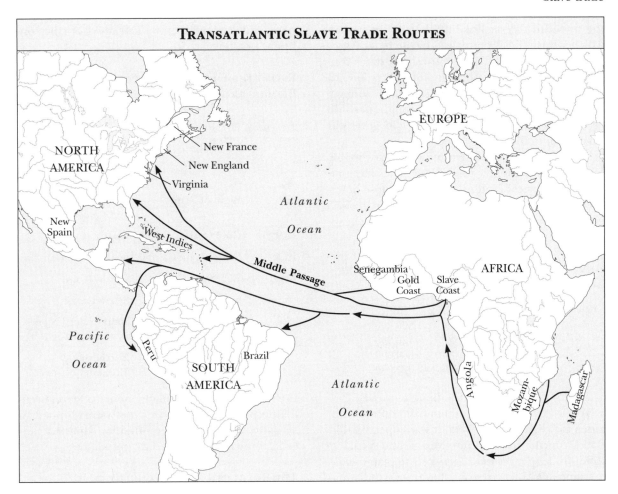

TRANSATLANTIC SLAVE TRADE ROUTES

The legalization of chattel slavery in the thirteen British colonies actually began in the northern colonies and occurred in this order:

- Massachusetts, 1641
- New Hampshire, 1645
- Connecticut, 1650
- Virginia, 1661
- Maryland, 1663
- Delaware, 1664
- New Jersey 1664
- New York, 1664
- North Carolina, 1669
- South Carolina, 1682
- Pennsylvania, 1700
- Rhode Island, 1700
- Georgia, 1750

Slavery had actually started in New York before 1664. When the Dutch founded their New Amsterdam colony in 1625, chattel slavery was almost immediately introduced. Therefore, when the English assumed control of the colony in 1664, they merely continued a system that the Dutch had already put in place. In Delaware, which had begun as New Sweden, chattel slavery of Africans was introduced as an accomplished fact in 1639 and was carried over through the Dutch occupation in 1655 and the English occupation in 1664.

PATTERNS AND STATISTICS

Generally, the pattern of trade in chattel slaves to the mainland of British North America followed at a steady but unspectacular pace, with the notable exception of South Carolina, through the seventeenth century and into the early years of the eighteenth century. Then followed a period of accelerated trade until the outbreak of the American Revolution during the 1770's. After the revolution, the trade steadily declined until 1808, the year in which it was officially outlawed by the federal government. After that date, the southern states continued a greatly diminished and illegal trade until 1862, when the U.S. Civil War put a halt to most southern maritime commerce. Throughout those years, however, a large internal trade in slaves was carried on in the South.

The total number of Africans who were forcibly brought to what is now the United States has long been the subject of intense debate. Because of imprecise and incomplete data, gaps between the lowest and highest modern estimates have been exceptionally wide, as this table shows.

RANGE OF TWENTY-FIRST CENTURY ESTIMATES OF HISTORICAL SLAVE IMPORTS

Period	Minimum	Maximum
Before 1786	275,00	1,500,000
1787-1808	70,000	420,000
1809-1861	54,000	1,000,000
Totals	151,500	2,920,000

When plantation owners bought slaves, they generally preferred to get them from different regions for reasons of security. It was expected that slaves from different cultures who arrived speaking different languages were less likely to plan escape attempts and insurrections. Favorable and unfavorable stereotypes of different African cultures sometimes also played roles in their sale. For example, Ibo men from what is now southeastern Nigeria were popularly regarded as being prone to defiance and therefore potentially dangerous. In contrast, Mandinke men from a large inland region of West Africa were thought to be more susceptible to discipline and thus more desirable as slaves. At the same time, however, slaveholders in different American colonies held different stereotypes. For example, Ibo men were considered desirable slaves in Virginia because of their presumed greater capacity for hard work. In Louisiana, Ibo women were sought because of their alleged propensity for greater fertility.

As was true in other parts of the Western Hemisphere, geographical proximity dictated that the majority of Africans transported to North America originated in West Africa. The most persuasive estimates show the largest number of Africans came from the west-central portion of the African conti-

nent, and the smallest number came from the continent's eastern coast.

ESTIMATED ORIGINS OF AFRICAN SLAVES BROUGHT TO NORTH AMERICA

Percentage	Historical region	Approximate modern location
24.5	West-central portion	Angola and Democratic Republic of Congo
23.3	Bight of Biafra	Southeastern Nigeria and Cameroon
15.9	Gold Coast	Ghana
13.3	Senegal and Gambia	Senegal and Gambia
11.4	Windward Coast	Cote d'Ivoire
5.5	Sierra Leone	Sierra Leone
4.3	Bight of Benin	Southwestern Nigeria, Benin, and Togo
1.6	East Africa	Northern Mozambique

Curiously, most of the small number of slaves originating on Africa's eastern coast were shipped to Virginia, where they accounted for some 4.1 percent of the total African slave population.

THE REVOLUTION, THE CONSTITUTION, AND 1808

At least a decade before the American Revolution began to raise questions about the compatibility of chattel slavery and principles of liberty and equality that were being bandied about, there arose a growing perception that both the slave trade and the institution of slavery itself were eventually destined for oblivion. In the northern and mid-Atlantic colonies, vestiges of slavery persisted, but the institution had never really taken root and was gradually being abolished. There, it was taken as common knowledge that slavery, even in the South, was becoming less profitable and would in time simply peter out of its own accord.

By 1787, four years after American independence was achieved, ten of the original thirteen states had outlawed the importation of slaves from Africa. The exceptions were North Carolina, South Carolina, and Georgia. Even among those who remained staunch in their support of slavery, there developed a concern that having too massive an influx of Africans enter the United States might lead to a perilous situation wherein someday free blacks and slaves would so far outnumber whites that a race war might happen, possibly with Native Americans allying with the Africans. This fear was certainly a powerful sentiment among Virginia planters.

The question of the slave trade, in conjunction with the larger issue of chattel slavery, was debated at the Constitutional Convention of 1787 in Philadelphia. Delegates of the three Deep South states that still allowed the slave trade remained so strong in their support of slavery that it was feared by other delegates that any firm moves against either the slave trade or slavery might result in one or more of those states refusing to ratify the Constitution. Consequently, a compromise was hammered out whereby the Constitution guaranteed that Congress would not prohibit the slave trade before the year 1808. Curiously, however, the Constitution does not use any form of the word "slave." According to Article I, section 9 of the document,

The Migration or Importation of such Persons as any of the States now existing shall think proper to admit, shall not be prohibited by the Congress prior to the Year one thousand eight hundred and eight, but a Tax or duty may be imposed on such Importation, not exceeding ten dollars for each Person.

Other clauses favorable to slave owners, such one that could be interpreted as requiring the return of fugitive slaves crossing state lines, were also inserted in the Constitution to appease southern sensibilities. The Constitution was afterward duly ratified and put into effect.

In 1807, an act of the British parliament made Great Britain the first nation officially to outlaw the slave trade. The following year, in accordance with the constitutional provision permitting such an act, the U.S. Congress passed a law prohibiting the importation of slaves from outside the United States.

A SLAVER DESCRIBES THE BEGINNING OF THE MIDDLE PASSAGE

Slaves in Benin bound for the New World were taken to ports such as Fida to await their ships. They were usually unaware of where they were going or even of whether they were to be executed or eaten by the alien, white-skinned men they encountered there. In the passage below, a slave merchant named John Barbot describes processing enslaved Africans who were about to embark on the Middle Passage.

As the slaves come down to Fida from the inland country, they are put into a booth, or prison, built for that purpose, near the beach, all of them together; and when the Europeans are to receive them, every part of every one of them, to the smallest member, men and women being all stark naked. Such as are allowed good and sound, are set on one side, and the others by themselves; which slaves so rejected are there called Mackrons, being above thirty five years of age, or defective in their limbs, eyes or teeth; or grown grey, or that have the venereal disease, or any other imperfection. These being set aside, each of the others, which have passed as good, is marked on the breast, with a red-hot iron, imprinting the mark of the French, English, or Dutch companies, that so each nation may distinguish their own, and to prevent their being chang'd by the natives for worse, as they are apt enough to do. In this particular, care is taken that the

women, as tenderest, be not burnt too hard.

The branded slaves, after this, are returned to their former booth, where the factor is to subsist them at his own charge, which amounts to about two-pence a day for each of them, with bread and water, which is all their allowance. There they continue sometimes ten or fifteen days, till the sea is still enough to send them aboard; for very often it continues too boisterous for so long a time, unless in January, February and March, which is commonly the calmest season: and when it is so, the slaves are carried off by parcels, in bar-canoes, and put aboard the ships in the road. Before they enter the canoes, or come out of the booth, their former Black masters strip them of every rag they have, without distinction of men or women; to supply which, in orderly ships, each of them as they come aboard is allowed a piece of canvas, to wrap around their waist, which is very acceptable to those poor wretches.

Source: From *A Description of the Coasts of North and South Guinea.* In *Collection of Voyages and Travels,* edited by Awnsham Churchill. Vol. 5. London: Churchill, 1746. UNESCO Slave Route Project. http://www.vgskole.net/prosjekt/slavrute/slavnarrative.htm. Accessed February 18, 2005.

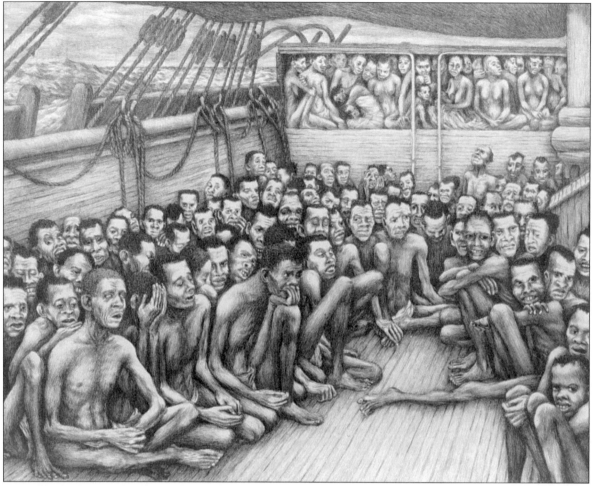

Imaginative depiction of the interior of a slave ship painted by Bernarda Bryson Shahn during the 1930's. (Library of Congress)

AFTER FORMAL ABOLITION OF THE TRADE

Both Great Britain and the United States outlawed the African slave trade, but enforcing this prohibition was a different matter. Indeed, American efforts to enforce the ban were practically ineffective. U.S. laws, such as the Piracy Act of 1820, which made slave trading subject to the death penalty, were not enforced and, consequently, widely ignored by both traders and law-enforcement officials.

Spain and Portugal, the two major colonial powers in the Western Hemisphere, made no pretence of their opposition to the British and American bans and showed their contempt for the ineffective Anglo-American enforcement measures. Nevertheless, Britain's powerful Royal Navy remained an intimidating force for any rogue slave trader to defy.

More effective perhaps than the ban in keeping down the trade in Africans to the United States was the fact that the natural population increase among the already resident slave population in the southern states was sufficient to meet the demands for slave labor on the plantations. The internal slave trade among the states flourished. In fact, the main sources of labor to southern cotton plantations during the years leading up to the Civil War (1861-1865) were the auction blocks in Virginia.

As the nation drifted into war in 1861, the avenues open to external slave traders rapidly closed. By early 1862, the Union's naval blockade of Southern ports effectively stopped new imports of African slaves. The symbolic end of the illicit slave trade occurred on February 21, 1862, when Captain Nathaniel Gordon became the first, and only, slave trader hanged under the Piracy Act of 1820. With the conclusion of the Civil War in 1865 and the subsequent ratification of the Thirteenth Amendment to the Constitution later that same year, slavery was completely and permanently abolished and with it the Atlantic slave trade to the United States.

Raymond Pierre Hylton

FURTHER READING

Curtin, Philip D. *The Atlantic Slave Trade: A Census.* Madison: University of Wisconsin Press, 1970. Landmark quantitative and statistical history of the slave trade. Although now somewhat dated in certain of its assumptions and conclusions, it provides a valid and enlightening picture of the actual numbers and geographical dispersal of slaves in the New World and remains a seminal and indispensable work on the subject.

Davis, David Brion. *Inhuman Bondage: The Rise and Fall of Slavery in the New World.* New York: Oxford University Press, 2006. Davis's work draws extensively on that of Eltis and Thomas, but it also effectively correlates portions of Africa to destinations in the New World and offers some different interpretations of existing records.

Du Bois, W. E. B. *The Suppression of the African Slave-trade to the United States of America, 1638-1870.* New York: Oxford University Press, 2007. First published in 1896, this classic study approaches the problem from the differing perspective of antislavery initiatives and provides documentation on continuing violations of the ban on slave importation into the United States after 1808.

Eltis, David, Stephen Behrendt, David Richardson, and Herbert S. Klein. *The Trans-Atlantic Slave Trade: A Database on CD-ROM.* New York: Cambridge University Press, 1998. Includes extensive documentation of more than 27,000 Middle Passage voyages that carries forward and enhances the earlier work of Philip Curtin and others.

Hashaw, Tim. *The Birth of Black America: The First African Americans and the Pursuit of Freedom at Jamestown.* New York: Carroll & Graf, 2007. Offers an iconoclastic and highly readable account of the coming of the first Africans on the Middle Passage and the eventual legalization of chattel slavery in Virginia.

Jewett, Clayton E., and John O. Allen. *Slavery in the South: A State-by-State History.* Westport, Conn.: Greenwood Press, 2004. Useful thumbnail guide to the local impact of the slave trade and the varied slave societies that were formed as a result.

Kulikoff, Allan. *Tobacco and Slaves: The Development of the Southern Cultures in the Chesapeake, 1680-1800.* Chapel Hill: University of North Carolina Press, 1986. Heavily quantitative work that is liberal in its application of statistical data while attempting to lay out the demography of slave settlement in the East Coast's Tidewater region.

Soodalter, Ron. *Hanging Captain Gordon: The Life and Trial of an American Slave Trader.* New York: Atria Books, 2006. This account of the only hanging administered for a violation of the anti-slave trading law provides valuable insights into the workings and effects of the illegal slave trade after 1808.

Thomas, Hugh. *The Slave Trade: The Story of the Atlantic Slave Trade, 1440-1870.* New York: Simon & Schuster, 1997. Substantial and nearly definitive study of the slave trade that focuses more deeply on the operation of the actual trade than its geo-demographic elements.

SEE ALSO: Abolitionist movement; African Americans and immigrants; African immigrants; *Clotilde* slave ship; Economic consequences of immigration; History of immigration, 1620-1783; History of immigration, 1783-1891; Indentured servitude; Liberia; Smuggling of immigrants.

SMUGGLING OF IMMIGRANTS

DEFINITION: Practice of illegally conveying undocumented aliens into the United States

SIGNIFICANCE: A 2007 report of the United Nations declared that human trafficking and smuggling of willing and unwilling persons into the United States and other affluent nations had become one of the largest international crime problems in the world. Only illegal drug trafficking of drugs was known to be a larger criminal business. Human smuggling has been practiced by small bands, organized street gangs, and large well-funded and -equipped crime syndicates. The ability of the U.S. government to combat human smuggling has been impeded by budget cuts, manpower shortages, and the sheer number of possible entry points along the nation's long coastlines and land borders.

The smuggling of immigrants into the United States has taken two primary forms: human trafficking and human smuggling. Although the two forms have points in common and the terms are not always used consistently, they also have significant differences. Human trafficking may be characterized as preying on impoverished individuals, particularly in countries disturbed by political unrest, famine conditions, warfare, or other problems that magnify economic problems.

HUMAN TRAFFICKING

Human traffickers lure individuals to emigrate to other nations with promises of good jobs and other inducements. However, after the traffickers convey the individuals to the other nations, they typically hold them hostage in order to exploit them economically. The most common victims whom traffickers bring to the United States are women, who may be made to work as exotic dancers, prostitutes, personal servants, or sweatshop employees in exchange for their travel to the United States. The common goal of the traffickers is to prey on defenseless parties and force them into sexual or labor exploitation into a modern-day form of slavery.

Victims of human traffickers generally have few freedoms, and the bulk of the earnings from their employment go to the individuals or groups responsible for bringing them to the country. During the early twenty-first century, worldwide human trafficking was estimated to involve almost 1 million victims a year. However, the U.S. government estimates that fewer than 5 percent of these victims are smuggled into the United States.

HUMAN SMUGGLING

Human smuggling differs from trafficking in that the people whom professional smugglers illegally convey into other countries are willing immigrants who voluntarily pay the smugglers for their services. Most immigrants who pay to be smuggled into the United States and other nations do so to seek economic opportunities not available in their own nations. Some smuggled immigrants are also motivated by the desire to be reunited with family members and friends who have preceded them.

All parties involved in human smuggling in the United States do so knowingly violating the criminal statutes of the United States. However, the risks of getting caught do not outweigh the potential rewards of succeeding. Smuggled immigrants who are apprehended in the United States are usually simply deported out of the country. In contrast, immigrants who are the involuntary victims of human traffickers are sometimes granted sanctuary in the United States. When smuggled immigrants find economic success in the United States, their expe-

Border Patrol agent inspecting a train for smuggled immigrants at the El Paso, Texas, border crossing in 1938. (Library of Congress)

riences often inspire more people in their homelands to attempt to follow their examples.

SMUGGLING OF IMMIGRANTS FROM MEXICO

Illegal immigration from Mexico, which shares a long border with the United States, has long been a major problem. Only a fraction of the millions of impoverished Mexicans who have wished to work in the United States have been permitted to entry the country legally, leaving the rest to consider ways of entering illegally. Smuggling has consequently become a popular option. Stopping illegal human crossings and drug smuggling at the border are daily concerns of U.S. Border Patrol agents.

Smuggling attempts begin with the groups that prepare to transport immigrants across the border. These groups are sometimes small and unorganized, but most are run much like organized crime elements such as the Italian Mafia. The smugglers are popularly known as "coyotes" because they prey on immigrants desperate to reach the United States. The means of conveyance they provide are usually not comfortable and may include overland walking and running, river crossings, and carriage in trucks and trains, sometimes within windowless compartments. The trips may take from days to weeks, during which time the travelers may be provided with little food, water, or rest. The goal of the coyotes is to conduct large numbers of eager immigrants as quickly and cheaply as possible. Moreover, it is not uncommon for the coyotes to abuse their charges. Women, and most often adolescent girls, are forced into sexual acts and may be beaten by their male handlers. Those too weak to continue may be left to die.

THE HUMAN TOLL

Because of the brutal conditions that smuggled immigrants are often forced to endure, injuries and deaths are common. In May of 2009, for example, the U.S. Coast Guard rescued twenty-six people, ten of whom died, who were being smuggled by sea from Haiti and the Bahamas. The deadliest smuggling accident on record, however, occurred in Victoria, Texas, in 2003, when nineteen immigrants abandoned inside a sweltering van perished from suffocation. During the early twenty-first century, smuggled immigrants have died because of suffocation, drowning, torture, dehydration, and starvation in New Mexico, Arizona, Texas, California, and many port cities along the Atlantic Ocean and Gulf of Mexico. Apprehension and prosecution of the smugglers responsible for these deaths has been difficult. The Victoria, Texas, case took more than five years to reach a conclusion, when one of the smugglers involved finally pleaded guilty.

Capturing human smugglers in the United States and other nations has been difficult in part because of the complexity of smuggling operations. Generally tightly centralized, the groups use safe houses for transporting immigrants and often change the location of these houses so frequently that law enforcement can never catch up with them. Cellular telephones, Global Positioning Systems, and other technological advances have helped smugglers work more quickly and stealthily.

SMUGGLING AND TRAFFICKING AS A WORLD PROBLEM

In 2008, the U.S. Department of State estimated that human smuggling, including trafficking, was a ten-billion-dollar-a-year enterprise. Smuggling is a world problem afflicting every populated region. After the collapse of the Soviet Union during the early 1990's, many former Soviet bloc nations such as Albania, Romania, Bulgaria, Belarus, and the Ukraine became hot spots for human trafficking and smuggling of women and young children. The sometimes willing participants are often tricked into prostitution and sexual exploitation and sold to barbaric handlers upon reaching their destination. Victims find themselves in unfamiliar countries without families, friends, or economic resources. Their problems are compounded by the fact that police agencies in the countries in which they find themselves may be on the take from the traffickers who have brought them there.

European nations, such as Great Britain, have made strides in combatting the smuggling and trafficking of immigrants within their own countries through new legislation, tougher enforcement, and stronger penalties.

Many Asian smuggling and trafficking groups have been known for transporting illegal immigrants by ship and using poorly guarded port cities as places of entry into the United States. The United States has worked closely with the Chinese and Japanese governments to combat the illegal transportation of immigrants on fishing vessels and cargo ships. By the early twenty-first century, other Asian countries were also enforcing stricter penalties for trafficking.

IMPACT ON CRIME RATES

Increased human smuggling in the United States has contributed to increases in other criminal activity. For example, immigrants attempting to elude capture have wounded and killed U.S. law-enforcement personnel. Western and southwestern states such as New Mexico, California, and Arizona have also seen increases in drug-related crimes, sexual assaults, robberies, burglaries, and murders in which immigrants have been the perpetrators. In 2004, Phoenix, Arizona, police estimated that an increase in the city's murder rate was largely a result of violence related to illegal immigration.

In response to increased human smuggling and international projections that the problem would continue to grow, the U.S. Congress passed the Intelligence Reform and Terrorism Prevention Act of 2004 to improve law enforcement at all levels. Under the new law, local, state, and federal agencies have worked together to combat human trafficking. These efforts have included more routine driver's license checks, sweeps of businesses to find illegal immigrants, and the increased federal efforts to detain and deport illegal immigrants. In addition, border southwestern states have set stronger penalties for illegal immigrants, including lengthy jail and prison terms. They have also provided more manpower to combat illegal smuggling. Creation of U.S. Immigration and Customs Enforcement in 2003 as an agency of the new Department of Homeland Security has also helped efforts to combat human smuggling.

Outside the United States, Interpol, which coordinates the law-enforcement agencies of more than 180 nations, has increased its efforts to combat the problem of smuggling and trafficking. Linking the crime to drugs and terrorist attacks, Interpol has listed human smuggling and trafficking as one of its six priority crime areas. In addition to trafficking and smuggling of humans, this area includes the use of Internet photos and transportation of children for sexual exploitation.

Keith J. Bell

FURTHER READING

Kyle, David, and Rey Koslowski. *Global Human Smuggling: Comparative Perspectives.* Baltimore: Johns Hopkins University Press, 2001. Examination of illegal immigration and those who profit from it, with attention to why more has not been done to suppress smuggling.

McGill, Craig. *Human Traffic: Sex, Slaves, and Immigration.* London: Vision Paperbacks, 2003. Details the stories of illegal immigrants from four different nations and the struggles the people involved have endured.

McMurray, David. *In and Out of Morocco: Smuggling and Migration in a Frontier Boomtown.* Minneapolis: University of Minnesota Press, 2001. Exploration of the lax laws for preventing smuggling and trafficking that some small nations, such as Morocco, have.

Ramos, Jorge. *Dying to Cross: The Worst Immigrant Tragedy in American History.* New York: Harper Paperbacks, 2006. Details the Victoria, Texas, tragedy involving the deaths of nineteen smuggled immigrants.

Uehling, Greta Lynn. "The International Smuggling of Children: Coyotes, Snakeheads, and the Politics of Compassion." *Anthropological Quarterly* 81, no. 4 (2008): 833-871. Examination of the growing problem of children who are illegally smuggled into the United States.

SEE ALSO: Asian immigrants; Border Patrol, U.S.; Bureau of Immigration, U.S.; Child immigrants; Crime; Drug trafficking; Economic consequences of immigration; Globalization; Immigration and Naturalization Service, U.S.; Mexican immigrants; Slave trade.

SNAKE RIVER MASSACRE

THE EVENT: Murder of Chinese gold miners by a gang of white men
DATE: May 25, 1887
LOCATION: Deep Creek Cove, Snake River Canyon, Oregon (later renamed Chinese Massacre Cove, Hells Canyon)

SIGNIFICANCE: The Snake River massacre represents one of the most vicious acts of brutality against Chinese immigrants in U.S. history.

In May of 1887, Chinese gold miners working along the Snake River in Oregon were brutally attacked and murdered by a band of horse thieves. Although robbery appeared to have been their murderers' primary motive, the viciousness of the attack and the subsequent failure to bring the perpetrators to justice are generally attributed to the racial bias harbored against Chinese immigrants in the western states and territories during the late nineteenth century.

Details of the incident have never been fully uncovered, in part because of the event's remoteness and the harshness of the location where the murders occurred. However, at least one scholar suggests that a cover-up also took place. What is known is that possibly as many as thirty-four Chinese miners from several small camps on the Snake River were murdered and whatever gold they had was stolen. An investigation paid for by a member of the Chinese Six Companies uncovered the names of the seven attackers. All seven were indicted, but the three ringleaders were never caught. Of the four remaining attackers, one turned state's evidence and was not tried, and the other three were acquitted, leaving little doubt that prejudice and discrimination played a role in the outcome of this event.

Christine M. Brown

FURTHER READING

Nokes, R. Gregory. "'A Most Daring Outrage': Murder at Chinese Massacre Cove, 1887." *Oregon Historical Quarterly* 107, no. 3 (2006): 326-353.

Stratton, David H. "The Snake River Massacre of Chinese Miners, 1887." In *A Taste of the West: Essays in Honor of Robert G. Ahearn*, edited by Duane A. Smith. Boulder, Colo.: Pruett Publishing, 1983.

SEE ALSO: Anti-Chinese movement; California gold rush; Chinese immigrants; Chinese Six Companies; Foreign miner taxes; Oregon.

SOCCER

DEFINITION: Ball game known as "football" to most of the world that pits eleven-member teams against each other on fields slightly larger than American football fields

ALSO KNOWN AS: Association football

SIGNIFICANCE: Although it is clearly the world's most popular team sport, soccer has historically been considered a "foreign" or "ethnic" sport in the United States because of its identification with European and Latin American immigrants. The game has grown to be one of the most widely played youth sports in American cities, suburbs, and rural areas alike but continues to be most strongly supported by immigrant communities.

Since its arrival in the United States, soccer has been associated with the immigrant experience. It was among the first games English settlers brought with them to the American colonies. Although the histories of soccer and American football in the United States can be traced to identical beginnings, soccer in the end lost out to its American cousin and was relegated to a game mostly enjoyed by Europeans and other immigrants.

The English colonists who settled in the United States brought one of their favorite pastimes with them: football. Historians agree that a form of the game was played in Virginia as early as 1609. Throughout the nineteenth century, scratch teams of British immigrants participated in the sport, along with some high school and college teams. By 1860, more than a dozen colleges located on the Atlantic seaboard had taken up the sport. After the rules of "association football" (from which the word "soccer" is taken) were formalized in Great Britain, Princeton and Rutgers universities played the first official game in the United States under these on November 6, 1869. At the time, it appeared that association football might become a major intercollegiate sport. However, a solely American form of football was then emerging that would soon displace it. This new game, which would become known as American football, evolved out of rugby football, which in turn had evolved from soccer. In contrast to soccer, both rugby and American football permitted players to carry the ball with their hands. American football eventually departed from rugby in allowing forward passes—a feature that would come to characterize the American game during the twentieth century.

Meanwhile, through the last quarter of the nineteenth century, soccer began a slow and painful climb to popularity outside the university and professional framework. Through the 1880's, newly arrived Irish, English, Scottish, and Welsh immigrants helped the game take root in New York, New Jersey, and New England. From there, soccer began moving westward. Soccer associations, mostly made up of immigrants, sprung up in cities such as Cincinnati and St. Louis. In 1883, the Pullman Railroad Car Company of Chicago built a soccer field for its immigrant employees—a testament to the popularity of the sport in Chicago and an early example of American business paternalism.

While these developments were unfolding in the United States, the British were planting the seeds of association football throughout Europe, where the game grew rapidly in popularity. As a result, the throngs of European immigrants who changed the face of the United States during the late nineteenth and early twentieth centuries also carried their newfound adoration of soccer to the New World. Ethnic football clubs and leagues such as the German American league, Greek Americans of New York, and Brooklyn Hispano played an essential role in promoting American soccer and socialization among immigrant groups.

PROFESSIONALIZATION, "AMERICANIZATION," AND NEW IMMIGRANTS

By the 1920's, soccer had become popular enough in the United States to form its first professional league, the American Soccer League (ASL). Industrial corporations behind the organization of this league imported European stars for the entertainment of newly arrived immigrant workers. The pattern of ethnic clubs fielding ASL teams became commonplace over the years among Irish, Scottish, Hispanic, Italian, German, Polish, and Ukrainian immigrants.

As international soccer competitions developed, the United States fielded teams, but these were made up predominantly of immigrants. The U.S. national team that competed in the first World Cup competition in Uruguay in 1930 consisted mainly of naturalized British and Scottish professional players. That was also the case when the United States achieved one of the most important victories in national team history—a win over world power England during the 1950 World Cup competition. After World War II, new immigrants and returning servicemen gave soccer a boost throughout the United States. As displaced persons arrived from Europe, they formed new soccer clubs, some of which sought admission to the ASL. At that time, it seemed that the American game would forever remain the diversion of immigrants.

Three decades after World War II, things began to change. In 1975, the recently formed North American Soccer League (NASL) imported some of the world's best player—such as Brazilian superstar Pelé—to play in the United States. This effort to popularize and legitimize the sport among broader segments of American society paid off. Interest in the game soared. In 1964, the American Youth Soccer Organization (AYSO) had begun in Southern California to foster the sport among suburban children. It and other youth soccer organizations grew slowly. However, by 1978, more than 350,000 American children were registered with these organizations, and 5,800 high schools fielded teams. White, middle-class suburbia provided the most fertile ground for this frenzied growth.

The Americanization of soccer appeared to have begun. NASL even began limiting the numbers of foreigners allowed on its teams, and U.S.-born players and coaches began to move up the professional ranks. NASL eventually folded, but during the 1990's, the U.S. men's national soccer team became a fixture in World Cup competitions and a regional powerhouse. The women's national team—built almost entirely on home-grown talent—did even better. It won the 1991 and 1999 World Cups and several Olympic gold medals. When the United States hosted the men's World Cup in 1994, the competition set new attendance and revenue records for the event. By the time a new professional soccer league, Major League Soccer (MLS), formed in 1996, soccer had grown from an immigrant game into the team sport with the most participation among children throughout the United States.

Despite the growing Americanization of the game, the love affair between soccer and immigrants in the United States never abated. Indeed, as most of the new immigrants entering the coun-

"THE GREATEST U.S. VICTORY"

One of the greatest upsets in international soccer history occurred during the 1950 World Cup competition in Brazil, where the United States defeated powerhouse England, 1-0, in a first-round game. Three important players on that U.S. team and its manager were immigrants. Joe Gaetjens, the center forward who scored the winning goal, shown here being carried off the field after the game, was a Haitian citizen. He was allowed to play for the United States because he had declared his intention to become an American citizen, but he never naturalized. He eventually returned to Haiti, where he was killed—apparently by one of President François Duvalier's death squads—in 1964. He was inducted in the U.S. Soccer Hall of Fame in 1976. (AP/Wide World Photos)

try during the twenty-first century are coming from soccer-crazed countries in Latin America, eastern Europe, Africa, and Asia, the numbers of immigrant soccer players and fans in the United States are becoming larger than ever. Their numbers are particularly evident at games played by visiting teams from Latin America, at which fans supporting the foreign teams generally outnumber those supporting the American teams.

Mauricio Espinoza-Quesada

FURTHER READING

Allaway, Roger. *Rangers, Rovers and Spindles: Soccer, Immigration and Textiles in New England and New Jersey.* Haworth, N.J.: St. Johann Press, 2005. History of how British workers in the textile mills popularized soccer in the late nineteenth century and early twentieth century.

Goldblatt, David. *The Ball Is Round: A Global History of Soccer.* New York: Riverhead Books, 2008. Up-to-date, comprehensive, and entertaining history of world soccer, with considerable attention given to the game in the United States.

Hollander, Zander, ed. *The American Encyclopedia of Soccer.* New York: Everest House, 1980. Comprehensive reference source that provides an overview of the sport's history, leagues, tournaments, and collegiate competitions in the United States.

Logan, Gabe. "The Rise of Early Chicago Soccer." In *Sports in Chicago,* edited by Elliot Gorn. Champaign: University of Illinois Press, 2008. Attempt to prove that Chicago immigrants embraced not only soccer but also such American sports as football and baseball.

Markovits, Andrei, and Steven Hellerman. *Offside: Soccer and American Exceptionalism.* Princeton, N.J.: Princeton University Press, 2001. Exploration of how the professionalization of sports such as football and baseball helped to marginalize soccer in the American sports scene.

Wangerin, David. *Soccer in a Football World: The Story of America's Forgotten Game.* London: WSC Books, 2006. Provides a history of soccer in the United States and explains why this sport has been considered "un-American."

SEE ALSO: African immigrants; Asian immigrants; British immigrants; European immigrants; German immigrants; Italian immigrants; Latin American immigrants; Latinos and immigrants; Mexican immigrants; Sports; World War II.

SOCIAL NETWORKS

DEFINITION: Also known as migrant networks, interpersonal ties between migrants and nonmigrants in both receiving and sending societies that provide social resources to those involved in such relationships; such ties are established through friendship, kinship, and community of origin

SIGNIFICANCE: Social networks serve a variety of functions in the migration process including providing information about the receiving society, offering sponsorship as a means of entry, and facilitating adaptation to the host society through social, economic, and psychological support. The study of social networks in migration reveals the importance of social relations in migratory behavior. It provides insight into the origins, composition, direction, and persistence of migration flows.

Social scientists have long been engaged in studying how individuals are connected and how action is constrained or achieved through interpersonal ties. The term used to refer to this social action is social networks. The concept of social networks is both seductive and intuitively simple. Unlike some other social science concepts, the idea of social networks seems to link readily with the way in which individuals routinely live and understand their lives. There are few individuals who are indeed truly isolated. Each individual can be linked, in a variety of ways and with varying degrees of significance, to a set of other people, and these, in turn, may sometimes be linked to others outside this original network.

In the literature on migration, social networks are viewed as critically important to the migration process. The existence of social networks linking migrants with each other across space and time challenges atomistic accounts of social action, where individuals act out of short-run self-interest with little regard for the situations of others. In contrast, the concept of social networks forces one to understand that migration decisions are seldom made by atomized individuals. Instead, the decisions to move or stay, and the choice of destination, are likely to occur within networks of kin and friends and to involve at least some degree of collective decision making. Social networks are indispensable in helping individuals provide aid to migrate, manage initial settlement, and find work.

AID TO MIGRATION

Social networks and the resources they provide can be drawn upon for many instrumental purposes, one of which is to aid migration. Since the first part of the twentieth century, studies have found that people with extensive social networks are more likely to migrate than those without. Social networks based on kinship, friendship, and community of origin allow migrants to draw upon obligations implicit in these relationships to gain access to assistance at their points of destination, thus helping to facilitate migration. Social networks act both as conduits of information and filters of that information, thus influencing who migrates and where they go.

Over time, as more and more individuals are involved in the migration process, the costs and risks associated with migration decline, which, in turn, enables more people to migrate. The development of a network makes migration a self-perpetuating phenomenon, with ties to settlers diffusing so broadly that almost everyone in the sending society enjoys access to a contact in the receiving society. In this way, migration builds momentum independent of the initiating conditions. Thereafter, ongoing migration is no longer dependent on the condition that initiated the migratory process.

MANAGING INITIAL SETTLEMENT

On arrival in the receiving society, migrants face many obstacles, and their hopes for a better life are usually unfulfilled in the short term. Social networks are fields both for linking back to the past and for beginning the process of managing initial settlement in a new society. Newly arrived migrants are completely unfamiliar with the institutions, laws, and people of the foreign country they choose as their destination. Seeing themselves alone in new surroundings and not being able to seek much help from the host society, migrants seek help from kin and friends who are already living in the receiving society.

Mutual aid through social networks is a significant dimension of communities among migrants. Communities with well-established networks provide newcomers with emotional and cultural support and various other practical resources, such as advice on initial housing and food; tips on the best places to shop; information on how to access support and formal services such as health providers, social services, and community organizations; knowledge of employment opportunities; and general information about the host society, its culture, its institutions, and much more. In these relationships, migrants and nonmigrants are connected to one another through dense network of reciprocal social relations that carry mutual obligations of assistance and support.

FINDING WORK

Social networks are useful not only in providing aid to migrate and settling in a new community, but also in helping new immigrants find employment. The majority of individuals who make the decision to migrate to a new destination society go with one objective in mind: to work. Migrants cross borders, risk their lives, leave loved ones behind, and are confronted with the combined stresses of migration to a new environment in order to find work. They rely on social networks to achieve that goal. Social networks can provide reliable and up-to-date information on the availability of jobs, and they often even provide personal references. These references by kin or friends help remove uncertainties associated with finding a job with an unfamiliar employer. For migrants, social networks are of much greater importance than for the general population because of the low levels of social and human capital that these individuals typically possess. By being enmeshed in a multifaceted social network, they are able to compensate for limitations of this nature.

There are a number of benefits for employers who use migrant networks to fill their labor needs. Aside from ensuring access to an ample low-cost workforce and having established workers train new workers, employers can count on a certain level of control because the permanent workers can actually control the behavior for those whom they refer.

Daniel Melero Malpica

FURTHER READING

Hagan, Jacqueline M. *Deciding to Be Legal: A Maya Community in Houston*. Philadelphia: Temple

University Press, 1994. This ethnographic study of Guatemalan immigrants living in Houston illustrates how community networks operate to limit women's ability to attain legal status in the United States while enhancing men's ability to do so.

Mahler, Sarah J. *American Dreaming: Immigrant Life on the Margins.* Princeton, N.J.: Princeton University Press, 1995. Study of Central and South American immigrants living in Long Island, New York, contending that poverty, marginality, and undocumented legal status influence the quantity of resources that can be shared among network ties.

Massey, Douglas, Rafael Alárcon, Jorge Durand, and Humberto Gonzalez. *Return to Aztlán: The Social Process of International Migration from Western Mexico.* Berkeley: University of California Press, 1987. Classic study on Mexican migration to the United States emphasizing the importance of social networks for sustaining migration flows.

Menjivar, Cecilia. *Fragmented Ties: Salvadoran Immigrant Networks in America.* Berkeley: University of California Press, 2000. Study provides an especially thought provoking explanation for why social networks may falter among Salvadoran immigrants living in San Francisco, highlighting that the context of reception must be taken into consideration.

Waldinger, Roger, and Michael Lichter. *How the Other Half Works: Immigration and the Social Organization of Labor.* Berkeley: University of California Press, 2003. Insightful study that contributes to the understanding of how and why immigrants gain employment in Los Angeles. Examining social networks reveals how immigrants obtain footholds in different industries and explains employers' rationale behind their hiring decisions.

SEE ALSO: Chain migration; Employment; Ethnic enclaves; Families; Family businesses; Illegal immigration; Immigration and Nationality Act of 1965; Settlement patterns.

SOCIEDAD PROGRESISTA MEXICANA

IDENTIFICATION: Mutual-aid organization serving Mexican immigrants
DATE: Founded in 1918
ALSO KNOWN AS: Sociedad Progresista Mexicana y Recreativa

SIGNIFICANCE: A mutual aid society, or *mutualista*, the Sociedad Progresista was established by Mexican immigrants to assist its members in times of financial need and of illness. The organization has also played an important role in the social life of the community and in maintaining community connections to Mexican culture. It still perpetuates Mexican culture and celebrations in the United States and is present as a local community or regional organization, especially in California.

In 1918, Mexican immigrants living in California formed the Sociedad Progresista Mexicana for the purpose of helping its members in time of need and to provide a means for organizing social events and festivals traditional to Mexico. Community solidarity and Mexican culture were important concerns of the organization. The immigrants had brought a sense of community from Mexico, where *mutualistas* were a part of the tradition of the towns and regions. The Sociedad Progresista Mexicana was modeled on the Mexican *mutualistas*.

Like other mutual aid societies, the society has been funded by dues or whatever amounts its members can afford to pay. Membership is limited to men, but the organization assists members' entire families. The assistance it has provided has included limited health insurance, funeral expenses, and expenses associated with births and weddings.

The society has also played an active role in planning traditional Mexican holiday celebrations and festivals. As a *mutualista*, it has discouraged assimilation and worked to maintain a strong sense of Mexican heritage among its members. Through the early years of the twenty-first century, it has continued to organize and support Mexican cultural events, especially annual Cinco de Mayo celebrations.

Shawncey Webb

FURTHER READING

Rodríguez, Havidán, Rogelio Sáenz, and Cecilia Menjivar. *Latinas/os in the United States: Changing the Face of America.* New York: Springer, 2008.

Tatum, Charles M. *Chicano Popular Culture: Que hable el pueblo.* Tucson: University of Arizona Press, 2001.

SEE ALSO: Bracero program; Farm and migrant workers; Immigrant aid organizations; Mexican American Legal Defense and Educational Fund; Mexican deportations of 1931; Mexican immigrants.

SOUTH AFRICAN IMMIGRANTS

SIGNIFICANCE: Although South Africans have accounted for a relatively small part of the immigrants to the United States, white South Africans began immigrating in increasing numbers after the early 1960's, as their homeland's apartheid policies raised political and social tensions.

The first South Africans known to immigrate to the United States arrived during the 1860's. Their numbers were small, however, and few of their countrymen followed them to the United States until the 1930's. The national origins quotas of the U.S. Immigration Act of 1924 limited South Africa to only 100 immigrants per year, and South Africans rarely filled their quota. Between 1924 and 1950, an average of only 61 South Africans immigrated to the United States each year. As late as 1960, only 5,300 people of South African descent were known to be living in the United States.

APARTHEID AND IMMIGRATION

After a half century of independence as the Union of South Africa, South Africa became a republic in 1961 and left the British Commonwealth. By this time, South Africa had become a pariah within the world community of nations because of its rigid system of government-supported segregation known as apartheid. Under that system, virtually all political power was in the hands of the approximately 20 percent of the country's popula-

tion who were white. Asians and mixed-race "Coloureds" enjoyed some political rights, while the nation's large black African majority had almost no power.

After South Africa began instituting its apartheid laws in 1948, immigration from that country began increasing. Some immigrants were nonwhite refugees leaving to escape the repressive segregation laws; others were white opponents of the new system.

The U.S. Immigration and Nationality Act of 1965 overturned the four-decade-old system of national origin quotas and allowed many more non-European immigrants entry into the United States. The numbers of South Africans admitted to the United States then increased to an average of 1,000 per year. The vast majority of these new immigrants were white, and they constituted 95 percent of the South Africans living in the United States in 1970.

POSTAPARTHEID TRENDS

In one of the most remarkable peaceful political transformations in world history, the South African government abandoned apartheid during the early 1990's and extended full civil and political rights to all its citizens, without regard to race or ethnicity. Under a new nonracial constitution, South Africans elected a new government in 1994.

PROFILE OF SOUTH AFRICAN IMMIGRANTS	
Country of origin	South Africa
Primary language	English
Primary regions of U.S. settlement	Midwest, East Coast, West Coast
Earliest significant arrivals	1860's
Peak immigration period	1990-2008
Twenty-first century legal residents*	26,979 (3,372 per year)

*Immigrants who obtained legal permanent resident status in the United States.
Source: Department of Homeland Security, *Yearbook of Immigration Statistics, 2008.*

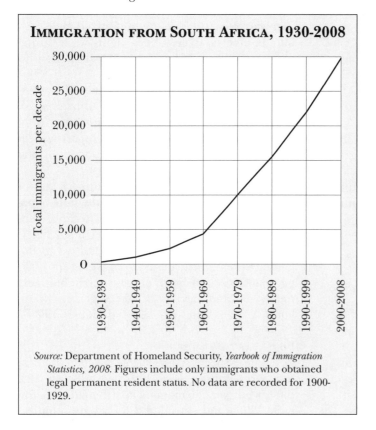

IMMIGRATION FROM SOUTH AFRICA, 1930-2008

Source: Department of Homeland Security, *Yearbook of Immigration Statistics, 2008.* Figures include only immigrants who obtained legal permanent resident status. No data are recorded for 1900-1929.

the national unemployment rate has steadily risen, reaching more than 23 percent in 2009.

SOUTH AFRICANS IN THE UNITED STATES

During the early twenty-first century, South African immigrants could be found living in major cities throughout the United States, most notably in York City, Los Angeles, Chicago, and Washington, D.C. As the vast majority of them are native English speakers, they have tended to assimilate quickly. South Africans have been among the most highly educated immigrants in the country, with nearly 58 percent of them holding college degrees.

Thousands of young professionals, including many doctors, teachers, and scientists, have left their country in search of employment opportunities, many in the United States. Not surprisingly, the large number of educated people leaving South Africa has caused the country to experience a "brain drain."

Bethany E. Pierce

Nelson Mandela—who had long been a political prisoner—became the country's first nonwhite president, and the African National Congress—which had long been banned as a subversive political organization—became the majority party in the country's parliament.

With the abolition of apartheid and the arrival of what was, in effect, black-majority rule, many people feared that South Africa would follow the example of its neighbor Zimbabwe and experienced a mass exodus of white people. Since that time, a large number of white South Africans have emigrated, but their numbers have not been as high as many predicted. Since 1995, approximately 800,000 white South Africans have left their country.

Political and social changes have not been the only factors driving South African emigration. Since the 1990's, the country has also been afflicted by rising crime and unemployment rates. Violent crimes have been a particular problem, with a rate of about fifty murders every day during the early years of the twenty-first century. Meanwhile,

FURTHER READING

Beck, Roger B. *The History of South Africa.* Westport, Conn.: Greenwood Press, 2000. General history of South Africa.

Botha, Ted, and Jenni Baxter, eds. *The Expat Confessions: South Africans Abroad Speak Out!* New York: Jented, 2005. Collection of interviews with South African expatriates.

Marrow, Helen B. "Africa: South Africa and Zimbabwe." In *New Americans: A Guide to Immigration Since 1965,* edited by Mary C. Waters and Reed Ueda. Cambridge, Mass.: Harvard University Press, 2007. Essay examining issues affecting recent immigrants from South Africa and its neighbor Zimbabwe, which experienced a massive flight of white settlers when Robert Mugabe's government began seizing their farms.

Mathabane, Mark. *Kaffir Boy in America: An Encounter with Apartheid.* New York: Macmillan, 1989. Memoir of a black South African college student in the United States.

Vigor, John. *Small Boat to Freedom: A Journey of Conscience to a New Life in America.* Guilford, Conn.: Lyons Press, 2004. Account of a journalist who fled South Africa and sailed for America during the 1980's to escape political oppression.

SEE ALSO: African immigrants; "Brain drain"; Economic opportunities; History of immigration after 1891; Immigration Act of 1921; Immigration and Nationality Act of 1965.

SOUTH CAROLINA

SIGNIFICANCE: South Carolina has been home to members of more different ethnic groups than any other southern state. Late in the twentieth century, many American northerners, as well as Germans and Canadians, moved to South Carolina. However, after 1990, Mexican immigrants far outnumbered those from any other country.

When Europeans made their first contact with the peoples of South Carolina during the early sixteenth century, the region was populated by Native Americans of the Iroquois, Algonquian, Sioux, and Muskogean cultures. The precise date of the first European settlement in South Carolina is uncertain, but it is believed that Spanish colonists established a settlement called San Miguel de Gualdape in what is now South Carolina in 1526. However, that failed settlement left so few traces that it is not even certain whether it was actually in South Carolina or Georgia. More certain is the fact that the French founded Charlesfort on Parris Island in 1562. That colony also failed quickly, as did the fort and village the Spanish established in its place five years later.

In 1663, England's King Charles II granted eight noblemen the rights to an area along the eastern seaboard that they named "Carolina" in his honor. In 1670, a ship with 130 men and women aboard, almost all of them English, arrived at the mouth of the Ashley River. They established a settlement several miles upriver, but ten years later they moved back to the coast, where Charleston is now situated. Through the next two decades, about one-half of the white settlers were from the West Indies island colony of Barbados, and many others also came from West Indies islands. Although the backgrounds of these early colonists were English, the colonists' cultural roots were in the Caribbean. Many brought slaves with them. Later, planters acquired additional slaves from Barbados and also from various parts of Africa, including the Congo region, Angola, Senegal, Gambia, and the Gold Coast.

The proprietors were eager to bring more white settlers into South Carolina. Some of the new immigrants were fleeing religious persecution, among them French Huguenots, German Moravians and Lutherans, and Jews from Spain and Portugal. Others had experienced political persecution, such as Scottish Highlanders who had fought for the Jacobite cause and the French Acadians whom the British had expelled from Nova Scotia. Still others simply wanted to better themselves. Immigrants also came from Ireland, Wales, and the Scottish lowlands. One of the largest groups, the Scotch-Irish from Ulster, settled South Carolina's upcountry region.

After the U.S. Civil War (1861-1865), economic hardships in South Carolina discouraged new

PROFILE OF SOUTH CAROLINA

Region	Southeast Atlantic coast
Entered union	1788
Largest cities	Columbia (capital), Charleston, North Charleston, Greenville
Modern immigrant communities	Mexicans, Canadians, Germans

Population	Total	Percent of state	Percent of U.S.	U.S. rank
All state residents	4,321,000	100.0	1.44	24
All foreign-born residents	176,000	4.1	0.47	29

Source: U.S. Census Bureau, *Statistical Abstract for 2006.*
Notes: The U.S. population in 2006 was 299,399,000, of whom 37,548,000 (12.5%) were foreign born. Rankings in last column reflect total numbers, not percentages.

immigrants from entering the state, and pervasive poverty, along with racial discrimination, drove many black South Carolinians to northern cities. By the 1920's, African Americans were no longer in the majority in South Carolina. Some returned to the state after the Civil Rights movement brought legal and social changes during the 1960's. Meanwhile, the state's African American cultural heritage had never been lost.

TWENTY-FIRST CENTURY TRENDS

During the second half of the twentieth century, South Carolina's rich history, ethnic diversity, and cosmopolitanism, along with its temperate climate, drew retirees from northern states to become permanent or part-time residents. New immigrants also came from various European countries and Canada. In 2006, 10 percent of the foreign-born population of South Carolina had been born in Germany or in Canada. Characteristically, these newcomers found homes in communities on or near the coast.

Europeans and Canadians were not, however, the most numerous immigrants living in South Carolina during the early twenty-first century. In 2006, almost 50 percent of the state's foreign-born residents were from Latin America. The majority of these immigrants were from Mexico, and many of them were undocumented. Because most of them were not well educated, Mexican immigrants took mostly poorly paid jobs and lived in substandard housing. Documentation problems caused many of them not to secure drivers' licenses, obtain health care, or even enroll in English-language courses. Because most of them did not use banks, they were frequently victimized and robbed. Most of them, especially those who had entered illegally, felt that they did not dare report crimes to the police or even complain to employers about their treatment. Moreover, many native-born South Carolinians did not hide their resentment of these new immigrants, who they believed were taking jobs from them as well as placing additional burdens on taxpayers.

Rosemary M. Canfield Reisman

FURTHER READING

Edgar, Walter B. *South Carolina: A History.* Columbia: University of South Carolina Press, 1998.

_____ *The South Carolina Encyclopedia.* Columbia: University of South Carolina Press, 2006.

Lacy, Elaine Cantrell. *Mexican Immigrants in South Carolina: A Profile.* Columbia: Consortium for Latino Immigration Studies, University of South Carolina, 2007.

Mohl, Raymond A. "Globalization, Latinization, and the *Nuevo* New South." In *Other Souths: Diversity and Difference in the U.S. South, Reconstruction to Present,* edited by Pippa Holloway. Athens: University of Georgia Press, 2008.

SEE ALSO: African Americans and immigrants; British immigrants; Canadian immigrants; French immigrants; Georgia; German immigrants; Irish immigrants; Jewish immigrants; Mexican immigrants; North Carolina; West Indian immigrants.

SOUTH DAKOTA

> **SIGNIFICANCE:** Like its northern namesake, South Dakota is an anomaly among U.S. states in having a small and highly homogenous population that has been little touched by modern immigration trends.

Until the mid-nineteenth century, the region that is now the state of South Dakota was populated almost entirely by Native Americans of the Lakota, or Sioux, culture—the people from whom the state takes its name. The region opened to outside immigration in 1858, when the Yankton Sioux signed a treaty that ceded most of present-day South Dakota to the United States, which established Dakota Territory over what in 1889 would become the states of North and South Dakota.

Enactment of the federal Homestead Act of 1862 opened land in South Dakota and other Great Plains states and territories to settlement by both Americans and immigrants from Europe by making land available to them for next to nothing. Among early immigrants to the region were the offspring of earlier immigrants to other states, especially New York and Wisconsin, who began coming during the 1870's and 1880's. The Homestead Act helped attract German, Scandinavian, and Irish immigrants to South Dakota. Norwegian settlers were especially prominent in South Dakota's eastern counties, where they accounted for two-thirds of the immigrants. The beliefs of these settlers created an atmo-

PROFILE OF SOUTH DAKOTA

Region	Upper Midwest
Entered union	1889
Largest cities	Sioux Falls, Rapid City, Aberdeen
Modern immigrant communities	Hispanics

Population	Total	Percent of state	Percent of U.S.	U.S. rank
All state residents	782,000	100.0	0.26	46
All foreign-born residents	17,000	2.2	0.05	48

Source: U.S. Census Bureau, *Statistical Abstract for 2006.*
Notes: The U.S. population in 2006 was 299,399,000, of whom 37,548,000 (12.5%) were foreign born. Rankings in last column reflect total numbers, not percentages.

populations in the United States. In 2005, the U.S. Census reported that almost 90 percent of the state's residents were of European ancestry. Fewer than 2 percent were Hispanic, about 2 percent were Asian, and the rest were Native American.

German Americans constituted the state's single-largest ancestry group, followed by Scandinavian Americans. South Dakota also had the nation's largest community of Hutterites, members of a communal Anabaptist sect that originated in Moravia during the late nineteenth century.

Gayla Koerting

sphere of experimentation with public ownership of certain businesses and help explain the political success of the Populist Party during the late 1890's and the popularity of the Progressive movement in the state during the early twentieth century.

The region's development was accelerated by the completion of a railroad to the territorial capital of Yankton in 1872 and the discovery of gold in the Black Hills that led to a rush two years later. The population of the entire Dakota Territory then increased quickly enough to bring statehood to North and South Dakota in 1889.

TWENTIETH AND TWENTY-FIRST CENTURY DEVELOPMENTS

South Dakota is typical of Great Plains states in having a population that has remained largely static and homogeneous in character. Through the twentieth century, the state ranked among the lowest in the union in both population and population density. Dust Bowl conditions during the 1930's helped begin a steady population decline.

Rural flight has been a common trend in South Dakota as well. During the 1990's alone, thirty of the state's counties lost population, as many educated young people and professionals moved to the largest cities of Sioux Falls and Rapid City or out of the state, leaving many counties with aging populations struggling to finance basic services.

During the early years of the twenty-first century, South Dakota had one of the least diverse

FURTHER READING

Blouet, Brian W., and Frederick C. Luebke. *The Great Plains: Environment and Culture.* Lincoln: University of Nebraska Press, 1979.

Gjerde, Jon. *The Minds of the West: The Ethnocultural Evolution of the Rural Middle West, 1830-1917.* Chapel Hill: University of North Carolina Press, 1979.

Schell, Herbert S. *History of South Dakota.* Lincoln: University of Nebraska Press, 1975.

Wishart, David J., ed. *Encyclopedia of the Great Plains.* Lincoln: University of Nebraska Press, 2004.

SEE ALSO: Czech and Slovakian immigrants; German immigrants; Iowa; Irish immigrants; Mexican immigrants; Missouri; Nebraska; North Dakota; Scandinavian immigrants; Westward expansion.

SPANISH IMMIGRANTS

SIGNIFICANCE: The bulk of immigration from Spain to the United States occurred during the second wave of mass European transatlantic migration during the late nineteenth and early twentieth centuries. Between 1880 and 1930, about 150,000 Spaniards crossed the Atlantic to the United States. Although few in number compared to Irish and Italian immigrants, the Spanish immigrants gained symbolic importance during the antifascist political movements during the 1930's.

Spaniards were the first Europeans to explore much of what are now the southern and western regions of the United States. Accordingly, the Spanish established some of the earliest European settlements in North America, including the oldest city in the continental United States, St. Augustine, Florida, which they established in 1565.

At various moments in history, Spain held authority over what are now Florida, parts of Louisiana, and a great swath of territory across the southwest from Texas to California. Because of the sparse populations in these areas, Spain set up military towns (*presidios*) and missionary towns (*misiones*) in a two-pronged effort to subdue Native American peoples and to establish Spanish authority. The legacy of the early Spanish presence in those regions is still visible in the names of numerous towns and geographical features, in remnants of Spanish colonial architecture and decorative arts, in historic sites scattered across the Southwest, and in the collections of dozens of museums. Classic American "cowboy" culture owes much to the Spanish legacy of cattle ranching. Among the many Spanish terms used in this culture are "corral," "lasso," "buckaroo," and "rodeo."

PROFILE OF SPANISH IMMIGRANTS

Country of origin	Spain
Primary language	Spanish
Primary regions of U.S. settlement	Northeast, Florida, and California
Earliest significant arrivals	1880's
Peak immigration periods	1900-1920's, 1960's-1970's
Twenty-first century legal residents*	12,386 (1,548 per year)

*Immigrants who obtained legal permanent resident status in the United States.
Source: Department of Homeland Security, *Yearbook of Immigration Statistics, 2008.*

During the American Revolutionary War, Spain supported the American colonies against Great Britain, only to lose most of its own colonies in the Americas during the early nineteenth century. In 1821, the United States took control over Florida. During that same year, Mexico won its independence from Spain, and Spanish Texas, California, and the American Southwest became Mexican provinces. Mexico, however, did not hold those territories for long. In 1836, American settlers in Texas won their own independence from Mexico, and Texas was incorporated into the United States in 1845. All the remaining territories of the Southwest were annexed by the United States after it won the Mexican War of 1846-1848. The Spanish and Mexican populations of these annexed territories were not large at the time the United States assumed control over them, but many of the people stayed and became American citizens. In 1898, the United States and Spain met head-on in the Spanish-American War. The American victory left Spanish Cuba and Puerto Rico under American control, along with Guam and the Philippines in the Pacific, and Spanish colonialism in the Western Hemisphere finally came to an end. The United States soon allowed Cuba to go its own way, but it has kept Puerto Rico in a semicolonial status into the twenty-first century.

ERA OF MASS EUROPEAN IMMIGRATION

Around the time the United States was winning control of Spain's last possessions in the Western Hemisphere in 1898, immigrants from Spain were beginning to arrive in the United States. In fact, most Spanish immigrants came to the United States during the short period between 1900 and 1921. This population movement was a small fraction of a much larger movement of Spaniards to Latin America and to Argentina and Cuba in particular. Of the estimated total of 3.5 million Spaniards who immigrated to the Western Hemisphere between 1880 and 1930, only about 150,000 ended up in the United States. However, these figures do not represent the total populations of Spaniards who *stayed* in the Americas because of the high percentage of return migration.

Seasonal migrations of some Spanish immigrants between Spain and the Western Hemisphere—commonly called *golondrina* migration—meant that many migrants were counted more

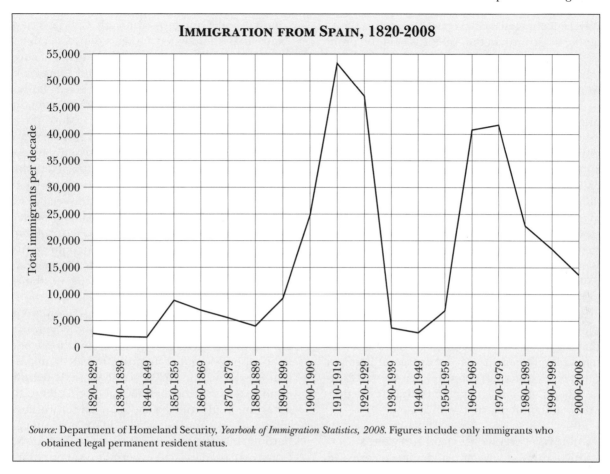

IMMIGRATION FROM SPAIN, 1820-2008

Source: Department of Homeland Security, *Yearbook of Immigration Statistics, 2008*. Figures include only immigrants who obtained legal permanent resident status.

than once as they traveled back and forth across the Atlantic. The luckiest migrants returned to Spain to stay after making their fortunes in the New World. During the 1920's and 1930's, however, many migrants returned to Spain because of diminished opportunities in the global economic downturn that led to the Great Depression. Of the 150,000 Spanish immigrants who came to the United States before the Depression, little more than one-half stayed.

MOTIVES FOR IMMIGRATION

The majority of Spanish immigrants to the United States were young, unmarried men of the lower class, and most of them were agricultural laborers by profession. The youthful character of Spanish immigrants and the predominance of young men reflected one of the motives immigrants had for leaving Spain: to avoid Spain's compulsory military service. Consequently, young men

of military age were also the most likely to emigrate illegally. Many emigrants left Spain without proper legal documents or with false papers, and some left from ports outside Spain. Smaller numbers of anarchist and syndicalist "undesirables" also took part in the legal and illegal flow of people out of Spain.

The most common Spanish motive for immigration during the early twentieth century, however, was to take advantage of better economic opportunities overseas. The agricultural modernization of Spain coupled with industrial underdevelopment to leave many young displaced agricultural workers with the choice of competing for limited jobs in Spanish cities or emigrating. Spain's urban centers failed to absorb workers displaced from traditional agricultural jobs. The pressures of the rapidly increasing population forced displaced workers to search for alternatives. The development of steamships and railroads that facilitated long-distance travel encouraged the flow of workers across the Atlantic. Wage work in the Americas held the promise of the possibility of both social and economic upward mobility that was often not present for workers within Spain.

As historian Jose Moya has pointed out, another important factor in deciding for transatlantic emigration was the implementation of liberal emigration laws such as the Spanish Emigration Law of 1907. This law upheld the basic freedom of Spanish citizens to emigrate. However, the law posed certain conditions, for example, it restricted the emigration of young men who had not performed military service and young women who did not have the permission of their guardians to emigrate. Women over the age of twenty-three who were legally autonomous could be denied the right to emigrate if it were suspected that they were prostitutes. The law also stipulated that married women had their husbands' permission to leave. Nevertheless, this law was permissive enough to allow most potential immigrants to take advantage of immigration laws in American countries that favored Europeans until the implementation of U.S. restrictions on immigration during the 1920's.

TRANSATLANTIC INFORMATION NETWORKS

Spaniards considering emigration received information about opportunities in the United States through various channels. As transportation of immigrants became big business, steamship agents often acted as recruiting agents and intermediaries between aspiring immigrants and their chosen destinations. Another fountain of information about life abroad, perhaps the most important, came from Spanish emigrants already living in foreign countries and those who had returned after living abroad. The figure of the *indiano* or *americano*, the successful immigrant, often spurred relatives or townspeople to try their luck at their own successful American experience. The attraction of joining family, friends, and neighbors also continued to draw people, often to the same concentrated areas in the same cities, well after other reasons for immigration disappeared.

The importance of informal networks is apparent in a breakdown of the regions from which Spanish emigrants came. The majority of Spanish immigrants came from the northern coast of Spain, comprising Galicia, Asturias, the Basque country, and Cantabria, although Galicians and Asturians predominated. Other groups also joined the Galicians, however, including the Valencians, Andalusians, Catalans, Castilians, and Canarians. Family, friends, and neighbors also affected choices of final destinations in the United States, often in connection with particular industries. Most Andalusians, for example, migrated first to Hawaii to work on sugar plantations and then continued on to California. Many Asturians were attracted to the cigar-making industry in Tampa, Florida, an extension of the cigar industry in Cuba. Industrial work in Pennsylvania, Ohio, West Virginia, and Michigan attracted Asturian miners and Galicians. However, nearly one-half of all Spanish immigrants ended up in the greater New York City region, which included southern Connecticut, northern New Jersey, and New York City itself.

Immigrants from Spain's Basque region are a special case. Basque sheepherders had begun migrating to the Pacific Northwest around 1910, but national origins quotas imposed in U.S. immigration law during the 1920's greatly slowed Spanish immigration. During the 1950's, however, the U.S. government identified a special need for workers willing to take on the solitary lifestyle of sheepherding. In order to obtain sheepherders, the U.S. Congress passed legislation permitting about 1,000 Basques to enter the United States outside the quota limits.

SPANISH CIVIL WAR AND THE RISE OF FRANCO

Although the Spanish immigrant community in the United States was small during the 1930's, it became a hotbed of activity through the years of the Spanish Civil War (1936-1939). In April of 1931, peaceful elections ushered in Spain's second attempt at a republican form of government. It was led by a coalition of socialists, republicans, and various cultural nationalist groups. The failure of these disparate groups to unite their causes into a single coherent vision spelled the ultimate failure of Spain's Second Republic and the eventual successful implementation of a right-wing nationalist dictatorship led by General Francisco Franco. During the Spanish Civil War, many Spaniards living in the United States mobilized behind the Republican and Nationalist causes.

Although Spanish social clubs and mutual aid societies existed in the United States before the war, the 1930's saw the creation of many new societies and the consolidation of some of those that already existed. For example, the umbrella organization called the Spanish Antifascist Committee started in Brooklyn in 1936 and then became a national organization under the name Confederated Hispanic Societies. This organization encompassed dozens of associated organizations, most of them from the greater New York City area and the East Coast, and became the major Hispanic organization responsible for organizing fund-raising efforts and an active pro-republican propaganda. Other vehicles for organization of Spanish immigrants were unions and political parties.

The Spanish community of the United States was not alone in its agitation over events in Spain. The Confederated Hispanic Societies would connect at times with a North American organization called the Medical Bureau and North American Committee to Aid Spanish Democracy for political rallies and fund-raising efforts. Some Spanish Americans fought in the Spanish Civil War on the Republican side, along with the International Brigades made up of volunteers from all over Europe and the Americas. However, the American contingent was made up of dozens of volunteers of all ethnicities.

Within the United States, General Franco found support for his Nationalist cause among the same kinds of groups that supported him in Spain—Roman Catholic organizations and members of the middle class. In 1937, several former members of the Spanish Chamber of Commerce in New York organized the Casa de España, which became the center of pro-Franco activity. It was led by Juan Francisco de Cardenas, the Spanish Nationalist government's representative to the United States. This organization pro-Franco propaganda was not intended solely, or even mainly, for the Spanish community in the United States. Many of the Casa de España's propaganda efforts were aimed at winning over North American conservatives, an endeavor in which it had some success. Franco's Spanish American supporters also established the National Spanish Relief Association to raise funds for Nationalist Spain.

Franco was installed as Spain's dictator in 1939 and remained in power until his death in 1975. Meanwhile, many of the small community of Spanish immigrants remained in the United States and other Western Hemispheric countries as political exiles.

SPANISH COMMUNITY OF THE UNITED STATES

As the number of immigrants coming from Spain diminished and descendants of earlier immigrants lost their ties to Spain, the Spanish community of the United States became increasingly identified with the vastly larger Hispanic communities made up of Latin American immigrants. As early as the 1930's, marriages of immigrants from Spain and Latin America were beginning to occur. Perhaps there is no greater sign of this melding of communities than the evolution of the Spanish newspaper *La Prensa* into the Hispanic newspaper *El Diario la Prensa*, the Spanish-language newspaper with the largest circulation in the United States.

Jahaira Arias

FURTHER READING

Gonzalez, Bernard. *Ironbound.* New York: Vantage Press, 2003. Memoir of a half-Spanish, half-Lithuanian man of Newark, New Jersey, and the transformations of this immigrant neighborhood in the second half of the twentieth century.

González, G. W., Mark Brazaitis, and Daniel F. Ferreras. *Pinnick Kinnick Hill: An American Story.* Morgantown: West Virginia University Press, 2003. Partly fictionalized memoir of a Spanish immigrant community in West Virginia. Memorializes the development of an Asturian community of industrial laborers in the first half of the twentieth century.

Lick, Sue Fagalde. *The Iberian Americans.* New York: Chelsea House, 1990. Part of a larger series on immigrant groups, this volume provides useful general information about the culture and history of Portuguese and Spanish American communities.

Weber, David J. *The Spanish Frontier in North America.* New Haven, Conn.: Yale University Press, 1992. Cultural history of Spanish society in North America prior to 1821.

SEE ALSO: California; European immigrants; Florida; Hawaii; Latin American immigrants; Louisiana; Montana; Nevada; New Jersey; New York City; Spanish-language press.

SPANISH-LANGUAGE PRESS

DEFINITION: Newspapers and magazines published for members of Hispanic communities in the United States

SIGNIFICANCE: The Spanish-language press has long played an important dual role in the lives of Hispanic immigrants by providing news in their native language and by helping them assimilate to American culture. The press also has played a significant role in fostering awareness of Hispanic heritage, and it continues to contribute to the maintenance of Hispanic culture and traditions. As a shared-language medium, it is one of the most important elements in molding the diverse Spanish-speaking communities in the United States into a single Hispanic American community.

The history of the Spanish-language press can be traced back to the early nineteenth century. Spanish-language newspapers have been published for a variety of reasons: as pure business ventures designed to generate profits, as culturally specific political tracts, and as media generated for both business and cultural reasons. The goals of the press have varied considerably over time—from providing news of readers' native homelands, to calling for political action, to serving as essentially American publications for Spanish-speaking readers. In all their forms, however, components of the Spanish-language press have consistently addressed the culture and traditions of Hispanics in the United States.

NINETEENTH CENTURY PUBLICATIONS

The first Spanish-language newspaper in the United States was published in 1804 in New Orleans, Louisiana. A four-page publication called *El Misisipí*, it targeted Spanish speakers who had come to the United States to escape political unrest in their homelands. It was published by the William H. Johnson Company, a non-Hispanic firm, as a purely business undertaking.

The true center of the early Spanish-language press, however, was in the American Southwest, a region populated during the early nineteenth century mostly by Mexicans who already had a strong tradition of reading papers published in their own language. For some time, after California and the Southwest were annexed by the United States during the 1840's, southwestern newspapers such as *El Crépusculo de la Libertad* and *La Verdad* continued to publish articles mostly about events in Mexico and their local communities. As local populations became more and more involved in American life, especially in seeking work and necessary services, and became more politically active, the focus of the newspapers shifted from Mexico to the condition of Mexican Americans in the United States. The weeklies and dailies published in the Southwest began a campaign to raise the residents' consciousness of their Hispanic heritage and to encourage active response to discrimination at work, poor working conditions, and low wages.

TWENTIETH CENTURY TRENDS

During the early twentieth century, the tradition of Spanish-language newspapers speaking out for the Hispanic community continued in California and in the Southwest. New publications also emerged in major metropolitan areas, such as Chicago, where many Mexicans had immigrated in response to the job opportunities created by World War I. This activism, which at times became militant, was not without risk for the journalists and publishers. For example, the Mexican-born journalist Ricardo Flores Magón, whose newspaper *Regeneracion* advocated the overthrow of the Mexican dictator Porfirio Díaz and labor reform in the United States, was jailed for violating neutrality laws in 1907. During World War I, he was imprisoned for espionage and died in Leavenworth's federal penitentiary.

After World War I ended in 1918, work opportunities for the Hispanic population changed. Jobs, especially in agriculture and government-sponsored employment, were often of short duration and required workers to develop a migratory lifestyle. The Spanish-language press was affected by this development, as many local papers were published only during the brief periods when substantial numbers of Spanish-speaking workers were in an area. Around this time, the papers tended to become less politically oriented.

After World War II, the Spanish-language press in general continued to follow a more conservative trend until about 1960. Many papers continued to promote Hispanic culture and traditions, as well as use of the Spanish language, but they also tended to place more emphasis on assimilation. *La Prensa* in San Antonio, Texas, and *La Opinión* in Los Angeles, California, were representative of such papers. However, there were also other papers whose editors and writers continued to encourage both social and political activism.

During the national Civil Rights movement of the 1960's, Spanish-language newspapers again spoke out strongly for rights of workers and condemned discrimination against Hispanics in the workplace, in the political arena, and in all aspects of life in the United States. Throughout the United States, Hispanic newspapers reflected this focus on political and social issues, a trend that continued through the 1970's.

From 1969 to 1976, the United Farm Workers union under the leadership of César Chávez published *El Malcriado,* demanding improved working conditions for agricultural laborers. From 1968 to 1980, the Crusade for Justice published *Le Gallo.* The Movimiento Estudiantil Chicano de Aztlán (MEChA) called for political and social action in *La Causa,* which was published from 1969 to 1972. From 1974 to 1978, with *Sin Fronteras,* the Centro de Acción Social encouraged the Mexican community to engage in both political and social action. The most radical of these papers was the prosocialist *El Grito del Norte.* Founded by Elizabeth Martínez and Beverly Axelrod in 1968 in Española, New Mexico, the semimonthly paper attacked the policies and activities of local government and worked to eradicate negative stereotypes of Mexican Americans that proliferated in the area. The paper ceased publication in 1973. During this period of intense social activism, other well-established Spanish-language newspapers, such as *La Opinión* in California and *La Prensa* in Texas, continued to serve the Hispanic community with articles emphasizing Hispanic culture and others addressing the rights of Hispanics but without the militancy of the activist papers.

Although the number of activist Hispanic newspapers declined dur-

ing the early 1980's, the Spanish-language press remained a significant force in the United States throughout the twentieth century. More than five hundred local Spanish-language newspapers were regularly published on a daily, weekly, or monthly basis. The 1990's began to see major newspaper companies replacing their weekly Spanish-language supplements with daily Spanish-language newspapers. Most important for the Hispanic community, these papers did not merely publish translations of articles in the companies' English-language papers; they were independent publications with their own Hispanic editors and journalists. In 1998, the Tribune Company founded *Hoy New York* in New York City as a daily newspaper serving the Hispanic community. Shortly afterward, the Tribune Company created *Hoy Chicago,* a daily Spanish-language paper, to replace its weekly Spanish-language supplement *Exito* in Chicago.

TWENTY-FIRST CENTURY DEVELOPMENTS

The trend toward daily Spanish-language newspapers has continued into the twenty-first century. Recognizing the ever-increasing growth of the country's Hispanic population, mainstream news-

Woman looking over a selection of Spanish-language newspapers and magazines at a downtown Los Angeles newsstand in 1986. (AP/Wide World Photos)

paper publishers have responded to the need to serve this market on a daily basis and as a primary target audience with newspapers written expressly for Spanish-speaking readers, not merely translations of English-language newspapers. The Tribune Company, ImpreMedia, and the McClatchy newspapers all publish daily Spanish-language newspapers that provide international, national, and local Hispanic community news. In 2005, El Paso, Texas, got its first daily Spanish-language newspaper, *El Diaro de El Paso*. It competes directly with the city's English-language *El Paso Times*, which it often publishes articles criticizing.

Despite the steady increase in daily Spanish-language newspapers into the twenty-first century, weeklies are still important segments of the national Spanish-language press. *La Voz*, a free weekly publication distributed in Phoenix and Tucson, Arizona, has continued to publish news of both political and social events in Mexico, helping to keep both Mexican and Mexican American readers in touch with their heritage. Several new weeklies have also been founded in the early twenty-first century. For example, in 2003, the Sun Sentinel Company of Fort Lauderdale added a Spanish-language weekly to its publications, *El Sentinel del Sur de la Florida*. In 2004, *El Latino Expresso* began publication on a weekly basis in Rhode Island, serving the Hispanic communities of both Rhode Island and southeastern Massachusetts.

ESPAÑOL MAGAZINES

Magazines also are a significant part of the Spanish-language press in the United States. In 2007, *People en Español* had the largest readership of any American Spanish-language magazine with 6.4 million readers. First published in 1996, the magazine was originally merely a Spanish-language version of the popular *People Magazine* in which about one-half the articles were translations of articles in the English-language edition. However, the magazine eventually evolved into a truly Hispanic publication with a Hispanic staff and about 90 percent original material. The remaining 10 percent consists of translated articles that are considered to have particular cultural significance for Hispanics. The magazine's editors maintain strict control over its language, avoid regionalisms and slang, and produce a magazine written in a Spanish common to the varied Hispanic populations in the United States.

Another Spanish-language magazine published in the United States, called *Alma*, targets all segments of the Hispanic population and contributes to the creation of a Hispanic American community. As a lifestyle magazine, it provides articles on culture, politics, and fashion.

Shawncey Webb

FURTHER READING

Kaniss, Phylis. *Making Local News*. Chicago: University of Chicago Press, 1997. Good for discussion of the importance and influence of newspapers generally in politics and society. Includes a detailed study of how Spanish-language newspapers in Miami, Florida, both serve and influence the local Hispanic community.

Kent, Robert B., and Maura E. Huntz. "Spanish-Language Newspapers in the United States." *Geographical Review* 86 (1996): 446-456. Useful article for statistics about circulation and facts about individual Spanish-language newspapers.

Meléndez, A. Gabriel. *Spanish-Language Newspapers in New Mexico, 1834-1958*. Tucson: University of Arizona Press, 2005. Reviews the history of Spanish-language newspapers in New Mexico, arguing that these papers established the tradition leading to the Chicano movements of the 1960's and 1970's and that they helped ensure the survival of Mexican culture in the Southwest.

Subervi-Vélez, Federico A. "Spanish-Language Daily Newspapers and the 1984 Elections." *Journalism Quarterly* 65, no. 3 (1988): 678-685. Close look at the impact of Spanish-language newspapers on politics and Hispanics during the 1980's.

_____, ed. *The Mass Media and Latino Politics: Studies of U.S. Media Content, Campaign Strategies and Survey Research, 1984-2004*. New York: Routledge, 2008. Excellent collection of articles that are especially useful for establishing the chronology of Spanish-language newspapers and their orientation.

SEE ALSO: Chicano movement; Civil Rights movement; German American press; Mexican immigrants; New Mexico; Presidential elections; Spanish immigrants; Telemundo; Univision.

SPORTS

SIGNIFICANCE: A long underestimated component of American culture, sports have long played an important role in American society, and they have also served as an integrative force that has helped immigrants to assimilate. It may be significant that the game of baseball, which has long been regarded as the most quintessentially American sport, has also become the team sport in which immigrants have become most prominent.

The involvement of immigrants in sports in the United States might best be understood by focusing on the country's most popular team sports—baseball, football, and basketball.

BASEBALL

One of the oldest and most deeply ingrained team sports in the United States is baseball. The game began its rise during the mid-nineteenth century, when it evolved from the British game of cricket. During the U.S. Civil War (1861-1865), combat troops often played the game during respites from fighting and traveling. After the war, the game began winning acceptance among working-class Americans. Codification of the game's rules helped standardize how the game was played and helped make baseball the first truly American game. Standardizing the rules helped the game spread more easily because teams could compete without having rules disputes.

The first people to play baseball regularly were laborers in metropolitan areas such as New York City and Philadelphia. The game found particular acceptance among the Irish and Italian immigrants who were flooding into the United States during the nineteenth century. Much as Civil War troops had done, members of these communities used baseball as a way to get away from work pressures.

What few people could have anticipated was that baseball games among different teams would grow into popular spectator events. Many of the earliest teams were formed on ethnic lines and were supported by fans from the same ethnic groups. However, as the quality of play improved and teams became professional, their rosters became more ethnically diverse as their managers selected players on the basis of their playing ability, rather than their ethnicity. This development broadened the fan bases of teams in their host cities.

Baseball can be seen as the sport that developed the idea of spectator sports in America, and it developed on the backs of blue-collar immigrant workers. By the late nineteenth century and the establishment of the National League, these players were being paid for their efforts. By the time that the American League had formed and Major League Baseball's World Series was inaugurated in 1903, the sport showed that a new avenue existed for immigrants to succeed in America. Throughout much of the twentieth century, Major League Baseball was dominated by native-born American players, but many of the game's stars were second- and third-generation members of immigrant families.

Among American sports, baseball has probably seen the biggest influx of immigrants. African American players were effectively banned from Major League Baseball through the first half of the twentieth century. In contrast, Hispanic players were admitted as early as 1902, when Luis Castro first appeared on a major roster. The first Hispanic players to earn all-star recognition were the Cuban pitcher Adolfo Luque and his Cuban catcher Miguel Angel González in 1911. Their achievement helped to ensure that more Hispanics would be welcomed to the major leagues.

Cuba was the biggest source of Hispanic players in Major League Baseball through the mid-twentieth century, but by the end of the century players from the Dominican Republic would have an impact on the game well out of proportion to the tiny size of their country. Whereas about 150 Cubans have played on American major league teams, between 1956 and 2009, more than 400 Dominicans were in Major League Baseball. Another Latin American country supplying a growing number of players to the American major leagues was Venezuela. By 2009, it had overtaken Cuba as a supplier of Major League Baseball talent, with more than 215 Venezuelan players in the major leagues since 1937.

By the late twentieth century, baseball was being played throughout the world; however, there were only three regions in which the game was being played at its highest level: in the United States; in

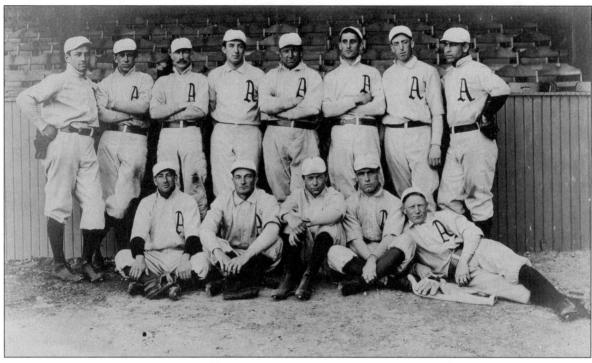

Philadelphia Athletics baseball team in 1902. The Colombian-born second baseman Luis Castro, sitting at far left, was the first Hispanic known to play major league baseball. (Library of Congress)

Latin America, especially in the Caribbean basin; and in Japan and Korea. Baseball had long held a high level of popularity in Japan, but there were few ties between American and Japanese baseball, apart from occasional goodwill tours by individual teams. Consequently, Americans had little knowledge of the caliber of Japanese baseball and tended to assume it was second-rate in comparison to American baseball.

That attitude began changing during the mid-1990's, after pitcher Hideo Nomo became the first Japanese baseball player to enter the American major leagues on a permanent basis in 1995. Nomo's successful career led to many more signings of Japanese and Korean pitchers. The next change in attitude came in 2001, when outfielder Ichiro Suzuki became the first Japanese position player (one who is not a pitcher) to sign with an American club. Winning both rookie of the year and most valuable player honors during his first season, Suzuki was an instant sensation. By 2009, more than forty Japanese players had played in Major League Baseball, and a dozen Korean players were on major league rosters.

FOOTBALL

As baseball gained in popularity, it spread out to other parts of the country from the major northeastern cities—the same pattern that American football would later follow. Football was also like baseball in another way, as it, too, evolved from a European game, rugby football. American football first became popular as a college sport during the late nineteenth century, which meant that many of its early players were privileged white students. However, the later popularity of the game would help it to grow beyond its narrow beginnings.

Professional football emerged during the early twentieth century. Formation of what would become the National Football League (NFL) in 1920 opened new opportunities for immigrant athletes. With many of the first professional teams based in midwestern states, players from these states had the best chance of making teams. As Germans and Poles were among the predominant immigrant groups in the Midwest, many of the early teams had German and Polish players on their rosters.

By the early twenty-first century, the modern game of football had yet to see a wave of immigrant influence similar to those in baseball and basketball. The major immigrant influence on football teams was usually at the placekicker position because many college teams recruited soccer players from Europe and other parts of the world for their exceptional kicking skills. Otherwise, the general scarcity of immigrant players in football was at least partly due to the failure of American football to catch on in other parts of the world. Between 1991 and 2007, the National Football League sponsored a professional football league in Europe. The experiment was undertaken partly to provide the NFL with a minor league in which to develop its own talent and partly to spread interest in the American game. However, the league proved unprofitable and was abandoned.

American football has, however, attracted the interest of one seemingly unlikely immigrant group: Pacific Islanders, particularly Samoans. By 2008, American college football teams—particularly in the West—had more than 200 American Samoans on their rosters, and more than two dozen Samoans were playing in the NFL. These are staggering numbers for a territory with a population of only about 65,000 people. Because of their tendency to grow to great sizes, Samoan men are physically well adapted for football. They are also exceptionally motivated, as the prospects of winning scholarships to American universities encourage many of them to take high school football very seriously.

BASKETBALL

In 1891, a doctor in Massachusetts named James Naismith looking for activities to keep his students physically in shape during the winter months invented the game of basketball. Much like football, most of the first players of this new sport were native-born white students. However, as the sport grew in popularity and moved into the professional realm, it attracted players of all ethnicities, particularly African Americans. Eventually, the game would embrace an ethnic diversity that would set it apart from other American team sports.

During the late twentieth century, professional basketball in the United States began taking on an international flavor. In contrast to baseball and football, basketball has become a truly international game. This is due in part to the introduction of the game to the Olympics during the early twentieth century and in part to the fact that game requires fewer players, less playing space, and less specialized equipment. In this regard, it compares to soccer, which is essentially a more two-dimensional version of basketball played on a larger field.

By the late twentieth century, professional leagues playing essentially the same version of basketball played in the United States were operating in virtually every region of the world, and international rivalries were being fiercely contested in the Olympic Games. As the caliber of basketball being played in other countries improved, increasing numbers of foreign players were recruited by American college teams. Many of these foreign players began being drafted by National Basketball Association (NBA) teams. By the late 1990's, NBA teams were drafting foreign players directly from their home countries, and number one draft picks were used on players from China, Australia, Italy, and Nigeria. By 2009, more than 300 foreign players had played in the NBA, and during some seasons, more than 75 foreign players were in the league—a figure equivalent to about 20 percent of all players. Meanwhile, foreign players were influencing the American game, helping it return to its roots by reemphasizing team play.

THE MODERN SPORTING CLIMATE

Professional sports in America have encouraged athletes to flourish in circumstances that they might otherwise have never have seen. Foreign athletes often come to the United States seeking opportunities for better lives. While most may remain tied to their home countries and never become American citizens, they do become part of American culture and help build bridges between the United States and other nations. As other sports rise to prominence in the United States, more ties are established and cultivated.

P. Huston Ladner

FURTHER READING

Bale, John, and T. Dejonghe. "Sports Geography: An Overview." *Belgeo* 2 (2008): 157-166. Brief but comprehensive survey of sports throughout the world.

Bale, John, and Joseph Maguire, eds. *The Global Sports Arena: Athletic Talent Migration in an Interdependent World.* London: Frank Cass, 1994. Broad overview of international sports with particular attention to athletes who move among different countries.

Cronin, Mike, and John Bale. *Sport and Postcolonialism.* Oxford, England: Berg, 2003. Examination of political issues relating to sports in the modern world.

Goldblatt, David. *The Ball Is Round: A Global History of Soccer.* New York: Riverhead Books, 2008. Comprehensive and often entertaining history of world soccer, with considerable attention given to the game in the United States, where the game has long been important to immigrant communities.

Nelson, Murry. "Sports History as a Vehicle for Social and Cultural Understanding in American History." *The Social Studies* 96, no. 3 (2005): 118-125. Interesting essay that finds connections between sports and broader cultural issues.

Sage, George. *Power and Ideology in American Sport.* 2d ed. Champaign, Ill.: Human Kinetics, 1998. Broad survey of social and cultural issues in American sports, with attention to the involvement of ethnic and immigrant communities.

SEE ALSO: Asian immigrants; Atlas, Charles; Cuban immigrants; Dominican immigrants; Immigration waves; Rockne, Knute; Schwarzenegger, Arnold; Soccer.

POEM FOR THE STATUE OF LIBERTY

American poet and scholar Emma Lazarus penned the poem "The New Colossus" in 1883 for an art exhibition that had been part of a fund-raising effort for the Statue of Liberty's final construction. Written in memory of Jewish immigrants from Russia, the poem, which won an award at the exhibition and then was soon forgotten, would be inscribed on a bronze plaque in 1903 and placed on the statue's second floor. In 1945, the plaque—and the poem—was moved to the statue's main entrance as an embracing gesture to Lazarus and her work.

Not like the brazen giant of Greek fame,
With conquering limbs astride from land to land;
Here at our sea-washed, sunset gates shall stand
A mighty woman with a torch, whose flame
Is the imprisoned lightning, and her name
Mother of Exiles. From her beacon-hand
Glows world-wide welcome; her mild eyes command
The air-bridged harbor that twin cities frame.
"Keep, ancient lands, your storied pomp!" cries she
With silent lips. "Give me your tired, your poor,
Your huddled masses yearning to breathe free,
The wretched refuse of your teeming shore.
Send these, the homeless, tempest-tost to me,
I lift my lamp beside the golden door!"

Source: National Park Service, Statue of Liberty National Monument.

STATUE OF LIBERTY

THE EVENT: Dedication of a monument given to the United States by France that would come to embody the ideal of America as a haven for new immigrants

DATE: Dedicated on October 28, 1886

LOCATION: Liberty Island, New York Harbor

SIGNIFICANCE: Originally intended to symbolize the concept of liberty in the French and American revolutions, during the twentieth century the Statue of Liberty would increasingly come to represent the possibility of new life in America for all immigrants passing by her, and the vision of America as a multicultural society strong because of its diversity.

The Statue of Liberty came to connect with the immigrant experience in two specific ways. Most directly and immediately, for all the millions passing into the United States through Ellis Island at the port of New York City, the statue's towering presence (305 feet high from the ground to the top of her torch) would have been an unforgettable image and symbol of the new land they were entering, at a moment when their expectations and anticipations were raised high after a long and perhaps difficult journey.

Even more significant, in the long run, would be the influence of a poem written in 1883 as a donation to a charity event raising money to pay for the pedestal upon which the Statue of Liberty would stand. For that auction, Emma Lazarus, an American-born Jew and recognized member of the New York literati, contributed "The New Colossus," a sonnet that would become one of the poems most widely memorized by American schoolchildren of the twentieth century. The poem alludes to the Statue of Liberty as the "Mother of Exiles." In its famous closing lines, Lazarus has the statue address the world directly, offering needy immigrants shelter, succor, and, most powerfully, the opportunity "to breathe free."

Lazarus herself became a strong advocate for Russian Jews fleeing pogroms and persecutions in their homeland, but she died of Hodgkin's disease at the age of thirty-eight on November 19, 1887, just over one year after the Statue of Liberty was dedicated. As a tribute to her in 1903, friends succeeded in having a plaque inscribed with "The New Colossus" and the poem placed inside the statue's pedestal itself, where visitors to the statue could read and reflect. That plaque has remained a significant component of the Statue of Liberty museum today.

During the 1930's, Louis Adamic and other writers and public speakers who championed America's pluralism helped promote the connection between the image of the Statue of Liberty and the ideas in "The New Colossus." Adamic recited the poem in radio addresses, reaching millions of listeners. With the advent of World War II, the idea of the great statue as a "Mother of Exiles" took on even deeper resonance for those fleeing totalitarian regimes and the Holocaust in Europe.

In 1965, Ellis Island, the former entry site for millions of nineteenth and twentieth century immigrants, was incorporated into the nearby Statue of Liberty National Monument. In 1984, in preparation for the 1986 centennial celebration of the Statue of Liberty, the United Nations named the statue a World Heritage site.

Scot M. Guenter

Before the Statue of Liberty was erected on what is now called Liberty Island, it was assembled in Manhattan. Frédéric-Auguste Bartholdi, the French sculptor who designed the statue, is shown in the cameo inset. (Library of Congress)

FURTHER READING

Moreno, Barry. *The Statue of Liberty.* Charleston, S.C.: Arcadia, 2004.

_____. *The Statue of Liberty Encyclopedia.* New York: Simon & Schuster, 2000.

Schor, Esther. *Emma Lazarus.* New York: Schocken, 2006.

SEE ALSO: Cultural pluralism; Ellis Island; European immigrants; History of immigration after 1891; *The Immigrant*; Immigration and Nationality Act of 1965; New York City; Pulitzer, Joseph.

STEREOTYPING

DEFINITION: Practice of assigning to all members of a group—particularly an ethnic or racial group—the same characteristics on the assumption that all members of the group share these traits

SIGNIFICANCE: Although ethnic stereotyping can be positive for less talented and weaker members of a favorably stereotyped group, the usual effect of stereotyping is an unfounded negative bias toward undeserving individuals that can contribute to making their lives more difficult. Members of certain immigrant groups—particularly Middle Easterners and Muslims generally—are popular targets of negative stereotypes in the United States. Because of stereotyping, immigrants are often perceived as undesirable and even potentially dangerous people to allow in the country, especially during times of national crises.

Stereotyping can be based on traits associated with race, cultural backgrounds, sexual orientations, age, gender, and even occupations and physical disabilities. Ethnic stereotyping pinpoints any category of people in the larger society who have the same national origin, common history, or religion, and who share similar physical, cultural, or social traits. The modern population of the United States is made up of people and their descendants from all over the world—a conglomeration of ethnic groups whose members have historically jockeyed for ascendancy over one another. Part of that jockeying has involved stereotyping—occasionally positive, but much more frequently negative.

When the independent republic of the United States emerged from more than a century and a half of British colonial rule during the late eighteenth century, the great bulk of its free citizens were culturally comparatively homogeneous, as most of them were of British ancestry. A half century later, the new nation began receiving great waves of newcomers, most of whom came from different cultural backgrounds.

As the young American nation spread out and built towns and cities, immigrants poured in to supply the labor. Generally, these newcomers were willing to work for less pay than their already established American counterparts; after all, even the low wages received in America were more than they could have earned in their homelands. Because they seemed satisfied with such compensation, employers were delighted to hire them—a fact that caused the American-born workers to resent the immigrants.

IRISH AND GERMAN STEREOTYPES

Many Irish immigrants who worked some of the nastiest and worst-paid jobs in the Pennsylvania coal mines were considered rabble and hated by Americans who may have had no greater abilities or ambition but who felt superior because they had been born in the United States. In their understandable dismay at such unfair perceptions and worn down by brutal working conditions, many Irish workers often found solace in heavy drinking. This tendency caused Americans who disparaged the Irish to promote a stereotype of Irish immigrants as drunken, potato-eating brawlers who lived with pigs in their parlors—a negative stereotype that stuck with the Irish far beyond the time when it might have had any relevance whatever. Ironically, perhaps, many Irish men capitalized on their reputations as fearless brawlers and convivial talkers to become policemen and politicians.

During the early nineteenth century, Irish men were prime targets for American comedy. They were often caricatured in periodicals and political cartoons as hairy, muscle-bound workmen with nearly simian features—protruding jaws, cheek whiskers, and small noses over thick upper lips. They were typically drawn wearing derby hats and clinching pipes in their teeth, when not downing whiskey.

The German immigrants who followed the Irish were seen in only a slightly better light than the Irish. They were typically labeled beer-guzzling, sauerkraut-swilling cheese eaters. They were grudgingly considered somewhat cleaner than the Irish, and because they were mostly Protestant, unlike Irish Catholics, they were therefore somewhat less objectionable. German Jews, however, being non-Christian, were viewed with greater suspicion. Although these people were usually well educated and nearly always established worthwhile, needed business enterprises in their communities, their stereotyping reflected disdain at their erudition and allegedly condescending attitudes toward non-Jews. They were perceived as overeducated and contemptuous.

OTHER ETHNIC STEREOTYPES

French Canadian immigrants were stereotyped as untrustworthy, largely because they moved about a great deal, returning to their homes in Canada with the wages they earned in the United States. Another of their traits that was held against them was the fact that they spoke French more than English. Also, they were Roman Catholics. The negative image that followed them for several years, however, gradually changed to a more respectful one when they were found to be both responsible and stable citizens and thrifty.

Chinese men who worked on the transcontinental railroad lines were seen as overly alien, with their yellow skins, oblique eyes, and long pigtails. Despite their diligent work ethic and personal cleanliness, the fact that they persisted in dressing and behaving very differently from their American coworkers made them subjects of mean-spirited name-calling and treatment. They were routinely accused of having a fondness for eating rats and dogs and being unable to distinguish in their speech between *l*'s and *r*'s. Moreover, they were rumored to be linked to crime syndicates and white slavery rings, to carry leprosy, to smoke opium, and to gamble obsessively. The fact that Chinese laborers were actually among the hardest-working, most steadfast, and most intrepid workers on the railroad lines and in the gold mines did little to change the negative preconceptions held by many Americans during the nineteenth century.

The immigration waves between the end of Reconstruction (1877) and beginning of World War I (1914-1918) brought large numbers of new immigrant groups to the United States. Increasing numbers of eastern and southern Europeans began arriving, looking for work and better lives, as their predecessors had done. These immigrants were non-Protestant for the most part and were consequently promptly disliked because of their religions. Some Americans believed rumors that many of these new immigrants had been expelled from their homelands because they were, at best, petty criminals. By the time World War I began, most new immigrants were being stereotyped as "slum-creating, soap-shy, illiterate, jargon-speaking, standoffish"

interlopers without civilized values. Depending on their specific origins, they were labeled as "dagos," "wops," "hunkys," "bohunks," "polacks," and "yids."

MODERN IMMIGRANT STEREOTYPES

Since passage of the U.S. Immigration and Nationality Act of 1965, many immigrants from non-European countries have flooded into the United States, causing Americans new concerns and generating new types of stereotypes. As in the past, most of the new immigrants from Asia, Africa, the Middle East, and Latin America have come looking for work. Others, however, have come to escape from natural disasters, persecution, and wars in their homelands. Despite the fact that many of these immigrants have been well educated, professionally trained, and even financially well off, they have been targets of damaging negative stereotypes.

One prevailing stereotype of immigrants who arrive with little money and with school-age children is that they drain America's health care system. They take advantage of emergency rooms in urban hospitals and most often do so without the ability to pay for the services they get. As more and more hospitals close their emergency rooms altogether, the reduction in medical care for all residents of the area is blamed on the inundation of immigrants seeking care that the taxpayers must pay for.

The stereotypes of immigrant workers who take jobs away from native-born Americans and contribute to lowering wage scales has continued to persist. Because of the notion that without the immigrants' ready acceptance of menial work and lower wages, American workers would command higher wages. Consequently, immigrants are often as "scabs" in the workplace.

Immigrants do in fact take jobs that most Americans do not want, such as fruit picking, lawn care and gardening, maid and child care, washing cars, and cooking—especially in fast food restaurants, Many of these jobs can be done "off the books," saving employers from having to withhold taxes or pay benefits, thereby making such workers even more attractive. American-born workers disparage immigrants for accepting such jobs because they themselves would take such jobs if the pay rates were higher.

Immigrants who have brought their families

with them or who marry in the United States and begin raising their children are accused of draining America's educational resources. Their children, who often speak no English when they start school, must first be taught enough English to permit them to assimilate into regular classes. The outlay of time and money to provide this extra instruction is obviously more than what the normal expenditures for a school system would be. So school boards must make budget adjustments to accommodate these necessary costs, which too often result in the elimination of other, popular academic programs. The idea that immigrants are thereby damaging the educational system is another common stereotype.

In addition to these drains on the nation's economy, some Americans level another charge that contributes to negative stereotyping: the idea that immigrants avoid paying taxes despite all the benefits they receive. If illegal immigrants do not pay taxes on their earnings, it is usually because doing so would bring them to the attention of the government and possibly lead to their deportation. On the other hand, legal immigrants have been found to pay more taxes and contribute more to the Social Security System than they receive in government benefits.

Jane L. Ball

FURTHER READING

Barkau, Eliot R. *And Still They Come: Immigrants and American Society, 1920 to the 1990's.* Wheeling, Ill.: Harlan Davidson, 1996. Broad history of twentieth century immigration with chapters dealing on anti-Semitism, refugee concerns, and wartime issues regarding ethnicity. Illustrated with photographs.

Berry, Gordon L., and Joy Asamen, eds. *Children and TV: Images in a Changing Socio-Cultural World.* Thousand Oaks, Calif.: Sage Publications, 1993. General work on the influence of television on children, with chapters devoted to stereotyping of members of specific ethnic groups in programs.

Browder, Laura. *Slippery Characters: Ethnic Impersonators and American Identities.* Chapel Hill: University of North Carolina Press, 2000. Discussion of the ways in which people have passed themselves off as being members of different ethnic groups throughout American history.

Ferrie, Joseph P. *Yankeys Now: Immigrants in the Antebellum United States, 1840-1860.* New York: Oxford University Press, 1999. Examination of early nineteenth century immigration, with chapters on discrimination against immigrants, particularly the Irish.

Hechinger, Kevin, and Curtis Hechinger. *Hechinger's Field Guide to Ethnic Stereotypes.* New York: Simon & Schuster, 2009. Humorously written and intriguing look at ethnic Americans, categorized as "Blacks," "Browns," "Whites," "Yellows," and "Exotic Breeds."

Lester, Paul M., and Susan D. Ross, eds. *Images That Injure: Pictorial Stereotypes in the Media.* Westport, Conn.: Praeger, 1996. Collection of essays about how visual images have helped to perpetuate misleading ethnic and other stereotypes and the societal consequences.

Shaheen, Jack. *Reel Bad Arabs: How Hollywood Vilifies a People.* New York: Olive Branch Press, 2001. Discusses twentieth century portrayals of Arabs and Muslims in eight hundred films, alphabetically arranged with descriptions of particular scenes in which negative stereotyping occurs.

Takaki, Ronald. *A Different Mirror: A History of Multicultural America.* Rev. ed. New York: Back Bay Books, 2008. Explores Anglo attitudes toward various other cultural and ethnic groups and races, and how those groups struggle to make a new life in America.

SEE ALSO: Anglo-conformity; Anti-Defamation League; Arab immigrants; Chinese immigrants; Crime; Films; Irish immigrants; Italian immigrants; Jewish immigrants; Mexican immigrants; "Model minorities"; "Undesirable aliens."

STRAUSS, LEVI

IDENTIFICATION: German-born American clothing manufacturer and philanthropist

BORN: February 26, 1829; Buttenheim, Bavaria (now in Germany)

DIED: September 26, 1902; San Francisco, California

SIGNIFICANCE: A civic-minded industrialist, Levi Strauss founded a large clothing business that was dedicated to the fair treatment of its workers, a large part of whom were immigrants.

Born in German Bavaria in 1829, Leob "Levi" Strauss was the youngest child of Jewish parents, Hirsch and Rebecca Strauss. His father earned a modest income as a dry-goods peddler but died from tuberculosis in 1845, when Levi was only sixteen. At that time, anti-Semitism was widespread in Bavaria, so Levi's two older brothers emigrated from the country to the United States. They settled in New York City, where they opened a dry-goods business in a large Jewish community. Two years later, Levi, his mother, and his sisters acquired exit visas and passports that enabled them to emigrate and join the brothers in New York City, where Levi initially peddled dry goods.

In 1853, Strauss became an American citizen at the age of twenty-four. During that same year, he traveled west to California's gold rush country to establish a West Coast branch of his brothers' dry-goods business. Near the wharves of San Francisco, he ran a shop with a brother-in-law, David Stern. Very soon he realized that one of the region's greatest needs was for durable pants suitable for gold mining work. To meet that demand, he designed heavy-duty overalls made with denim fabric that rapidly became popular.

In 1863, the family company was renamed "Levi Strauss & Co." By 1870, Strauss himself was already a millionaire. He teamed with an immigrant tailor, Jacob Davis, contributing the sixty-eight dollar filing fee on a patent to add copper rivets to stress-points on the pants' seams. They received the patent on May 20, 1873.

Eager to share his good fortune, Strauss helped build a synagogue and establish an orphanage. As a member of the California Immigrant Union he encouraged immigration and promoted California products. He died in 1902 at the age of seventy-three, leaving bequests to Hebrew, Roman Catholic, and Protestant charities.

Lisa A. Wroble

FURTHER READING

Ford, Carin T. *Levi Strauss: The Man Behind Blue Jeans.* Berkeley Heights, N.J.: Enslow, 2004.

Henry, Sondra, and Emily Taitz. *Everyone Wears His Name: A Biography of Levi Strauss.* New York: Dillon Press, 1990.

SEE ALSO: California; California gold rush; Garment industry; German immigrants; Jewish immigrants; San Francisco.

SUPREME COURT, U.S.

DEFINITION: Highest court in the United States

> **SIGNIFICANCE:** Judgments and interpretations of the U.S. Supreme Court have been crucially important in the development of immigration law, including issues such as the constitutional powers of Congress, the legal rights of resident noncitizens, and the rules for deportation proceedings.

Immigration law is primarily a function of statutes and executive regulations. Armed with its established power of judicial review, the Supreme Court makes binding rulings on both the meanings and constitutionality of such statutes and regulations. Although the Constitution does not directly mention either immigration or the rights of aliens, it delegates to Congress the powers to regulate "commerce with foreign nations" and to establish a "uniform rule of naturalization." Another relevant provision is the supremacy clause, which recognizes that federal statutes and treaties are equally part of the "supreme law of the land," so long as they are not in conflict with the Constitution. Combining these provisions with legal traditions, the Supreme Court held in *Chae Chan Ping v. United States* (1889) that the authority to exclude foreigners was "an incident of sovereignty belonging to the government of the United States as a part of those sovereign powers delegated by the Constitution."

Based on this "plenary power doctrine," the Supreme Court has recognized that foreigners seeking to enter the United States have almost no constitutional rights that Congress must respect. Noncitizens legally residing in the country, however, are entitled to at least some of the legal rights that are enjoyed by citizens. In deportation proceedings, the federal government is bound by the due process clause of the Fifth Amendment. However, because deportation is classified as a civil sanction rather than a criminal punishment, the Court has held that most constitutional protections—including the Sixth Amendment's right to counsel and the Fifth Amendment's privilege against self-incrimination—are generally not applicable to the proceedings.

CONGRESSIONAL POWERS AND FEDERALISM

Immigration laws and regulations, by their nature, raise delicate questions concerning federalism—that is, the sharing of powers between the national government and the states. Before the 1880's, the national government did little to regulate immigration. The coastal states with large ports, therefore, established institutions and procedures for the admission of foreigners. Although state governments tended to be liberal in their admission policies, they attempted to restrict the number of persons who were indigent, diseased, or mentally disabled.

In order to help finance these needy immigrants, New York and a few other states required ships' captains to pay a head tax and maintain control over each passenger. The Supreme Court in *New York v. Miln* (1837), its first major immigration decision, sustained the law as a legitimate application of the state's police power. Justice Philip P. Barbour avoided the issue of the congressional powers, instead focusing on the need for the state legislature to protect citizens from the problems and costs associated with paupers and other undesirable persons.

Slightly more than a decade later, the Supreme Court essentially reversed the *Miln* decision in the *Passenger Cases* (1849), prohibiting the states from placing taxes on immigrants. This was followed by *Cooley v. Board of Wardens of the Port of Philadelphia* (1852), which explicitly recognized Congress's exclusive power to regulate interstate commerce and prohibited the states from interfering with a system of national uniformity. Expanding on these two rulings in *Henderson v. Mayor of the City of New York* (1875), the Supreme Court overturned state laws requiring ships to post bonds on entering immigrants in order to help pay the costs of those needing assistance. Because the decision made it clear that almost all state laws restricting immigration would be ruled unconstitutional, the states began to abolish their institutions for regulating immigration.

The dismantling of state regulatory agencies took place at the same time when the "new immigration" from Europe was beginning. In response, in 1882 Congress enacted its first major immigration law, which imposed a head tax of fifty cents on each immigrant and prohibited the admittance of those who were paupers, insane, or suffering from a contagious disease. When shipping companies challenged the constitutionality of the tax, the Supreme Court upheld its constitutionality in the *Head Money Cases* (1884). Reaffirming the federal government's plenary power over foreign commerce, the Court held that the head tax was actually a "mere incident of the regulation of commerce." Acknowledging that the law was in conflict with a foreign treaty, moreover, the Court held that Congress had the unfettered power to override treaties by way of legislation.

CHINESE EXCLUSION LAWS

Between 1882 and 1902, Congress enacted a series of Chinese exclusion laws. The first such statute, passed in 1882, prohibited Chinese laborers and miners from entering the country. An amendment of 1884 required Chinese laborers leaving the country to have a reentry certificate in order to return. Later that year, the Supreme Court ruled on the enforcement of the legislation in *Chew Heong v. United States* (1884). Chew Heong, a Chinese laborer who had left the country in 1881, was denied reentry because of his lack of a certificate. By a 7-2 majority, the Court overturned the refusal as a violation of Heong's legal rights. Justice John Marshall Harlan's opinion for the Court addressed two major arguments. First, Heong was qualified to obtain a certificate, and he could not be required to do what was impossible for him to do. Second, the denial of his right to return contradicted a treaty with China. Since Congress had not clearly and unambiguously expressed its intent to repeal the treaty, Harlan explained, the Court was required to reconcile the provisions of the treaty with those of the legislation.

In 1888, Congress enacted the more stringent Scott Act, which included a provision prohibiting Chinese residents from returning to the United States if they traveled abroad. Chae Chan Ping had left for a visit to China in 1887, and he attempted reentry a few days after the Scott Act went into effect. Chae challenged the constitutionality of the law, based on its incompatibility with U.S. treaties with China. In the resulting *Chae Chan Ping v. United States* (1889), the Supreme Court unanimously rejected Chae's challenge and upheld the law, based on the inherent power of a sovereign nation to establish its own immigration policies. The opinion for the Court also reaffirmed the authority of Congress to repeal or to modify a treaty as it deemed appropriate.

The Geary Act of 1892 continued the earlier restrictions and also required that all Chinese laborers had to have residency certificates or face deportation. When Fong Yue Ting and two other Chinese residents were found not to have certificates, they were ordered to be deported. In the resulting case of *Fong Yue Ting v. United States* (1893), the Supreme Court upheld the deportations and recognized that the government's power to deport foreigners "is as absolute and unqualified as the right to prohibit and prevent their entrance into the country." The next year, Congress authorized immigration officials to make final decisions concerning which aliens to exclude from admission, without the privilege of habeas corpus relief in the federal courts. The Supreme Court upheld this limit on due process rights in *Lem Moon Sing v. United States* (1895), which meant that immigration officials no longer had to worry about being overruled by judges.

STATE GOVERNMENTS AND ALIENAGE

The rights guaranteed under the Fourteenth Amendment's due process clause and equal protection clause apply to "any person" within a state's jurisdiction, which includes aliens legally residing in the country. The Supreme Court's first important case involving the states' regulations of such persons was *Yick Wo v. Hopkins* (1886), which struck down a San Francisco ordinance requiring laundries in wooden buildings to obtain a license from city authorities. Although the ordinance appeared to be neutral on its face, the Court determined that its application was so grossly discriminatory against Chinese laundries that it violated the Fourteenth Amendment. The opinion in the case was somewhat unclear about the specific ways in which aliens enjoy equal rights.

The Supreme Court clarified this issue in *Truax v. Raich* (1915), striking down an Arizona law requiring citizenship for 80 percent of the employees in most businesses. In writing the opinion for the Court, Justice Charles Evans Hughes focused on the law's effect of depriving alien residents of their right to earn a livelihood. The right to work in the common occupations, he declared, was "the very essence of the personal freedom and opportunity

Under Chief Justice Earl Warren, the Supreme Court began one of its most activist periods. Members of the court during the late 1960's included (clockwise from upper left) Abe Fortas, Potter Stewart, Byron R. White, Thurgood Marshall, William J. Brennan, Jr., William O. Douglas, Warren, Hugo L. Black, and John Marshall Harlan II. (Harris and Ewing/Collection of the Supreme Court of the United States)

that it was the purpose of the Fourteenth Amendment to secure." In addition, the power to admit or to exclude immigrants was vested exclusively in the federal government. State legislation that deprived such persons of their right to earn a livelihood was "tantamount to denying their entrance and abode." The Arizona law, therefore, violated principles of federalism under the supremacy clause.

The Supreme Court, nevertheless, has sometimes authorized significant limitations on the rights of immigrants as a class. In the case of *Patsone v. Pennsylvania* (1914), for example, the Court upheld a state law forbidding noncitizens from hunting wild game. Justice Oliver Wendell Holmes wrote that it was reasonable for a state to reserve its limited natural resources for the exclusive use of its citizens. Holmes even allowed the state to prohibit noncitizens from owning shotguns and rifles, because such weapons were presumably not necessary for purposes other than hunting. In a similar ruling, *Terrace v. Thompson* (1923), the Court upheld a Washington State law that severely restricted the right of aliens to own or lease land for agriculture. Such a right, in the Court's view, was not necessary for earning a livelihood, and the states had a strong interest in controlling which persons use large portions of farming land. Although acknowledging that a treaty with Japan authorized immigrants to lease land as necessary to "carry on trade," the Court concluded that trading activities were different from agricultural production.

STANDARDS OF REVIEW FOR ALIENAGE

After World War II, the Supreme Court began developing different standards of review for examining governmental classifications that are challenged as violating persons' rights to equal protection. The Court gradually arrived at three main standards: ordinary scrutiny, strict scrutiny, and intermediate scrutiny. In *Korematsu v. United States* (1944), which upheld the constitutionality of the relocation of persons of Japanese ancestry, Justice Hugo L. Black wrote in the majority opinion that racial classifications were "inherently suspect" and therefore subject to the "most rigid scrutiny." The classification, therefore, could be justified only by a compelling government interest. In the *Korematsu* case, the need to protect against espionage outweighed the rights of the individual. When the classification is based on age, the Court has used

ordinary scrutiny, asking only if the policy is reasonable. In gender classifications, the Court has usually used intermediate scrutiny.

During the early 1970's, the Supreme Court explicitly applied strict scrutiny to governmental regulations that discriminated against aliens in public benefits and employment opportunities. The landmark decision was *Graham v. Richardson* (1971), which overturned Arizona's law denying welfare benefits to aliens. Recognizing that such aliens are a discrete and politically powerless minority, the Court refused to accept the state's argument that giving funds to them would make it impossible to provide citizens with adequate benefits. The Court also applied strict scrutiny in *In re Griffiths* (1973), which held that the Fourteenth Amendment prohibited the states from denying noncitizens the right to practice law.

A few years later, however, in *Foley v. Connelie* (1978), the Supreme Court applied a lesser standard of review in upholding a New York law that required U.S. citizenship in order to serve on the state's police force. A 6-3 majority of the justices accepted the theory that states need only show a rational relationship between a valid governmental interest and a classification limiting the rights of aliens. In evaluating such criteria, the majority opinion referred to the citizenship role of police offices and to the states' long-standing precedents of excluding "aliens from participation in its democratic political institutions," "the basic functions of government." In the case of *Ambach v. Norwick* (1979), the majority of the justices accepted *Foley's* "political function" rationale in upholding a state law that barred aliens from teaching in the public schools.

In the case of *Bernal v. Fainter* (1984), however, the Court, by an 8-1 majority, explicitly returned to the standard of strict scrutiny, which resulted in the invalidation of a Texas law that barred aliens from working as notary publics. In an attempt to reconcile the *Foley-Ambach* precedents with *Bernal*, Justice Thurgood Marshall argued that the former decisions had been based on a "political function" exception, which referred to positions clothed with significant discretion and authority to promote the values of democratic citizenship.

In the controversial 5-4 ruling in *Plyler v. Doe* (1982), the Supreme Court struck down a Texas law denying undocumented children the free public education available to other children in the state. Because undocumented aliens were in the country in violation of federal law, Justice William J. Brennan acknowledged that they were not a suspect class. Rather than strict scrutiny, therefore, the majority applied an intermediate standard of heightened scrutiny. In order to justify the denial of educational opportunity to innocent children under this standard, the majority required the state to show that such denial would promote a "substantial state interest," and they concluded that the state had failed to meet this burden. In 1994, the *Plyler* decision would provide part of the rationale for the federal courts to forbid California from enforcing Proposition 187, which would have denied most nonemergency benefits to illegal immigrants.

REVIEWS OF DEPORTATION ORDERS

The Supreme Court has rarely overturned the procedures used in the deportation of persons illegally residing in the country. The case of *Immigration and Naturalization Service v. Lopez-Mendoza* (1984), for example, dealt with the challenge of two undocumented Mexican immigrants who had been arrested contrary to the Fourth Amendment's prohibition against unreasonable searches and seizures. The two men argued that their confessions were the fruit of an illegal arrest, so that the confessions should be suppressed according to the exclusionary rule. The Supreme Court, however, ruled that the rights of Fourth Amendment apply only minimally to civil deportation procedures. The Court found that the Immigration and Naturalization Service (INS) maintained an acceptable oversight program to monitor constitutional compliance. Deportation hearings, unlike criminal trials, were designed to prevent continuing violations of the law, and the minor benefits of the exclusionary rule would not justify releasing a defendant whose mere presence is a violation of the laws.

In 1996, Congress enacted the Anti-terrorism and Effective Death Penalty Act (AEDPA) and the Illegal Immigration Reform and Immigrant Responsibility Act (IIRIRA), both of which limited the role of the courts to provide judicial review of deportation orders. In *Reno v. American-Arab Anti-Discrimination Committee* (1999), the Supreme Court examined the application of the law toward eight resident aliens who belonged to an organiza-

tion believed to support terrorism and communism. None of the eight had been accused of a crime, and they claimed to be victims of selective enforcement, in violation of their rights to free speech and association under the First Amendment. After the lower courts denied their petition for review, the Supreme Court upheld the deportations. Justice Antonin Scalia wrote in the majority opinion that "an alien unlawfully in this country has no constitutional right to assert selective enforcement as a defense against his deportation."

The *American-Arab Anti-Discrimination Committee* decision failed to clarify whether federal courts might have jurisdiction for habeas corpus relief in some other instances of deportation orders. In *Immigration and Naturalization Service v. St. Cyr* (2001), the Court by a 5-4 majority decided that the AEDPA and IIRIRA did not eliminate opportunities for such relief in most situations. Claiming that the language in the legislation was ambiguous, Justice John Paul Stevens asserted that the terms "judicial review" and "habeas corpus" had different meanings, and since denying a person the opportunity to seek a writ of habeas corpus probably violated the Constitution, the legislation should be interpreted in a manner that avoided examination of the constitutional issue.

In *Zadvydas v. Davis* (2001), the Supreme Court put a limit on the time during which immigration officials are allowed to keep deportable aliens in custody while attempting to relocate them. When the INS ordered the deportation of Kestutis Zadvydas because of his criminal record, officials could not find a country willing to accept him. In balancing his liberty interest against possible threats to the community, the Court disallowed detention for more than nine months, except when the government could present strong evidence that civil confinement was justified.

NATURALIZATION AND DENATURALIZATION

Because Article I of the Constitution authorizes Congress to establish universal rules concerning the naturalization process, the Supreme Court has very rarely questioned congressional judgment in the matter. In *United States v. Macintosh* (1931), the Court underscored congressional discretion when it upheld a law requiring applicants to pledge unconditionally to take up arms in defense of the country. The majority opinion defined naturalization as "a privilege, to be given, qualified, or withheld as Congress may determine." The Court has never challenged the constitutionality of discriminatory regulations that deny naturalization on grounds such as extremist political affiliations, continuing polygamy, prior criminal records, or lack of English proficiency.

Since naturalized citizens are considered equal to native-born citizens, however, the Supreme Court has placed an extremely high burden of proof for denaturalization. In *Schneiderman v. United States* (1943), the Court held that the federal government could not revoke the citizenship of a naturalized citizen because he had worked as an active member of the Communist Party after entering the country. The opinion for the Court insisted that denaturalization would require compelling and clear justification, such as treason or renunciation of citizenship. In *Afroyim v. Rusk* (1967), the Court overturned the provision in the Nationality Act of 1940 that authorized loss of citizenship for having voted in a foreign election. In several cases, however, the Court has allowed the government to revoke citizenship if there is proof that dishonest information was given in the naturalization process. In *Fedorenko v. United States* (1981), for example, the Court upheld the denaturalization of a person who had falsely claimed not to have participated in Nazi activities during World War II.

Thomas Tandy Lewis

FURTHER READING

Aleinikoff, Thomas, et al. *Immigration and Citizenship: Process and Policy.* 6th ed. St. Paul, Minn.: West Group, 2008. Comprehensive resource with good summaries and readable discussions of major laws and court decisions.

Bosniak, Linda. *The Citizen and the Alien: Dilemmas of Contemporary Membership.* Princeton, N.J.: Princeton University Press, 2006. Addresses the complex issues of alienage law and the sociological aspects of outsider status.

Epstein, Lee, and Thomas Walker. *Constitutional Law for a Changing America.* 6th ed. 2 vols. Washington, D.C.: CQ Press, 2006-2007. Readable and interesting textbook written primarily for undergraduate students, with one volume devoted to constitutional rights and the other volume discussing the institutional powers of the government.

Hull, Elizabeth. *Without Justice for All: The Constitutional Rights of Aliens.* Westport, Conn.: Greenwood Press, 1985. Critical examination of the limited constitutional rights of resident noncitizens, temporary visitors, and undocumented aliens.

Hyung-chan, Kim, ed. *Asian Americans and the Supreme Court: A Documentary History.* Westport, Conn.: Greenwood Press, 1992. Critiques of major decisions relating to the admissions, civil rights, and deportations of Asian Americans during the last 150 years.

Neuman, Gerald L. *Strangers to the Constitution: Immigration, Borders, and Fundamental Law.* Princeton, N.J.: Princeton University Press, 1996. Dependable study of the controversies, laws, and court decisions concerning the rights of aliens and their children from the debates of 1798 until the late twentieth century.

Salyer, Lucy. *Laws as Harsh as Tigers: Chinese Immigrants and the Shaping of Modern Immigration Law.* Chapel Hill: University of North Carolina Press, 1995. Interesting account of the social and legal restrictions on Chinese immigration to the United States from 1891 until 1924.

SEE ALSO: Congress, U.S.; Constitution, U.S.; Due process protections; Frankfurter, Felix; Immigration law; Naturalization.

SWEATSHOPS

DEFINITION: Term originally applied to crowded urban workplaces in which piecework farmed out by manufacturers was done by low-wage employees; in modern usage, the term has come to be applied to almost any crowded workplace with unsafe and unsanitary working conditions

SIGNIFICANCE: Since the term "sweatshop" was coined in America during the 1890's, immigrants and other urban poor, including children, have made up the bulk of sweatshop workers. The term was originally associated with the garment industry but has been broadened to encompass many other small-scale manufacturing and assembling industries. The central common characteristics of sweatshops have been crowded and unhealthy working conditions and low pay and long hours. In 2000, the U.S. Department of Labor defined "sweatshops" broadly as workplaces that violate at least two federal or state labor laws pertaining to child labor, overtime pay and minimum wages, safety and health standards, workers' compensation, and other matters.

From their first emergence in American cities, sweatshops have been associated with public moral indignation. Attempts to eliminate them have taken many forms, but reformers have agreed that whether sweatshops are located in private homes or factories in the United States or other countries producing items for sale in the United States, they represent a danger to society and should be eliminated.

EARLY SWEATSHOPS

Sweatshops first arose in American cities—most notably New York City—during the nineteenth century and were made possible by the large numbers of impoverished immigrants willing to endure poor working conditions for low wages. The earliest sweatshops serviced the garment industry, in which making clothes involved many separate operations that could easily be farmed out to pieceworkers. Working in usually close quarters, each worker in a garment sweatshop typically performed only one or two operations for each garment, which was passed from worker to worker. Many early sweatshops attracted eastern European Jewish immigrants. Later, large numbers of immigrants from Italy and other European regions, such as Bohemia, joined the ranks of sweatshop workers.

During the nineteenth century, criticisms of sweatshops took many forms. Some reformers attempting to close down sweatshops regarded them as alien institutions that had no place in American industry, which they believed should be built on large factories. They also criticized sweatshops for retarding the assimilation of immigrants into American life. Other critics saw sweatshops as threats

Garment workers in a New York City sweatshop in 1908. (Library of Congress)

to families because they employed women who should have been taking care of their homes and children. They also complained about the close proximity in which men and women in sweatshops worked, especially in hot weather, when workers often removed their outer garments. Still other critics feared that workers in such close conditions would breed diseases and worried that the garments the workers produced would spread those diseases, especially tuberculosis, to member of the middle class who bought them.

Wages paid in the sweatshops tended to be extremely low. Employers often paid as little as possible so as to maximize their profits. Nevertheless, despite low pay and poor working conditions, many eastern European Jewish immigrants worked in sweatshops run by other Jews because they preferred to work under Jewish bosses, could speak Yiddish freely while working, and could take off Saturdays, the Jewish Sabbath. Some immigrants saw working in sweatshops as the first small step toward becoming rich in the New World. Others, however, saw them as inescapable traps. As the work in the sweatshops became increasingly routine, demanding less in the way of skilled labor, immigrants without skills were drawn to work in them.

MODERN SWEATSHOPS

The International Ladies' Garment Workers' Union eventually managed to unionize many sweatshops and factories and strove to improve their working conditions. However, despite union and legislative efforts to end sweatshop conditions, sweatshops have survived into the twenty-first century.

During the 1950's, Puerto Rican and other Latin American, African, and Asian immigrants to the United States became associated with the sweatshop's return. At the same time, sweatshops engaged in producing clothes for American markets began appearing in many of the countries from which the immigrants were coming. Labels in clothes sold in American retail stores reveal the wide range of countries in which they are made—from Central America to Africa to Southeast Asia.

Modern sweatshops in the United States tend to operate on the fringes of the law, ignoring legal workplace standards and hiring both documented and undocumented immigrants. As in the nine-teenth century, sweatshops have been particularly common in the garment industry. Occasionally, they make headlines when federal immigration officers raid them to round up undocumented immigrants and discover horrible working conditions in them.

Richard Tuerk

FURTHER READING

Bender, Daniel E. *Sweated Work, Weak Bodies: Anti-Sweatshop Campaigns and Languages of Labor.* New Brunswick, N.J.: Rutgers University Press, 2005. Examination of the ways in which the antisweatshop movement and antisweatshop rhetoric have both helped and hurt workers.

Bender, Daniel E., and Richard A. Greenwald, eds. *Sweatshop USA: The American Sweatshop in Historical Perspective.* New York: Routledge, 2003. Set of essays that treat political, social, cultural, and economic aspects of sweatshops from their beginnings in the United States to their overseas manifestations in the twenty-first century.

Fung, Archon, Dara O'Rourke, and Charles Sabel. *Can We Put an End to Sweatshops?* Boston: Beacon Press, 2002. Critical study of modern sweatshops throughout the world that is concerned with finding ways to make them unnecessary.

Hapke, Laura. *Sweatshop: The History of an American Idea.* New Brunswick, N.J.: Rutgers University Press, 2004. Examination of the words used to describe sweatshops to find out what the term "sweatshop" means to the American imagination.

SEE ALSO: Captive Thai workers; Child immigrants; Economic opportunities; Employment; Garment industry; Infectious diseases; International Ladies' Garment Workers' Union; Jewish immigrants; Labor unions; Triangle Shirtwaist fire.

SWISS IMMIGRANTS

SIGNIFICANCE: Among the earliest non-English peoples to settle in the United States, the Swiss have always constituted a comparatively small immigrant group who have settled throughout the United States. Despite their relatively small numbers, they have

Swiss-born politician Albert Gallatin served in the U.S. Senate and was secretary of the treasury under Presidents Thomas Jefferson and James Madison. (Library of Congress)

made significant contributions to American industry, politics, science, religion and other fields.

Although the Swiss were among the first non-English peoples to enter what is now the United States, they have never constituted a large immigrant group. Indeed, they have seldom accounted for more than 1 to 2 percent of all incoming immigrants. Nevertheless, their impact as a group has been noticeable—from midwestern agricultural landscapes to the denominational landscaping of American Christianity. Moreover, they have also contributed more than their numerical share of distinguished public figures, such as the Jeffersonian politician and diplomat Albert Gallatin, the pioneer of American psychiatry Adolf Meyer, and the self-taught engineer and entrepreneur Louis Chevrolet, for whom an American automobile was named.

The majority of Swiss immigrants to the United States have been German speakers, but members of Switzerland's French- and Italian-speaking minorities have also come in substantial numbers. Speakers of Romansh, a tiny minority within Switzerland, have, however, never immigrated to the United States in significant numbers.

COLONIAL ERA

Swiss immigration to British North America began before the eighteenth century on a very small scale. The first Swiss person known to have visited the continent was the Bernese Diebold von Erlach, a young member of a failed French Huguenot settlement in Florida during the mid-sixteenth century. The first Swiss to participate in English colonial schemes were probably the several "Switzer" craftsmen who joined the initial wave of settlers at Jamestown, Virginia, in 1619. In the century that followed, some notable immigrants from Switzerland settled in the British colonies. These included the wealthy Jean François Gignilliat of Vevey, who in 1687 received a grant of three thousand acres from the proprietors of South Carolina, where he settled the following year.

The eighteenth century witnessed a surge in Swiss immigration to America, with 25,000 immigrants coming to British America before 1776. Religious persecution, social unrest, and the frail economic position of an early modern society with a paucity of arable land and few natural resources were major push factors that helped prompt their emigration from Switzerland. Reports circulated by colonial promoters and returning Swiss immigrants of the fertile soils, low taxes, and boundless opportunities in the New World helped attract new immigrants.

Swiss immigrants settled in a number of British colonies, but North Carolina's New Bern settlement, founded in 1710, and South Carolina's Purrysburg, founded in 1734, were important sites of early Swiss settlement in the southern colonies. Pennsylvania drew the largest number of immigrants from Switzerland. Many were pietist dissenters, such as the Swiss Brethren, who became known as Mennonites in America. These people were strongly attracted by Pennsylvania's reputation for religious toleration. Most other Swiss immigrants were members of the state Reformed Church who came to the colony primarily for economic reasons.

EARLY NATIONAL PERIOD

While Swiss immigrants continued to trickle into the new United States during the last decades of the eighteenth century and the first decades of the nineteenth century, the next great surge of Swiss immigration came after 1820. Between that year and 1900, about 200,000 Swiss came to the country. The main cause of this immigration wave was the contrast between the severely contracted economic opportunities in Switzerland and the reportedly abundant opportunities in America.

About 60 percent of Swiss immigrants settled in rural areas—especially in the Midwest, where the first significant Swiss settlement of the century, Nouevelle Vevey, was established in Indiana by French-speaking Swiss viticulturists. This trend continued during the second half of the nineteenth century, when Ohio, Indiana, Missouri, Illinois, Iowa, and Wisconsin were favored destinations for Swiss immigrants. However, significant numbers of immigrants continued to settle in Pennsylvania and neighboring states, and small colonies of Swiss also appeared in states such as Kentucky, West Virginia, and Tennessee during this period. California also attracted Swiss settlers, especially Italian-speaking laborers from Canton Ticino, who began arriving

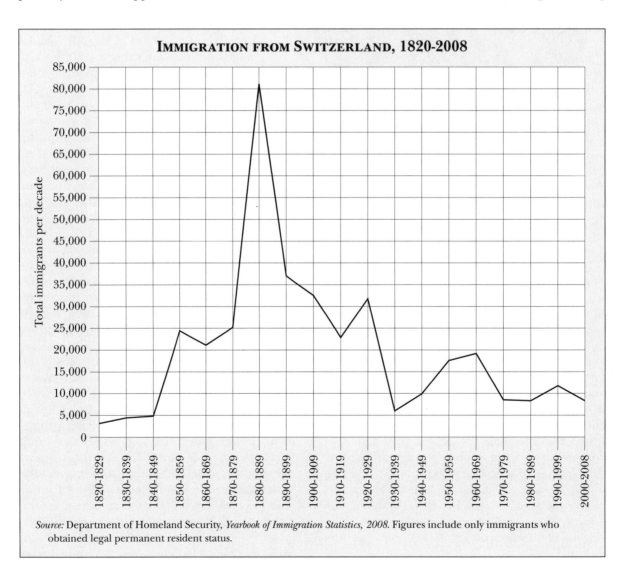

IMMIGRATION FROM SWITZERLAND, 1820-2008

Source: Department of Homeland Security, *Yearbook of Immigration Statistics, 2008.* Figures include only immigrants who obtained legal permanent resident status.

in significant numbers during the last two decades of the nineteenth century.

Immigration was often encouraged by letters from immigrants in America to family and friends back in Switzerland, and it was maintained by the social and economic support networks created by chain migrations of communities. In some cases, Switzerland's cantonal governments—eager to purge poor rolls and dispose of "undesirables"—subsidized some emigration from Switzerland. In at least one case, a canton directly financed the establishment of a major Swiss settlement in the United States: New Glarus (named after its government benefactor, Canton Glarus) in Wisconsin.

Nineteenth century Swiss immigrants were religiously diverse, with both Roman Catholics and Protestants well represented. Members of the Swiss Brethren continued to arrive in America, and they sometimes joined with their Swiss Mennonite cousins, whose forebears had come in colonial times. American Mormon missionaries in Europe helped create a new category of Swiss immigrants, as about 1,000 of their faithful converts settled in Utah and Idaho.

TWENTIETH CENTURY

Swiss immigration followed similar patterns during the first two decades of the twentieth century. Although the peak decade of the 1880's, during which more than 80,000 Swiss arrived in the United States, would never be repeated, the numbers were still substantial. Between 1901 and 1920, more than 58,000 Swiss immigrated to the United States. However, the rate of immigration gradually diminished after the Immigration Act of 1924 set quotas. Swiss immigration nearly stopped during the Great Depression of the 1930's. However, during the last decades of the twentieth century, Swiss immigration again became steady, although still demographically almost insignificant, with fewer than 1,000 immigrants per year arriving between 1971 and 2000.

Jeremiah Taylor

FURTHER READING

Commetti, Elizabeth. "Swiss Immigration to West Virginia, 1864-1884." *Mississippi Valley Historical Review* 47 (1960): 66-87. Interesting account of Swiss settlement in Appalachia during the peak years of their immigration.

PROFILE OF SWISS IMMIGRANTS	
Country of origin	Switzerland
Primary languages	German, French
Primary regions of U.S. settlement	Pennsylvania, Wisconsin, Ohio, California, Oregon, and New York City
Earliest significant arrivals	1608
Peak immigration period	1880's-1890's
Twenty-first century legal residents*	7,289 (911 per year)

*Immigrants who obtained legal permanent resident status in the United States.
Source: Department of Homeland Security, *Yearbook of Immigration Statistics, 2008.*

Grueningen, J. P. von. *The Swiss in the United States.* Madison, Wis.: Swiss-American Historical Society, 1940. Older but still indispensable starting point for any study of Swiss immigration. Based on extensive use of U.S. Census data.

Hale, Frederick. *Swiss in Wisconsin.* Madison: Wisconsin Historical Society Press, 2007. Brief examination of the Swiss experience in one of the most popular nineteenth century destinations for German-speaking immigrants.

Haller, Charles R. *Across the Atlantic and Beyond: German and Swiss Immigrants to America.* Bowie, Md.: Heritage Books, 1993. Intended as a sourcebook for genealogists, this volume also contains much useful information for students and historians, including bibliographies.

Schelbert, Leo, ed. *America Experienced: Eighteenth and Nineteenth Century Accounts of Swiss Immigrants.* Camden, Maine: Picton Press, 1996. Excellent collection of primary documents on Swiss immigration to the United States.

SEE ALSO: Chain migration; Einstein, Albert; European immigrants; French immigrants; German immigrants; Guggenheim, Meyer; Pennsylvania; Religions of immigrants; Wisconsin.

T

TAIWANESE IMMIGRANTS

SIGNIFICANCE: During the late twentieth century, Taiwanese became one of the largest and most prosperous immigrant groups from Asia, settling in new Chinatowns and suburbs.

Following the course of Chinese history, immigration from the island of Taiwan to the United States was primarily a late twentieth century phenomenon. Almost no immigrants came from Taiwan until after Chiang Kai-shek established the Republic of China on the island. In earlier centuries, Taiwan was a remote island belonging to the Chinese Empire and populated mostly by Austronesian aborigines and Han Chinese who had come from Fujian

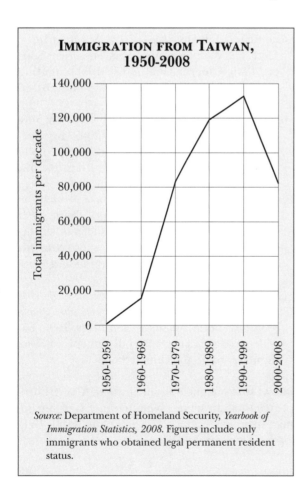

IMMIGRATION FROM TAIWAN, 1950-2008

Source: Department of Homeland Security, *Yearbook of Immigration Statistics, 2008.* Figures include only immigrants who obtained legal permanent resident status.

Province on the Chinese mainland. In 1895, Japan wrested control of the island, which it retained until it was defeated in World War II.

MAINLAND CHINESE IMMIGRATION TO THE UNITED STATES

In contrast to later Taiwanese immigration, large numbers of Chinese from mainland China immigrated to the United States during the second half of the nineteenth century. Most of them came from Hong Kong and Guandong (Canton) Province and settled in and near San Francisco. By the time the U.S. Congress enacted the first Chinese exclusion laws during the 1880's, approximately 300,000 Chinese had immigrated to the United States and lived in Chinatowns throughout the nation. Chinese immigration was sporadic in the following decades until Chinese Exclusion was repealed in 1943. This change was, to some extent, due to the U.S. speaking tour of Soong Mei-ling, the wife of the president of the Republic of China, Chiang Kai-shek. With the end of World War II, China reclaimed Taiwan from Japan. After Mao Zedong's communists took power in China in 1949, Chiang's Nationalist forces found refuge on Taiwan, where Chiang set up a quasi-independent government. As a result of these calamitous events, the first wave of immigration of Chinese from Taiwan began slowly. Meanwhile, emigration from mainland China was forbidden by the new communist government.

LATE TWENTIETH CENTURY IMMIGRATION FROM TAIWAN

With the Republic of China ensconced on the island of Taiwan, Taiwanese immigration to the United States began in earnest. This immigration included two groups of Chinese. The first consisted of ethnic Chinese who were native to Taiwan. These were people whose families had arrived in Taiwan from the mainland in previous centuries and who spoke a language derived from the southern Fujian dialect. The second group comprised Chinese who had more recently arrived with Chiang Kai-shek in response to the communist takeover and spoke Mandarin.

Immigration from Taiwan was prompted by several factors. Because U.S. immigration quotas for Asia had grown less restrictive, Chinese immigrants began coming from all parts of China. At the same time, the looming threat of Taiwan's being invaded by the vastly larger People's Republic of China prompted emigration. Also, the great economic prosperity that Taiwan attained during the 1960's and 1970's also made it economically feasible for many Taiwanese to send their children to study in the United States.

The first stage of immigration from Taiwan occurred between the years immediately after World War II ended until 1965. This stage consisted mostly of students coming to the United States to study for higher degrees. Massachusetts's Wellesley College was a particularly attractive destination for elite Taiwanese women, as it was Madame Chiang Kai-shek's alma mater. Three-quarters of these Taiwanese students remained in the United States after graduating, often taking well-paying jobs.

The second stage of Taiwanese immigration began after U.S. passage of the Immigration and Nationality Act of 1965 (also known as the Hart-Celler Immigration Reform Act). This law eliminated national quotas for immigration and instituted preferences for skilled workers. As a result, many Taiwanese professionals and technical workers

PROFILE OF TAIWANESE IMMIGRANTS	
Country of origin	Taiwan
Primary languages	Chinese (Mandarin), English
Primary regions of U.S. settlement	California
Earliest significant arrivals	1950's
Peak immigration period	1970's-2008
Twenty-first century legal residents*	73,162 (9.145 per year)

*Immigrants who obtained legal permanent resident status in the United States.
Source: Department of Homeland Security, *Yearbook of Immigration Statistics, 2008.*

NOTABLE TAIWANESE IMMIGRANTS

- Elaine Chao, U.S. secretary of labor
- Steve Chen, founder of YouTube
- Madame Chiang Kai-shek, widow of Chiang Kai-shek
- David Ho, AIDS researcher
- Mei-ling Hopgood and Stephen Lo, writers
- Min Kao, billionaire businessman
- Ang Lee, film director
- David Lee, founder of Qume Corporation
- Henry Lee. forensic scientist
- Wen Ho Lee, nuclear physicist
- Chang-Lin Tien, chancellor of the University of California's Berkeley campus
- Samuel Ting and Yuan Tseh Lee, Nobel Prize winners
- David Wu, Oregon congressman
- Jerry Yang, founder of Yahoo!

immigrated to the United States with their families. After arriving in the United States, Taiwanese immigrants helped to create new and more spacious Chinatowns in New York City's Flushing and Queens neighborhoods and in Monterey Park, California. Many of them settled in prosperous new suburban neighborhoods in other cities.

In 1979, the United States switched from recognizing Taiwan as the official government of China to recognizing the People's Republic. However, the Taiwan Relations Act passed during that same year allowed entry for up to 20,000 Taiwanese starting in 1982. With the Republic of China liberalizing its own emigration policy in 1980, a third stage of Taiwanese immigration began.

During the 1980's, American newspapers began reporting on a new kind of Taiwanese immigrants—"parachute children"—children whose parents remained in Taiwan to continue their successful businesses while sending their children to attend public schools in the United States while living on their own. A 1990 study undertaken by the University of California at Los Angeles estimated that as many as 40,000 Taiwanese "parachute kids" were studying in the United States. Most lived in wealthy California suburbs.

TWENTY-FIRST CENTURY TRENDS

By the early twenty-first century, Chinese immigrants from Taiwan were almost equally divided between native Taiwanese and Chinese from the mainland who had arrived in Taiwan after World War II. Divisions between these groups have lessened within Taiwan and are little evident in the Taiwanese communities of the United States.

Between 1984 and 1999, an estimated 200,000 Taiwanese immigrated to the United States, at a rate of about 13,000 per year. By the year 2008, the total number of Taiwanese immigrants in the United States was estimated at about 500,000.

Howard Bromberg

FURTHER READING

Chang, Iris. *The Chinese in America: A Narrative History.* New York: Penguin Books, 2004. History written by the acclaimed author of *The Rape of Nanking* (1997), who was herself the daughter of immigrants from Taiwan. Building from her own experience, Chang tells the story of the Chinese, including Taiwanese, settling in the United States.

Chang, Shenglin. *The Global Silicon Valley Home: Lives and Landscapes Within Taiwanese American Trans-Pacific Culture.* Stanford, Calif.: Stanford University Press, 2006. Scholarly study of Taiwanese-born engineers who commute between homes in Silicon Valley and Taiwan.

Chee, Maria. *Taiwanese American Transnational Families: Women and Kin Work.* New York: Routledge, 2005. Research on Taiwanese immigrant families in which the husbands remain in Taiwan to work based on questionnaires, interviews, and "snowball" sampling.

Chen, Hsiang-shui. *Chinatown No More: Taiwan Immigrants in Contemporary New York.* Ithaca, N.Y.: Cornell University Press, 1992. Case studies of Taiwanese immigrant life in Queens, New York.

Gu, Chien-juh. *Mental Health Among Taiwanese Americans: Gender, Immigration, and Transnational Struggles.* New York: LFB Scholarly Publishing, 2006. Sociological study of mental health experiences of recent Taiwanese immigrants.

Ng, Franklin. *The Taiwanese Americans.* Westport, Conn.: Greenwood Press, 1998. Part of the *New American* series, covering the experiences of Taiwanese Americans in the United States.

SEE ALSO: Asian immigrants; California; Chinatowns; Chinese Exclusion Act of 1882; Chinese immigrants; Hong Kong immigrants; Immigration and Nationality Act of 1965; Parachute children; Yang, Jerry.

TAMMANY HALL

IDENTIFICATION: One of the earliest and most powerful urban political machines, based largely on its ability to deliver the New York City immigrant vote in elections

DATE: Founded in 1789

LOCATION: New York, New York

SIGNIFICANCE: Political machines are organizations designed to keep certain parties or factions in power. One of the earliest political machines to develop in the United States, New York City's Tammany Hall exerted a powerful influence over the city's politics from the mid-nineteenth to the early twentieth centuries. The machine's power was largely built upon its ability to deliver to the Democratic Party the rising immigrant vote in the city.

Tammany Hall took its name from a Delaware Indian chief whose name was variously transcribed as Tammany, Tammend, or Tamanend. Chief Tammany was widely celebrated in the folklore of colonial America as a wise and powerful leader, and he was sometimes called Saint Tammany. In 1789, shortly after the new constitutional form of government had gone into operation, William Mooney, a small businessman in New York City, organized the Society of St. Tammany, which in its early days was also known as the Columbian Order. One purpose of the organization was to provide a kind of people's democratic opposition to what were perceived to be the aristocratic tendencies of the Federalist Party. In its early days, the Society of St. Tammany used many Indian symbols and terms as a way of caricaturing the aristocratic airs of their opponents. Beginning in 1798, Aaron Burr helped to turn the organization into a powerful political force, and the society helped to deliver the New York vote for the Democratic-Republican ticket of Thomas Jefferson and Burr in the 1800 presiden-

"Boss" William Marcy Tweed was one of the most crooked politicians in U.S. history but in his drive to buy and solicit votes, he did much to help immigrants in New York City. (Library of Congress)

tial election. In 1805, the Society of St. Tammany was formally incorporated as a benevolent organization. In 1830, a headquarters building named Tammany Hall was built on East Fourteenth Street. Soon the name of the headquarters became the colloquial name for the political organization.

TAMMANY HALL AND THE IMMIGRANT VOTE

Originally, Irish immigrants and all Roman Catholics were barred from membership in Tammany Hall, but in 1817 Irish militants invaded the organization's offices to protest the group's failure to recognize the rising influence of Irish voters in the city. Irish immigrants to the United States had a significant advantage over many other immigrants because they generally spoke English. With their strong sense of community solidarity and great interest in politics, they quickly became a force to be reckoned with in America. By 1820, the Irish were being accepted as members of Tammany

Hall. Irish leaders came to dominate the machine, helped in part by the flood of Irish immigrants into the city during the potato famine in Ireland (1845-1852). By 1850, more than 130,000 Irish-born people were living in New York City, accounting for about one-quarter of the entire population. By 1855, the Irish made up 34 percent of the city's voters.

Many of these recently arrived Irish immigrants were desperately poor. Tammany Hall perfected the system of delivering votes by providing services for these poor immigrants. The ward boss in each of the city's political wards kept a close eye on his neighborhood. At a time when any public welfare from the state or local government was virtually unknown, the machine gave people in need many kinds of assistance. For example, a man looking for work would be given a referral to a job, or those in legal trouble would be provided a lawyer. If a family's main breadwinner was sick or injured, the machine provided groceries or financial help. In return, those who received this aid were expected to vote for the machine's candidates. The machine also helped immigrants proceed through the naturalization process, and it sometimes fraudulently arranged for an immigrant to be naturalized much earlier than the law allowed. By the end of the 1850's, Irish politicians in New York City were moving into state politics, and their attentions were being courted by national Democratic administrations.

The first New York City mayor backed by the Tammany Hall machine was Fernando Wood, who was elected in 1855. The machine would dominate city hall for the next seventy years, with only minor interruptions. Perhaps the most notorious leader of Tammany Hall was William M. "Boss" Tweed, who came to power in 1868. Tweed, who also held a seat in the New York State senate, presided over a city administration rife with corruption; estimates of the total cost of the various kinds of graft during his ascendancy are between $40 and $200 million. In 1871, Tweed was finally brought down and sent to jail by a reform-minded prosecutor, Samuel J. Tilden, who ironically had gotten his political start in the machine.

DECLINE OF TAMMANY HALL

After Tweed's fall, the power of Tammany Hall was diminished for a time, but during the late

1870's Irish leaders such as "Honest" John Kelly and Richard Croker brought the machine back to prominence. Vestiges of Tammany Hall remained into the 1960's, but much of its power and influence was broken during the 1930's through attacks by President Franklin D. Roosevelt and the reform mayor of New York City, Fiorello La Guardia.

Mark S. Joy

FURTHER READING

Ackerman, Kenneth D. *Boss Tweed: The Rise and Fall of the Corrupt Pol Who Conceived the Soul of Modern New York*. New York: Carroll & Graf, 2005. Well-written narrative of the career of William M. Tweed and the journalists who helped bring about his downfall.

Allen, Oliver E. *The Tiger: The Rise and Fall of Tammany Hall*. Reading, Mass.: Addison-Wesley, 1993. Study of the era and political machine that spawned Boss Tweed.

Callow, Alexander B., Jr. *The Tweed Ring*. New York: Oxford University Press, 1966. Detailed, thoroughly documented history of Tweed and the men he handpicked to defraud the city of New York.

Erie, Steven P. *Rainbow's End: Irish-Americans and the Dilemmas of Urban Machine Politics, 1840-1985*. Berkeley: University of California Press, 1988. Focuses specifically on Irish involvement in several American big-city machines.

Hershkowitz, Leo. *Tweed's New York: Another Look*. Garden City, N.Y.: Doubleday, 1977. Reevaluation of the impact that Tweed and Tammany Hall had on New York City.

Mandelbaum, Seymour J. *Boss Tweed's New York*. New York: John Wiley & Sons, 1965. Study of machine politics that credits Tweed with exerting strong leadership at a time of chaos and change in the growing metropolis of New York City.

Welch, Richard F. *King of the Bowery: Big Tim Sullivan, Tammany Hall, and New York City from the Gilded Age to the Progressive Era*. Madison, N.J.: Fairleigh Dickinson University Press, 2008. Detailed study of one of the most important Tammany Hall figures, Tim Sullivan, and his rise to power.

SEE ALSO: Irish immigrants; Machine politics; New York City; Political parties.

TELEMUNDO

IDENTIFICATION: Spanish-language television network

DATE: Launched on March 28, 1954

ALSO KNOWN AS: WKAQ-TV, Telemundo Canal 2

SIGNIFICANCE: Telemundo provides Spanish-language programming to Hispanic households in the United States, offering cultural shows, entertainment, and world news. The network's bilingual captioning also enables English-only speakers to become familiar with various aspects of Hispanic culture.

Based in Hialeah, Florida, Telemundo originated in San Juan, Puerto Rico, in March of 1954 as the television station WKAQ-TV. It was founded by Ángel Ramos, who also owned Puerto Rico's first radio station, WKAQ-FM, known as Radio El Mundo, and its major newspaper at that time, *El Mundo*. Ramos established continuity between his radio and television stations by hiring Ramón Rivero (Diplo), the famous Puerto Rican comedian and actor, to produce shows for Telemundo. Radio El Mundo broadcasted Rivero's popular comedy show *El Tremendo Hotel*, and Rivero created similar comedy-variety shows for Telemundo. Two of his shows, *La Taberna India* and *La Farándula Corona*, earned top ratings for Telemundo.

During the 1970's and 1980's, Telemundo became known for its Puerto Rican Spanish-language soap operas, better known as telenovelas, and was known as Telemundo Canal 2. Its logo was the number 2 with the silhouette of two upright fingers inside the number; thus, Telemundo was called "El canal de los dedos" (the channel of the fingers). The station changed its logo in 1993 and again in 2000.

During the 1980's and 1990's, the Telemundo network expanded as a result of acquisitions and mergers. It was launched in the continental United States in 1987. The Telemundo Communications Group was formed and eventually became part of NBC Universal on April 12, 2002. By 2009, Telemundo owned and managed sixteen stations located throughout the United States and was also associated with one independent Spanish-language station. In addition to its own stations, it had thirty-six broadcast affiliates and seven hundred cable affiliates. The Telemundo network is available to 93 percent of Hispanic households in the United States.

Telemundo is the only Spanish-language network in the United States that offers a prime-time program schedule of its own original programming, including talk shows, news programs, sports, music programs, reality shows, and telenovelas such as *Doña Bárbara*. The network is also the only one in the United States that produces original telenovelas. In addition to its original programming, Telemundo broadcasts major events such as the Miss Universe Pageant and the Macy's Thanksgiving Day Parade in New York City in Spanish and a variety of Hollywood films dubbed in Spanish. The network is the only one in the United States that provides closed captions in both Spanish and English. Second only to Univision in size among Spanish-language networks in the United States, Telemundo also ranks second worldwide as the largest producer of Spanish-language programming.

Shawncey Webb

FURTHER READING

Dávila, Arlene. *Latinos, Inc.: The Marketing and Making of a People.* Berkeley: University of California Press, 2001.

Rivero, Yeidy. *Tuning Out Blackness: Race and Nation in the History of Puerto Rican Television.* Durham, N.C.: Duke University Press, 2005.

SEE ALSO: Cultural pluralism; Language issues; Latin American immigrants; Mexican immigrants; Spanish-language press; Television and radio; Univision.

TELEVISION AND RADIO

DEFINITION: Broadcasting designed primarily for immigrant communities

SIGNIFICANCE: Since the early twentieth century inventions of radio and television, broadcasting media for immigrant communities in the United States have gained importance in forging and maintaining cultural identities, meeting the specific needs of immigrant groups, promoting acculturation, and fostering ethnic enterprises.

Television and radio broadcasting for immigrant communities in the United States—which might be called "ethnic broadcasting"—targets specific groups with unique cultural and ethnic identities, which are defined by common languages, histories, religious faiths, traditions, and, often, countries of origin. The broadcasting media play a significant role in the development and maintenance of group identities by facilitating the preservation of immigrant languages and traditions. They also provide information on medical services, cultural performances, financial services, and other topics of interest to specific ethnic groups. In addition to news from and about the communities, the ethnic media disseminate information about events occurring in the homelands of immigrants, thus fortifying the immigrants' bonds with their parent societies.

Immigrant broadcasting may also have a surveillance function in trying to protect communities from external threats. For example, it provides information about the legal rights of immigrants, such as civil rights violations, changes in U.S. immigration laws, and crimes against immigrants, and often serves as a channel for mobilization. At the same time, the broadcast media facilitate the process of acculturation and assimilation of the immigrant communities in American society. Radio and television programming often offers English-language lessons. It also provides information on the values and norms of the host society and promotes citizenship and naturalization. Finally, ethnic broadcasting creates platforms for the development of economic enterprises in the ethnic enclaves.

EARLY HISTORY

Radio broadcasting developed at such a fast pace at the beginning of the twentieth century that a number of unregulated business arrangements between manufacturers of radio equipment and broadcasters arose. The threat of a broadcasting market monopoly developing prompted the U.S. government to pass a series of regulations designed to assign broadcast wavelengths and licenses, starting with the Radio Act of 1927. As a result of the government's antitrust actions, four major radio networks were created—the National Broadcasting Company (NBC), the Columbia Broadcasting Company (CBC), the Mutual Broadcasting System,

One of the most successful sitcoms of all time, I Love Lucy *(1951-1957) starred real-life couple Lucille Ball and Desi Arnaz, a Cuban-born bandleader who played Ricky Ricardo, a Cuban bandleader much like himself. The series frequently called attention to Ricardo's Cuban origins and found humor in cultural misunderstandings.* (AP/Wide World Photos)

and the American Broadcasting Company (ABC). Television broadcasting emerged around this same time. NBC launched a television station in 1928. However, significant television broadcasting did not begin until shortly after World War II, when CBS and ABC started their television networks.

During the early days of radio broadcasting, there were several programs with an emphasis on the immigrant experience—the documentary series *Americans All, Immigrants All,* the comedy series *The Goldbergs* (or *The Rise of the Goldbergs*), the situation comedies *Abby's Irish Rose* and *Life with Luigi.* Throughout the 1940's and 1950's, television shows addressing the immigrant experience included the situation comedies *I Remember Mama, I*

Love Lucy, and *Hey, Jeannie!* Television versions of the radio series *Life with Luigi* and *The Goldbergs* gained popularity during the early 1950's. The emphasis of these series changed gradually from the economic conditions of immigrants during the Great Depression to their lives within the exigencies of consumer society in the 1950's. Toward the end of the 1950's, American television slowly began to replace immigrant-oriented sitcoms with white, middle-class family situation comedies.

SPECIAL PROGRAMMING FOR IMMIGRANTS IN RADIO

The major modifications in U.S. immigration law brought by the Immigration and Nationality Act of 1965 prompted the broadcast media to introduce programming aimed at a number of specific ethnic and foreign-language groups. These programs mostly targeted African Americans, Spanish speakers, Native Americans, and some groups of European descent. American radio stations began offering "special programming" for groups from Asia and the Caribbean. Between 1965 and 2000, the number of radio stations offering ethnic and foreign-language formats rose from 170 to 877. At the same time, the number of hours of such programming rose from 4,384 per week in 1965 to 8,500 hours per week in 2000.

Since the 1960's, commercial radio for immigrants has increasingly responded to the tastes of particular communities. Similar preferences in the radio programming often act as a reconciliatory mechanism that unite audiences from different ethnic and racial communities. For example, despite the inherent conflict-based relationship among Asian Indians, Pakistanis, Nepalese, Bangladeshis, and Sri Lankans in Asia, immigrants from all these societies consume the same media products in the United States.

Because public radio receives substantial funding from the federal government, it is subject to governmental regulations written to ensure that "special programming" is provided for immigrant communities. According to the Public Telecommunications Act of 1988, the only radio services required by law are those that respond to the needs of immigrants and other minority groups. Since 1986, the Radio Program Fund of the Corporation for Public Broadcasting (CPB) has funded programs designed to increase diversity on public radio. As a result, independent producers whose programs target minority communities have received about 75 percent of the radio production awards from the CPB radio fund. In addition, the incentive of public radio to educate competent journalists and improve its human resources was extended during the 1980's to include a special program that addressed minority employees—Minority Recruitment and Specialty Development Initiatives.

TELEVISION PROGRAMMING FOR IMMIGRANTS

Throughout 1970's and 1980's, the federal government's deregulation of cable channels and the development of satellite television challenged the dominance of the three major broadcast television networks—ABC, NBC, and CBS. The emergence and increasing popularity of new channels reflected the need of commercial television to address specific cultural groups of the society. Consequently, during the 1990's, special networks targeting particular ethnic communities emerged, such as the Black Entertainment Television (BET), the Spanish-language Univision and Telemundo.

Two special challenge facing television have been portraying members of ethnic and immigrants groups properly and ensuring representation of immigrant communities on television—both objectives that have proven difficult to regulate. One of the first bodies to address proper representation of minority groups was the Kerner Commission, which was created in 1967 in response to social disorders arising from racial issues. It concluded that broadcasting played an important role in perpetuating the discriminatory attitudes toward African Americans and members of other minorities. The commission strongly recommended that the broadcasting media do more to reflect the nation's racial and ethnic diversity. However, the federal government was constrained from taking stronger action by the First Amendment to the U.S. Constitution, which effectively prohibits government from directly influencing the content of programs on commercial television. Despite this constraint,

the Federal Communications Commission (FCC), the principal federal agency involved in the regulation of broadcasting in the United States, has established regulations that have an indirect influence on minority employment, ownership, and advertising in the media.

The case of American public television is completely different. Since its inception, it has striven to maintain a programming scheme that represents the full ethnic and racial diversity in the nation. In fact, it is the only television service in the United States required by law to serve minority communities. Public television has produced such programming in all its programming categories: children's, public affairs and news, education, cultural documentaries, performing arts, and science and nature. Examples from children's programming on public television have included such popular shows such as *Sesame Street*, and *Mr. Roger's Neighborhood*.

AFRICAN AMERICAN RADIO AND TELEVISION

Throughout the 1920's, 1930's, and 1940's, African American radio played an important role in the establishment of black communities emerging in the midwestern and northeastern regions of the United States. Although it was not addressing the needs of African Americans in its early days, commercial African American radio contributed significantly to the acculturation and cultural transmission of the community and to its resistance to racism. Music programming was its main early format. During the 1960's, black radio broadcasting reflected the radical changes then taking place in the African American community. As a result of the Civil Rights movement, more African Americans became owners of radio stations and produced their programs. In 2000, 140 African American-owned radio stations were operating through the country. Listeners also associated specific music genres with black radio: jazz, urban contemporary, blues, gospel, and hip-hop.

During the 1970's, African Americans finally gained positive representation on television. An outstanding example was the 1977 miniseries *Roots*, which strengthened the identity of the black community and helped improve attitudes toward minority racial and ethnic groups generally throughout the country. During the 1980's and 1990's, the exposure of African American issues became more prevalent. Talk shows addressing problems of people of color emerged, as did popular series starring African Americans, such as *The Cosby Show*, *Different World*, and *In Living Color*. Meanwhile, entertainment programming began offering more information about African Americans.

However during the early 1990's, the representation of African Americans on commercial television actually decreased. Moreover, some shows with African American characters, such as *Out All Night* and *Rhythm and Blues*, tended to contribute to fortifying rather than destroying negative stereotypes of African Americans. In 1979, a special network emerged to address the needs of African American audience—Black Entertainment Television (BET).

ASIAN RADIO AND TELEVISION

Since the 1990's, the Asian community has been the fastest-growing immigrant population in the United States. In 2000, 10.5 million people of Asian descent were living in America. The Asian broadcasting media have served many different ethnic groups—Chinese, Japanese, Koreans, South Asians, Filipinos, Vietnamese, Cambodians and Laotians, Pacific Islanders, and some groups from the Middle East. In 2000, twelve mainly AM stations had formats that targeted the Asian community, and eighty-one other stations provided 254 hours of special programming for Asian-speaking groups in the United States. During the early 1990's, the dominant format on Asian radio was music programming, along with some ethnic advertisements. Asian Indian radio, serving a community of at least 1 million listeners during the late 1990's, offered more diverse programming formats: music, talk shows, drama, news and information programs.

As the Asian American population has grown rapidly, so too has the number of television channels targeting Asian viewers. In 1995, only six national cable networks catered to Asian immigrants. By 2001, that number had risen to eight. During the early 1990's, the International Channel Networks (ICN) launched via different cable operators the International Channel, which targeted speakers of Asian Pacific languages. ICN later offered programs in seventeen different languages.

SPANISH-LANGUAGE RADIO AND TELEVISION

As with the Asian community, the rapid growth of the Spanish-speaking population in the United States that began during the last decades of the twentieth century has increased demand for broadcast media in Spanish. Between 1990 and 2002, the number of radio stations offering primarily Spanish-language programming grew from 261 to 687. Most of the stations operated in areas with large Spanish-speaking populations, particularly in Texas, California, Florida, Arizona, and New Mexico. The dominant format in Spanish-language radio has been music programming, which have accounted for more than 80 percent of all programs. Music programming is more cost-effective than other formats, but more importantly, it appeals to all segments of the diverse Spanish-speaking population in the United States. Some radio stations, however, have targeted much narrower audiences. For example, Caracol Radio in Miami, Florida, broadcasts to South Florida's small Colombian immigrant community amid a local Spanish-language broadcasting industry dominated by Cuban immigrants.

In 2006, about 165 U.S. television stations offered programming primarily in the Spanish language. Like Spanish-language radio stations, the television stations are concentrated in states with large Hispanic populations. Univision Communications is the leading Spanish-language broadcast television network in the United States, with about twenty-three stations that reach 97 percent of the country's Hispanic households. The next-largest Spanish-language network is Telemundo, whose stations reach about 88 percent of Hispanic households. It is followed by the TeleFutura Network and several small networks, such as Azteca America. In addition to these mainstream broadcast networks, the American Hispanic community also has access to other Spanish-language networks that transmit signals over cable lines and satellites.

RADIO AND TELEVISION IN THE INTERNET AGE

The information revolution of the 1990's and the subsequent rapid development of information technologies have marked a significant change in the delivery of radio and television services to the immigrant communities in the United States. Satellite and cable services have considerably improved the TV and radio choices of the ethnic groups. The emergence of the World Wide Web and other new communication technologies has provided immigrants with an array of ways to gather information about their homelands. Today, immigrants can watch television and listen to radio stations from their country of origin on the Internet. In addition, a number of companies sell equipment that provides users with access to satellite bandwidth unavailable from the geographic position of the United States, thus giving diverse immigrant communities an opportunity to watch channels and listen to radio stations produced in their homeland.

Elitza Kotzeva

FURTHER READING

Cambridge, Vibert C. *Immigration, Diversity, and Broadcasting in the United States, 1990-2001*. Athens: Ohio University Press, 2005. Historical analysis of how broadcasting catered to the multicultural environment in the United States during the late twentieth century.

Gumpert, Gary, and Susan J. Drucker, eds. *The Huddled Masses: Communication and Immigration*. Cresskill, N.J.: Hampton Press, 1998. Collection of articles examining the social implications of immigration using a multidisciplinary approach.

Kamalipour, Yahya R., and Theresa Carilli. *Cultural Diversity and the U.S. Media*. Albany: State University of New York Press, 1998. Detailed analysis of the relationship between culture, media, and communication with a focus on race and ethnicity and their representation in American media.

Nuñez, Luis V., ed. *Spanish Language Media After the Univision-Hispanic Broadcasting*. New York: Novinka Books, 2006. Overview of the Spanish-language media in the United States, with a detailed survey of the patterns of the U.S. Hispanic viewers and an analysis of relevant public policy issues.

Torres, Sasha, ed. *Living Color: Race and Television in the United States*. Durham, N.C.: Duke University Press, 1998. Collection of essays exploring representations of race on American television utilizing media studies, cultural studies, and critical race theory.

Wilson, Clint C., and Félix Gutiérrez. *Race, Multiculturalism, and the Media: From Mass to Class Communication*. Thousand Oaks, Calif.: Sage Publications, 1995. Collection of essays investigating the representation of racial minorities and the construction of racial identity in mainstream American media.

SEE ALSO: Chinese American press; Filipino American press; Films; Globalization; Huffington, Arianna; *I Remember Mama*; Japanese American press; Jennings, Peter; Telemundo; Univision.

TENNESSEE

SIGNIFICANCE: The basic structure of Tennessee's population was set during the colonial era, when most of its residents were British settlers and African slaves. Other Europeans immigrated then and during the nineteenth century, but their numbers were never great. During the last decades of the twentieth century, the state began undergoing a transformation, as substantial numbers of Asians and Hispanics began entering the state.

The earliest European settlers of Tennessee were primarily of Scotch-Irish and English ancestry. However, Germans and other Europeans were also among the early settlers, along with substantial numbers of African slaves. Throughout the nineteenth and much of the twentieth century, however, Tennessee attracted few new foreign immigrants. Many of those who did come during this period were drawn to urban developments in the state. During the 1850's, for example, Memphis was one of the fastest-growing cities in the United States. Standing on the Mississippi River, it was well positioned to attract both immigrants and commerce moving up the river. Not surprisingly, Memphis drew many of the Irish and German immigrants who were fleeing famine and political turmoil in Europe.

Other immigrants sought more bucolic attractions. During the 1840's, dozens of German and Swiss families settled in Wartburg, an east Tennessee community developed by out-of-state businessmen. The settlement did not prosper, however, so most of its settlers eventually moved on to other towns, such as nearby Knoxville. During the post-Civil War era, several colonization companies and immigration societies—including one spearheaded by Germans already living in Nashville—attempted to encourage Swiss and German settle-

PROFILE OF TENNESSEE

Region	South
Entered union	1796
Largest cities	Memphis, Nashville-Davidson (capital), Knoxville, Chattanooga, Clarksville
Modern immigrant communities	Koreans, Mexicans, Kurds, other Hispanics

Population	Total	Percent of state	Percent of U.S.	U.S. rank
All state residents	6,039,000	100.0	2.02	17
All foreign-born residents	237,000	3.9	0.63	24

Source: U.S. Census Bureau, *Statistical Abstract for 2006.*

Notes: The U.S. population in 2006 was 299,399,000, of whom 37,548,000 (12.5%) were foreign born. Rankings in last column reflect total numbers, not percentages.

ment in Tennessee. Their efforts met with mixed success, but several small but enduring immigrant communities did result.

MODERN IMMIGRATION

Substantial foreign immigration to Tennessee has been largely a late twentieth century development. Indeed, much occurred during the 1990's and first decade of the twenty-first century, particularly during the economic boom of the 1990's. In contrast to earlier eras, many of the new immigrants have been nonwhite—a trend that has challenged Tennessee's image as a predominately white and black society.

A large portion of Tennessee's most recent immigrants have been Asians. Skilled and well-educated Vietnamese immigrants, for example, have found high-tech employment in the state's Oak Ridge area. Between 1990 and 2000, Tennessee's Korean population increased by 64 percent—one of the South's largest proportional gains for that Asian group. However, many of these arrivals came not from Asia but from West Coast states.

An increasingly diverse city, Nashville has become noted for its Kurdish refugee population from the Middle East. The city's 10,000-resident "Little Kurdistan" district is home to the largest Kurdish community in the United States.

As in earlier times, most of the growth in immigrant populations has been in Tennessee's large cities. However, there have been exceptions to this pattern. For example, Hmong immigrants from Southeast Asia have preferred to settle in smaller communities. These people originated in remote rural areas of Laos and its neighboring countries. Many of them settled in big northern cities when they came to the United States and later relocated to smaller towns in southern states after having had their fill of inner-city life in the North. By 2008, Tennessee had the fifth-largest Hmong population among the southern states.

During the first decade of the twenty-first century, Tennessee also had one of the nation's fastest-growing Hispanic populations. Indeed, between 1990 and 2000, the state's 278 percent increase in Hispanic residents ranked it fourth in the South in the rate of increase. Most of Tennessee's Hispanic immigrants have been Mexicans, but representatives of other Latin American nationalities have also come to the state. Most Hispanic residents have been employed in agriculture, the construction trades, and in the distribution and service sectors. The increase in the Hispanic population has been especially evident in some rural areas, in which the immigrants have found agricultural work. For example, Hamblen County in east Tennessee saw its Hispanic population triple between 1990 and 2000. By 2008, Hispanic residents constituted 5.7 percent of the country's total population. The largest concentration of Hispanics, however, has been in Middle Tennessee, around the Nashville-Davidson County Metropolitan Area. A large but unknown number of these immigrants are undocumented.

Jeremiah Taylor

FURTHER READING

Berkeley, Kathleen C. "Ethnicity and Its Implications for Southern Urban History: The Saga of Memphis, Tennessee, 1850-1880." *Tennessee Historical Quarterly* 50 (1991): 193-202.

Dykeman, Wilma. *Tennessee: A History.* New York: W. W. Norton, 1984.

Ray, Celeste, ed. *The New Encyclopedia of Southern Culture.* Vol. 6. *Ethnicity.* Chapel Hill: University of North Carolina Press, 2007.

Van West, Carol, ed. *The Tennessee Encyclopedia of History and Culture.* Nashville: Tennessee Historical Society, 1998.

SEE ALSO: Asian immigrants; British immigrants; Economic opportunities; European immigrants; German immigrants; Irish immigrants; Korean immigrants; Mexican immigrants; Vietnamese immigrants.

TERRACE V. THOMPSON

THE CASE: U.S. Supreme Court decision on immigrant rights
DATE: Decided on November 12, 1923

> **SIGNIFICANCE:** A major setback for legally admitted immigrants from Asia, the *Terrace* decision upheld the validity of state laws prohibiting Asians from owning or leasing land for the purpose of agriculture.

In 1921, the Washington State legislature enacted a law that prohibited aliens from buying or selling land for agricultural purposes unless they had "in good faith declared their intention to become citizens of the United States." The law, which was enforced by severe criminal sanctions, did not make any exception for Asian residents who were legally disqualified from becoming naturalized citizens. Terrace, an alien Japanese farmer wanting to lease land, argued in court that the law violated both the Fourteenth Amendment and a treaty with Japan that guaranteed the right of Japanese citizens to participate in trade on an equal basis with U.S. citizens.

The U.S. Supreme Court, however, rejected Terrace's arguments. Although the Court in *Truax v. Raich* (1915) had recognized the constitutional right of a resident alien to earn a livelihood in a common occupation, it concluded that this right did not extend to "the privilege of owning or controlling agricultural land within the state." The police power of the state included discretionary regulation of the "quality and allegiance" of persons who might exercise this important privilege that

affected "the safety and power of the state itself." Defining agricultural production as distinct from trade or commerce, moreover, the Court concluded that the law was not inconsistent with the applicable treaty.

Thomas Tandy Lewis

FURTHER READING
Chuman, Frank. *The Bamboo People: The Law and Japanese Americans.* Del Mar, Calif.: Publisher's Inc., 1976.

Hyung-chan, Kim, ed. *Asian Americans and the Supreme Court: A Documentary History.* Westport, Conn.: Greenwood Press, 1992.

SEE ALSO: Asian immigrants; Constitution, U.S.; Due process protections; Japanese immigrants; *Oyama v. California*; *Ozawa v. United States*; Supreme Court, U.S.; *Truax v. Raich.*

TESLA, NIKOLA

IDENTIFICATION: Serbian American engineer and inventor
BORN: July 9, 1856; Smiljan, Austro-Hungarian Empire (now in Croatia)
DIED: January 7, 1943; New York, New York

> **SIGNIFICANCE:** Tesla's work on magnetism and electricity led to the development and introduction of alternating current (AC) electricity systems that revolutionized the electric power industry.

Born in a Croatian village in the Austro-Hungarian Empire, Nikola Tesla was the son of a priest in the Serbian Orthodox Church. His mother was an amateur inventor who created simple devices, such as a mechanical eggbeater, to help with home duties. Tesla would later credit her with inspiring his inventive mind. As a youth, he saw a metal engraving of Niagara Falls and imagined that he would one day travel to America and develop a way to capture the energy of the falling water. In 1875, Tesla enrolled in the Austrian Polytechnic School in Graz, where he studied engineering and began working with alternating electric currents. After graduating, he moved to Budapest and later Paris. When his attempts to persuade European electric compa-

Nikola Tesla. (Library of Congress)

nies to switch from direct current (DC) to alternating current (AC) failed, he left for New York in 1884 with the hope of finding support for his ideas with American power companies.

When he arrived in America, Tesla brought a letter of recommendation from a former employer addressed to Thomas Alva Edison that read: "My Dear Edison: I know two great men and you are one of them. The other is this young man!" Edison had little knowledge or interest in alternating current, but he was impressed with Tesla and hired him immediately. However, the two had a falling-out and Tesla resigned. Through the following year, Tesla worked as a day laborer to support himself in his new country. His confidence in the New World proved to be justified when he began working with George Westinghouse to develop a system for long-distance AC electrical transmission. Westinghouse's company also succeeded in using AC power to harness the energy of Niagara Falls, realizing Tesla's childhood dream. Although Tesla became wealthy,

he invested his money in unrealistic projects, suffered a nervous breakdown, and died in poverty.

Nicholas C. Thomas

FURTHER READING

Cheney, Margaret. *Tesla: Man Out of Time.* New York: Simon & Schuster, 2001.

O'Neill, John J. *Prodigal Genius: The Life of Nikola Tesla.* New York: Adventures Unlimited Press, 2006.

Seifer, Marc. *Wizard: The Life and Times of Nikola Tesla—Biography of a Genius.* New York: Citadel Press, 2001.

Tesla, Nikola. *My Inventions: The Autobiography of Nikola Tesla.* Radford, Va.: Wilder, 2007.

SEE ALSO: Czech and Slovakian immigrants; Industrial Revolution; Science.

TEXAS

> **SIGNIFICANCE:** With its policy of welcoming immigrants, Texas has contributed to creating the rich multicultural diversity of the United States. The various immigrant groups have not only maintained their own traditions but have blended them together in an artistic and cultural multiplicity.

Throughout most of its history, Texas has welcomed immigrants. During the brief period when Texas was under Mexican rule, between 1821 and 1836, the empresario plan implemented contracts and granted land to individuals who brought groups of immigrants to the area. Immigrants came from both Europe and the United States until 1830 when the Mexican government prohibited further immigration from the United States.

During the 1830's, the first German settlers immigrated to Texas and established homes in the south central part of the future state. During the following decade, with which began when Texas was an independent republic, another wave of Germans arrived. These two groups were peasant farmers fleeing religious persecution and poverty. In 1848, a group of better educated and more affluent Germans arrived and contributed significantly to the establishment of towns. While Mexico was fighting the United States in the Mexican War of 1846-1848, a number of Irish immigrants entered Texas with the U.S. Army and stayed. Some of the Irish became merchants and farmers; others worked in coal mines.

The major immigration wave into Texas occurred after the Civil War (1861-1865). With a vast amount of cheap land and a sparse population, Texas offered an abundance of economic opportunities for farming, ranching, and employment. The state government, private companies, and individuals actively sought immigrants to populate the state. An extensive written campaign of pamphlets and letters encouraged immigrants from most European countries to come to Texas. A few Texans, mostly planters, even traveled to Europe to entice people to immigrate to the state. The major stipulation was that the new arrivals be hardworking and eager to prosper through their own efforts. In 1870, Texas created the Texas Bureau of Immigration. The campaign for settlers came at a time when Europe was plagued by economic hardships, food shortages, and religious persecution. Consequently, substantial numbers of immigrants from many European countries heeded Texas's invitation.

EUROPEAN IMMIGRANTS

From 1866 to 1880, a steady flow of German immigrants, attracted by religious freedom and the availability of land, arrived in Texas. In 1866 alone, they bought more than 10,000 acres of land. Other European immigrants included Bohemians, Poles, Swedes, Norwegians, English, Irish, Scots, and Italians. Members of each of these groups tended to settle close together. The St. Louis, Iron Mountain, and Southern Railroad set up a land immigration office and played an important role in helping immigrants set up homes in the state.

The first immigrants from Poland had actually begun arriving in Texas as early as 1854-1855. In 1870, a large number of them came to Texas due to escape the imposition of Prussian culture on their politically dismembered homeland. Many of these Poles had owned property in Poland

and were relatively affluent. Those who lacked funds worked as sharecroppers, saved their earnings, and soon became landowners themselves. They founded new Texas towns and also helped to settle the state's frontier regions. From 1880 to 1920, Italians immigrated to Texas. Many of them initially worked in the coal mines of the Thurber area or as laborers for the New York, Texas and Mexican Railroad. As they prospered, many of them purchased land and became farmers, growing corn and cotton. Others opened businesses.

Significant European immigration continued into the twentieth century. After World War II ended in 1945, Germans began immigrating to Texas, and substantial German immigration continued into the 1980's. By then, a considerable number of Polish immigrants were coming to Texas, fleeing the policies of the Poland's communist regime.

ASIAN IMMIGRANTS

By the end of the twentieth century, the majority of immigrants coming to Texas—as in other states—were no longer coming from Europe. While substantial immigration from Mexico continued, large numbers of immigrants were beginning to come from Asia. The first Asians to arrive in Texas were Chinese. During the mid-nineteenth century, many Chinese had immigrated to Califor-

---

PROFILE OF TEXAS

Region	South
Entered union	1845
Largest cities	Houston, Dallas, San Antonio, Austin (capital), El Paso, Fort Worth, Arlington, Corpus Christi
Modern immigrant communities	Mexicans, Vietnamese, Asian Indians

Population	Total	Percent of state	Percent of U.S.	U.S. rank
All state residents	23,508,000	100.0	7.85	2
All foreign-born residents	3,741,000	15.9	9.96	3

Source: U.S. Census Bureau, *Statistical Abstract for 2006.*
Notes: The U.S. population in 2006 was 299,399,000, of whom 37,548,000 (12.5%) were foreign born. Rankings in last column reflect total numbers, not percentages.

nia to work in the gold mines. There they faced an ever-increasing resentment and prejudice that made their lives both unpleasant and dangerous. During the 1880's, many Chinese workers were entering Texas to work as laborers on construction of the Southern Pacific Railroad. After that railroad was completed, about 300 Chinese workers stayed in El Paso, where they created a Chinatown enclave. There they opened laundries and restaurants, worked as house servants, and raised and sold vegetables. As some of them prospered, they purchased property.

Japanese immigrants have also made important contributions to Texas. During the early twentieth century, Japanese began immigrating to the state's Rio Grande Valley, where they grew rice and prospered, as they doubled their crop yields in only three years. They also grew vegetables and citrus fruits. These immigrants were initially welcomed into the state and treated well, but the entry of the United States into World War II in 1941 inflamed anti-Japanese sentiment in Texas and throughout the United States. After the war ended in 1945, many of the Japanese settled in Texas's cities, where they sought employment in business and the professions. By 1990, more than two-thirds of the Japanese living in the state resided in or near major cities, such as Houston and Dallas-Fort Worth. Among the cultural contributions of the Japanese to Texas are the Japanese gardens in most of the state's major cities.

Between 1975 and 1990, many Vietnamese immigrants came to Texas. The first to arrive were mostly well-educated individuals fleeing the communist government that took over South Vietnam when the Vietnam War ended in 1975. The larger groups of refugees who followed them had mostly been farmers in Vietnam. Many of them became fishermen in Texas. By the 1980's, most of Texas's Vietnamese immigrants had become U.S. citizens. In 1981, Texas had the second-largest Vietnamese population in the United States.

Texas has also gained a large community of Asian Indians. They are well educated as a group, and most came with university degrees. During the early twenty-first century, about one-quarter of the state's Asian Indians worked in the field of information technology. Many others were employed as physicians, engineers, and scientists or were business professionals.

MEXICAN IMMIGRANTS

Texas's largest immigrant community is Hispanic, primarily Mexican. The state's diverse Hispanic community includes families tracing their roots back to residents of Texas while it was still under Mexican rule, people who immigrated and became citizens after Texas became a state, and modern immigrants who have entered the United States illegally. During the early years of the twentieth century, many Mexicans immigrated to the United States to escape to the political unrest and economic disturbances of the Mexican Revolution. At that time, Mexicans were welcomed to come to the state to work on farms and ranches, in the mines, and on the railroads. Between 1910 and 1930, the immigrant Mexican population in Texas tripled.

During the early years of the Great Depression of the 1930's, many Mexicans were deported back to Mexico. However, in 1942, the U.S. and Mexican governments set up the bracero program, a cooperative guest-worker venture that sent Mexican workers into the United States on a temporary basis until 1964. In addition to the Mexicans brought in by the program, others also entered illegally. This situation resulted in Operation Wetback in 1954 that deported many illegal immigrants back to Mexico. Mexicans have continued to immigrate to Texas seeking employment and a better standard of life for themselves and their families.

From 1970 to 1990, Texas experienced a growth in its foreign-born population that was four times greater than the national average. Both the Hispanic and the Asian populations more than doubled during the period. From 2000 to 2006, the number of illegal immigrants in Texas increased at a faster rate than anywhere else in the United States.

Shawncey Webb

FURTHER READING

Brady, Marilyn Dell. *The Asian Texans.* College Station: Texas A&M University Press, 2004. Useful source for the social and cultural contributions of Asian immigrants.

Gomez, Luis. *Crossing the Rio Grande: An Immigrant's Life in the 1880's.* Translated by Guadalupe Valdez. College Station: Texas A&M University Press, 2006. Excellent detailed account by a Mexican immigrant to Texas that offers insights into relationships between early immigrants and their American employers. Also provides a look at Mexican lifestyles in Texas.

Gutiérrez, David G. *Walls and Mirrors: Mexican Americans, Mexican Immigrants, and the Politics of Ethnicity*. Berkeley: University of California Press, 1995. Good for understanding the effects of the continuous immigration from Mexico. Also examines U.S. government programs that encouraged the immigration of workers and discusses Mexican resistance to assimilation.

Konecny, Lawrence, and Clinton Machann, eds. *Czech and English Immigrants to Texas in the 1870's*. College Station: Texas A&M University Press, 2004. Excellent source for understanding the rhetoric used to bring immigrants to Texas and the lives of immigrants in Texas as well as the dangers they encountered in reaching Texas.

McKenzie, Phyllis. *The Mexican Texans*. College Station: Texas A&M University Press, 2004. Good coverage of Mexican social and work environments in Texas and the contributions made by Mexicans.

Rozek, Barbara J. *Come to Texas: Attracting Immigrants, 1865-1915*. College Station: Texas A&M University Press, 2003. Excellent history of efforts of the Texas government and private companies and individuals to lure immigrants to Texas, emphasizing printed sources.

Tang, Irwin A., ed. *Asian Texans: Our Histories and Our Lives*. Austin, Tex.: It Works, 2008. Well-researched and detailed study of the history of Texas's various Asian immigrants and the discrimination and exploitation they have encountered. Excellent for both hard facts and statistics and anecdotal personal stories.

SEE ALSO: Border fence; Bracero program; Dallas; El Paso incident; Empresario land grants in Texas; Farm and migrant workers; German immigrants; Houston; Mexican immigrants; Operation Wetback; Texas Cart War.

TEXAS CART WAR

DATE: 1857

LOCATION: South Texas

THE EVENT: Anglo-Americans physically attacked Mexican immigrant teamsters to discourage their freight operations between the Gulf of Mexico coast and San Antonio, Texas

SIGNIFICANCE: These hostilities reduced one of the few employment opportunities for Mexican immigrants in Texas and impaired relations between the Anglo and Mexican populations in the state.

From the time the Spanish established settlements in Texas during the eighteenth century, through the era when Mexico controlled Texas (1821-1836), immigrant teamsters—freighters known as *carreteros*—provided transport services essential to the existence of these settlements. The teamsters used enormous carts laden with essential goods, pulled by teams of oxen to supply these scattered settlements. As commerce increased in Texas in the two decades following the Texas Revolution in 1835-1836, increasing numbers of Mexican immigrant *carreteros* emigrated from Mexico to Texas.

During the 1850's, the leading occupation of Mexicans in San Antonio was reportedly freighting. At that time, Mexican immigrant labor dominated this increasingly lucrative trade. Mexican freighters were able to provide exceedingly low-cost services because their operations were highly efficient. Although no statistics are available on the magnitude of the Texas cart trade during the 1850's, various estimates place the amount at several million dollars annually. Undoubtedly, the substantial financial rewards that accrued to the immigrant *carreteros* caught the attention of Anglo-Texan traders. Anglo-Texan teamsters tried unsuccessfully to establish competing freight operations.

During the summer and fall of 1857, Anglo-Texan freighters who found themselves unable to compete with the more efficient Mexican immigrant teamsters employed lawless bands of hooligans to initiate attacks on the Mexican *carreteros* to intimidate and discourage them. The *carreteros* were threatened, harassed, beaten, and murdered. Most of the hostile attacks on the Mexican freighters were on the cart road linking San Antonio and the Gulf coast. Although attacks occurred at various locations along the cart road, the most barbarous assaults occurred in Goliad and Karnes counties. Caravans of Mexican carts were repeatedly waylaid and many carts destroyed. Oxen were either driven off or killed and valuable cargos pillaged and confiscated. Some seventy-five *carreteros* may have died in the wanton attacks, although the exact number of deaths remains in dispute. While the immigrant *carreteros* endeavored to protect themselves and their cargo, few Anglo-Texan attackers were injured or killed in the conflicts. It is worth noting that in addition to cart trade issues, deeply rooted Anglo ethnic and racial prejudices contributed to the animosity toward Mexicans.

By the end of 1857, the attacks on the immigrant Mexican teamsters had ended. The abrupt termination to the "Cart War" is most attributable to severe economic hardships Anglo merchants and businesses experienced when the Mexican freight operations were curtailed by the attacks. Anglo merchants and businesses suffered significant financial losses when freight deliveries ceased. Affected merchants complained to authorities in Austin. Simultaneously, word of the attacks reached the Mexican ambassador in Washington, D.C., who lodged a complaint with the U.S. secretary of state in October, 1857. The secretary of state then appealed to Texas governor Elisha Pease to take action to prevent the harassment of the Mexican freighters. Governor Pease responded by creating and dispatching a company of Texas Rangers to patrol the San Antonio-Gulf cart road.

Although some Anglo-Texan teamsters gained a foothold in the South Texas freight business and several immigrant Mexican freighters ceased to operate because of the attacks, many Mexican teamsters continued their trade for several decades. Reports from the Civil War era suggest that Mexican teamsters prospered from increased trade.

Robert R. McKay

FURTHER READING

De León, Arnoldo. *They Called Them Greasers: Anglo Attitudes Toward Mexicans in Texas, 1821-1900.* Austin: University of Texas Press, 1983.

Navarro, Armando. *Mexicano Political Experience in Occupied Aztlán: Struggles and Change.* Walnut Creek, Calif.: AltaMira Press, 2005.

SEE ALSO: Employment; Empresario land grants in Texas; Mexican immigrants; Texas; Xenophobia.

THAI IMMIGRANTS

SIGNIFICANCE: As one of the most stable of the Southeast Asian states, Thailand has served as a conduit for thousands of immigrants fleeing communist governments in other countries. However, immigration of Thai nationals to the United States has been limited, making Thais one of the smallest and least noticed Asian American populations.

Prior to the twentieth century Thailand, or Siam as it was long known, was a political backwater, a country that had avoided colonialism and had limited contacts with the West. In absence of significant knowledge about the Western world or the United States, few Thais had compelling reasons to come to the United States. Not until the United States became involved in Vietnam's civil war during the 1960's did Thais become exposed to American culture. Many of them soon saw the United States as a potential refuge from political and economic turmoil. Thailand was the only Southeast Asian country to escape destruction during the ensuing Vietnam War. Its own military government allied with the United States during the war but managed to keep the conflict from crossing its borders or bringing a destructive communist insurgency like those that devastated its eastern neighbors.

PROFILE OF THAI IMMIGRANTS

Country of origin	Thailand
Primary language	Thai
Primary regions of U.S. settlement	Southern California
Earliest significant arrivals	1960's
Peak immigration period	1960's
Twenty-first century legal residents*	48,475 (6,059 per year)

*Immigrants who obtained legal permanent resident status in the United States.

Source: Department of Homeland Security, *Yearbook of Immigration Statistics, 2008.*

Throughout the Vietnam War, American servicemen used Thailand as a haven for rest and recreation from the fighting. Thais were thereby introduced to American culture, and a few thousand Thais began immigrating to the United States every year. Among the most numerous Thai immigrants were wives of American soldiers and sailors. They contributed to a growing concentration of Thai Americans around military bases in California, Texas, and Georgia, but this initial immigration wave was too small to create a substantial Thai community in the United States.

Marriages between American military personnel and Thai women produced two of the most accomplished and famous athletes of early twenty-first century America: baseball player Johnny Damon of the Boston Red Sox and New York Yankees, and golfer Tiger Woods. The fathers of both served in the U.S. military during the Vietnam War.

The Thai American community remained small through the 1970's, as large numbers of Vietnamese, Cambodians, and Laotians were admitted to the United States as political refugees. Because Thailand had a pro-Western government, Thais wanting to go to the United States could not claim refugee status. Consequently, the number of Thais in the United States remained a small fraction of the numbers of other Southeast Asian immigrants. The already small rate of Thai immigration became even slower during the 1980's and 1990's, as Thailand's increasing political stability brought democratic reforms and economic growth that promised better lives for most Thais. However, the Asian financial crisis of 1997 and a new military coup in Thailand in 2006 spurred increased immigration to the United States.

THAI AMERICANS

The 2000 U.S. Census reported that more than 110,000 Thais were living in the United States—a figure one-tenth that of Vietnamese residents and barely 1 percent of the total Asian American population. Because of its small size, the Thai American community has received much less attention than most other Asian American commu-

---

THE MOST FAMOUS THAI IMMIGRANTS

The first-known Thai immigrants to the United States may be the most famous Thais in history: Chang and Eng, better known as the "Siamese Twins." Born in Siam (Thailand) in 1811, the brothers came to the United States as touring entertainers during the 1830's, when they were already world famous. Having already accumulated enough money to retire, they settled in North Carolina in 1839, took the surname Bunker and became American citizens. They also married American sisters and raised large families.

What made Chang and Eng famous was the fact that they were the first physically conjoined twins at whom the world got a close look. During their time, it was rare for conjoined twins to survive to adulthood, let alone perform stunts on stage before dazzled audiences. So closely did Chang and Eng become associated with conjoined twins that "Siamese twins" became synonymous with conjoined twins. Ironically, however, Chang and Eng themselves were not ethnic Siamese (Thai). They were actually ethnic Chinese born into one of Thailand's own immigrant communities. Before they began their international career, they were known in Thailand as the "Chinese twins."

---

nities. The few Thais living in the United States are also spread too thinly across the country to maintain strong cultural ties. Los Angeles, California, is the only American city to develop a "Thai Town."

According to 2007 census data, Thai Americans rank among the middle of Asian groups in their education level; nearly 40 percent of adult Thais had college degrees. Their income levels were the average for all Americans. As a group, Thai Americans are much older than most Asian communities, with only 15 percent of the community below the age of eighteen.

Two specialized forms of Thai immigration are typically associated with underground economies: mail-order brides and undocumented workers. With poverty widespread in parts of rural Thailand, some women see an attractive path to prosperity in marriages to Americans, which can earn them quick American citizenship with all its benefits and new lives in the United States. Although the numbers of Thai women who become mail-order brides have been much smaller than those of Filipino and Russian women, they nevertheless account for a significant number of immigrants.

Smuggling workers into the United States to work in sweatshops is also part of the story of Thai immigration.

Douglas Clouatre

FURTHER READING

Larsen, Wanwadee. *Confessions of a Mail Order Bride: American Life Through Thai Eyes.* Far Hills, N.J.: New Horizon Press, 1989. Memoir of a Thai woman who came to the United States to marry an American.

Ng, Franklin. *The History and Immigration of Asian Americans.* New York: Garland, 1998. Wide-ranging examination of how Asians immigrated to the United States, their role in the country's economic and political system, and their continued influence in the modern United States.

Osborne, Milton. *Southeast Asia.* 9th ed. St. Leonards, N.S.W.: Allen & Unwin, 2005. History of modern Southeast Asia through the aftermath of the Vietnam War and the refugee movement from the region.

Portes, Alejandro, and Rubén Rumbaut. *Immigrant America.* Berkeley: University of California Press, 2006. Collection of personal stories of immigrants, their struggles within their home country, their struggles to reach the United States, and their lives in their new country.

Zia, Helen. *Asian American Dreams.* New York: Farrar, Straus and Giroux, 2001. Details the creation of an Asian American community in the United States by a once isolated immigrant group.

SEE ALSO: Asian immigrants; Burmese immigrants; Cambodian immigrants; Captive Thai workers; Hmong immigrants; Indonesian immigrants; Laotian immigrants; Malaysian immigrants; "Marriages of convenience"; Vietnam War; Vietnamese immigrants.

TOCQUEVILLE, ALEXIS DE

IDENTIFICATION: French political scientist and historian whose book *Democracy in America* surveys the state of American society during the 1830's
BORN: July 29, 1805; Paris, France
DIED: April 16, 1859; Cannes, France

SIGNIFICANCE: Publication of Tocqueville's *Democracy in America* during the early nineteenth century helped Americans of that era better appreciate the value of the work of the nation's Founders. Tocqueville's writings—which comment at length about the roles of immigrants—have been much quoted and remain as popular as when they were first published in 1835.

It has been said that the most important event in the life of Alexis de Tocqueville occurred before he was born. The French Revolution, which began in 1789, forever changed the French aristocratic world in which Tocqueville's family was rooted. His great-grandfather was a liberal aristocrat who was killed in the revolution, and his parents favored a return to the Bourbon monarchy, whose final end in 1830 created a crisis in the life of Tocqueville, then twenty-five years old. With the realization that France was turning toward democracy, he wanted to learn more about that form of government, of which the best exemplar of his age was the United States. Using the excuse of wanting to study American prison reform, he received permission to sail to America.

With his traveling companion Gustave de Beaumont, Tocqueville arrived in New York City on May 10, 1831, and left the United States ten months later. On their arrival, the travelers were immediately impressed by the apparent social equality, which Tocqueville attributed in part to the diverse European immigrant communities being molded into one society. When he later wrote up his observations, he began with the British immigrants of the early seventeenth century but also included the French and Spanish, as well as other smaller groups. All of them, in his view, shared the goal of making American democracy work. In his analysis of this process, Tocqueville felt compelled to include the divine purpose of God preparing a new land where the suffering masses of Europe could transplant the embryos of democracy being created by European philosophers, but also being opposed by the old states of Europe.

From these embryos, Tocqueville observed three principles at work in the United States. The first was equality of conditions. He noted there was no superiority of one class over others and that poverty and hardship were the best guarantees of equality. With the exception of New England, whose early inhabitants came primarily for religious reasons, the equality was enhanced by the common lack of education and resources among the immigrants. The second principle he observed was popular sovereignty. With European traditions of aristocracy and monarchy being broken, Tocqueville declared that Anglo-Americans were the first to establish and maintain the popular sovereignty being defined by European philosophers.

Combined with Tocqueville's first two principles was public opinion, which he defined as the force that put democracy into action. He noted the complete freedom of public discussion that was carried into the legislative assemblies. Any conflicts that arose would be settled by a judiciary, which—unlike European judicial systems—was free from legislative or executive manipulation.

Tocqueville published *De la démocratie en Amérique* in two volumes in 1835 and 1840, and the English-language editions were published almost simultaneously as *Democracy in America*. His companion book, *On the Penitentiary System in the United States and Its Application in France* (1833), coauthored by Beaumont, addresses the stated purpose of his American visit. Both works give credit to the impact of the thirteen million European immigrants then spreading into the interior of America.

Glenn L. Swygart

WHY TOCQUEVILLE WROTE *DEMOCRACY IN AMERICA*

In his introduction to Democracy in America, *excerpted below, Alexis de Tocqueville explained the source of his fascination with U.S. society and his motives for writing a book about that society.*

Amongst the novel objects that attracted my attention during my stay in the United States, nothing struck me more forcibly than the general equality of conditions. I readily discovered the prodigious influence which this primary fact exercises on the whole course of society, by giving a certain direction to public opinion, and a certain tenor to the laws; by imparting new maxims to the governing powers, and peculiar habits to the governed. I speedily perceived that the influence of this fact extends far beyond the political character and the laws of the country, and that it has no less empire over civil society than over the Government; it creates opinions, engenders sentiments, suggests the ordinary practices of life, and modifies whatever it does not produce. The more I advanced in the study of American society, the more I perceived that the equality of conditions is the fundamental fact from which all others seem to be derived, and the central point at which all my observations constantly terminated.

I then turned my thoughts to our own hemisphere, where I imagined that I discerned something analogous to the spectacle which the New World presented to me. I observed that the equality of conditions is daily progressing towards those extreme limits which it seems to have reached in the United States, and that the democracy which governs the American communities appears to be rapidly rising into power in Europe. I hence conceived the idea of the book which is now before the reader. . . .

Source: Alexis de Tocqueville, *Democracy in America*, translated by Henry Reeve. (New York: D. Appleton, 1904). Introduction.

FURTHER READING

Brogan, Hugh. *Alexis de Tocqueville: A Life.* New Haven, Conn.: Yale University Press, 2007.

Heckerl, David K. "Democracy in America." In *American History Through Literature, 1820-1870*, edited by Janet Gabler-Hover and Robert Sattelmeyer. Detroit: Charles Scribner's Sons/Thomson Gale, 2006.

Tocqueville, Alexis de. *Democracy in America*. Translated by Arthur Goldhammer. New York: Library of America, 2004.

Welch, Cheryl. *De Tocqueville*. New York: Oxford University Press, 2001.

SEE ALSO: Alien and Sedition Acts of 1798; Assimilation theories; British immigrants; Dutch immigrants; German immigrants; History of immigration, 1783-1891; Irish immigrants; Literature.

TRANSIT ALIENS

DEFINITION: Noncitizens who are permitted to travel through the United States with or without visas

SIGNIFICANCE: Transit aliens are exempt in many important ways from the requirements for other immigrant travelers in the United States.

Transit aliens are defined as non-U.S. citizens who are permitted to travel through the United States with or without regular visas. They include foreign nationals who are entitled to pass to and from the United Nations Headquarters District in New York City as well as diplomats and officials of foreign governments, along with their spouses and unmarried dependent children who are passing through the United States on their way to other countries. According to the statutory provisions of the U.S. Department of State Foreign Affairs Manual, these travelers must provide documentation indicating that they are in the United States for official business with the United Nations. Alternatively, they must be able to show that they possess tickets with common carriers to final destinations outside the United States and adequate funds to complete their journeys.

Travelers designated as transit aliens are automatically awarded one of three visa types. Holders of the C-1 transit visa are allowed to enter into the United States while transitioning to other countries. To be eligible for this type of visa, travelers must be able to show visas to their ultimate destinations and appropriate travel reservations.

C-2 visas are provided to foreign citizens and family members traveling to or from the United Nations Headquarters District. C-3 visas are issued to representatives of foreign governments and their immediate family members who are passing through the United States on their way to other countries. Although these travelers have been largely exempt from many of the security measures enacted after September 11, 2001, they are still subject to providing adequate documentation regarding the nature of their travel to officials of the U.S. Department of Homeland Security.

William Carney

FURTHER READING

Anosike, Benji O. *How to Obtain Your U.S. Immigration Visa for a Temporary Stay: The Non-Immigrant Visa Kit.* Newark, N.J.: Do-It-Yourself Legal Publishers, 2003.

Beshara, Edward C., et al. *Emigrating to the U.S.A.: A Complete Guide to Immigration, Temporary Visas, and Employment.* New York: Hippocrene Books, 1994.

Gania, Edwin T. *U.S. Immigration Step by Step.* 3d ed. Naperville, Ill.: Sphinx Sourcebooks, 2006.

SEE ALSO: Deportation; Green cards; Immigration law; Passports; Permanent resident status; Resident aliens.

TRANSPORTATION OF IMMIGRANTS

DEFINITION: Modes of transportation historically used by immigrants to reach destinations in the United States

SIGNIFICANCE: Before the modern era of giant ocean liners and international passenger planes, most immigrants from overseas countries had to endure arduous and often dangerous voyages to the reach the United States.

The earliest European immigrants crossed the Atlantic Ocean on wooden sailing ships to reach what is now the United States. Advances in ship design between the early seventeenth and early nineteenth centuries improved the speed of sailing ships and their ability to sail closer to the wind and made them larger. However, these changes made only incremental differences to passengers, for whom transatlantic crossings remained long, arduous, and often dangerous.

EUROPEAN TRAVEL

After the United States became independent in the late eighteenth century, immigrants coming from Europe sailed on merchant ships that began their voyages from seaports along the coastlines of continental Europe and the British Isles. Most immigrants during that period were peasants with little money for travel who had to make their way from inland homes to the ports any way they could. Before railroads were developed, the fastest and most comfortable methods of inland travel in Europe were canal and river boats. However, their fares were often prohibitively expensive for immigrants, as were fares on public stagecoaches. Consequently, travelers walked, unless they owned carts and animals that they could sell when they reached their seaport destinations. Some immigrants had to travel overland more than three hundred miles, spending a month or more braving the dangers of the road—bad weather, con men eager to cheat them, bandits, and even wild animals.

During the early nineteenth century, overland travel in Europe became even more difficult, as governments put ever more bureaucratic obstacles in the way of travelers, especially those crossing national borders. Rights of transit were required in every country through which travelers passed. If the travelers lacked sufficient documentation to identify themselves, show they had paid their taxes in their home countries, or prove they had not evaded compulsory military service, or if they could not prove they had neither physical disabilities or diseases, they could be stopped and even turned back.

When immigrants finally reached seaports, there were no guarantees they would find passage on ships sailing to North America. Because many vessels had no firm sailing schedules, immigrants might have to wait in the port towns for weeks or even months to board departing ships. To complicate travel further, the ships' captains often were not even certain to which ports in the New World they would be sailing, as their routes depended on the cargoes they would be carrying. Finally, after the ships loaded their cargoes and their captains determined their destinations, the captains would decide which passengers they would allow to sail with them.

TRANSATLANTIC VOYAGES

After negotiating and paying their fares, the immigrants were allowed to board the ships. The poorest travelers were given accommodations in the ships' steerage sections—the most crowded, least comfortable, and least desirable quarters, which were usually well below deck, toward the stern. Until the mid-nineteenth century, no government regulations dictated any health and safety standards for passenger accommodations aboard ships. As transatlantic crossings could take from six to ten weeks, steerage passengers generally faced exhausting ordeals.

In many ships, the steerage accommodations were located in parts of ships that were originally built to contain cargoes, not human beings. Individual quarters were tiny, with little light or ventilation. During stormy weather conditions, when the ships' hatches were battened down, passengers often feared suffocating more than they did drowning, and went above deck, where they risked being washed overboard in heavy seas.

In some ships, as many as 400 to 1,000 men, women, and children were crowded in steerage sections as small as seventy-five long, twenty-five feet wide, and only five and one-half feet high—a total area of only eighteen hundred square feet. Passengers were provided with stoves and a few tables on which to cook and consume meals. The ships were supposed to supply food and drinking water, but inefficient and miserly management sometimes left passengers unsupplied for days at a time. Passengers aware of this possibility usually had the foresight to bring food supplies with them. Less provident passengers went hungry. Occasionally, they went so long without food they went mad.

Facilities for sanitary needs were limited. Enclosed water closets provided for female passengers were usually situated at the ends of steerage areas. Male passengers were expected to go above deck when they needed to relieve themselves. Water for washing was practically nonexistent. Rows of five-foot-long plank bunks lined the bulkheads, but many passengers simply slept on the decks. Some were wise enough to bring straw on which to sleep. To add to their discomfort, passengers were allowed above decks only infrequently, and typically at the captains' whims. In bad weather, passengers could be kept belowdecks, without sunlight or fresh air, for days at a time.

A serious hazard of traveling by steerage was the fact that some passengers carried communicable diseases that could spread easily within the cramped steerage quarters. Smallpox, yellow fever, measles, cholera, dysentery, and other diseases could all be brought on board through carelessness or indifference. Stifling heat during warm-weather voyages and bitter cold during the winter voyages further aggravated health hazards. On one early voyage, 500 of 1,100 Germans on a single ship died before reaching America. That high mortality rate was exceptional, but mortality rates of 10 percent were common. After 1855, governments began regulating passenger ships, limiting the crowding, requiring medical doctors on ships with more than 300 passengers, and inspecting food supplies before ships sailed to make sure they were adequate for the voyages.

STEAM-POWERED OCEAN TRAVEL

The introduction of steam-powered oceangoing ships during the 1840's began an era during which transatlantic travel conditions gradually began to improve for impoverished immigrants. As the earliest steam-powered passenger ships catered to wealthy travelers, immigrants found the obsolescent wooden sailing ships competing for their business. These ships lowered their fares, improved their accommodations, and began adhering to more regular departure schedules. By the 1870's, steerage fares on steamships were even lower than those on sailing ships. In addition to cheaper fares, the steamships provided reliable meals. Even more important, however, was their speed. They could cross the Atlantic in as few as ten days, and they were largely immune to the vagaries of the winds that propelled sailing ships. By the last decades of the nineteenth century, hundreds of thousands of European immigrants crossed the Atlantic on steamships every year. About 90 percent of them came by steerage.

PACIFIC OCEAN TRAVEL

The first significant numbers of Asians who immigrated to the United States began arriving in California during the early 1850's, by which time steamships were beginning to displace sailing ships on transpacific routes. The steamships that brought Asians to the West Coast were often owned by the same Americans who hired them to work on railroads and in gold mines. Because employers wanted their immigrant workers to be healthy and relatively strong when they arrived, the Asian immigrants were typically provided with less oppressive accommodations than those of Europeans arriving on the East Coast by steerage. American employers sometimes paid the Asian workers' fares, but the immigrants were expected later to repay their transportation costs out of their wages.

By 1867, a regular transpacific steamship service connecting Asian ports to California was making transpacific travel more efficient. The Pacific Mail Steamship Company became the principal carrier of Chinese and Japanese immigrants to California. Its early steamships were built mostly of wood. Propelled by side paddle wheels, the ships also carried auxiliary sails.

Print made in 1882 depicting the various forms of transportation by which immigrants reach their destinations in America. (Library of Congress)

EARLY INLAND TRAVEL

As the American western frontier opened up for settlement, many immigrants arriving on the East Coast soon headed west. Most had lived off the land in their home countries and were more familiar with farm life than with urban conditions. Those longing to own their own land set out on foot or on horseback. Those who had livestock and draft animals drove them ahead or had them pull their wagons loaded with their belongings. Some dragged or pushed crude, homemade three-wheeled carts piled high with their possessions.

Because few establishments along the immigrants' overland routes offered meals and overnight accommodations, travelers had to carry their own supplies with them. Many travelers began their journeys on the National Road. Started in 1811 with federal funding, it ran from Cumberland, Maryland, to Wheeling on the Ohio River and was one of the few all-weather roads in the United States at that time. By 1833, it reached mid-Ohio, and by the 1850's, it reached Illinois and the Mississippi River. Stagecoach routes began opening as the frontier was pushed west, but the services they provided were not suitable for most immigrants. The coaches were fast, but they charged high fares and had severely limited carrying capacities.

INLAND WATERWAYS

While stagecoaches were more comfortable and convenient than the kinds of overland conveyances that most immigrants used in their westward treks, travel by canal boats and riverboats was comparatively luxurious. Barges, flatboats, packet boats, keelboats, and large steamboats were all used on inland waterways and offered easier, faster, and less punishing transportation than most forms of land transportation before railroads were developed. Another advantage of boats was that they generally adhered to reliable schedules.

The packet boats used on canals were often as narrow as only fourteen feet, but they could be from seventy to ninety feet in length. The boats had cabin space for as many as sixty passengers, along with space to carry mail and freight. They moved up and down artificial canals, pulled by two or three horses or mules walking along the adjacent banks. The provided generally smooth rides, and they were almost always considerably faster than most forms of surface travel. The great era of canal

boat traveling lasted from 1784 to the 1850's, when the rise of railroads revolutionized inland travel.

The development of steamboats had an even greater impact on inland travel than canals. One of the most outstanding geographical features of the United States is its Mississippi River system, which drains an area of more than 1,250,000 square miles encompassing all or parts of thirty-one states between the Rocky and Allegheny mountains. Virtually all 2,350 miles of the Mississippi itself between Minnesota and the Gulf of Mexico are navigable, as are long stretches of the dozens of rivers feeding into the Mississippi. Before the development of steam-powered boats in the early nineteenth century, the Mississippi was useful for transporting large cargoes and passengers in only one direction: downriver. Timber cut in the upper Midwest could easily be floated down the river, as could boats and rafts carrying other cargoes, but upriver voyages were too difficult to make carrying cargo or large numbers of people practical.

The introduction of steamboats to American waterways was one of the first great revolutions in inland travels. The first commercial passenger steamboats actually starting operating on the rivers of New England and other East Coast states, but they had their great impact on the Mississippi River system. By the 1830's, several hundred steamboats were carrying passengers on the Mississippi and its major tributaries. By the 1850's, arguably the golden age of steamboating, more than 1,000 boats were in service. Until railroads began supplanting them after the Civil War (1861-1865), steamboats became one of the major conveyances of immigrants to the frontier regions. Many European immigrants entered the United States at New Orleans, from which they could begin steamboat voyages into dozens of states. It was even possible to ride steamboats as far inland as Montana. Many immigrants rode steamboats to St. Joseph, Missouri, which they could continue farther west by overland routes.

RAILROADS

The second great revolution in inland travel was the development of railroad networks across the country. By the end of the nineteenth century, no other form of passenger transportation could compete with the railroads for speed and carrying capacity. Major construction of railroad lines in the

United States began during the 1840's, when about 2,800 miles of tracks were laid—primarily in eastern states. By the 1860's, more than 30,000 miles of tracks were in use, and work was beginning on the first transcontinental line, which would connect western Missouri with California. Other transcontinental lines would soon follow.

As American railroads expanded, immigrants gladly took advantage of this new form of travel to reach the Midwest to the lands west of the Mississippi River. Railroad companies were direct participants in the sale of undeveloped land to settlers, and they encouraged immigrants to ride their trains to inspect land for possible purchase. They often offered immigrants such inducements as cut-rate tickets and free carriage of household goods. Sometimes, they went so far as to offer financing to help immigrants buy land.

The trains on which the typically cash-strapped immigrants rode differed greatly from those catering to more prosperous travelers. Immigrants generally rode in what were essentially crowded and stuffy cars with narrow wooden benches, poor ventilation, and windows that could not be opened.

These cars were railroad equivalents of steerage quarters. Passengers wishing to eat had to prepare their own meals, and facilities for any kind of washing were often absent. Sleeping accommodations were fashioned from boards stretched across aisles between benches. Despite these spartan conditions, such railroad cars were a cut above the real boxcars often used to transport immigrants. Loaded with as many as sixty 60 or seventy passengers each, the boxcars were attached to freight and cattle trains and were often filthy because they were also used to transport cattle.

Jane L. Ball

FURTHER READING

Bettmann, Otto L. *The Good Old Days—They Were Terrible*. New York: Random House, 1974. This volume's chapter on travel during the post-Civil War era discusses conditions faced by immigrants traveling by steerage on ships and by train. Illustrated.

Calkins, Carroll, ed. *The Story of America*. Pleasantville, N.Y.: Reader's Digest Association, 1975. Illustrated general history of the United States containing chapters discussing how immigrants traveled.

Davidson, Marshall. *Life in America*. 2 vols. Boston: Houghton Mifflin, 1974. Generously illustrated work on U.S. history with chapters devoted to both travel and immigrants.

Dublin, Thomas, ed. *Immigrant Voices: New Lives in America, 1773-1986*. Champaign: University of Illinois Press, 1993. Collection of accounts of immigrants' lives in America that includes immigrant travel narratives.

Flayhart, William. *The American Line: Pioneers of Ocean Travel*. New York: W. W. Norton, 2001. History of the early disasters and triumphs of the American Steamship Company, the first American transatlantic line that competed directly with European lines. Includes lengthy discussions of shipboard conditions for immigrants.

Levy, Janey. *Erie Canal: A Primary Source History of the Canal That Changed America*. New York: Rosen, 2003. Discusses both the building of the Erie Canal and the canal's impact on the transportation of goods and people into Louisiana Territory.

Portes, Alejandro, and Rubén Rumbaut. *Immigrant America: A Portrait*. Berkeley: University of California Press, 2006. Broad study of immigration containing chapters devoted to immigrant movements to and within the United States.

Ray, Kurt. *New Roads, Canals, and Railroads in Early Nineteenth-Century America: The Transportation Revolution*. New York: Rosen, 2004. Discusses how new forms of transportation opened the frontiers and changed life in America. Most suitable for juvenile readers.

SEE ALSO: Asian immigrants; European immigrants; Freedom Airlift; Haitian boat people; Hamburg-Amerika Line; Illegal immigration; Mississippi River; National Road; Pacific Mail Steamship Company; Railroads; Smuggling of immigrants.

TRIANGLE SHIRTWAIST FIRE

THE EVENT: Industrial disaster resulting in the deaths of about 146 workers, many of whom were young female immigrants
DATE: March 25, 1911
LOCATION: New York, New York

SIGNIFICANCE: The Triangle Shirtwaist Factory fire was one of the worst workplace disas-

A VOICE FOR THE WORKERS

After the Triangle Shirtwaist Factory fire, a memorial meeting held at New York City's Metropolitan Opera House attracted uneducated workers, middle-class reformers, and social leaders. Discord among the various factions was evident until Polish immigrant Rose Schneiderman touched the crowd with these words:

I would be a traitor to those poor burned bodies, if I were to come here to talk good fellowship. We have tried you good people of the public—and we have found you wanting.

The old Inquisition had its rack and its thumbscrews and its instruments of torture with iron teeth. We know what these things are today: the iron teeth are our necessities, the thumbscrews are the high-powered and swift machinery close to which we must work, and the rack is here in the firetrap structures that will destroy us the minute they catch fire.

This is not the first time girls have been burned alive in this city. Every week I must learn of the untimely death of one of my sister workers. Every year thousands of us are maimed. The life of men and women is so cheap and property is so sacred! There are so many of us for one job, it matters little if 140-odd are burned to death.

We have tried you, citizens! We are trying you now and you have a couple of dollars for the sorrowing mothers and brothers and sisters by way of a charity gift. But every time the workers come out in the only way they know to protest against conditions which are unbearable, the strong hand of the law is allowed to press down heavily upon us.

Public officials have only words of warning for us—warning that we must be intensely orderly and must be intensely peaceable, and they have the workhouse just back of all their warnings. The strong hand of the law beats us back when we rise—back into the conditions that make life unbearable.

I can't talk fellowship to you who are gathered here. Too much blood has been spilled. I know from experience it is up to the working people to save themselves. And the only way is through a strong working-class movement.

Source: Quoted in Leon Stein, *The Triangle Fire* (New York: Carroll & Graf, 1962).

---

ters in American history. The disaster exposed the horrible working conditions of many immigrants and helped spur union organization and occupational safety laws.

Located in Manhattan's Greenwich Village, the Triangle Shirtwaist Factory was a typical turn-of-the-century sweatshop. Many of the employees were young female immigrants, primarily Russian Jews, Italians, Hungarians, and Germans. They worked long hours in dangerous working conditions for low wages. Shortly before the 4:45 P.M. closing time on Saturday, March 25, 1911, a fire broke out on the eighth floor of the ten-story Asch Building where they worked. The company occupied the eighth, ninth, and tenth floors.

The fire rapidly spread throughout the building, and most of the workers on the eighth and tenth floors were able to escape; many on the tenth floor made it safely to the roof, where they made their way to an ajoining building. Employees on the ninth floor, however, discovered that one of the two exits had been locked—a routine precaution

management felt was necessary to keep employees from stealing from the company. The single fire escape quickly buckled and collapsed under the weight of the workers. One of the two elevators in the building was not operating, and the other elevator shaft was later found clogged with the bodies of thirty girls who had unsuccessfully tried to escape. Some workers waited for rescue workers, but the ladders and water hoses that were brought were too short to reach the upper floors. In desperation, some workers leapt from the ninth floor to their deaths. By time the fire was extinguished, about half an hour after it had started, an estimated 146 of the nearly 600 employees had died. Many had burned to death.

Following the tragedy, there was public outcry for reform of fire safety laws and working conditions. The fire led to increased support for labor unions, including the International Ladies' Garment Workers' Union, of which some Triangle Shirtwaist employees were members. At the end of April that year, the governor of New York appointed a Factory Investigating Commission to collect information and conduct hearings, resulting in important factory safety legislation.

The owners of the Triangle Shirtwaist Company were Isaac Harris and Max Blanck. Both men were in the building at the time the fire started but escaped. Blanck, his children, and his governess fled the area when the fire broke out. Although the building had experienced four fires before the 1911 disaster and had been reported by the city fire department as an unsafe workplace with insufficient exits, Blanck and Harris were acquitted of any wrongdoing in the disaster. Twenty-three families then filed civil suits against the owners. Two years after the fire, in March of 1913, Harris and Blanck settled the suits by paying settlements of only seventy-five dollars for each employee who had been killed.

Kathryn A. Cochran

FURTHER READING

De Angelis, Gina. *The Triangle Shirtwaist Company Fire of 1911.* Philadelphia: Chelsea House, 2001.

Sherrow, Victoria. *The Triangle Factory Fire.* Brookfield, Conn.: Millbrook Press, 1995.

Von Drehle, David. *Triangle: The Fire That Changed America.* New York: Atlantic Monthly Press, 2003.

SEE ALSO: Employment; Garment industry; International Ladies' Garment Workers' Union; Labor unions; New York City; Sweatshops; Women immigrants.

TRUAX V. RAICH

THE CASE: U.S. Supreme Court decision on immigrant rights

DATE: Decided on November 1, 1915

SIGNIFICANCE: Holding that a law restricting employment of noncitizens was unconstitutional, the *Truax v. Raich* decision explicitly held that the equal protection clause protected their equal right to earn a livelihood in the common occupations of the state.

In early 1914, the Arizona legislature enacted a law requiring that at least 80 percent of the employees of every business operating within the state had to be American citizens. At the time, Mike Raich, an Austrian citizen who was a legally admitted alien, was working as a cook in a Bisbee, Arizona, restaurant. His employer, William Truax, discharged him solely because of the penalties that could be incurred under the new law. Filing suit in a U.S. district court, Raich asserted that the law denied him the equal protection of the law and was therefore contrary to the Fourteenth Amendment.

By an 8-1 vote, the U.S. Supreme Court upheld Raich's challenge. In unambiguous language, Justice Charles Evans Hughes wrote that the "right to work for a living in the common occupations of the community is of the very essence of the personal freedom and opportunity that it was the purpose of the Fourteenth Amendment to secure." The Arizona statute, moreover, violated the principles of federalism. Because the power to admit or exclude aliens was vested exclusively in Congress, the states "may not deprive aliens so admitted of the right to earn a livelihood, as that would be tantamount to denying their entrance and abode."

Thomas Tandy Lewis

FURTHER READING

Aleinikoff, Thomas A., et al. *Immigration and Citizenship: Process and Policy.* 6th ed. St. Paul, Minn.: Thomson/West, 2008.

Epstein, Lee, and Thomas Walker. *Constitutional Law for a Changing America: Rights, Liberties, and Justice.* 6th ed. Washington, D.C.: CQ Press, 2006.

SEE ALSO: Citizenship; Due process protections; History of immigration after 1891; Supreme Court, U.S.; *Terrace v. Thompson.*

TURKISH IMMIGRANTS

SIGNIFICANCE: Although Turkey has a moderately large population, the numbers of Turks who have immigrated to the United States have never been great, and by the early twenty-first century, the Turkish American population remained small. The community is made of immigrants and their descendants who came during the time of the former Ottoman Empire as well as people who came after the Turkish Republic was founded in 1923. Most of the immigrants settled in large cities, seeking better economic opportunities.

The first wave of Turkish immigration to the United States occurred between 1860 and 1920. During that period, 400,000 people from the Ottoman Empire were recorded as entering the country. However, only 10 to 15 percent of them identified themselves as ethnic Turks. Most were Greeks, Armenians, Christian Arabs, Jews, and Slavs from Macedonia and other parts of the Balkan Peninsula. The total number of Muslims among these first newcomers was estimated at 15,000-20,000, approximately 85-90 percent of whom were men. Most Turkish immigrants from the Ottoman Empire came to the United States intending eventu-

ally to return to their homeland, and it has been estimated that about 84 percent of them actually did go back to Turkey.

Turkish immigration slowed considerably during World War I, in which the Ottoman Empire fought on the side of the Central Powers. During the 1920's, as Turkey was undergoing a political revolution under the leadership of Mustafa Kemal Atatürk, restrictive quotas added to U.S. immigration law continued to keep Turkish immigration figures down.

Turkish immigration resumed during the 1950's. The immigrants who came during this period were different from their predecessors in having a sense of national belonging. Unlike subjects of the old Ottoman Empire, they consciously identified them-

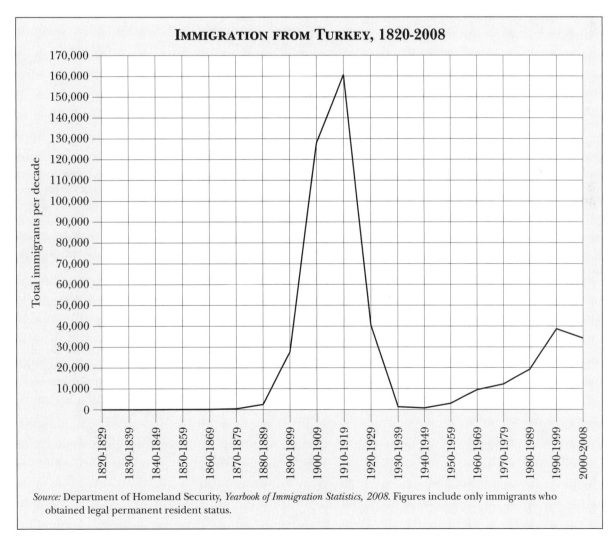

IMMIGRATION FROM TURKEY, 1820-2008

Total immigrants per decade

Source: Department of Homeland Security, *Yearbook of Immigration Statistics, 2008*. Figures include only immigrants who obtained legal permanent resident status.

PROFILE OF TURKISH IMMIGRANTS

Country of origin	Turkey
Primary language	Turkish
Primary regions of U.S. settlement	East Coast cities
Earliest significant arrivals	c. 1900
Peak immigration period	1890's-1920's
Twenty-first century legal residents*	31,644 (3,956 per year)

*Immigrants who obtained legal permanent resident status in the United States.
Source: Department of Homeland Security, *Yearbook of Immigration Statistics, 2008.*

selves as Turks because of Atatürk's nationalist movement to promote Turkish ethnicity in the new republic. Again, most of the Turkish immigrants were male, but unlike the early immigrants, these newcomers included professionals, particularly engineers and physicians. The Turkish Republic offered attractive employment incentives to Turks educated overseas to return to their homeland, and some of the immigrants did return.

The next wave of Turkish immigrants started coming during the 1970's. During the 1960's and early 1970's, most Turks who immigrated to the United States had come for educational and economic opportunities. During the late 1970's and 1980's, a set of political conflicts evolving in Cyprus, eastern Turkey, and Bulgaria motivated Turks to leave their homeland.

The Turkish Republic's policy was to build a secular state and a society with new identity for its citizens that merged modernity with Turkish ethnicity, while rejecting the religious culture and Ottoman past. Consequently Turks who immigrated to America during the late twentieth century arrived with a new attitude, fostered by a mixture of national solidarity and openness to modern life. Unlike their predecessors, they managed to establish Turkish American communities by adapting their values and sense of Turkishness to the society and economy of the United States.

Passage of the Immigration and Nationality Act of 1965 abolished the national quotas of the 1920's, opening the way for increased numbers of Turks to come to the United States. During the 1970's, about 1,300 Turks immigrated each year. By the 1990's, that figure had risen to 3,800 immigrants a year. During the early years of the twenty-first century, the annual average leveled off to about 3,000 immigrants per year. During the early twenty-first century, the largest concentrations of ethnic Turks were living in New York City, Rochester, New York, Washington, D.C., and Detroit, Michigan.

Elitza Kotzeva

FURTHER READING

Ahmed, Frank. *Turks in America: The Ottoman Turk's Immigrant Experience.* Greenwich, Conn.: Columbia International, 1993.

Balgamis, A. Deniz, and Kemal H. Karpat. *Turkish Migration to the United States: From Ottoman Times to the Present.* Madison: Center for Turkish Studies at the University of Wisconsin, 2008.

DiCarlo, Lisa. *Migrating to America: Transnational Social Networks and Regional Identity Among Turkish Migrants.* London: Tauris Academic Studies, 2008.

Lewis, Bernard. *The Emergence of Modern Turkey.* New York: Oxford University Press, 2002.

SEE ALSO: Economic opportunities; Employment; European immigrants; Greek immigrants; Immigration and Nationality Act of 1965; Immigration waves; Muslim immigrants; Return migration.

U

"UNDESIRABLE ALIENS"

DEFINITION: Term for foreign immigrants who are judged to be unsuitable for admission to the United States because of their presumed low morals, poor health, objectional political or religious views, or other reasons

SIGNIFICANCE: An essential irony of U.S. immigration history has been the propensity of Americans to stigmatize members of certain groups and categories. Although the types of immigrants who have been denigrated have changed from era to era, a fundamental cause for their stigmatization has generally been some form of fear, such as fear of loss of hegemony by the majority groups, fear of cultural change, or fear of criminal behavior.

Unlike some countries, such as the Philippines, the United States does not have a legal definition for "undesirable alien." In America, the concept of undesirable aliens derives from popular, not legal parlance, primarily in journalism and in the rhetoric of speakers and writers opposed to immigration by members of certain groups. The closest equivalent in law, one that turns up in statutes and court cases having to do with immigration, naturalization, and deportation, is the term "undesirable resident." However, even this term seems to lack a clear definition. Moreover, it might be applied to native-born citizen as well as foreigners.

Outside the legal community, the term "undesirable aliens" has traditionally been leveled against a wide range of groups for an equally wide range of reasons, with race and religion perhaps prompting its most frequent application. For example, from the days of the early republic through the early twentieth century, French, German, Irish, and Italian immigrants were often stigmatized simply because many of them were Roman Catholics. Inevitably, religious intolerance led to sadly ironic mistakes, such as U.S. attacks on French Huguenots, whose ancestors had fled to America because they were Protestants weary of living under Roman Catholic rulers.

Discrimination against immigrants based on race has a long legal history in the United States as well. Through much of the nineteenth and early twentieth centuries, various laws prohibited or severely rigidly restricted immigration from eastern and southern Europe and non-European countries. Anti-Chinese sentiment was especially vitriolic, resulting in such discriminatory legislation as the Chinese Exclusion Act of 1882, which all but ended immigration from China for decades, and such atrocities as the 1887 massacre of nearly three dozen Chinese workers at Snake River, Oregon. The perception of nonwhites as "undesirables" also led to some of the most shameful court cases in American history, such as 1922's *Ozawa v. United States*, in which Japanese were declared not to be "white" and the 1923 *United States v. Bhagat Singh Thind* ruling, in which a World War I veteran of Punjabi origin was denied U.S. citizenship because people from the Indian subcontinent were judged to be neither "white" nor "Caucasian."

BEYOND RACE AND RELIGION

Numerous other factors have led certain groups of immigrants to be tagged as undesirable in America. One of the most obvious is the fear of political subversion or sabotage. The first instance of such a fear resulting in legislation happened early in the republic, when tensions between the United States and France moved legislators to pass the Alien and Sedition Acts of 1798, which allowed authorities to deport noncitizens who were deemed threats to the government.

Similar worries of officials and the public led to discrimination against Germans during both World War I and World War II. During the latter conflict, the state of Minnesota passed a law forbidding the speaking of German. However, the most glaring example of fear causing an immigrant population to be seen as "undesirable" because they threatened national security was the internment of more than 100,000 Japanese Americans during World War II.

Fear of political subversion spread in the aftermath of President William McKinley's assassination in 1901 by a Polish American anarchist. That same fear, refocused on communists, increased after World War II during the Cold War between the

United States and the Soviet Union. During the early twenty-first century, in the wake of the attacks of September 11, 2001, fear of subversion by Islamic militants surged, resulting in acts of prejudice against both aliens and citizens of Middle Eastern descent.

After race, religion, and political persuasion, perhaps the most prominent force that creates circumstances in which members of alien groups come to be perceived as "undesirable" is fear of submersion. In these instances, Americans who see themselves as "mainstream" or "typical" fear the loss of their way of life because of a large influx of immigrants with cultures and folkways different from theirs. For example, Irish and Italian people had been present in small numbers before the American Revolution, but xenophobic attitudes toward them as groups did not emerge on a large scale until large waves of them came, first with the Irish during the Great Irish Famine during the mid-nineteenth century and then when similar economic disasters befell Italy in the latter half of the century. Only after these groups appeared in great numbers did anti-Irish and anti-Italian rhetoric appear and violence occur: for example, the notorious signs reading "No Irish Need Apply" in windows of businesses and the slaying of eleven Italian Americans in the streets of New Orleans in 1890 because of their suspected but totally unproven connection to the killing of a local police chief. Likewise, much xenophobic propaganda about Latinos stresses the large number of recent immigrants and feeds on the fear that "Anglo" culture will be subsumed and English will be replaced by Spanish.

Thomas Du Bose

Anti-immigrant cartoon published in 1913 in which eastern and southern European immigrants are dressed in Japanese kimonos, suggesting that the principle applied to keeping Japanese immigrants out of the country might be used to keep out other undesirables. (Library of Congress)

FURTHER READING

Bernard, William, Carolyn Zeleny, and Henry Miller, eds. *American Immigration Policy.* Port Washington, N.Y.: Kennikat Press, 1969. Thorough review of U.S. immigration legislation, including discriminatory laws and rulings.

Curran, Thomas J. *Xenophobia and Immigration, 1820-1930.* Boston: Twayne, 1975. Provides a wealth of detail on one of the most colorful periods of immigration in America and the negative stereotypes that members of various immigrant groups faced.

Dalla, R. L., John Defrain, Julie Johnson, and Douglas A. Abbott, eds. *Strengths and Challenges of New Immigrant Families.* Lanham, Md.: Lexington Books, 2008. Interesting collection of essays on how immigrant families cope with such problems as negative stereotyping.

Daniels, Roger. *Coming to America: A History of Immigration and Ethnicity in American Life.* New York: HarperCollins, 1990. One of the best books on the subject of the role of ethnicity in immigration history.

Vellos, Diana. "Immigrant Latina Domestic Workers and Sexual Harassment." *American University Journal of Gender and the Law* 407 (Spring, 1997): 414-418. The first four pages of this article contain a pithy summary of the history of discrimination against various immigrant groups in America.

SEE ALSO: Alien and Sedition Acts of 1798; American Protective Association; Anglo-conformity; Chinese Exclusion Act of 1882; Criminal immigrants; Deportation; Infectious diseases; "Moral turpitude"; Stereotyping.

UNITED FARM WORKERS

IDENTIFICATION: Agricultural labor union movement
DATE: Established on September 30, 1962, as the National Farm Workers Association
LOCATION: Fresno, California
ALSO KNOWN AS: UFW; United Farm Workers of America

SIGNIFICANCE: The first successful American farm labor union, the United Farm Workers used civil disobedience and a social justice platform to win wage concessions, collective bargaining rights, and better working and living conditions from growers, as well as legal protection for previously powerless and unorganized agricultural laborers.

In 1942, wartime labor shortages in the United States led to the establishment of the bracero program, which contracted Mexican citizens as temporary guest workers. Through the next twenty-two years, more than 4 million of the bracero workers who entered the United States worked in California agricultural fields. One consequence of the bracero program was that Mexican American farmworkers suffered job losses because of their inability to compete with Mexican braceros, who were willing to endure worse working conditions. During the early 1960's, most agricultural workers in California lived in temporary, insect-infested hous-

ing, without clean drinking water, electricity, cooking facilities, or sanitary facilities. Average wages for workers were ninety cents per hour, without benefits of any kind. The average life expectancy of farmworkers was only forty-nine years. Although the federal government terminated the bracero program at the end of 1964, Mexican American farmworkers continued to be impoverished.

FOUNDING OF THE UNION

Born in Arizona in 1927, César Chávez was ten when his father died and his family lost its farm. Forced into migrant farmwork, Chávez attended thirty-seven different schools as his family moved throughout the Southwest, ever looking for work. After completing the eighth grade, Chávez became a full-time migrant worker. In 1948, he married fellow farmworker Helen Fabela, with whom he settled in an impoverished barrio in San Jose, California. There Chávez met Father Donald McDonnell, an outspoken advocate of fair wages, better treat-

César Chávez in 1966. (Library of Congress)

ment of farmworkers, and universal education. Under McDonnell's guidance, Chávez studied the nonviolent activism of Mohandas Gandhi and Martin Luther King, Jr.

In 1952, Chávez became an organizer with the Community Service Organization (CSO), a Latino civil rights group conducting successful voter registration drives and urban campaigns. Within six years, he was CSO's executive director; however, what he most wanted to do was to create an organization whose primary mission was to protect farmworkers, a vision shared by fellow CSO organizer Dolores Huerta. A native-born Californian, Huerta was an effective lobbyist and negotiator who understood the plight of agricultural workers. In 1862, Huerta and Chávez both resigned from the CSO so they could establish the National Farm Workers Association (NFWA).

On September 30, 1962 in Fresno, California, several hundred workers attended the first convention of the NFWA, which would be renamed the United Farm Workers of America (UFW) ten years later. Members set union dues at $3.50, adopted the slogan *Viva La Causa* (long live the cause), and unveiled an official flag with a black eagle symbol over a white circle within a red field.

The First Strike

In September 1965, Filipino grape pickers from the Agricultural Workers Organizing Committee (AWOC) invited NFWA members to join their strike for decent wages in Delano, California. At that time, the NFWA had 1,200 member-families but only one hundred dollars in its treasury, so it joined the strike on September 16 in order to raise awareness of farmworker concerns. About 5,000 workers picketed more than 30 vineyards in the San Joaquin Valley. Although the growers beat the strikers and sprayed them with chemicals, Chávez insisted on strikers responding nonviolently.

As the strike continued into 1966, it won the support of churches, universities, civil rights activists, community organizations, and labor groups. Strikers called for a consumer boycott of the products of Schenley Industries, a major wine grape grower. In March, Chávez and hundreds of strikers began a historic 340-mile, twenty-five-day march from Delano to Sacramento, California's state capital. By the time they reached the capitol building on Easter Sunday, April 10, they were 10,000

strong. Meanwhile, Schenley had agreed to sign the union's first contract.

In August, 1966, NFWA and AWOC merged to become the United Farm Workers Organizing Committee, AFL-CIO (UFWOC). In 1967, the union boycotted Giumarra Vineyards, California's largest table grape grower. When it was learned that Giumarra grapes were being shipped under other growers' labels, Chávez called for a consumer boycott of all California table grapes in January, 1968. Volunteers, major supermarket chains, local governments, labor unions in Sweden and Great Britain, and others joined to make the boycott successful. By September, 1970, most California grape growers had signed three-year union contracts covering more than 20,000 jobs and more than 10,000 union members. These contracts provided wage increases to $1.80 per hour, restrictions on use of dangerous pesticides, health care benefits, provision of field toilets, and other benefits.

Continuing the Work

In 1972 the UFW became the United Farm Workers of America, chartered as an independent affiliate by the AFL-CIO. The UFW won the 1975 passage of the landmark California Agricultural Labor Relations Act, establishing collective bargaining for farmworkers. By the 1980's, about 45,000 farm laborers were protected by UFW contracts. The UFW continued efforts in the wine, lettuce, strawberry, vegetable, and other industries. After Chávez died in 1993, Arturo Rodriguez became the union's president. Between 1994 and 2005, the UFW bargained on behalf of workers in California, Florida, Washington State, Arizona, and Texas. Since 2000, the UFW has used the Internet to help mobilize massive grassroots support. The UFW has had a significant impact on Latino, labor, and immigrant rights movements.

Alice Myers

Further Reading

Dalton, Frederick John. *The Moral Vision of César Chávez.* Maryknoll, N.Y.: Orbis Books, 2003. Exploration of how Chávez's deep religious faith shaped his activism and the UFW.

Ferriss, Susan, Ricardo Sandoval, and Diana Hembree. *The Fight in the Fields: César Chávez and the Farmworkers Movement.* New York: Harcourt Brace, 1997. A companion volume to a public television documentary, this biography includes contemporary eyewitnesses accounts of the farmworker movement.

Ganz, Marshall. *Why David Sometimes Wins: Leadership, Organization, and Strategy in the California Farm Worker Movement.* New York: Oxford University Press, 2009. A former colleague of Chávez in the UFW, Ganz documents the initially powerless UFW's victory over California's powerful grape industry.

Levy, Jacques E. *César Chávez: Autobiography of La Causa.* Minneapolis: University of Minnesota Press, 2007. Prize-winning journalist's portrait of Chávez and the UFW.

Shaw, Randy. *Beyond the Fields: César Chávez, the UFW, and the Struggle for Justice in the Twenty-first Century.* Berkeley: University of California Press, 2008. Study of how the UFW helped shape modern movements for immigrant and labor rights.

SEE ALSO: Arizona; Bracero program; California; Chicano movement; Civil Rights movement; Farm and migrant workers; Filipino immigrants; Mexican immigrants; Mexican Revolution.

UNITED STATES V. BHAGAT SINGH THIND

THE CASE: U.S. Supreme Court decision concerning naturalization
DATE: Decided on February 19, 1923

SIGNIFICANCE: In an interpretation of the immigration laws, the Supreme Court held that immigrants from India were ineligible to become naturalized citizens, and since the decision classified Indians as Asians, it eliminated a number of legal rights that immigrants from India had previously enjoyed.

Bhagat Singh Thind, a resident of Oregon, was an immigrant from the Punjab region of northwestern India. When he applied for naturalization in the United States, he appeared to have a good chance of having his application accepted. Al-

though U.S. immigration law had since 1790 restricted naturalization to "white persons," in the previous year's case of *Ozawa v. United States* the U.S. Supreme Court had defined the term as synonymous with the word "Caucasian." Anthropologists at the time classified people of northwestern India as belonging to the "Caucasian race." It was also relevant that Thind was a person of light complexion and a member of a high caste, which meant that his ancestors had presumably been Aryans who spoke an Indo-European language.

Nevertheless, in Thind's case the U.S. Supreme Court held unanimously that immigration laws did not permit any persons of Indian ancestry to become naturalized citizens. In the official opinion for the Court, Justice George Sutherland wrote that such an individual was not a "white person" as used in the "common speech . . . interpreted in accordance with the understanding of the common man." Although high-caste Indians in the Punjab had historically attempted to preserve the "purity of Aryan blood," Sutherland wrote that they had not been entirely successful, so that there had been an "intermixture of blood" with Asian races. Because the decision classified Indians as Asians, they henceforth fell under the restrictions of the California Alien Land Law, making it illegal for them to own land in the state. In addition, A. K. Mozumdar, the first person of Indian origin to have been naturalized, had his citizenship revoked. The *Thind* ruling was overturned by the Luce-Celler Bill of 1946, insofar as it extended the privilege of naturalization to Indians.

Thomas Tandy Lewis

FURTHER READING
Hyung-chan, Kim, ed. *Asian Americans and the Supreme Court: A Documentary History.* Westport, Conn.: Greenwood Press, 1992.
Rangaswamy, Padma. *Indian Americans.* New York: Chelsea House, 2007.

SEE ALSO: Asian immigrants; Asian Indian immigrants; Citizenship; Congress, U.S.; Naturalization Act of 1790; *Ozawa v. United States*; Supreme Court, U.S.; "Undesirable aliens."

UNITED STATES V. JU TOY

THE CASE: U.S. Supreme Court decision on
habeas corpus relief and due process
DATE: Decided on May 8, 1905

SIGNIFICANCE: The *Ju Toy* decision held that
the due process clause of the Fifth Amendment does not always require a judicial procedure for denial of benefits, even when a person claims to be a U.S. citizen. Congress,
therefore, may authorize an executive department to make the final determination on
a person's claim to citizenship.

When Ju Toy arrived at the port of San Francisco,
he claimed to be a U.S. citizen returning from a
temporary visit to China. Immigration officials,
however, rejected his claim of citizenship and denied him permission to enter the country. The ruling was upheld on administrative appeal by the
secretary of commerce and labor. When Toy petitioned the U.S. district court for a writ of habeas
corpus, his petition was rejected. In earlier cases,
the Supreme Court had upheld a federal law authorizing executive departments to make the final
determination concerning the admission of persons affected by the Chinese Exclusion Act of 1882,
but the Court had never ruled on whether the U.S.
Constitution permitted a denial of habeas corpus
relief for a person claiming to be a U.S. citizen by
birth.

By a 6-3 vote, the U.S. Supreme Court endorsed
the district court's decision. Writing for the majority, Justice Oliver Wendell Holmes referred to a series of precedents holding that judicial proceedings were not necessary in every assertion of legal
rights, but that determinations by the executive
branch were usually sufficient when mandated by
Congress. He defended the procedures used in determining Toy's status, particularly since it had included an administrative appeal. He suggested,
nevertheless, that district courts should grant habeas corpus relief whenever there was good evidence that officers had abused their discretion or
committed prejudicial error. In a strong dissent,
Justice David Brewer argued that claims of citizenship should be decided by the courts.

Thomas Tandy Lewis

*Associate Justice Oliver Wendell Holmes, who wrote the
majority opinion in* United States v. Ju Toy. *(Library
of Congress)*

FURTHER READING

Aleinikoff, Thomas A., et al. *Immigration and Citizenship: Process and Policy.* 6th ed. St. Paul, Minn.:
Thomson/West, 2008.

Hyung-chan, Kim, ed. *Asian Americans and the Supreme Court: A Documentary History.* Westport,
Conn.: Greenwood Press, 1992.

SEE ALSO: *Chinese Exclusion Cases*; Citizenship; Congress, U.S.; Due process protections; History of immigration after 1891; Supreme Court, U.S.

UNITED STATES V. WONG KIM ARK

THE CASE: U.S. Supreme Court decision about citizenship

DATE: Decided on March 28, 1898

SIGNIFICANCE: Based on the Fourteenth Amendment, the *Wong Kim Ark* decision held that any person born on American soil is a citizen of the United States. Before this decision, jurists had disagreed about the citizenship status of babies born in the country to alien parents.

Wong Kim Ark was born in San Francisco to Chinese parents. When he attempted to return to the United States after a visit to China, U.S. Customs officials refused him entry on the basis of the federal Chinese exclusion laws, which severely limited Chinese immigration and prohibited persons of Chinese ancestry from becoming naturalized citizens. The position of the executive branch at the time defined citizenship based on the nationality of parents (jus sanguinis) rather than the place of birth (jus soli). Referring to the Chinese exclusion laws, government lawyers argued that persons of Chinese parentage were not eligible for citizenship because they were under the jurisdiction of the emperor of China.

However, the U.S. Supreme Court recognized, by a 6-2 margin, that Wong Kim Ark was a U.S. citizen because of his place of birth. Writing for the majority, Justice Horace Gray based the decision primarily on a literal reading of the citizenship clause of the Fourteenth Amendment: "All persons born or naturalized in the United States, and subject to the jurisdiction thereof, are citizens of the United States." Even though the primary intent of the Fourteenth Amendment had been to guarantee citizenship for the former slaves and their descendants, Gray insisted that the comprehensive phrase "all persons" made it unconstitutional to exclude anyone because of race or national origin.

In regard to the phrase "subject to the jurisdiction thereof," a person living in the country "owes obedience to the laws of that government, and may be punished for treason or other crimes." The English common law, moreover, had long recognized only two exceptions to granting citizenship based on jus soli: children of foreign diplomats and children of enemy forces occupying a part of the country's territory. Finally, Gray emphasized that the Fourteenth Amendment was "the supreme law of the land," so that congressional legislation "cannot control its meaning, or impair its effect, but must be construed and executed in subordination to its provisions."

The application of the *Wong Kim Ark* ruling went far beyond persons affected by the Chinese exclu-

---

UNITED STATES V. WONG KIM ARK

Justice Horace Gray delivered the opinion of the majority in United States v. Wong Kim Ark. *His decision was based upon the precedents set by international law, as well as statements made by U.S. senators while debating the language and meaning of the Fourteenth Amendment, who had explicitly considered the case of children born to Chinese immigrants.*

The fourteenth amendment affirms the ancient and fundamental rule of citizenship by birth within the territory, in the allegiance and under the protection of the country, including all children here born of resident aliens, with the exceptions or qualifications (as old as the rule itself) of children of foreign sovereigns or their ministers, or born on foreign public ships, or of enemies within and during a hostile occupation of part of our territory, and with the single additional exception of children of members of the Indian tribes owing direct allegiance to their several tribes. The amendment, in clear words and in manifest intent, includes the children born within the territory of the United States of all other persons, of whatever race or color, domiciled within the United States. Every citizen or subject of another country, while domiciled here, is within the allegiance and the protection, and consequently subject to the jurisdiction, of the United States. . . .

To hold that the fourteenth amendment of the constitution excludes from citizenship the children born in the United States of citizens or subjects of other countries, would be to deny citizenship to thousands of persons of English, Scotch, Irish, German, or other European parentage, who have always been considered and treated as citizens of the United States.

sion laws. The Naturalization Act of 1790 stipulated that only "free white persons" were eligible to become naturalized citizens, and the law continued for some ethnic groups until 1952. In addition, many illegal immigrants have given birth to babies on American soil, and they continue to do so. The *Wong Kim Ark* ruling clarified the legal status of all such children.

Thomas Tandy Lewis

FURTHER READING

Aleinikoff, Thomas A., et al. *Immigration and Citizenship: Process and Policy.* 6th ed. St. Paul, Minn.: Thomson/West, 2008.

Salyer, Lucy. *Laws as Harsh as Tigers: Chinese Immigrants and the Shaping of Modern Immigration Law.* Chapel Hill: University of North Carolina Press, 1995.

SEE ALSO: Arab immigrants; Chinese Exclusion Act of 1882; Citizenship; Constitution, U.S.; History of immigration after 1891; Naturalization Act of 1790; Supreme Court, U.S.

UNIVERSAL NEGRO IMPROVEMENT ASSOCIATION

IDENTIFICATION: Organization created to promote the condition of black people around the world

DATE: Established in 1914

ALSO KNOWN AS: UNIA

SIGNIFICANCE: Founded by Marcus Garvey, the UNIA was created to promote racial unity and uplift among peoples of the African diaspora and to foster a back-to-Africa movement for African Americans.

Marcus Garvey established the Universal Negro Improvement Association in Jamaica in August of 1914 to encourage self-pride, unity, and the advancement of black people around the world. Using the motto, "One God! One Aim! One Destiny," the movement had as one of its objectives the return of Americans of African descent to Africa.

After traveling to various Central and South American countries, England, and parts of Africa,

Garvey was displeased with the living conditions and hardships of the black people whom he encountered and decided to work to improve their lot. After returning to Jamaica, he organized the UNIA with the intention of building an international movement. In 1916, he relocated to the United States. After traveling throughout the southern states and witnessing the injustices that black Americans faced, he became convinced that achieving economic independence was the key to improving the political and social condition of black people. The following year, he formed a chapter of the UNIA in New York City, which became his movement's headquarters.

From the UNIA's Liberty Hall in New York City's Harlem district, Garvey delivered his message to audiences of thousands. His movement's goals included promoting racial pride, assisting the deprived, establishing schools and universities, promoting economic independence through black-owned commercial endeavors, and assisting people of African descent to return to Africa. Millions of African Americans were stirred by Garvey's message, but the actual number of dues-paying UNIA members was never more than a few tens of thousands.

The UNIA reached many of Garvey's followers through its weekly newspaper, the *Negro World*, which had a worldwide circulation. The UNIA also formed such uniformed auxiliary groups as the African Legion, the Black Cross Nurses, and the Universal Motor Corps. These groups served to organize and unite the people to help build self-esteem and promote self-reliance among adults as well as the youth. For Garvey, the swiftest and efficient way to economic liberation was through black-controlled trade and industrial success. The UNIA launched a shipping line called the Black Star Line to carry cargo and transport passengers to Africa; however, faulty management and unwise purchases of ships led to its collapse. The UNIA itself ceased to be an international organization after Garvey was imprisoned in 1925 on mail-fraud charges relating to the mismanagement of the shipping line.

The UNIA continued to operate for several years but lost its impetus and gradually splintered into a few vestigial bodies. The UNIA operated as a mass movement for only a brief period, but it was the first organization in the United States to gather an enormous membership of people of African descent. The association was determined to offer people of African descent a sense of racial pride, Garvey was the first to publicly announce "black is beautiful," for the sake of instilling a sense of pride among black people.

Diana Pardo

FURTHER READING

Cronon, Edmund David. *The Black Moses: The Story of Marcus Garvey and the Universal Negro Improvement Association.* Madison: University of Wisconsin Press, 1969.

Garvey, Marcus. *Selected Writings and Speeches of Marcus Garvey.* Edited by Bob Blaisdell. New York: Dover, 2004.

Grant, Colin. *Negro with a Hat: The Rise and Fall of Marcus Garvey.* New York: Oxford University Press, 2008.

Hill, Robert A., ed. *The Marcus Garvey and Universal Negro Improvement Association Papers.* 9 vols. Berkeley: University of Californa Press, 1983-1996.

SEE ALSO: African Americans and immigrants; American Colonization Society; Garvey, Marcus; Latin American immigrants; Mexican immigrants.

UNIVISION

IDENTIFICATION: Spanish-language media company

DATE: Founded in 1962 as the Spanish International Network

ALSO KNOWN AS: Univision Communications Incorporated

SIGNIFICANCE: The leading Spanish-language media company in the United States, Univision operates radio and television stations and cable networks and has recorded music and Internet divisions. Its services provide broad-based programming content that competes effectively with English-language media, providing important sources of information and entertainment for Hispanic Americans and Spanish-speaking immigrants.

Univision began in 1962 as the Spanish International Network (SIN) through the facilities of flagship station KWEX-TV, San Antonio, Texas. During that same year, KMEX-TV in Los Angeles, went on the air, followed by other SIN-owned and operated stations to form the first foreign-language broadcast television network in the United States.

As SIN was partly foreign owned, the Federal Communications Commission (FCC) ordered its sale in 1986. Hallmark Cards bought the network, changed its name to Univision, and developed programming to attract a broader national audience, while still addressing Hispanic viewers. In 1992, Hallmark sold Univision to an American-Venezuelan-Mexican consortium. In 2006, the network again went on sale. The private equity investors Broadcast Media Partners, Incorporated, purchased it the following year. Since then, Univision Communications, Inc., has been headquartered in New York City, and its primary television production center has been located in Miami, Florida.

Following the example of other national networks that owned multiple services, Univision launched and acquired media properties providing new markets, the first of which was America's first Spanish-language cable service, Galavision Network, with was launched in 1979. The Univision Online division was launched in 2000, creating Univision.com., which would become the most frequently accessed Spanish-language site on the World Wide Web. In 2008, the division was renamed Univision Interactive Media, which added Univision Movil to deliver mobile interactive content.

In 2002, Univision acquired USA Broadcasting, along with its thirteen broadcast television stations, to form a second Spanish-language television service called TeleFutura Network that reached more than 85 percent of all U.S. Hispanic households. In 2003, Univision acquired Hispanic Broadcasting Corporation and established Univision Radio, the largest Spanish-language radio group in America, with more than seventy radio stations that reached about 75 percent of the U.S. Hispanic population, as well as Puerto Rico.

By the early twenty-first century, Univision Network was maintaining an audience-share advantage over its main competitor, Telemundo, largely through imported programming produced in Mexico by Televisa, the world's largest producer of Spanish-language television shows. Televisa's long-term arrangement to supply programs to Univision has served as an important cultural link between Mexican immigrants in the United States and their homeland. Central American immigrants are also familiar with Televisa programs broadcast on Univision. Access to familiar television programming has helped Latin American immigrants adjust to life in the United States.

As a multimedia conglomerate reaching millions of people, Univision has also helped to promote voter education and raise awareness of immigration issues. Together with other Spanish-language media, Univision has played an activist role by mobilizing Hispanics to social action. In 1994, when California's Proposition 187 went on the ballot to limit government benefits for undocumented immigrants, Univision contributed $100,000 to oppose the measure. In 2006, a group of activists enlisted Univision and other Hispanic broadcasters to help mobilize more than 500,000 people in a peaceful national protest against proposed federal immigration policy reforms.

In 2008, Univision received a prestigious Peabody Award for its *Ya Es Hora* (it's time) public service campaign, an effort to inform, educate and motivate Hispanic participation in citizenship and political matters. The campaign included public service announcements that encouraged eligible permanent legal residents to apply for U.S. citizenship and supported get-out-the-vote efforts.

Dennis A. Harp

FURTHER READING

Cambridge, Vibert C. *Immigration, Diversity, and Broadcasting in the United States, 1990-2001*. Athens: Ohio University Press, 2005.

Nuñez, Luis V., ed. *Spanish Language Media After the Univision-Hispanic Broadcasting*. New York: Novinka Books, 2006.

Rodriguez, America. *Making Latino News*. Thousand Oaks, Calif.: Sage Publications, 1999.

Rodriguez, Clara. *Latin Looks: Images of Latinas and Latinos in the U.S. Media*. Boulder, Colo.: Westview Press, 1997.

SEE ALSO: Latin American immigrants; Mexican immigrants; Spanish-language press; Telemundo; Television and radio.

UTAH

SIGNIFICANCE: The region that now forms the state of Utah was inhabited almost entirely by Native Americans as late as 1847, when Brigham Young led followers of the Mormon Church into the valley of the Great Salt Lake. Since that time, the state's immigration has been has been colored by the powerful presence of the church, which has maintained an aggressive worldwide missionary program to find new converts, many of whom have come to Utah. The state has also attracted large numbers of American-born Mormons and has one of the most homogenous populations of any American state.

Prior to the arrival of Mormon pioneers in Great Salt Lake Valley, the Native American Ute nation dominated the region now known as Utah. Soon after the establishment of Salt Lake City in 1847, more than 70,000 Americans migrated to Utah. Most of these immigrants were Mormon followers of the Church of Jesus Christ of Latter-day Saints (LDS). The vast majority of these early settlers were white Americans from the eastern United States. However, as they were moving into the region and establishing new settlements along the Wasatch Mountains range, other new immigrants were also beginning to enter the region.

LATE NINETEENTH CENTURY IMMIGRATION

In 1850, only fifty African Americans were known to be living in Utah; half of them had come as slaves. In 1870, Italian immigrants established a small community near Ogden, and an even smaller Chinese community was beginning to develop in Rock Springs. Soon, however, a series of anti-Chinese riots in Carbon County drove out most of the Chinese settlers, who were soon replaced by Japanese immigrants who were happy to take over jobs that become vacant.

The main impetus for foreign immigration into Utah was the work of Mormon missionaries in other countries. Shortly after Joseph Smith organized the Mormon Church during the 1830's, he began sending missionaries abroad to find new converts. From that time to the twenty-first century, the church has continued to maintain a strong missionary presence abroad. Early missionary efforts of the church focused on Canada, western Europe, and Australia, and the church assisted foreign converts who wished to come to Utah.

TWENTIETH CENTURY ARRIVALS

The early twentieth century saw the beginnings of heavy industry in Utah with the establishment of large coal and salt mines throughout the state. The mines frequently hired immigrant labor as they proved to be both cost-effective and less likely to organize unions. By 1903, the Castle Gate Mine alone employed 356 Italians and 108 Austrians. Meanwhile, Greek, Scandinavian, and Russian immigrants were beginning to settle in the state. They established small communities in the main urban centers of Salt Lake City, Provo, and Ogden.

Most immigrants coming to Utah sought land suitable for farming, while they followed the teachings of the Mormon Church. By the early twentieth century, Utah's economy was centered on agriculture and the development of sustainable food crops for livestock. Many Japanese immigrants farmed, but others who could not afford to buy land worked on railroad construction. In 1920, more than 3,000 Japanese were living in Utah. By 1970, that figure had risen to almost 5,000.

By the early twenty-first century, Utah's population had become more diverse, but 90 percent of the state's residents were white. The large percentage of white residents was partly due to the high rate of natural increase among Mormons, whose church encourages early marriage and large families. A similar percentage of residents were born in the United States. Thanks in part to the Mormon Church's past policy of excluding people of African

descent from enjoying full membership, Utah's African American population was very small, but Hispanics constituted about 8 percent of the state's total population.

Robert D. Mitchell

PROFILE OF UTAH

Region	Rocky Mountains
Entered union	1896
Largest cities	Salt Lake City (capital), West Valley City, Provo, Sandy, Orem
Modern immigrant communities	Japanese, Hispanics

Population	Total	Percent of state	Percent of U.S.	U.S. rank
All state residents	2,551,000	100.0	0.85	34
All foreign-born residents	211,000	8.3	0.56	25

Source: U.S. Census Bureau, *Statistical Abstract for 2006.*

Notes: The U.S. population in 2006 was 299,399,000, of whom 37,548,000 (12.5%) were foreign born. Rankings in last column reflect total numbers, not percentages.

FURTHER READING

Alexander, Thomas G. *Mormons and Gentiles: A History of Salt Lake City.* Boulder, Colo.: Pruett Publishing, 1984.

Mulder, William. *Homeward to Zion: The Mormon Migration from Scandinavia.* Minneapolis: University of Minnesota Press, 2000.

Stegner, Wallace. *The Gathering of Zion: The Story of the Mormon Trail.* New York: McGraw-Hill, 1964.

Stipanovich, Joseph. *The South Slavs in Utah: A Social History.* San Francisco: R&E Research Associates, 1975.

SEE ALSO: Chinese immigrants; Economic opportunities; Employment; History of immigration after 1891; Idaho; Italian immigrants; Mormon immigrants; Pacific Islander immigrants; Railroads.

V

VERMONT

SIGNIFICANCE: A small and comparatively homogenous state, Vermont has the fewest foreign-born residents of any New England state. Its percentage of foreign-born residents was only about 4 percent during the early twenty-first century, but it was rising rapidly, thanks to a growing influx of Mexican workers, many of whom were undocumented.

In 1609, the French explorer Samuel de Champlain claimed the area that is now Vermont for France, giving its mountains the name *Verd Mont* (green mountains). The French built a few military posts to protect their claims and established a fur trade with the local Algonquian people. However, they did little else to develop the region, which later passed into English hands and became known as New Hampshire Grants. Dutch immigrants settled in the southwest part of the region in 1724, but significant immigration did not begin until around 1750. With the help of the British crown, local settlers resisted the efforts of New York to absorb the region. In 1777, they declared their independence from both New York and Great Britain and renamed their territory Vermont. In 1791, Vermont became the first state after the original thirteen British colonies to join the union.

NINETEENTH CENTURY IMMIGRATION

Because Vermont shares a border with French-speaking Quebec, it has a long history of immigration from the north. The first significant influx of French Canadians came in 1837 and 1838 as a result of a British campaign in Quebec to curtail French influence.

As the only New England state without an Atlantic coastline, Vermont attracted fewer immigrants from overseas, but the composition of European immigrants who did come was similar to that of other New England states. The first

group to come in significant numbers were Irish immigrants, who tended to settle in the state's railroad towns of Bellows Falls, Northfield, Rutland, Burlington, and St. Albans. As early as 1846 Irish railroad workers staged the first strike ever in Vermont. Irish women also found wage employment, primarily as peddlers, mill workers, and domestic and farm servants. Most of these immigrants were Roman Catholics, and their presence helped candidates of the nativist Know-Nothing Party to get elected to the Vermont legislature during the 1850's.

Post-Civil War immigration into Vermont was characterized by the arrival of new immigrants from southern and eastern European countries. Russian Jews contributed to the business life of Burlington, the largest city, during the 1870's. Other immigrants from southern and eastern Europe found work in Vermont's urban centers. These new arrivals include small numbers of Greeks, many of whom worked as peddlers and in the restaurant industry. Many Russian, Polish, and Italian immigrants worked in the state's granite and marble industries. Vermont also had a thriving textile industry, and agents of a mill in Springfield that reprocessed old wool went to New York City to recruit workers from among Russian immigrants already living there. Russians also constituted an important part of the workforce in another Springfield

---

PROFILE OF VERMONT

Region	New England
Entered union	1791
Largest cities	Burlington, Essex, Rutland
Modern immigrant communities	Chinese, Mexicans

Population	Total	Percent of state	Percent of U.S.	U.S. rank
All state residents	624,000	100.0	0.21	49
All foreign-born residents	24,000	3.9	0.06	45

Source: U.S. Census Bureau, *Statistical Abstract for 2006.*
Notes: The U.S. population in 2006 was 299,399,000, of whom 37,548,000 (12.5%) were foreign born. Rankings in last column reflect total numbers, not percentages.

factory that produced turret lathes that revolutionized the machine tool industry.

TWENTIETH CENTURY TRENDS

The peak moment in Vermont immigration history came in 1910, when U.S. Census figures show that the state's foreign-born population was 14 percent. The bulk of these immigrants were French Canadians. By the early years of the Great Depression of the 1930's, Franco-Americans made up 75 percent of the workforce in Vermont's cotton and woolen mills. However, they were slower to assimilate than Irish and Jewish immigrant communities.

The predominantly Anglo-Protestant population of Vermont was never comfortable with the influx of eastern and southern European settlers. During the 1920's, one of its U.S. senators, William P. Dillingham, led a congressional movement against immigration from eastern and southern Europe and Asia and helped to enact laws restricting immigration from those regions. Since that time, Vermont has attracted few new immigrants from those parts of the world.

Despite nativist tendencies in Vermont history, the state has generally succeeded in accommodating foreign immigrants. For example, its educational system has ranked above national averages in all levels of education, reflecting the fact that immigrant children have not caused a decline in standards. Another measure of Vermont's success in accommodating immigrants has been its high rate of immigrant naturalization.

Robert P. Ellis

FURTHER READING

Brault, Gerard J. *The French-Canadian Heritage in New England.* Hanover, N.H.: University Press of New England, 1986.

Gallagher, Nancy L. *Breeding Better Vermonters: The Eugenics Project in the Green Mountain State.* Hanover, N.H.: University Press of New England, 1999.

Graffagnino, J. Kevin, et al. *Vermont Voices, 1609 Through the 1990's: A Documentary History of the Green Mountain State.* Montpelier: Vermont Historical Society, 1999.

Woolfson, A. Peter. *The French in Vermont: A Civil Rights Perspective.* Burlington: University of Vermont Center for Research on Vermont, 1983.

SEE ALSO: Canadian immigrants; Illegal immigration; Immigration Act of 1924; Jewish immigrants; Maine; New Hampshire.

VIETNAM WAR

THE EVENT: Military conflict in which the United States provided large-scale military assistance to the South Vietnamese government's unsuccessful effort to repel a takeover by North Vietnam's communist regime
DATE: Early 1960's to 1975
LOCATION: Southeast Asia

SIGNIFICANCE: American military involvement in the internal war in Vietnam spread to the adjacent countries of Laos and Cambodia, and the eventual communist victories in all three countries triggered a massive exodus of peoples, more than 2 million of whom immigrated to the United States. As the United States had experience almost no immigration from Southeast Asia before the war, the assimilation of these immigrants presented new challenges to both the immigrants and the United States.

During the long years of the Cold War, the United States defended noncommunist governments throughout the world. After France withdrew from its Southeast Asian colonies in 1954, an international agreement partitioned the former French Indochina into Laos, Cambodia, and North and South Vietnam. The division of Vietnam was intended to be temporary, but the fact that the North had a communist government and the South had a pro-Western government almost guaranteed future conflict. During Operation Passage to Freedom from August, 1954, to May, 1955, the U.S. Navy transported 310,000 primarily Roman Catholic Vietnamese from North to South Vietnam. After this time, a civil war developed in which the North sent troops into South Vietnam in an attempt to take over the entire country by force.

IMMIGRATION DURING THE VIETNAM WAR

American military involvement in the war in Vietnam began during the early 1960's and escalated gradually until the United States itself was one of the primary combatants. By 1969, the peak year of direct American military involvement, 541,000 American soldiers were serving in Southeast Asia, along with thousands of civilian support personnel. In 1964, before American military involvement began in earnest, only 603 Vietnamese were known to be living the United States. By the time the United States withdrew from Vietnam in 1975, that figure had risen to about 20,000. Most of these immigrants were Vietnamese women who had married American military personnel. However, that large increase in Vietnamese immigration to the United States was only a fraction of the numbers of immigrants who would arrive after the war.

Meanwhile, as communist North Vietnamese troops moved through Laos and Cambodia to reach South Vietnam, the governments of both neighboring countries became involved in the war. These developments help trigger communist insurgencies in Laos and Cambodia that helped lead both countries into economic and political chaos, but few Laotians and Cambodians who fled the disorders found their way to the United States. This was partly because direct American involvement in those countries was initially slight.

Postwar Immigration

Recognizing that it had become immersed in an unwinnable war, the United States began withdrawing its combat troops from Southeast Asia in early 1973. As American troops were leaving, the war continued and communist victories in Vietnam, Laos, and Cambodia, soon followed. On April 17, 1975, the fervently communist Khmer Rouge faction captured Phnom Penh, the capital of Cambodia, and began a murderous campaign against its political rivals. Two weeks later, North Vietnamese troops occupied Saigon, the capital of the South Vietnamese government, which then collapsed, ending the Vietnam War. In December, communists completed their conquest of Laos.

The communist victories in Southeast Asia triggered a massive exodus of people who had supported the anticommunist regimes and cooperated with

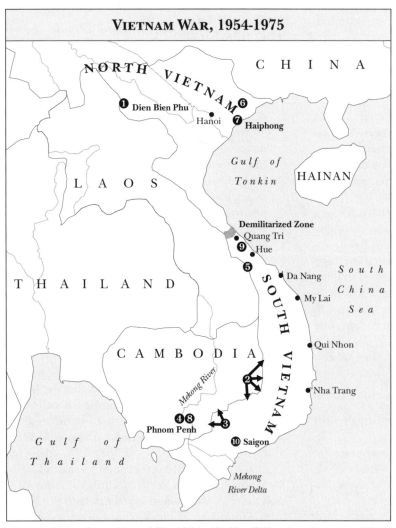

VIETNAM WAR, 1954-1975

(1) Last French position falls, 1954. (2) Tet Offensive, January, 1968. (3) Cambodian invasion, April-May, 1970. (4) Sihanouk falls, April, 1970. (5) Laotian incursion, February, 1971. (6) Areas of U.S. bombing, 1972. (7) Mining of Haiphong Harbor, May, 1972. (8) Lon Nol falls, April, 1975. (9) North Vietnamese offensive, spring, 1975. (10) South Vietnam surrenders, April 20, 1975.

South Vietnamese Marines leaping aboard an American naval vessel helping to evacuate Da Nang in April, 1975. (AP / Wide World Photos)

the American military. Many of these refugees eventually found their way to the United States. The biggest wave of refugees, by far, to reach America came from Vietnam. As the war was ending, the U.S. government helped evacuate about 65,000 Vietnamese on airplanes and on naval vessels anchored off South Vietnam. Another 65,000 Vietnamese reached American ships and bases on their own. Much smaller numbers of refugees from Laos and Cambodia succeeded in escaping. In 1975, about 4,600 Cambodians made it to the United States. Escaping from landlocked Laos was more difficult, and only about 800 Laotian refugees reached the United States. However, many Laotian Hmong who had fought against the communists alongside Americans fled into neighboring Thailand. From there, 10,200 of the Hmong refugees reached the United States in 1976.

In response to the growing refugee crisis in Southeast Asia, the U.S. Congress passed the Indochina Migration and Refugee Assistance Act shortly after the Vietnam War ended. Under this law, resettlement assistance was granted to some 130,400 refugees in 1975 alone. Most of these refugees were Vietnamese.

CONTINUING POSTWAR IMMIGRATION

Southeast Asia's postwar refugee exodus did not end in 1975. Because of the harsh and sometimes murderous policies of the region's communist governments, refugees continued to flee the region. This exodus accelerated in late 1978, and many refugees risked their lives by attempting to leave by sea on small boats. In response to this new crisis, the United States again lent assistance to the refugees by supporting the efforts of the United Nations High Commissioner for Refugees (UNHCR). In May, 1979, the UNHCR worked out an agreement with the Vietnamese government to establish what was called the Orderly Departure Program (ODP), which was designed to assist Vietnamese who wished to emigrate to Western countries. The United States accepted about one-half of the people leaving Vietnam under this program, as well as many of the boat people. Moreover, in July, 1979, the United States agreed to take in anticommunist refugees from the countries of their first arrival, such as Thailand. More U.S. legislation designed to assist refugees followed.

The Refugee Act of 1980 established the Office of Refugee Resettlement in the United States. To address the plight of Amerasians, children of American fathers and Asian mothers, the U.S. Congress passed both the Amerasian Immigration Act of 1982 and the Amerasian Homecoming Act of 1987. Through these two programs, some 25,000 Vietnamese Amerasians and 60,000-70,000 of their real or paper relatives immigrated to the United States.

In November, 2005, the United States and Vietnam agreed to a new program to facilitate the immigration to the United States of Vietnamese who had been interned in communist reeducation camps. Called the Humanitarian Resettlement Program, this venture expired on June 25, 2008, but one year later, the United States was still accepting immigrants whose processing had been delayed.

SUMMARY

As a direct result of the Vietnam War, about 770,000 Vietnamese, 260,000 Lao and Hmong people, and 146,000 Cambodians immigrated to America as refugees between 1975 and 2008—a total of about 1,176,000 people. In addition, more than 753,000 nonrefugee immigrants were accepted from Southeast Asia—about 623,000 from Vietnam, 77,000 from Cambodia, and 53,000 from Laos. It can thus be fairly argued that the approximately 2,300,000 million people of Vietnamese, Cambodian, and Lao heritage living in the United States in 2007 owe their ties to America to the Vietnam War.

R. C. Lutz

FURTHER READING

Desbarats, Jacqueline. "Indochinese Resettlement in the United States." In *The History and Immigration of Asian Americans*, edited by Franklin Ng. New York: Garland, 1998. Good overview of first Southeast Asians who came to the United States after the Vietnam War and their adjustment to American society.

Detzner, Daniel. *Elder Voices: Southeast Asian Families in the United States.* Walnut Creek, Calif.: AltaMira Press, 2004. Studies of forty leaders of Southeast Asian immigrant communities in the United States that illuminate postwar immigration issues.

Le, Cuong Nguyen. *Asian American Assimilation.* New York: LFB Scholarly Publishing, 2007. Includes concise description of how the Vietnam War led to Southeast Asian immigration to the United States, using census data to assess factors helping the immigrants adapt successfully to life in the United States. Excellent bibliography.

Schulzinger, Robert D. "The Vietnamese in America." In *A Time for Peace: The Legacy of the Vietnam War.* New York: Oxford University Press, 2006. This chapter in Schulzinger's book offers a sympathetic description of Vietnamese refugees in America and discusses their paths to assimilation and success.

Vo, Nghia M. *Vietnamese Boat People, 1954 and 1975-1992.* Jefferson, N.C.: McFarland, 2006. Focusing on the waves of Vietnamese immigration immediately after the Vietnam War, this book discusses how the immigrants adapted to life in the United States.

SEE ALSO: Amerasian children; Amerasian Homecoming Act of 1987; Cambodian immigrants; Freedom Airlift; Hmong immigrants; Indochina Migration and Refugee Assistance Act of 1975; Korean War; Laotian immigrants; Orderly Departure Program; Refugees; Vietnamese immigrants.

VIETNAMESE IMMIGRANTS

SIGNIFICANCE: Before the United States entered the Vietnam War during the early 1960's, fewer than 1,000 Vietnamese people lived in the United States. By the time the war ended in 1975, the number of Vietnamese residents had risen to 20,000, most of whom were spouses of American military personnel serving in Vietnam. Immediately after the war ended, tens of thousands of desperate refugees were admitted to the United States. Over the next three decades, even larger numbers of immigrants came in a more orderly fashion. By the early twenty-first century, more than 1.6 million Vietnamese were living in the United States. Although these people constituted one of the most recent immigrant groups, they were also one of the most successful groups.

When the Southeast Asian country of Vietnam finally gained its full independence from France in 1954, it was partitioned into a communist North called the Democratic Republic of Vietnam and a noncommunist South, which became the Republic of Vietnam in 1955. These two ideologically opposed nations soon began a civil war for mastery of all of Vietnam. Following its Cold War precepts, the U.S. government supported South Vietnam against its northern communist enemy.

Before this period, Vietnamese immigration had been practically nonexistent. Between 1950 and 1959, only 290 people from Vietnam became permanent residents of the United States. Most of these people were language teachers and students, along with a few people in commercial businesses. As late as 1964, only 603 Vietnamese were living in the United States.

THE VIETNAM WAR

The war in Vietnam intensified during the 1960's, when the North began working to topple the South's government in Saigon by force. To prevent a communist takeover of South Vietnam, the U.S. government committed increasing amounts of military equipment and personnel to the South's defense. This was not an easy task, as the South Vietnam government was both unstable and unpopular among its own people. By early 1965, the United States was sending substantial numbers of combat troops to fight for South Vietnam.

Although the U.S. military frowned on U.S. military personnel becoming involved with Vietnamese women, many soldiers married them. Many Americans also fathered children with Vietnamese women, who then automatically became eligible for U.S. citizenship when the fathers acknowledged their paternity or married the children's mothers. Gradually, the Vietnamese wives and children of Americans immigrated to the United States. By 1969, 2,949 Vietnamese were living in the country.

This slow immigration trend continued after American forces began withdrawing from South

PROFILE OF VIETNAMESE IMMIGRANTS	
Country of origin	Vietnam
Primary language	Vietnamese
Primary regions of U.S. settlement	California, Texas, Gulf coast states, Washington, Virginia, northeastern seaboard
Earliest significant arrivals	1950's
Peak immigration period	1975-2008
Twenty-first century legal residents*	246,256 (38,782 per year)

*Immigrants who obtained legal permanent resident status in the United States.
Source: Department of Homeland Security, *Yearbook of Immigration Statistics, 2008.*

Vietnam in early 1973, while leaving behind Americans who continued acting in advisory, diplomatic, and business roles. As Le Ly Hayslip, the Vietnamese wife of an American contractor in Vietnam, describes in her powerful 1989 memoir, *When Heaven and Earth Changed Places*, Vietnamese dependents of Americans sometimes faced hostility from Americans anxious to forget their nation's discredited role in the Vietnam War. By the end of the war in 1975, about 20,000 Vietnamese immigrants were living in the United States.

THE END OF THE WAR

In March, 1975, when it was clear that South Vietnam would fall to invading North Vietnamese communist forces, the U.S. government prepared for the evacuation of the 3,839 American citizens and their dependents still in South Vietnam. The government also planned to evacuate 17,000 of its South Vietnamese allies. However, a much larger number of Vietnamese also wanted to leave the country. The first step in evacuation program, Operation Babylift, was designed to take war orphans and other infants out of the country. The maiden evacuation flight crashed on April 4, killing more than 150 evacuees. The crash was a tragedy, but it helped to focus international attention on the plight of the South Vietnamese, who were about to be conquered by possibly murderous enemies.

On April 17, U.S. president Gerald R. Ford established the Interagency Task Force to launch Operation New Life. U.S. ships were sent to the coast of South Vietnam to accept refugees, and relocation centers were set up in Guam, the Philippines, Thailand, Wake Island, and Hawaii.

Meanwhile, as communist forces encircled Saigon, Operation Frequent Wind began on April 29. The United States sent in helicopters to collect Americans and refugees from various landing zones in Saigon. When the mission ended, 1,373 U.S. citizens and 5,595 others, primarily Vietnamese, had been rescued. After the communists occupied Saigon on April 30, many South Vietnamese tried to reach the waiting U.S. fleet by boats. South Vietnamese navy captain Kiem Do refused to surrender the vessels under his command and instead used them to rescue about 30,000 Vietnamese refugees. Overall, the United States saved about 65,000

Vietnamese directly, with about another 65,000 making it to U.S. ships on their own in the final week of April, 1975.

RESETTLEMENT IN THE UNITED STATES

In late spring of 1975, about 125,000 Vietnamese refugees arrived in the United States in one of the single largest short-term influxes of immigrants in the nation's history. On May 23, 1975, President Ford signed the Indochina Migration and Refugee Assistance Act, which established a sound legal basis for the resettlement of the refugees in the United States and the provision of special aid to them. The refugees were processed in four American resettlement centers.

Government officials originally intended to disperse the refugees through out the United States to avoid large concentrations in any individual areas. The refugees were assigned sponsors—both institutions and individuals—to help them ease into American life. Quickly, however, the refugees took

Vietnamese orphans being evacuated aboard an American airliner in 1975. (AP/Wide World Photos)

advantage of their freedom by relocating to live close together in new communities. Many moved to California's Orange County and to the Gulf Coast of Texas and Louisiana—places with climates somewhat similar to that of South Vietnam. After it became clear that communist control over their homeland was firm, the refugees realized they had become immigrants. On July 2, 1976, Vietnam was reunited as the Socialist Republic of Vietnam.

Members of the first wave of Vietnamese immigrants tended to be better educated than average. Many came from the middle class. A substantial number could speak some English and already had some familiarity with American culture. Most of these refugees were aided by the fact that they came as families, not as individuals. Consequently. the numbers of men and women were nearly balanced, and the immigrants enjoyed the company and support of relatives of all ages.

BOAT PEOPLE

As the communists were consolidating their power throughout Vietnam, only a trickle of new Vietnamese refugees arrived in the United States—4,100 in 1976 and 1977 together. Another 8,859 Vietnamese immigrated to the United States as nonrefugees during these two years. In 1978, the Vietnamese government was becoming more repressive and many Vietnamese were finding life increasingly bleak, with little prospect of economic betterment. At the same time, Vietnam was becoming involved in new military conflicts. Its government invaded Cambodia to topple the murderous Khmer Rouge regime and also had to defend itself against a Chinese incursion in 1979. The latter conflict brought Vietnamese reprisals against ethnic Chinese living in southern Vietnam.

Both ethnic Chinese and Vietnamese living in the south began trying to flee from Vietnam on hardly seaworthy boats in late 1978. During the following year, the world noticed the plight of these refugees, who were being called "boat people." Risking their lives on the open sea in order to reach freedom, they were often brutally attacked by Thai pirates and found they were unwelcome in other Asian countries. International concern led to an agreement in Geneva in June, 1979, that Western countries such as the United States would take in Vietnamese refugees from their Pacific Rim countries of first asylum.

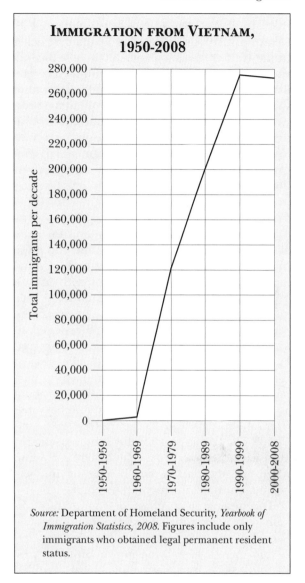

IMMIGRATION FROM VIETNAM, 1950-2008

Source: Department of Homeland Security, *Yearbook of Immigration Statistics, 2008.* Figures include only immigrants who obtained legal permanent resident status.

In response to growing international pressure, Vietnam agreed in late 1979 to establish the Orderly Departure Program under the auspices of the United Nations High Commissioner for Refugees (UNHCR). The program set up its office in Bangkok, Thailand, in January, 1980, under American leadership and UNHCR authority. However, it got off to a slow start and the flow of boat people and their sufferings at sea abated only gradually during the mid 1980's.

The United States began resettling about half of all the surviving boat people in the United States. In 1979, the first 44,500 Vietnamese refugees of this second wave were admitted. As result, the U.S. Census of 1980 showed 261,729 Vietnamese living in the United States, up from 3,000 only one decade earlier. Passage of the 1980 Refugee Act established the Office of Refugee Resettlement within the U.S. Department of Health and Human Services. This help was needed very much by second-wave refugees, who tended to be poorer and from less well-educated backgrounds than earlier refugees, and who also had haunting memories of perilous journeys to safety.

Continuing Immigration

Despite promises of Vietnam's government to allow more people to leave the country, no more than 5,000 Vietnamese immigrated to the United States during any year between 1980 and 1985. In 1986, however, the number tripled to 15,256, only go down again afterward. Congress's passage of the Amerasian Homecoming Act of 1987 opened an avenue to the United States for children fathered by Americans in Vietnam who were still living in that country. Refugees and immigrants from Vietnam reached a third wave peak from 1989 to about 1993, when their combined annual numbers rose from about 48,000 to 72,000 (1991, 1992) and 61,000. The last big peak of refugees was reached in 1994 and 1995 with more than 32,000 each year. Afterward, the refugee and immigrant numbers declined through the rest of the decade.

The demographic effect of continuing Vietnamese immigration and flight to America was reflected in the U.S. Census of 1990 that counted 614,547 Vietnamese living in the United States. By the 2000 Census, their number had doubled to 1,122,528. Census respondents who described themselves as only part Vietnamese added another 101,208 people to that figure.

In May, 1995, the United States and Vietnam established full diplomatic relations, a change that facilitated Vietnamese immigration to the United States. By the twenty-first century, the numbers of Vietnamese entering the country as regular immigrants exceeded those of refugees for the first time since the Vietnam War had ended. Between 2004 and 2008, about 30,000 new immigrants were entering the United States each year. The vast majority of them were relatives of Vietnamese already living in the United States. Of the 31,497 new Vietnamese who received permanent resident status in

the United States during 2008, 28,316 were family members and relatives of existing residents, and only 2,404 were classified as refugees.

Vietnamese in the United States

According to the 2007 American Community Survey, there were 1,642,950 Vietnamese Americans, 95 percent of whom reporting being of purely Vietnamese heritage. Their male-female ratio was balanced, and they were, as a group, slightly younger than the American national average. About 77 percent of them resided within family households, compared to the national average of 67 percent, and they lived with significantly more relatives than the average American.

The Vietnamese trend to live in large households contributed to their average annual household incomes of $54,871 exceeding the national average of $50,740, even though the average incomes of Vietnamese American individuals were lower than the national average. As a very recent immigrant group, they were remarkable in having a rate of home ownership that matched the national average of 67 percent. However, their average household size was 3.6 persons, compared to the national average of 2.7.

Vietnamese Americans have generally done well in education, reflecting the traditional emphasis on education in their culture. Of those in school, 30 percent were in college, compared to the national average of 26 percent. The percentage of Vietnamese Americans with college degrees was also a little higher than the national average. However, a troubling trend in the Vietnamese community has been a lower-than-average high school graduation rate. This trend reflects findings that many Vietnamese at the bottom of the socioeconomic scale have been failing in society.

Overall, however, Vietnamese immigrants have shown remarkable upward mobility and achievement in the United States. In 2007, their employment rate reached the average of 65 percent. Vietnamese women were employed at the same 59 percent level as the national female population. Vietnamese held to 32 percent managerial or professional positions, compared to 35 percent on average. With 25 percent, more than the average 17 percent were employed in service professions. There was a lag of Vietnamese in educational and government services. In general, with some unfortunate exceptions, Vietnamese immigrants have succeeded well in American society. In 2008, Louisiana Republican Joseph Cao became the first Vietnamese American elected to Congress, signaling a significant civic accomplishment.

R. C. Lutz

FURTHER READING

Do, Hien Duc. *The Vietnamese Americans.* Westport, Conn.: Greenwood Press, 1999. Written by a Vietnamese refugee, this book focuses on the experiences of Vietnamese immigrants and refugees resettling in the United States.

Do, Kiem. *Counterpart: A South Vietnamese Naval Officer's War.* Annapolis, Md.: Naval Institute Press, 1998. Memoir of the man who used navy craft to help rescue 30,000 Vietnamese boat people after the fall of Saigon.

Hayslip, Le Ly. *When Heaven and Earth Changed Places.* New York: Doubleday, 1989. This book, along with Hayslip's second book, *Child of War, Woman of Peace* (1993), provides a harrowing account of one Vietnamese immigrant woman's journey to America, revealing many facets of the Vietnamese immigrant experience.

Le, Cuong Nguyen. "Vietnamese Americans: History and Context." In *Asian American Assimilation.* New York: LFB Scholarly Publishing, 2007. Concise description of factors leading to Vietnamese immigration to the United States.

Saito, Lynne Tsuboi. *Ethnic Identity and Motivation: Socio-Cultural Achievement of Vietnamese American Students.* New York: LFB Scholarly Publishing, 2002. Sociological study of the fates of first- and second-generation Vietnamese immigrant children and how they have done academically.

Schulzinger, Robert D. "The Vietnamese in America." In *A Time for Peace: The Legacy of the Vietnam War.* New York: Oxford University Press, 2006. Sympathetic description of Vietnamese refugees in America and their path to assimilation and success.

SEE ALSO: Amerasian children; Amerasian Homecoming Act of 1987; Asian immigrants; Cambodian immigrants; Freedom Airlift; Indochina Migration and Refugee Assistance Act of 1975; Laotian immigrants; *Nguyen v. Immigration and Naturalization Service*; Orderly Departure Program; Refugees; Vietnam War.

VIRGINIA

SIGNIFICANCE: The first of the original thirteen British North American colonies, Virginia began its existence as an immigrant society populated primarily by British settlers. After achieving statehood when the United States became independent, it received little significant new immigration for almost two centuries, until economic growth and a new national immigration policy brought waves of new, often nonwhite, residents during the 1960's and 1970's. Like many southern states, it had a growing population of Hispanics during the early twenty-first century.

As the site of the first permanent English colony in North America in 1607, Virginia was the first future state to receive a substantial stream of immigrants from Europe. The eastern part of Virginia was settled primarily by English immigrants—and these mostly from England's Midland and southern counties. Many of Virginia's seventeenth century immigrants were poor, young and single men who came as indentured servants. Mortality rates were high through the colony's first several decades, but by 1660, the colony's population had achieved a degree of stability. During the governorship of William Berkeley (1641-1676), many English royalists also immigrated to Virginia.

Although the English were a majority of the settlers in Virginia's seaboard settlement, they were not alone. As early as 1619, French Huguenots arrived in the colony. During the eighteenth century, they were being joined by Welsh and others. During the same year in which the first Huguenots arrived, a Dutch ship unloaded at Jamestown the colony's first contingent of African slaves. The importation of involuntary immigrants from Africa gained increasing importance during the late seventeenth century. Members of many African cultures came to Virginia, but Ibos from what is now southeastern Nigeria and peoples from the Senegambia region were especially well represented in the colony.

Although people of English and other nationalities would also contribute large numbers to the settlement of western Virginia, Germans, and Scotch-Irish people played a pioneering role in peopling the colony's backcountry. By the mid-eighteenth century, more members of both these groups were moving from Pennsylvania into the Great Valley of Virginia. From there they moved farther west into the extremities of the colony or into new western lands farther afield. Some went south into the Carolina backcountry, others east into the Virginia Piedmont.

NINETEENTH CENTURY TRENDS

Following the late eighteenth century American Revolution and throughout the nineteenth century and well into the twentieth century, Virginia exported many more people than it imported. Large numbers of white Virginians moved to other states, and many of the state's African slaves were sold to out-of-state buyers. Meanwhile, Virginia offered few economic inducements to potential foreign immigrants, and the very fact that it was a slave state deterred many Europeans from coming.

As elsewhere in the South, however, the exception to Virginia's net emigration trend was its chief city. Indeed, the state capital of Richmond may have had the largest immigrant population in the entire region. By the end of the colonial period, it was already a fairly diverse society, with a mixture of European nationals, native-born whites, black slaves, and free blacks. Its development into the South's major manufacturing center during the first half of the nineteenth century did little to lessen its demographic diversity. Even during the post-Civil War Reconstruction era, when sociopolitical instability discouraged new immigration into many parts of the South, new arrivals poured into Richmond—Germans and Irish in particular. However, after Reconstruction ended in 1877, new immigration into Richmond slowed to a trickle, and the city became less cosmopolitan and more of a distinctively regional city, albeit a major one.

TWENTIETH CENTURY

By the 1960's Virginia was experiencing major urban growth—especially in the Hampton Roads cluster of cities by the mouth of the James River on Chesapeake Bay and in northern Virginia. Passage of the federal Immigration and Nationality Act of 1965 removed restrictions on the immigration of many nationalities, permitting a flood of new immigrants to come into the United States from parts of the world that had not supplied many immigrants since the nineteenth century. Like most other states, Virginia then began receiving increased numbers of immigrants. In 1970, Virginia's long-negligible foreign-born population was only 2 percent. By 2000, it had risen to 8 percent. Moreover, within only a few decades, Virginia's almost entirely white and black population was undergoing visible changes: By the early twenty-first century, 4.3 percent of the state's total population were Asians. That percentage exceeded the national average, and Virginia was the only state in the South that could make that claim.

Some of Virginia's new Asian residents have been refugees. After the Vietnam War ended in 1975, a number of Vietnamese immigrants entered the state. Many of these people were professional and middle-class people who had had ties with the American-backed former government of South Vietnam. Most of Virginia's Vietnamese immigrants chose to live in the rapidly developing northern part of the state,

---

PROFILE OF VIRGINIA

Region	Atlantic coast
Entered union	1788
Largest cities	Virginia Beach, Norfolk, Chesapeake, Richmond (capital), Arlington, Newport News
Modern immigrant communities	Vietnamese, Koreans, Salvadorans

Population	Total	Percent of state	Percent of U.S.	U.S. rank
All state residents	7,643,000	100.0	2.55	12
All foreign-born residents	774,000	10.1	2.06	11

Source: U.S. Census Bureau, *Statistical Abstract for 2006.*

Notes: The U.S. population in 2006 was 299,399,000, of whom 37,548,000 (12.5%) were foreign born. Rankings in last column reflect total numbers, not percentages.

near the heart of American political power in nearby Washington, D.C. By the early twenty-first century, about 43,709 Vietnamese were residing in the greater District of Columbia area. As elsewhere in the South, Vietnamese Americans tend to be suburbanites and have a strong sense of community cohesion. Many work in education, scientific research and other specialized, white-collar professions.

By the year 2000, Virginia also had a substantial Korean community, with more than 45,000 Koreans living in the state. In contrast to the Vietnamese, the Koreans have been more evenly dispersed about the state. Most of them came after passage of the 1965 federal immigration law. They have also been joined by Korean Americans from western states. Most have gravitated toward Virginia's urban areas because their occupations tend to be centered in urban-oriented professions and industries, support work, and sales and small-business enterprises.

One of the largest immigrant groups to enter Virginia since the early 1990's has been Latinos, who by 2008 constituted about 35 percent of the state's entire immigrant population. Most have come from Mexico and El Salvador. Many are concentrated in heavily developed areas such as Hampton Roads and northern Virginia, where they tend to engage in construction trades, light fabrication and other manual labor. Many more work as agricultural laborers throughout the state, and others are routinely employed by the meat-packing and other agricultural industries. A large but unknown number of these Latino workers are undocumented. Although Virginia has seen less growth in its Latino population than some other southern states, illegal immigration has become a hotly debated topic in Virginia.

Jeremiah Taylor

FURTHER READING

Ayers, Edward, and John C. Willis, eds. *The Edge of the South: Life in Nineteenth-Century Virginia.* Charlottesville: University Press of Virginia, 1991. Provides a fascinating glimpse of Virginia during the period from the Revolution to the Civil War.

Fischer, David Hackett, and James C. Kelly. *Bound Away: Virginia and the Westward Movement.* Charlottesville: University Press of Virginia, 2000. Study of three stages of historical migration to, from, and within the state.

Larson, Chiles. *Virginia's Past Today.* Charlottesville, Va.: Howell Press, 1998. Examines the legacy and meaning of Virginia's historic past.

Rubin, Louis D., Jr. *Virginia: A History.* New York: W. W. Norton, 1984. Solid history with excellent discussions of the colonial period, the Civil War and Reconstruction, and economic and cultural developments following 1900.

Steger, Werner H. "German Immigrants, the Revolution of 1848, and the Politics of Liberalism in Antebellum Richmond." *Yearbook of German-American Studies* 34 (1999): 19-34. Study of the German community living in Virginia's state capital.

SEE ALSO: British immigrants; Economic opportunities; European immigrants; German immigrants; Korean immigrants; Mexican immigrants; Salvadoran immigrants; Vietnamese immigrants; Washington, D.C.; Westward expansion.

W

WAR BRIDES

THE EVENT: Immigration of foreign-born spouses of Americans serving abroad during World War II, most of whom entered the United States either as nonquota immigrants under provisions of the War Brides Act of 1945 or as nonimmigrants under provisions of the Fiancées Act of 1946

DATE: 1945-1950

LOCATION: Western Europe; East Asia; Australia

SIGNIFICANCE: Throughout U.S. history, American military personnel and civilians serving abroad during times of foreign wars have returned home with foreign spouses. Not surprisingly, the conflict that brought home the largest number of "war brides"—a term encompassing both wives and husbands—was World War II. Indeed, so large was the number of war brides that the U.S. Congress enacted special legislation to accommodate their immigration. Precise statistics on their numbers are not available. However, under provisions of the War Brides Act of 1945 alone, 114,691 women and 333 men immigrated to the United States between 1945 and 1950. Thousands more immigrated under other immigration laws.

On December 28, 1945, a little more than four months after World War II officially ended, the U.S. Congress passed the War Brides Act. Six months later, it passed the Fiancées Act. Both laws were designed to facilitate the immigration of spouses of Americans who had served abroad during the war. Under the War Brides Act, visa requirements for foreign-born spouses were waived, with the exception of foreign-born spouses from South and Southeast Asia. Records kept by the U.S. Immigration and Naturalization Service (INS) provide statistics on the numbers of war brides who came from different countries under the provisions of the War Brides Act. However, because many spouses immigrated under provisions of other laws, the INS figures do not tell the entire story.

EUROPEAN WAR BRIDES

British-born spouses and their children were by far the largest cohort of war brides to enter the United States after World War II. The reasons are readily evident.

The U.S. Immigration and Naturalization Service (INS) recorded a total of 35,469 people who entered the United States between 1945 and 1950 under the provisions of the War Brides Act. These figures included 34,944 wives, 53 husbands, and 472 children. Other sources, however, have estimated that as many as 70,000 British women may have married American serviceman.

The first group of them left for the United States from Southampton aboard the SS *Argentina* on January 26, 1946. The average age of the women was about twenty-three. Most were from working-class and lower-middle-class families and had attended school only through the age of fourteen.

Although France, like Great Britain, was an American ally during World War II, it had a vastly different relationship to the American military. Most of France was occupied by Nazi Germany throughout the war, and American troops did not begin encountering French women until after the Allied invasion of France began in June, 1944. Over the ensuing year, millions of American servicemen contributed to France's liberation from German occupation. Some of them took up relationships with French women, who were popularly perceived in the United States as being sexually debauched "oh-la-la girls." According to INS records, between 1945 and 1950, 8,581 French-born wives of Americans with 140 children and 23 French-born husbands of American women entered the United States under provisions of the War Brides Act.

German war brides were a special case, as they were nationals of an enemy power. In September, 1944, the U.S. military officially banned servicemen from fraternizing with German women after the war. The underlying reason was a fear of Nazi sympathizers. Despite this ban, many Americans formed romantic liaisons with German women after the war. As early as 1944, some of these servicemen petitioned the military to allow them to marry their German sweethearts.

In 1946, twenty-three-year-old Robert J. Lauenstein became the first American serviceman to receive permission to marry a German-born fiancé. Lauenstein reportedly exploited a loophole in the Fiancées Act of 1946 to obtain an exit permit for his fiancé. His highly publicized marriage to the woman in November, 1946, effectively set a precedent for other American servicemen to marry German-born women. In December, the U.S. Army revoked its ban on marriages to Germans. By 1949, as many as 20,000 German war brides appear to have immigrated to the United States.

Italy, Germany's primary European ally during the war had a very different wartime experience. It was the first Axis territory to be occupied by Allied troops, who began entering it from the south in 1943. However, the large number of American troops in the Allied occupation force resulted in comparatively few Italian war brides. According to INS figures, only 9,728 Italian-born spouses of Americans immigrated to the United States between 1945 and 1950.

AUSTRALIAN WAR BRIDES

The Pacific theater of the war took many American service personnel to Australia, from which operations against Japanese positions in Southeast Asia were mounted. As in Europe, many American personnel took up relations with Australian citizens. According to INS records, during the five years after the war, 6,853 Australians entered the United States under provisions of the War Brides Act. All were wives of Americans, except for 7 husbands and 175 children. Other sources, however, suggest that the number of Australian wives coming to the United States could have been as high as 15,000.

Like the French wives of American servicemen, the Australian wives were negatively stereotyped as morally loose, money-hungry "good-time girls," who were suspected of marrying Americans merely to go to the United States. Responding to a request by the U.S military in 1942, the American Red Cross investigated the backgrounds of potential Australian and British brides until public objec-

British war brides departing for the United States shortly after World War II. (Popperfoto/Getty Images)

MALE "WAR BRIDES"

Because the numbers of foreign-born men who married American servicewomen were minuscule in comparison to those of foreign-born women who married American men, the term "war brides" was loosely applied to both husbands and wives who entered the United States after World War II.

In 1949, the Hollywood film *I Was a Male War Bride*, starring Cary Grant in the title role, helped draw attention to the fact that not all "war brides" were women. The film was based on the real-life story of Belgian army officer Henri Rochard (also known as Dr. Roger H. Charlier), who married an American woman serving with the U.S. military in Europe. A popular hit, the film won the Writers Guild Award for best American comedy of 1949.

tions brought an end to the investigations ended before the conclusion of World War II.

ASIAN WAR BRIDES

U.S. involvement in the Pacific theater of the war also took many American service personnel to China. At the beginning of the war, almost no Asian immigration to the United States was permitted under U.S. immigration laws enacted during the 1920's. A law enacted in 1943 eased restrictions on Chinese immigration but only slightly. Consequently, most postwar female Chinese immigrants to the United States had to be admitted under the War Brides Act.

During World War II, 12,041 Chinese Americans were drafted into the U.S. military, and many of them served in China. Under the terms of a special federal law that allowed servicemen to bring home alien wives, 2,317 Chinese women immigrated to the United States between 1947 and 1950. Another 5,132 women immigrated under the War Brides Act. These Chinese immigrants were, on average, older than war brides from other countries. Fully 85 percent of them were at least twenty-six years old.

The major combatants in World War II, Japan provided the smallest number of war brides to immigrate to the United States. Between 1945 and 1950, only 758 Japanese came to the United States under the War Brides Act.

SOCIAL, CULTURAL, AND POLITICAL IMPLICATIONS

The War Brides Act expired in December, 1948, but it had a lingering impact on immigration. which included the delayed transportation of many foreign-born dependents of American service personnel to the United States. An acute shortage of seafaring passenger ships slowed the transportation of war brides. Moreover, restrictive U.S. immigration laws complicated some marriages and delayed the arrival of many war brides. Japanese war brides were particularly affected, as they were not permitted entry into the United States until 1952.

An ironic effect of the War Brides Act was its impact on the gender balance of foreign immigrants. Although the law itself was gender-neutral, it facilitated the immigration of women far more than it did men. Before the war, male immigrants had greatly outnumbered female immigrants. This shift was particularly evident in postwar immigration from China, more than half of whose immigrants were women for the first time.

Nicole Anae

FURTHER READING

Esser, Raingard. "'Language No Obstacle': War Brides in the German Press, 1945-49." *Women's History Review* 12, no. 4 (December, 2003): 577-603. Study of depictions of German war brides in German newspapers and magazines published in the American and British zones during the late 1940's.

Hibbert, Joyce, ed. *The War Brides.* Toronto, Ont.: PMA Books, 1978. Broad survey of World War II era war brides.

Kaiser, Hilary. *French War Brides in America: An Oral History.* Westport, Conn.: Praeger, 2008. Collection of oral histories, detailing the destinies of fifteen French war brides from both World War I and World War II.

Shukert, Elfrida Berthiaume, and Barbara Smith Scibetta. *War Brides of World War II.* Novato, Calif.: Presidio Press, 1988. General overview of World War II war brides.

Virden, Jenel. *Good-bye, Piccadilly: British War Brides in America.* Champaign: University of Illinois Press, 1996. Often cited study arguing that British war brides represented the largest single group of female immigrants to the United States in the immediate post-World War II years.

Zhao, Xiaojian. *Remaking Chinese America: Immigration, Family, and Community.* New Brunswick, N.J.: Rutgers University Press, 2002. Examination of changes to American culture in the wake of postwar immigration legislation favoring family reunification for Chinese American service personnel.

See also: Families; Fiancées Act of 1946; Intermarriage; Mail-order brides; Marriage; Picture brides; Quota systems; War Brides Act of 1945; Women immigrants; World War II.

War Brides Act of 1945

The Law: Federal law allowing foreign-born spouses and children of U.S. military personnel to enter the United States after World War II
Date: 1945

Significance: The War Brides Act represented a change not only in the number of immigrants allowed entry to the United States but also in the gender make-up of total immigration, as it allowed far more women than men to immigrate. The law also allowed many Asians to enter the country at a time when national quota restrictions were still blocking the entry of Asian immigrants.

The War Brides Act of 1945 was passed to allow U.S. military personnel to bring their newly wed spouses and other family members from Europe and Japan to the United States for a temporary period without regard to national origins quotas or other restrictions in U.S. immigration law. Before 1945, U.S. immigration policy conformed with the quotas set by the Immigration Act of 1924. That law's national origins provision limited the number of immigrants allowed entry to the United States to 2 percent of the number of people from any given country who had been living in the United States in 1890. The law also forbade virtually all Asian immigration, with very limited exceptions, and effectively limited immigration from southern and eastern Europe because few people from those regions were residing in the United States at the time of the 1890 U.S. Census.

By the time World War II ended in 1945, a significant number of U.S. military personnel had married or had children with women from European nations and Japan. The War Brides Act passed in 1945 gave these servicemen temporary permission to bring spouses and family members to the United States. The Bureau of Immigration and Naturalization worked with the U.S. Department of State, the U.S. Army, and the American Red Cross to develop official transportation networks for these foreign-born spouses and family members to enter the United States.

The official number of foreign-born war brides was listed at 115,000 in 1945, but many scholars believe that the actual number was much higher because many of U.S. service personnel who had British, Germany, and Italian spouses had arranged on their own for their spouses to come to the United States, thereby causing them not to be counted in official U.S. Army estimates.

The War Brides Act of 1945 also allowed large numbers of Japanese women to enter the United States. This was a major change, as Japanese immigration had been almost completely disallowed for decades. General Douglas MacArthur, who led the U.S. occupation government in postwar Japan, embraced the War Brides Act and encouraged international press coverage of Japanese wives who joined their American-born husbands in the United States. For MacArthur, the War Brides Act symbolized what he hoped would become a permanent American presence in Asia, with the United States liberating Japanese women from formerly oppressive social relationships.

Meanwhile, the act brought Japanese-born spouses and family members to many American cities and towns, particularly on the West Coast. These immigrant women and their families were instrumental in helping to reinvigorate Japanese American communities that had been devastated by the experience of internment camps during World War II. These new immigrants also represented a dramatic shift in Asian immigration patterns. Prior to 1945, the few Asian immigrants who had been allowed entry to the United States were predominantly male laborers who lived in bachelor communities, apart from the mainstream of American life. The new Japanese immigrants and their families became a group that would seek full participation in American institutions even as they

Washington, D.C.

retained aspects of their culture. In many ways, they became models of assimilation for members of later Asian immigrant groups.

William Carney

FURTHER READING

Hibbert, Joyce, ed. *The War Brides.* Toronto, Ont.: PMA Books, 1978.

Kaiser, Hilary. *French War Brides in America: An Oral History.* Westport, Conn.: Praeger, 2008.

LeMay, Michael C., and Elliott Robert Barkan, eds. *U.S. Immigration and Naturalization Laws and Issues: A Documentary History.* Westport, Conn.: Greenwood Press, 1999.

Shukert, Elfrida Berthiaume, and Barbara Smith Scibetta. *War Brides of World War II.* Novato, Calif.: Presidio Press, 1988.

Virden, Jenel. *Good-bye, Piccadilly: British War Brides in America.* Champaign: University of Illinois Press, 1996.

SEE ALSO: Asian immigrants; Australian and New Zealander immigrants; British immigrants; German immigrants; Italian immigrants; Japanese immigrants; War brides; World War II.

WASHINGTON, D.C.

IDENTIFICATION: Administratively autonomous capital city of the United States

SIGNIFICANCE: As its nation's capital, Washington, D.C., is more a seat of government than an industrial or commercial center. Consequently, during the nineteenth century fewer Europeans immigrated there, relative to other mid-Atlantic metropolitan areas. However, Washington did attract large numbers of African Americans from the South after the U.S. Civil War ended in 1865, and more immigrants came from Africa and Latin America during the late twentieth century.

Thanks to the natural resources of the Potomac and Anacostia rivers, Piscataway Indians used the region that would later become Washington, D.C., as a trade center long before the arrival of European settlers during the seventeenth century. In 1790, sections of Maryland and Virginia—populated largely by persons of British ancestry and enslaved African Americans—were ceded to establish the District of Columbia. However, Virginia's portion was returned to the state in 1846.

After the seat of the federal government officially moved from Philadelphia in 1800, Washington's population grew accordingly. Slaves, along with Irish artisans and laborers, helped construct the most important buildings, including the White House and the Capitol Building. Many more Irish arrived when famine struck Ireland during the late 1840's, making them the largest immigrant group in Washington—peaking at 58.1 percent of the city's foreign-born population (or 10.1 percent of the total population) in 1860.

Additional groups from Europe immigrated to Washington during the late nineteenth and early twentieth centuries. Germans were the most numerous, many of them refugees from the revolutions of 1848, laboring as artisans, merchants, and servants; the population of Germans peaked in 1890, when they represented 30.8 percent of the city's foreign-born population (or 2.5 percent of the total). Other significant immigrant groups, especially between 1890 and World War I, included Greeks, who sought entrepreneurial jobs in barbershops, restaurants, and retail produce; Italians, many working as stonemasons and craftsmen on new government buildings; and Jews, primarily from eastern Europe and Russia, many starting as peddlers before opening businesses of their own.

In 1860, African Americans constituted 19.1 percent of the District's population; 22.2 percent of them were enslaved. Following the Civil War, many more African Americans arrived in the nation's capital, seeking a fresh start. This trend continued throughout the nineteenth century; by 1900, 86,702 inhabitants (or 31 percent of Washington's population) were black, thus forming the largest urban community of African Americans anywhere in the United States. The population peaked in 1970, when 71.1 percent of the District was African American. Although this percentage has since decreased—to 55.5 percent in 2007—Washington remains a center of African American culture, with many blacks working in the federal government (including, in 2009, the first African American president, Barack Obama).

PROFILE OF DISTRICT OF COLUMBIA

Region	Atlantic coast
Status	Federal administrative capital
Modern immigrant communities	Africans, Hispanics, Vietnamese

Population	Total	Percent of district	Percent of U.S.
All district residents	515,000	100.0	0.17
All foreign-born residents	74,000	2.7	0.20

Source: U.S. Census Bureau, *Statistical Abstract for 2006.*
Notes: The U.S. population in 2006 was 299,399,000, of whom 37,548,000 (12.5%) were foreign born.

As the district's African American population declined, their place was taken by new immigrants, primarily from Latin America and Africa. During the 1970's and 1980's, many Spanish-speaking immigrants moved into the Mount Pleasant and Adams Morgan neighborhoods, forging a distinct Latino identity. The civil war in El Salvador during the 1980's was a particularly powerful push factor. Similarly, conflicts in Eritrea, Ethiopia, Nigeria, and Sierra Leone from the 1960's to the 1990's led thousands of political refugees from those countries to Washington. In 2000, the District had the highest percentage of any state of African-born residents: 1.6 percent of the population.

In 2006, 13.0 percent of the District's population was born outside the United States. This represents the highest percentage ever recorded—topping previous highs enumerated in the United States decennial censuses: 12.9 percent in 2000, 12.6 in 1870, 10.7 in 1850, and 9.7 in 1990. Of Washington's foreign-born residents in 2006, 48 percent came from Latin America, 18.7 percent from Asia, 15.5 percent from Europe, 14.4 percent from Africa, and 3 percent from other world regions. As a result, Washington, D.C., is truly an international city during the twenty-first century.

James I. Deutsch

FURTHER READING

Cary, Francine Curro, ed. *Washington Odyssey: A Multicultural History of the Nation's Capital.* Washington, D.C.: Smithsonian Institution Press, 2003.

Gittens, Anthony, et al. "Washington, D.C.: It's Our Home." In *Smithsonian Folklife Festival 2000*, edited by Carla M. Borden. Washington, D.C.: Smithsonian Institution Press, 2000.

Smith, Kathryn Schneider. *Washington at Home: An Illustrated History of Neighborhoods in the Nation's Capital.* Northridge, Calif.: Windsor, 1988.

SEE ALSO: African Americans and immigrants; African immigrants; Ethiopian immigrants; German immigrants; Irish immigrants; Latin American immigrants; Maryland; Salvadoran immigrants; Virginia.

WASHINGTON STATE

SIGNIFICANCE: Like the state of Oregon to its south, Washington appealed to early pioneers from the East. Unlike Oregon, it lacked racially exclusionary land laws. Consequently, it also attracted Asian immigrants, and Filipinos became one of the state's largest immigrant groups. By the turn of the twenty-first century, Mexican had become the state's fastest-growing immigrant group, thanks in part to Washington's agriculture industry, which poses a draw for undocumented immigrants.

Although similar to Oregon geographically and economically, Washington has drawn many more immigrants not of European stock. During the first several decades of statehood, hundreds of Chinese, Japanese, and Filipino immigrants came to Washington for work. The first Filipinos in the Seattle area worked in lumber mills, which employed many Filipinos during the early years of statehood. Fishing and canning were also typical jobs for Filipino workers.

After the United States took the Philippines from Spain in the 1898 Spanish-American War, Congress passed the Pensionado Act in 1903 to provide funds for Filipinos to study in the United States. By 1912, 209 Filipino students had graduated from American college or university programs, and the University of Washington had enrolled more Filipinos than studied in any other state.

In 1906, the city of Seattle hired forty Filipino workers to lay a cable in the Pacific; several decided to become permanent residents of Seattle. Federal immigration laws that excluded Asian workers from the United States did not apply to the Philippines, which was regarded as an American colony. Consequently, the number of Filipinos in Washington increased rapidly. They were drawn by the promise of work and economic security and quickly took the places of Chinese and Japanese laborers on railroads, in canneries, and on farms.

During the early decades of the twentieth century, Washington's Filipino population continued to grow through ongoing immigration and natural increase. However, in 1934, the federal Tydings-McDuffie Act changed the status of Filipinos from "nationals" to "aliens" and limited the number of them who would be permitted to enter the United States to fifty per year. The Filipino Repatriation Act of 1935 sent more than 1,000 Filipino residents of Washington back to the Philippines.

Through World War II and afterward, Washington's Filipino community again grew larger, particularly after 1965, when a new federal immigration law removed national-origins quotas. During the war, Washington's ethnic Japanese residents, along with those of other West Coast states, were rounded up and interned. After the war, the state's ethnic Japanese population increased. By 1950, 6.8 percent of the state's total population were of Japanese ancestry.

By 2003, Washington was home to 631,500 foreign-born residents, who constituted 10.3 percent of the state's entire population. An estimated 100,000 of these people were illegal immigrants. By this time, the single-largest immigrant group was Mexicans. Most Mexican immigrants, both documented and undocumented, worked as migrant farmworkers in the southeast-central part of the state and as laborers in western Washington. A legacy of its immigrant heritage, Washington has the

PROFILE OF WASHINGTON

Region	Northwest Pacific coast
Entered union	1889
Largest cities	Seattle, Spokane, Tacoma, Vancouver, Bellevue
Modern immigrant communities	Filipinos, Mexicans

Population	Total	Percent of state	Percent of U.S.	U.S. rank
All state residents	6,396,000	100.0	2.14	14
All foreign-born residents	794,000	12.4	2.11	10

Source: U.S. Census Bureau, Statistical Abstract for 2006.
Notes: The U.S. population in 2006 was 299,399,000, of whom 37,548,000 (12.5%) were foreign born. Rankings in last column reflect total numbers, not percentages.

fourth largest Asian American population of any state, and immigration from the Philippines and Vietnam has increased dramatically since 1980. The Filipino American community in Washington is one of the largest in the United States.

Melissa A. Barton

FURTHER READING

Daniels, Roger. *Asian America: Chinese and Japanese in the United States Since 1850.* Seattle: University of Washington Press, 1988.

Gruenewald, Mary Matsuda. *Looking Like the Enemy: My Story of Imprisonment in Japanese American Internment Camps.* Troutdale, Oreg.: NewSage Press, 2005.

Lambert, Dale A. *Washington: A State of Contrasts.* Edited by Dustin W. Clark and Kathleen A. Lambert. 2d ed. East Wenatchee, Wash.: Directed Media, 2007. Examines the complex past and present history of Washington and its unique geographic regions.

Ritter, Harry. *Washington's History: The People, Land, and Events of the Far Northwest.* Portland, Oreg.: WestWinds Press, 2003. Explores the events and people who helped in the development of Washington State.

SEE ALSO: Alaska; *Asakura v. City of Seattle*; Bellingham incident; Chinese immigrants; Farm and migrant workers; Filipino immigrants; Filipino Repatriation Act of 1935; Japanese American internment; Japanese immigrants; Mexican immigrants.

WELFARE AND SOCIAL SERVICES

DEFINITION: Tax-supported cash payments provided to the eligible needy by government agencies and government programs designed to improve residents' lives

SIGNIFICANCE: Welfare benefits paid out to poor people have long been contentious issues in the United States. Many Americans believe that individuals should take care of themselves. As the United States developed elements of a welfare state between the 1930's and the 1960's, legal immigrants were considered future Americans and were generally eligible for benefits. However, that notion changed in 1996, when reforms in public welfare systems began restricting the access of immigrants to most means-tested federal welfare programs. Giving immigrants access to social services such as education and public health programs has been less contentious.

FEDERAL WELFARE PROGRAMS

The concept of government "welfare" has generally been applied to cash assistance provided to poor people. Major federal welfare programs began during the Great Depression. In 1935, the federal government created what became the Aid to Families with Dependent Children (AFDC) program to provide direct cash assistance to mothers of young children who had low incomes. Recipients of these payments were expected to stay home and care for their children.

The federal Personal Responsibility and Work Opportunity Reconciliation Act of 1996 (PRWORA) fundamentally changed the welfare system in three major ways. First, it ended a guarantee that eligible poor residents would receive cash assistance by converting an open-ended entitlement program into a fixed grant of $16.8 billion to the individual states, which were permitted to end payments to poor people after their funds ran out. Second, PRWORA introduced limits on how long recipients could receive cash assistance, generally five years in a lifetime and two years without working. Third, PRWORA marked a major change in the

relationship between immigrants and the social safety net, shifting U.S. policy from generally making immigrants eligible for welfare benefits to making them generally ineligible.

PRWORA converted the Aid to Families with Dependent Children program into a block grant to states and renamed AFDC Temporary Assistance for Needy Families (TANF). States have used these federal funds, as well as their own funds, to provide cash assistance to poor people. In 1997, the United States had 12.6 million welfare cases—typically family units of single mothers with two children. By 2007, there were only 4.1 million welfare cases.

PRWORA limits "lifetime" cash assistance to five years, requires most welfare recipients to work after two years of cash assistance, and prohibits persons convicted of drug felonies from obtaining cash benefits. PRWORA is a work-first or A-B-C program (*A* job leads to a *B*etter job leads to a *C*areer), that is, adult TANF recipients are encouraged to work.

Enacted at a time of concern over rising federal budget deficits, PRWORA was expected to save about $54 billion over six years, with 40 percent of the savings coming from denying benefits to noncitizen immigrants. PRWORA's provisions affecting immigrants were widely seen as the culmination of anti-immigrant efforts that began with the approval of Proposition 187 in California in 1994. That voter initiative proposed to create a state-run system to prevent undocumented immigrants from obtaining tax-supported welfare benefits. A court ruling blocked implementation of the Proposition 187 plan, but some of its provisions were included in PRWORA.

PRWORA introduced two major changes for immigrants. First, most legal immigrants who arrived in the United States after August 22, 1996, became ineligible for most means-tested benefits until they had worked ten years in the United States, or had became naturalized U.S. citizens after five years. Second, to prevent new immigrants from needing assistance, PRWORA and the Illegal Immigration Reform and Immigrant Responsibility Act of 1996 required the American sponsors of immigrants to prove, by showing tax and other records, that they had the resources to support the persons they were sponsoring in the United States. Moreover, they also had to sign legally binding affidavits promising to support those immigrants.

In 2009, the federal government defined the

poverty line for a family of four as an annual income of $22,050. For example, if an American couple were to sponsor two immigrant parents, they had to show they themselves had an income at least as high as 125 percent of the poverty-line figure, or $27,562. If the immigrant parents who were being sponsored applied for and received welfare assistance, the government could then sue the sponsoring couple to recover whatever benefits it had paid out. PRWORA required state and local agencies that provide welfare benefits to use the Systematic Alien Verification for Entitlements (SAVE) system to verify the legal status of noncitizen applicants for welfare benefits.

PRWORA has been called the third major change in U.S. immigration policy during the twentieth century. The first change was the introduction of national origins quotas during the 1920's. The second change was the elimination of national quotas in 1965. The third change, therefore, was the introduction of a sharp distinction between U.S. citizens and immigrants in access to welfare in 1996. In each case, policy changes reflected the dominant political mood of the times—nativism and political isolationism after World War I, the Civil Rights movement of the 1960's, and the quest for a balanced budget during the 1990's.

During the U.S. economic boom of the late 1990's, eligibility for welfare benefits was restored for most legal immigrants who had been resident in the United States before August 22, 1996. The rationale was that the U.S. government should not

President Bill Clinton signing the Personal Responsibility and Work Opportunity Reconciliation Act in August, 1996. (AP/Wide World Photos)

change the rules for immigrants midway through the game. President Bill Clinton urged restoration of eligibility, arguing

> We passed welfare reform. We were right to do it. But . . . we must restore basic health and disability benefits when misfortune strikes immigrants who came to this country legally, who work hard, pay taxes, and obey the law. To do otherwise is simply unworthy of a great nation of immigrants.

SOCIAL SERVICES

Social services are government-provided services that range from education to health care, and from housing to Social Security. Some are mandatory, such as the requirement that all young children attend school. Some are work related, such as participation in the government Social Security program. Some are means-tested, such as eligibility for housing subsidies.

EDUCATION

Education and cash welfare assistance frame the extremes of the immigrant-eligibility spectrum. All children, regardless of their legal immigration status, are not only eligible to attend public schools but also required to do so—at no charge. At the other end of the spectrum, both legal and undocumented immigrants are generally barred from receiving cash assistance. In between are work-related benefits such as employer-provided health insurance benefits, which can be provided to and used by both legal and undocumented workers. Other programs draw distinctions between legal and undocumented workers. Workers compensation insurance, for example, which covers the costs of job-related injuries, pays for hospital and doctor care for all workers but does not provide continued wage-replacement benefits to undocumented workers because they are not legally allowed to work in the United States. Similarly, employers and legal and undocumented workers contribute to Social Security, but only legal immigrants receive Social Security benefits.

Most social service issues involving immigrants focus on education, health, and social security. Schools are the most expensive taxpayer-supported service used by young immigrant families with children. They are also the key to ensuring that the children of immigrants obtain the education they need to succeed in the United States. At issue is whether the education of non-English-speaking immigrant children should be in their native languages, should be bilingual, or should be in English. Also at issue is what services should be offered to adult immigrants, such as English as a second language courses. Many researchers look at immigrant children in American schools and see a half-full glass, as some immigrant children excel, even though their parents have not completed elementary school educations themselves. Others look at immigrant high school dropout rates of up to 50 percent and despair.

HEALTH CARE

Unlike workers in countries with national health insurance programs, most American workers obtain health and other social service benefits from their employers. However, employers are not legally required to provide health insurance, and many smaller employers who employ recently arrived immigrants usually do not. Children of immigrant parents with low incomes and no employer health insurance benefits are often covered by Medicaid and the State Child Health Insurance Program. However, because legal immigration status may vary among family members, so also does eligibility for social services. Consequently, some American-born children within immigrant families may be eligible for publicly provided health insurance benefits for which their parents and foreign-born siblings are not.

Other work-related social services can be even more complicated. Social Security provides an example. In 2009, employers and their employees each contributed 7.65 percent of the employees' first $106,800 in annual earnings to cover the cost of Social Security and Medicare. However, only legal U.S. residents were eligible to collect Social Security benefits. However, undocumented workers who legalize their status can receive credit for the time worked while their status was illegal. During the late 1980's, millions of immigrants did exactly that after a federal law legalized them.

IMMIGRANTS AND THE SAFETY NET

When the U.S. government was creating the welfare state between the 1930's and 1960's, it made few distinctions between U.S. citizens and immigrants. However, as immigration rates were increasing during the 1980's and 1990's, and illegal migration was becoming a political issue, federal and state governments began to require applicants for means-tested benefits to prove they were in the United States legally.

The federal welfare reforms of 1996 marked a turning point in welfare policy for all Americans, but especially for immigrants. A five-year time limit was placed on cash assistance for all adults, legal immigrants were barred from receiving cash assistance for at least five years, and barriers between social services and unauthorized foreigners were raised.

The national health care reform debate launched by President Barack Obama in early 2009 seemed to signal that U.S. policy would continue to exclude especially unauthorized foreigners from receiving social services. By 2009, the United States was spending about two trillion dollars a year on health care, but 46 million U.S. residents still lack health care coverage, including 7 million unauthorized foreign residents. Obama and other leaders have said that legal immigrants would be covered but unauthorized foreigners would be excluded from universal health care plans, indicating that policy makers will continue to make distinctions between U.S. citizens, legal immigrants, and unauthorized foreigners.

Philip L. Martin

FURTHER READING

Fix, Michael, ed. *Securing the Future: U.S. Immigrant Integration Policy—A Reader.* Washington, D.C.: Migration Policy Institute, 2007. Articles in this book discusses the fact that although the United States had admitted one million immigrants per year through the previous two decades, it remained one of the few industrial countries without an immigrant integration policy. Compared to European countries, the United States had nevertheless been successful in integrating low-skilled immigrant workers into its labor force, but they have wound up among the working poor, without health insurance. The contributors urge more government assistance for education, health care, and other social services to ensure successful integration.

Krikorian, Mark. *The New Case Against Immigration: Both Legal and Illegal.* New York: Sentinel, 2008. This book argues against large-scale immigration on grounds ranging from the changing U.S. economy to their potential welfare costs. Krikorian contends that because the U.S. economy has changed, it no longer needs large numbers of low-skilled newcomers, and that social norms and government policies have changed to reduce the incentives of newcomers to integrate. Krikorian emphasizes that there were few social services except education provided by government during the last major wave of immigration at the beginning of the twentieth century.

Martin, Philip. *Importing Poverty? Immigration and the Changing Face of Rural America.* New Haven, Conn.: Yale University Press, 2009. Explores the process of moving poor Mexicans—who are the most numerous immigrants in the United States—into rural and agricultural areas of the United States, and what these newcomers mean for welfare and social service systems in these areas.

Myers, Dowell. *Immigrants and Boomers: Forging a New Social Contract for the Future of America.* New York: Russell Sage Foundation, 2007. Argues that aging baby boomers need to ensure that immigrants and their children get the education and skills needed to succeed in the United States so that their taxes can support the boomers in their old age.

Smith, James P., and Barry Edmonston, eds. *The New Americans: Economic, Demographic, and Fiscal Effects of Immigration.* Washington, D.C.: National Research Council, 1997. This book is the result of a yearlong study by a panel of social scientists conducted in the aftermath of Proposition 187 in California and welfare reform in 1996. It reviews the impact of immigration on the evolution of the U.S. population and economy and on taxes paid and the value of tax-supported services received.

SEE ALSO: Commission on Immigration Reform, U.S.; Economic consequences of immigration; Economic opportunities; Employment; Federation for American Immigration Reform; Illegal Immigration Reform and Immigrant Responsibility Act of 1996; Immigration Reform and Control Act of 1986; Proposition 187; Select Commission on Immigration and Refugee Policy.

West Indian immigrants

SIGNIFICANCE: Although West Indians have made up a relatively small part of immigrants who have come to the United States, notable West Indian communities have arisen in New York and Florida. Their places of origin are close to the southernmost part of the United States and they have a comparatively long history of immigrating to the United States.

The many small countries of the Caribbean make up the West Indies. There are some variations in the use of the term "West Indian," but the expression most frequently describes people in the English-speaking Caribbean islands. This region encompasses inhabitants of Anguilla, Antigua, Bahamas, Barbados, Belize, Cayman Islands, Dominica, Grenada, Jamaica, St. Kitts, St. Lucia, Montserrat, Trinidad, St. Trinidad, and the British and American and Virgin Islands. The term sometimes also encompasses people from Bermuda, which is north of the Caribbean, and Guyana, which is on the South American mainland. Moreover, many immigration authorities also include people from the French West Indies, notably Guadeloupe and Martinique, under the category "West Indian." Information presented here describes immigrants from both the English and French West Indies.

Although West Indians have constituted one of the smaller immigrant groups in the United States, they have a fairly long history of immigration as a result of the geographic proximity of the Caribbean. Between 1900 and 1920, immigrants from the West Indies living in the United States increased from only about 10,000 to more than 53,000. One of the best-known West Indians who immigrated during this period was the black nationalist leader Marcus Garvey, who arrived in the United States in 1916 and settled in New York City, which was already home to the largest concentration of immigrants from the West Indies in the United States. In 1920, close to one-half the West Indians in the United States lived in New York. Other, smaller, but significant communities of West Indians lived in New Orleans and Miami, Florida.

The West Indian population of the United States grew to nearly 79,000 by 1930. It then dropped dramatically to around 26,000 in 1940, and rose back up to about 38,000 in 1950. Numbers of West Indians increased over the 1950's to just over 100,000 in 1960 and then to 165,000 in 1970. The numbers of West Indians again increased rapidly after the early 1970's. By 1980, the West Indian immigrant population was close to 377,000. In 1990, the total reached 697,000, 1 million in 2000, and 1,174,000 in 2007.

Jamaicans made up the single-largest West Indian group in the United States, numbering an estimated 600,000 in 2007. New York City was still

PROFILE OF WEST INDIAN IMMIGRANTS

Countries of origin	Anguilla, Antigua-Barbuda, Aruba, Bahamas, Barbados, Bermuda, British Virgin Islands, Cayman Islands, Cuba, Dominica, Dominican Republic, Grenada, Guadeloupe, Haiti, Jamaica, Martinique, Montserrat, Netherlands Antilles, St. Kitts-Nevis, St. Lucia, St. Vincent and the Grenadines, Trinidad and Tobago, Turks and Caicos, U.S. Virgin Islands
Primary languages	English, Spanish, French
Primary regions of U.S. settlement	New York City, Florida
Earliest significant arrivals	1830's
Peak immigration periods	1900-1920's, late 1960's-2008
Twenty-first century legal residents*	868,416 (108,552 per year)

*Immigrants who obtained legal permanent resident status in the United States. Note that figures do not include Puerto Ricans.
Source: Department of Homeland Security, *Yearbook of Immigration Statistics, 2008.*

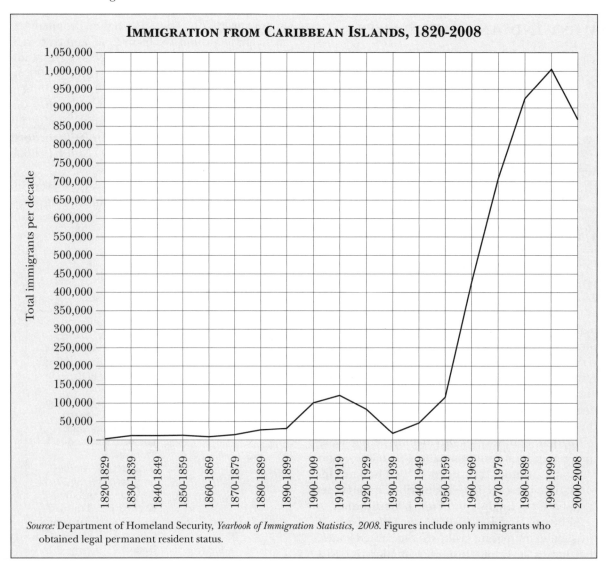

IMMIGRATION FROM CARIBBEAN ISLANDS, 1820-2008

Source: Department of Homeland Security, *Yearbook of Immigration Statistics, 2008*. Figures include only immigrants who obtained legal permanent resident status.

home to the greatest number of West Indian immigrants in the twenty-first century, holding close to one-third of the total. Florida, the state closest to the Caribbean, was home to nearly one-quarter of the West Indian immigrants in the United States. Most of Florida's West Indians settled in the Fort Lauderdale-Hollywood-Pompano Beach metropolitan area and the Miami-Hialeah metropolitan area.

West Indians worked in a variety of occupations during the early twenty-first century. They were especially well represented in medical and health services. About one of every ten West Indians in the American labor force worked as a hospital or other institutional attendant in 2007, and nearly one in twenty worked as a nurse.

Most West Indians are of African ancestry, but some are descendants of people from India who settled in the Caribbean during the era of the British Empire. The Indian presence in the Caribbean is most evident in Trinidad and Tobago. Immigration studies of this group are often concerned with the influence of racial prejudice on their adaptation to life in the United States. Relations between African Americans and black West Indians have generally been good, but some tensions have arisen between members of the two groups.

Carl L. Bankston III

FURTHER READING

Alvarez, Julia. *How the Garcia Girls Lost Their Accents.* Chapel Hill, N.C.: Algonquin Books, 1991.

Foner, Nancy, ed. *Islands in the City: West Indian Migration to New York.* Berkeley: University of California Press, 2001.

Vickerman, Milton. *Crosscurrents: West Indian Immigration and Race.* New York: Oxford University Press, 1999.

Waters, Mary C. *Black Identities: West Indian Immigrant Dreams and American Realities.* Cambridge, Mass.: Harvard University Press, 1999.

SEE ALSO: African Americans and immigrants; Cuban immigrants; Dominican immigrants; Florida; Garvey, Marcus; Haitian immigrants; Miami; New York City; Puerto Rican immigrants; Universal Negro Improvement Association.

WEST VIRGINIA

SIGNIFICANCE: This small, mountainous state has attracted little foreign immigration; however, modest numbers of northern Europeans came during the nineteenth century and larger numbers of southern and eastern Europeans came to work in its coalfields during the early twentieth century. By the early twenty-first century, West Virginia had one of the nation's smallest foreign-born populations.

The region that has become West Virginia was settled by Pennsylvania Germans, who established their first settlement at Shepherdstown on the Potomac River in 1731. Later influxes of Germans settled in more scattered patterns, but German-speaking peoples were sufficiently numerous into the early nineteenth century for public documents occasionally to be printed in both German and English. Most of the state's other early settlers were of English and Scotch-Irish extraction. A number of northern and western Europeans entered the area during the mid-nineteenth century. By 1863, the year in which West Virginia separated from Virginia to become a Union state, 4 percent of its residents were from Germany, Switzerland, Great Britain, Belgium, and Scandinavia.

West Virginia's small population at statehood worried many of its political and business leaders, as more people were needed to develop the state's natural resources and farmlands. In 1864, the state legislature created the office of immigration commissioner and made the energetic Swiss immigrant Joseph H. Diss Debar the first commissioner. His main interest—and that of his backers—was to attract farmers of northern European extraction. However, although Debar began his work with energy, he faced many problems, including a confusing tangle of land titles that disillusioned new, land-hungry immigrants and prevented others from coming. His successors as immigration commissioner proved to be both inactive and underfunded. West Virginia's office of immigration was also plagued by both disorganization and the presence of unscrupulous employees who sought to profit from credulous immigrants. Nevertheless, the office was a modest success. By the turn of the twentieth century, the foreign-born population of the state had risen to 22,451, of whom 6,537 Germans constituted the largest portion.

Meanwhile, the opening of new railroads and the development of coalfields in the southern part

PROFILE OF WEST VIRGINIA

Region	East
Entered union	1863
Largest cities	Charleston (capital), Huntington, Parkersburg
Modern immigrant communities	Canadians, Mexicans, Germans

Population	Total	Percent of state	Percent of U.S.	U.S. rank
All state residents	1,819,000	100.0	0.61	37
All foreign-born residents	22,000	1.2	0.06	46

Source: U.S. Census Bureau, *Statistical Abstract for 2006.*
Notes: The U.S. population in 2006 was 299,399,000, of whom 37,548,000 (12.5%) were foreign born. Rankings in last column reflect total numbers, not percentages.

of the state after 1880 brought new immigrants, The mines needed more workers than the state's native white black communities could provided, so they sought workers from Europe—especially southern and eastern Europe. In 1900, the U.S. Census counted 2,921 Italians and 810 Hungarians in West Virginia. By 1920, Italians, Hungarians, and Poles were among the largest groups of foreign laborers in West Virginia's mines. A number of Syrian and Lebanese suppliers and shopkeepers were also attracted to the region by the coal boom. During the Great Depression of the 1930's, the coalfields went into a slump, and many foreign workers left the state. However, several thousand immigrants remained to raise families in West Virginia.

West Virginia has not shared the economic and demographic growth that many southern states have had since the early 1990's. It has also seen little growth in its immigrant population. In 2000, only 1.1 percent of state residents were foreign born—a figure far below the national average. Indeed, the total number of foreign-born residents in West Virginia has increased little since the late nineteenth century.

In 2006, the largest number of immigrants in the state were of Mexican origin. They were followed by Canadians and Germans. West Virginia also has smaller communities of Asians and Europeans of various nationalities. Another aspect of West Virginia's small immigrant community has been a small rate of illegal immigration. In 2006, fewer than 10,000 undocumented immigrants—mostly Latinos—were estimated to be in the state.

Jeremiah Taylor

FURTHER READING

Fones-Wolf, Ken, and Ronald L. Lewis. *Transnational West Virginia: Ethnic Communities and Economic Change, 1840-1940*. Morgantown: West Virginia University Press, 2002.

Hennen, John C. *The Americanization of West Virginia: Creating a Modern Industrial State, 1916-1925*. Lexington: University Press of Kentucky, 1996.

Sullivan, Ken, ed. *The West Virginia Encyclopedia*. Charleston: West Virginia Humanities Council, 2006.

Williams, John Alexander. *West Virginia: A History*. Rev. ed. Morgantown: West Virginia University Press, 2001.

SEE ALSO: British immigrants; Economic opportunities; European immigrants; German immigrants; Hungarian immigrants; Italian immigrants; Mexican immigrants; Polish immigrants; Swiss immigrants; Virginia.

WESTWARD EXPANSION

THE EVENT: Settlement of the American West by foreign immigrants
DATE: Late sixteenth to late nineteenth century
LOCATION: Continental United States

SIGNIFICANCE: Except during the colonial period, foreign immigrants did not constitute a majority of those settling the western fringes of the expanding United States. Still, many did arrive during the nineteenth century, bringing unique traditions and aiding in the economic development of the regions they pioneered.

In settling western lands, immigrants added their numbers and energies to the cause of American nation building, but they also sought their own dreams and interests in the American hinterlands. More often than not, their goals were economic— whether desire for wealth or, more commonly, sufficient land or income to ensure a family competency and economic security for children. Others sought an escape from religious, ethnic, and political oppression, and a few saw the "virgin" West as the perfect place for building the world anew and realizing lofty social and spiritual visions. These sundry goals were not necessarily mutually exclusive.

COLONIAL ORIGINS

Appropriately, the history of American westward expansion and American immigration begin together. The westward expansion of Europe across the Atlantic necessarily involved immigration, for all who came were strangers to the New World.

By the mid-sixteenth century, several countries had established claims as well as a physical presence in North America. The colonial populations of the non-English colonies were never large, but

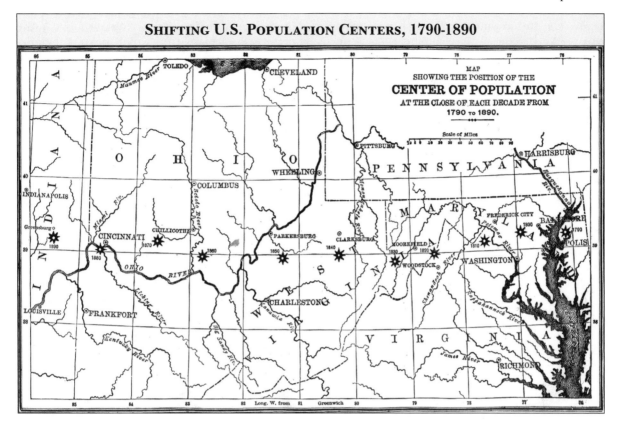

SHIFTING U.S. POPULATION CENTERS, 1790-1890

MAP
SHOWING THE POSITION OF THE
CENTER OF POPULATION
AT THE CLOSE OF EACH DECADE FROM
1790 TO 1890.

some of them were surprisingly diverse. That of New Sweden numbered only about three hundred men, women, and children when it was absorbed by the Dutch in 1655, and many of these "new Swedes" were the very Finnish farmers whom some scholars credit with introducing log architecture to North America. New Netherland had a population of about five thousand in 1660, and thanks to Dutch religious tolerance, it was even more diverse. French Huguenots, English Puritans, Flemings, Walloons, Scandinavians, Germans, and Jews (altogether, about half the population) rubbed elbows with Dutch settlers and African slaves.

The British North American colonies and their peoples proved numerically superior and ultimately prevailed over their competitors. The majority of their inhabitants were English. About 60.9 percent of those living in the future United States on the eve of the American Revolution were of English origin. They came for different reasons. During the seventeenth century, the average English immigrant to this "New West" was poor, single, and male. They responded more to the push factors at

home than to the pull factors of an uncertain existence in the United States.

Economic woes and a growing population in England meant that many desperately poor men preferred to risk the life of an indentured servant in North America (where they might one day acquire land) rather than live as a beggar at home. Those who came to New England during the same century—especially during the Great Migration of the 1630's—were a very different set. Usually from an economically independent middle-class background, these English immigrants came in family groups. While profit was not unimportant to them, economics was not their sole purpose for immigrating. They were religious dissenters who, despairing of purifying the English Church of extrabiblical corruptions, wished to build an exemplary Christian commonwealth in the wilderness.

As economic conditions in England improved during the eighteenth century, fewer English people thought the journey to the colonies worthwhile. Their place was mostly taken by large numbers of Scots, Scotch-Irish, Germans, and others. Ger-

1059

mans, who began entering Pennsylvania (where they would become the "Pennsylvania Dutch") during the 1680's and who continued migrating there well into the eighteenth century, would come to constitute about 8.7 percent of the colonial population. Most came from the Rhineland, from whose demographic pressures, economic woes, wars, and authoritarian princes they fled. They were also encouraged by colonial promoters. The Scotch-Irish, so often identified with the frontier in American history, were mostly the descendants of Protestant Lowland Scots and northwestern English border folk who had been transplanted to Ulster as tenants in seventeenth century. In response to push factors such as rising rents and pull factors such as promotional literature, many moved to the Pennsylvania frontier during the eighteenth century. From

there they pushed southward into the Great Valley of the Appalachians, from which they and their descendants would later move into the trans-Appalachian West. In this great and piecemeal migration, they were joined by Germans, English, and others.

TRANS-APPALACHIAN WEST

Most late colonial and early national migration into the lands beyond the Appalachians was international in character. The descendants of colonial America's first immigrants—and these included many slaves of African descent—were the rank and file of American westering. There were exceptions to this rule. Some exceptions were relatively small, such as those French immigrants who chose homes in Kentucky and elsewhere in the West during the turbulence of the French Revolution and Napole-

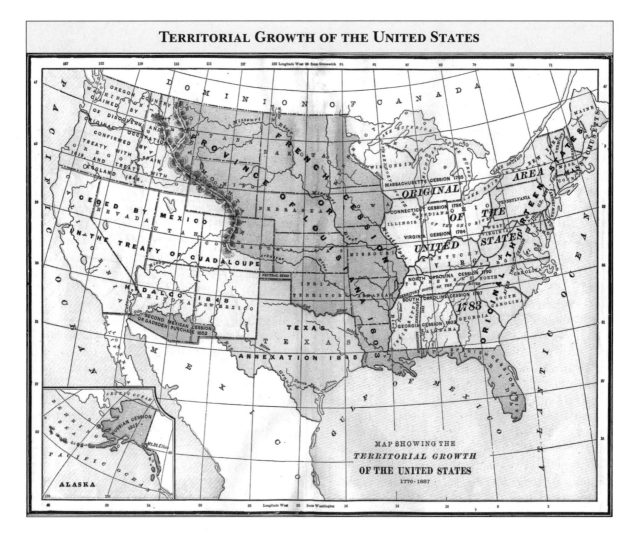

TERRITORIAL GROWTH OF THE UNITED STATES

MAP SHOWING THE
TERRITORIAL GROWTH
OF THE UNITED STATES
1776-1887

onic Wars. Other exceptions were unusual: planned communities, for example, such as that founded by a communal sect of German pietists at New Harmony, Indiana, in 1814. By the mid-nineteenth century, however, there were mass movements of immigrants into trans-Appalachia. These were largely restricted to the Midwest.

During the 1840's, Europeans began flooding into the Old Northwest. Norwegians, Irish, and others came, but Germans were the most numerous. Wisconsin and especially Milwaukee—whose culture and beer still owe something to this mass migration—was a favored destination for Germans arriving in New York during this period. By 1850, foreign-born residents in Wisconsin actually outnumbered native-born Americans by 107,000 to 63,000. Settlement continued during the 1850's and after the U.S. Civil War, bringing Belgians and new Scandinavian settlers in addition to preexisting streams of immigration. Poles, Czechs, and other Slavs came as well, but they mostly gravitated toward Chicago. Nearly all immigrants to the South during this period were city-bound—principally to New Orleans. Excluding these urban populations, by 1860 around 10 to 15 percent of the population of trans-Appalachia was foreign-born.

Push-pull factors worked in tandem to bring this flood of foreigners into the trans-Appalachian West. Guidebooks and other literature were freely available in Europe during the nineteenth century. These touted America—and especially its extensive, newly opened lands—as a place of unlimited opportunity. Positive letters from friends and family members already living in the United States also fanned the ardent desire of many Europeans to emigrate. If they required a bit of push, they had only to look at the world of uncertainty and flux around them. In 1845, the population of Europe had increased about 80 percent since 1750. Arable lands were at a premium—and this was especially true of Norway, where only 3 to 4 percent of the land was tillable. Industrialization had displaced many, including skilled artisans—and this process was nowhere more sharply felt than in Germany. Political upheavals drove many away. The failed revolutions of 1848, for example, were an especially potent factor in driving Germans across the Atlantic. The potato famine that stalked Ireland and fueled emigration from its shores also affected many on the Continent.

TRANS-MISSISSIPPI WEST

Postwar migration beyond the Mississippi River displayed similar patterns. Germans, for example, continued to be a dominant immigrant group. Large numbers of them settled the plains—especially Texas and the upper Midwest. They were joined by Scandinavians, the greatest number of whom were Norwegians, but they were accompanied by many Swedes and Danes as well. By 1914, some 2 million Scandinavians had come to the United States, mostly to the Dakotas, Minnesota, Wisconsin, and Nebraska. Slavs, especially Czechs, immigrated in great numbers, too. Many settled in cities such as Chicago and St. Louis, but a number of them also chose the rural frontier. Nebraska especially was a popular destination. These immigrants were joined on the plains by German Mennonites from Russia, Irish ex-laborers, and European Jews. The latter founded more than forty farming colonies in the trans-Mississippi West between 1881 and 1915. Beginning in the 1880's, new agricultural frontiers were reached when the push of transcontinental railroads opened the fecund valleys of the Pacific Northwest to both native-born American and foreign migration. A number of specialist agriculturalists, including Italian and French vintners and Armenian fig and date farmers, were drawn to the valleys of California.

Not all newcomers to the West were tillers of the soil. After the U.S. Civil War, Basque immigrants took up sheepherding beyond the Rockies, and by the last decades of the century, men from many nations were engaged in the logging industry of the Pacific Northwest. San Francisco itself was a great locus of immigration. By 1880, 50 percent of its people had been born abroad. Western mines invited foreign laborers, too. Cornish men, for example, toiled in Utah's lead mines, while Croats, Slovenes, and Serbs dug for coal in Montana. British, Italians, Mexicans, Greeks, Irish, and many others also chased livelihoods by various means in the trans-Mississippi West.

Nonwhite immigration to America occurred for the first time on a large scale during the settlement of the Far West. About 300,000 Chinese came to the United States between 1848 and 1882, where they labored in western cities, mined for western minerals, and built western railroads. By the mid-1890's, Japanese immigrants were entering the western United States in significant numbers. Most worked

Pioneer family working their way west during the mid-1880's. (Getty Images)

as agricultural laborers—especially in California—but some also worked on the railroads and in other occupations. Because of their race and their perceived threat to free, white labor, both Chinese and Japanese immigrants faced bitter nativist opposition and, finally, official federal policies of discrimination.

As was the case with the colonial and trans-Appalachian frontiers, most people came to the trans-Mississippi West in the name of socioeconomic betterment. Promotional literature—sometimes distributed by purely speculative government or private concerns, and at other times by companies of immigrants eager to draw their countrymen to the New World—circulated widely and praised the manifold opportunities in the United States. Agents sometimes recruited abroad, and news from friends and family already in the United States continued to be a potent factor. Some immigrants—including many Chinese—did not come to stay, but to work toward "nest eggs" and eventually return home. Others wished to construct ideal religious or social

communities. In one such (failed) experiment in 1870's Kansas, a group of aristocratic English immigrants endeavored to create a community that would embody the ideal lifestyle of their nation's landed gentry. Some immigrants readily mixed nonmaterial and material motives. That twenty-thousand Danish Mormons migrated to Utah in the second half of the nineteenth century might have been due in part to the exemplary efforts of American missionaries, but it is also notable that most of the convert-immigrants were families of modest means and that the Mormon Church funded their emigration.

In the far western United States, immigrants eventually made up only about 5.6 percent of the white population. As was the case with the trans-Appalachian West, the foreign-born (with certain exceptions, as in the above-mentioned cases of Wisconsin and San Francisco) remained a minority within the westering population. The importance of their presence, however, should not be underestimated. Of those groups who stayed in the United

States, most have long since acculturated and entered the mainstream of American life. There remain, however, distinctive cultural markers in the places they pioneered—be they architectural styles or religious denominations. Moreover, these immigrants, to the benefit of their new nation (if often to the detriment of the Amerindians they frequently helped displace), built infrastructure and assisted at all levels of western economic development. They built railroads, harvested crops, tended stock, felled trees, mined minerals, and helped carve farms, ranches, and towns from the raw stuff of expanding American empire. In this way, they shared many of the same basic activities and essential goals with those seventeenth century pioneers of westward expansion, all of whom were immigrants.

Jeremiah Taylor

FURTHER READING

Billington, Ray Allen. *Land of Savagery, Land of Promise: The European Image of the American Frontier in the Nineteenth Century.* New York: W. W. Norton, 1981. Offers insights into what immigrants expected to find on the American frontier.

Griffin, Patrick. *The People with No Name: Ireland's Ulster Scots, America's Scots Irish, and the Creation of a British Atlantic World, 1689-1764.* Princeton, N.J.: Princeton University Press, 2001. Thorough examination of an important eighteenth century immigrant-pioneer group, examining their history on both sides of the Atlantic.

Korytova-Magstadt, Stepanka. *To Reap a Bountiful Harvest: Czech Immigration Beyond the Mississippi, 1850-1900.* Iowa City, Iowa: Rudi, 1993. Standard account of one of the largest Slavic ethnicities to settle the American West.

Milner, Clyde A. II, Carol A. O'Connor, and Martha A. Sandweiss, eds. *The Oxford History of the American West.* New York: Oxford University Press, 1994. Standard survey covering immigration and much more.

Noble, Allen G., ed. *To Build in a New Land: Ethnic Landscapes in North America.* Baltimore: Johns Hopkins University Press, 1992. Covers westering immigrants' cultural impact upon the American landscape.

Stellingwerff, Johan. *Iowa Letters: Dutch Immigrants on the American Frontier.* Translated by Walter Lagerwey. Grand Rapids, Mich.: William B. Eerdmans, 2004. This large collection of primary

documents allows a fascinating glimpse into immigrant life on the nineteenth century midwestern frontier.

SEE ALSO: British immigrants; California; California gold rush; Chinese immigrants; Homestead Act of 1862; Nativism; New Harmony; Railroads; Scandinavian immigrants; Wisconsin.

WISCONSIN

SIGNIFICANCE: Like other upper midwestern states, received the bulk of its nineteenth century immigrants from northern and western Europe. Germans were especially numerous, and they left a lasting imprint on the state.

Between the time of American independence and 1830, Wisconsin remained sparsely populated, with small numbers of Native Americans and French along the Mississippi River. Lead mining in the southwest part of the state brought a mix of southern American, Cornish, and Welsh miners. Wars with the Winnebago and other tribes, including the brutal Black Hawk war of 1832, drove most Indians from the state except for those remaining on reservations in the far north. Completion of the Erie Canal in 1832 linked the Great Lakes with the East Coast ports of entry, and Wisconsin's population began to grow. In 1848, it became a state; two years later, the U.S. Census counted 300,000 people living in Wisconsin.

GERMAN IMMIGRANTS

Substantial numbers of Germans began immigrating into Wisconsin after the failed European revolutions of 1848, which gave these German immigrants the nickname "Forty-eighters." However, some significant German settlement had actually begun earlier, mostly along the west bank of Lake Michigan. By the time of the 1850 census, Germans already made up almost one-sixth of Wisconsin's population. In Milwaukee, Germans actually outnumbered native-born American residents, with 38 percent of the city's population, against only 33 percent for the Americans.

The cultural imprint of Germans was evident for years in Wisconsin. Milwaukee hosted German op-

PROFILE OF WISCONSIN

Region	Upper Midwest
Entered union	1848
Largest cities	Milwaukee, Madison (capital), Green Bay, Kenosha, Racine
Modern immigrant communities	Mexicans, Hmong

Population	Total	Percent of state	Percent of U.S.	U.S. rank
All state residents	5,557,000	100.0	1.86	20
All foreign-born residents	245,000	4.4	0.65	23

Source: U.S. Census Bureau, *Statistical Abstract for 2006.*

Notes: The U.S. population in 2006 was 299,399,000, of whom 37,548,000 (12.5%) were foreign born. Rankings in last column reflect total numbers, not percentages.

eras and beer gardens. TurnVerein clubs in Milwaukee and Madison encouraged the development of gymnastic and artistic skills; Germans were also active in Wisconsin politics, and they quarreled in the state legislature with nativists over the use of German in public schools. After the Civil War (1861-1865), the state elected to the U.S. Senate Carl Schurz, a German immigrant who had served as a brigadier general in the Union Army during the war. For a time, German-language public schools and teacher-training academies flourished. German immigration declined during the twentieth century, but a German presence remained in Wisconsin. The 2000 U.S. Census counted 48,300 Wisconsin residents who reported that they spoke German at home.

POLISH IMMIGRANTS

Poles seeking economic opportunities began arriving in Wisconsin around the middle of the nineteenth century. In 1855, they founded a farming community named Polonia, in which they grew what was then the principal Wisconsin crop, wheat. Later Polish immigrants, however, came seeking political freedom from Prussian domination of Poland and conscription into the Prussian army. Polish immigrants continued to seek farmland and helped to populate the far north, but other Poles were more attracted to industrial jobs in the Milwaukee area, where their strong prolabor sentiments worried employers.

Polish immigration declined during the twentieth century, but more Poles came to Wisconsin during after World War II—first as refugees from Nazi Germany's occupation of Poland and later from Soviet domination. In the census of 2000, more than 12,000 Wisconsin residents reported speaking Polish at home.

OTHER IMMIGRANT GROUPS

Significant Hispanic immigration was slow to reach Wisconsin. During the 1970's, economic crises in Mexico and increasing poverty in the other parts of Latin America caused a surge of Hispanic immigration into the United States, and Wisconsin got a substantial share. Between 1990 and 2000, the state's Hispanic population more than tripled—to 168,780 residents who reported they spoke Spanish at home. Most of these new immigrants were Mexicans.

In Wisconsin's western counties, along the Mississippi River, some Norwegian immigrants settled during the nineteenth century, although they were much more numerous across the river in Minnesota. Swiss immigrants settled in New Glarus and Monroe. At the beginning of the twenty-first century, New Glarus remained a tourist attraction, with Swiss restaurants and hotels, often staffed by Swiss nationals. Wisconsin also received its share of refugees from Southeast Asia after the Vietnam War. In 2000, Wisconsin's 30,570 Hmong constituted one of the largest Hmong communities in the United States.

Timothy C. Frazer

FURTHER READING

Blashfield, Jean F. *Wisconsin.* New York: Children's Press, 2008. Good overview of the state's geography, history, natural resources, economy, culture, and people for younger readers.

Frazer, Timothy C., ed. *"Heartland" English: Variation and Transition in the American Midwest.* Tuscaloosa: University of Alabama Press, 1993. Collection of essays describing the impact immigrants and settlement had on the spoken English of several midwestern states, including Wisconsin.

Jensen, Joan M. *Calling This Place Home: Women on the Wisconsin Frontier, 1850-1925.* St. Paul: Minnesota Historical Society Press, 2006. Study of how women helped shape the state's history and how broader developments shaped their lives.

Loew, Patty. *Indian Nations of Wisconsin: Histories of Endurance and Renewal.* Madison: Wisconsin Historical Society Press, 2001. Collection of brief histories of twelve indigenous groups who have maintained their presence in Wisconsin from the point of European contact to the present.

McClelland, Ted. *The Third Coast.* Chicago: Chicago Review Press, 2008. Includes a humorous chapter on Milwaukee's beer tradition and another on Washington Island and its Icelandic immigrants.

Risjord, Norman K., ed. *The WPA Guide to Wisconsin: The Federal Writers' Project Guide to 1930's Wisconsin.* 1941. Reprint. St. Paul: Minnesota Historical Society Press, 2006. Compiled by writers who traveled the state during the Depression, this work includes descriptions of Wisconsin's ethnic groups.

SEE ALSO: German immigrants; Language issues; Mexican immigrants; North American Free Trade Agreement; Polish immigrants; Schurz, Carl; Westward expansion.

WOMEN IMMIGRANTS

SIGNIFICANCE: A gendered understanding of immigrants reveals that women have often migrated under circumstances that differ from those of men, and they have typically become involved in specifically female occupations on their arrival in the United States. During the late twentieth century, scholars in many fields began studying women's documented and undocumented immigration and have found that the patterns of female immigration that were previously subsumed within general studies of immigration were often very different from those of men.

The study of women's immigration is a developing field of research that is receiving increased attention from anthropologists, economists, geographers, and other scholars. With increased scrutiny and more attention to data-gathering, it has become apparent that the motivations, pathways, and ultimate destinations of women immigrants have often been determined by criteria that differ from those of male immigrants. These patterns went long unnoticed because scholars assumed that gender differences played no role in migration. Women were generally considered only in their dependent roles as wives, mothers, or daughters, rather than as self-sufficient immigrants and workers in their own right.

Among issues that specifically affect women's immigration patterns have been the desire to escape from gendered hardships, such as domestic violence, educational and employment opportunities that are lower for women than for men, religious and political inequities, and other privations that weigh more heavily on women than men. The United States has exercised a special attraction to female immigrants because women in the United States possess many freedoms that are not available to women in other nations, as evidenced by legislation, law enforcement, and courts that support women's rights. Many women also may immigrate to the United States to fill certain jobs that are held mostly by women, such as child care and other domestic work, which draw many immigrants from developing countries. Some immigrants also take advantage of the American demand for foreign-born wives by finding prospective husbands online in chat rooms or through relationship brokers.

The fact that the decisions of male and female immigrants are influenced by different push-pull factors was not fully recognized until scholars began comparing the data on men with data on women. Moreover, inattention to gender issues also meant that most scholars were long unaware that women, rather than men, dominated legal immigration flows from the 1930's until 1980. Coding problems in immigration data for 1980-1984 make gender comparisons in the United States almost impossible, but the international facts are instructive. At the start of the 1980's, 157 of the world's countries produced census data that enumerated approximately 78 million people living outside their countries of birth. Of this total, 48 percent were women. During this same time period, in the developed nations, women immigrant populations outnumbered those of male immigrants.

Between 1985 and 1992, women immigrants to the United States outnumbered men, though by a smaller margin than in previous decades. However, some of the 1990's data were skewed in favor of men by the legalization of undocumented immigrants already living in the United States because large numbers of male agricultural workers took advantage of the Immigration Reform and Control Act of 1986 to gain legal immigration status.

Data from the early twenty-first century have shown a continued preponderance of female over male immigrants. For example, in 2008, 54.2 percent of the more than 1 million new legal permanent resident documents granted were granted to women. Gender ratios for 2002 through 2007 were similar.

The predominance of women in U.S. immigration data is somewhat surprising, given the emphases found in most national and state histories on contributions of male immigrants to national and regional events. Less attention has been paid to women's achievements, even though female immigrants outnumbered male immigrants in most years since the 1930's.

WOMEN, RELATIONSHIPS, AND DOMESTIC VIOLENCE

A challenge for immigration scholars has been to figure out how all these disparate data fit together and to document women's divergent immigration strategies and patterns. Many women have immigrated to the United States under family reunification programs. The War Brides Act of 1945, which served to unite non-American wives with their American husbands after World War II, is one example.

As late as 1972-1979, 10 percent of all immigrants to the United States were foreign women

Cooking class in Chicago's Hull-House. (University of Illinois at Chicago, University Library, Jane Addams Memorial Collection)

New York City garment workers demonstrating their solidarity with the victims of the Triangle Shirtwaist Factory fire.
(AP/Wide World Photos)

married to American men who chose to immigrate using the spousal preferment option. The trend of American men seeking wives in other nations has continued and has developed in new directions, especially with the expansion of the Internet, which has become increasingly available in developing nations. Some men in more developed countries find women using online mail-order bride services or other e-mail connections. During the early twenty-first century, as many as 4,000-6,000 marriages resulted from such connections every year. However, the data are unreliable, and it is unclear how many such marriages last beyond the acquisition of American passports and settlement in the United States.

A special problem faced by mail-order brides is that many of them lack U.S. documentation in their own right, which leaves them open to manip-

ulation and abuse by others. Moreover, they may fear deportation if they object to being poorly treated. Battered women's shelters across the United States have assisted immigrant women requesting help. Domestic violence is challenging to all women who are victims, and even native-born American women may be reluctant to ask for help for reasons such as feelings of shame, the risk of further harm, or financial difficulties.

The challenges of family abuse are especially difficult for immigrant women, who may have poor English-language skills, few local friends, and meager understandings of services and legal help available to them. In addition to dealing with the stresses of domestic violence, women naturally fear the prospect of being returned to their homelands with few resources to aid their reintegration into their native communities. The laws can be bewildering, and immigration officials are not always helpful to the impoverished and those who lack English skills and legal understanding.

For all of these reasons, in the United States, there has been increasing attention to providing immigrant victims of family violence with specialty services. For example, some battered women's centers cater to women from immigrant communities by providing translators and other services that enhance the women's safety and ability to remain in the United States legally. Spanish-language serves have become available in most major American cities, but many immigrants speak other languages for which translators may not be available. Language and culture also play important roles in immigrant women's employment opportunities.

WOMEN'S WORK

In the United States, women doing the same work as men have almost always been paid less than men, and immigrant women are paid less than American-born women. Consequently, women immigrants have typically faced severe struggles to house and feed themselves and their families. As early as the late nineteenth century, these inequities were challenged by women philanthropists, such as Jane Addams and Ellen Gates Starr, who established Hull-House in Chicago in 1889. Hull-House and other settlement houses were founded on humanitarian principles, and offered housing, education, and other services to poor women, typically newcomers.

Immigrant women who have been desperate for employment have often accepted jobs requiring them to endure hazardous working conditions. Historically, the general public became aware of these conditions when horrible industrial accidents occurred, such as New York City's Triangle Shirtwaist Factory disaster in 1911, when 146 sweatshop employees, who were mainly young immigrant women, were killed in a fire because they could not get out of an unsafe building. The aftermath of that disaster brought some reforms in occupational safety, but many immigrants continued to work in unsafe conditions.

A large number of immigrant women work in domestic situations, providing daily household labor for families with whom they often live. They often tend children and clean homes for their employers. Such tasks are not highly remunerated,

and because many of these women are undocumented, they have limited ability to push for higher wages or to obtain health care and other benefits.

Other fields in which many immigrant women are concentrated include the garment industry, family-run businesses in ethnic enclaves, and skilled service work, such as nursing. Undocumented immigrant women are often excluded from skilled employment by their insecure legal status, and may accept lower wages in return for piecework or employment with small businesses.

Susan J. Wurtzburg

FURTHER READING

Danquah, Meri Nana-Ama, ed. *Becoming American: Personal Essays by First Generation Immigrant Women.* New York: Hyperion, 2000. Collection of twenty-three memoirs by immigrant women telling their own immigration stories.

Hondagneu-Sotelo, Pierrette. *Doméstica: Immigrant Workers Cleaning and Caring in the Shadows of Affluence.* Berkeley: University of California Press, 2001. Extensive study based on interviews with thirty-seven employers and twenty-three immigrant employees in Los Angeles County.

McGill, Craig. *Human Traffic: Sex, Slaves and Immigration.* London: Vision Paperbacks, 2003. Chilling accounts of sex trafficking of women in all areas of the world, with considerable information on the United States.

Parreñas, Rhacel Salazar. *Children of Global Migration: Transnational Families and Gendered Woes.* Stanford, Calif.: Stanford University Press, 2005. Study of gender and its impact on Filipino families with members living in the United States.

Pedraza, Silvia. "Women and Migration: The Social Consequences of Gender." *Annual Review of Sociology* 17 (1991): 303-325. Overview of the academic debates about women immigrants.

Tyler, Anne. *Digging to America: A Novel.* New York: Alfred A. Knopf, 2006. Beautifully written fiction about immigrant families in the United States, foreign adoptions, and the challenges for women immigrants.

Warrier, Sujata, and Jennifer Rose. "Women, Gender-Based Violence, and Immigration." In *Social Work with Immigrants and Refugees: Legal Issues, Clinical Skills, and Advocacy,* edited by Fernando Chang-Muy and Elaine P. Congress. New York: Springer, 2009. Article presenting information about domestic violence and immigrant women, including strategies for assisting women.

SEE ALSO: Families; Immigration waves; International Ladies' Garment Workers' Union; Mailorder brides; "Marriages of convenience"; Picture brides; Settlement houses; Triangle Shirtwaist fire; War brides; War Brides Act of 1945; Women's movements.

WOMEN'S MOVEMENTS

DEFINITION: Campaigns and organizations dedicated to principles and agendas that promote the empowerment of women

SIGNIFICANCE: Two goals have driven the involvement of women's movements in issues affecting women immigrants. The first issue has been supporting affirmative action legislation that benefits women. The second has been overturning gender stratification that has benefited the interests of men over those of women.

Advocates of the rights of immigrant women trace global developments emerging in the last quarter of the twentieth century to the presence of growing numbers of women in international migration flows and their identification as immigrants. They argue the economic and cultural shifts in many less-developed nations have reduced employment opportunities for populations of men and women generally, but have contributed to individuals finding alternatives to traditional means of making a living. The concept of the "feminization of survival" emphasizes both the public and domestic contributions of women to state and household in an era of acute economic hardship and an increasingly global demand for women's work. One consequence of the "feminization of survival" phenomenon has been a growing proportion of women in migration flows across the globe, including those to North America.

SPECIAL PROBLEMS OF WOMEN IMMIGRANTS

Studies of immigrant women coming to the United States have found that these women typically enter as wives and dependents of men who sponsor their admission. Research has also shown that one effect of gender stratification has been that women are usually less likely than men to enter the United States on humanitarian or economic grounds. Immigrant women have also faced a gender-stratified labor market in which they typically occupy positions regarded as "women's jobs," such as seamstresses, nannies, domestic workers, caregivers, and nurses. Moreover, such studies have revealed that the negative impacts of gender stratification have combined with those of being immigrants. For this reason, many women's movements have argued that immigrant women are doubly disadvantaged and consequently more likely to occupy marginal occupations that are poorly paid and unregulated by labor laws.

Established to protect the rights of women, including immigrants, the Equal Employment Opportunity Commission (EEOC) is a federal government agency that administers, interprets, and enforces Title VII of the Civil Rights Act of 1964. That law prohibits employment discrimination based on race, color, religion, sex, or national origin. Although the EEOC is not part of any women's movement, it has been influenced by women's movements.

THE MOVEMENTS

Women's movements have developed in a variety of forms. They have included community organizations that bring immigrant women and other members of a community together to confront the various forms of oppression immigrant women experience. Women's movements also come in the form of advocacy groups that attempt to represent the interests of individuals in government agencies as well as groups calling for benefits and lobbying for social and political change. Other groups have been involved in public education and awareness campaigns that aim to inform immigrants of their rights as well as to challenge generalizations and cultural stereotypes about immigrant women that tend to develop in their receiving communities.

One of the most urgent imperatives for movements concerned with immigrant women has been ensuring the human rights of both legal and illegal immigrant women. As such, various organizations have mobilized to combat human rights abuses including violence against immigrant women along U.S. borders, sexual abuse by employers, inhuman conditions in refugee camps, and domestic violence perpetrated by American spouses. Additionally, sex trafficking has become one of the largest international industries in the underground global economy. The gender inequality of many women around the globe has enhanced the vulnerability of women. Women's movements argue that sex trade traffickers use the low status of women and stereotypes of women as sexual commodities to fuel the industry and perpetuate the extreme marginalization and exploitation of many women and girls.

SOCIAL, CULTURAL, AND POLITICAL IMPLICATIONS

Although immigration to the United States has continued to offer women social and economic opportunities, these opportunities have not been evenly distributed, especially in employment. Moreover, nonwhite immigrants have faced additional hurdles. Indeed, some immigrant women may be said to have been triply disadvantaged in the labor market by virtue of being female, foreign born, and nonwhite.

One of the most serious criticisms leveled against the feminist movement, even by feminists themselves, has been that women's movements have focused largely on the needs of middle- and upper-class white women, to the exclusion of lower-class women, especially members of racial or ethnic minorities. Some feminists have argued the need for a more inclusive feminist strategy that focuses less on less on gender and more on the complex interrelationships among race, ethnicity, and class.

Advocates for immigrant women have called for women's movements to define "woman" in ways that go beyond class, race, and other categories. They further argue that a word such as "immigrant" is itself restrictive in that an immigrant woman can have many identities. Such advocates have also argued that human rights and immigrant women's movements should be more closely integrated. They also suggest that immigrant women should be more proactive in speaking out for their

Poster issued by the Young Women's Christian Association (YWCA) in 1919 to call attention to the contributions of women immigrants. (Library of Congress)

own interests. Only then, they argue, will they become less marginalized in that their concerns will be represented by voices that do include them.

POLITICAL REFORM

Despite criticisms of the limited scope of some women's movements, many feminists and women's organizations dedicated to legal reform have successfully advocated on behalf of low-income and marginalized women through campaigning for decisive civil rights legislation. For example, the Violence Against Women Act (VAWA) of 1994 was arguably the most significant of these efforts. In addition to providing financial support to a wide variety of violence prevention programs and agencies serving victims of violence—including shelters for abused women and a nationwide help hotline—VAWA has allowed victims of gender-motivated violent crimes to seek redress against their abusers in civil courts.

Nicole Anae

FURTHER READING

Dutt, Mallika, Leni Marin, and Helen Zia, eds. *Migrant Women's Human Rights in G-7 Countries: Organizing Strategies.* San Francisco: Family Violence Prevention Fund and Center for Women's Global Leadership, 1997. Collection of articles examining how immigrant women in the United States and other developed nations have raised public concern about such issues as domestic violence, worker's rights, and xenophobia.

Fitzpatrick, Ellen. *Endless Crusade: Women Social Scientists and Progressive Reform.* New York: Oxford University Press, 1990. Examination of the lives of four progressive women who played a crucial role in the establishment of settlement houses and social reform.

Kamm, Richard. "Extending the Progress of the Feminist Movement to Encompass the Rights of Migrant Farmworker Women." *Chicago-Kent Law Review* 75, no. 765 (2000): 765-783. Essay on how the needs of immigrant female farmworkers might best be served by a more inclusive feminist movement originating at the grassroots level.

Pikkov, Boyd, and Deanna Pikkov. "Gendering Migration, Livelihood, and Entitlements: Migrant Women in Canada and the United States." *Policy Report on Gender and Development: Ten Years After Beijing.* New York: United Nations Research Institute for Social Development, 2005. Comparative study of immigrant women's experiences in the United States and Canada.

SEE ALSO: Families; Goldman, Emma; Immigration Act of 1924; Immigration and Nationality Act of 1952; Intermarriage; Marriage; Settlement houses; Women immigrants.

WONG WING V. UNITED STATES

THE CASE: U.S. Supreme Court decision on the deportation of noncitizens
DATE: Decided on May 18, 1896

> **SIGNIFICANCE:** The *Wong Wing* ruling prohibited Congress from imposing criminal punishments on noncitizens without permitting them jury trials and other constitutional rights. At the same time, however, the decision reaffirmed Congress's unfettered authority to mandate the deportation of aliens without jury trials.

The Chinese Exclusion Act of 1882 imposed deportation and imprisonment for a maximum of one year at hard labor for Chinese persons found guilty of illegally entering or residing in the United States. The law specified that a hearing was sufficient for sentencing, and either a judge or a U.S. commissioner was authorized to render the sentence. Soon after the law went into effect, a commissioner for the Circuit Court of eastern Michigan determined that Wong Wing and three other Chinese men were illegal immigrants, and he sentenced them to sixty days at hard labor to be followed by deportation to China.

The Supreme Court unanimously held that the imprisonment provisions of the legislation were void because they violated constitutional guarantees. Speaking for the Court, Justice George Shiras, Jr., emphasized that the necessity for due process applied to "persons," not simply citizens. Although Congress had the authority to legislate the deportations of aliens without jury trials, when the issue was punishment for an infamous crime, principles of due process required a grand jury indictment and a jury trial, as well as the other provisions in the Fifth and Sixth Amendments. Justice Stephen J. Field wrote a concurring opinion. The four Chinese petitioners, therefore, were deported without first having to serve a prison term.

Thomas Tandy Lewis

FURTHER READING

Hyung-chan, Kim, ed. *Asian Americans and the Supreme Court: A Documentary History.* Westport, Conn.: Greenwood Press, 1992.

McClain, Charles J. *In Search of Equality: The Chinese Struggle Against Discrimination in Nineteenth-Century America.* Berkeley: University of California Press, 1994.

SEE ALSO: Chinese Exclusion Act of 1882; Congress, U.S.; Constitution, U.S.; Deportation; Due process protections; History of immigration after 1891; Immigration law; Supreme Court, U.S.

WORLD MIGRATION PATTERNS

DEFINITION: Trends and patterns in international migrations in modern world history

SIGNIFICANCE: Although the United States has had a unique immigration history, many elements of immigration into the country fit into broad patterns affecting other parts of the world, particularly western Europe. U.S. immigration history cannot, therefore, be fully understood without reference to its place in a global context.

In his 1995 study of global migration, Myron Weiner identified five distinct eras of immigration that had occurred since the Renaissance. The United States has featured centrally in each, although perhaps less so than Europe. The first two eras stretched from the seventeenth century through World War I (1914-1918). Those eras encompassed Europe's acquisition of colonies in the Americas, Australia, and New Zealand during the seventeenth, eighteenth, and very early nineteenth centuries and the settlement of those colonies through the nineteenth century. North America in general and the United States in particular benefited from the arrival of immigrants from Great Britain, France, Ireland, Germany, Italy and their neighboring "donor" states in southern and eastern Europe.

The same eras also saw European governments shape the travel of non-Europeans to distant regions, most aggressively through the slave trade. During Weiner's three subsequent eras of twentieth century global migration, the United States continued to become an ever more ethnically diverse country of immigrants, and Europe itself was profoundly reshaped by immigrant flows.

THE AGE OF COLONIALISM

History, and the spread of humanity across the globe, is to no small extent the story of ancient migrations. However, Weiner and most modern historians and sociologists date the modern waves of migration from those of the sixteenth to eighteenth centuries, when European governments in their search for wealth and power sent their peoples to remote lands, first to find goods of value and then to secure their holdings with settlements. Most of these early settlements were merely coastal affairs, under the protective cannons of their homeland's warships. European firearms were primitive by the standards that would develop during the nineteenth century, but even the single-shot, muzzle-loading weapons that earlier empire builders brought with them from Europe were superior to most weapons of the native peoples whom they encountered in the Americas, Australasia, Asia, and Africa, and the numbers in which they eventually arrived were overwhelming to the aborigines. However, neither their numbers nor their weaponry were great enough to enable them to move far from their initial settlements and the protective cover they enjoyed there.

The numbers of settlers involved during the long initial era of modern migration were not insignificant by the European standards of the time. Before 1820, an estimated 240,000 Europeans migrated to North America alone. Some came as indentured servants, and many sought to escape the religious and political persecution they experienced in Europe. To these must be added the large number of forced immigrants who were imported into North America from Africa during the slave trade that emerged during this period. Above all, perhaps, this early wave of migration established the three patterns that were to characterize international migration into the twentieth century.

First, the flow of migrants was largely unrestricted until the consolidations of European borders during the eighteenth and nineteenth centuries would cut down on movements of groups within Europe. During the nineteenth century, several countries in the Americas would pass laws prohibiting the entry of the diseased and Gypsies at the same time that European states were trying to expel them. Nevertheless, for the most part, transoceanic movements of peoples were unaffected by laws restricting immigration.

Secondly, despite some settlements that were established in the Southern Hemisphere, human migrations were essentially north-north movements, in which most migrations occurring within the Northern Hemisphere across an east-west axis—most frequently, from Old World Europe to the receiving areas of the New World of North America.

Finally, the arrival of immigrant European communities frequently displaced the native populations. The latter, in turn, often found it expedient to move deeper into the interior of their lands or were forced to do so.

FIRST MODERN ERA OF MASS MIGRATION

These patterns permeated global migrations through the nineteenth century. The era of forced migration of African slaves came to its conclusion in midcentury, but between 1820 and 1914 more than 44 million Europeans voluntarily migrated to the United States alone—a total number 6 million people higher than the total population of France at the time when it was the most populous country in western Europe. Still other people emigrated from Asia, this time from the East to the West, across the axis, but still within the globe's Northern Hemispheric corridors. With their arrival, native populations shrank, not only as percentages of the total populations but also in absolute numbers, as they perished from alien diseases and were often pushed into less hospitable parts of continents they once controlled. In the United States, many Native Americans were shoved westward into what was called Indian Territory during the 1830's, ahead of incoming settlers from Europe; others were confined to reservations during the 1880's.

The factors accounting for this mass wave of migration were both sociopolitical and scientific-technological. The middle of the nineteenth century was a particularly turbulent time in Europe, as whole societies were shaken by the revolutions of 1832 and 1848. Large numbers of people began to consider journeying to the Americas to seek better lives and greater freedom. Meanwhile, reforms introduced in Ireland by the British government combined in midcentury with a fungal infection in the potato crop to produce the Great Famine in Ireland between 1845-1852, and the beginnings of a mass flight of hundreds of thousands from that island to the United States.

Technological changes also helped further this

movement. The emergence of steam-powered ships made the transportation of large numbers from Europe and Asia to American ports cheaper, safer. and above all swifter. They cut travel time for transatlantic voyages from as many as five weeks in 1700 to fewer than eight days by the advent of World War I (1914-1918). Likewise, the development of transcontinental railroads in the United States after the Civil War provided a means of moving large numbers into the American Midwest and eventually the Far West, where land was free. Industrializing cities needed laborers, and federal troops could provide safety from hostile threats on the frontier by availing themselves of the rapidly evolving weapon technologies to which these troops had easy access. In 1840, breech-loading rifles revolutionized combat by replacing muzzle-loading muskets, which for two centuries had limited soldiers to firing only one round per minute, while requiring them to stand and expose themselves to enemy fire while reloading. With breech loaders, soldiers or settlers could fire seven rounds per minute from behind cover, and the rifles were more powerful and more accurate than muskets. By the time of the Civil War, Gatling guns raised firing rates to more than one hundred rounds per minute. It was not a coincidence that shortly afterward Indian wars came to their end in North America.

The product of all these developments was a growing tide of migration to the Americas that transformed the U.S. population from its overwhelming British-based stock at the time of independence into the multiethnic and multiracial mixture out of which the multicultural American nation would emerge in the twentieth century. Indeed, the influx reached its peak during the early years of the twentieth century, when approximately 3 million immigrants entered the United States every year. The number would have been even higher, had not the unification of Germany between 1860 and 1870, and the resultant growth there of pride and identification with Imperial Germany, slowed significantly what had previously been a major point of origin of migration to the United States.

Finally, scientific discoveries and technological changes had another noteworthy effect during the second half of the nineteenth century that would profoundly affect the nature of global migration a century later. Simply stated, these developments helped lead to the age of world empires. The revolutionary changes in weaponry allowed European forces easily to subdue native peoples armed only with spears, arrows, bladed weapons, and occasionally obsolete firearms. Moreover, the emergence of steam-powered riverboats allowed Europeans to carry their weapons deep into the interiors of regions where previously only coastal areas could be protected. The discovery of quinine as a preventative against malaria allowed Europeans to penetrate tropical regions protected from a disease that previously was a greater threat to European armies than hostile tribes.

Meanwhile, the invention and development of the telegraph and telephone, coupled with the laying of transoceanic cables, allowed heads of states, their generals, and field commanders to be in constant communication. Packaged for empire building, these discoveries, technologies, and inventions changed the nature of politics around the world, and the portion of the earth's land surfaces peopled by Europeans or under European control jumped from approximately 30 percent in 1820 to more than 80 percent by the time of World War I. By the start of the next world war in 1939, increasing numbers of the non-European subjects of these empires would begin their own south-to-north migrations to the capitals of their imperial rulers.

WORLD WAR I THROUGH THE COLD WAR

The shift from a predominantly north-to-north to a largely south-to-north pattern of immigration was not the only change involving patterns of global migration during the early years of the twentieth century. The door to largely unrestricted entry into the United States that was beginning to close slowly near the end of the nineteenth century was nearly completely shut. The process began with the passage of U.S. laws forbidding the admission of the Chinese and the insane. After President William McKinley was assassinated in 1901, anarchists were excluded. A 1917 immigration law required literacy tests. In 1921, a quota system was imposed on immigrants from individual countries, based on the percentages of people from each country who had been resident in the United States in 1910. Three years later, a new law made the quota system even more restrictive by pushing the baseline year back to 1890—a time when very few

eastern and southern European immigrants had been in the country. The quota laws naturally favored future immigrants from northern and western Europe, but they also sharply curtailed the total numbers of immigrants permitted to enter the country legally. Meanwhile, by the first decades of the twentieth century, aboriginal peoples of North America and Australia no longer had to be relocated to make room for new immigrants from abroad. The native peoples still trying to live in traditional ways had long since been moved to Australia's Outback and to tribal reservations in the United States and Canada.

Even without the enactment of U.S. quota restrictions, immigration from Europe to the United States would likely have slackened considerably during the years between the end of World War I and the commencement of World War II. Wartime dislocations, a plague that traveled through Europe after World War I, and the deprivations wrought by the Great Depression contributed to widespread poverty that left few Europeans with sufficient resources to afford transatlantic passage at the same moment the Great Depression was raising unemployment levels to unprecedented heights the United States. During some Depression years, the United States actually experienced negative net immigration.

Meanwhile, within Europe and neighboring regions, the revolutions of 1917 and subsequent civil war in Russia and the collapse of the Ottoman Empire following World War I produced significant population movements within Europe. An estimated 3 million Russians, Poles, and Germans left the collapsing Russian Empire amid its political unrest. Significant numbers of Russian nationals relocated in France. Meanwhile, in the Balkans, Muslims moved in sizeable numbers to Turkey. Likewise, the postwar decision of the newly created League of Nations to make Palestine a homeland destination for Jewish people led to the movement of approximately 400,000 European Jews to that British mandate territory in the Middle East.

The end of World War II produced even more significant movements of peoples, especially on the European continent. Many of the several hundred thousand Eastern European Jews who survived the Holocaust left Europe to migrate to Palestine even before the independent state of Israel was carved out of it in 1948. Still others emigrated there after 1948, stripping Eastern Europe of its once large and prosperous Jewish community. Meanwhile, under the terms of the Potsdam Agreement signed by the principal victors in World War II in 1945, massive, largely forced migrations had already occurred within Europe, when approximately 16 million ethnic Germans were sent west from Czechoslovakia and other Eastern European countries. Millions of Poles were also driven west from what had been the eastern Kresy region of Poland, which the Soviet Union acquired as part of its 1939 nonaggression pact with Germany.

The flow of migrants within Europe was not only from east to west. During the same period, hundred of thousands of ethnic Ukrainians, Lithuanians, Estonians, and Poles were expelled from neighboring states to the Soviet Union and parts of its rapidly forming empire in Soviet-occupied Eastern Europe. As the Cold War developed between the Soviet Union and its former wartime allies in the West, other population movements occurred. When the Western Allies decided to unify their zones in occupied Germany and create the independent Federal Republic of Germany, approximately 7 million Germans fled from Soviet-controlled East Germany into what would become known as West Germany.

GLOBAL MIGRATION AFTER 1950

Significant as these wartime and postwar migrations were in reshuffling the peoples of Europe, the migration that would most dramatically affect Europe, and to a lesser extent North America, and which has most profoundly broken from the pattern of previous migrations, developed elsewhere. It is the one involving the peoples who have migrated from culturally and often religiously different areas in the developing world into the economically more advanced and democratic states of

Turkish women praying in a community center in a predominantly Muslim district of Berlin, Germany. Like many other western European nations, Germany has experienced a large influx of Muslim immigrants since the late twentieth century. (AP/Wide World Photos)

Europe and North America during the second half of the twentieth century.

The origins of this development Europe lay largely in that region's need to rebuild after World War II, which forced much of Western Europe to import large numbers of workers from abroad to fill needed positions. Germany recruited its own "guest workers" in the less economically advanced states of southern Europe—most notably, secular Muslims from Turkey. France turned initially to its possessions in Africa and imported large numbers of foreign workers from Tunisia, Morocco, and Algeria. Britain looked to nations from its former empire in Asia, chiefly in India, from which former British subjects were entitled to immigrate to the United Kingdom as members of the British Commonwealth until, that is, controversy surrounding Britain's growing "foreign population' eventually caused Britain to pass more restrictive immigration laws.

By the 1950's, the worldwide process of decolonization of European empires was coinciding with Europe's sustained postwar economic recovery, and its need for still more imported labor. Consequently, ever more immigrants from Europe's former colonial world were journeying legally to European countries in pursuit of far better earnings than they could receive in their newly independent nations. This trend continued until a worldwide recession that began in 1973 resulted in most European countries restricting further entry. However, by then, workers who had been recruited as temporary employees were becoming permanent members of many European countries' workforces.

For the most part, the more restrictive European immigration laws did not so much stop immigrant flows as increase the numbers of immigrants entering European countries illegally. Most continued to come from developing countries in Africa and Asia, and a very high percentage of these people were Muslim, not Christian, in their religious faiths. By the turn of the twenty-first century, it was conservatively estimated that Europe's Muslim population numbered more than 20 million, and was growing at a much faster rate than the indigenous population because of family unification programs that allowed immigrants' spouses and children to join them. Moreover, the average sizes of Muslim families were sometimes were much larger than those of European families.

The population of the United States was also becoming noticeably more multicultural in the period following World War II. Many American soldiers serving in occupied Japan between 1945 and 1955 returned home with Japanese spouses. The advent of the Korean War in 1950 had a similar social outcome, with many American service personnel returning home with Korean spouses. Still later, the Vietnam War that stretched from the mid-1960's to 1975 further enlarged the Asian community in the United States. After the war ended, the U.S. Congress made room in the United States for large numbers of Vietnamese refugees whose service to the United States during the war placed their lives in danger after the fall of Saigon and the withdrawal of American forces.

However, it was the south-to-north pattern in later twentieth century immigration that had the greatest impact on American society. As a result of the steady emigration of peoples from Mexico and other countries in Central and South America and the Caribbean, Hispanics eclipsed African Americans as the largest minority group in the United States by the turn of the twenty-first century. Moreover, by the early years of the new millennium, the illegal Hispanic immigrant population in the United States was being conservatively estimated to be in the range of between 10 and 12 million people, making the country's growing Hispanic population a central political issue. This new wave of immigrants from the developing world was becoming politically controversial even before the terrorist attacks on the United States of September 11, 2001, the attack by homegrown Muslim suicide bombers on London's public transit system in 2005, and the attack by Muslim terrorists on the railroad system of Madrid, Spain, the previous year. The presence of these "foreign" populations in the modern Western world has become more controversial over time as their numbers have continued to grow and as the security concerns of home-grown terrorists and insecure borders have been added to the list of concerns that their presence entails.

Joseph R. Rudolph, Jr.

FURTHER READING

Barkan, Elliott Robert. *From All Points: America's Immigrant West, 1870s-1952*. Bloomington: Indiana University Press, 2007. Ideal for advanced research on world migration, this lengthy work covers the many waves of immigrants that settled west of the Mississippi River between the last days of the frontier and the early days of the Cold War.

Hatton, Timothy J., and Jeffrey G. Williamson. *Global Migration and the World Economy: Two Centuries of Policy and Performance.* Cambridge, Mass.: MIT Press, 2006. Outstanding analysis of the history and economic impact of the great nineteenth century and post-1950 waves of immigration that transformed and continue to transform the developed democratic world.

McClain, Paula D., and Joseph Stewart, Jr. *"Can We All Get Along?" Racial and Ethnic Minorities in American Politics.* 5th ed. Boulder, Colo.: Westview Press, 2009. Up-to-date edition of a widely used basic undergraduate text on American minorities and the political process.

Moch, Leslie Page. *Moving Europeans: Migration in Western Europe Since 1650.* Bloomington: Indiana University Press, 2003. Though a briefer study, Moch's work is for Europe very much the equivalent of Barkan's study of the American West and is equally good.

Vertovec, Steven, ed. *Migration and Social Cohesion.* Cheltenham, England: Edward Elgar, 1999. Collection of essays covering the developed world, from Australia to Europe to America, treating a broad range of topics related to the integration and nonintegration of immigrants into their host societies and political processes.

Weiner, Myron. *The Global Migration Crisis: Challenge to States and to Human Rights.* New York: HarperCollins, 1995. Useful starting point for research on the topic, complete with an extensive bibliography of useful materials for additional reading on immigrants, refugees, and government policies toward the waves of immigrants still entering the Western world during the 1990's.

SEE ALSO: Asian immigrants; Chinese immigrants; European immigrants; History of immigration, 1620-1783; History of immigration, 1783-1891; History of immigration after 1891; Latin American immigrants; Slave trade.

WORLD WAR I

THE EVENT: Global military conflict in which most major European powers and the United States were the principal combatants

DATE: Began in Europe in August, 1914; United States entered in April, 1917; armistice signed on November 11, 1918

LOCATION: Primarily Western Europe

SIGNIFICANCE: American entry into World War I brought about major changes in the U.S. government's immigration policy that infringed on the civil liberties of many people during and after the war and led to new immigration restrictions.

Beginning in the 1880's, new immigrants from southern and eastern Europe and Japan arrived at American ports of call in great numbers. Fleeing from poverty, religious persecution, and disease, they poured into the East and West coasts searching for employment and a better life. The America they encountered, however, was less than welcoming. Fearful that the immigrants, largely uneducated, would not assimilate, vocal citizens advocated immigration restriction.

GROWING NATIVISM

Nativism—an attitude that favored the interests of native inhabitants over those of immigrants, often accompanied by hostility toward foreigners—had always been present in American history. Following the second great wave of immigration of the 1880's, however, nativism assumed a new posture. In the large cities, industrialists welcomed the newcomers, who became the major source of unskilled, cheap labor. Native-born workers, fearing competition, and New England patricians railing against the degradation of America formed an unlikely alliance to restrict immigration. By imposing a literacy test, they hoped to eliminate any future influx of illiterate peoples to their shores.

First introduced in 1887 by economist Edward W. Bemis, the literacy test gained ground after the newly formed Immigration Restriction League began, in 1897, to lobby for a bill that would require immigrants to take such a test. The bill failed passage several times, since presidents from Grover Cleveland to Woodrow Wilson, eyeing reelection, considered the literacy test too controversial. Nonetheless, the intellectual climate of the country began to change with the outbreak of World War I in Europe in August, 1914. The test was added to the Immigration Act of 1917.

GOVERNMENT ACTION

Progressive Era reform efforts encouraged the humanitarian work of reformers such as Frances Kellor and Jane Addams, who fought for the education of the foreign-born. Novelist Edith Wharton also kept the reform spirit alive by founding the American Hostels for Refugees, which assisted French and Belgian refugees in Paris, in 1914. However, the U.S. government, as a neutral power during the war, offered little assistance to overseas refugees on the whole, despite individual petitions from Armenian deportees during the Armenian genocide perpetrated by the Ottoman Turkish government from 1915 to 1923. America's declaration of war in April, 1917, offered only one concession to the refugees—a provision in the Immigration Act of 1917 exempting from the literacy test those fleeing religious persecution.

With American shipping threatened, President Wilson demanded uncompromising Americanism, considering it essential for the survival of the republic. By 1915, nativist sentiment had shifted from the anti-Roman Catholism and anti-Semitism of the Progressive Era to anti-German hysteria. Innumerable hardships were inflicted on the once-lauded German Americans, now regarded as potentially treacherous. As a result, approximately three thousand Germans and Austro-Hungarian nationals were held in military camps. In 1918, near St. Louis, a German immigrant was lynched.

Ironically, despite the repressive atmosphere of the period, the war Americanized some immigrants. After Wilson called for a Selective Service Act in 1917, immigrants, exempt from service since they were not officially citizens, volunteered and were placed in select battalions where they could learn English. However, the plan was short-lived, and many were eventually placed in segregated units. For Slavic refugees fleeing from the Austro-Hungarian Empire, Congress sanctioned the formation of a Slavic Legion in July, 1918. The war's conclusion four months later, however, abruptly ended the arrangement.

Despite the patriotism of many newcomers who served their adopted country, a resistant America supported the passage of the Immigration Act of 1917 or the Asiatic Barred Zone Act, which required all newcomers over the age of sixteen to submit to a literacy test in English or their native tongue. The act further restricted admission of other Asian peoples not previously excluded, such as Indians and Southeast Asians. Passed over President Wilson's veto, the act set the stage for further limits on immigration. Ironically, however, the bill did not succeed in restricting the desired number, since only 1,450 of the 800,000 immigrants who arrived that year failed the test.

AFTERMATH

Following the war, millions of Germans and Jews sought refuge in the United States. Anticipating the strain on America's resources, Congress passed the Immigration Act of 1921, followed by the Immigration Act of 1924 (or the Johnson-Reed Act), the latter setting a 2 percent quota on incoming foreigners. The resulting decline in immigrants from southern and eastern Europe produced a shortage of workers in America's factories, causing Immigration Commissioner Anthony Caminetti to fill vacancies with Mexicans.

Wary of the dislocation that war had brought, the United States turned inward, especially against radical ideas from abroad, and strove to divorce itself from foreign influence. The country rejected internationalism, especially the League of Nations—and Attorney General A. Mitchell Palmer conducted raids aimed at purging the United States of foreign socialist influence. Thus, under the Alien Act of 1918, foreign-born members of the Socialist Party could be deported without trial.

On a positive note for native-born and immigrant women, the war resulted in the ratification of the Nineteenth Amendment, which granted suffrage to all women. The Cable Act of 1922 (also known as the Married Woman's Act) granted women outright citizenship regardless of the status of their husbands but denied citizenship to women married to Asians. While immigrant women had finally received recognition as individuals, immigrants as a whole continued their arduous journey to equality.

Debra A. Mulligan

FURTHER READING

Barkan, Elliott Robert. *From All Points: America's Immigrant West, 1870's-1952*. Bloomington: Indiana University Press, 2007. Scholarly study detailing American immigration history in the West and its peculiar set of problems.

Bennett, Marion T. *American Immigration Policies: A History*. Washington, D.C.: Public Affairs Press, 1963. Invaluable narrative that focuses on how immigration legislation affected America.

Higham, John. *Strangers in the Land: Patterns of American Nativism, 1860-1925*. New York: Atheneum, 1963. Preeminent historian's groundbreaking study of immigration, labeling the height of nativism "the tribal twenties."

Kennedy, David M. *Over Here: The First World War and American Society*. 1980. Reprint. New York: Oxford University Press, 2004. History of the World War I home front. Important evaluation of how immigration affected America during and following the war.

LeMay, Michael, and Elliott Robert Barkan, eds. *U.S. Immigration and Naturalization Laws and Issues: A Documentary History*. Westport, Conn.: Greenwood Press, 1999. Compilation of major documents relating to immigration history. Includes a handy chronology and a brief introduction.

SEE ALSO: Dillingham Commission; Ellis Island; Espionage and Sedition Acts of 1917-1918; European immigrants; History of immigration after 1891; Immigration Act of 1917; Immigration Act of 1921; Literacy tests; Military conscription; Nativism; Red Scare; World War II.

WORLD WAR II

THE EVENT: Global military conflict in which the United States, Great Britain, and the Soviet Union were the principal allies against Nazi Germany, Italy, Japan, and their allies

DATE: Began in Europe in September, 1939; United States entered in December, 1941; war ended on all fronts in August, 1945

LOCATION: Throughout Europe, parts of East and Southeast Asia, and North Africa

SIGNIFICANCE: Although millions of people were forced into mass migration by the war,

the U.S. government maintained most of its restrictions on immigration despite a national labor shortage. Presidential executive orders allowed some refugees to enter the United States, and Congress passed some laws allowing limited numbers of wartime refugees, Mexican laborers, and Chinese nationals to enter. After the war ended, the United States admitted substantial numbers of refugees.

Until Japan launched its surprise attack on Pearl Harbor, the great U.S. naval base in Hawaii, on December 7, 1941, the majority of Americans had wanted their country to stay out of the growing world conflict. The previous decade had been of low, sometimes even negative, immigration into the United States because the entire world was suffering under the Great Depression. Millions of Americans had been unemployed, and immigrants posed the threat of competing with them for scarce jobs. After the United States declared war on Japan, Germany, and Italy immediately after Pearl Harbor, the number of immigrants entering the country fell even lower because transocean shipping was devoted almost entirely to the war effort, and international flights were not available to civilians.

Another reason that immigration rates were low was the persistent anti-immigration feelings of substantial portions of the American voters who feared competition from newcomers. Some of this feeling reflected nativist attitudes about the alleged inferiority of peoples from regions other than northern and western Europe, from which most early American immigrants had originated. Most Americans were opposed to lifting national immigration quotas, even as tragic circumstances in Europe were increasing the numbers of homeless refugees. Congressional leaders who wanted to take in more refugees saw their legislative measures fail. Only President Franklin D. Roosevelt's executive orders could open the doors wider for some of the refugees.

ENEMY ALIENS IN THE UNITED STATES

At the moment that the United States entered the war, significant numbers of citizens of the principal enemy nations—Germany, Italy, and Japan—were residing in the United States. Moreover, huge

During World War II, Asian entrepreneurs such as this Filipino farmer advertised their non-Japanese ethnic identities in order to do business safely. (NARA)

numbers of American citizens traced their ancestry to immigrants from these same nations. Many Americans turned their suspicions on people who were obviously of German, Italian, and Japanese ancestry. However, perhaps because of their more distinctive physical appearance, people of Japanese ancestry were treated most harshly.

Indeed, the treatment of Japanese—both Japanese nationals and American citizens—became one of the most shameful episodes in American history. More than 110,000 of these people were taken from their homes on the West Coast and interned in bleak relocation camps in remote interior regions. About 70,000 of these people were American-born citizens, called Nisei. The rest were first-generation immigrants, called Issei, who had been barred from American citizenship, along with other Asians, by federal immigration laws. Public and government fear that these people might be disloyal to the United States by collaborating with a rumored Japanese invasion of the West Coast prompted the internments. Ironically, although the Hawaiian Islands, which were home to

more than 200,000 persons of Japanese heritage, were a much more likely target for Japanese invasion than the U.S. mainland, they were not affected by the internment order. Because the islands' Japanese residents constituted about one-half the territory's entire population, interning them would have brought economic chaos.

Despite the federal governments' harsh treatment of Japanese residents, thousands of Nisei—many from the internment camps—patriotically volunteered for military service and formed one of the most decorated combat units in the U.S. Army during the war. Others served in the Pacific theater of the war as translators. Some left the camps to work in factories. Although the internment program disrupted the lives of the internees and caused many of them to lose their homes and businesses, it helped to disperse the Japanese community geographically and introduce them to many economic opportunities outside their traditional work in agriculture.

Members of other alien communities within the United States were treated less harshly. When the war began, at least 1 million enemy aliens were living in the United States, and millions more people from Germany and Italy were naturalized citizens. Of these people, only a few thousand German and Italian nationals and an even smaller number of naturalized citizens from enemy nations were deemed sufficiently dangerous to require internment during the war. Most were held in camps in North Dakota and Montana. Before the war was over, President Roosevelt canceled the designation of enemy aliens for Italians in the United States.

WARTIME AND POSTWAR MASS MIGRATIONS

Wartime migration within the United States involved internal population shifts rather than waves of immigration. Fifteen million Americans left their homes for military training, and three-quarters of them went overseas. One in five Americans migrated during the war, and 8 million of them became permanent residents in other states. The main flows were toward West and East Coast defense industries and factories in the upper Midwest. In contrast, the rural South and Midwest saw sharp population declines. Most notably, African American migrants left the South in large numbers in order to work on jobs under federal contracts in northern factories that required equal wages and fair treatment. Many Puerto Ricans came to the mainland and many Native Americans left their reservations in order to work in wartime industries.

In contrast, migrations within Europe were brought on by a series of catastrophes. When German armies advanced to the east, millions of German settlers followed them. When the Soviet armies countered from the east, ethnic Germans from all over eastern Europe fled westward. Throughout the war, Germany conscripted workers in conquered areas and moved them about. After the war ended, these people swarmed through Central Europe seeking passage home. Large numbers of surviving prisoners of war were similarly on the move. During the early stages of the war, Jews fled from German domains—many to Palestine in the Middle East. By the end of the war, not many of Europe's Jewish peoples were left alive, and only a remnant were on the move. At the war's end, Central Europe resembled an anthill that had been kicked.

SPECIAL CATEGORIES OF WARTIME IMMIGRANTS

The term "displaced persons," or DPs, was applied to people driven out of their countries by war. The total number of persons displaced by World War II may never be known, but estimates have ranged from 8 to 20 million. By 1945, only a few thousand displaced persons had been admitted to the United States. President Harry S. Truman issued a directive to admit more, and his order was followed by Congress's Displaced Persons Act of 1948, which eventually allowed 400,000 war refugees to immigrate to the United States directly from the camps in which they were temporarily residing. Until then, U.S. law did not officially recognize refugees as an immigrant category and had no provisions for offering them asylum.

German scientists constituted another special category of wartime immigrants, and many of them were admitted to the United States after the war ended. Operation Paperclip slipped hundreds of German scientists and their families out of Germany and into the United States. Germany's rocket scientist Wernher von Braun became the most famous of these when he later played a major role in the American space program.

Another special category comprised tens of thousands of war brides, war fiancés, their babies, and a few war husbands. All of these individuals had become attached to American military personnel serving overseas. Most came from Britain, but many were of French, Italian, Dutch, Australian, and New Zealand origin. After the war, German and Japanese nationals joined this category. Under the provisions of the War Brides Act of 1945, national quotas did not apply to spouses of American military personnel.

REFUGEES AND DISPLACED PERSONS

Europe's largest prewar concentrations of Jewish populations were in Nazi-occupied eastern Europe, especially in Poland and Russia. Not many survived the Nazi death camps to which Jews from all over Europe were sent. Their victims included German Jews who had held the false hope that the Nazis would become more civilized after spending some time in power. The mass genocide against Jews and other minorities is known as the Holocaust. However, despite evidence, most Americans during the war did not believe what was going on, treating information as mere rumors.

Jewish refugees from the Holocaust posed a moral dilemma for Americans before, during, and after the war. The failure of the United States to grant them asylum in their time of greatest need has been a matter of controversy ever since. Between 1945 and 1950, the United States finally admitted 700,000 refugees, many of them Jewish, but by then the war and Germany's mass slaughter of Jews were over. Adolf Hitler had come to power in 1933, and through the following years, his Nazi regime was an escalating campaign against Jews. Discriminatory laws placed ever greater restrictions on the Jews, and violence was increasingly used against them. Soon, those who sought to flee could not take their money out of the country. Immigration to the United States was problematical because there was a prohibition against immigrants regarded as likely to become public charges.

The number of German Jews who were admitted to the United States in 1936-1937 was small. President Franklin D. Roosevelt stretched the limits of his presidential authority to allow some German and Austrian Jews to come. About 50,000 did so before the European war broke out. He also allowed the visas of German and Austrian Jews who were already resident in the United States to be extended. During the war, President Roosevelt ordered the U.S. State Department to issue visas to individual European refugees deemed especially important, such as Albert Einstein, Enrico Fermi, Thomas Mann, and Marc Chagall. A dozen of these people had already received Nobel Prizes, and most of them made significant contributions to scientific research and the arts in the United States.

In 1944, President Roosevelt established the War Refugee Board that eventually allowed some thousands of rescued refugees to enter the country under his presidential executive orders. Many of the immigrants who came under this arrangement were from the middle class with experience in business and the professions. They generally prospered after arriving in the United States.

OTHER WARTIME MIGRANTS

World War II substantially increased Mexican immigration to the United States because of the nationwide shortage of workers. In 1942, the United States and Mexico formed an agreement to create the bracero program, which brought temporary Mexican contract workers into the United States. Many of these workers did not return, and other Mexican immigrants came into the United States on their own. Most Mexican immigrants worked in agriculture in the Southwest; others worked on railroad maintenance. By the end of the war, they were beginning to relocate to other parts of the country.

World War II also brought a significant change for Chinese immigration to the United States. The Chinese Exclusion Act of 1882 was repealed by a new act of 1943. For the first time, the United States allowed a small number of Chinese to naturalize and become citizens. This change was in recognition of China's role as an important wartime ally.

Henry G. Weisser

FURTHER READING

Divine, Robert A. *The Reluctant Belligerent: American Entry into World War II.* 2d ed. New York: John Wiley & Sons, 1979. Valuable source of information about the political climate in the United States at the dawn of World War II.

Gamboa, Erasmo. *Mexican Labor and World War II: Braceros in the Pacific Northwest, 1942-1947.* Austin: University of Texas Press, 1990. Detailed history of the life, conditions, and social policy affecting Mexican guest workers who began coming to the United States early during World War II.

Gilbert, Martin. *The Holocaust: A History of the Jews of Europe During the Second World War.* New York: Henry Holt, 1985. Study of the European Holocaust that places U.S. immigration policies in the context of a tragic history.

Kennedy, David M. *Freedom from Fear: The American People in Depression and War, 1929-1945.* New York: Oxford University Press, 1999. Describes how Americans responded to the deprivations of the Great Depression, the recovery period of the New Deal, and the country's entrance into World War II. Considers immigration issues within the broader context of the war.

Ng, Wendy. *Japanese American Internment During World War II: A History and Reference Guide.* Westport, Conn.: Greenwood Press, 2002. Comprehensive reference source on all aspects of the internment of Japanese people during World War II. Includes a selection of primary documents.

Shukert, Elfrieda Berthiaume, and Barbara Smith Scibetta. *War Brides of World War II.* Novato, Calif.: Presidio Press, 1988. Comprehensive study of war brides that includes many interviews with brides.

SEE ALSO: Bracero program; Displaced Persons Act of 1948; German immigrants; History of immigration after 1891; Holocaust; Japanese American internment; Jewish immigrants; Prisoners of war in the United States; War brides; War Brides Act of 1945; World War I.

WYOMING

SIGNIFICANCE: Wyoming was one of the last states to be settled by peoples other than Native Americans. Always one of the smallest states in the union, it has experienced far less foreign immigration than most states. Moreover, many of the immigrants who did come to Wyoming did not stay. Consequently, by the early twenty-first century, the state still had a relatively homogenous population.

The history of immigration into Wyoming is peppered with numerous immigrant groups and communities that made their home in the vast state, but did not establish a permanent presence. The region that is now Wyoming was settled originally by the Crow, Arapaho, Lakota, and Shoshone peoples. Europeans first entered the area during the early nineteenth century, but they did not establish significant population centers until after the Union Pacific Railroad reached them during the 1860's. This major transportation link to the rest of the country hastened Wyoming's development, and the state's first major European town, Cheyenne, was established in 1867.

The railroad helped to bring in new settlers, including foreign immigrants, but the their numbers were never large. In 1894, Wyoming had slightly fewer than 15,000 foreign-born residents. English, German, and Irish immigrants made up almost one-half of this group. In contrast to other Rocky Mountain states, Wyoming never attracted a significant number of Chinese. As late as the early twenty-first century, the state's Chinese population has remained very small.

The rise of a coal-mining industry during the late nineteenth century created a need for labor. However, rather than risk bringing in cheap foreign workers who might organize unions that would demand higher wages and shorter hours, the mines around Hanna hired 200 African American workers in 1890. The mines then operated relatively efficiently until a general economic downturn struck them later in the decade.

During the early 1940's, Wyoming became the host to 11,000 people of Japanese ancestry who had been living in West Coast states. These people, most of whom were American citizens, were interned for the duration of World War II because of government fears that some of them might support Japanese attempts to occupy the West Coast. The internees were housed at the Heart Mountain Relocation Center in Park County, which was selected as the camp's site because of its remoteness from major population centers and because Wyoming lacked a sizeable Japanese population of its own that might cause problems at the camp. Very few citizens of Wyoming protested the internment of the Japanese. However, several officials, including Wyoming governor Nels Smith, expressed concern that some of the internees might try to stay in Wyoming after they were released at the conclusion of the war. However, almost all the internees eventually returned to their home states.

At the beginning of the twenty-first century, Wyoming continued to have a relatively small population, with slightly more than 500,000 residents. This population includes few sizeable ethnic communities. In the 2000 U.S. Census, 92 percent of the state's residents identified themselves as "white Americans." Fewer than 1 percent called themselves either African American or Asian American. The state's Native American residents constituted another 4 percent. The Wind River Indian Reservation in the west-central region of the state is home to the Eastern Shoshone and Northern

PROFILE OF WYOMING

Region	Rocky Mountains
Entered union	1890
Largest cities	Cheyenne (capital), Casper, Laramie
Modern immigrant communities	Hispanics

Population	Total	Percent of state	Percent of U.S.	U.S. rank
All state residents	515,000	100.0	0.17	50
All foreign-born residents	14,000	2.7	0.04	49

Source: U.S. Census Bureau, *Statistical Abstract for 2006.*
Notes: The U.S. population in 2006 was 299,399,000, of whom 37,548,000 (12.5%) were foreign born. Rankings in last column reflect total numbers, not percentages.

Wyoming

Arapaho nations, who together numbered about 7,500.

As in most other states, Wyoming's Hispanic population was its fastest growing. In 2000, Hispanics accounted for about 4 percent of the state's residents. Most of them have settled in the southern portion of Wyoming that include the cities of Cheyenne and Laramie.

Robert D. Mitchell

FURTHER READING

Larson, T. A. *History of Wyoming.* Lincoln: University of Nebraska Press, 1965.

———. *Wyoming: A Bicentennial History.* New York: W. W. Norton, 1977.

Wolff, David A. *Industrializing the Rockies: Growth, Competition and Turmoil in the Coalfields of Colorado and Wyoming, 1868-1914.* Boulder: University of Colorado Press, 2003.

SEE ALSO: African Americans and immigrants; Economic opportunities; Employment; History of immigration after 1891; Japanese American internment; Japanese immigrants; Labor unions; Railroads.

X

XENOPHOBIA

DEFINITION: Fear, hatred, or distrust of
foreigners

SIGNIFICANCE: Fear and suspicion of immigrants inspired discrimination and persecution of immigrant groups in the United
States long before the term "xenophobia"
was coined during the early twentieth century. Xenophobia is distinguished from bigotry and prejudice
in that the latter denote disrespect
and contempt based on one's belief in another group's alleged cultural or even biological inferiority,
whereas xenophobia is prompted
by a perceived threat to the culture
and mores of the group to which
one feels one's greatest allegiance.

Xenophobic behavior in the United
States has been made manifest in many
ways throughout the nation's history
and often involved the nativist notion
of "America for Americans," an ironic
slogan given that those who used the
phrase were themselves descendants
of immigrants. Many xenophobic activities over the years have been carried out by secret organizations such as
the Ku Klux Klan, which terrorized not
only African Americans but also Roman Catholics and Jews—all of whom
Klan members regarded as deemed
"foreign" and "un-American." Other
manifestions of xenophobia have included secret, unofficial rules, such as
gentlemen's agreements, that kept immigrants, especially Jewish and Catholic ones, out of certain neighborhoods,
businesses, and clubs.

Xenophobic acts were also conducted by aboveboard, highly public
organizations such as the Asiatic Exclusion League, founded in 1905 by labor leaders to fight against what they
saw as a Chinese menace to American business,
and the American Protective Association of the late
nineteenth century, which militated against the
perceived threat to American society and Protes-
tantism posed by the surge in Irish Catholic immigration. The popular Know-Nothing Party of the
mid-nineteenth century was virulently opposed to
the Irish and Italian Catholic immigrants; in some
states, such as Arkansas, the party incited church

*This turn-of-the-twentieth century advertisement for rat poison carried
a double message: It used the negative stereotype of a Chinese "coolie"
eating rats to make its point about the effectiveness of the product, while
pointing a finger at the Chinese figure above the words, "They must go!"*
(Asian American Studies Library, University of California at
Berkeley)

burnings and attacks on Roman Catholic clergy. Some of the worst examples of xenophobic actions in the United States were spontaneous: vicious riots, such as those against Irish immigrants in Philadelphia in 1844. Other xenophobic measures were carefully planned and scrupulously drawn up: for example, the Chinese Exclusion Act of 1882, which implemented a ten-year moratorium on the immigration of Chinese laborers. One of the worst examples of a violent outburst of xenophobia in American history was the slaughter of almost three dozen Chinese miners along the Snake River in Oregon in 1887.

During the late twentieth and early twenty-first centuries, American xenophobia began to manifest in subtler ways, as civil rights laws now militated against the sorts of violent outrages that had taken place in the past. From the 1970's onward, fear of foreigners and foreign influence often took the form of calls for strict quotas and other restrictions on immigration and a concern for the preservation of the English language as a particularly American institution. Across the nation, cities, counties, and entire states considered implementing laws declaring English the official language and re-stricting the appearance of other languages on public signs, on ballots, and in legal documents. Some even sought to ban the public use of languages other than English.

Thomas Du Bose

FURTHER READING

Anbinder, Tyler. *Nativism and Slavery: The Northern Know Nothings and the Politics of the 1850's.* New York: Oxford University Press, 1992.

Caldwell, Wilber W. *American Narcissism: The Myth of National Superiority.* New York: Algora, 2006.

Curran, Thomas J. *Xenophobia and Immigration, 1820-1930.* Boston: Twayne, 1975.

Schildkraut, Deborah. *Press "One" for English: Language Policy, Public Opinion, and American Identity.* Princeton, N.J.: Princeton University Press, 2005.

SEE ALSO: American Protective Association; Anti-Catholicism; Anti-Chinese movement; Anti-Semitism; Asiatic Exclusion League; Chinese Exclusion Act of 1882; English-only and official English movements; Know-Nothing Party; Nativism; Philadelphia anti-Irish riots; Snake River Massacre.

Y

YANG, JERRY

IDENTIFICATION: Taiwanese-born American entrepreneur
BORN: November 6, 1968; Taipei, Taiwan
ALSO KNOWN AS: Chih-Yuan Yang

SIGNIFICANCE: While working on a doctorate in electrical engineering at California's Stanford University, Jerry Yang cofounded Yahoo!, which provided one of the first and most popular Internet search engines and became one of the most successful companies to ever to do business on the World Wide Web.

Jerry Yang speaking at a consumer electronics trade show in 2007. (Getty Images)

Jerry Yang's father was born on mainland China but died when Yang himself was only two. His mother moved his family from Taiwan to San Jose, California, when he was eight and changed his first name from Chih-Yuan to Jerry. Yang graduated from Piedmont Hills High School, where he was his class valedictorian and senior class president, and nearby Stanford University, where he majored in electrical engineering.

After earning a master's degree, Yang was working on his doctorate in 1994, when he and David Filo created a Web site that consisted of a directory of other Web sites. Initially called "Jerry's Guide to the World Wide Web," it was later renamed "Yahoo!," an acronym for "Yet Another Hierarchical Officious Oracle." Yahoo! became so popular that Yang and Filo left graduate school to incorporate Yahoo! in 1995.

Yahoo! became one of the earliest and commercially most successful Internet search engines and web portals. Yang stepped down from active management of Yahoo! in 2009 but remained on its board of directors.

Thomas R. Feller

FURTHER READING

Angel, Karen. *Inside Yahoo! Reinvention and the Road Ahead.* New York: John Wiley & Sons, 2002.
Hillstrom, Kevin. *Defining Moments: The Internet Revolution.* Detroit: Omnigraphics, 2005.
Sherman, Josepha. *Jerry Yang and David Filo: Chief Yahoos of Yahoo!* Brookfield, Conn.: Twenty-First Century Books, 2001.

SEE ALSO: Asian immigrants; Brin, Sergey; California; Chinese immigrants; Economic opportunities; Taiwanese immigrants.

"YELLOW PERIL" CAMPAIGN

THE EVENT: Nativist anti-Asian immigration campaign focusing on Japanese immigrants along the West Coast
DATE: 1890's to 1940's
LOCATION: West Coast states, particularly California

SIGNIFICANCE: One of several nativist movements directed against Asian immigration, the "yellow peril" campaign attempted to restrict and remove Japanese immigrants from the United States. The movement strengthened anti-Asian feeling in the United States, strained relations between the U.S. and Japanese governments, and contributed to public support for the federal government's internment of Japanese Americans during World War II.

In 1890, only about 2,000 Japanese were living in North America. Most worked as laborers and farmhands in California and the Pacific Northwest. Despite their minuscule numbers, the use of Japanese to break a labor strike in British Columbia coal mines began what was to become a widespread anti-Japanese campaign. During the ensuing decade, Japanese immigrants began to arrive in large numbers in California. Prior to this, most of the small number of Japanese immigrants were temporary residents. The shortage of labor caused by the exclusion of Chinese immigrants made these early Japanese immigrants welcome. However, with this influx of Asian immigrants who intended to settle permanently, there arose an almost immediate anti-Japanese movement.

ORIGINS OF "YELLOW PERIL"

As a derogatory description of Asian immigrants, the expression "yellow peril" gained wide currency in the United States during the early twentieth century, particularly in newspapers published by William Randolph Hearst, who, perhaps ironically, was noted for "yellow journalism." However, the precise origins of the expression are uncertain.

In 1893, C. H. Pearson, a British journalist and educator, discussed the possibility of a "yellow peril" arising within Europe in his book *National Life and Character*. However, his use of the expression had nothing to do with Asians. A more likely possibility comes from Germany, where Kaiser William II called Japan a "yellow peril" in 1895, when he feared Japan might wage war on Germany. A few years later, Homer Lea, an American writer on geopolitics who would later become a general in the Chinese army, began applying "yellow peril" to an Asian threat that was both foreign and domestic—the sense in which the expression was typically used in the twentieth century.

COMPARING THE JAPANESE TO THE CHINESE

With the surge of Japanese immigration during the 1890's, the new century brought increased scrutiny of Asian immigrants. In 1900, new Japanese and Chinese immigrants were quarantined on their arrival on the West Coast on the pretext of health concerns. To protest this action, Japanese businessmen formed the Japanese Association of America. Their action provoked an anti-Japanese meeting in San Francisco that discussed why Japanese were a problem. Among the charges made against them was the claim that the Japanese were not assimilating to American culture. Also, because they worked for less money than Americans, they took jobs from American workers. That charge tied into a third charge: That the Japanese had lower standards of living that created health, moral, and legal problems. Finally, it was charged that the Japanese would never understand American democracy and would always remain loyal to the Japanese emperor.

EARLY TWENTIETH CENTURY DEVELOPMENTS

As California's state government became concerned with the sudden rise in Japanese immigration, it began investigating the question of whether the Japanese were, in fact, a potential problem. In an effort to forestall some of the difficulties that Chinese immigrants had faced in the United States, the Japanese government limited the number of its subjects who could emigrate to American. Meanwhile, fear of the "yellow peril" continued to grow in the eyes of American labor. Both the Exclusion League and the American Federation of Labor asked that Japanese immigration be limited. Anti-Japanese agitation also figured into local politics. In San Francisco, for example, both major political parties sought to exploit the anti-Japanese feeling in the city during a mayoral race.

Through the first few years of the twentieth century, the anti-Japanese movement had focused on the dangers Japanese immigrants posed to American labor. In 1905, a shift occurred that caused the Japanese to be seen a threat to the security of the United States. In the immediate aftermath of the Russo-Japanese War of 1905, in which Japan defeated the much larger Russia, the anti-Japanese movement began warning that the "yellow peril" would soon be threatened the shores of the United States. Armed with this new argument, the anti-Japanese forces pushed even harder to limit the impact of new immigrants as much as possible.

SAN FRANCISCO SCHOOL BOARD

On October 11, 1906, San Francisco's city school board ordered students of Japanese descent to attend a school that had been created during the 1870's for the Chinese. Although this event was little reported elsewhere in the United States, it elicited a strong response from the Japanese government that provoked President Theodore Roosevelt to persuade San Francisco to withdraw its order. This action, however, merely irritated groups such as the Asiatic Exclusion League and increased anti-Japanese feelings in California. Anti-Japanese feelings were further strengthened by the growth of the Native Sons of the Golden West (not to be confused with the Chinese immigrant advocacy organization "Native Sons of the Golden State"). This organization limited its membership to white persons born in California. From its founding in 1907 until World War II, it advocated a strong anti-Japanese platform, which it used to its is own political advantage. The segregation issue always raised support for the anti-Japanese feeling among southern congressmen, who saw a connection between their own attitudes toward African Americans and Californian attitudes toward the Japanese.

CONTINUED RESENTMENT

Although Japanese immigrants were never numerically significant along the West Coast, the fear that they represented a threat to the United States continued to grow. One area of Japanese immigrant control that came under attack was their ability to own land. In 1913, California passed a law denying Japanese the right to own land within the state. Supporters of this law hoped not only to prevent Japanese from owning land but also to drive them from the state. The yellow peril campaign continued through the 1920's and 1930's and finally came to a head with the entrance of the United States into World War II and the internment of more than 110,000 West Coast Japanese during the war.

David R. Buck

FURTHER READING

Chan, Sucheng. *Asian Americans: An Interpretive History.* Boston: Twayne, 1991. Broad survey of Asian American history that examines aspects of Asian immigration from the 1850's to 1990. Excellent college-level overview of the subject, with photos, maps, chronology, and bibliography.

Daniels, Roger. *Asian America: Chinese and Japanese in the United States Since 1850.* Seattle: University of Washington Press, 1988. Well-written, scholarly account of the experiences of Japanese and Chinese immigrants in America.

_____. *Prisoners Without Trial: Japanese Americans in World War II.* New York: Hill & Wang, 1993. Analyzes the decision of the federal government to intern Japanese Americans from the West Coast during the war.

Takaki, Ronald. *Strangers from a Different Shore: A History of Asian Americans.* Boston: Little, Brown, 1988. Highly readable history of all Asian American communities by a leading Japanese American scholar who drew upon a variety of primary sources, from newspapers to court cases.

SEE ALSO: Anti-Japanese movement; Asiatic Exclusion League; Japanese American internment; Japanese immigrants; Native Sons of the Golden State; San Francisco.

YEZIERSKA, ANZIA

IDENTIFICATION: Polish-born novelist
BORN: c. 1880; Plinsk, Russian Poland (now in Poland)
DIED: November 21, 1970; Ontario, California

SIGNIFICANCE: Yezierska's writings center on Jewish immigrants, especially women, in New York City and stands in stark contrast to earlier immigrant literature that depicted seamless integration from the Jewish community. Her most popular novel, *Bread Givers* (1925), focuses on a young woman whose struggle for independence is hampered by her father's old-world rabbinical sexism and America's patriarchal attitudes.

Anzia Yezierska was probably about thirteen years old when her large family immigrated to the

United States from Poland during the early 1890's. The family had been subject to harsh anti-Semitism in Poland, and the move to the Jewish ghettos of Manhattan's lower East Side in New York City was really a step forward, if a meager one. As was customary for immigrants at the time, the family Anglicized its name, and the young woman became Harriet (Hattie) Meyer, an identity she would later reject, changing back to Anzia Yezierska in her late twenties. Her father followed Jewish traditions, encouraging his sons toward education but requiring his daughters to work and support the family. Like many immigrant girls and women, Anzia worked in sweatshops, but, unlike many, she left home at the age of seventeen and attended night school and college.

Yezierska was drawn to writing, and she focused on the squalor and struggles of immigrant life. She often depicted the efforts of Jewish women to find self-identity in New York City, but her first short story was not published until 1915, as publishers were wary of such subject matter. Many of her works are semiautobiographical, including *Bread Givers* (1925) and *Red Ribbon on a White Horse* (1950). By far, *Bread Givers* is considered her most accessible and is her most studied work. Yezierska's protagonists often confront paternalistic snobbery with the stubborn insistence that they can be more than menial houseworkers. They experience poverty and squalor in the ghettos and struggle to achieve an American identity without erasing their pasts or denying their womanhood.

Stories such as these proved to be the forerunners of immigrant stories to follow. They contrasted sharply with previous depictions of Jewish immigrant life published by the likes of Mary Antin that had implied that the New World welcomed all and that these immigrants universally assimilated with ease. Yezierska wanted instead to build a bridge between her heritage and her American home. Her characters seek to Americanize, but they experience serious difficulty in doing so, because they clash with the expectations of their families, of the nonimmigrant populations, and of a paternalistic American culture. Americans and wealthy Jews (whether immigrant or American-born) are depicted in her work as repressed by outside expectations. In contrast, her ghetto dwellers live in chaos, but their lives are richer. Toward the end of her life, Yezierska shifted her focus away from the Jewish population to examine the experience of immigrant Puerto Ricans in a series of short stories.

Jessie Bishop Powell

FURTHER READING

Schoen, Carol. *Anzia Yezierska*. Boston: Twayne, 1982.
Wirth-Nesher, Hana. *Call It English: The Languages of Jewish American Literature*. Princeton, N.J.: Princeton University Press, 2005.
Yezierska, Anzia. *Bread Givers*. 1925. Reprint. New York: Persea Books, 2003.

SEE ALSO: Antin, Mary; Anti-Semitism; Jewish immigrants; Literature; Marriage; New York City; Religion as a push-pull factor; Russian and Soviet immigrants; Women immigrants; World War I.

YICK WO V. HOPKINS

THE CASE: U.S. Supreme Court decision on racial discrimination
DATE: Decided on May 10, 1886

SIGNIFICANCE: The *Yick Wo* ruling was the first case in which the Supreme Court held that a racially neutral law applied in a discriminatory manner violates the equal protection requirement of the Fourteenth Amendment. Of limited influence during the nineteenth century, the decision became an important precedent during the twentieth century Civil Rights movement.

In 1885, San Francisco began enforcing a municipal ordinance that required operators of laundries in wooden buildings to obtain a license from the city's board of supervisors. The ordinance did not apply to laundries in brick or stone buildings. Because fires were a true danger to the city, the ordinance appeared to be a reasonable application of the police power granted to states and cities. At the time, about two hundred of the city's laundries in wooden buildings were owned by persons of Chinese ancestry, and approximately eighty were owned by non-Chinese. Among the applicants, only one Chinese owner was awarded a license, although seventy-nine non-Chinese owners were approved.

Yick Wo had operated his laundry for more than twenty years, and local inspectors had deemed it safe the previous year. After his application was denied, he continued to operate his business, resulting in a ten-dollar fine and a jail sentence of ten days. His petition to the California Supreme Court for a writ of habeas corpus was refused.

When the case reached the Supreme Court, the justices unanimously agreed that the city's enforcement of the ordinance violated both the equal protection clause and the due process clause of the Fourteenth Amendment. Writing for the Court, Justice Thomas Stanley Matthews observed that operating a laundry was "a harmless and useful occupation" that provided the livelihood for Yick Wo's family, and based on the facts of the case, he concluded that city officials had been motivated by hostility to the Chinese race and nationality. Even though the ordinance appeared to be reasonable and impartial in appearance, it had been administered "with a mind so unequal and oppressive as to amount to a practical denial" of the "equal justice" secured to persons by the Fourteenth Amendment.

Thomas Tandy Lewis

FURTHER READING

McClain, Charles J. *In Search of Equality: The Chinese Struggle Against Discrimination in Nineteenth-Century America.* Berkeley: University of California Press, 1994.

Salyer, Lucy. *Laws as Harsh as Tigers: Chinese Immigrants and the Shaping of Modern Immigration Law.* Chapel Hill: University of North Carolina Press, 1995.

SEE ALSO: Chinese immigrants; Chinese laundries; Due process protections; History of immigration, 1783-1891; San Francisco; Supreme Court, U.S.

YUGOSLAV STATE IMMIGRANTS

SIGNIFICANCE: The history of Yugoslav state immigration divides into three distinct eras: the period before Yugoslavia was formed in 1918, the period during which Yugoslavia was an independent nation, and the period after the early 1990's, when Yugoslavia began breaking into new, ethnically based independent states. Yugoslav immigration is further complicated by the large number of distinct ethnic groups that made up Yugoslavia, including Bosniaks, Croats, Kosovo Albanians, Macedonians, Montenegrins, Serbs, Slovenes, and others. Although immigrants and their descendants from former Yugoslavia do not quite represent even one-half of 1 percent of the whole population of the United States, they can be found throughout the North American continent. Descendants of the original immigrants from Yugoslavia are among important inventors, and they have made themselves valued in all fields in the United States.

The earliest identifiable Yugoslav immigrants to arrive in what is now the United States came during the 1680's. They were among the early explorers and Roman Catholic missionaries in the regions along what would become the Mexican border region. During the 1830's, some small Croatian settlements were founded in California. Croatians were employed as farmers and also worked in the fields of commerce and fishing and oyster industries. Around the same time, Slovene Catholic missionaries labored among North American Indians in the regions on the Great Lakes, and the first Serbs were starting to arrive.

LATE NINETEENTH THROUGH EARLY TWENTIETH CENTURIES

From 1890 to 1914, the largest wave of Slovene, Croatian, Serbian, Montenegrin, and Macedonian immigrants came to the United States. According to U.S. Census data of 1910, among immigrants and their children there were 183,431 Slovenes, 1,460 Wends (Slovenes from the Hungarian part of Austria-Hungary), 93,036 Croats, 5,505 Dalmatians, 26,752 Serbs, and 3,961 Montenegrins. These immigrants founded settlements in the mining communities and industrial centers in Pennsylvania, Illinois, Michigan, Ohio, Minnesota (Iron Range), Indiana, Colorado, and California. Within those early settlements, the immigrants organized fraternal benefit organizations; built Catholic, Protestant, and Orthodox Christian churches in which, at first, they worshiped in their ancestral languages; and built national homes in which they gathered for meetings of their cultural and fraternal lodges and for dances and wedding parties.

Most immigrants from the territories of former Yugoslavia came from the agrarian and economically undeveloped regions that were then part of Austria-Hungary—regions that were part of Slovenia and Croatia during the early twenty-first century. Within these regions, almost everyone depended on income from the land. Because more than half these regions were situated on porous limestone (karst) areas in which fertile land was scarce, the immigrants looked for additional sources of income. Many turned to handicrafts and transportation services. However, after the mid-

nineteenth century, their incomes from these occupations declined because they could not compete with developing factory industries and the expanding railroads.

The loss of the additional sources of income affected small farms the most, as they were heavily taxed. Large families could not survive off their farms. An already bad economic situation became even worse due to natural disasters, such as floods, heavy frosts, and droughts. At the beginning of the twentieth century, the political situation in then European Turkey worsened and this was followed by the Balkan Wars. Serbs, Montenegrins, and Macedonians then began following the Slovene and Croatian immigrants to the United States.

By 1910, about 230,000 people from the regions that would later make up Yugoslavia were living in the United States. About 85 percent of them were men. About 93 percent were between fourteen and forty-five years of age, and roughly equal numbers were younger and older. The bulk of these immigrants had been small farmers and farm laborers at home. After they arrived in the United States, most worked in mines and other industries. The majority intended to save money and later return to their homelands, but that rarely happened.

Most of these immigrants were deeply concerned about the condition of their homelands. During World War I (1914-1918), many hoped that Austria-Hungary would be defeated. Serbs and Montenegrins opposed Austria-Hungary because their ancestral homelands were at war with it. Slovenes and Croats opposed it because of its pressure to Germanize and Hungarianize their homelands.

After Italy entered the war in 1915, many Slovenes and Croatians feared that it might annex substantial parts of their territory. Not surprisingly, therefore, most of the immigrants wanted a Yugoslav state to be established. Views differed on whether the future state should be a kingdom or a republic, a federal or a centralized state. Before the end of the war, however, the immigrants united in their endeavors to help the Yugoslav state be formed and to ensure it would have "fair borders."

PROFILE OF YUGOSLAV STATE IMMIGRANTS

Countries of origin	Bosnia-Herzegovina, Croatia, Former Yugoslav Republic of Macedonia, Kosovo, Montenegro, Slovenia, and Serbia
Primary languages	Bosnian, Croatian, Serbian
Primary regions of U.S. settlement	California, East Coast, Midwest
Earliest significant arrivals	1680's
Peak immigration periods	1890-1914, 1920's, 1970's-2008
Twenty-first century legal residents*	149,099 (18,637 per year)

*Immigrants who obtained legal permanent resident status in the United States.
Source: Department of Homeland Security, *Yearbook of Immigration Statistics, 2008.*

INTERWAR PERIOD

After World War I, tens of thousands of immigrants left the United States and returned to their homelands, where were now part of the newly established Kingdom of Serbs, Croats, and Slovenes—

Refugees fleeing the civil war in Bosnia in August, 1995. (AP/Wide World Photos)

which in 1929 was renamed the Kingdom of Yugoslavia. However, most of the immigrants were unable to find work in Yugoslavia. Between 1919 and 1924, 24,409 of them returned to the United States. Many of these people wisely feared that changing U.S. immigration laws might prevent them from returning if they waited too long.

In 1920, the U.S. Census counted 411,012 residents of the United States whose mother tongues were among the languages spoken in Yugoslavia. Among them were 208,552 Slovenes, 140,559 Croats, 52,208 Serbs, 4,535 Montenegrins, 3,119 Dalmatians, and 2,039 Wends.

New U.S. immigration laws enacted in 1921 and 1924 drastically reduced the numbers of immigrants permitted into the country from southern and eastern Europe, causing the migration currents to change the course they had taking for several decades. The entire nation of Yugoslavia was permitted fewer than 1,000 immigrants per year. However, loopholes in the quota system allowed many more immigrants to enter the United States

legally. Between 1920 and 1938, for example, about 70,000 people from Yugoslavia came to the country.

By this time, the composition of the immigrants from Yugoslavia was changing. For the first time, more than one-half (55 percent) of the newcomers were women. Another change was a substantial increase in the proportion of immigrants who were children. U.S. Census data for 1940 recorded 342,700 residents of the United States whose mother tongues were Yugoslavian languages. The bulk of these people were Slovenes (184,420), Croats (119,360), and Serbs (38,920).

WORLD WAR II

Yugoslavia's entry into World War II (1939-1945) again virtually stopped movement between it and the United States. During the war, the only Yugoslavians who traveled abroad were politicians, diplomats, and businessmen. Between 1941 and 1945, fewer than 1,000 Yugoslavs took refuge in the United States.

The April 6, 1941, Axis invasion of Yugoslavia

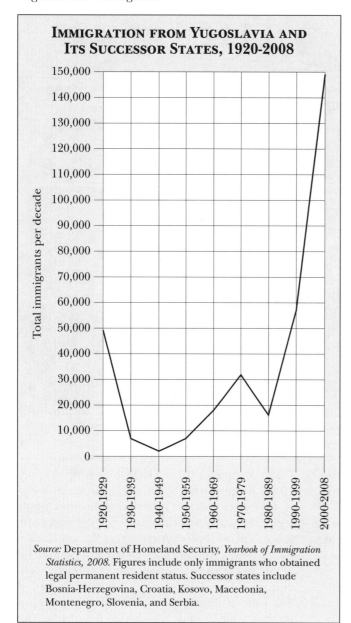

IMMIGRATION FROM YUGOSLAVIA AND ITS SUCCESSOR STATES, 1920-2008

Source: Department of Homeland Security, *Yearbook of Immigration Statistics, 2008*. Figures include only immigrants who obtained legal permanent resident status. Successor states include Bosnia-Herzegovina, Croatia, Kosovo, Macedonia, Montenegro, Slovenia, and Serbia.

federated Yugoslavia. The leaders organized the United Committee of South Slavic Americans to coordinate their activities. In 1944, they began gathering relief supplies for Yugoslavia and established a special organization for that purpose. Yugoslav Americans eventually collected about 20 million dollars for Yugoslavia's relief efforts. During late 1944 and early 1945, Yugoslav American leaders directed their activities toward favorable solutions for Yugoslavs in resolving postwar border issues among Yugoslavia, Italy, and Austria.

MID TO LATE TWENTIETH CENTURY TRENDS

After World War II, immigration from Yugoslavia to the United States resumed as changing U.S. immigration laws allowed in more immigrants from eastern Europe. By this time, many Yugoslavians wished to escape from the rising communist influence in eastern Europe. After the mid-1960's, many qualified for refugee status and could seek political asylum in the United States. Most were refugees from communist suppression of liberal movements within Croatia and Serbia. After the mid-1980's, suppression of the Albanian minority in Kosovo forced thousands of ethnic Albanians to flee Slobodan Milošević's regime to seek asylum.

Between 1950 and 1989, approximately 73,000 people immigrated to the United States from Yugoslavia. The 1990 U.S. Census counted 544,270 Croatians, 116,795 Serbians, 124,437 Slovenes, 20,365 Macedonians, and 257,994 people designated simply as "Yugoslavs."

POST-YUGOSLAVIA IMMIGRATION

During the 1990's, immigrants from the territories of former Yugoslavia played important roles in the process of dissolving Yugoslavia. The goal of transforming Yugoslavia's major ethnic regions into separate independent republics became popular during the mid-1980's. Most Slovene, Croat, and Macedonian immigrants in the United States supported the efforts of their homelands to establish independent states. Most Serb immigrants sup-

mobilized Yugoslavian immigrants. Until the end of 1942, they supported the Yugoslav people's fight against the Axis through correspondence with important world leaders, members of the Yugoslav regime, and later its representatives in exile. Between December, 1942, and April, 1943, American Slovene, Croat, and Serb leaders called for unity among all Yugoslav Americans in the war effort. They also issued resolutions in which they tried to find solutions for their "national questions" in a ported the policy of Slobodan Milošević and Serbia, which meant that initially they supported centralization of the Yugoslav federation and, later, "Great Serbia."

Many immigrants wrote letters and petitions to newspaper editors, heads of world governments, and legislators in the United States. A war of words developed among members of the different ethnic communities during the early 1990's. Members of each community hoped to receive support for their requests, especially from American politicians with the same ethnic backgrounds, such as Helen Delich Bentley, a Maryland congresswoman who worked to aid the "Serb cause." Minnesota congressman James Obersta and Ohio, congressman Dennis Eckart supported the "Slovene cause." Diaspora communities established several organizations in support of independence and recognition of their countries of origin, and these groups were often active in collecting economic and humanitarian aid. Among these organizations were the United Americans for Slovenia, the Serb National Federation, the Croat Congress, the United Macedonian Organization, and the Macedonian Patriotic Organization.

As Yugoslavia was breaking apart during the early 1990's, bloody civil wars within several former Yugoslav territories prompted many people to flee to the United States. By the year 2000, about 107,000 Bosnian refugees had been admitted to the United States. Much small numbers of refugees came from Croatia (4,500) and Serbia and Montenegro (15,000). Most of the latter were Serbs from Kosovo who immigrated after the North Atlantic Treaty Organization (NATO) began intervening in Bosnia's civil war, and it was becoming clear that Kosovo would not remain part of Serbia.

The 2000 U.S. Census counted 374,241 Croats, 176,691 Slovenes, 140,337 Serbs, 38,051 Macedonians, and 328,547 "Yugoslavs" residing in the United States. After that year, the number of refugees from the former Yugoslav region decreased quickly. However, the number of immigrants petitioning for green cards increased. During 2000-2006 alone, permanent residency was granted to approximately 122,000 persons from the region of former Yugoslavia. Two-thirds of them were from Bosnia and Herzegovina.

Matjaž Klemenčič

FURTHER READING

Čizmić, Ivan, Ivan Miletić, and George J. Prpić. *From the Adriatic to Lake Erie: A History of Croatians in Greater Cleveland.* Eastlake, Ohio: American Croatian Lodge, 2000. Brief but useful survey of Croatian immigration into the region around Cleveland, Ohio.

Čolaković, Branko Mita. *Yugoslav Migrations to America.* San Francisco: R&E Research Associates, 1973. Broad overview of Yugoslavian immigration to the United States written at a time when Yugoslavia appeared to be a strong unitary state.

Coughlan, Reed, and Judith Owens-Manley. *Bosnian Refugees in America: New Communities, New Cultures.* New York: Springer, 2005. Study of immigrants who came from the troubled nation of Bosnia and Herzegovina after the breakdown of Yugoslavia during the early 1990's.

Gorvorchin, Gerald G. *Americans from Yugoslavia.* Gainesville: University Press of Florida, 1961. Now badly dated but still useful scholarly study of Yugoslavian immigration to the United States.

Klemenčič, Matjaž. *Slovenes of Cleveland: The Creation of a New Nation and a New World Community Slovenia and the Slovenes of Cleveland, Ohio.* Novo Mesto, Slovenia: Dolenjska Založba, 1995. Useful study complementing Čizmić, Miletić, and Prpić's study of Croats in Cleveland.

Prpić, George J. *South Slavic Immigration in America.* Boston: Twayne, 1978. Overview of immigration from the eastern European nations by southern Slavs, who include many of the peoples of the former Yugoslavia.

SEE ALSO: European immigrants; Greek immigrants; Italian immigrants; Muslim immigrants; Russian and Soviet immigrants.

Z

ZADVYDAS V. DAVIS

THE CASE: U.S. Supreme Court decision on detention of deportable aliens

DATE: Decided on June 28, 2001

> **SIGNIFICANCE:** In cases in which no country is willing to accept a noncitizen who is under order of deportation, the controversial *Zadvydas* decision restricted the length of time of detentions, except when the government can demonstrate aggravating circumstances that require additional detention.

A resident alien in the United States, Kestutis Zadvydas had been born to Lithuanian parents in a German camp for displaced persons. However, after he acquired a long criminal record, the Immigration and Naturalization Service (INS) ordered his deportation. Both Germany and Lithuania refused to admit him because he was not a citizen of either country, and no other country could be found to accept him. According to applicable U.S. law, following a final deportation order, an alien was to be held in custody for a period of up to ninety days. If the alien was still in the country after the removal period had expired, INS personnel would conduct an administrative review to decide between further detention or supervised release.

After Zadvydas's custody had lasted longer than ninety days, he petitioned a U.S. district court for a writ of habeas corpus. The court ruled in Zadvydas's favor, based on the theory that the government would never deport him, thereby resulting in permanent confinement without a criminal trial, which violated constitutional requirements of due process. The court of appeals, however, reversed the decision, based on the theory that an eventual deportation was not impossible, thereby providing a rationale for continuing the administrative detention.

In a 5-4 opinion, the U.S. Supreme Court held that the "the statute, read in light of the U.S. Constitution's demands, limits an alien's post-removal-period detention to a period reasonably necessary to bring about that alien's removal from the United States." Writing the opinion for the Court, Justice Stephen G. Breyer explained that since indefinite detention of aliens without trials would raise serious constitutional objections, the federal courts were obligated to construe the statute as containing an "implicit reasonable time limitation."

Although deportation proceedings were "civil and assumed to be nonpunitive," the government's two justifications did not appear adequate to an indefinite civil detention. First, the possibility of flight appeared weak, since no country wanted to accept Zadvydas; second, the use of preventive detention to protect the community was only allowed for individuals judged to be especially dangerous. Balancing Zadvydas's "liberty interests" with the risk of his committing crimes, Breyer wrote that the INS could detain him for an additional six months, after which it would have to demonstrate strong proof to justify further detention.

Justices Antonin Scalia and Anthony Kennedy both expressed strong dissenting opinions. They argued that Justice Breyer had misread the relevant statute, and also that he had failed to give adequate consideration to several precedents, especially *Shaughnessy v. United States ex rel. Mezei* (1953), which appeared to put no time limit for detaining an alien under an order of detention. Describing the majority opinion as a claim for the "right of release into this country by an individual who concededly has no legal right to be here," Scalia declared, "There is no such constitutional right."

Thomas Tandy Lewis

FURTHER READING

Kanstroom, Daniel. *Deportation Nation: Outsiders in American History.* Cambridge, Mass.: Harvard University Press, 2007.

Welch, Michael. *Detained: Immigration Law and the Expanding I.N.S. Jail Complex.* Chicago: University of Chicago Press, 2002.

SEE ALSO: Congress, U.S.; Constitution, U.S.; Deportation; Due process protections; Supreme Court, U.S.

APPENDIXES

BIOGRAPHICAL DIRECTORY OF NOTABLE IMMIGRANTS

This list is merely a representative sampling of the many thousands of immigrants who have made notable contributions to American history. Full essays can be found in the main text on immigrants whose names are asterisked (*) below.

AGASSIZ, LOUIS (1807-1873). Scientist and academic. Born in Motier, Switzerland, Agassiz already had a distinguished academic career—which included a doctorate from the University of Erlangen and a professorship at Neuchatel University—before going to Massachusetts's Harvard University in 1848 to chair the department of natural history. Opposed to Charles Darwin's theory of natural selection, Agassiz pioneered the study of the ice age and glaciology in such works as *Natural History of the United States* (1847-1862) and *Geological Sketches* (1866, 1876).

ALBRIGHT, MADELEINE* (1937-   ). Czechoslovakian-born scholar of international relations who became the first female U.S. secretary of state.

ALEXANDERSON, ERNST FREDERICK WERNER (1878-1975). Inventor and longtime electrical engineer for General Electric. Born in Uppsala, Sweden, Alexanderson became a graduate of the Swedish Royal Institute of Technology. Strongly influenced by the writings of Charles Proteus Steinmetz, he journeyed to the United States in 1901 to work under Steinmetz at General Electric. He remained with that company and with the Radio Corporation of America (RCA) through most of the rest of his life. His most notable invention was the Alexanderson (high-frequency) alternator, which enabled the transmission of global radio broadcasts. Alexanderson held patents and made groundbreaking discoveries in the areas of facsimile (FAX) transmission, radio, television, and transportation electronics.

ALLENDE, ISABEL (1942-   ). Journalist and novelist born in Lima, Peru. Allende's father, a Chilean diplomat, vanished—probably murdered—when Allende was two. After her cousin, Chilean president Salvador Allende, was overthrown and perished during a military coup, she was threatened and fled into exile, first to Venezuela, then to the United States. She transitioned from a journalistic to a literary career in 1982, with the publication of *The House of the Spirits*, followed by works such as *Eva Luna* (1987), *Paula* (1995), and *The Sum of Our Days* (2008).

ANTIN, MARY* (1881-1949). Russian-born author and political activist.

ARNAZ, DESI (1917-1986). Musician and film and television personality. Arnaz was born in Santiago, Cuba, to a wealthy family that lost almost everything when Fulgencio Batista took over as dictator in 1933. The family went into exile in Florida, where they had to subsist on whatever employment was at hand. Arnaz learned English from scratch and eventually formed his own Cuban musical band. Fellow immigrant and bandleader Xavier Cugat helped him to get his first break, a role in a Broadway musical. Afterward, Arnaz began appearing in Hollywood films. From 1951 to 1960, he and his first wife, Lucille Ball, starred in the popular television situation comedy *I Love Lucy*. He and Ball also founded Desilu Studios in 1950 and produced many other television shows through the 1950's and 1960's.

ASTOR, JOHN JACOB* (1763-1848). German-born American businessman.

ATLAS, CHARLES* (1892-1972). Italian American physical fitness expert.

AUDUBON, JOHN JAMES (1785-1851). Painter and naturalist born in Les Cayes, Haiti. After being sent to France, Audubon immigrated to the United States in 1803 to avoid being drafted for service in the Napoleonic Wars. He was self-taught in ornithology and painted birds as a hobby while running a dry-goods business. After going bankrupt in 1819, he undertook wilderness treks while his wife tutored. From 1827 to 1838, he illustrated and published *The Birds of America* and other works on natural history.

BAEKELAND, LEO HENDRIK (1863-1944). Chemist and inventor born in Ghent, Belgium. Baekeland earned his doctoral degree in 1884, at the age of twenty-one. While he was in New York on a graduate fellowship in 1889, he accepted a chemist's position with Anthony Photographic Company and remained in the United States. While struggling through the economic depression of 1893 and bouts of ill health, he suddenly became wealthy in 1898 by selling his patented Velox photographic paper to Eastman Kodak Company. He later invented a plastic that was named Bakelite for him.

BALANCHINE, GEORGE (1904-1983). Ballet master, choreographer, and composer born in St. Petersburg, Russia. After graduating from the Petrograd Conservatory, Balanchine was so harassed by the new Soviet's regime's censorship and manipulated that he left the country in 1924. After a brilliant, though erratic, career in Europe, Balanchine was recruited to come to the United States in 1933. After forming several ballet companies, he established the New York City Ballet. Balanchine worked closely with a fellow Russian immigrant, composer Igor Stravinsky, many of whose works he choreographed. He also produced retrospectives in Stravinsky's honor.

BANNISTER, EDWARD MITCHELL (c. 1828-1901). Landscape painter born in St. Andrew's, New Brunswick, Canada, of African and European parentage. Bannister was orphaned at the age of sixteen, and he immigrated to Boston around 1848. There he established himself within the African American community, joined the Crispus Attucks Choir and Histrionics Club, and married the wealthy Christina Carteaux. He became a noteworthy Victorian-era painter who specialized in dreamlike landscapes. After relocating to Providence, Rhode Island, he cofounded the Rhode Island School of Design.

BELL, ALEXANDER GRAHAM* (1847-1922). Scottish inventor of the telephone and educator.

BERLIN, IRVING* (1888-1989). Russian-born songwriter.

BLACKWELL, ELIZABETH (1821-1910). Physician, abolitionist, and suffragette born in Bristol, England. When Blackwell's father got in deep financial trouble, he took his wife and daughters to Cincinnati, Ohio, in 1832, only to die shortly afterward, leaving his family destitute. Elizabeth Blackwell became a teacher and helped her mother manage a school. She then studied medicine at Geneva Medical College in Geneva, New York, and became the first woman in the United States to earn a medical degree, in 1849. While enduring prejudice and ridicule, she opened a New York City dispensary that in 1857 became the New York Infirmary for Women and Children. While not practicing medicine, she plunged herself into the abolition and suffrage movements, and she founded other medical facilities in both the United States and Britain.

BOAS, FRANZ (1858-1942). Trailblazing anthropologist born in Minden, Germany. After earning a doctorate in physics from Kiel University in 1881, Boas undertook a scientific voyage to study the Inuit peoples. Drawing on this experience, he published *The Central Eskimo* (1888). Meanwhile, in 1887, he was offered the assistant editorship of the journal *Science*, which was published in New York, so he took up residence in the United States. From 1896 to 1937, he held a faculty position at Columbia University, where he established an anthropology program. Combative by nature, he resigned in disgust from an assistant curatorship at the American Museum of Natural History in 1905, and he was an ardent crusader against racism and anti-Semitism.

BOIARDI, ETTORE "HECTOR" (1897-1985). Chef, caterer, and entrepreneur born in Piacenza, Italy. After immigrating to the United States through Ellis Island in 1914, Boiardi eventually acquired such a reputation as a chef in New York hotel restaurants that he was offered the position of head chef at Cleveland's Hotel Winton in 1917. Four years later, he opened his own Italian restaurant in Cleveland. Soon, his sauces were in such demand that he established a factory for bottling and distributing them that grew into a nationwide million-dollar company that took the homonymic name "Chef Boy-Ar-Dee" (later Boyardee). In 1946, Boiardi sold the company to American Home Foods, but the Boyardee brand name and Boiardi's image have remained on the products into the twenty-first century.

BRIN, SERGEY* (1973-   ). Russian-born cofounder of Google.

CABRINI, FRANCES XAVIER, MOTHER (1850-1917). Roman Catholic missionary born in Sant'Angelo Lodigiano, Italy. In 1880, Cabrini founded and became the mother superior-general of the Missionary Sisters of the Sacred Heart of Jesus. Dispatched by Pope Leo XIII to the United States in 1889, she overcame her frail health to minister to Italian immigrant communities and found schools, hospitals, and orphanages. While working in Seattle, Washington, in 1909, she became an American citizen. In 1946, the Roman Catholic Church made her the first American citizen to be canonized as a saint.

CHANDRASEKHAR, SUBRAHMANYAN (1910-1995). Academic and physicist born in Lahore, in what was then British India. The son of a civil servant, Chandrasekhar earned a doctorate at England's Cambridge University in 1933. Academic disputes over his astrophysical theories led to his leaving England to accept a faculty post at the University of Chicago in 1937. Noted for his work on stellar phenomena, he won the Nobel Prize in Physics in 1983. His publications include *An Introduction to the Study of Stellar Structure* (1939), *The Mathematical Theory of Black Holes* (1983), and *Newton's Principia for the Common Reader* (1995).

CLAIBORNE, LIZ* (1929-2007). Belgian-born fashion designer and entrepreneur.

CLEBURNE, PATRICK RONAYNE (1828-1864). Controversial Confederate general born in Ovens, County Cork, Ireland. After a three-year stint as a corporal in the British army, Cleburne emigrated to the United States and settled in Arkansas as a pharmacist and lawyer. In 1861, he joined the Confederate Army, in which he rose to the rank of major general and commanding a division in December, 1863. The following year, he caused a stir by proposing that the South's best chance of victory lay in emancipating all its slaves and inducting them to fight for the Confederacy. Confederate president Jefferson Davis quickly rejected Cleburne's suggestion, and Cleburne received no further promotions, despite his exceptional command record. He was killed at the Battle of Franklin in Tennessee on November 30, 1864.

COLOSIMO, JAMES "DIAMOND JIM" (1878-1920). Mobster born in Cosenza, Italy. Colosimo arrived in the United States at the age of seventeen with practically nothing to his name. After settling in Chicago, he quickly became involved in political and racketeering activities, moving rapidly from small-time operations, through an advantageous marriage in 1902, to the control of a criminal empire revolving around prostitution, gambling, and the protection racket. He was

known as "Diamond Jim" because of his opulent lifestyle. He was assassinated in 1920, apparently by his lieutenants, Al Capone and Johnny Torrio, possibly because he opposed a business expansion into the lucrative bootleg liquor market. Colosimo's gang formed the core of Capone's future crime empire.

CUGAT, XAVIER (1900-1990). Latin songwriter and bandleader born in Gerona, Spain, and taken to Cuba as a child. In 1915, Cugat's family came to New York. For a period, Cugat drew cartoons for the *Los Angeles Times* while playing in musical bands in the evenings. He soon focused on music and formed several Latin bands until one of his groups achieved fame for its 1931 performances at New York's Waldorf-Astoria Hotel. Over the next forty years, Cugat composed and directed musical performances and recorded in such Latin genres as the rumba, the tango, the mambo, and the conga.

DANTICAT, EDWIDGE* (1969-   ). Haitian-born author.

DAVIS, JAMES JOHN* (1873-1947). Welsh-born politician who served as U.S. secretary of labor under three presidents.

DE KOONING, WILLEM (1904-1997). Painter and sculptor born in Rotterdam in the Netherlands. De Kooning entered the United States illegally in 1926 and settled at Newport News, Virginia. He worked at irregular carpentry and house- and sign-painting jobs, and from 1935 to 1937, he was employed on the art project of the New Deal Works Progress Administration (WPA) program. Thereafter, he gained fame as a leader of the abstract expressionist movement. He legally naturalized as an American citizen in 1962.

DU PONT, ELEUTHÈRE IRÉNÉE (1771-1834). Chemical and explosives manufacturer born in Paris, France. Du Pont's family was persecuted by the French Revolutionary government for their conservative views. After the government shut down their printing firm in 1797, the family immigrated to the United States. At the age of thirty, du Pont set up a gunpowder manufacturing company while he was living in a crude log cabin near Wilmington, Delaware. By the time of his death, E. I. Du Pont de Nemours had become one of the most prosperous corporations in the United States.

EINSTEIN, ALBERT* (1879-1955). German-born physicist.

EL-BAZ, FAROUK (1938-   ) space and geological scientist born in Zagazig, Egypt. Upon receiving a bachelor of science degree in Egypt in 1958, El-Baz was awarded a fellowship at the Missouri University of Science and Technology, where he received a doctorate in 1964. Three years later, he joined the National Aeronautics and Space Administration (NASA) as a special trainer for astronauts and contributed to the success of the first manned moon landing in 1969. A recognized authority on lunar geology, El-Baz left NASA to join the staff of the Smithsonian Institution in 1972. A decade later, he joined the faculty of Boston University.

ERICSSON, JOHN (1803-1889). Maritime engineer and inventor born in Langbanshyttan, Sweden. Though Ericsson's father went bankrupt and his own finances were tight, Ericsson secured engineering credentials and gained some reputation as an inventor in England before he accepted an invitation by Captain Robert Stockton to travel to New York in 1839. Ericsson designed the innovative warship USS *Princeton* in 1843, but his reputation suffered a reverse when a cannon aboard the vessel exploded, killing two federal government cabinet secretaries. Although Ericsson was personally exonerated of wrongdoing, he was never paid for his work and only reluctantly undertook the commission that led to his greatest invention—the pioneer ironclad warship USS *Monitor,* which saved the Union Navy from the Confederate ironclad CSS *Virginia* during the Civil War battle of Hampton Roads on March 9, 1862. Ericsson later tinkered with solar-powered engines and with torpedoes.

FACTOR, MAX (1877-1938). Pharmacist and cosmetics manufacturer born in Lodz, Poland. Factor was already well known in the Russian Empire as the makeup specialist for the Royal Ballet in 1904, when he immigrated to the United States to escape anti-Jewish pogroms. After a slow start in New York and St. Louis, he moved to Los Angeles, where in 1909 he founded the cosmetics company that still bears his name. Factor became the leading cosmetics supplier for the Hollywood film industry, and the Max Factor company grew into a multimillion-dollar international concern.

FERMI, ENRICO (1901-1954). Physicist born in Rome, Italy. A scientific prodigy, Fermi rose to hold a professorship at the University of Rome. Feeling threatened by the Fascist government, he took his family to the United States in 1938—the same year that he received the Nobel Prize in Physics for originating the theory of nuclear fission. He helped devise the first nuclear reactor at the University of Chicago in 1942 and actively participated in the Manhattan Project that developed the first atomic bomb at Los Alamos, New Mexico.

FLANAGAN, EDWARD J., FATHER* (1886-1948). Irish-born social activist and humanitarian who founded Boys Town in Nebraska.

FRANKFURTER, FELIX* (1882-1965). Austrian-born law professor and political activist who became a U.S. Supreme Court justice.

GALLATIN, ALBERT (1761-1849). Politician and diplomat born in Geneva, Switzerland. Gallatin was born into a wealthy family but was orphaned at an early age. In 1780, he traveled to Boston, Massachusetts, out of a sense of adventure while he was still a teenager. After suffering some financial reverses, he entered politics in 1789. In 1795, he became a U.S. congressman. A strong supporter of Thomas Jefferson's Democratic-Republican Party, he served as secretary of the treasury in the Jefferson and Madison administrations from 1801 to 1814. In 1814, he helped negotiate the Treaty of Ghent that ended the War of 1812. Afterward, he served as U.S. diplomatic minister to France (1815-1823) and Great Britain (1826-1827).

GARVEY, MARCUS* (1887-1940). Jamaican immigrant, social activist, and journalist who founded a worldwide organization for peoples of African descent.

GENEEN, HAROLD (1910-1997). Businessman born in Hampshire, England. Geneen immigrated to the United States as a child. After studying accounting at New York University, he rose to senior vice president of Raytheon (1956-1959) and then moved to International Telephone and Telegraph (ITT), of which he eventually became president. Over nearly two decades, he built the modest-sized company into a multinational conglomerate with close ties to the federal government and its intelligence community. The growth of ITT was fueled by Geneen's purchase of a variety of other businesses in eighty countries, including rental car agencies, commercial and residential real estate, and hotels.

GIBRAN, KAHLIL (1883-1931). Author, poet, and artist born in Besharri, Lebanon. After Gibran's father was accused of corruption and imprisoned by the Ottoman government, his destitute family made its way to New York in 1895. The members of the family survived in modest circumstances by undertaking menial jobs and engaging in door-to-door sales. Gibran himself began selling his illustrations when he was only fifteen. His poetry is highly religious in its tone and content; his first notable publication in English was *The Madman* (1918). His most-acclaimed book was *The Prophet* (1923).

GODKIN, EDWIN LAWRENCE (1831-1902). Author and journalist born in Moyne, county Wicklow, Ireland. During the mid-1850's, Godkin served as war correspondent for the *London Daily News* in the Crimean War. Afterward, he sailed for New York. While writing for various New York publications, he branched out on his own in 1865 to found and edit *The Nation*. From 1883 to 1899, he edited the *New York Evening Post*.

GOLDMAN, EMMA* (1869-1940). Lithuanian-born anarchist and feminist.

GOMPERS, SAMUEL* (1850-1924). English-born labor leader.

GROVE, ANDREW* (1936-   ). Hungarian-born chief executive officer of Intel.

GUGGENHEIM, MEYER* (1828-1905). Swiss-born industrialist.

HAYAKAWA, S. I.* (1906-1992). Japanese Canadian immigrant who became a college president and one of California's U.S. senators.

HILL, JAMES JEROME (1838-1916). A railroad magnate dubbed the "Empire Builder," Hill was born in Rockwood, Ontario, where he received limited schooling. His father's early death and his family's impoverished circumstances compelled him to seek work at various odd jobs— and he was further hindered by blindness in one eye from an arrow wound. In 1856, he relocated to St. Paul, Minnesota, where he later purchased the St. Paul & Pacific Railroad in 1878. Over the next twelve years, he built it into the conglomerate Great Northern Railroad. In 1901, he allied with J. P. Morgan to form the mammoth Northern Securities Company.

HILLMAN, SIDNEY (1887-1946). Labor leader born into a Jewish family in Zagare, Lithuania, which was then part of the Russian Empire. Hillman became active in the revolutionary labor movement and was twice imprisoned. After the 1905 Russian Revolution, he escaped from the right-wing terror of the Black Hundreds and found his way to Chicago. Active from the beginning in trade unionism, he served as president of the radical Amalgamated Clothing Workers of America from 1914 to 1946,. Hillman was instrumental in delivering the political support of organized labor behind the administrations of Franklin D. Roosevelt and Harry S. Truman. He also helped found the Congress of Industrial Organizations (CIO) in 1935.

HUFFINGTON, ARIANNA* (1950-   ). Greek-born author and journalist.

JENNINGS, PETER* (1938-2005). Canadian-born television journalist.

KISSINGER, HENRY* (1923-   ). German-born scholar who became U.S. secretary of state.

KUNIYOSHI, YASUO (1889-1953). Artist born in Okayama, Japan. After coming to the United States in 1906, Kuniyoshi lived in Seattle, Washington, and Los Angeles, California, where he studied art and earning money as a photographer and by doing odd jobs. After relocating to New York, he pursued advanced studies in art under master artists Robert Henri and Kenneth Hayes Miller and was mounting one-man shows in both Japan and in the United States by 1922. His work is generally seen as a synthesis of Eastern and Western elements. While supporting the American war effort from 1941 to 1945, he served as designer and Japanese-language broadcaster for the War Information Office.

LAHIRI, JHUMPA* (1967-   ). British-born author of Asian Indian descent.

LATROBE, BENJAMIN HENRY (1764-1820). Architect born in Fulneck, England. Latrobe was educated in architecture, surveying, and engineering. After his wife died and he went bankrupt, he sailed to Norfolk, Virginia, in 1795. His first architectural commission in the United States was the Virginia state penitentiary in Richmond. This was followed by the Bank of Philadelphia, the Capitol Building in Washington, D.C., the New Orleans customs house, and Baltimore's Roman Catholic basilica. Latrobe is credited with bringing the Neoclassical Revival in architecture to the United States.

LENNON, JOHN* (1940-1980). English musician and political activist most famous as a member of the Beatles rock band.

LIM, SHIRLEY GEOK-LIN* (1944-   ). Malaysian author and academic.

LIPMANN, FRITZ ALBERT (1899-1986). Biochemist and academic born in Königsberg, Germany. After earning his doctoral degree at the University of Berlin, Lipmann faced increasing danger as Adolf Hitler's Nazi regime intensified its persecution of Jews. He spent time conducting research in New York and in Copenhagen, Denmark, before deciding in 1939 to reside in the United States permanently. After working at Cornell University and Massachusetts General Hospital, he taught at Harvard Medical School from 1949 to 1957 and then spent three decades at Rockefeller University in New York City. Lipmann is noted for his research in the field of oncology, phosphates, and the discovery of co-enzyme A, for which he was awarded the 1953 Noble Prize in Physiology or Medicine.

LOON, HENDRIK WILLEM VAN (1882-1944). Prolific historian and illustrator born in Rotterdam in the Netherlands. From 1902 to 1905, Loon attended Cornell University, where he later taught history. Naturalized in 1919, he authored—and also often illustrated—forty-four books between 1913 and 1944. Among the best known are *The Fall of the Dutch Republic* (1913), *The Story of Mankind* (1921), and *Van Loon's Lives* (1942).

LYON, MATTHEW (1750-1822). Revolutionary soldier and legislator born in county Wicklow, Ireland. After arriving in Connecticut in 1765, Lyon worked as a printer and farm laborer and later moved to Vermont. There he served in the Continental Army from 1775 until 1778, when he won election to Vermont's legislature (1779-1796). During 1797-1801 and 1803-1811, he served in the U.S. House of Representatives.

MEAGHER, THOMAS FRANCIS (1823-1867). Military commander and government administrator born in Waterford, Ireland. His involvement during an 1848 Irish uprising against British rule led to his transportation to a prison colony in Tasmania. However, he escaped to New York in 1852. There he put himself through law school, started a legal practice, and published newspapers. During the U.S. Civil War, he formed and led the Irish Brigade as a brigadier general in the Union army. In 1865, he became acting governor of Montana Territory.

MERGENTHALER, OTTMAR (1854-1899). Inventor born in Germany and apprenticed to a watchmaker. In 1872, Mergenthaler immigrated to Baltimore, Maryland, where he worked in a machine shop of which he eventually became a partner. At the age of thirty-two, he created a prototype of his first linotype composing machine, in which type could be set and cast in one step by entering letters on a keyboard similar to a typewriter. His invention revolutionized the printing and publishing industries and earned him the nickname "Second Gutenberg," for the inventor of movable type.

MUIR, JOHN* (1838-1914). Scottish-born writer, naturalist, and conservationist.

MUKHERJEE, BHARATI* (1940-   ). Indian-born teacher and author.

NABOKOV, VLADIMIR (1899-1977). Author and zoologist born in St. Petersburg, Russia. Nabokov was born into a wealthy family, but the Russian Revolution sent his family into exile in Berlin, where Nabokov's father was murdered in 1922. After fleeing from the Nazis to the United States in 1940, Nabokov secured a position at Harvard University's Museum of Comparative Zoology, where he could pursue his passion for studying butterflies. He also taught literature at Cornell and Wellesley universities and founded the latter's Russian language department. His first English-language novel was *The Real Life of Sebastian Knight* (1941), which was followed by *Bend Sinister* (1947) and a 1964 translation of Alexander Pushkin's *Eugene Onegin* (1825-1832). However, it was Nabokov's 1955 novel *Lolita* that secured his fame.

PEI, I. M.* (1917-). Chinese-born architect.

PINKERTON, ALLAN* (1819-1884). Scottish-born founder of a detective agency.

PONZI, CHARLES* (1882-1949). Italian-born swindler who gave his name to fraudulent "Ponzi schemes."

PULITZER, JOSEPH* (1847-1911). Hungarian-born newspaper publisher.

PUPIN, MICHAEL IDVORSKY (1858-1935). Inventor born in the village of Idvor in Serbia. Pupin took care of his father's cattle until he was sixteen, when his father's untimely death impelled him to board a ship to America. Broke and unable to speak English, he spent five years working at a variety of menial jobs while he learned English, and he saved until he could attend Columbia University in 1879. He then obtained a scholarship to the University of Berlin, where in 1889 he received a doctoral degree. From 1889 to 1931, he served on the Columbia University faculty and achieved wealth and fame for his invention of the Pupin long-distance induction coil, which was bought by American Telephone and Telegraph. Pupin also developed sonar and X-ray photography. His autobiography, *From Immigrant to Inventor* (1924), won a Pulitzer Prize.

RAND, AYN (1905-1982). Philosophical novelist who originated Objectivism, born in St. Petersburg, Russia. After the Russian Revolution, Rand fled from repressive conditions in the Soviet Union and went to America in 1926. She had to learn English and worked in a series of part-time jobs in Hollywood. In 1936, she published her first novel, *We the Living*. It and *Anthem* (1938) and *The Fountainhead* (1943) established her literary reputation. Her capstone novel, *Atlas Shrugged* (1957), elevated her to near-cult status on college campuses.

RAPP, GEORGE* (1757-1847). German-born founder of the Rappite religious community.

RICKOVER, HYMAN* (1900-1986). Polish-born U.S. Navy admiral.

RIIS, JACOB (1849-1914). Journalist, author, photographer, and social activist born in Ribe, Denmark, One of fifteen children in his Danish family, Riis immigrated to the United States in 1870 and spent three years enduring harsh conditions in New York slums and flophouses. He finally escaped the poverty of the tenements and poorhouses by securing a position as reporter for the *New York Evening Sun* and later the *New York Tribune*. He specialized in photojournalistic essays on life in the most impoverished, crime-infested areas of the city and was among the first photographers to use flash cameras. His most notable publications include *How the Other Half Lives* (1891), *The Children of the Poor* (1892), *The Battle with the Slum* (1902), and his autobiography, *The Making of an American* (1901).

ROCKNE, KNUTE* (1888-1931). Norwegian-born football coach at the University of Notre Dame.

ROEBLING, JOHN AUGUSTUS (1806-1869). Engineer born in Mulhausen, Germany. Roebling studied civil engineering at the Royal Polytechnic Institute in Berlin, where he graduated in 1826. With the economic situation in Germany worsening and the political climate becoming increasingly repressive, Roebling left for the settlement of Saxonburg, Pennsylvania, in 1831. He tried his hand at farming until 1837, then returned to engineering. Among his most significant commissions were the Allegheny aqueduct bridge in Pittsburgh (1844), the Niagara Falls suspension bridge (1854), the Roebling suspension bridge in Cincinnati (1867), and New York City's Brooklyn Bridge (1883). This last project was completed by his son, Washington Roebling.

SCHURZ, CARL* (1829-1906). German-born journalist, lawyer, social activist, Civil War general, and statesman.

SCHWARZENEGGER, ARNOLD* (1947-). Austrian American bodybuilder and film star who became governor of California.

SIDHWA, BAPSI* (1938-). Pakistani-born author.

SIGEL, FRANZ (1824-1902). Civil War general born in Sinsheim, in what was then the Grand Duchy of Baden, Germany. Sigel served as an officer in Baden's army from 1843 to 1847 and during the German revolution of 1848, as a colonel in the insurgent forces. After the revolt was suppressed in 1849, he fled Germany. Three years later, he became a professor and school administrator in St. Louis, Missouri. In 1861, he joined the Union Army as a colonel. Because of his influence within Missouri's large German community, he played an important role in keeping Missouri from falling under Confederate control. After the war, he became involved in politics and journalism.

SINGER, ISAAC BASHEVIS (1904-1991). Author born in Leoncin, Poland. The son of a village rabbi, Singer went to Warsaw to take up a career in journalism; however, the threat posed by Adolf Hitler's rise to power in Germany led him to come to the United States in 1935. Initially dismayed by the stresses of adjusting to a new environment, he turned to writing novels in Yiddish. When his works began to be translated into English he achieved an international reputation and won the 1978 Nobel Prize in Literature. Among his major works are *The Family Moskat* (1950), *Satan in Goray* (1955), *Enemies: A Love Story* (1972), and *Yentl: The Yeshiva Boy* (1983).

STEINMETZ, CHARLES PROTEUS (1865-1923). Inventor and electrical engineer born in Breslau, Germany. Steinmetz's activities in Germany's socialist movement brought down government repression that motivated him to emigrate to the United States in 1889. When he arrived in New York with neither money nor any knowledge of English, he was nearly turned back at Ellis Island. He first worked for the Eikenmeyer Transformer Company, then for General Electric beginning in 1893. Steinmetz's most influential discoveries lay in the field of alternating currents, artificial lightning, and induction motors.

STRAUSS, LEVI* (1829-1902). German-born clothing manufacturer and philanthropist.

STRAVINSKY, IGOR FEDOROVITCH (1882-1971). Musical composer born in Oranienbaum, Russia. Stravinsky immigrated to the United States in 1939, shortly after the deaths of his mother, wife, and daughter, and the start of World War II. When he arrived, he already had a well-established reputation as a composer in Europe. He became an American citizen in 1946 and lived in Los Angeles and New York. His best-known compositions include the symphony *Orpheus* (1947), the opera *The Rake's Progress* (1951), and *The Flood* (1962), a made-for-television opera.

TELLER, EDWARD (1908-2003). Nuclear scientist born in Budapest, Hungary. Teller was studying physics in Germany when Adolf Hitler came to power. In 1935, he emigrated to the United States and settled in Washington, D.C. During

World War II, he worked on the Manhattan Project that developed the first atomic bomb. After 1945, he continued his work in nuclear physics, turning his attention to fusion, and was the driving force behind the development of the hydrogen bomb during the 1950's.

TESLA, NIKOLA* (1856-1943). Serbian-born engineer and inventor.

TRAPP, MARIA AUGUSTA (1905-1987). Teacher and musician born in the Tyrol, Austria. Orphaned at an early age, Trapp entered the Benedictine Order of nuns and became a tutor to the family of the aristocrat Georg Von Trapp, whom she married in 1927. After her husband lost his fortune in 1935, Trapp organized her large family into a singing troupe that became known as the Trapp Family Singers. After Germany occupied Austria in 1938, the Trapps left Europe. They eventually settled in Vermont and continued to perform as a musical troupe. A highly romanticized version of Trapp's story was made into the Broadway musical *The Sound of Music* (1959), which was later adapted to the screen.

UNDERWOOD, JOHN T. (1857-1937). Born in London, Underwood emigrated to the United States in 1873 and later founded the Underwood Typewriter Company, which produced typewriter ribbons. When Remington, his company's principal buyer, decided to produce its own ribbons, Underwood decided to manufacture his own brand of typewriters. He purchased the patent for an innovative front-stroke model that allowed operators to see the letters as they were typed. Underwood later opened a typewriter factory in Hartford, Connecticut, which by 1915 was the largest of its kind in the world, producing five hundred machines per day.

VON NEUMANN, JOHN (1903-1957). Mathematician and nuclear scientist born in Budapest, Hungary. A mathematical prodigy, Von Neumann earned his doctorate in mathematics from Pazmany Peter University in 1925. After his father's death he immigrated with his family to the United States in 1930. Three years later he was appointed to the faculty of Princeton University, where he taught for twenty-four years. Von Neumann is renowned for his innovative set and game theories, his work in quantum mechanics, and contributions to computer and nuclear science, including the crucial role he played during the Manhattan Project.

WAKSMAN, SELMAN ABRAHAM (1888-1973). Biologist born in Pryluky in Ukraine. Waksman left for the United States in 1910. He worked his way through Rutgers University and the University of California at Berkeley, receiving his doctorate from the latter institution in 1918. Afterward, he devoted himself to teaching and research as a faculty member at Rutgers from 1918 to 1958. He coined the term "antibiotic" and developed actinomycin, neomycin, and streptomycin—for which he was awarded the Nobel Prize in Physiology or Medicine in 1952.

WHIPPLE, PRINCE (c. 1750-1784). Soldier and abolitionist born in Africa, possibly in what is now the nation of Ghana. His well-to-do parents paid a ship's captain to take him to be educated in the United States. The captain betrayed them and sold the young man into slavery. He was purchased by William Whipple, a businessman in Portsmouth, New Hampshire. William Whipple became a general in the Continental Army and a signer of the Declaration of Independence, and his slave Prince accompanied him into combat. In 1779, Prince Whipple petitioned for his freedom on the basis of the Declaration of Independence, but he was not manumitted by General Whipple until 1784. The long-accepted legend that he was the black soldier depicted in Emanuel Gottlieb Leutze's painting of George Washington crossing the Delaware has of, late, been disputed.

WIESEL, ELIE (1928-   ). Holocaust survivor, author, and human rights advocate born in Sighet, Romania. In May, 1944, Wiesel was sent to the Nazis' Auschwitz concentration camp, along with the entire Jewish community of Sighet. Both of Wiesel's parents and a sister died in the camp, but Wiesel survived. In 1955, he came to the United States, where he worked as a journalist. During that same year, he published his autobiography, *Un di Velt hot geshvign*, in Yiddish. A French edition appeared in 1958, but it was the 1960 English edition, titled *Night*, that won Wiesel international renown as an author. In 1986, he received the Nobel Peace Prize.

WIRZ, HENRY (1823-1865). Confederate prison warden born in Zurich, Switzerland. Wirz immigrated to the United States in 1849. He practiced medicine in Kentucky and Louisiana before joining the Confederate Army in 1861. After being promoted to captain, he served as commandant of the notorious prisoner-of-war camp at Andersonville, Georgia, from February, 1864, until May, 1865. After the war, he was tried for war crimes for his complicity in the deaths of nearly 13,000 Union prisoners under his charge. He was convicted and hanged.

YANG, JERRY* (1968-   ). Taiwanese-born entrepreneur who cofounded Yahoo!

YEZIERSKA, ANZIA* (c. 1880-1970). Polish-born novelist.

ZWORYKIN, VLADIMIR (1889-1982). Inventor born in Murom, Russia. Zworykin graduated from the St. Petersburg Institute of Technology in 1912 and served briefly in the Russian army. After siding with the unsuccessful White Russian movement during the Russian Civil War, he emigrated to the United States. While working as an engineer for Westinghouse Corporation, he built upon research he had done in St. Petersburg to develop the prototype for television. In 1929, he went to work for the Radio Corporation of America (RCA), in which he rose to a vice presidency and remained until retiring in 1954. At RCA, he completed his work on television by inventing the iconoscope picture tube.

Raymond Pierre Hylton

U.S. SUPREME COURT RULINGS ON IMMIGRATION

Cases covered in full essays are marked with asterisks (*).

1824
Osborn v. Bank of the United States
22 U.S. 738

Decision in which Chief Justice John Marshall ruled there is no legal difference between citizenship by birth and citizenship by naturalization.

1837
*New York v. Miln**
38 U.S. 102

Authorized the states to regulate immigrants entering through state ports, based on the doctrine of state police power. Twelve years later, however, the Court would reverse this ruling in the *Passenger Cases.*

1847
License Cases
46 U.S. 504

ALSO KNOWN AS: *Thurlow v. Massachusetts; Fletcher v. Rhode Island*

Held that Congress's broad authority to regulate foreign and interstate commerce was limited by the police powers of the individual states.

1849
*Passenger Cases**
48 U.S. 283

ALSO KNOWN AS: *Norris v. Boston; Smith v. Turner*

Held that the individual states did not have constitutional authority to tax immigrants entering the country, overturning *New York v. Miln* (1837).

1852
Cooley v. Port of Pennsylvania
53 U.S. 299

Established the pragmatic compromise called "selective exclusiveness," which allowed the states to regulate commerce in local matters, while prohibiting state regulations that interfered with aspects requiring national uniformity.

1875
*Chy Lung v. Freeman**
92 U.S. 275

Held that fees and restrictions by the states on aliens entering the country were unconstitutionally unless absolutely necessary and reasonable.

1875
*Henderson v. Mayor of the City of New York**
92 U.S. 259

Recognized that the exclusive power of Congress to regulate international commerce included the landing of passengers, thereby striking down state immigration laws interfering with national uniformity.

1884
*Chew Heong v. United States**
112 U.S. 536

This first of the Chinese exclusion cases affirmed that a Chinese citizen had the benefit of rights promised in treaties with China that had not been clearly and explicitly repealed by Congress.

1884
*Head Money Cases**
112 U.S. 580

Upheld a federal tax on immigrants as "a mere incident of the regulation of commerce," thereby helping to consolidate federal control over immigration.

1886
*Yick Wo v. Hopkins**
118 U.S. 356

First case in which the Court held that a racially neutral law applied in a discriminatory manner violates the Fourteenth Amendment's equal protection clause.

1889

*Chae Chan Ping v. United States**

130 U.S. 581

ALSO KNOWN AS: Chinese Exclusion Case

Recognized the sovereign power of Congress to exclude any group from immigration and to abrogate or modify treaties.

1892

*Nishimura Ekiu v. United States**

142 U.S. 651

Upheld enforcement of the Immigration Act of 1891, which authorized local immigration officials to exclude categories of undesirable immigrants without any right of appeal.

1893

*Fong Yue Ting v. United States**

149 U.S. 698

Upheld the Geary Act of 1892, which provided Congress with almost unlimited discretion to establish rules for alien registration and deportation.

1895

*Lem Moon Sing v. United States**

158 U.S. 538

Upheld a federal law prohibiting district courts from reviewing habeas corpus petitions by alien immigrants, thereby empowering immigration officials to exclude or deport without any judicial review.

1896

*Wong Wing v. United States**

163 U.S. 228

Prohibited criminal punishment of noncitizens without a jury trial and other constitutional rights, but reaffirmed the authority of Congress to authorize their deportation without trials.

1898

*United States v. Wong Kim Ark**

169 U.S. 649

Ruled that under the Fourteenth Amendment's citizenship clause any person born on American soil is a U.S. citizen, even when parents are illegal aliens and ineligible for citizenship.

1902

*Chin Bak Kan v. United States**

186 U.S. 193

Authorized vigorous enforcement of the Chinese Exclusion Act of 1882 and its amendments and disregarded minor procedural defects in the deportation of persons who entered the country illegally.

1904

Turner v. Williams

194 U.S. 279

Upheld the expulsion of an immigrant because of his advocacy of anarchism, thereby approving the Immigration Act of 1903, which excluded aliens simply because of their political beliefs.

1905

*United States v. Ju Toy**

198 U.S. 253

Authorized officials of the executive branch to make the final determination of a resident Chinese's claim to citizenship without any review by the federal courts.

1914

Patsone v. Pennsylvania

232 U.S. 138

Upheld a state law that prohibited noncitizens from hunting wild game in the state.

1915

*Truax v. Raich**

239 U.S. 33

Struck down a state law that required eighty percent of workers in most businesses to be citizens, based on the equal right of noncitizens to earn a livelihood in common occupations.

1922

*Ozawa v. United States**

260 U.S. 178

Defined the word "white" in U.S. naturalization law as meaning a person of European racial ancestry—thus disqualifying all persons of Asian ancestry from naturalization.

U.S. Supreme Court Rulings on Immigration

1923
*Terrace v. Thompson**
263 U.S. 197

Upheld the validity of a state law that prohibited noncitizens from owning or leasing land for the purpose of agriculture.

1923
*United States v. Bhagat Singh Thind**
261 U.S. 204

Held that the word "white" in immigration law did not refer to light-skinned immigrants from India, thus making them ineligible for naturalized citizenship.

1924
*Asakura v. City of Seattle**
265 U.S. 332

Gave relatively liberal interpretations to foreign treaties that guaranteed the civil rights of particular aliens in the United States.

1925
*Chang Chan v. Nagle**
268 U.S. 346

Upheld a law disallowing some foreign wives of U.S. citizens from entering the country.

1925
*Cheung Sum Shee v. Nagle**
268 U.S. 336

Held that treaties with foreign countries guaranteeing rights for their citizens were legally binding unless they had clearly and explicitly been abrogated by Congress.

1928
*Jordan v. Tashiro**
278 U.S. 123

Held that treaties with Japan guaranteed the right of Japanese citizens to operate trading businesses in the United States—overruling limited parts of the California Land Law.

1931
United States v. Macintosh
283 U.S. 605

Upheld a law prohibiting naturalization for persons not promising to bear arms in U.S. wars and recognized the broad discretion of Congress to establish such restrictions.

1943
Schneiderman v. United States
320 U.S. 118

Held that denaturalization requires "clear, unequivocal, and convincing" evidence of disloyalty or fraud in the application for citizenship.

1944
Korematsu v. United States
323 U.S. 214

Upheld the emergency relocation of persons of Japanese ancestry following Japan's attack on Pearl Harbor, but declared that racial classifications were "inherently suspect" and must be judged by the "most rigid scrutiny."

1946
Knauer v. United States
328 U.S. 654

Upheld a denaturalization order for an immigrant from Germany who had intended to promote Nazism when applying for citizenship and had taken a false oath of allegiance.

1948
Ludecke v. Watkins
335 U.S. 160

Recognized that an alien resident could not be deported without a deportation proceeding, which included reasonable notice, a fair hearing, and an order based on adequate evidence.

1948
*Oyama v. California**
332 U.S. 633

Overturned the portions of the California Alien Land Laws that discriminated against Asian Americans who were citizens by birth, but without any affect on Asian immigrants.

1950

United States ex rel. Knauff v. Shaughnessy
338 U.S. 537

Upheld the government's inherent authority to disallow the return of an alien of permanent resident status who had lived abroad for nineteen months.

1950

Wong Yang Sung v. McGrath
339 U.S. 33

Reaffirmed the constitutional right of aliens to a fair hearing before deportation, except for those who had recently entered the country illegally.

1952

Carlson v. Landon
342 U.S. 524

Upheld the detaining of five aliens awaiting determination of deportability for Communist membership, without any right of judicial review.

1952

Harisiades v. Shaughnessy
342 U.S. 580

Upheld the constitutionality of the Alien Registration Act of 1942, which authorized the deportation of legally resident aliens holding membership in the Communist Party.

1954

*Galvan v. Press**
347 U.S. 522

Upheld the deportation of a resident alien who had belonged to the Communist Party after entry, despite a lack of evidence that he had been aware of the party's advocacy of violent revolution.

1964

Schneider v. Rusk
377 U.S. 163

Struck down the provision in federal law that had revoked the citizenship of naturalized citizens who returned to their country of origin for three years.

1967

*Afroyim v. Rusk**
387 U.S. 253

Established that U.S. citizenship may not be re-voked involuntarily for actions such as voting in a foreign country.

1967

*Boutilier v. Immigration and Naturalization Service**
387 U.S. 118

Based on congressional intent and psychiatric ideas of the time, the Supreme Court upheld the government's policy of classifying gays and lesbians as ineligible for immigration.

1971

*Graham v. Richardson**
403 U.S. 365

Landmark decision holding that alienage is a suspect classification and that states may not deny welfare benefits to alien residents.

1973

In Re Griffiths
413 U.S. 717

Permitted the states to prohibit resident aliens from practicing law.

1973

Matthews v. Dias
426 U.S. 67

Upheld the constitutionality of a provision in the Social Security Act of 1935 that denied supplementary Medicare insurance to aliens unless they had been permanent residents for five years.

1973

Sugarman v. Dougall
413 U.S. 634

Recognized that aliens may be excluded from elective positions and from nonelective positions that involve the formation or execution of public policy—a major exception to *Graham v. Richardson* (1971).

1974

*Lau v. Nichols**
414 U.S. 563

Required school districts to provide compensatory training for students with limited English proficiency, but allowed school districts to decide the methods of instruction.

1975

United States v. Brignoni-Ponce
422 U.S. 873

Required that before "roving patrols" near the Mexican border stop vehicles to question occupants, their officers must have reasonable grounds to think that the vehicles contain passengers who are in the country illegally.

1976

*Hampton v. Mow Sun Wong**
426 U.S. 88

Held that federal agencies may not refuse to employ noncitizens except when the Congress expressly establishes the policy based on an overriding national interest.

1977

Castaneda v. Partida
430 U.S. 482

Concluded that there was sufficient evidence to demonstrate unconstitutional racial discrimination in jury selections by Texas border counties.

1977

Fiallo v. Bell
430 U.S. 787

Upheld gender discrimination in the Immigration and Nationality Act of 1952 that applied to foreign-born children whose parents were unmarried and only one of whom was a U.S. citizen.

1978

*Foley v. Connelie**
435 U.S. 291

Upheld a New York law prohibiting noncitizens from serving as police officers and undertaking other kinds of work involving discretion in administering public policy.

1979

Ambach v. Norwick
441 U.S. 68

Upheld a New York State law that disallowed aliens who were eligible for citizenship from teaching in the public schools.

1980

Vance v. Terrazas
444 U.S. 252

Held that a person's citizenship status can be revoked when the government demonstrates, by a preponderance of evidence, that the person intended to surrender the status.

1981

*Fedorenko v. United States**
449 U.S. 490

Allowed the revocation of naturalized citizenship because a person had intentionally provided false information to enter the country and apply for naturalization.

1982

Cabell v. Chavez Salido
454 U.S. 432

Expanding *Foley v. Connelie* (1978), the Court allowed California to require citizenship for "peace officers" who exercise discretion as part of their duties.

1982

*Plyler v. Doe**
457 U.S. 202

Held that the Fourteenth Amendment prohibited states from denying a public education to any child residing in the country illegally.

1983

*Immigration and Naturalization Service v. Chadha**
462 U.S. 919

Prohibited legislation authorizing one house of Congress to override a decision made by the executive branch.

1984

*Bernal v. Fainter**
467 U.S. 216

Struck down a state law prohibiting aliens from working as notary publics and held that laws discriminating against resident aliens must be justified by compelling governmental interests.

1984

*Immigration and Naturalization Service v. Lopez-Mendoza**
468 U.S. 1032

Upheld deportation proceedings without full Fourth Amendment rights, thereby allowing immigration officials to introduce some improperly acquired evidence in the proceedings.

1993

*Sale v. Haitian Centers Council**
509 U.S. 155

Allowed the government to capture fleeing refugees before they reached the shores of the United States and to return them to Haiti, even if the refugees faced political persecution.

1998

Miller v. Albright
523 U.S. 420

Upheld a federal law making acquisition of citizenship more difficult for a foreign-born, illegitimate child when the father is a U.S. citizen than when the mother is a citizen.

1999

*Reno v. American-Arab Anti-Discrimination Committee**
525 U.S. 471

Upheld a federal statute that severely restricted the rights of alien residents to challenge deportation orders in federal court, even in cases with an alleged violation of constitutional rights.

2000

Bond v. United States
529 U.S. 334

Held that a Border Patrol agent in Texas violated the Fourth Amendment when he physically manipulated a bus passenger's bag, based on the owner's reasonable expectation of privacy.

2001

Calcano-Martinez v. Immigration and Naturalization Service
533 U.S. 348

Held that federal circuit courts did not have jurisdiction to review cases of permanent residents subject to removal, but that petitioners may seek relief in district courts.

2001

*Immigration and Naturalization Service v. St. Cyr**
533 U.S. 289

Held that immigration law had not removed the jurisdiction of federal courts to review habeas corpus petitions from resident aliens deportable because of felony convictions.

2001

*Nguyen v. Immigration and Naturalization Service**
533 U.S. 53

Reaffirmed the constitutionality of federal gender-based preferences in the citizenship rights of illegitimate, foreign-born children who have one parent who is a U.S. citizen.

2001

*Zadvydas v. Davis**
533 U.S. 678

Restricted the length of time for detaining noncitizens awaiting deportation, except when the government can demonstrate aggravating circumstances.

2002

Hoffman Plastic Compounds, Inc. v. National Labor Relations Board
535 U.S. 137

Held that the Immigration Reform Act of 1986 did not authorize the awarding of back pay to an undocumented immigrant who had illegally worked in the country.

2006

Fernandez-Vargas v. Gonzales
548 U.S. 30

Held that the immigration law of 1996 did not apply retroactively to an alien who had illegally reentered the country before 1996.

2006

Lopez v. Gonzales
549 U.S. 47

Disallowed removal proceedings against a legally permanent resident because of a felony conviction in state court, when the offense is only a misdemeanor under federal law.

2008

*Dada v. Mukasey**

551 U.S.

A complex interpretation of immigration law, holding that an alien has the right to withdraw a motion of voluntary departure and to present new arguments for remaining in the U.S.

2009

Flores-Figueroa v. United States

556 U.S.

Held that to prosecute an illegal immigrant for identity theft felony, prosecutors must show that the user knew that the false social security number belonged to another person.

Thomas Tandy Lewis

FEDERAL GOVERNMENT AGENCIES AND COMMISSIONS

This list summarizes information on the past and present federal government bodies that have been most concerned with immigration issues. Those marked with asterisks (*) are subjects of full essays in the main text.

CABINET-LEVEL DEPARTMENTS

DEPARTMENT OF AGRICULTURE

DATE: Established in 1862; became a cabinet-level department in 1889

The Department of Agriculture is one of the U.S. government's largest cabinet offices with a budget of nearly $100 billion and more than 100,000 employees. The department's primary mandate is to aid both large and small producers, but it also offers aid to agricultural workers—many of whom are immigrants. Through its numerous subdepartments and agencies, the department touches the lives of virtually everyone in the United States, including immigrants. Most of what the department does affects immigrants only indirectly; however, it played a direct role in the controversial bracero program that began during World War II and continued until 1964.

DEPARTMENT OF DEFENSE

DATE: Established in 1947

In both manpower and budget, the Department of Defense is the largest of all cabinet-level departments. It oversees not only the Army, Navy, and Air Force but also many intelligence-gathering agencies, some of which maintain surveillance over immigrants. The department also manages programs dealing with immigrants and naturalized citizens in the United States. For example, in January, 2008, the National Defense Authorization Act modified parts of the Immigration and Nationality Act so that military spouses could be naturalized at overseas posts where American personnel are stationed, instead of having to wait until they were physically within the United States.

*DEPARTMENT OF HOMELAND SECURITY

DATE: Established in 2003

After the terrorist attacks of September 11, 2001, national security and public safety concerns led to the establishment of this new omnibus department, which consolidated functions that previously had been spread widely across several cabinet departments. With more than 200,000 employees and a budget of more than $45 billion in 2009, this department addresses the safety of all those living in the United States—including immigrants.

DEPARTMENT OF JUSTICE

DATE: Established in 1870

This department has a number of regulatory functions that affect everyone on U.S. soil. The most notable of these is the Federal Bureau of Investigation (FBI), the department's principal investigative arm. From 1940 to 2003, the Bureau of Immigration was housed under the Department of Justice, during which time its name was changed to the Immigration and Naturalization Service (INS). In 2003, the INS was terminated and most of its functions were transferred to the new Department of Homeland Security's U.S. Citizenship and Immigration Services.

DEPARTMENT OF STATE

DATE: Established in 1789

State is the cabinet department in charge of U.S. foreign policy, and the first dealings of legal immigrants to the United States are usually with its Consular Service, which grants visas to enter the country through its embassies and consulates across the globe. Historically, the State Department performed many functions pertaining to immigrants that were later transferred to other agencies and departments of the federal government.

DEPARTMENT OF TREASURY

DATE: Established in 1789

In addition to collecting taxes for the federal government, the Treasury Department performs vital economic regulatory functions in maintaining integrity of U.S. currency and guaranteeing the government's solvency. As such, the department directly affects immigrants as well as those born in the United States. From 1891 until 1903, the Bureau of Immigration was housed under this department.

OTHER FEDERAL AGENCIES

BORDER PATROL, U.S.

DATE: Established in 1924

Created during the Prohibition era to combat the smuggling of liquor into the United States, the Border Patrol later evolved into the federal law-enforcement agency with primary responsibility of protecting U.S. borders against unlawful crossings by undocumented immigrants. In 1933, it was placed under the jurisdiction of the Immigration and Naturalization Service. After the terrorist attacks of September 11, 2001, it was moved to the new Department of Homeland Security. Combined with several other agencies, it became the U.S. Customs and Border Protection.

*BUREAU OF IMMIGRATION

DATE: Established in 1891

The first federal government body to standardize immigration procedures in the United States, the Bureau of Immigration passed under the control of several cabinet departments throughout its history. In 1903, Congress decided that greater emphasis should be placed on attracting immigrants to fill jobs in the United States, so it transferred the bureau to the newly created Department of Commerce and Labor. In 1914, the bureau was moved to the new Department of Labor. In 1933, it was reunited with the Bureau of Naturalization in a single agency, the U.S. Immigration and Naturalization Service.

BUREAU OF THE CENSUS, U.S.

DATE: Established in 1903

The U.S. Constitution required the federal government to conduct a national census every ten years, but censuses were conducted on an ad hoc basis until the Bureau of the Census was created in 1903 as a part of the newly established Department of Commerce and Labor. The bureau has remained within the Commerce Department since the Labor Department was separated in 1914 and has gathered various classes of data on residents of the United States and on the national economy. Throughout its existence, the bureau has collected increasingly detailed information on immigrants that has been used by government policy makers to formulate immigration policies.

*COAST GUARD, U.S.

DATE: Established in 1790 as the Revenue Cutter Service; formed as the Coast Guard in 1915

Although never permanently part of the Department of Defense, the Coast Guard is the smallest of the five military services. In addition to its military functions during wartime, the Coast Guard is permanently involved in enforcing maritime law and offering assistance to vessels in coastal and interstate waters. Originally under the Department of the Treasury, the Coast Guard was later moved to the Department of Transportation. In 2003, it was placed under the new Department of Homeland Security. As the primary law-enforcement agency protecting national ports and waterways, the Coast Guard has a key role in combatting smuggling and illegal immigration.

*COMMISSION ON CIVIL RIGHTS, U.S.

DATE: Established in 1957

This commission investigates complaints about abuses of civil rights, such as citizens being deprived of their right to vote by reason of their race, color, religion, sex, age, disability, or national origin. The commission also studies and collects information on discrimination or denial of equal protection of the laws under the U.S. Constitution and serves as a national clearinghouse for information regarding discrimination or denial of equal protection of the laws based on the same criteria. Lacking direct enforcement powers, the commission submits reports and recommendations to the president and Congress. Although the commission's primary mandate is to protect the rights of American citizens, its investigations sometimes reveal abuses of immigrants' rights.

*COMMISSION ON IMMIGRATION REFORM, U.S.

DATE: Operated from 1990 to 1997

Created by Congress to investigate the implementation and impact of U.S. immigration policies, this bipartisan commission initially focused on problems associated with illegal immigration but later broadened its agenda to cover other issues, such as family unification and employment needs.

DILLINGHAM COMMISSION

DATE: Operated from 1907 to 1911
ALSO KNOWN AS: U.S. Immigration Commission

Under intense threats from nativist elements, Congress created the joint House and Senate U.S. Immigration Commission to study the origins and results of immigration. Because of the political impetus behind the commission's creation, it is not surprising that the commission found recently arrived immigrants from the southern and eastern Europe to be a threat to American society. The commission demanded a strict English reading and writing test as the best means to block undesirable immigrants and called for greatly reduced immigration from southern and eastern Europe. The commission's findings were used for decades as justification for restrictive immigration laws.

FEDERAL MARITIME COMMISSION, U.S.

DATE: Established in 1961

President John F. Kennedy persuaded Congress to create he Federal Maritime Commission to regulate U.S. oceanic transportation of foreign commerce. An earlier body had also managed the U.S. Merchant Marine, but this function was given to another agency and subsequently to the Department of Transportation. The commission regulates shipping lines, cruise ship lines, and other passenger ship lines to ensure they have sufficient resources to pay compensation for personal injuries. It also monitors international agencies to protect American shipping from unfair competition. Because many immigrants are involved in maritime transportation, this agency is of special important to them.

IMMIGRATION AND NATURALIZATION SERVICE (INS)

DATE: Operated from 1933 until 2003

A branch of the Department of Justice, the INS was the principal U.S. agency in charge of immigration and immigrants for seventy years, until it was superseded by the U.S. Citizenship and Immigration Services. It granted permanent residence, naturalization, and asylum to immigrants—functions similar to those of its successor agency. Throughout its tenure, the INS was criticized from all sides. Nativist elements thought its treatment of illegal immigrants was too lenient. Many business eager to hire immigrants thought its regulations were too tough. Many people thought it treated immigrants too coldly. Almost all its critics regarded it as inefficient.

PUBLIC HEALTH SERVICE, U.S.

DATE: Established in 1798

Over its long history—during which it has undergone many changes in name and organization—the Public Health Service has had the primary goal of protecting and promoting the health of all residents of the United States, including immigrants. One way in which it has worked to achieve its goal has been through helping to regulate the entry of new immigrants. Health service personnel have examined newly arrived immigrants to prevent persons carrying communicable diseases from entering the country. Immigrants found to have such diseases are either quarantined before being permitted entry or returned to their homelands.

*SELECT COMMISSION ON IMMIGRATION AND REFUGEE POLICY (SCIRP)

DATE: Operated from 1978 to 1981

Congress created this commission to evaluate federal laws and policies concerning immigrants and refugees. Made up mostly of members appointed by Democratic president Jimmy Carter, the commission submitted its final report to the newly installed administration of Republican president Ronald Reagan in early 1981. The commission presented a cautious call for a slight increase in the annual rate of legal immigration, while acknowledging the possible need to limit immigration in the future.

SOCIAL SECURITY ADMINISTRATION

DATE: Established in 1935

This branch of the Department of Health and Human Services administers the Social Security, Medicaid, and Medicare programs. The Social Security system covers all persons—including immigrants—who are employed in jobs that pay Social Security taxes. Immigrants who pay Social Security taxes for at least ten years enjoy the same benefits from the program as citizens. However, those who pay into the system for fewer than ten years forfeit benefits. Many undocumented immigrants who pay Social Security taxes do not claim benefits for fear of having their illegal immigration status discovered.

*U.S. Citizenship and Immigration Services (USCIS)

Date: Established in 2003

When the Department of Homeland Security was created, U.S. Citizenship and Immigration Services was made one of its branches to replace the widely criticized Immigration and Naturalization Service (INS). However, the new agency inherited most of the functions and personnel of its prede-cessor—a fact that raised serious questions about how much real reform or change had taken place. The new agency's officially stated priorities were to promote national security, eliminate immigration-case backlogs, and improve client services. Like the INS, the agency processes immigrant visa applications, including asylum and refugee applications, and evaluates naturalization petitions. One change that directly affected immigrants was a large increase in fees it charged. Like the INS, the USCIS pays for the bulk of its operations through its fees.

Richard L. Wilson

FEDERAL LAWS PERTAINING TO IMMIGRATION

The official modern compilation of federal laws, organized by subjects, is the United States Code (USC). Many libraries contain an annotated version of this code that includes references to cases and other legal sources interpreting the laws, together with the laws themselves. This annotated version is known as the United States Code Annotated (USCA). Copies of the code may be found at several sites on the World Wide Web, including the FedLaw site operated by the Center for Regulatory Effectiveness (http://www.thecre.com/). This site's link to the USC is http://www.thecre.com/fedlaw/default.htm. In addition, Cornell Law School, which maintains an immense and important collection of legal materials on the Web, also maintains an online copy of the USC at http://www.law.cornell.edu/uscode. The best places to find printed copies of the USC and USCA are public libraries and law libraries. Most courthouses also have law libraries with copies of the USC or USCA.

TITLES AND CITATION NUMBERS

The United States Code is organized into fifty sections—each of which is called a "title"—that correspond to fifty subject areas. Since 1926, most federal immigration laws have been classified under Title 8, "Aliens and Nationality." The USC titles are subdivided into chapters, and the chapters are divided into sections. However, one need know only the title and the section of a particular law to find it. Before 1926, federal laws were generally given "United States Statute at Large" numbers, such as "22 Stat. 214." The first number designates a volume, the second a page.

When an act of Congress is incorporated into the code, provisions of the act may be dispersed across several sections of the code, and these sections themselves may be scattered throughout several titles of the code. Thus, a given act may amend previously existing code sections, and its language might therefore be codified under the various sections it amends. These realities of legislative codification sometimes make it difficult to refer to a specific section of the code as locating a particular act. Whenever possible in the list below, code references are to the first of a series of sequential sections of the code or to some general statements of purpose of an act.

COVERAGE

The following chronologically arranged list of federal laws does not exhaustively catalog all immigration laws. Its purpose is merely to refer readers to especially important immigration laws, to laws with relatively well-known popular names, and to laws of general interest to those interested in immigration. Readers in need of more comprehensive lists of immigration laws should consult the United States Code itself. A useful tool for looking up particular federal laws is the *USC Table of Popular Names*, which indexes federal laws according to the names generally assigned to them when they become law. This table is included in the volumes of the USCA and is available on the World Wide Web (http://www.law.cornell.edu/uscode/topn). The FedLaw site operated by the Center for Regulatory Effectiveness (http://www.thecre.com/) also includes a useful collection of federal laws organized by topic.

Laws covered in full essays are marked with asterisks (*).

NATURALIZATION ACT OF 1790*

ALSO KNOWN AS: An Act to Establish an Uniform Rule of Naturalization

CITATION: 1 Stat. 103

First federal law to establish procedures for naturalization under the U.S. Constitution. Although it required only two years' residence prior to naturalization, less time than any succeeding law, it restricted the right of naturalization to white male immigrants.

ALIEN AND SEDITION ACTS OF 1798

CITATION: 1 Stat. 566 (Naturalization Act), 1 Stat. 570 (Alien Act), 1 Stat. 577 (Alien Enemies Act), 1 Stat. 596 (Sedition Act)

The four laws collectively known as the Alien

and Sedition Acts—the Alien Act, the Alien Enemies Act, the Naturalization Act, and the Sedition Act—were ostensibly passed to avoid war with France but led to a debate regarding the function of the Bill of Rights during wartime, the role of the federal government in legislating for the states, and the process of judicial review. The acts allowed the president to deport any alien he deemed dangerous, extended the period for naturalization from five to fourteen years, and allowed enemy aliens to be detained during wartime. These acts were repealed under Thomas Jefferson, who became president three years after their passage.

STEERAGE ACT OF 1819
CITATION: 3 Stat. 489

First major regulation controlling conditions on incoming immigrant ships. It required the submission of passenger lists and set limits on how many people could be carried within certain amounts of space.

PRE-EMPTION ACT OF 1841
CITATION: 5 Stat. 456

Allowed squatters on government land to stake claims to it and pay very low prices, regardless of whether they had a right to be occupying the land in the first place. Claimants did not have to be citizens but did have to intend to be naturalized. Repealed in 1891.

HOMESTEAD ACT OF 1862*
CITATION: 12 Stat. 392

Accelerated settlement of western lands in the United States by making public lands available to both citizens and immigrants who were willing to establish residence, make improvements, and cultivate crops.

CONTRACT LABOR LAW OF 1864
CITATION: 13 Stat. 386

Designed to deal with the labor shortage that arose during the Civil War by creating an office to recruit workers from other countries. Because many workers left before their contracts were up, this system did not work effectively, and it was opposed by domestic workers. Repealed in 1868.

PAGE LAW OF 1875*
ALSO KNOWN AS: Act Supplementary to the Acts in Relation to Immigration
CITATION: 18 Stat. 477

Originally designed to prohibit Chinese contract workers and prostitutes from entering the United States, this federal law eventually excluded Asian women in general.

CHINESE EXCLUSION ACT OF 1882*
CITATION: 22 Stat. 58

Banned all immigration from China. Initially written to be enforced for ten years, the law was extended in 1892 and made permanent in 1902. This ban was subsumed into the general ban on Asian immigration that was part of the Immigration Act of 1924 and subsequent legislation.

IMMIGRATION ACT OF 1882*
CITATION: 22 Stat. 214; 8 USC

Setting the basic course of U.S. immigration law and policy, this law established categories of foreigners deemed "undesirable" for entry and gave the U.S. secretary of the treasury authority over immigration enforcement.

ALIEN CONTRACT LABOR LAW OF 1885*
ALSO KNOWN AS: Contract Labor Law
CITATION: 23 Stat. 332

Banned employers from hiring workers in other countries and bringing into the United States under contracts. However, some categories of workers were exempted, such as actors, singers, domestic servants, and certain skilled laborers.

SCOTT ACT OF 1888
CITATION: 25 Stat. 476; 8 USC § 261-99

Refined the ban on Chinese immigration by disallowing Chinese laborers who had already been in the United States legally from returning after they left the country.

IMMIGRATION ACT OF 1891*
CITATION: 26 Stat. 1084; USC 101

Assigned responsibility for enforcing immigration policy to the federal government and centralized all immigration functions under the U.S. Immigration and Naturalization Service. The act also expanded the list of excludable and deportable aliens.

GEARY ACT OF 1892*

CITATION: 27 Stat. 25; 8 USC

Amended the Chinese Exclusion Act of 1882 by requiring all Chinese to have residential permits. The penalty for failing to abide by the act was deportation. This act was amended the following year by the McCreary Amendment.

McCREARY AMENDMENT OF 1893*

ALSO KNOWN AS: McCreary Act
CITATION: 28 Stat. 7

Amended the previous year's Geary Act and gave Chinese people living in the United States an additional six months to acquire residential permits.

IMMIGRATION ACT OF 1903*

CITATION: 32 Stat. 1213

Expanded the federal government's power to regulate immigration, codified immigration law, refined the existing classes of inadmissible immigrants, and added two new inadmissible classes: persons involved in prostitution and anarchists.

IMMIGRATION ACT OF 1907*

CITATION: 34 Stat. 1213

Created the Dillingham Commission to collect data used in future immigration laws, further narrowed Asian immigration, limited Muslim immigration, and expanded the definition of undesirable women immigrants. The law also allowed the U.S. president to detain immigrants if their entry into the country might be detrimental to American workers.

ESPIONAGE ACT OF 1917*

CITATION: 18 USC § 2388

Banned all speech and activities intended to harm the U.S. war effort in World War I.

IMMIGRATION ACT OF 1917*

CITATION: 39 Stat. 874

First federal law to impose a general restriction on immigration in the form of a literacy test. It also broadened restrictions on the immigration of Asians and persons deemed "undesirable" and provided tough enforcement provisions.

SEDITION ACT OF 1918*

CITATION: 18 USC § 2388

Strengthened the Espionage Act of 1917 by eliminating the element of intent required, thereby making it easier to prosecute offenders. Both laws were used to prosecute and deport immigrants judged to have written or spoken anything critical of the war effort. Repealed in 1920.

IMMIGRATION ACT OF 1921*

ALSO KNOWN AS: Johnson Act; Emergency Quota Act of 1921
CITATION: 42 Stat. 5

First federal law to limit immigration from Europe. By specifying that the number of people allowed to immigrate from any country during a year could be no greater than 3 percent of the number of people from the same country who had been living in the United States in 1910, the law had a particularly strong impact on immigration from southern and eastern Europe. Modified by the Immigration Act of 1924.

CABLE ACT OF 1922*

ALSO KNOWN AS: Married Woman's Act
CITATION: 42 Stat. 1021

Changed the status of married immigrant women so that not all of them would automatically obtain the citizenship of their husbands. The law had the effect of denying American citizenship to Asian women.

IMMIGRATION ACT OF 1924*

ALSO KNOWN AS: National Origins Act; Johnson-Reed Act; Asian Exclusion Act
CITATION: 43 Stat. 153

Created a quota system of determining eligibility to enter the United States legally by one's national origin. For Europeans and Africans, it allowed 2 percent of the number of people from each country who had been living in the United States in 1890 to enter. The law had the effect of favoring immigrants from northern and western Europe. Asian immigration was wholly banned. Repealed in law by the Immigration and Nationality Act of 1952 and in spirit by the Immigration and Nationality Act of 1965.

LABOR APPROPRIATION ACT OF 1924

CITATION: 8 USC § 1101

Created the U.S. Border Patrol as a federal law-enforcement agency.

FILIPINO REPATRIATION ACT OF 1935*

CITATION: 49 Stat. 478; 8-9 USC

Designed to send Filipino immigrants back to the Philippines, this law paid for their return passage but did not allow them reentry. In 1943, a small quota was given to the Philippines each year for immigration, and controls were loosened.

IMMIGRATION ACT OF 1943*

ALSO KNOWN AS: Magnuson Act; Chinese
    Exclusion Repeal Act
CITATION: 8 USC § 2040

Legalized Chinese immigration into the United States for the first time since 1882 but allowed only a small number each year. Effectively repealed by the Immigration and Nationality Act of 1965.

WAR BRIDES ACT OF 1945*

CITATION: 8 USC § 232

Enacted to facilitate the immigration of foreign spouses of Americans who served overseas during World War II, this law represented a change, not only in the number of immigrants allowed entry to the United States but also in the gender makeup of total immigration with far more women being allowed entry. It also allowed increased numbers of Asian immigrants entry into the United States.

FIANCÉES ACT OF 1946*

ALSO KNOWN AS: G.I. Fiancées Act
CITATION: 50 App. USC § 1851

Extension of the War Brides Act of 1945 that granted fiancés of American service personnel a special exemption from established immigration quotas.

LUCE-CELLER BILL OF 1946*

ALSO KNOWN AS: Immigration Act of 1946;
    Filipino Naturalization Act
CITATION: 60 Stat. 416

Overturned several decades of federal immigration laws that discriminated against specific Asian nationalities by reopening immigration from India and the Philippines and granting the right of naturalization to immigrants from those countries.

DISPLACED PERSONS ACT OF 1948*

CITATION: 50 App. USC § 1951

Enacted to facilitate the immigration of persons forcibly displaced from their homelands by World War II. Among the largest groups helped were Jewish refugees who had survived the Holocaust. The act also helped refugees from communist persecution during the Cold War.

McCARRAN INTERNAL SECURITY ACT OF 1950*

ALSO KNOWN AS: Subversive Activities Control Act
CITATION: 50 USC § 781

An outgrowth of anticommunist hysteria during the early Cold War. this law prohibited individuals who had ever been members of registered communist organizations from entering the United States. It also allowed for the deportation of communists and other individuals deemed subversive by the federal government.

IMMIGRATION AND NATIONALITY ACT OF 1952*

ALSO KNOWN AS: McCarran-Walter Act
CITATION: 8 USC § 1101

Significantly revamped the national origins system that had been in place since the 1920's. It abolished racial restrictions that had existed but retained bans on holders of certain ideologies. The law also combined all previous immigration restrictions into a single bill and created a preference system for immigrants. Replaced by the Immigration and Nationality Act of 1965.

REFUGEE RELIEF ACT OF 1953*

CITATION: 50 App. USC § 1971

Following the Displaced Persons Act of 1948, this law allowed anticommunist refugees entry into the United States under a special set of regulations. Ethnic Germans who had previously resided in non-German countries but who had been expelled after the collapse of Nazi Germany, war orphans, and members of military forces who had fought on the Allied side during World War II were also eligible for immigration to the United States under special quotas. With the exception of war orphans, these refugees had to prove that they would be subject to government persecution if they were not allowed to immigrate.

MUTUAL EDUCATIONAL AND CULTURAL EXCHANGE ACT OF 1961

CITATION: 22 USC § 2454

Permitted cultural exchanges between the United States and other countries with an eye toward promoting greater understanding on the part of participating nations.

IMMIGRATION AND NATIONALITY ACT OF 1965*

ALSO KNOWN AS: Hart-Celler Act

CITATION: 8 USC § 1101

Technically a revision of the Immigration and Nationality Act of 1952, this landmark law removed the national origins quotas that had existed since the 1920's, replacing them with hemispheric limits. The new limits were accompanied by a preference system that favored spouses, immigrants related to persons already living in the United States, and certain skilled workers.

BILINGUAL EDUCATION ACT OF 1968*

ALSO KNOWN AS: Title VII of the Elementary and Secondary Education Act of 1965

CITATION: 20 USC § 1703

First federal law to address the special educational needs of students with limited English-speaking ability by providing funding to school districts to develop bilingual education programs.

INDOCHINA MIGRATION AND REFUGEE ASSISTANCE ACT OF 1975*

CITATION: 22 USC § 2601

Established a resettlement assistance program for Southeast Asian refugees and allowed the United States to join the International Organization for Migration.

AMERASIAN IMMIGRATION ACT OF 1982

CITATION: 8 USC § 1151

Provided an immigration preference to the Amerasian children of American soldiers who had fathered them during the Vietnam War. Amended in 1988 by the Amerasian Homecoming Act.

IMMIGRATION REFORM AND CONTROL ACT OF 1986*

ALSO KNOWN AS: Simpson-Mazzoli Act; Simpson-Rodino Act; IRCA

CITATION: 8 USC § 1324a

First federal law to impose sanctions on employers who hired undocumented immigrants, while also providing amnesty for undocumented aliens already in the country.

AMERASIAN HOMECOMING ACT OF 1987*

CITATION: 8 USC § 1151

Built on the Amerasian Immigration Act of 1982, this law made it easier for children of American military personnel who had served in the Vietnam War to come to the United States.

CIVIL LIBERTIES ACT OF 1988

CITATION: 50 USC § 1989

Provided for reparations for persons of Japanese heritage who had been interned during World War II. It provided up to twenty thousand dollars for each person who had been forcibly resettled and also allowed for those who had been convicted for offenses related to their internment to have their convictions reviewed for possible pardons.

IMMIGRATION ACT OF 1990*

CITATION: 8 USC § 1101

Significantly eased restrictions on immigration in what has been seen as a return to the old open-door immigration policy. In additional to allowing an increase in the numbers of immigrants, the law waived many rules previously used to exclude immigrants.

CHINESE STUDENT PROTECTION ACT OF 1992*

CITATION: 8 USC § 1255

Permitted Chinese students and scholars to remain in the United States and apply for permanent residency.

IMMIGRATION AND NATIONALITY TECHNICAL CORRECTIONS ACT OF 1994

CITATION: 8 USC § 1448

Dropped requirement that immigrants swear they would stay in the United States permanently when they naturalized as citizens. The law also disallowed taking away citizenship from naturalized citizens who did not spend enough time in the United States.

ILLEGAL IMMIGRATION REFORM AND IMMIGRANT RESPONSIBILITY ACT OF 1996*

ALSO KNOWN AS: IIRIRA
CITATION: 8 USC § 1631

Designed to reduce illegal immigration, the law created waiting periods for prospective immigrants to remain outside the United States after they were found to have entered the country illegally. The law also made deportation processes easier.

INTERCOUNTRY ADOPTION ACT OF 2000

CITATION: 42 USC § 14901

Enacted to implement the Hague Convention on Protection of Children and Co-operation in Respect of Intercountry Adoption, this convention was adopted to regulate adoption practices and prevent child trafficking. It also aimed to ensure that the interests of the children themselves are adequately addressed.

AVIATION AND TRANSPORTATION SECURITY ACT OF 2001*

CITATION: 49 USC § 40101

Established the Transportation Security Administration (TSA) to enforce security in transportation systems throughout the United States, with particular emphasis on airport security.

PATRIOT ACT OF 2001*

ALSO KNOWN AS: Uniting and Strengthening America by Providing Appropriate Tools Required to Intercept and Obstruct Terrorism Act (USA PATRIOT Act)
CITATION: 8 USC § 1189

Passed in the wake of the September 11, 2001, attacks on New York City and Washington, D.C., this law significantly expanded the ability of U.S. Citizenship and Immigration Services (USCIS) to investigate immigrants with terrorist ties by giving the USCIS greater access to intelligence information regarding terrorist suspects. The act also made it more difficult for non-U.S. citizens to gain citizenship, visas, permanent residency, and work permits.

ENHANCED BORDER SECURITY AND VISA REFORM ACT OF 2002

CITATION: 8 USC § 1701

Designed to increase border and gateway security, this law required that fingerprints be collected from more people and more stringent visa requirements be met. It also created stricter requirements for foreign students studying in the United States.

Scott A. Merriman

FILMOGRAPHY

America, America (1963): Directed by Elia Kazan, this film is based on the life of Kazan's uncle Stavros, a Greek youth living in the Ottoman Empire during the late nineteenth century. He is sent to Constantinople, Turkey, because his family believes he will have a better life, but he dreams only of coming to America. Stavros eventually immigrates to New York, where his family and young nephew Elia later join him. Some little-known history, the plight of the minority Greeks within the Ottoman Empire, is spotlighted. These people, along with members of the empire's other ethnic minorities, such as the Armenians, were severely discriminated against in their home countries. Many thousands found emigration their only hope for better lives. The Academy Award-winning Ottoman-born director Kazan was himself a shining example of a successful adjustment to a new country.

An American Tail (1986): By means of clever animation, the journey of an immigrant from Russia to the United States is sometimes amusingly—but often darkly—portrayed in this film directed by Don Bluth. In a parody of the immigrant belief that the streets of America were paved with gold, a mouse named Fievel Mousekewitz believes that there are no cats in the United States, whose streets are paved with cheese. However, Fievel discovers that cats (stand-ins for murderous Cossacks in Russia) are, in fact, present in his new country, though they now represent other kinds of adversaries. The fact that this film is animated makes it no less illustrative of the hardships, including poverty and discrimination, that Jews and other immigrants encountered when they came to America.

Avalon (1990): Directed by Barry Levinson, this film realistically portrays the tensions created by the gradual disintegration of a once close-knit nuclear family after it immigrates to America. A Russian Jewish family that has immigrated to Baltimore during the early part of the twentieth century begins to drift apart over time, despite the efforts of its stern and increasingly unyielding patriarch to keep it together. He finds his control over the family is dissipating as younger members adopt values that he cannot accept. In his view, they have become too Americanized. His desire to retain the values of his native land creates tensions with his descendants, who no longer want to obey their elders or live in the way their parents wish them to live.

The Betrayal (*Nerakhoon*) (2008): This Oscar-nominated documentary that took more than twenty years to bring to the screen depicts a Laotian family fleeing their homeland after the father was arrested by Laos's communist government for helping the American military during its Vietnam War-era clandestine operations. Ultimately, the man's wife and ten children make their way to a United States that they have been led to believe is "one step away from heaven." However, they find that their hoped-for refuge is a dangerous and divisive place for their family. Their first home in Brooklyn is adjacent to a crack house. The film presents a convincing picture of how culture shock can affect an immigrant family. One of the sons (the codirector of the film, Thavisouk Phrasavath) worries that "in living in America we are losing ourselves."

The Black Legion (1937): A blue-collar machinist (Humphrey Bogart) becomes enraged when a Polish immigrant gets the foreman job that he wants. He joins an anti-immigrant hate group called the Black Legion—modeled on the Ku Klux Klan—that terrorizes the immigrant and his family into leaving town. Eventually the xenophobic machinist's involvement in this organization leads to his own downfall. This exciting Warner Bros. film tackles the consequences of anti-immigrant prejudice in the hard-hitting, gritty style for which the studio was famous during the 1930's.

The Border (1982): Over the years, a border guard (Jack Nicholson) has grown callous about the treatment of Mexican immigrants attempting to cross the border illegally. He gradually regains his humanity in the face of a young Mexican woman's tragedy. A realistic and sensitive depiction of the vast problems faced by both sides in what is frequently an immigration nightmare, the film shows how immigrants frequently rely on paid "coyotes" to get them across the border undetected. They are sometimes injured or killed in the attempt. Faced with a torrent of undocumented immigrants, border guards struggle to retain their humanity and accomplish a most difficult job at the same time.

Born in East L.A. (1987): A native-born Mexican American (Cheech Marin) is caught up in a raid on a factory by immigration authorities and is sent to Mexico when he cannot prove his U.S. citizenship. His attempts to return to the United States are dealt with largely through comic means, including his inability to speak Spanish. During his struggle to return he finds solace in helping Mexican nationals seeking to enter the United States and learns that the apparent ethnicity of persons is frequently the basis for how others judge them. Although basically a comedy, the film is also a poignant account of the protagonist's growing understanding of the tribulations that immigrants face. *See also full essay in main text.*

Bread and Roses (2000): Two sisters from Latin America who are in Los Angeles illegally are victimized in their workplace by being denied decent wages, working conditions, and benefits. They lead an attempt to unionize cleaning women and janitors in the face of mounting threats from exploitive managers. There is the ever-present threat of being denounced to *la migra* (the immigration authorities) and being deported, but they continue their struggle. Although a fictionalized treatment, the film is realistic in its account of how immigrants, particularly those who do not possess the "papers" to live legally in the United States, are often exploited.

Catfish in Black Bean Sauce (1999): An African American couple adopts a Vietnamese brother and sister. The boy assimilates quickly into his new milieu, but his sister misses the home she knew as a child and contacts their tradition-bound birth mother. When the mother arrives in the United States, she attempts to reassert her authority over her children. As the film's symbolic title suggests, admixtures of cultures may sometimes result in different cultures blending easily. However, in this case the mix does not prove to be so easy. The Vietnamese mother's arrival shows the discomfited adoptive parents just how wide ethnic differences can be.

Crossing Over (2009): A veritable laundry list of immigration-related issues is dealt with in the several plot lines of this film. Immigrants of different nationalities experience problems ranging from obtaining green cards to seeking political asylum and experiencing culture clashes. The work of customs and immigration officials (one played by Harrison Ford) is portrayed both sympathetically and unsympathetically.

A Day Without a Mexican (2004): Although this is a broad comic satire that sometimes misses the mark, it is nonetheless thought provoking. One day Californians awaken to find they can neither communicate beyond the state's borders nor leave California. They then discover that all the Mexicans have vanished from the state, leaving the state's economy to grind to a halt. Only then do Californians appreciate what Mexican laborers and professionals—both legal and undocumented—have contributed to their lives.

El Norte (1983): A Guatemalan brother and sister undergo a harrowing trek to the United States as illegal immigrants after their village is destroyed by a government that seeks to destroy the native Indian population. The siblings make their way with the help of "coyotes" (smugglers). After a journey that includes crawling through a rat-infested tunnel, they arrive in the United States. At first, it appears the illiterate pair will succeed in the United States against considerable odds; however, they ultimately endure tragedy. This is a powerful film that graphically depicts the hazards to undocumented aliens of both reaching the United States and what may happen after they arrive. Directed by Gregory Nava, the film was selected by the Library of Congress as part of its prestigious National Film Registry.

Ellis Island (1984): With the effective support of such high-powered actors as Richard Burton, Liam Neeson, and Faye Dunaway, this appealing television miniseries follows the saga of four immigrants from the turn of the twentieth century through World War I. An Italian, a Russian Jew, and two Irish sisters all experience dire poverty and eventually rise to lead successful lives, but at what cost? Although sometimes melodramatic, the program shows the sacrifices and struggles that immigrants endure to succeed in a strange country, even if they have to compromise some of their "old country" values.

The Emigrants (*Utvandrarna*) (1971) and *The New Land* (*Nybyggarna*) (1972): Together, these masterfully produced Swedish films encompass the saga of a family's life in Sweden and subsequent emigration to the United States. Both star the distinguished actors Max Von Sydow and Liv Ullmann. *The Emigrants* depicts the family's bare existence on a small Swedish farm during the 1850's until hunger finally forces them to emigrate. After a grueling ten-week voyage on a sailing ship, they reach America and establish themselves on the unforgiving Minnesota prairie. In *The New Land* they find life has improved for them, but hard times, including family tragedies, continue to be their lot. Directed by Jan Troell, the beautifully photographed films are almost epochal in their portrayal of the lives of poor immigrant farmers striving to cope with life in a strange country.

Far and Away (1992): Directed by Ron Howard, this occasionally improbable film depicts the hardships that a pair of immigrants (Tom Cruise and Nicole Kidman) undergo to realize their dreams in the United States. The hopelessness of his life impels a poor Irish tenant farmer to emigrate during the 1890's. However, even after he is settled in Boston, he remains mired in poverty. Ultimately, his lifelong dream to possess his own land leads him to the Oklahoma land rush of 1893. With a sometimes epic sweep, the film tries to encapsulate much of the immigrant saga, effectively utilizing the landscapes of Ireland and the American Southwest.

Forbidden Passage (1941): An entry in MGM's popular *Crime Does Not Pay* series, this Oscar-nominated short film purports to show how the Immigration and Naturalization Service strove to put a halt to the illegal smuggling of immigrants from Europe before the United States entered World War II. A boatload of European refugees is being smuggled to Florida via Central America. (One their number is played by Hugh Beaumont of *Leave It to Beaver* fame.) When the ship is challenged by American customs officials, the villainous smugglers toss many of the immigrants overboard to drown. Although it is melodramatic, the film documents a little-remembered aspect of World War II: the desperate efforts of many Europeans to escape the war and reach the United States.

Gangs of New York (2002): The slums of mid-nineteenth century New York are colorfully reproduced by director Martin Scorsese in this highly charged story of gang warfare between native-born New Yorkers and Irish immigrants, which stars Leonardo DiCaprio, Daniel Day Lewis, and Liam Neeson. It begins in 1846, during one of the peaks of anti-immigrant sentiment in the United States, and concludes almost twenty years later during the U.S. Civil War. It records the violence that was often used against immigrants by so-called nativists who feared, among other things, the economic impact of the new arrivals.

The Gatekeeper (2002): A racist border guard is frequently brutal with the undocumented immigrants he deals with at the border with Mexico. He even joins a vigilante group that is involved in drug activities. Eventually he reconnects with his own unacknowledged Hispanic heritage and realizes that the immigrants are as much human beings as he is. The film depicts the sometimes deplorable treatment of undocumented immigrants by "coyote" smugglers and border guards. Directed by John Carlos Frey, who also wrote the film's script and played the lead role.

The Girl Who Spelled Freedom (1986): A Cambodian immigrant girl finds personal success in the United States when she becomes a champion in school spelling bees. Her family, having survived Cambodia's horrific communist regime, was sponsored to immigrate to the United States. The family's older members find it difficult to adjust and learn English, but the children thrive in a free environment. This television drama may be somewhat sentimental, but its portrayal of immigrant children working ceaselessly to succeed rings true.

The Godfather (1972), *The Godfather, Part 2* (1974), and *The Godfather, Part 3* (1990): This trilogy offers a sweeping epic of the American immigrant dream perverted. *The Godfather* and its first sequel, *The Godfather Part 2*, delve into the lives of Italian immigrant Vito Corleone and his three sons (played by James Caan, Al Pacino, and John Cazale). Vito Corleone (Marlon Brando in the first *Godfather* and Robert De Niro in *Part 2*) immigrates to the United States from Italy and after many years becomes a top crime figure. He continues to adhere to the so-called "honor" code he has brought from his native country, but it eventually leads to his family's destruction.

Part 2 shifts back and forth in time, between the periods preceding and following the narrative of the first film. Beginning in 1901, it shows young Vito's arrival at Ellis Island, his first years as a poor immigrant in Manhattan's Little Italy, and his ultimate rise to power. *Part 3* depicts the downfall of the dynasty with the lonely demise of Michael Corleone (Al Pacino), Vito's youngest son, in Italy. The family history has now come full circle. The impact of the first two films is stunningly dramatic; they have been aptly compared to the Greek tragedies. One of the most powerful aspects is the irony that America has opened its doors to a friendless immigrant and he repays the boon by unloosing murder and corruption on his adoptive country. *See also full essay in main text.*

The Golden Venture (2006): This documentary film deals with a subject not often seen on theater screens. In 1993, the ironically named ship *Golden Venture* went aground near New York City and was found to be carrying 276 Chinese men trying to enter the United States illegally. They had each paid at least $30,000 to be smuggled into the United States. Possibly because this incident occurred shortly after the first World Trade Center bombing, the Immigration and Naturalization Service (INS) seemed particularly punitive in this case. Some of the passengers were detained for up to four years or deported back to China to face unknown fates. The film is not objective, but it does provoke viewers to think about the fairness of American immigration policy.

Gran Torino (2008): When a curmudgeonly Korean War veteran (Clint Eastwood, who also directed) sees his Michigan city become a haven for Hmong immigrants from Southeast Asia, all his prejudices come to the fore. He believes that these newcomers and their "strange" customs have no place not only in his neighborhood, but also in the United States. When the immigrants try to befriend him, he responds with racial epithets. A crisis finally brings him to the realization that his neighbors share a common humanity. Although the film is somewhat far-fetched at times, it deals with an immigrant group that is not often in the spotlight, and it respectfully depicts the culture of their native regions.

Green Card (1990): An obstacle facing many immigrants who wish to reside in the United States is obtaining the "green card" that legally sanctions their residency. One such would-be immigrant's challenge is presented in this hit romantic comedy directed by Peter Weir. A Frenchman (Gérard Depardieu) is offered a job in the United States; to get his green card so he can take that job, he fraudulently marries an American woman (Andie MacDowell). The woman has her own reason for marrying him: renting an apartment that is available only to married couples. The INS becomes rightfully suspicious of the marriage, and complications ensue while the couple actually do fall in love with each other. *See also full essay in main text.*

Green Card Fever (2003): In this small-budget version of 1990's popular *Green Card*, a young man from India has overstayed his visa and is seeking a wife so he can obtain a green card to remain in the United States. After tangling with shady immigration lawyers and the INS, he finds true romance with an American woman of Indian heritage.

Hester Street (1975): Films depicting the Jewish immigrant experience were relatively rare when this picture was made. Set around the turn of the twentieth century, it shows the growing division between an Americanized immigrant (Steven Keats) and his newly arrived "greenhorn" wife (Carol Kane), who retains the ways of Russia. It realistically depicts the tensions that develop in the marriage when neither partner seems willing to get used to the "foreign" ways of the other—an apparently common occurrence in immigrant communities of that era.

House of Sand and Fog (2003): This poignant, highly dramatic film depicts the results of an extreme clash of cultures precipitated when a proud Iranian immigrant (Ben Kingsley) buys the home of a woman (Jennifer Connolly) who has lost it because of unpaid taxes. The man's cultural upbringing leads him to treat her problem as unimportant. She, in turn, lacks understanding of the immigrant's desire to better his life. This conflict leads to a denouement of almost Greek tragedy proportions. Enhancing the drama is a strong undercurrent of anti-immigrant prejudice. Shoureh Aghdashoo, who plays the immigrant's wife, was nominated for an Academy Award for her performance.

I Remember Mama (1948): A warmhearted and memorable film about a family of Norwegian immigrants living in San Francisco around the year 1910, starring Irene Dunne as the indomitable matriarch of the film's title and ventriloquist Edgar Bergen. The film's strength lies mainly in the portrayal of Mama's daily struggle to keep her family financially afloat while coping with the inevitable generational differences that are developing. This feel-good film led to an equally popular television series. *See also full essay in main text.*

The Immigrant (1917): Charles Chaplin starred in and directed this famous comedy short, which mixes slapstick comedy and sentimentality in equal measures. A bedraggled group of apparently eastern European immigrants is approaching the Statue of Liberty on a tub-like ship that is fiercely pitching and rolling. Chaplin's tramp character helps a young woman and her mother; over the course of the film, he falls in love with the younger woman. Although played for comedy, the portrayal of the distressed passengers seems quite authentic, given that the great wave of immigration had ebbed not many years before the film was made. Chaplin himself had immigrated from England only a few years earlier so was undoubtedly empathetic in his sensitive handling of the immigrants' plight. *See also full essay in main text.*

In America (2002): Many films depict Irish immigrants from earlier times; this is one of the few set in the modern era. An actor who hopes to work in the United States and his family enter the United States from Canada illegally. Already riven by family tragedy, they end up in a run-down tenement and are befriended by an African immigrant. They initially instinctively fear this man but eventually come to recognize they have a great deal in common with him as fellow strangers in a strange land. Directed by the well-respected Irishman Jim Sheridan.

The Joy Luck Club (1993): Based on the bestselling novel of the same title by Amy Tan, this film examines the generation gap between parents who have immigrated from China and their American-born offspring in San Francisco. Exacerbating the usual generational stresses between mothers and daughters is the elders' insistence that the children adhere to the rigid Chinese customs that they have brought with them. An ultimately positive portrait, it nevertheless is a sharp-eyed look at what happens when old-country mores clash with American culture.

Lana's Rain (2004): This small, independent film depicts the dark side of an immigrant's American dream. To escape the war raging in Bosnia during the mid-1990's, a brother and sister stow away on a ship and settle in Chicago illegally. Because their undocumented status prevents them from working in the open, they turn to crime, including prostitution, to survive. The only minimally bright spot is their friendship with a Chinese immigrant with whom they can barely communicate.

Lost Boys of Sudan (2003): A well-received documentary film that records the improbable saga of two young orphaned Sudanese boys as they transition from life in a war-torn country to suburban America. After surviving a cross-country trek in Africa of hundreds of miles, a lion attack, and rogue militias, the boys join thousands of other children in a refugee camp. It is from there that the boys are chosen to immigrate to Houston, Texas, and eventually separate. The culture of their new country is so alien to them that they face unanticipated problems, including racial discrimination.

Made in L.A. (2007): Like *Bread and Roses*, this film concerns three Latina immigrants working under sweatshop conditions in Los Angeles; however, it is a documentary about their struggle for workplace improvements. The three women labor in a factory that makes clothing for an up-market retailer that exploits its employees. One of the film's major strengths is its intimate depiction of each woman and the changes each undergoes during their fight for better working conditions.

Mississippi Masala (1992): When a well-off Indian family is expelled from Uganda by dictator Idi Amin during the 1970's, they immigrate to a Mississippi town to start over. Among their problems is acculturating to a southern society that regards them as merely another undesirable minority—the same attitude they had faced in East

Africa. When the daughter falls in love with an African American working man (Denzel Washington), many forms of prejudice come out into the open.

The Molly Maguires (1970): During the mid-1870's, a secret society of Irish immigrant coal miners, whose ringleader is played by Sean Connery, deal with exploitative mine owners by sabotaging the mines. Another Irish immigrant is sent to infiltrate the group and bring them to justice. The question is whether he will carry out his assignment or fall in with the saboteurs. Based on events that actually occurred in the Pennsylvania coalfields.

Moscow on the Hudson (1984): Robin Williams plays a Russian circus musician who defects in a New York department store while the circus is on an American tour. Aided by some unlikely friends, he eventually attempts to establish a musical career in New York. His life after he defects is better than it was in Russia but far from what he dreamed it might be.

My Boy (1921): A young boy (Jackie Coogan) is orphaned when his mother dies on the ship bringing them to New York as immigrants. He escapes deportation when he is accidentally released from Ellis Island with another family group. After being tracked down by his wealthy grandmother and helped by sympathetic immigration officials, he eventually finds happiness. This film is interesting for its portrayal of Ellis Island during the second decade of the twentieth century, when the last major wave of European immigration was coming to a close.

My Family/Mi Familia (1995): Directed by Gregory Nava and featuring actors Jennifer Lopez and Jimmy Smits, this film follows the lives of three generations of Mexican Americans living in the barrios of East Los Angeles, beginning with the grandparents, who immigrate during the 1930's and immediately encounter the anti-immigrant prejudices of that time.

My Girl Tisa (1948): In 1905, a young Hungarian immigrant (Lilli Palmer) works in a New York garment factory to earn enough money to bring her father to the United States. Her boss is studying for his citizenship test. When the girl's deportation is ordered, no less a personage than President Theodore Roosevelt steps in to save her. Although it contains some dramatic license, this little-known film provides a fairly realistic look at the daily lives of poor immigrants in turn-of-the-century New York.

The Namesake (2006): Lavishly produced, this absorbing film is based on a bestselling novel of the same title by Jhumpa Lahiri. Following an arranged marriage, two young immigrants from India settle in the United States and have a son whose nickname is Gogol. The story then focuses on Gogol's attempts at being completely American. His priorities shift with the death of his father and reel him back into his parents' first-generation experience. The film ends ambiguously, however, as Gogol's traditional marriage falls apart, clearly demonstrating that he cannot find his footing in either culture.

Picture Bride (1994): During the late nineteenth and early twentieth centuries, thousands of Japanese women came to Hawaii and the United States to marry Japanese men they had never seen. In this film, a young women arrives in Hawaii to discover that her intended husband is much older and poorer than he has led her to believe in his letter. She spends a long time trying to save enough money to return to Japan before realizing that her new life might work out after all. This is an interesting portrayal of an aspect of immigration history that is seldom portrayed onscreen.

Popi (1969): This heartwarming film gently satirizes U.S. immigration policies of the late 1960's. A Puerto Rican father (Alan Arkin) struggles to make a bare living for his two young sons. Upon hearing how well refugees from Cuba are being treated in the United States, he arranges to have his sons pose as Cubans who have been washed ashore, hoping they will be showered with American bounty. When the real-life Cuban refugee Elián González made news some thirty years later, the similarities of his case to the story of *Popi* were remarked upon.

Saved (2009): A young man who is being held in detention by the INS claims to be an Iranian who was persecuted in his own country. He is seeking asylum, but U.S. immigration authorities are suspicious of his claim and are ready to deport him. He is finally released to a young couple willing to sponsor him but who themselves begin to doubt his story. This television drama, while tending to the melodramatic, does illustrate the seemingly hopeless binds in which many immigrants find themselves when they cannot prove their status.

Sentenced Home (2007): Cambodians are not often featured on American film screens. This compelling documentary follows three Cambodian youths who are brought to the United States during the 1980's as permanent residents in the wake of the massacres by their homeland's communist government. Because they become involved in minor crimes, the INS deports two of them, as the third fights to remain in the United States. Their stories make for a riveting film that is ultimately critical of American immigration policies.

Sewing Woman (1983): In this Oscar-nominated short documentary film, filmmakers Arthur and Lisa Dong recount their mother's difficult journey from a village in rural China to the garment factories of San Francisco. Her arduous experiences with both Chinese authorities upon her departure and the U.S. immigration authorities on her arrival are related, as well as her attempts to cope with the culture of a strange country. The incorporation of rare home movies and footage of rural China and San Francisco's Chinatown combine to make this a noteworthy film that has remained highly regarded.

The Stars Are Singing (1953): Italian singer Anna Maria Alberghetti plays a Polish girl who jumps ship to enter the United States illegally. As INS officers search for her, she finds sanctuary with an opera singer (Lauritz Melchior) and a pop vocalist (Rosemary Clooney). However, just as she receives her first big break, she is discovered by the immigration authorities and is threatened with deportation back to communist Poland. This tune-filled film is a rare musical film with an immigration theme.

Strangers in a Promised Land (1984): Narrated by former California governor George Deukmejian, himself of Armenian descent, this hour-long documentary traces Armenian settlement in Fresno, California, through the previous century. Beginning with the first Armenians to arrive in Fresno during the 1880's, the film effectively depicts their initial hardships, including contending with prejudice, and their eventual realization of the American Dream.

Sweet Land (2005): A young German mail-order bride arrives in Minnesota in 1919 to marry a Norwegian farmer who does not know her background. When he and other members of their small community discover her nationality, the marriage is jeopardized as the woman becomes a victim of the antipathy toward Germans following World War I. This beautifully photographed and poignant film deals with an era and a situation not often pictured onscreen.

Telling Lies in America (1997): A teenage Hungarian immigrant to Cleveland (Brad Renfro) is having problems adjusting to American culture during the 1970's, so he models himself on a popular but unscrupulous radio disc jockey (Kevin Bacon) to appear "cool" to his peers. Eventually, he realizes that he is on the wrong track. This is an unusual but sometimes worthwhile look at the problem of acculturation.

The Terminal (2004): Steven Spielberg directed this film about an early twenty-first century man (Tom Hanks) who is suddenly and literally a man without a country. When he arrives at a New York airport he learns that his unnamed eastern European country no longer exists. This fact voids his passport, so he cannot enter the United States. However, because he cannot be deported anywhere, he appears to be doomed to remain at the airport forever. This is a thought-provoking film about the nature of citizenship and, in somewhat exaggerated fashion, mirrors the plight of some immigrants who can spend years in legal limbo.

Under the Same Moon (*La Misma Luna*) (2007): The depiction of the dislocation and heartbreak caused by family separation and unfeeling immigration policy is the major strength of this film. A Mexican woman is working illegally in the United States as a housecleaner. Her young son crosses the border illegally, after several misadventures, to find her. They are under the "same moon" but may as well be a million miles apart.

The Visitor (2007): A college professor (Richard Jenkins) finds an undocumented couple—a Syrian man and a Senegalese woman—living in his seldom-visited New York apartment. At first indifferent to their plight, he eventually befriends and tries to help them. However, he is unable to keep the young man from being deported by the immigration authorities. This film has a very definite viewpoint in its portrayal of U.S. Citizenship and Immigration Services as a cold and bureaucratic institution unmoved by humane considerations. Jenkins received an Oscar nomination for his performance.

West Side Story (1961): Adapted from a Broadway musical loosely based on William Shakespeare's play *Romeo and Juliet* (1595-1596), this Oscar-winning film revolves around the rivalry of two New York City street gangs—the Anglo-American Jets and the Puerto Rican Sharks. Tensions between the gangs become lethal at the same time Tony (Richard Beymer) a former member of the Jets is falling in love with Maria (Natalie Wood), the sister of the Sharks leader who is recently arrived from Puerto Rico. The film pays considerable attention to the challenges faced by Puerto Rican immigrants, whose love-hate relationship with the United States is given a poignant musical voice in "America," a call-and-response song in which multiple characters compare life in America with life in Puerto Rico. The film's ten Oscars included best picture and a best-supporting-actress award for Rita Moreno, who is herself a Puerto Rican immigrant.

Roy Liebman

BIBLIOGRAPHY OF GENERAL WORKS ON IMMIGRATION

1. GENERAL STUDIES

Alba, Richard, and Victor Nee. *Remaking the Mainstream: Assimilation and Contemporary Immigration*. Cambridge, Mass.: Harvard University Press, 2003. Compares the experiences of immigrants of the late nineteenth century European and East Asian wave of immigrants and the late twentieth century wave of Latin Americans and Asians, and West Indians.

Aneesh, A. *Virtual Migration: The Programming of Globalization*. Durham, N.C.: Duke University Press, 2006. Defines virtual immigration as the flow of software information to replace actual migration of people. Explores practical and theoretical ramifications of virtual migration.

Baron, Dennis. *The English-Only Question: An Official Language for Americans?* New Haven, Conn.: Yale University Press, 1991. Traces the history of why the United States has never had an official English-language policy, although immigrants must take an English test. Points out that statehood was generally withheld from territories until their populations contained English-speaking majorities, with the exception of Louisiana. Finds that many immigrants are not being served adequately by American schools and concludes that a constitutional amendment cannot force people to adopt English if they are unwilling or unable to do so.

Beasley, Vanessa. *Who Belongs in America? Presidents, Rhetoric, and Immigration*. College Station: Texas A&M Press, 2006. Asks why early immigrants were lionized as the foundations of American character, while modern immigrants have been demonized as threats to national stability and safety. Also explores how U.S. presidents have dealt with immigration issues.

Beck, Roy. *The Case Against Immigration*. New York: W. W. Norton, 1996. Presents the moral, economic, social, and environmental reasons for advocating the reduction of U.S. immigration back to earlier levels. Argues that America needs substantially fewer than 100,000 immigrants a year.

Geyer, Georgia Anne. *Americans No More*. New York: Atlantic Monthly Press, 1996. Exposes practices and policies, some following the enactment of the Immigration Act of 1990, "the most comprehensive reform of our immigration laws in sixty-six years," that demonstrate how far America has strayed from its origins. Most notably, cites the new 1986 citizenship test and the naturalization process, while holding out hope that measures will be taken to preserve the best of the past, the present, and the future.

Golab, Caroline. *Immigrant Destinations*. Philadelphia: Temple University Press, 1977. Attempts to account for the geographic distribution of immigrants to the United States from 1870 to 1920, the period of their greatest influx. Focuses on Philadelphia and analyzes the forces that accounted for the city's immigrant population.

Hoskin, Marilyn. *New Immigrants and Democratic Society: Minority Integration in Western Democracies*. Westport, Conn.: Praeger, 1991. Discusses public opinion about new immigrants as well as economic, social, and political factors associated with immigration.

Kennedy, John F. *A Nation of Immigrants*. New York: Harper & Row, 1964. Traces the history of immigration to the United States and provides a chronology of immigration from 1607 to 1963.

Lansford, Jennifer, Kirby Deater-Deckard, and Marc H. Bornstein, eds. *Immigrant Families in Contemporary Society*. New York: Guilford Press, 2007. Discusses the family circumstances and health of children in immigrant families and their development of ethnic identity and acculturation. Essays on various aspects of educational development among immigrants and the role of law as it affects American concepts viewed differently in other cultures.

Levitt, Peggy, and Mary C. Waters, eds. *The Changing Face of Home: The Transnational Lives of the Second Generation*. New York: Russell Sage Foundation, 2002. The first part of this book addresses the content, meaning, and consequences of transnational practices of the second generation of immigrants. Writers in the second part suggest ways of bridging the transnational divide, and those in the third part analyze the second-generation experience.

Long, Robert Emmet, ed. *Immigration to the U.S.* New York: H. W. Wilson, 1992. Collection of articles addressing issues affecting refugees from the Caribbean, Central America, and Vietnam. Contains a section on immigration policy.

Meissner, Doris, Deborah W. Meyers, Demetrios G. Papademetriou, and Michael Fix. *Immigration and America's Future: A New Chapter.* Washington, D.C.: Migration Policy Institute, 2006. Asks and responds to such questions about immigration as why it is important, what is wrong with policy and practice, how the United States may attract the kinds of immigrants it needs, and how to enforce existing immigration laws.

Portes, Alejandro, and Rubén G. Rumbaut. *Immigrant America: A Portrait.* 2d ed. Berkeley: University of California Press, 1996. Discusses origins of immigrants and motives for immigrating; continues with patterns of settlement, occupational and economic adaptation, ethnic identity and political participation, mental health and acculturation, and language and education. Concludes with a chapter on immigration and public policy.

Riley, Jason L. *Let Them In: The Case for Open Borders.* New York: Gotham Books, 2008. Offers rebuttals to anti-immigrationists and argues for a practice of regulating cross-border labor flows, rather than stopping them, and maintains that the United States has more to gain than to lose from immigrants seeking better lives.

Williamson, Chilton, Jr. *The Immigration Mystique: America's False Conscience.* New York: Basic Books, 1996. Develops the thesis that America's immigration problem is better addressed by insights from moral and religious philosophy, from history and international relations, and from the science of ecology than from economics and politics.

Wright, Russell O. *The Chronology of Immigration in the United States.* London: McFarland, 2008. Traces the chronology of immigration issues from 1607 to 2007. Two appendixes show immigration data by decade and by period and source. Appendixes on key immigration legislation, the bracero program, immigration and population, and eugenics and the Immigration Act of 1924.

2. REFERENCE SOURCES

Bankston, Carl L., III, and Danielle Antoinette Hidalgo, eds. *Immigration in U.S. History.* 2 vols. Pasadena, Calif.: Salem Press, 2006. Wide-ranging collection of articles on immigration, with particular emphasis on culture and intergroup relations.

Bayor, Ronald H. *The Columbia Documentary History of Race and Ethnicity in America.* New York: Columbia University Press, 2004. Documents the history of immigration in the United States. Each of eight chronologically organized chapters provides a survey essay, an annotated bibliography, and a number of source documents.

Blake, Barbara. *A Guide to Children's Books About Asian Americans.* Hants, England: Scolar Press, 1995. Gives some historical background on the Chinese, Filipino, Japanese, Asian Indian, Korean, and Vietnamese. Organizes recommended books according to genre and age or grade. Appendixes provide listings by author, title, culture, genre, and grade level.

Fellows, Donald Keith. *A Mosaic of Ethnic Minorities.* New York: John Wiley & Sons, 1972. Historical and cultural background for African American, Mexican, Chinese, Japanese, and Puerto Rican immigrants. Discussion of the imprint and future of each of these groups. Review and discussion topics.

Hoglund, A. William. *Immigrants and Their Children in the United States: A Bibliography of Doctoral Dissertations, 1885-1982.* New York: Garland, 1986. Listing of 3,543 dissertations from all disciplines dealing with aspects of immigrants and their children who have come to the United States. An appendix lists another 64 dissertations that treat ethnic groups that came to the United States before 1789. Index of ethnic and nationality groups.

Hyman, Paula E., and Deborah Dash Moore. *Jewish Women in America: An Historical Encyclopedia.* 2 vols. New York: Routledge, 1997. Biographical sketches of the lives, experiences, and achievements of Jewish women in the United States. Photographs and bibliography.

Lee, Kenneth K. *Huddled Masses, Muddled Laws: Why Contemporary Immigration Policy Fails to Reflect Public Opinion.* Westport, Conn.: Praeger, 1998. Attempt objectively to analyze why United States immigration policy no long reflected public opinion, as it had done before the mid-1960's.

Mageli, Paul D. *The Immigrant Experience: An Annotated Bibliography.* Pasadena, Calif.: Salem Press,

1991. Following entries on general studies, Mageli organizes this bibliography by motives; difficulties of immigration; repatriation and re-migration; immigration groups; assimilation and acculturation; issues of the economy, urban ills, education, cultural life, politics, and ethnic conflict; and the immigrant experience as depicted in literature.

3. Economic Issues

Bean, Frank D., and Stephanie Bell-Rose, eds. *Immigration and Opportunity: Race, Ethnicity, and Employment in the United States.* New York: Russell Sage Foundation, 1999. Examines the relationship of immigration and race in the United States at the end of the twentieth century. Focuses on labor market and economic implications for African immigrants, though some of the analyses look at other ethnic or racial minorities as well.

Borjas, George J. *Friends or Strangers: The Impact of Immigrants on the U.S. Economy.* New York: Basic Books, 1990. Deplores a perceived decline in labor market performance of post-1965 immigrants. Denies the likelihood that immigration law changes can attract immigrants most likely to succeed economically.

Fine, Janice. *Worker Centers: Organizing Communities at the Edge of the Dream.* Ithaca, N.Y.: ILR Press, 2006. Examines the origins and development of immigrant worker centers, their methods of outreach and recruitment, models of service delivery, and strategies used for raising wages and improving work conditions. Other chapters discuss public policy, and partnerships with government entities to enforce labor laws. Presents an overall assessment of worker centers, identifying weaknesses and strengths. Appendix contains contact list of centers.

Hatton, Timothy J., and Jeffrey G. Williamson. *The Age of Mass Migration: Causes and Economic Impact.* New York: Oxford University Press, 1998. Following chapters on cycles of immigration, discusses issues of absorption, the labor market, and inequality trends. Extensive bibliography.

Jones, Richard C. *Ambivalent Journey: U.S. Migration and Economic Mobility in North-Central Mexico.* Tucson: University of Arizona Press, 1995. Based on extensive research, questionnaires, and interviews, draws conclusions regarding how immigration to the United States affects the livelihoods of families in Zacatecas, a poor mining and grazing area of central Mexico and Coahuila, a dynamic industrial and agribusiness area in northern Mexico.

_____, ed. *Immigrants Outside Megalopolis: Ethnic Transformation in the Heartland.* New York: Lexington Books, 2008. Focuses on the changing cultural and social geography of immigration. Prior to the 1990's, immigrants tended to live in large American cities; since then, a major shift toward smaller places has occurred. This book investigates interaction between the creation of new cultural landscapes and the social adjustments that these changes necessitate.

Parmet, Robert D. *Labor and Immigration in Industrial America.* Boston: Twayne, 1981. Following an introductory chapter, Parmet discusses historical attitudes and treatment of certain immigrant groups such as the Chinese, various European groups, and Russians. Looks at the situations of immigrants in specific industries, such as the steel, coal mining, and garment industries. Discusses relationships of various ethnic groups with labor unions. Cites the victory of restrictionism over free immigration.

Waldinger, Roger, and Michael I. Lichter. *How the Other Half Works: Immigration and the Social Organization of Labor.* Berkeley: University of California Press, 2003. Three sections provide overviews followed by discussion of the nature of work in the low-skill labor segment and how ethnicity affects the social organization of labor; the ways in which social networks and formal hiring practices affects who get jobs; and prejudice, discrimination, and ethnic conflict in the workplace. Addresses the question of competition between immigrant and African American workers.

4. Ethnicity and Nationality Issues

Chiswick, Barry R., ed. *Immigration, Language, and Ethnicity: Canada and the United States.* Washington, D.C.: AEI Press, 1992. Four sections discuss immigration history and policy, immigrants' demographic characteristics and earnings, the economics of language, and language, women, and minorities. Each part is followed by commentaries, tables, and notes.

Coppa, Frank J., and Thomas J. Curran, eds. *The Immigrant Experience in America.* Boston: Twayne,

1976. Discusses various aspects of the immigrant experience for German, Norwegian, Irish, Italian, Jewish, African slave, and Asian immigrants. A final chapter treats the Immigration and Nationality Act of 1952 and the conflict over immigration policy during the Truman administration.

Daniels, Roger. *Coming to America: A History of Immigration and Ethnicity in American Life.* New York: HarperCollins, 1990. Traces immigration to America from colonial times to the "century of immigration" between 1820 and 1924, when Europeans, Asians, and French Canadians flocked to the United States. The final section, "Modern Times," discusses immigration during the Depression and World War II as well as new immigrants from Asia, the Caribbean, Central America, and the Soviet Union who arrived after immigration laws changed.

Drachsler, Julius. *Democracy and Assimilation: The Blending of Immigrant Heritages in America.* Westport, Conn.: Negro Universities Press, 1970. Discusses the impact of World War I and a rise of nationalism in the United States on more than one million immigrants. Argues for a comprehensive immigration law that synthesizes the policies of selection, distribution, and incorporation of immigrant groups. Maintains that the process of Americanization is too one-sided by requiring new immigrants to shed their personalities, rather than adapt American life to themselves and grow in the process.

Fuchs, Lawrence H. *The American Kaleidoscope: Race, Ethnicity, and the Civic Culture.* Hanover, N.H.: University Press of New England, 1990. Documents inclusion of white immigrants from various countries and exclusion of Africans, Native Americans, Asians, and Mexicans. Expresses hope for America's political future as it concerns post-1965 Latin American and Asian immigrants.

Haddad, Yvonne Yazbeck, Jane I. Smith, and Kathleen M. Moore. *Muslim Women in America: The Challenge of Islamic Identity Today.* New York: Oxford University Press, 2006. Discusses the situations of Muslim women in the United States and Canada before and after the September 11, 2001, attack. Suggests that the tensions between Muslims and American society should not be exaggerated. Discusses both the problems encoun-tered and the opportunities that many Muslim women enjoy as they try to define their identities.

Min, Pyong Gap, ed. *Asian Americans: Contemporary Trends and Issues.* Thousand Oaks, Calif.: Sage Publications, 1995. Following an overview, identifies issues such as underemployment; underrepresentation in managerial positions and politics; misinterpretation of class homogeneity, ethnic solidarity, family ties, and mental health statistics; and discrimination among Chinese, Japanese, Filipino, Asian Indian, Korean, Vietnamese, Laotian, and Cambodian Americans. Discusses future prospects of Asian Americans.

Olson, James Stuart. *The Ethnic Dimension in American History.* New York: St. Martin's Press, 1979. Part 1, "Colonial Origins," discusses cultural confrontations between Native Americans and Europeans from 1607 to 1776. Part 2, "American Adolescence" (1776-1890), treats the arrival of British Protestants, Irish Roman Catholics, Dutch, Germans, Scandinavians, French, African Americans, Mexicans, and Chinese. Part 3, "America in Transition" (1877-1945), focuses on the immigration of Mediterranean, eastern European, Russian and other Eastern Orthodox groups, Jewish groups, Mexicans, and Japanese. Part 4, "Conflict and Continuity" (after 1945), looks at issues involving Africans, Hispanics, Asian Americans, Native Americans, and members of various religious groups. Discusses impact of the Civil Rights movement.

Pedraza, Silvia, and Rubén G. Rumbaut, eds. *Origins and Destinies: Immigration, Race, and Ethnicity in America.* New York: Wadsworth, 1996. Introduces historical and contemporary aspects of the subject. Discusses various topics related to color and caste among the African, Latin American, and Asian immigrants; pre-World War I waves of immigrants from northwestern, southern, and eastern Europe; the Civil Rights movement as a watershed; modern waves of Latin American and Asian immigrants; New York, Los Angeles, Miami, and Washington, D.C., as urban strongholds for immigrants; and language and racial matters.

Reimers, David M. *Other Immigrants: The Global Origins of the American People.* New York: New York University Press, 2005. Traces the history of immigration to the United States from 1492 to

1940, identifying the countries of origin of Europeans, Africans, and Asians. Treats the history of large numbers of immigrants from new countries who, under new laws, were allowed to come in.

Seller, Maxine. *To Seek America: A History of Ethnic Life in the United States.* New York: Jerome S. Ozer, 1977. Defines ethnicity and discusses its importance. Traces ethnic communities from colonial days in America through the post-World War II era and finds an ethnic revival developing after the war.

Simon, Rita James, and Caroline B. Brettell, eds. *International Migration: The Female Experience.* Totowa, N.J.: Rowman & Allanheld, 1986. Provides a demographic overview of the international migration of women. Discusses immigrant women and the labor force as well as family adaptation and cultural adjustment. Tables and bibliography.

Sowell, Thomas. *Migrations and Cultures: A World View.* New York: Basic Books, 1996. Looks at migration patterns around the world, then focuses on specific groups: Germans, Japanese, Italians, Chinese, Jews, and Asian Indians.

Takaki, Ronald. *Strangers from a Different Shore: A History of Asian Americans.* Boston: Little, Brown, 1989. Traces Asian American presence in the United States. Recalls the hope and optimism of early waves of immigrants, to be replaced during the nineteenth century by a feeling of being strangers used for cheap labor. Discusses discrimination suffered by the Japanese on the United States mainland and the gradual development of ethnic solidarity and enterprise. Records discrimination experienced by Koreans and isolation felt by Asian Indians, Filipinos, and Vietnamese who, as refugees, did not choose to immigrate.

Wheeler, Thomas C., ed. *The Immigrant Experience: The Anguish of Becoming American.* New York: Dial Press, 1971. Chronicles the stories of the joys and sorrows of immigrants from Ireland, Italy, Norway, Puerto Rica, China, England, and Poland. Also has chapters on African American and Jewish immigrants.

5. LAW AND LAW-ENFORCEMENT ISSUES

Andreas, Peter. *Border Games: Policing the U.S.-Mexico Divide.* Ithaca, N.Y.: Cornell University Press, 2000. Traces the politics and practice of policing the flow of immigrants and drugs across the U.S.-Mexico border.

Cornelius, Wayne A., Philip L. Martin, and James F. Hollifield, eds. *Controlling Immigration: A Global Perspective.* Stanford, Calif.: Stanford University Press, 1994. Comparative study of immigration policy and policy outcomes in the United States, Canada, Britain, France, Germany, Belgium, Italy, Spain, and Japan. Concludes that there are growing similarities among the policies of industrialized, labor-importing countries and that gaps between goals and outcomes of national immigration laws remain wide and are growing wider.

Haerens, Margaret, ed. *Illegal Immigration.* Farmington Hills, Mich.: Greenhaven Press, 2006. Considers opposing viewpoints on four issues: how illegal immigration harms America, how fairly the United States treats undocumented immigrants, how the United States should protect its borders, and how the United States should enforce its immigration policies. Also contains a directory of organizations to contact on immigration issues.

Maril, Robert Lee. *Patrolling Chaos: The U.S. Border Patrol in Deep South Texas.* Lubbock: Texas Tech University Press, 2004. Offers insights into the border patrol personnel, the immigrants south of the border, the dynamics of the landscape itself, and the implications of certain public and national immigration policies.

Motomura, Hiroshi. *Americans in Waiting: The Lost Story of Immigration and Citizenship.* New York: Oxford University Press, 2006. Explores the subject of permanent residency status, focusing on such issues as voting, taxes, and availability of public benefits. Also looks at ways in which lawful immigrants are not equals of U.S. citizens and discusses earlier eras when immigrants could file intent to become citizens.

Rudolph, Christopher. *National Security and Immigration: Policy Development in the United States and Europe Since 1945.* Stanford, Calif.: Stanford University Press, 2006. Contrasts national security and immigration issues in the United States with those of Germany, France, and Great Britain; discusses the complex interplay that exists between national security and immigration and how immigration affects the national economy, labor force, wealth, and manpower for defense.

Tannedo, Tom. *In Mortal Danger: The Battle for America's Border and Security.* Nashville, Tenn.: WND Books, 2006. Discusses a perceived weakening of American roots and a broken immigration system. A final section suggests steps for reform and reiterates the necessity for preserving Americans' national existence.

Weissinger, George. *Law Enforcement and the INS: A Participant Observation Study of Control Agents.* New York: University Press of America, 1996. Using perceptions gleaned from interviews with Immigration and Naturalization Service (INS) investigators, this study describes the structure of the INS in its social context. Many of the problems identified appear to be related to the fact that the INS was a dual-mandate agency.

Williams, Mary E., ed. *Immigration: Opposing Viewpoints.* Farmington Hills, Mich.: Greenhaven Press, 2004. Considers opposing viewpoints on four issues: whether immigration should be restricted, whether immigration is a serious problem, how the United should address illegal immigration, and how U.S. immigration policy should be reformed. Includes a directory of organizations that provide information on these issues.

Zolberg, Aristide R. *A Nation by Design: Immigration Policy in the Fashioning of America.* Cambridge, Mass.: Harvard University Press, 2006. Traces the history of immigration from a time when immigrants were needed for the economic well-being of the United States to a point of inclusive/exclusive policy. Discusses the security challenges and suggests practical methods for determining who should enter the United States.

Victoria Price

GLOSSARY

abolitionist movement. Early nineteenth movement seeking to end slavery in the United States.

accent discrimination. Negative discrimination against persons with foreign-sounding accents.

acculturation. Process whereby immigrants adopt the culture of their new country, altering but not obliterating their original cultural patterns.

acquired citizenship. Citizenship conferred on children born overseas to parent(s) holding U.S. citizenship.

affirmative action. Policies applied by government agencies, educational institutions, private businesses, and other organizations to increase representation of members of specified minority groups.

alien land laws. State laws limiting land ownership by noncitizens, particularly Asian immigrants.

aliens. Noncitizens within a country.

Amerasians. Persons born to mothers in Asian countries whose fathers are Americans. Under U.S. law, certain Amerasians are given preference for admission into the country.

amnesty. Permission for an illegal or undocumented immigrant to legally remain in the United States.

Anglo-conformity. Tendency of immigrants to subordinate their native cultural heritage to the core Anglo-Protestant culture of the United States.

antimiscegenation laws. Laws banning interracial marriages.

assimilation. Process whereby members of immigrant groups gradually replace their original cultures with those of their new homelands.

asylum. Legal status of foreigners, or asylees, in the United States who cannot or will not return to their home countries because of persecution or reasonable fear of persecution. Such persons are eligible to apply for permanent resident status after one year of continuous residence.

au pairs. Foreign nationals—typically young women—who live in the homes of American families, caring for children and performing light household chores in exchange for room and board and the opportunity to learn the English language and become familiar with American culture.

barrios. Predominantly Hispanic neighborhoods. See also *ghettoes.*

bilingual education. Classroom instruction in two different languages, either as a means of assisting students not yet conversant in the primary language of instruction or as a method of cultivating bilingualism in all students.

birth rule. Legal principle holding that an individual's origins are determinable by birthplace and not by last place of residence.

boat people. Asylum-seekers or refugees who desperately flee their home countries in what are often makeshift or otherwise unseaworthy boats. The term is especially associated with Haitians, Cubans, and Southeast Asians.

Border Patrol, U.S. Principal federal law-enforcement agency responsible for policing U.S. borders.

braceros. Mexican farm laborers employed as guest workers in the United States between 1942 and 1964, as part of the Labor Importation Program, commonly known as the bracero program.

brain drain. Also called human capital flight, the phenomenon in which educated, skilled persons emigrate from underdeveloped to developed countries.

capitation taxes. Fixed-rate direct taxes on individuals; also known as poll taxes and head taxes.

certificates of citizenship. Documents issued to naturalized and derivative citizens as proof of their American citizenship.

chain migration. Process whereby members of a certain community eventually follow other members of that community to a new locale, often encouraged by positive reports sent and social-economic-cultural support networks established by the pioneering immigrants.

Chicano. Mexican American. *Chicana* is the feminine form.

citizenship. Membership in a political community, usually conferring rights such as suffrage and obligations such as taxes. Citizenship is usually determined by place of birth but can be acquired through naturalization.

coolies. Historic term for manual workers from Asia.

During the nineteenth century United States it specifically denoted Chinese laborers and had racist connotations.

coyotes. Slang for persons paid to smuggle immigrants into the United States from Mexico.

creoles. Persons of mixed European, Native American, or African ancestry, often evincing a hybridized culture.

cultural pluralism. Concept holding that members of individual ethnic groups should be able to live on their own terms within the larger society while retaining their unique cultural heritages.

deportable alien. Alien subject to deportation for any number of violations of United States immigration law.

deportation. Legal process whereby an alien is removed from the United States for certain violations of United States immigration law. Also currently called removal.

derivative citizenship. U.S. citizenship conferred on children through the naturalization of their parents or through adoption by citizens.

displaced persons (DPs). Refugees who are forced to leave their homelands. The term was used extensively in reference to European refugees of the World War II era.

domestic workers. Persons who work in private households, performing cooking, cleaning, child care, gardening, and other tasks.

dual citizenship. Condition in which one holds citizenship in two countries.

due process of the law, procedural. Application of fair and established procedures.

due process of the law, substantive. Protecting the substance of liberty and property.

emigration. Leaving one country in order to immigrate to another.

émigrés. Persons residing outside their native countries.

employer sanctions. Civil fines or criminal penalties against employers who hire undocumented workers.

English as a second language (ESL). Language-instruction programs for immigrants whose native languages are not English.

ethnic enclaves. Neighborhoods that are populated primarily by members of single ethnic groups, whose native communities they tend to resemble.

ethnic group. Group of humans who share and accept a common identity because of cultural affinities and real or perceived common ancestry.

eugenics. Theory and practice of attempting to improve the overall genetic quality of a human population through selective breeding.

exclusion. Official denial of entry into the United States, after due process as defined by current immigration law.

exiles. Persons prevented from returning to their homelands for political or legal reasons.

expansionist. Within modern political debate over immigration in the United States, a person who wants to maintain or increase the numbers of visas granted to permanent residents.

expatriates. Any persons residing in countries other than their own homelands.

foodways. Term used by social scientists to describe the many social, cultural, and economic practices associated with the production, preparation, and consumption of food.

genocide. Systematic attempt to annihilate all members of a race, ethnicity, or nation.

Gentlemen's Agreement. Informal 1907 agreement between Japan and the United States regarding Japanese immigration to the United States.

ghettoes. Italian term originally applied to districts within European cities in which Jews were required to live. In modern usage, the term is applied to any depressed urban neighborhood that is occupied predominantly by members of a single minority group.

Great Irish Famine. Blight that wiped out most of Ireland's potato crop from 1845 to 1852.

green card. Common name for a permanent resident card, an identification card issued to permanent residents by the U.S. Citizenship and Immigration Services and formerly by the Immigration and Naturalization Service.

guest worker. Foreigner who works in another country—usually legally—as a temporary resident.

Hispanic. Term denoting persons from Spanish- or Portuguese-speaking countries, especially Latin American countries. From the Latin word *Hispania* for the Iberian Peninsula, which encompasses both Spain and Portugal. See also *Latinos.*

Holocaust. Systematic attempt by Germany's Nazi regime to exterminate European Jews from the late 1930's to the end of World War II in 1945.

host country. Country in which a person stays without being a national of that country.

identificational assimilation. Late stage of assimilation in which members of a minority group, such as newly arrived immigrants, develop a sense of peoplehood based exclusively on their host society.

illegal immigrants. Colloquial term for aliens who circumvent or break national immigration laws to enter, reside in, or work in another country.

immigrant. Any person who has moved from an original homeland to another state or country.

immigrant advantage. Term used within sociology to describe distinctions among minority groups within a larger society and those peoples who immigrate to these societies voluntarily from other nations.

immigrant removal/immigrant return. Official federal government terms for deportation.

immigration. Incoming movement of peoples and individuals across international boundaries, usually with intention of establishing permanent residence.

immigration lawyers. Attorneys who specialize in representing immigrants.

immigration wave. Period during which the level of immigration increases markedly—either for all immigration or for the immigration of a single group or category.

inadmissible. Status of an alien who does not meet the criteria for entry into the United States. Formerly classified as "excludable."

indentured servants. Immigrants who bind themselves as servants for specified periods of time after their arrival—either to pay for their transportation or to work off penalties for legal infractions.

integration. Process whereby immigrants find places for themselves within the cultural, social, and economic fabrics of their new homeland.

Issei. First-generation Japanese immigrant.

Latinos. Persons of Hispanic background. Most commonly applied to nonimmigrants but also often applied to immigrants. *Latinas* is the feminine form. See also *Hispanic.*

"likely to become a public charge" test (LPC). One of the standards that immigrants seeking permanent resident status in the United States must meet, by proving that they have sufficient means of financial support so they are not likely to require extensive government assistance in the future.

literacy tests. Tests of reading and writing fluency administered to immigrants seeking to attain U.S. citizenship.

loyalty oaths. Required expressions of allegiance to a country or government that are often employed to test the loyalty of immigrants.

machine politics. Political system in which influential "bosses" or a group of politicians maintain their positions and power by distributing patronage and other rewards to their supporters.

mail-order brides. Women who advertise themselves as available for marriage to eligible men in other countries, often for the purpose of immigration. See also *marriages of convenience; picture brides.*

marriages of convenience. Marriages entered into, not for love, but for the financial, social, or legal benefits for one or both parties. In the context of immigration, such marriages—between nationals and aliens—are entered into to improve the legal immigration status of the latter, a practice that is illegal in many countries.

melting pot. Term—now often considered outdated and oversimplified—for the process whereby diverse immigrant groups are transformed culturally, socially, and politically into Americans.

middleman minority. Immigrant or minority population whose members perform specialized "middleman" roles in an economy, often serving as economic intermediaries between dominant and subordinate populations.

migrant superordination. Process through which immigrants use force to overwhelm and subdue the original inhabitants of the territories they settle.

migration. Movement of individuals and peoples from one location to another, though not necessarily across international boundaries.

miscegenation. Marriage or sexual relations between members of groups regarded as different races.

model minority. Minority group that achieves—or is perceived to achieve—a higher degree of success than the population at large. Often applied to the Asian American community, many members of which regard the designation as a stereotype.

mongrelization. In certain nativist ideologies, the alleged process whereby unchecked immigration leads to the debasement of a native population's culture and racial "purity."

moral turpitude. Broad class of crimes, which under United States immigration law might lead to the curtailment of certain immigration benefits or even to the deportation of an alien or permanent resident. These are normally crimes of dishonesty, such as tax evasion; immorality, such as drug violations; or violence, such as sexual assault.

multiculturalism. Ideology or policy that stresses the acceptance and full incorporation in society of a multiplicity of cultures.

nationality. Formal relationship between a person and a state, the latter of which exercises jurisdiction over the former. Nationality does not necessarily imply citizenship, which generally confers the right to participate in political processes.

nativism. Political ideology that holds that immigration—or immigration from certain countries—is economically, politically, socially, and/or culturally detrimental to a native-born population.

naturalization. Process of conferring citizenship upon an alien.

naturalization court. Any court authorized to confer American citizenship on an alien.

9/11. Terrorist attacks on the United States of September 11, 2001.

Nisei. Second-generation Japanese immigrant.

nonimmigrant. Alien who seeks temporary entry into the United States for a particular purpose, such as tourism or participation in a guest-worker program.

padrone. Italian term for an exploitative employer or manager of immigrant workers. Especially associated with Italian immigration in North America during the late nineteenth and early twentieth centuries.

paper sons. Chinese immigrants who took advantage of the destruction of government birth records during the San Francisco earthquake of 1906 to claim they were American citizens because they had been born in the United States.

parachute children. Informal term for the children of wealthy foreign—usually East Asian—parents, who are sent to schools in the United States, where they live on their own with little or no adult supervision.

parolee. Generic term for any person paroled from jail or detention. In the context of immigration law, an alien who would normally be inadmissible to the country who is permitted to enter the United States for humanitarian reasons or for reason of the public good.

passport. Document issued by a national government for the purpose of facilitating international travel by its nationals that attests to the identity and nationality of the holder.

Pennsylvania Dutch. German-speaking immigrants who first settled in Pennsylvania. "Dutch" is an English corruption of the German word for German, *Deutsche.*

peripheral nations. Term used by some social scientists for poor, less economically diversified countries, heavily influenced by the policies and economic needs of core nations.

permanent resident. Alien permitted to reside and work indefinitely in the United States.

permanent resident card. See *green card.*

picture brides. Japanese and Korean women who married fellow countrymen who preceded them to the United States during the late nineteenth and early twentieth centuries. The men typically selected their brides from sets of photographs. See also *mail-order brides.*

port of entry. Any location in the United States designated as an official point of entry and processing for aliens and U.S. citizens.

pull factors. Factors outside a person's own homeland that tend to encourage emigration—for example, economic opportunities or the presence of a sympathetic religious community at the target destination.

push factors. Factors within a person's own homeland that tend to encourage migration—for example, limited economic opportunities or religious persecution.

quota system. Limits placed on the number of United States visas issued to aliens of certain nationalities.

racial profiling. Controversial practice in which law-enforcement officials use ethnic/racial characteristics as indicators of potential criminality.

Red Scare. Brief period after World War I when public hysteria fueled by Russia's Bolshevik Revolution led to government harassment of radicals, trade unionists, and political dissidents—particularly those of foreign birth.

redemptioners. Indentured servants during the colonial era who sold themselves into servitude upon reaching their destinations in order to pay for their transatlantic passages. Redemptioners' indentures were sometimes purchased by relatives or friends already in the colonies.

refugee fatigue. Reluctance of countries to host ever-growing numbers of refugees and asylees.

refugees. Emigrants who flee their homelands to escape from wars, various forms of persecution, famines, or other dire circumstances.

remittance. Money sent by immigrants to friends and relatives in their home countries.

removal. Expulsion of aliens from the United States after they are adjudged inadmissible or deportable. Those removed cannot apply for readmission for five years. Formerly—and still informally—called deportation.

resettlement. Permanent relocation of refugees within a host country.

resident aliens. Term informally applied to immigrants who reside in the United States for long periods without obtaining citizenship.

restrictionist. Within the context of modern political debate over immigration in the United States, a person who wants to reduce the numbers of visas granted to permanent residents.

return immigrants. Immigrants who return to their countries of origin permanently or for indefinite periods.

sanctuary movement. Underground humanitarian movement of the 1980's—mostly centered in churches—in which Central American refugees were sheltered from the INS.

seasoning. Period of adjustment to the climate and sicknesses of a new country—often used in reference to immigrants in colonial America.

segmented assimilation. Process whereby immigrants absorb select elements of their new country's culture while retaining certain elements of their original culture.

selective inclusion. Process whereby a native population permits immigrants to occupy certain socioeconomic positions while purposefully excluding them from others.

settlement houses. Neighborhood centers that provided community services to residents of economically depressed areas of cities during the late nineteenth and early twentieth centuries.

snakehead. Slang for a person paid to smuggle Asian immigrants into the United States.

social mobility. Ability to move from one socioeconomic level to another, generally in an upward direction.

special immigrants. Classes of immigrants who are, under U.S. law, free from quota limitations, such as physicians and former employees of the U.S. government.

sponsors. Petitioners to the U.S. government on behalf of immigrants or prospective immigrants. Typically family members, friends, or employers, sponsors sometimes file affidavits of support, attesting that they personally will ensure that the immigrants do not become public charges.

stateless person. Person without a specific nationality.

stereotyping. Practice of assigning to all members of a group—particularly an ethnic or racial group—the same characteristics on the assumption that all members of the group share these traits.

stowaways. Persons who attempt to travel secretly on ships, planes, or other forms of transportation, often for the purpose of entering other countries illegally.

sweatshop. Term originally applied to crowded urban workplaces in which piecework farmed out by manufacturers was done by low-wage employees; in modern usage, the term has come to be applied to almost any crowded workplace with unsafe and unsanitary working conditions.

temporary protected status (TPS). Temporary refugee status granted to aliens by the U.S. attorney general. TPS generally lasts six to eighteen months, although extensions may be granted. Any removal procedures are usually suspended in cases of TPS.

terrorism. Acts of violence designed to terrorize or coerce members of a community or nation.

trafficking (in persons). Inveigling or forcing of persons into traveling to other countries where they are exploited as prostitutes or made to endure other forms of slavery.

transit aliens. Nonimmigrant aliens—traveling with or without visas—who are merely passing through the United States. Such aliens are prohibited by law from lingering in the country beyond short, specified periods of time.

transnationalism. Phenomenon or process in which immigrants retain close economic, political, and social ties with their country of origin.

unauthorized alien (or immigrant). Alternative official term for an undocumented alien.

undesirable aliens. Aliens considered inadmissible or removable for one or more reasons, such as carrying communicable diseases, having mental deficiencies, or presenting high probabilities of becoming public charges or engaging in criminal behaviors.

undocumented alien (or immigrant). Immigrant residing in the United States without proper legal documentation. Preferred alternative to "illegal alien," a term that some people believe conveys negative connotations.

visa. Legal document, or, more commonly, endorsement stamped on passports, permitting an alien to enter other countries.

voluntary departure. Voluntary departure of a removable alien from the United States without an order of removal. Such a person may reapply for admission into the country at any time.

war brides. Women who marry foreign service personnel stationed in their countries during and immediately after times of war and who typically immigrate to their spouses' countries. Immigration laws pertaining to "war brides" also encompass husbands.

wetbacks. Obsolete pejorative term for immigrants—particularly Mexicans—who entered the United States illegally. The expression derives from Mexicans who entered by the United States by wading across the Rio Grande.

xenophobia. Fear of foreigners.

yellow peril. Racist metaphor for the alleged threat that East Asian—and especially Chinese—immigrants posed to white, Western civilization during the late nineteenth and early twentieth centuries. Also applied to Japan and the Japanese during the World War II era.

Jeremiah Taylor

Time Line of U.S. Immigration History

All legislative acts mentioned below are federal laws unless otherwise noted.

c. 15,000 B.C.E. Ancestors of Native Americans begin crossing the Bering Strait into North America.

1003-1008 Norse explorers make tentative attempts to establish settlements in North America.

1492 Christopher Columbus's first voyage to the New World opens the Western Hemisphere to immigration from the Old World.

1521 Spanish conquest of the Aztec Empire begins permanent European settlement of the North American continent.

1534 The French start to explore Canada, founding fisheries but little else.

1565 Spanish found St. Augustine in Florida—the earliest permanent European settlement in what will become the United States.

1607 (April) English settlers arrive in Chesapeake Bay and found Jamestown colony.

1619 First Africans in North America arrive in Virginia as indentured servants.

1620 (November) Earliest Pilgrims land at Plymouth.

1624 Dutch settlers found New Amsterdam on Manhattan Island, which will become part of the future New York City.

1630-1640 Puritan Great Migration to New England takes place.

1634 Sephardic Jews found the first recorded settlement of Jewish immigrants in North America in Maryland.

1638 First recorded settlement of Scandinavian immigrants is founded along the Delaware River.

1654 First Jewish immigrants begin arriving in New Amsterdam from Brazil.

1664 Dutch cede control of the colony of New Netherlands to England.

1680's German immigrants who are beginning to arrive in Pennsylvania become known as the "Pennsylvania Dutch" as their settlement continues into the eighteenth century.

1681 William Penn receives proprietorship of Pennsylvania from King Charles II of England.

1685 King Louis XIV expels from France the Huguenots, many of whom go British North America.

1695 Scotch-Irish immigrants begin arriving in North America.

1713 Great Britain's occupation of formerly French Nova Scotia leads to expulsion of the Acadians, many of whom go to Louisiana.

1784 Russians begin settling in Alaska.

1789 (March 4) U.S. Constitution goes into effect.

1790 Naturalization Act of 1790, the first federal law addressing naturalization issues, stipulates that any "free white person" may obtain U.S. citizenship after two years of residency.

1790 Federal government conducts the first national census.

1790 Revenue Marine and Cutter Service, the forerunner of the U.S. Coast Guard, is established.

Time Line of U.S. Immigration History

1795   Second Naturalization Act increases the length of time immigrants must wait to be naturalized to five years.

1798   Naturalization law is revised to require fourteen years of residence before becoming a citizen.

1798   Passage of the Alien and Sedition Acts gives the U.S. president the authority to deport all foreigners who are regarded as dangerous.

1799   (February) Riot in Philadelphia is the first mass public reaction to the Alien and Sedition Acts.

1800   Led by the Federalist Party, the U.S. Congress passes the Alien Acts. These include the Nationalization Act, which lengthens the residency requirement for citizenship and makes citizenship more difficult for immigrants to acquire; the Alien Act, which gives the president the authority to deport any noncitizen thought to be dangerous; and the Alien Enemies Act, which permits the capture and imprisonment of enemy aliens in time of war.

1801   Congress repeals the parts of the Alien and Sedition Acts that have not already expired.

1802   Congress reduces the residency requirement for becoming a citizen to five years.

1808   Congress bans the importation of slaves, but holding and trading American-born slaves continues to be legal, and small numbers of foreign-born slaves continue to be smuggled into the United States from Africa and the Caribbean.

1818   Maryland enacts a law regulating indentured-servant contracts that prohibits some abuses; this law discourages ship companies from transporting indentured servants, thereby helping to end indentured servitude.

1819   Federal government begins to collect data on immigrants by requiring ships' captains and others bringing in immigrants to keep records and submit manifests.

1833   British parliament passes the first Passenger Act, which makes it cheaper to immigrate to Canada than to the United States.

1834   Inventor Samuel F. B. Morse's anti-Roman Catholic tract *Foreign Conspiracy Against the Liberties of the United States* calls for the formation of the Anti-Popery Union to resist the influence of Catholic immigrants.

1837   (February) U.S. Supreme Court's *New York v. Miln* decision gives individual states power over arriving immigrants by allowing them to regulate passengers on ships entering their ports under the doctrine of the states' police powers.

1839   Ohio and Pennsylvania pass laws permitting dual-language instruction in their public schools, primarily to accommodate German immigrants.

1844   (May-July) Anti-Irish riots in Philadelphia express anti-immigrant sentiments of nativism.

1845   Ireland experiences a potato crop failure, beginning the Great Irish Famine, which prompts almost 500,000 people to migrate from Ireland to North America between 1845 and 1850.

1848-1849   Failed political revolutions throughout Europe stimulate a new wave of immigration to the United States.

1848   (February) Treaty of Guadalupe Hidalgo ends the Mexican War; Mexico cedes its northern territories to the United States, and about 100,000 Mexicans living in the region suddenly become citizens of the United States.

1849   California gold rush begins and attracts a wave of Chinese immigrants to the United States.

Some of these immigrants settle in San Francisco, where they build the first American Chinatown.

1849   (February) U.S. Supreme Court's rulings in the *Passenger Cases* hold that only the federal government has the right to regulate immigration; states are not allowed to tax immigration for any purpose, but they may still undertake public health measures, such as quarantines of immigrant ships and passengers.

1850   Church of Jesus Christ of Latter-day Saints sets up a travel bureau in Europe to help new converts immigrate to the United States.

1852   Know-Nothing Party emerges to promote nativist, anti-immigrant agenda.

1854   Chinese district associations in the United States join together to form the Chinese Six Companies, which becomes the primary organization representing Chinese residents.

1854   Anti-immigrant Native American Party, also known as the "Know-Nothing Party," wins every statewide office and a majority of seats in the state legislature in Massachusetts elections.

1857   William Marcy Tweed becomes a leader of New York City's Tammany Hall and uses his influence in machine politics to assist arriving immigrants while soliciting their political support.

1857   Anglo-Americans assault Mexican immigrant teamsters to discourage their freight operations between the Gulf of Mexico coast and San Antonio, Texas.

1859   *Clotilde* slave ship is the last American ship to deliver involuntary African immigrants to the United States.

1861-1865 U.S. Civil War disrupts immigration from Europe.

1862   (May) Passage of the Homestead Act accelerates immigration by making western lands freely available to settlers, including foreign immigrants.

1865   (December) Ratification of the Thirteenth Amendment to the U.S. Constitution abolishes slavery and brings a final end to the importation of African slaves.

1866   Ku Klux Klan is founded in Tennessee.

1868   (July) To encourage Chinese immigrants to settle on the West Coast, the United States persuades China's government to ratify the Burlingame Treaty, which allows people to leave China for America.

1868   (July) Ratification of the Fourteenth Amendment to the U.S. Constitution establishes the principle that all persons born on U.S. soil are American citizens, regardless of the citizenship of their parents.

1869   (May) First transcontinental railroad is completed, releasing large numbers of immigrant workers, many of them Chinese, into the general job market, especially in California. Completion of the railroad also makes settlement of the Far West faster and easier.

1870   Naturalization Act of 1870 extends naturalization rights to people of African descent but excludes other nonwhites.

1875   (March) Passage of the Page Law prevents Chinese contract workers and prostitutes from entering the United States.

1875   (October) U.S. Supreme Court's *Henderson v. Mayor of New York* decision holds that cities and states have no power over immigration, even in such matters as public health regulations.

Time Line of U.S. Immigration History

1875	(October) In *Chy Lung v. Freeman*, the U.S. Supreme Court limits the extent to which individual states can restrict the admission of persons into the country.
1880	*In re Tiburcio Parrott*, a U.S. district court ruling in California, disallows application of a state constitutional amendment to prohibit employment of Chinese persons.
1880	Italian immigrants begin entering the country in large numbers, signaling a shift in immigration patterns from northern and western Europe to southern and eastern Europe; this change also brings a shift from primarily Protestant to predominantly Roman Catholic and Jewish immigrants.
1882	(May) Chinese Exclusion Act bans the entry of Chinese laborers into the United States for a period of ten years; the act is later renewed.
1882	(August) Immigration Act of 1882, the first comprehensive federal immigration law, imposes the first "head tax" on immigrants.
1884-1893	Constitutionality of the Chinese Exclusion Act is tested in the *Chinese Exclusion Cases*.
1884	(December) U.S. Supreme Court approves taxing immigrants in the so-called *Head Money Cases*.
1885	(February) Congress passes Alien Contract Labor Law, which prohibits the importation of immigrant workers under contract; the law is later frequently revised.
1886	(May) *Yick Wo v. Hopkins* is the U.S. Supreme Court case holding held that a racially neutral law applied in a discriminatory manner violates the equal protection requirement of the Fourteenth Amendment.
1886	(October 28) Statue of Liberty is dedicated in New York Harbor.
1887	Federal government bans the Perpetual Emigration Fund of the Church of Jesus Christ of Latter-day Saints as part of its campaign against Mormon polygamy.
1887	(March) American Protective Association is founded to combat growing influence of Roman Catholic immigrants.
1887	(May 27) Horse thieves murder Chinese miners in Snake River Canyon, Oregon.
1888	(October) Scott Act amends the Chinese Exclusion Act by imposing a complete prohibition on reentry of Chinese laborers who leave the United States, even if they have legal certificates guaranteeing reentry.
1889	(May) In *Chae Chan Ping v. United States*, the U.S. Supreme Court recognizes the power of Congress to exclude any groups from immigration.
1889	(September) Jane Addams establishes Hull-House in Chicago, helping to begin the settlement house movement.
1890's	Anti-Asian "yellow peril" campaign develops on the West Coast.
1891	(March) Bureau of Immigration—the forerunner of the Immigration and Naturalization Service—is established, and Congress sets health qualifications for new immigrants.
1892	First newspaper for Arab immigrants is started in New York City.
1892	Quarantine station for immigrants opens on the northwest side of Angel Island in San Francisco Bay.
1892	(January) Ellis Island, the largest and most famous immigrant station in the United States,

opens. During the turn-of-the-century wave of immigration, from 1892 to 1924, three-quarters of all the immigrants arriving in the United States pass through Ellis Island.

1892	(January) U.S. Supreme Court's *Nishimura Ekiu* decision recognizes constitutionality of a federal law authorizing immigration officials to refuse admission to aliens, with no opportunities for habeas corpus relief.
1892	(May) Geary Act extends the Chinese Exclusion Act for an additional ten years and requires Chinese already in the United States to obtain certificates of residence.
1893	(May) In *Fong Yue Ting v. United States*, the U.S. Supreme Court upholds the constitutionality of the Geary Act of 1892, conceding that Congress has almost unlimited discretion to establish all aspects of the nation's immigration policy.
1894	(December) United States and China sign Gresham-Yang Treaty, which suspends immigration of Chinese laborers to the United States for ten years, while allowing conditional readmission of immigrants visiting China.
1895	Native Sons of the Golden State is formed in San Francisco; in 1915; it will be chartered as the Chinese American Citizens Alliance.
1895	(May) In *Lem Moon Sing v. United States*, the U.S. Supreme Court upholds a federal law authorizing immigration authorities to exclude or deport immigrants without any concern that judges might find fault with their procedures.
1896	(May) In *Wong Wing v. United States*, the U.S. Supreme Court prohibits Congress from imposing criminal punishments on noncitizens without permitting them jury trials and other constitutional rights.
1898	(March) In *United States v. Wong Kim Ark*, the U.S. Supreme Court rules that children born in the United States are American citizens, regardless of the status of their parents.
1898	(April-December) Spanish-American War leaves the United States in control of Cuba, Puerto Rico, and the Philippines.
1898	(July) United States annexes Hawaii, making it a U.S. territory.
1902	(May) Cuba becomes independent, while Puerto Rico remains a U.S. dependency.
1902	(June) In *Chin Bak Kan v. United States*, the U.S. Supreme Court endorses vigorous enforcement of the Chinese Exclusion Act.
1903	(March) Immigration Act of 1903 increases federal regulation of immigration by enlarging the number of categories of inadmissible aliens.
1904	Congress extends the Chinese Exclusion Act indefinitely.
1905	(May) In *United States v. Ju Toy*, the U.S. Supreme Court holds that the Fifth Amendment's due process clause does not always require a judicial procedure for denial of benefits, even when a person claims to be a U.S. citizen.
1905	(July) Chinese nationalists begin a boycott of American goods to protest mistreatment of Chinese immigrants in the United States.
1906	American Jewish Committee is formed as an advocacy group for Jewish immigrants.
1906	Hawaii Sugar Planters Association hires attorney A. F. Judd to travel to the Philippines to recruit field-workers and make arrangements for bringing the workers to Hawaii. By 1930, three-quarters of the agricultural workers in Hawaii will be Filipinos.

Time Line of U.S. Immigration History

1906	Upton Sinclair's novel *The Jungle* exposes harsh conditions of immigrants working in Chicago.
1906	(April) Earthquake and fire level much of San Francisco, and the destruction of official birth records makes it possible for many Chinese "paper sons" to claim American birth when they enter the United States with forged documents.
1906	(October) Segregation of California schools begins when the San Francisco school board orders Japanese pupils to attend a separate school.
1907	(February) Immigration Act of 1907 increases the head tax on immigrants and authorizes the president of the United States to deny admission to any immigrants he believes have a negative influence on labor conditions.
1907	(March) United States and Japan reach the Gentlemen's Agreement, under which the United States allows Japanese residents to attend San Francisco public schools, and Japan agrees to stop emigration of its workers to the United States.
1907	(September) White residents of Bellingham, Washington, attempt to keep Sikh laborers out of the region.
1908	Israel Zangwill's play *The Melting Pot* introduces the term "melting pot" to the English language.
1910	Angel Island Immigration Station begins operating in San Francisco Bay; it will continue processing immigrants arriving on the West Coast until 1940.
1910	Mexican Revolution begins a decade of political and economic chaos that drives an estimated 900,000 Mexicans to cross the border into the United States.
1911	(March) Triangle Shirtwaist Company fire kills 146 garment workers—mostly women immigrants—in New York City.
1913	California passes its first Alien Land Law, which denies land ownership rights to Asians and to other immigrants ineligible for American citizenship.
1914	Birth control movement begins to emerge.
1914	(August) Opening of World War I in Europe severely retards immigration into the United States.
1915	(November) U.S. Supreme Court decision holding that a law restricting employment of noncitizens was unconstitutional.
1916	Naturalist Madison Grant advances the idea of "mongrelization" in *The Passing of the Great Race*, which classified national and ethnic groups as "races."
1916	Jamaican immigrant Marcus Garvey founds the Universal Negro Improvement Association in New York City.
1917	Congress passes the Jones Act, making all Puerto Ricans American citizens, thereby further decreasing barriers between the mainland and Puerto Rico.
1917	(April) United States enters World War I, and President Woodrow Wilson establishes regulations on enemy aliens, restricting the movements and rights of people from the countries with which the United States is at war. Federal agents will intern 6,300 people under these regulations, and anti-German prejudice will rise throughout the United States.
1917	(May) Immigration Act of 1917 bars the entry of immigrants who cannot read or write in

English or in their own languages, as well as immigrants from what is called the "Asiatic Barred Zone."

1917	(October) Russian Revolution begins period of increasing Russian emigration.
1919-1920	Under the direction of U.S. attorney general A. Mitchell Palmer, federal agents round up and deport foreign radicals with state and local police assistance in a series of purges known as the Palmer raids.
1920	California's second Alien Land Law increases restrictions imposed by its 1913 law by ruling that Asian immigrants cannot transfer their land to their citizen children.
1920	(November) Election of Warren G. Harding as president signals a shift in U.S. policy away from the internationalism and international involvement promoted by President Woodrow Wilson.
1921	(May) Immigration Act of 1921 creates the first national origins quota law. This limits immigrants from any particular country to 3 percent of the number of people from that country in the United States in 1910. The act also places a ceiling of 350,000 immigrants per year.
1921	(May-July) First trial of Nicola Sacco and Bartolomeo Vanzetti reveals depth of American prejudice against Italian immigrants.
1922	(September) Cable Act changes the status of married immigrant women so that not all of them automatically obtain the citizenship of their husbands.
1922	(November) In *Ozawa v. United States*, the U.S. Supreme Court rules that Japanese aliens are not "white" and cannot be naturalized as citizens.
1923	(February) In *United States v. Baghat Singh Thind*, the U.S. Supreme Court holds that because Asian Indians are not white, they are ineligible for American citizenship.
1924	(May) Immigration Act of 1924, also known as the National Origins Act, tightens the national origins quotas by limiting immigration from any given country to 2 percent of the number of people from that country living in the United States in 1890. The annual ceiling on immigrants is lowered to 165,000. The act also creates the U.S. Border Patrol.
1924	(May) *Asakura v. City of Seattle* provides a liberal interpretation of treaties with foreign countries that guarantee the civil rights of their citizens residing in the United States.
1924	(November) U.S. Supreme Court's *Terrace v. Thompson* decision upholds validity of state laws prohibiting Asians from owning or leasing land for the purpose of agriculture.
1925	(May) In *Chang Chan v. Nagle*, the U.S. Supreme Court upholds a law disallowing the entrance of some foreign wives of U.S. citizens.
1927	(November) Jamaican immigrant Marcus Garvey is declared an undesirable alien and is deported.
1929	Congress makes annual immigration quotas by national origin permanent and sets the annual ceiling on immigrants at roughly 150,000. The restrictions of the 1920's bias immigration heavily in favor of northern and western Europe, which receive 83 percent of the visas to enter the United States as immigrants. Southern and eastern Europe receive 15 percent of the visas, and only 2 percent of the visas go to the rest of the world.
1929	League of United Latin American Citizens is founded as an advocacy organization for Latinos.

Time Line of U.S. Immigration History

1929	(August) Japanese American Citizens League is founded.
1929	(October 24) White farmers attack Filipino farmworkers in Exeter, California.
1929	(October 29) Crash of the American stock market triggers the Great Depression.
1931	Congress amends the Asian provision of the Cable Act to allow American women who marry noncitizens to keep their citizenship.
1931	(January) Federal government begins Mexican deportations to conserve jobs for American citizens.
1933	(January) Adolf Hitler's Nazi Party comes to power in Germany, beginning a period of anti-Jewish persecution that will develop into the Holocaust and drive many Jews and others to emigrate from Europe.
1934	(March) Tydings-McDuffie Act places the Philippines on track toward independence from the United States, reclassifies Filipinos from American nationals to aliens, and restricts the admission of Filipino immigrants to the United States to only fifty per year.
1935	(July) Filipino Repatriation Act is passed to help Filipino immigrants return to their homeland.
1938	Sociologist Marcus Lee Hansen publishes *The Problem of the Third Generation Immigrants*, which introduces the concept of the Hansen effect.
1938	President Franklin D. Roosevelt allows Holocaust refugees already in the United States to have their visas extended indefinitely. This helps roughly 15,000 people remain in the United States.
1939	SS *Louis*, carrying more than 900 German Jewish refugees, is met off the coast of Florida by a U.S. Coast Guard patrol boat sent to prevent refugees from swimming ashore.
1939	John Steinbeck's novel *The Grapes of Wrath* chronicles the internal migrations of Americans fleeing the Oklahoma Dust Bowl.
1939	(September 2) World War II begins in Europe when Germany invades Poland.
1940	In response to war in Europe and Asia, the Alien Registration Act requires the registration and fingerprinting of all noncitizens in the United States. About 5 million noncitizens register.
1941	(December 7) Japan's surprise attack on the Pearl Harbor naval base near Honolulu, Hawaii, brings the United States into World War II.
1942	(February) The internment of all persons of Japanese descent on the West Coast of the United States begins when President Franklin D. Roosevelt signs Executive Order 9066.
1942	(August) Wartime labor needs lead the United States to establish the bracero program, which brings Mexican laborers, primarily in agriculture, to the United States. The program continues through 1964 and helps to establish a pattern of labor migration from Mexico.
1943	(December) Immigration Act of 1943 repeals Asian exclusion laws.
1945	(May) End of World War II in Europe leaves many Europeans homeless.
1945	(December) War Brides Act enables foreign-born wives and children of U.S. service personnel to enter the country on a nonquota basis.

1946	(June) Fiancées Act permits American servicemen to bring their foreign-born fiancés into the United States.
1946	(July) Luce-Celler Bill eases immigration sanctions on Asian Indians and Filipinos.
1948	In response to urging by President Harry S. Truman, Congress passes the Displaced Persons Act to deal with the problem of refugees and displaced people in Europe following the war. Truman is criticized for excluding more than 90 percent of displaced Jews. When the act is revised in 1950, most passages discriminating against Jewish refugees are removed.
1948	(January) U.S. Supreme Court's *Oyama v. California* ruling overturns portions of California's Alien Land Laws that discriminate against U.S. citizens on the basis of race but does not address the constitutionality of similar discrimination against noncitizens.
1948	(October) A dispute over wages of bracero workers leads to the U.S. Border Patrol allowing four thousand other Mexicans to enter the United States illegally through El Paso, Texas, to harvest the cotton crop.
1950	(June) Korean War begins.
1950	(September) McCarran Internal Security Act requires the registration of communist organizations and prohibits persons who have been members of registered communist organizations from entering the United States.
1950	(December) United Nations General Assembly creates the office of High Commissioner for Refugees to deal with the problem of refugees left by World War II.
1952	(April) In *Sei Fujii v. State of California*, California's supreme court strikes down the state's Alien Land Law as a violation of the equal protection clause of the Fourteenth Amendment.
1952	(June) Immigration and Nationality Act of 1952, also known as the McCarran-Walter Act, becomes the new basis of U.S. immigration policy. It establishes a four-category preference system, makes it easier for Asians to immigrate, and makes it tougher for communists to enter the United States. The act retains the national origins quota system.
1953	(August) President Harry S. Truman's appeal to Congress to help escapees from the communist countries of Eastern Europe leads to the passage of the Refugee Relief Act of 1953, which allows 200,000 more visas than are authorized under national immigration quotas.
1954	(May) U.S. Supreme Court's *Galvan v. Press* decision upholds the authority of the federal government to order the deportation of persons who have been members of the Communist Party.
1954	(June-September) U.S. government deports thousands of Mexican laborers in Operation Wetback.
1954	(November) Ellis Island closes after having processed more than 12 million immigrants since 1892.
1956	President Dwight D. Eisenhower authorizes the admission of 38,000 refugees from Hungary's failed anticommunist uprising.
1957	Congress passes the Refugee-Escapee Act, which defines refugees as persons escaping from communist or communist-dominated countries.
1958	Future president John F. Kennedy publishes *A Nation of Immigrants,* calling attention to the contributions made by immigrants.

1153

Time Line of U.S. Immigration History

1959	(January) Fidel Castro's revolutionary movement takes power in Cuba.
1959-1962	First Cuban refugees from Castro's new government arrive in the United States and settle primarily in South Florida.
1960's	United States begins gradual involvement in Vietnam's civil war.
1960	U.S. government creates the Cuban Refugee Program to handle the processing and resettlement of Cuban refugees.
1963	Miami-Dade County, with its growing population of Cubans and other Hispanics, becomes the location of the first bilingual education program in U.S. public schools.
1964	Milton Gordon publishes *Assimilation in American Life*, a major study of the assimilation of immigrants into American society.
1965	President Lyndon Johnson makes the long-closed and decaying immigrant station at Ellis Island part of the Statue of Liberty National Monument. Planning begins for the restoration of the island.
1965	(October) Immigration and Nationality Act of 1965, also known as the Hart-Celler Act, expands the preference system adopted by the 1952 Immigration and Nationality Act. The new law repeals the national origins quota system and makes family reunification the primary basis of immigration law. The act also establishes a ceiling of 170,000 on immigration from the Eastern Hemisphere and 120,000 from the Western Hemisphere.
1965	(December) Freedom Airlift begins the transporting of more than 260,000 Cuban refugees to the United States in a program that will continue until 1973.
1966	(January) Expression "model minority" first appears in a *New York Times Magazine* article by sociologist William Petersen.
1967	(May) U.S. Supreme Court's *Afroyim v. Rusk* ruling establishes that American citizenship may not be revoked involuntarily for actions such as voting in a foreign country.
1967	(May) In *Boutilier v. Immigration and Naturalization Service*, the U.S. Supreme Court approves the government's policy of classifying gays and lesbians as ineligible for immigration.
1968	Mexican American Legal Defense and Education Fund is formed in San Antonio, Texas, to promote Latino rights.
1968	(January) Bilingual Education Act, which is passed as Title 7 of the Elementary and Secondary Education Act, provides funds for special programs for speakers of minority languages.
1971	(June) In *Graham v. Richardson*, the U.S. Supreme Court strikes down discriminatory state laws denying public benefits to noncitizens.
1972-1980	About 50,000 Haitian refugees from the dictatorship of Jean-Claude Duvalier begin arriving illegally on the coasts of Florida in hastily constructed, overcrowded boats. In response, the U.S. government begins the practice of interdiction, stopping the Haitian boats at sea and returning most of their passengers to Haiti.
1973	(April) Cuban president Fidel Castro ends the Freedom Airlift flights.
1974	Jackson-Vanik Amendment to the U.S. Trade Act of 1974 penalizes the Soviet Union and other countries that do not allow their citizens to emigrate peacefully. The law pressures the Soviet government to permit dissidents and members of minority religious communities to leave.

1974	Asian American Legal Defense Fund is formed to defend and promote the legal rights of Asian Americans.
1974	(January) In *Lau v. Nichols*, the U.S. Supreme Court rules that public schools must provide bilingual education to limited-English-speaking students.
1975	(April) After the fall of the Saigon government ends U.S. involvement in the Vietnam War, President Gerald Ford authorizes the admission of 130,400 refugees from Vietnam, Laos, and Cambodia. Most of those in this first wave of refugees are Vietnamese immigrants, and the numbers of Southeast Asian immigrants increase.
1975	(May) Indochina Migration and Refugee Assistance Act establishes a resettlement assistance program for Southeast Asian refugees.
1976	First Hmong immigrants begin arriving in the United States.
1976	(June) In *Hampton v. Mow Sun Wong*, the U.S. Supreme Court severely restricts the extent to which the federal government and its agencies may refuse to employ noncitizens.
1977	U.S. attorney general Griffin Bell uses his parole authority to allow thousands of people from Cambodia, Laos, and Vietnam to resettle in the United States. President Jimmy Carter signs legislation permitting these refugees to become permanent residents.
1978	Helsinki Watch is established as a nongovernment body to monitor U.S. compliance with an international agreement signed by thirty-five countries pledging to respect basic human and civil rights.
1978	Federal government adopts a new worldwide ceiling of 290,000 immigrants per year, replacing the Eastern and Western Hemisphere ceilings established in 1965.
1978	(March) In *Foley v. Connelie*, the U.S. Supreme Court upholds a state law discriminating against aliens.
1979	(January) Islamic revolution in Iran leads to large increase in the numbers of Iranian immigrants to the United States and other nations.
1980's	Civil wars in El Salvador, Nicaragua, and Guatemala create an estimated 1 million political and economic refugees, most of whom flee north to the United States.
1980's	Liberalization of Soviet emigration laws under Mikhail Gorbachev increases the numbers of Soviet Jewish immigrants who come to the United States.
1980	In response to the large numbers of immigrants that have begun to arrive from Southeast Asia and other locations, Congress passes the Refugee Act. This places refugees in a category separate from other immigrants and provides a definition of refugees as people fleeing their countries because of persecution on grounds of race, religion, nationality, or political opinion. The president is authorized to establish the number of refugees to be allowed into the United States.
1980	(April-September) Fidel Castro opens the port of Mariel to Cubans who want to leave the country. More than 115,000 people take advantage of the Mariel boatlift to cross to Key West, Florida.
1981	Congress sets an annual quota of 20,000 Taiwanese immigrants.
1981	(January) In *Fedorenko v. United States*, the U.S. Supreme Court establishes that the citizenship of naturalized citizens may be revoked if they are found to have intentionally provided false information to enter the country or to obtain citizenship.

Time Line of U.S. Immigration History

1982   (June) In *Plyler v. Doe*, the U.S. Supreme Court extends the Fourteenth Amendment's equal protection clause to give noncitizens the right to public social services.

1983   (June) The U.S. Supreme Court's *Immigration and Naturalization Service v. Chadha* ruling on deportation has wide-ranging political ramifications.

1984   (May) The U.S. Supreme Court's *Bernal v. Fainter* ruling strikes down a state law prohibiting aliens from working as notary publics.

1984   (July) In *Immigration and Naturalization Service v. Lopez-Mendoza*, the U.S. Supreme Court upholds minimal application of Fourth Amendment rights to deportation proceedings.

1984   (December) The United States and Cuba agree that Cuba will take back nearly 3,000 criminals and mental patients who have arrived with the Mariel boatlift, and the United States will issue visas to political prisoners and others wishing to leave Cuba.

1986   Concerns over illegal immigration into the United States lead Congress to pass the Immigration Reform and Control Act of 1986. This raises the annual ceiling on legal immigration from the 270,000 established six years earlier to 540,000. To decrease the jobs drawing illegal aliens into the country, the act introduces stiff penalties for employers of those in the country illegally. The act also offers amnesty to illegal aliens who can prove that they have resided in the United States since January 1, 1982.

1987   (December) Amerasian Homecoming Act is passed to ease the immigration of Vietnamese Amerasian children and their close relatives to the United States.

1988   Civil Liberties Act authorizes each internee of a wartime relocation camp for Japanese Americans to receive twenty thousand dollars and a formal apology from the United States. About 60,000 Japanese Americans apply for and receive these reparations.

1989   (June) Helsinki Watch report on U.S. refugee policy criticizes American treatment of refugees.

1990   (September) National Immigration Museum opens at Ellis Island.

1990   (November) Immigration Act of 1990 raises the worldwide ceiling on immigration to 700,000 for 1992 through 1994, with the ceiling to go down to 675,000. The act revises the 1952 Immigration Act so that immigrants can no longer be excluded because of political beliefs or affiliations.

1992   President George H. W. Bush issues Executive Order 12807, directing the U.S. Coast Guard to interdict undocumented aliens at sea and to return them to their places of origin.

1992   (May) Asian Pacific American Labor Alliance is formed to promote the interests of Asian and Pacific Islander immigrants.

1992   (October) Chinese Student Protection Act is passed to allow Chinese students and scholars to remain in the United States and apply for permanent residency.

1993   (February 26) A bomb in the subterranean garage of one of New York City's World Trade Center towers kills six people and injures one thousand more. The bomb is later found to have been planted by a Middle Eastern immigrant who entered the United States illegally.

1993   (June) U.S. Supreme Court's *Sale v. Haitian Centers Council* decision allows the U.S. government to apprehend Haitian refugees at sea, before they reach the United States, and return them to Haiti.

1993   (June 26) Freighter *Golden Venture* runs aground off Queens, New York; federal authorities take into custody 276 Chinese passengers who were attempting to enter the United States illegally.

1994   (January) North American Free Trade Agreement (NAFTA) goes into effect to reduce barriers to trade among the United States, Canada, and Mexico. The agreement also requires the three countries to ease restrictions on the movement of business executives and professionals. This promotes professional migration from Canada to the United States, in particular.

1994   (April) In an illegal-immigrant suit, the state of Florida demands restitution from the federal government for its expenditures on illegal immigrants.

1994   (June) Congressional Commission on Immigration Reform, also known as the Jordan Commission, calls for limiting legal immigration to 500,000 per year, with 100,000 slots to be granted to immigrants with needed job skills; the commission's report also calls for strict controls on the hiring of illegal immigrants wherever necessary.

1994   (August) Responding to the large numbers of Cubans attempting to leave their country after Fidel Castro declares that he is not opposed to people leaving, the United States changes its Cuban refugee policy when President Bill Clinton declares that Cuban refugees will no longer be allowed automatic entry to the United States.

1994   (November) California voters approve Proposition 187, a voter initiative designed to limit public services available to undocumented immigrants.

1995   (August) The enslavement of garment workers in Southern California is revealed when captive Thai immigrants are freed.

1996   Welfare Reform Act denies public assistance services to resident aliens for a period of time.

1996   (March) Immigration and Naturalization Service creates a self-petitioning process for immigrants who are battered spouses and battered children of U.S. citizens and legal permanent residents. If approved, the petitions enable immigrants to remain in the United States after separating from abusive spouses.

1996   (September) Illegal Immigration Reform and Immigrant Responsibility Act is enacted to stop the flow of undocumented aliens into the United States with increased border patrol staffing, strong enforcement and penalties against alien smuggling, and tougher sanctions for undocumented immigrants caught inside the United States.

1997   Czechoslovakian-born Madeline Albright is appointed U.S. secretary of state.

1998   (June) California voters approve Proposition 227, a voter initiative designed to end bilingual education in public schools.

1999   (February) In *Reno v. American-Arab Anti-Discrimination Committee*, the U.S. Supreme Court upholds a federal statute severely restricting the rights of alien residents to challenge deportation orders in court.

1999   (November) Rescue of youthful Cuban refugee Elián González off Florida's coast touches off a diplomatic conflict between the United States and Cuba.

2001   (June) In *Zadvydas v. Davis*, the U.S. Supreme Court rules that the government may not detain deportable aliens indefinitely simply because no other country accepts them.

Time Line of U.S. Immigration History

2001   (June) In *Immigration and Naturalization Service v. St. Cyr*, the U.S. Supreme Court holds that recent federal laws do not eliminate the federal courts' jurisdiction to consider habeas corpus petitions from resident aliens who are deportable because of felony convictions.

2001   (June) In *Nguyen v. Immigration and Naturalization Service*, the U.S. Supreme Court rules on the citizenship of children born abroad and out of wedlock who have only one American parent.

2001   (September 11) Nineteen Middle Eastern terrorists hijack four American airliners; they fly two planes into the towers of New York's World Trade Center, killing thousands of people. A third plane hits the Pentagon building near Washington, D.C., and a fourth crashes in Pennsylvania after an apparent struggle between passengers and hijackers. Nine days later, U.S. president George W. Bush reacts to the events of "9/11" by creating the Office of Homeland Security. The following January, the new office is upgraded to a cabinet department. Meanwhile, national suspicion and resentment of immigrants—particularly Middle Eastern Muslims—mounts.

2001   (October) Congress passes Public Law 107-56, known as the USA Patriot Act. The act includes new reasons for denying entry into the United States, gives a broader definition to the concept of terrorist activity, and increases the causes for deporting visitors and immigrants.

2001   (November) Congress passes the Border Security Act, authorizing more funds for immigration and customs staff, providing for the sharing of information on deportation cases among federal agencies, tracking foreign students, and tightening oversight in other ways.

2001   (November) Aviation and Transportation Security Act is enacted to improve security of transportation systems throughout the United States, with particular emphasis on airport security.

2003   (March) Functions and offices of the Immigration and Naturalization Service are transferred to U.S. Citizenship and Immigration Services (UCIS), a bureau of the new Department of Homeland Security.

2003   (October) Austrian bodybuilder and actor Arnold Schwarzenegger is elected governor of California in a special election.

2006   Secure Fence Act authorizes construction of a 700-mile fence between the United States and Mexico.

2008   (June) In *Dada v. Mukasey*, the U.S. Supreme Court recognizes the right of immigrants to petition to reopen their cases after they have already agree to leave the country.

2009   Thirty-eight million immigrants are estimated to be living in the United States.

Scott A. Merriman
Carl L. Bankston III

INDEXES

CATEGORIZED LIST OF ARTICLES

List of Categories

IMMIGRATION REFORM

INTERNATIONAL AGREEMENTS

JOURNALISM

COURT CASE INDEX

LAW AND TREATY INDEX

PERSONAGE INDEX

SUBJECT INDEX

668; miners, 136, 223, 321, 478, 1063; music of, 748; and soccer, 956; Virginia, 1041; Wisconsin, 1063

Wesley, John, 898

West, Benjamin, 316

West Indian immigrants, 651, 1055-1057; and Florida, 382; Haitians, 448-452; in literature, 670; New York City, 785; remittances, 900; and voodoo, 894

West Side Story (film), 1132

West Virginia, 101, 1057-1058; coal mines, 223; Spanish immigrants, 968; Swiss immigrants, 990

Westward expansion, 1058-1063; and land distribution, 640-644; and railroads, 562

"Wetbacks," 806-807, 1144

Wetbacks (film), 375

Wharton, Edith, 1078

Wheatley, Phillis, 334

Wheeler, William, 279

When Heaven and Earth Changed Places (Hayslip), 71

When I Was Puerto Rican (Santiago), 922

Where Is My Child? (film), 375

Whig Party, 1, 851, 858-859

Whipple, Prince, 1107

Whistler, James, 316

White, Byron R., 546-547, 983

White Russians. *See* Belorussian immigrants

Whitfield, George, 898

Wiesel, Elie, 1107

Wigner, Eugene, 506, 933-934

Wilder, Billy, 96

Williams, Robin, 1130

Williams, Roger, 891, 895, 899

Wilmington, Delaware, 273

Wilson, James, 762

Wilson, Pete, 866

Wilson, Woodrow, 44, 82, 531, 533, 535, 645, 665; and eugenics, 340; and Poland, 849; and World War I, 716, 1077-1078

Wine industry, 1024, 1061; Italian immigrants, 595, 675

Winthrop, John, 132, 469

Wirz, Henry, 1107

Wisconsin, 101, 108, 476, 643, 846, 1062-1065; Canadian immigrants, 157; Canton Glarus, 991; draft riots, 716; Dutch immigrants, 293; German immigrants, 321, 476, 928, 1061; Polish immigrants, 849; prisoner of war camps, 863; Puerto Rican immigrants, 869; Scandinavian immigrants, 924, 1061; schools, 331; Swiss immigrants, 990-991

Wise, Isaac Mayer, 617

Wise Up!, 226

"Wobblies." *See* Industrial Workers of the World

Woman Warrior, The (Kingston), 70, 668

Women, 1065-1069; Chinese, 200; European immigrants, 342; in garment industry, 405; and Immigration Act of 1907, 530; indentured servants, 560; Iranian, 581; Italian, 597; Japanese, 1047; Latin American immigrants, 325; occupations, 324; Polish, 849; returning immigrants, 904; Scandinavians, 927; Spanish, 968; war brides, 1044-1047; War Brides Act of 1945, 1047-1048; in workforce, 354

Women's movements, 1069-1071

Wong, Jade Snow, 69

Wong, Kent, 81

Wong, Mow Sun, 454

Wong, Shawn Hsu, 70

Wong Kim Ark, 291, 1027

Wong Kim Ark, United States v., 213, 290, 1027-1028, 1109

Wong Wing v. United States, 1071, 1109

Wong Yang Sung v. McGrath, 1111

Woods, Tiger, 1009

World Cup (soccer), 956-957

World Trade Center, 281, 831. *See also* September 11, 2001, terrorist attacks

World Trade Organization, 405

World War I, 1077-1079; aftermath, 390; and Mary Antin, 49; and Irving Berlin, 105; conscription, 716, 1078; and Czech and Slovak immigrants, 268; Espionage and Sedition Acts, 333-334; and German immigrants, 420, 804; influenza pandemic, 572; and intelligence testing, 574; and language issues, 645; and Mexico, 705; and passports, 828; and Polish immigrants, 849; and Red Scare, 882-883; and shipping, 452; and Yugoslavia, 1092

World War II, 1079-1082; aftermath, 390; and Australia, 91; and Austria, 95; and Irving Berlin, 105; and Border Patrol, U.S., 117; and bracero program, 124; and Canada, 158; and China, 210; displaced persons, 282-283, 324, 884-886, 1074; and Dutch immigrants, 294; 442d Regimental Combat Team, 603; and German immigrants, 420, 1021; and Holocaust, 487-490; and Immigration and Naturalization Service, 545; Japanese American internment, 601-606; and Mexico, 124; and Peru, 613-614; and the Philippines, 370; and Polish immigrants, 849; prisoners of war, 861-864; and Russian immigrants, 910; and Soviet Union, 395; war brides, 1044-1047; war criminals, 258; and Yugoslavia, 1093

World Wide Web, 646; federal laws on, 1119; Google, 131; Arianna Huffington, 503; and mail-order brides, 577, 687; missionary sites, 722; Spanish-

FOR REFERENCE

Do Not Take From This Room